Rational-Emotive Approaches to the Problems of Childhood

Rational-Emotive Approaches to the Problems of Childhood

Edited by
Albert Ellis
Institute for Rational-Emotive Therapy
New York, New York

and
Michael E. Bernard
University of Melbourne
Parkville, Victoria, Australia

PLENUM PRESS • NEW YORK AND LONDON

Library of Congress Cataloging in Publication Data

Main entry under title:

Rational-emotive approaches to the problems of childhood.

Includes bibliographical references and index.
1. Rational-emotive psychotherapy. 2. Child psychotherapy. I. Ellis, Albert, 1913– . II. Bernard, Michael Edwin, 1950– . [DNLM: 1. Psychotherapy —In infancy and childhood. 2. Psychotherapy—In adolescence. 3. Child behavior disorders—Therapy. 4. Mental disorders—Therapy. WS 350.2 R236]
RJ505.R33R37 1983   618.92′8914   83-19172
ISBN 0-306-41331-0

© 1983 Institute for Rational-Emotive Therapy

Plenum Press, New York is a Division of
Plenum Publishing Corporation
233 Spring Street, New York, N.Y. 10013

All rights reserved

No part of this book may be reproduced, stored in a retrieval system, or transmitted in any form or by any means, electronic, mechanical, photocopying, microfilming, recording, or otherwise, without written permission from the Publisher

Printed in the United States of America

TO

Dr. Janet L. Wolfe, my esteemed associate
and co-builder of RET for the past eighteen years
(Albert Ellis)

Patricia C. Bernard, my closest companion and friend
(Michael E. Bernard)

Contributors

JAMES A. BARD	Department of Psychology, Cleveland State University, Cleveland, Ohio
MICHAEL E. BERNARD	Department of Education, University of Melbourne, Victoria, Australia
JOHN D. BOYD	Institute of Clinical Psychology, University of Virginia, Charlottesville, Virginia
RAYMOND DIGIUSEPPE	Institute for Rational-Emotive Therapy, New York, New York
ALLEN ELKIN	Department of Psychology, Empire State College on Long Island, State University of New York, Clinical Psychologist in Private Practice, 110 E. 36 St., New York, New York
ALBERT ELLIS	Executive Director, Institute for Rational-Emotive Therapy, New York, New York
GARY L. FISCHLER	Department of Psychology, University of Minnesota, Minneapolis, Minnesota
HAROLD R. FISHER	Clinical Psychologist in Private Practice, Cleveland Institute for Rational Living, Beachwood, Ohio

JOHN P. FOREYT	Department of Medicine, Baylor College of Medicine, Houston, Texas
RUSSELL M. GRIEGER	Clinical Psychologist in Private Practice, Institute of Clinical Psychology, University of Virginia, Charlottesville, Virginia
W. KIM HALFORD	Department of Psychology, Brisbane College of Advanced Education, Queensland, Australia
PAUL A. HAUCK	Clinical Psychologist in Private Practice, Rock Island, Illinois
MARIE R. JOYCE	Department of Education, University of Melbourne, Victoria, Australia
PHILIP C. KENDALL	Department of Psychology, University of Minnesota, Minneapolis, Minnesota
WILLIAM J. KNAUS	Psychologist in Private Practice, 113 Arlington Road, Longmeadow, Massachusetts
ALBERT T. KONDO	Department of Psychology, University of Houston, Houston, Texas
JOHN F. MCINERNEY	Director of Pre-School Programs for the Handicapped, Cape May County Schools for Special Services, District of Cape May County, New Jersey
PAMELA M. ROSEWARNE	Counseling, Guidance and Clinical Services, Victoria Education Department, Victoria, Australia
KAREN SUTTON-SIMON	Department of Psychology, Oberlin College, Oberlin, Ohio
GLORIA K. VANDERHORST	Psychologist in Private Practice, Baltimore, Maryland

CONTRIBUTORS

ANN VERNON
Department of Educational Administration and Counseling, University of Northern Iowa, Cedar Falls, Iowa

SUSAN R. WALEN
Department of Psychology, Towson State University, Towson, Maryland

NINA WOULFF
Dartmouth Branch of the Atlantic Child Guidance Centre, Dartmouth, Nova Scotia, and Division of Family Medicine and Department of Psychiatry, Dalhousie University, Halifax, Nova Scotia

HOWARD S. YOUNG
Hibbard Psychiatric Clinic, Huntington, West Virginia

Preface

This book was planned during Dr. Bernard's visit to the Institute for Rational-Emotive Therapy in New York City, while he was on sabbatical leave from the University of Melbourne in Australia. In discussing the practice of rational-emotive therapy (RET) with younger populations, it became apparent to both editors that the time had come for a work that could set down in some detail how RET was currently being employed to resolve different problems of childhood. The project was greeted with enthusiasm by those at the Institute including Ray DiGiuseppe, Karen Sutton-Simon, and Richard Wessler. With their helpful suggestions, a tentative list of topics to be covered and potential contributors who had demonstrated expertise in a particular area was drawn up. Telephone calls were placed to all contributors and, with few exceptions, all contributors expressed delight in being asked and readily accepted. Within a two-week period, the manuscript was conceived. Midway along in the planning of this book, its emphasis and general contents were discussed with Leonard Pace, senior editor at Plenum. We were especially encouraged by his excitement, support, and interest, which continued throughout the project.

We have divided this book into three sections. Part I consists of three chapters that present the history of and rationale for the application of RET to the childhood period as well as methods and techniques for using RET with children and adolescents. Part II focuses on how RET can be employed to tackle specific childhood disorders (conduct disorders; low frustration tolerance; impulsivity; fears, phobias, and anxieties; underachievement; shyness; obesity; and sexual problems). Part III deals with the many ways RET can be applied within the family and the school. A chapter that discusses research perspectives for the practitioner concludes the book.

Most of the contributors to this book are recognized as pioneers in the application of RET to the problems of childhood. During the past 15 years, a small number of RET practitioners, such as Paul Hauck, Ray DiGiuseppe, Howard Young, William Knaus, James Bard, and Harold Fisher, have shown how the complexities of rational thinking can be introduced to younger populations in a more simplified form. We have also represented in this book a number of practitioners (John McInerney, Ann Vernon, and Nina Woulff) who are making significant advances in applying RET with parents and teachers as well as with groups of children (Allen Elkin).

The contributors to this book are not all rational-emotive therapists. Some, no doubt, associate themselves with cognitive-behavior therapy (CBT). As we indicate in Chapter 1, RET and CBT share many similarities. Therefore, we felt it appropriate to invite people like Philip Kendall and John Foreyt, who have established themselves as leaders in applying cognitive-behavioral approaches to the treatment of a specific childhood disorder (e.g., impulsivity or obesity), even though they might not practice all aspects of RET.

We believe that this book can be employed in university and college settings to train psychologists, counselors, social workers, nurses, and other mental and community health workers interested in the problems of children and adolescents. We also see the book as being of immense value to practitioners who are already working with younger populations, as well as with their parents and teachers.

We would like to acknowledge the diligence of the contributors who kept to chapter deadlines. Their conscientiousness made the process of editing a book in both New York and Melbourne surprisingly straightforward and manageable. We would also like to mention the creative efforts of Virginia Waters, Director of Children's Services at the Institute. At the time of writing this book, Virginia was not in a position to be able to make a contribution. We wish to recognize her extensive influence on the practice of RET with children in general, and on the development of ideas presented in Chapters 1 and 2 in particular.

ALBERT ELLIS
MICHAEL E. BERNARD

Contents

I: INTRODUCTION, RATIONALE, AND BASIC ISSUES 1

Chapter 1

AN OVERVIEW OF RATIONAL-EMOTIVE APPROACHES TO THE PROBLEMS OF CHILDHOOD.................... 3

ALBERT ELLIS AND MICHAEL E. BERNARD

The Emergence of Cognitive Restructuring	4
The Cognitive Perspective	7
The RET Approach to Children and Adolescents...............	16
Allied Cognitive-Behavioral Approaches	27
The Future...	35
References...	36

Chapter 2

PRINCIPLES OF ASSESSMENT AND METHODS OF TREATMENT WITH CHILDREN: SPECIAL CONSIDERATIONS 45

RAYMOND DIGIUSEPPE AND MICHAEL E. BERNARD

Theoretical Assumptions	47
Special Considerations with Children	53
Assessment Guidelines..	60
Methods of Treatment..	67
Case Illustration	78
References...	87

Chapter 3

PRINCIPLES OF ASSESSMENT AND METHODS OF
TREATMENT WITH ADOLESCENTS: SPECIAL
CONSIDERATIONS 89

HOWARD S. YOUNG

Relationship Building 90
Problem Defining 92
Problem Intervention 94
Problem Solving 99
Other Methods 101
Case Illustration 103
References 107

II: PROBLEMS OF CHILDHOOD 109

Chapter 4

RATIONAL-EMOTIVE THERAPY AND CONDUCT
DISORDERS 111

RAYMOND DIGIUSEPPE

Diagnosis 111
Behavioral Approaches 115
Cognitive Approaches 116
Steps in Treatment 121
Assessing the Parents 125
Cognitive-Behavioral Interventions with Children 133
References 136

Chapter 5

CHILDREN AND LOW FRUSTRATION TOLERANCE 139

WILLIAM J. KNAUS

Frustration: A Complex Process 139
Action Strategies 146

Case Application: REE With a Battered Child 153
References 156

Chapter 6

TEACHING RATIONAL SELF-TALK TO IMPULSIVE
CHILDREN 159

PHILIP C. KENDALL AND GARY L. FISCHLER

Definition of the Problem 160
Treatment Approaches 163
Cognitive-Behavioral Interventions 168
A Clinical Case Example 174
Philosophical Issues 176
References 185

Chapter 7

A RATIONAL-EMOTIVE APPROACH TO ACADEMIC
UNDERACHIEVEMENT 189

JAMES A. BARD AND HAROLD R. FISHER

Defining Academic Underachievement 189
Explaining Academic Underachievement 191
The Rational-Emotive Approach 195
Prevention 207
References 209

Chapter 8

CHILDHOOD ANXIETIES, FEARS, AND PHOBIAS: A
COGNITIVE-BEHAVIORAL-PSYCHOSITUATIONAL
APPROACH 211

RUSSELL M. GRIEGER AND JOHN D. BOYD

Definition of the Problem 212
A Cognitive-Behavioral-Psychosituational Model of Childhood
    Psychopathology 213
Cognitive Distortions in Children's Anxiety Problems 218
Cognitive-Behavioral-Psychosituational Assessment 227

Cognitive-Behavioral-Psychosituational Therapy of Anxiety
    Disorders 232
Conclusion 237
References 237

Chapter 9

TEACHING RATIONAL SELF-TALK TO HELP SOCIALLY ISOLATED CHILDREN AND YOUTH 241

W. KIM HALFORD

The Significance of Social Isolation in Children and Youth 241
The Role of Cognitions in Social Isolation 245
Assessment of Social Withdrawal 252
Treatment Methods 259
Special Considerations in Applications of Cognitive
    Procedures with Children and Youth 265
References 266

Chapter 10

COGNITIVE-BEHAVIORAL TREATMENT OF CHILDHOOD AND ADOLESCENT OBESITY 271

JOHN P. FOREYT AND ALBERT T. KONDO

Definition and Problem 271
Etiology 273
Obesity Assessment 276
A Model of Treatment 277
Behavioral Bases of Treatment 288
Cognitive Interventions 292
Summary 305
References 305

Chapter 11

A RATIONAL-EMOTIVE APPROACH TO CHILDHOOD SEXUALITY 311

SUSAN R. WALEN AND GLORIA K. VANDERHORST

When Does Sex Education Begin? 312
How Do Children and Adults Think about Sexuality? 314

Sexuality in Therapy 319
Who Presents the Problem: Whose Problem Is It? 322
Cognitive Therapy and Sexuality 323
Correcting Misconceptions... 324
Suggested Readings... 327
References... 329

III: APPLICATIONS 331

Chapter 12

WORKING WITH PARENTS 333

PAUL A. HAUCK

The Rationale for Working with Parents........................ 334
The Rational-Emotive Approach................................... 335
Nonmanipulative Behavior 340
Manipulative Behavior 353
Parent Case Conference 360
Summary... 364
References... 365

Chapter 13

INVOLVING THE FAMILY IN THE TREATMENT OF THE CHILD: A MODEL FOR RATIONAL-EMOTIVE THERAPISTS ... 367

NINA WOULFF

Rationale for REFT... 368
Conceptual Schemata for REFT.................................... 369
Stages of REFT 370
Characteristics of REFT Therapists............................... 382
Hazards and Pitfalls of REFT...................................... 383
Summary... 384
References... 385

Chapter 14

WORKING WITH THE PARENTS AND TEACHERS OF
EXCEPTIONAL CHILDREN 387

JOHN F. MCINERNEY

Introduction... 387
Parents of Exceptional Children 388
Teachers of Exceptional Children............................ 408
Future Directions 413
References... 413

Chapter 15

HELPING TEACHERS COPE WITH STRESS: A RATIONAL-
EMOTIVE APPROACH 415

MICHAEL E. BERNARD, MARIE R. JOYCE, AND PAMELA M.
ROSEWARNE

The Stresses of Teaching 416
RET Analysis of Teacher Stress.............................. 418
A Stress Reduction Program for Teachers 424
Introducing RET to Teachers: Background Concepts for the
    Program Leader 427
Sample RET and REE Methods, Activities, and Techniques for
    Teacher Education 446
References... 466

Chapter 16

RATIONAL-EMOTIVE EDUCATION 467

ANN VERNON

Rationale for Emotional Education Programs................. 467
A Description of Emotional Education 468
Rational-Emotive Education.................................. 469
Conclusion... 483
References... 483

Chapter 17

WORKING WITH CHILDREN IN GROUPS 485
ALLEN ELKIN

A Cognitive-Behavioral–Skills-Training Approach 486
Forming the Group 490
Assessment Strategies and Procedures 493
Treatment Strategies and Procedures 499
Working with Younger Children 506
The Challenge 507
Suggested Readings 507
References 507

Chapter 18

RESEARCH PERSPECTIVE FOR THE MENTAL HEALTH PRACTITIONER 509
KAREN SUTTON-SIMON

Introduction 509
Review of Research 510
Areas for Research 512
Cognitive-Behavioral Interventions as Education and for
 Prevention 526
Conducting Research in Clinical Settings 528
Traditional Clinical Research Strategies and Guidelines 529
Conclusion 533
References 533

INDEX 537

I

Introduction, Rationale, and Basic Issues

The first three chapters of this book set the stage for the deployment of RET and allied cognitive-behavioral approaches with school-age children. It will be seen that the ancient history of cognitive restructuring with children and youth can be traced to Socrates, and its contemporary origins lie in the work of Alfred Adler. During the past 20 years, the practice of rational-emotive therapy (RET) and cognitive-behavior therapy (CBT) with young clients has evolved to the point where it no longer represents an inelegant approximation to an adult model. Cognitive practitioners know which questions to ask of the young client, how they are to be expressed, and how to go about eliciting relevant information. Cognitively oriented therapeutic and counseling methods for use with a younger client abound and are continuing to grow. It will be demonstrated throughout this book that practitioners are increasingly aware of the importance of taking into account the child's linguistic-cognitive developmental repertoire in both deciding if a problem exists as well as analyzing and treating the problem. The significant role of parents and teachers is being recognized and, in particular, the importance of assessing the involvement of their faulty cognitions, emotions, and behavior.

In Chapter 1, we discuss the emergence of cognitive restructuring and how the cognitive perspective can characterize childhood maladjustment. The history of RET with children and youth provides a background to a consideration of principles of assessment and methods of treatment. Allied cognitive-behavioral approaches that can be combined with RET are also reviewed.

Raymond DiGiuseppe and Michael E. Bernard provide in Chapter 2 an overview with extensive practical illustrations of how RET and other cognitive and behavioral interventions can be used with children. A great deal of attention is devoted to discussing special considerations that practitioners had better take into account in working with very young populations. Of particular interest in this chapter is a detailing of the various levels and types of cognitive disputational and other strategies that can be employed to change cognitions in children.

In Chapter 3, Howard Young documents his extensive experience in applying RET with adolescents. It will be seen how the complex RET conceptual-linguistic system can be concretely simplified and communicated to adolescents. Specifically, he demonstrates how the nature and consequences of irrational thinking can be made meaningful to an adolescent and how irrational concepts and beliefs can be rationally restated and reformulated.

1

An Overview of Rational-Emotive Approaches to the Problems of Childhood

ALBERT ELLIS AND MICHAEL E. BERNARD

The history of cognitive restructuring with children and youth doubtless goes back many centuries and may be traced to early philosophers and religious preachers. Socrates, let us remember, was persecuted by the Athenians for supposedly corrupting the youth of that ancient city. And the Greek-Roman Stoic Epictetus, who is often acknowledged as the main philosophical father of rational-emotive therapy (RET) and cognitive-behavior therapy (CBT), pioneered in conveying significant cognitive teachings to the young people as well as the adults of his time. Because of his influence, some 2,000 years ago, the Roman Emperor Marcus Aurelius was raised from childhood in the Stoic tradition and consequently was later led to write his famous *Meditations,* one of the most influential books of all time, outlining the principles and practice of cognitive restructuring.

In modern times, methods of teaching children and adolescents to talk more sensibly to themselves, and thereby to make themselves individually and socially more effective, were pioneered by Alfred Adler. Not only was Adler (1927) probably one of the first cognitive therapists to specialize in direct psychological approaches to youngsters, but he and his associates, starting in the 1920s, saw the importance of using cognitive approaches in the school system and of teaching them to parents to employ in the rearing of children.

ALBERT ELLIS • Executive Director, Institute for Rational-Emotive Therapy, New York, New York 10021.   MICHAEL E. BERNARD • Department of Education, University of Melbourne, Victoria, 3052 Australia.

The Emergence of Cognitive Restructuring

As a background to our discussion of applications of cognitive restructuring to the problems of children and adolescents, we present a brief historical overview of contemporary RET and CBT. Readers interested in a full history are referred to the writings of Ellis (1962, 1979), Kazdin (1978), Kendall and Hollon (1979), Mahoney (1974, 1977), Mahoney and Arnkoff (1978), Meichenbaum (1977), and Murray and Jacobson (1978).

Science Lags Behind

Science has had to "catch up" with the wisdom that has been handed down by those who have recognized the importance of thinking in all aspects of human functioning. One of the main reasons that science has lagged behind advances in thinking in this area is that it has been only within recent times that an experimental methodology for studying nonobservable cognitive phenomena has developed in and been accepted by the scientific community. It has also been the case that cognitive theory and research have taken some time to influence practice, largely because of the scientist–practitioner split and the absence of an appropriate *applied* methodology that could be employed to examine the effectiveness of cognitive and other counseling and therapeutic approaches.

At present, it is still difficult to design and conduct research that will answer the question of which approach is best suited to individuals who may demonstrate problems that are embedded within different personality and cognitive makeups expressed within different life contexts. The constraints and lack of control that are inherent in naturalistic settings continue to make the ruling out of both sources of internal invalidity, when employing single-subject time-series designs, and sources of external invalidity, when employing group designs, a difficult problem. Indeed, it was not until the early 1980s that the first volumes devoted to cognitive assessment appeared (Kendall & Hollon, 1981; Merluzzi, Glass, & Genest, 1981).

The substantial advances that have been made in experimental methodology in the past 20 years have enabled cognitive researchers to demonstrate the role of mediation in explaining (and modifying) human emotion and behavior. Such findings have been of increasing interest to practitioners. Moreover, the advent of applied research methodologies in general, and methodological behaviorism in particular, has enabled cognitively and semantically oriented practitioners to demonstrate empirically the utility of their respective approaches.

Contemporary Approaches

There are a number of distinct sources of influence that underlie cognitive restructuring. Primary among these is the work of Albert Ellis, a psychoanalytically trained therapist, who in the 1950s revolutionized the field of psychotherapy both by analyzing psychological maladjustment in terms of cognitive distortion and by advocating an action-oriented and educational-didactic method of therapy. Independently of Ellis's clinical work and theorizing, Aaron T. Beck, in the mid-1960s, formulated an approach to the treatment of depression that also emphasized the role of cognitive interpretation and faulty thinking patterns. As a consequence of these developments, of advances in other branches of cognitive psychology (information processing, Piaget), and of *self-control* as a concern of behavioral investigation (and with it an acceptance of reciprocal determinism), leading authorities in the behavior therapy movement began to acknowledge that humans do indeed mediate their environment (Bandura, 1969; Franks, 1969).

Since the late 1960s, many experimenters and clinicians—such as Albert Bandura, Joseph Cautela, Gerald Davison, Marvin Goldfried, Fred Kanfer, Alan Kazdin, Philip Kendall, Arnold Lazarus, Michael Mahoney, Donald Meichenbaum, Ray Navaco, George Spivack, and Myrna Shure, along with Ellis and Beck—have been developing the theoretical and practical school of cognitive-behavior therapy. They have been adapting, refining, and developing cognitively oriented strategies, techniques, and methods that are based on their own research and practice and that derive from a variety of sources, including earlier therapeutic practice and personality theory (Adler, 1927; Horney, 1942; Kelly, 1955; Mischel, 1973; Rotter, 1954); Soviet psychology (Luria, 1961; Vygotsky, 1962); research dealing with the roles of cognitive factors in classical and operant conditioning (e.g., awareness of reinforcement contingencies); empirical work that has found a relationship between emotional (psychological) arousal and cognitive factors (R. Lazarus, 1966; Schacter, 1966); and theories of cognitive psychology that emphasize cognitive activity and cognitive structuring as primary learning processes (Miller, Galanter, & Pribram, 1960).

The 1970s saw the appearance of procedural "how-to-do-it" texts and clincal manuals written by the proponents of different cognitive approaches. The dissemination of these works allowed "cognitively oriented" practitioners to begin to spell out and examine more carefully the effectiveness of various aspects of their approaches. Operational definitions of independent variables became more possible and with the refinement of methodological behaviorism, applied researchers began increasingly to document the clinical utility of RET and CBT. The marriage of cognitive practice and empirical accountability was formally consummated in 1977 with the first issue of a journal called *Cognitive Therapy and Research*. University and other professional training programs have increasingly incorporated the cognitive restructuring approach, and it would seem that the cognitive school is one of the most important in its field and will play a major role in the shaping of mental health practice in the 1980s and beyond.

Adult "Bias"

The greatest amount of cognitive theory, research, and practice has been directed at studying problems of older adolescent and adult populations. It has been only recently that the utility of cognitive approaches for both preventing and treating the problems of childhood have been fully realized. Indeed, practitioners are demonstrating increasingly how cognitive methods can be used with parents and teachers. Although there have been a few books, articles, chapters, and manuals that illustrate how a specific cognitive approach can be used preventatively as a part of an affective education or developmental counseling program (e.g., rational-emotive education—Knaus, 1974), how this approach can be applied to a specific problem (e.g., impulsivity—Kendall & Finch, 1976), or how cognitive procedures can be used with children (e.g., DiGiuseppe, 1981), adolescents (e.g., Bedrosian, 1981), parents (e.g., Hauck, 1967), and teachers (e.g., Forman & Forman, 1978), there has not been a work until this one (and Bernard & Joyce, 1984) that presents practical guidelines and techniques for illustrating how RET and allied cognitive-behavioral approaches are employed directly with children and youth to resolve a *variety* of childhood problems as well as indirectly with parents and teachers.

As we briefly indicate in a later section, there is increasing evidence that cognitive restructuring can be effectively employed to alleviate the emotional distress and enhance the behavioral functioning of school-age children. We believe that the chapters in this volume represent the collective and accumulated wisdom of a growing number of professionals who employ cognitive procedures with children of different ages. It is our wish and expectation that, with the appearance of this book, the clinical utility of the cognitive view of psychological adjustment and disturbance for younger populations will receive the empirical scrutiny (and validation) it deserves.

The Cognitive Perspective

Before discussing the practice of RET and CBT as it relates to younger populations, we would like to bring to light some conceptual distinctions within the field that will, it is hoped, illuminate subtle differences that exist across different cognitive approaches and that also make the specification of a unifying cognitive model of psychological (mal)adjustment a problem. A clarification of what the differences are between RET and CBT, how "cognition" and "beliefs" can be defined, and how treatment goals differ across cognitive approaches will, we hope, enable the material presented in this book to be more readily assimilated.

The RET and the CBT approach can be classified together in that each defines emotional disorders and behavioral maladjustment as well as therapeutic targets in terms of *cognitive-mediational dysfunctions.* Cognitive approaches can be differentiated, however, on the basis of (1) whether their focus is primarily on emotions or behavior and (2) whether dysfunctional cognition is viewed either in terms of an individual's inadequate, faulty, and, at times, excessive linguistic-conceptual (system which leads to a distorted view of the world) or in terms of the individual's failing to generate the mediators necessary for self-control and guidance of emotion and behavior.

Common Characteristics

We are in agreement with Mahoney and Arnkoff (1978) that "the 'cognitive perspective' continues to be a relatively diversified amalgam of principles and procedures that have yet to be formalized into a monolithic system or model" (p. 692). These authors list three fundamental assumptions that seem to underly the loose aggregate of cognitive approaches (p. 692):

1. Humans develop adaptive and maladaptive behavior and affective patterns through cognitive processes (selective attention, symbolic coding, etc.).
2. These cognitive *processes* can be functionally activated by procedures that are generally isomorphic with those of the human learning laboratory (although there may be other procedures which activate the cognitive processes as well).

3. The resultant task of the therapist is that of the diagnostician-educator who assesses maladaptive cognitive processes and subsequently arranges learning experiences that will alter cognitions and the behavior and affect patterns with which they correlate.

Although theoretical incompatibilities do exist across different cognitive approaches, it is nonetheless apparent that the methods marry quite nicely in practice.

Cognitive approaches attempt to assess and alter the cognitive activity of the client and while they may differ in terms of the goals of treatment and the cognition to be changed:

> The distinguishing feature of cognitive learning therapies is their simultaneous endorsement of the importance of cognitive *processes* and the functional promise of experimentally developed (and often behavioristic) *procedures*. (Mahoney & Arnkoff, 1978, p. 703)

RET versus CBT

Is the use of RET synonymous with the use of CBT when they are employed with children and adolescents? Not exactly, because, as has been shown in a paper, "Rational-Emotive Therapy and Cognitive Behavior Therapy: Similarities and Differences" (Ellis, 1980c), although general or nonpreferential RET is virtually synonymous with CBT, specific or preferential RET is not. Preferential RET is what RET practitioners usually prefer to use, particularly with relatively bright, neurotic, and reasonably well-motivated clients. It includes a deep philosophical emphasis, a humanistic outlook, the seeking of a profound and maintained personality change, the use of active disputing techniques, the teaching of clients how to give up *any* kind of rating of their egos or their selves (and, instead, only how to rate their acts and performances), and the getting at and eliminating of secondary as well as primary sources of anxiety and depression.

Although preferential RET is highly suitable for many bright adolescents, it may require too much philosophical analysis and more of an application of rigorous scientific method than many average youngsters, not to mention most younger children, are capable of fulfilling. In the case of younger children, nonpreferential RET, or general cognitive-behavior therapy, is usually employed. These clients are shown how they upset themselves with irrational and unrealistic beliefs; and they are sometimes taught how to actively dispute these beliefs, and to figure out more rational philosophies by which to run their lives. But as they often resist this kind of teaching, and especially the internalization of a thoroughgoing scientific way of thinking, they are frequently provided with rational or coping statements (as is explained in several of the succeeding chapters of this book) and are encouraged and reinforced for believing these more sensible beliefs.

CBT subsumes a variety of methods that attempt to modify cognitive content and processes that support problem behavior. The main difference between CBT and RET is that CBT does not attempt to modify the overall philosophy and assumptive world of clients through the use of disputational methods. It appears that CBT is more problem-focused (or behavior-focused) and defines goals of treatment in terms of specifiable behavior change. RET views problem behavior (and emotions) as symptomatic of an underlying belief system that constitutes the core of maladjustment. An elegant RET solution is conceived of as having been achieved when the client has adopted a more flexible, relativistic, and conditional outlook on life, which manifests itself in a more objective and empirically based reality-testing approach, in emotional reactions that are consistent with reality, and in self-enhancing, goal-directed behavior. An elegant CBT solution involves the client's acquiring cognitive and metacognitive strategies not only for dealing with a presenting problem, but also for dealing with a range of stressful situations that may confront the client in the future. These general and conceptually based strategies may involve the client's learning to think (and act) more reflectively and to adopt a more systematic problem-solving approach to life's difficulties.

Cognitive restructuring, in other words, has many forms, some of them abstruse and elegant and some of them much simpler and less elegant. When used with children and adolescents, less elegant specific problem-oriented methods are often employed instead of some of the more elegant methods of cognitive restructuring. But the basic goal of RET and CBT remains the same: helping youngsters with emotional and behavioral problems to internalize a *philosophy of life/cognitive strategy* that is more rational and realistic than the one they commonly abide by when they get into difficulties.

As emphasized in *Rational-Emotive Therapy and Cognitive Behavior Therapy* (Ellis, 1984), RET is not only a form of psychological treatment (or training) that is comprehensive and multimodal, and that is cognitive, emotive, and behavioral (and not *strictly* cognitive) in its methods, but it is also wedded to an interactional theory of human personality and personality disturbance. It emphasizes that humans, especially when they once acquire language and internalized speech, almost never experience *pure* thoughts, feelings, or actions. What we (somewhat arbitrarily) *call* their thinking, their emoting, and their behaving invariably seem to coalesce and interact, so that their ideations influence their feelings and behaviors, their emotions influence their thoughts and behaviors, and their behaviors influence their thoughts and feelings. Therefore, to help effect both moderate symptom removal and profound personality transformation, RET encourages the use of a wide variety of intellectual, affective, and activity-oriented techniques. And it assumes that although youngsters, because of their relatively immature stage of development, are especially influenceable by affective and behavioral interventions, they are also highly susceptible to didactic, persuasive, information-giving, and other cognitive appeals. Showing the reader how to understand and use children's and adolescents' intellectual susceptibility to change is one of the main—though hardly the only—purposes of the material in this book.

The Nature of "Cognition"

The term *cognition* can be defined in a variety of ways and at a number of levels, depending on the particular psychological theory from which it derives. The different conceptions of the term *cognition* vary in terms of how abstract they are and whether they refer to covert processes or content. Marzillier (1980) indicated three ways in which *cognition* is employed. *Cognitive events* refer to thoughts and images occurring in the individual's stream of consciousness. *Cognitive processes* include ways in which external stimuli are appraised and transformed. *Cognitive structure* is the most embracing of all applications of the term:

> These are constructs used to account for more general, long-standing cognitive characteristics such as beliefs and attitudes. Kovacs and Beck (1978, p. 526) have termed such structures "schemata," which they have described variously as "relatively enduring aspects of a person's cognitive organization," "organized representation of prior experience," and "systems for classifying stimuli." These structures form the rules and principles that regularize and govern an individual's interpretation of events and his behavior, and describe more fundamental and deep-seated cognitive aspects. A similar view of cognitive structure is provided by Meichenbaum (1977) who writes of that organizing aspect of thinking that seems to monitor and direct the strategy, route, and choice of thoughts (p. 213). (p. 252)

Another conception of cognition that we believe helps to clarify the role of cognition in human emotion and behavior is what has variously been referred to as *inner speech, self-talk, automatic thoughts, covert self-instructions, private thought, primal whispers*, etc.. (The idea of inner speech originates in part from Soviet research that deals with the "second signaling" properties of language.) Inner speech is speech for oneself. It has been described elsewhere as having an "idiosyncratic and semantic system which is really only intelligible to the individual (except when the person is getting ready to communicate to another or is rehearsing a speech). Inner speech may also vary in the degree to which the individual is aware of what it is she is saying to herself" (Bernard & Joyce, 1984).

Inner speech can be seen as serving two distinct and largely independent functions. When people are using their inner speech to think about, plan, and carry out a course of action, we can say that inner speech is serving an *instrumental and cognitive self-guiding function*. When people talk to themselves about how they are feeling about what they are planning and/or doing, have done, or will do, we designate inner speech as serving an affective function. The affective-instrumental distinction is important insofar as, although differing cognitive approaches tend to be geared to either emotional or behavioral change, clients do not make this distinction (see Bernard, 1981, for a detailed discussion of inner speech).

When the practitioner assesses the cognitions of a client, it is useful to have in mind not only the affective-instrumental distinctions that surround the function of inner speech, but also the level of generality at which the assessment will take place (e.g., covert stimuli, inner speech, or cognitive structures/beliefs), and whether the assessment is to be focused more on affective or instrumental cognitions. Such distinctions help organize the cognitive assessment component of problem analysis.

Defining "Beliefs"

In RET, the terms *belief* and *belief system* refer to that aspect of human cognition that is responsible for the mental health and the psychological well-being of the individual. Beliefs are a central explanatory construct of RET, and it is important that the meaning of the term be as clear as possible.

Ellis (e.g., 1977) has elaborated an ABC(DE) theory of emotional disturbance that describes how a person becomes upset. RET starts with an emotional and behavioral consequence (C) and seeks to identify the activating event (A) that appears to have precipitated (C). While the commonly accepted viewpoint is that (A) caused (C), RET steadfastly maintains that it is the individual's beliefs (B) about what happened at (A) that more directly "create" (C). Disputation (D), one of the cornerstones of the RET practice of therapeutic change, involves employing the scientific method of challenging and questioning antiempirical and untenable hypotheses, as well as imperative and absolutistic assumptions (irrational beliefs) that individuals may hold about themselves, about others, and about the world, which lead to the particular interpretations and appraisals that the individual forms about the activating event. When individuals who hold irrational beliefs begin to change their unsound assumptions, to reformulate them into more empirically valid statements, and to believe strongly in the validity of the new ideas, they wind up with new cognitive (philosophical), emotive, and behavioral effects (E's).

As a reading of the chapters in this book will illustrate, there is no consensus among RET theorists and therapists about the exact meaning of *beliefs*. That is to say, the term *belief* has been used to refer to various characteristics and aspects of the thinking activity that are seen to cause dysfunctional emotion and behavior. We now offer a contemporary formulation concerning the nature of beliefs (adapted from Bernard & Joyce, 1984).

Belief may be viewed as a very broad hypothetical construct that embraces at least three distinct subclasses of cognitive phenomena: (1) thoughts that an individual is thinking and is aware of at a given time about A; (2) thoughts about A that the individual is not immediately aware of; and (3) more abstract beliefs that the individual may hold in general (Bernard, 1981). Eschenroeder (1982) was in essential agreement with this analysis when he wrote that the ABC scheme is a simplification of the complex processes of the perception, interpretation, and evaluation of events and the activation of emotional reactions and behavioral responses:

> The B-element of the ABC refers to rather different phenomena: (1) *thoughts* and *images*, which can be observed through introspection by the individual; (2) *unconscious processes*, which can be inferred post hoc from the individual's feelings and behavior ("unconscious verbalizations"); (3) the *belief system* underlying the person's thoughts, emotions, and behaviors. (p. 275)

The more abstract beliefs that people hold are unspoken and constitute the assumptive framework by which they evaluate, appraise, and form conclusions about what they observe to be happening to themselves, to others, and in the world around them. These abstract beliefs are not expressed in the self-talk of people but can be considered relatively enduring personality traits that affect people's interpretations of reality and often, in so doing, guide subsequent behavior. They are inferred from the types of thought statements that clients are able to articulate both to themselves and to the practitioner as well as from their pattern of behavior. For example, people who strongly hold the belief that they desperately need others to depend and rely on tend to interpret situations in terms of whether they offer particular sorts of personal security and also search for environments and relationships that satisfy this self-perceived need.

Abstract beliefs can be differentiated on the basis of whether they reflect absolutistic and imperative qualities (irrational) or relativistic and conditional qualities (rational). Those beliefs that lead to self-defeating emotional and behavioral consequences are almost always expressed as unqualified should's, ought's, must's, command's, and demand's and are deemed "irrational." Ellis, who has referred to these beliefs as a form of "musturbatory thinking," has indicated that if people hold rigid views and beliefs about how they, others, and the world should or must be under all circumstances, then they are likely to experience some form of disturbance. Beliefs that are expressed not as commands but as preferences and that are viewed as conditional on and relative to a set of circumstances are defined as *rational* and lead to more adaptive levels of emotionality and appropriate behavior.

In terms of the ABC model, rational beliefs generally lead to moderate emotions that enable clients to achieve their future goals by facilitating constructive behavior, although rational beliefs may result in extreme levels of some emotions that are appropriate, such as extreme sadness and regret. Irrational beliefs lead to extremely stressful emotional consequences (intense anxiety, anger, or depression) and behavioral reactions (aggression or withdrawal), which make it quite difficult for the individual to improve the situation.

The main irrational beliefs that people tend to hold and that very frequently lead to dysfunctional emotional and behavioral consequences can be categorized under three major ones each with many derivatives (Ellis, 1980b):

1. I must do well and win approval for my performances, or else I rate as a rotten person.
2. Others must treat me considerately and kindly in precisely the way I want them to treat me; if they don't society and the universe should severely blame, damn, and punish them for their inconsiderateness.
3. Conditions under which I live must get arranged so that I get practically everything I want comfortably, quickly, and easily, and get virtually nothing that I don't want. (pp. 5–7)

RET stresses that there are three main forms of thinking that are "logical" derivatives of the basic irrational "must" that lead to psychological upset:

(1) *Awfulizing* ("It is awful, or terrible, or horrible that I am not doing as I must"); (2) *I can't stand-it-itis* ("I can't stand, can't bear the things that are happening to me that must not happen!"); (3) *Worthlessness* ("I am a worthless person if I don't do as well and win as much approval as I must") (Ellis, 1980b, p. 8).

Irrational beliefs sometimes have been described as dysfunctional thinking processes in which disturbances in cognitive operations result in illogical and distorted thoughts (see Sutton-Simon, 1981, for further discussion). We prefer to confine the meaning of *irrational beliefs* to absolutistic and imperative personal philosophies rather than to faulty information-processing and illogical reasoning (e.g., selective abstraction, overgeneralization, or arbitrary inference). Although the latter are of great importance in understanding and assessing disturbance, we do not believe that they have to be included within the rubric of *irrationality*.

Abstract beliefs are often an expression of the values of people and as such play an important role in explaining (to therapist and client alike) the basic goals and purposes of people's behavior. People come to value such things as love and approval from others and achievement, and it is the degree to which these goals are valued that will influence the behavior and the sense of well-being of people. Extreme valuations of, for example, security would be likely (but not always) to lead to needless unhappiness and therefore may constitute "irrationality."

Beliefs refer generally to our appraisals and evaluations of our interpretations of reality, rather than to the interpretations themselves. This distinction is a rather sticky one that generates some disagreement among RET theorists. The basic notion here is that RET chooses to designate only certain aspects of cognitive content that deal with how the individual interprets reality as beliefs. For example, consider Bill, who is sitting at home feeling depressed because his woman friend has not called when she was supposed to. Bill interprets the situation as follows: "She is not going to call, and if she doesn't, that will really show that she doesn't like me anymore." While these interpretations may be true or false, they are in and of themselves (even if they are true) insufficient to trigger Bill's extreme upsettedness. For Bill to become really upset, it would be necessary for him to appraise (make an affective judgment about) his interpretations. His belief that he needs (must have) Jane's love and his appraisal that he could not stand it (or himself) without it is irrational and leads to depression. One of RET's distinctive contributions to psychotherapy is the separation of interpretations of reality from appraisals and the systematic delineation of irrational beliefs that lead to emotional upset (for a further discussion of these distinctions, see Ellis, 1977, 1980a; Bard, 1980; Hauck, 1980; Walen, DiGuiseppe, & Wessler, 1980; Wessler & Wessler, 1980).

The term "assumption" within RET theory refers to both interpretations of reality that people make and that can be empirically tested as being true or false and to the appraisals and evaluations of those interpretations (beliefs) whose rationality and irrationality can be examined. The notion here is that what we assume to be true (what we think to ourselves) may refer to our interpretation or to our belief.

Irrational beliefs have been referred to by some RET theorists as antiempirical assumptions that people hold about themselves and the world around them.

These assumptions (strictly speaking, they are not beliefs) often serve as a basis for guiding behavior, and sometimes they may lead to self-defeating behavior without an accompanying emotional upset (a cognitive-behavior link). An example can be seen in the assumption held by some parents that severe and harsh punishment is the best way to correct a child's misbehavior. When a child does not comply with parental requests, he or she may be dealt with in a harsh way by the parents, who are not particularly upset, but who know of no other way to handle a situation. Such child-management approaches are frequently counterproductive, and it is one of the tasks of the RET practitioner to assess and correct antiempirical assumptions.

These differences in the meanings of beliefs will, we hope, help the reader more fully to distinguish and organize the different types of dysfunctional cognitions that the contributors to this volume believe cause undue emotional and behavioral problems of children and adolescents as well as their significant others (e.g., parents and teachers).

Goals of Treatment

Cognitive restructuring approaches strongly endorse the position that (1) emotional disturbance and behavioral maladjustment can be understood from an analysis of the *cognitive-mediational repertoire* of the individual and (2) emotional and behavioral change can be brought about by modification of the mediational competence of the individual. RET and CBT involve the utilization of a wide range of cognitive, emotive, and behavioral methods to bring about these changes.

The target of cognitive change depends on both the presenting problem and the preferred RET and CBT approach of the practitioner. A useful distinction to bear in mind is that certain cognitive procedures (e.g., RET, Beck's cognitive therapy, and stress inoculation) are used primarily to teach, modify, or replace dysfunctional *cognitive-emotive links*, whereas other cognitive approaches (self-instructional training [SIT], and interpersonal cognitive problem-solving) are directed more to establishing adaptive *cognitive-behavior links*. That is not to say that RET does not bring about behavioral changes. It is only that it generally does so via emotional change. Similarly, although SIT does not generally (except when employed for the specific purpose of anxiety, anger, or pain management) target emotional change, emotional change can be brought about indirectly and often at the same time as behavior changes.

As we indicated in our discussion of RET and CBT, the degree and type of change that is targeted for younger clients varies both within and across different cognitive approaches. The goals vary on a continuum of specific "problem-focused" change to general, pervasive, personality and cognitive change. When working with younger and less cognitively mature children, cognitive methods can be used on a short-term basis to bring about the removal of the specific problem.

The focus of treatment is obviously guided by whether a presenting problem is embedded in a relatively "stable" or "neurotic" personality. Although cognitive approaches are especially useful for providing "brief" counseling, they can also be employed to deal with more pervasive, enduring, and debilitating problems. That is, both RET and CBT can teach clients concrete and direct solutions for solving specific emotional and behavioral problems as well as providing clients with more general and conceptually based skills and strategies for solving both a wide range of difficulties that occur during treatment and novel ones that may arise in the future.

THE RET APPROACH TO CHILDREN AND ADOLESCENTS

It is interesting to note that although many behavior therapists (e.g., Craighead, 1982) appear to date the beginnings of the cognitive-behavioral movement around the late 1960s and the early 1970s, the application of cognitive methods in the form of RET to parenting and to the psychological treatment of youngsters was pioneered by Ellis in the mid-1950s. Soon after he started to use RET with adults, at the beginning of 1955, he saw that it could also be employed with children either directly by a therapist or indirectly by a RET practitioner working with the children's parents. He therefore included some cognitive parenting techniques in his first book on RET, *How to Live with a "Neurotic"* (Ellis, 1957). When he began making tape recordings of RET sessions, he recorded a series of sessions with an 8-year-old female bedwetter (Ellis, 1959), which were widely circulated and encouraged many other therapists to use RET methods with children. In the 1960s, cognitive restructuring with youngsters was promoted by a number of RET-oriented writers who showed how it could be effectively employed by therapists, parents, and school personnel (Doress, 1967; Ellis, 1967; Ellis, Wolfe, & Moseley, 1966; Glicken, 1967, 1968; Hauck, 1967; Lafferty, 1962; Lafferty, Dennell, & Rettich, 1964; McGory, 1967; Wagner, 1966).

By and large, the only cognitive restructuring approach being employed with school-age children through the late 1960s was RET. By the late 1960s, behavior therapists began to open their minds to cognition, and as a consequence, widely practiced and researched behavioral methods of helping youngsters overcome their emotional and behavioral problems began to be combined with RET and other cognitive methods.

It is in a sense surprising that the 1970s did not see more of a union of RET and other cognitive-behavioral approaches. Indeed, the development of RET and CBT as each applied to younger populations was relatively independent.

Recent reviews of cognitive-behavioral approaches for school-age children (e.g., Kendall, 1977; Urbain & Kendall, 1980; winter edition of the *School Psychology Review*, 1982) fail to credit RET with any significant contributions to the area.

During the 1970s, a large number of articles, chapters, and manuals appeared that explained the use of RET with children and adolescents (Bedford, 1974; Blanco & Rosenfeld, 1978; Brown, 1974, 1977, 1979; Daley, 1971; DiGiuseppe, 1975a,b; Edwards, 1977; Ellis, 1971a,b, 1972a, 1973a, 1975a,b, 1980b; Grieger, Anderson, & Canino, 1979; Hauck, 1974, 1977; Knaus, 1974, 1977; Knaus & McKeever, 1977; Kranzler, 1974; Maultsby, 1974, 1975; McMullin, Asafi, & Chapman, 1978; N. J. Miller, 1978; Muirden, 1976; Nardi, 1981; Protinsky, 1976; Rand, 1970; Rossi, 1977; Sachs, 1971; Shibles, 1978; Smith, 1979; Staggs, 1979; Tosi, 1974; Waters, 1980a,b, 1981; Young 1974a,b, 1977). Indeed, because of the observed success of RET that was found in early clinical and experimental investigations, the Institute for Rational-Emotive Therapy in New York started the Living School in 1970, a small private grade school where all the children were taught RET along with the usual elementary-school curriculum. The school flourished for five years, in the course of which it was found that teachers (not therapists) could teach young children RET in the regular classroom situation and thereby help them (and their parents) to improve their emotional health and to live more happily and efficiently. Publications on the use of RET in this school setting have been published by DiNubile and Wessler (1974), Ellis (1971a,b, 1972b, 1973b, 1975b), Gerald and Eyman (1981), Knaus (1974), Sachs (1971), and Wolfe (1970). In order to have a greater impact in classrooms both in the community and across the country, the Living School was transformed in 1975 into the Rational-Emotive Education Consultation Service, which provides (1) in-service workshops for teachers and counselors; (2) consultations to schools, classes, and teachers wishing to implement a program of RET; and (3) materials and techniques for use in classrooms and/or school counseling settings (Waters, 1981).

During the past 15 years, a large number of case studies and quasi-experimental and experimental outcome studies have appeared in the RET literature (Agosto & Solomon, 1978; Albert, 1972; Bernard, 1979;

Block, 1978; Boker, 1972; Brody, 1974; Cangelosi, Gressard, & Mines, 1980; Costello & Dougherty, 1977; D'Angelo, 1977; DeVoge, 1974; DiGiuseppe, 1975a; DiGiuseppe & Kassinove, 1976; Harris, 1976; Jacobs, 1977; Katz, 1974; Knaus & Boker, 1975; Kujoth, 1976; Maes & Heinman, 1970; Maultsby, Knipping, & Carpenter, 1974; Miller, 1978; Patton, 1978; Ritchie, 1978; Sharma, 1970; Solomon, 1978; Sydel, 1972; Taylor, 1975; Wagner, 1966; Warren, Deffenbach, & Broding, 1976; Zelie, Stone, & Lehr, 1980). A review of many of these studies by DiGiuseppe, Miller, and Trexler (1979) led to the following conclusion:

> The studies described in this section provide support for the hypothesis that elementary school children are capable of acquiring knowledge of rational-emotive principles and that the modification of a child's self-verbalizations or irrational self-statements can have a positive effect on emotional adjustment and behavior. Certain critical factors relevant to rational-emotive therapy procedures have not been thoroughly investigated. These include the specification of the relative contributions of the behavioral components within rational-emotive therapy (i.e., behavioral rehearsal and written homework assignments) and the degree to which a child's intellectual ability is related to his acquisition of the cognitively oriented principles of rational-emotive therapy. (p. 225)

With the spiraling growth of RET during the past few years (four major books on RET were published in 1980 alone), research interest and methodological sophistication in the RET area are also on the increase. It is obvious that much instrumentation that is required to measure the full range of attitudinal and emotive changes brought about by RET interventions is not yet available. It is hoped that, with advances in experimental methodology and with more research-trained practitioners entering the field, the utility of RET with younger populations—which RET therapists and counselors have known for many years to exist—will be documented.

As this volume and other recent works (Bernard & Joyce, 1984; DiGiuseppe, 1981; Grieger & Boyd, 1982; Waters, 1982a,b) attest, the practice of RET has evolved over the years into a sophisticated and functional counseling and therapeutic approach to the problems of childhood. Indeed, it will be seen that a RET model of child treatment has arrived and offers distinctive contributions to the field. Here, we briefly touch on the defining characteristics of the RET model. A more thorough analysis is presented in Bernard and Joyce (1984), and the deployment of the model is described in the chapters of this book.

The RET Perspective on Childhood Maladjustment

A principle that is beginning to be emphasized within the RET perspective toward maladjustment is *interactionism.* Some RET practitioners believe that emotional disorders and abnormal behavior in childhood can be best understood in terms of an interaction between "person" and environmental variables. Bernard and Joyce (1984) characterized this perspective as follows:

> People demonstrate characteristic ways of thinking about and relating to their environment which exert an influence on their environment. Similarly, situations themselves modify the behavior and attitudes of people by both providing (or not providing) appropriate learning experiences and enrichment opportunities as well as rewarding and punishing consequences for behavior within certain contexts. We believe that there is an almost inexorable reciprocal relationship between abnormal behavior and a deviant environment such that abnormalities in either the person or the environment of the person tend to bring out abnormalities in the other. It would seem, therefore, necessary to determine how persons and environments interact and covary together in analyzing psychopathology.

RET has also recognized the importance of cognitive-developmental factors in the treatment of children. On the assessment side, a recognition of child development enables the practitioner to judge whether a presenting problem is a transient and/or a normal developmental phenomenon (i.e., fear of the dark) or whether it represents something more serious. The level at which the RET intervention is used (rational self-statements, irrational concepts, or irrational beliefs) depends on the linguistic and cognitive maturity of the young client.

RET views a young client's presenting problem in the context of three major dimensions that potentially contribute to childhood maladjustment: *cognitive-affective developmental status, psychological conditions,* and *environmental conditions* (Bernard & Joyce, 1984). This contextual perspective enables the RET practitioner to determine the degree of severity of the problems, who owns the problems, and what factors seem to be maintaining the problems.

Cognitive-Affective Developmental Status

RET recognizes, as do the proponents of many different approaches to childhood psychopathology that there is a reciprocal relationship between mental and emotional development. When children are very young, the quality of their subjective emotional experience is very much limited by their capacity to think about and understand the meaning of experience. The cognitive limitations of the early childhood period can often result in children's acquiring beliefs about themselves and their surrounding world that are untrue and irrational and that, if not corrected, can have an extremely deleterious effect on their future well-being. That is, children construct their own theories and arrive at their own conclusions based on inferences from what they have observed.

The child's conception of the world is idiosyncratically organized and derives from the child's limited capacity to make observations and draw logical conclusions.

In working with children, we are struck by the pervasive influence that their ideas and beliefs have on their behavior. These beliefs are often implicit and frequently result from the child's having formed a conclusion based on limited evidence and having used the conclusion as an "unquestioned" rule for guiding subsequent behavior. The beliefs, be they rational or irrational, that are formed early in life may become firmly fixed, and they represent part of the phenomenological framework of children that provides the basis for self-evaluation, for the demands they place on others, and for the interpretation they make of the behavior of others. Children's capacity for rational and logical thought limits the types of ideas that they acquire and frequently reinforces a variety of irrational beliefs which take many years to overcome.

A cognitive analysis of maladjustment in adolescents frequently reveals beliefs about themselves, others, and the world, as well as logical reasoning processes, that appear to be either a holdover from or a regression to more immature levels of thinking and primitive belief systems. Moreover, the advent of formal operational thought capacities in adolescents also brings with it its own problems. Adolescents in their early teens begin to experience a form of egocentrism, a "naive idealism" (not dissimilar in effect from the egocentrism of the early childhood period), that frequently leads to a variety of emotional and behavioral problems. The struggle for a personal identity and for new definitions of social relationships that accompanies the increased capacity for reflective and abstract thought often results in adolescents' acquiring sets of beliefs concerning themselves (self-rating) and others (demandingness) that accompany some people throughout life.

RET practitioners are beginning to rely more heavily on Piaget's theory of intelligence and stage-related levels of cognitive development not only for understanding the characteristics of thought and emotion across the childhood period, but also for adapting RET methods to the developmental level of the child. Indeed, there are a number of interesting overlaps between the theories of Ellis and those of Piaget. Both share the assumption of *constructivism*. They also place great "faith" in the scientific method of investigation and the power of formal logical reasoning. Both appear to be in agreement concerning the importance of cognition in the experience and expression of emotions. Piaget (1952) wrote that "it is, in fact, only a romantic prejudice that makes us suppose that affective phenomena constitute immediate givens or innate and ready-made feelings similar to Rousseau's 'conscience'" (p. 12).

We shall not review Piaget's four-stage conceptual model, which describes the general cognitive organizational structure that regulates the child's conception of the world. Piaget's theory and its implication for RET practice have been discussed elsewhere (Bernard & Joyce, 1984). There are relationships between a child's level of cognitive development, as defined by Piaget's stages, and RET therapeutic methods. Whereas we employ rational self-statements with children of all ages, we generally do not cognitively dispute irrational concepts with children who are less than 7 years old, and we do not often dispute irrational beliefs with children much below the age of 11 or 12.

Psychological Conditions

Internal personality and cognitive variables that exert a direct and contemporaneous influence on emotion and behavior can be considered psychological conditions. Although they may vary in the degree to which they are removed from observable data, they are considered conditions that serve as the basis for mediation and self-control. As such, they are in principle capable of being modified and are seen as having a controlling influence. An analysis of psychological conditions involves determining those conditions within the organism that are related to the manifestation of maladjustment.

Whereas the cognitive-affective developmental status of children and adolescents characterizes the types of thinking and emotional experience they are capable of, psychological conditions are the type of mental operations that are actually employed or brought to bear by them in problem situations. These conditions are seen as developing in complexity over time as a function of the progressive development and differentiation of psychological functioning.

It is possible to enumerate a variety of psychological concepts that influence emotions and behaviors. Those that are of most interest to RET are those that are defined cognitively and that have a direct link to emotions and behavior. It would appear that there are at least five reasonably distinct psychological conditions that provide some understanding of the dysfunctional cognitive activity of the young person (from Bernard & Joyce, 1984):

1. The term *attention processes* refers to children's patterns of selective attention to certain aspects of both their external and their internal worlds (Mahoney, 1974).

2. *Mediational processes*, which are frequently but not always verbal, range from the store of concepts that the child has available for representing and understanding experience (Klausmeier, Ghatala, & Frayer,

1974) to those processes that aid basic learning, such as attention and memory (Kendler & Kendler, 1959). The covert verbalizations (Vygotsky, 1962) and images (A. Lazarus, 1972) of children, that play an important role in controlling affective and instrumental responses, can also be subsumed in this category.

3. *Logical-reasoning processes* are the manner in which children interpret and draw generalizations and conclusions from personal observation, as well as the way in which they employ premises, assumptions, and beliefs deductively to arrive at conclusions (Beck, Rush, Shaw, & Emery, 1979).

4. *Beliefs* are the understandings and assumptions that children hold about themselves and about the world around them. There appear to us to be at least two different types of beliefs that children evolve: (a) beliefs concerning their individual desires, how others and themselves "should" behave, the manner in which they characterize the qualities of events and experience (e.g., "awfulize"), and the rules that they apply and the conclusions that they draw in judging the worth of themselves and others (Ellis & Grieger, 1977); and (b) beliefs that children hold concerning the extent to which they view themselves as being the cause of the events that occur in their lives (internal locus of control) or whether they consider outside environmental factors responsible for their successes and misfortunes (external locus of control) (Seligman, 1975).

5. *Cognitive strategies* are broad constructs dealing with the capacity of children to generate plans and solutions to novel problems (Gagné, 1977) and can be seen, for example, in the variety of ways in which they employ the scientific method of problem solving (D'Zurilla & Goldfried, 1971) for dealing with impersonal and interpersonal problems (Spivack & Shure, 1974).

We believe that these five psychological conditions are broad enough to enable us to conceptualize different aspects of childhood maladjustment from a cognitive viewpoint. The clinical and incremental utility of these conditions in practice has yet to be systematically assessed.

Environmental Conditions

This third dimension refers to those aspects of the immediate environment of children that provide stimulation, enrichment, and reinforcement. Stimulation of different kinds and intensities is seen as facilitating the cognitive-affective development of children:

> The environment of the child not only creates the conditions for normal cognitive-affective development, it also provides the basis for the child learning situation-specific adaptive behavior as well as acquiring mediational con-

trol of emotions. An examination of *antecedent stimuli* and *reinforcing consequences* which surround children's emotional and behavioral reactions provides extensive insights as to the role the environment plays in either creating or maintaining maladjustment. Antecedent stimuli can be analyzed to determine why they are not occasioning adaptive behavior as can the density, quality, and consistency of the rewards and punishments which operate. (Bernard & Joyce, 1984)

The delimitation of the importance of environmental conditions in childhood disorders is obviously not a distinctive contribution of RET. We would hope that any practitioner working with younger populations has a thorough grasp of behavioral principles. The distinctive contribution of proponents of RET in describing environmental conditions has been their description of the styles of parenting and child management that may have a deleterious influence on children. It is our view that irrational parental beliefs often create inappropriate levels of emotionality that manifests themselves in maladaptive parent–child interaction.

It appears that parents as role models and reinforcing-punishing agents play a major part in preventing, minimizing, or exacerbating emotional and behavioral problems in their children. This is not to say that poor parenting is the only cause of psychological maladjustment in children. We frequently see children experiencing emotional strife who have parents who appear to be reasonably well adjusted, who have positive attitudes toward their child, and whose child-rearing practices appear to be sound. And we do not receive referrals for well-adjusted children whose parents, because of their problems, one would back at long odds to produce disturbed offspring. There appear to be temperamentally difficult children who, as a result of their frustrating behavior, literally create conditions that drive their parents to distraction. We agree with Bard's (1980) comments:

> Some children seem especially prone to make themselves miserable about their parent's relatively minor imperfections. I emphasize this point at the onset to attack the myth that parents are always to blame and to alert practitioners to the fact that parent-child problems may be extremely complex. (p. 93)

Ellis (1962) has consistently maintained that the worst thing that parents can do to their children is to blame them for their mistake making and wrongdoing. Such blaming encourages children to continue to blame themselves and inevitably leads to chronic feelings of anxiety, guilt, and low self-esteem for some children and hostility and bigotry in others. Ellis (1973c) wrote:

> Parents or other early teachers usually help a child plummet down the toboggan slide toward disturbed feelings and behavior by doing two things when

> he does something that displeases them: (a) they tell him that he is wrong for acting in this displeasing manner; and (b) they strongly indicate to him that he is a worthless individual for being wrong, and that he therefore deserves to be severely punished for his wrongdoing. . . . For if they were really sensible about bringing up their children, they would obviously show their child that: (a) she is wrong when she engages in activities that displease them and other members of their social group, and that (b) she is still a highly worthwhile individual who will merely, if she wants to get along well in the community, eventually have to discipline herself and learn to be less wrong in the future. (pp. 239–240)

Paul Hauck (1967, 1977) is an RET practitioner who has written extensively regarding irrational beliefs that underlie ineffective parenting. As is demonstrated in the chapters of this book, RET practitioners have followed his lead in identifying a number of erroneous parental beliefs concerning child management that are irrational not only because they are inaccurate and empirically unsupportable, but also because they lead to destructive emotions and self-defeating behavior in themselves as well as their children.

Irrational beliefs of parents can influence their behavior in two basic ways. One is through their emotions.

> Parents frequently get very upset when their child breaks a rule because they believe that: (a) "My child must be good all the time"; (b) "I find it awful or horrible when my child is not—I can't stand it," and (c) "My child deserves punishment because he has made me so angry and for being such a bad child." The belief that children must never break a rule leads to extreme anger which produces intense and non-constructive disciplinary action. (Bernard & Joyce, 1984)

Alternatively, parents may employ inappropriate and counterproductive methods of child management because of ignorance. That is, they believe that what they are doing is the correct thing to do, and often, it is the only way that they can conceptualize relating to their children. Their maladaptive behavior is not associated with extreme emotional arousal but motivated directly by their "unjustified" and "outdated" assumptions. Bernard and Joyce (1984) have noted:

> We have worked with several fathers who would administer physical consequences to their children whenever they caught them misbehaving. At these times, they were not particularly angry though they may have felt mildly irritated. These fathers held the simple belief that "children who break rules need to be punished severely to learn a lesson" and employed this rule as a basis for knowing what to do in problematic situations.

Irrational beliefs of parents can, therefore, lead directly to behavior without the intervention of significant emotional arousal. The practitioner can help objectively to dispute the rationality and adaptiveness of these beliefs without considering the emotional involvement. This is not to say, of course, that there are not more pervasive, absolutistic beliefs underlying these parenting beliefs that do occasion high degrees of emotionality, such as, "To be a perfect parent and a worthwhile person, my child must be totally obedient at all times." Both types of influences had better be considered in understanding the role of parental beliefs.

Different RET practitioners are becoming increasingly cognizant of these three dimensions of childhood adjustment in their work with children. Assessing the current personality and cognitive makeup of the child in the context of her or his developmental status as well as her or his family circumstances is recognized as sound RET practice.

Principles of Assessment

RET assessment can be seen as being composed of a *problem identification* and a *problem analysis* phase. Problem identification involves determining whether, in fact, a problem exists and, if it does, who owns it. Children and adolescents are frequently referred to a practitioner by their parents (or teachers). The initial task of the practitioner is to determine whether the youngster, the parents, and/or the teachers are actually demonstrating an emotional or a behavioral problem. During problem identification, it is important for the practitioner to be aware of developmental, peer, and cultural-familial norms in the area of concern. It is quite common for the problem to be shared by both a child and his or her significant others.

Once it has been established that a problem does exist and the problem ownership has been determined, the problem analysis phase of RET assessment takes place. The practitioner may interview the children, the parents, and the teachers to determine the extent of their respective cognitive, emotive, and behavioral dysfunction.

A distinctive aspect of RET assessment is the separation of emotional from practical (behavioral) problems. Waters (1982b) differentiates among these types of problems as follows:

> Emotional problems are generated by self and goal defeating belief systems, and are characterized by extremely uncomfortable, stagnated feelings, while practical problems are realistic difficulties in the environment resulting in unsatisfactory situations, which one wishes to change. . . . When one is in the midst of an emotional problem, it is analogous to creating a dense fog which obscures one's view of the practical problem, and also renders any logical or reasonable thinking about the problem virtually impossible. In order to clear up the emotional fog so that practical problem-solving can proceed, it is necessary to identify the beliefs generating the fog and replace them with more rational beliefs. Practical problem solving is best attempted when emotions are appropriate to the situation. (p. 233)

Typical emotional problems include inappropriately high levels of anger, anxiety, or depression (self-downing), which are generated by irrational beliefs and which lead to extreme reactions that prevent goal attainment. Practical problems are revealed in either aggressive or avoidant behavior and stem from the youngster's not knowing how to behave appropriately in a situation (i.e., being teased). Emotional problems often precede practical problems, although children may upset themselves emotionally about their practical problems.

In assessing dysfunctional cognitions in both children and their parents and teachers, interpretations of reality as well as appraisals of interpretations are examined. Waters (1982b) suggested four main problem areas to assess:

1. Is the client distorting reality?
2. Is the client evaluating situations in a self-defeating way?
3. Does the client lack appropriate cognitions?
4. Does the client lack practical problem-solving skills?

The chapters that follow reveal a variety of elicitational techniques that child-oriented RET practitioners have developed to assess problem cognitions, emotions, and behavior of children as young as 4 years old (for a comprehensive review, see Bernard & Joyce, 1984). Problem identification and analysis result in a specification and ordering of the goals of therapy; of the types of cognitive, emotive, and behavioral changes to be made; and of who will participate in therapy (one or both parents, child, parents and child) (Waters, 1982b).

TREATMENT GOALS AND METHODS

RET is primarily oriented to teaching skills for the solving of emotional problems. Its aim is to have clients of all ages acquire an attitude of emotional responsibility, that is, to take control of their feelings through the operation of rational thinking and problem-solving skills. The main goal of emotional problem solving is to teach children and adolescents how to change inappropriate to appropriate feelings.

RET accomplishes this goal for younger children by helping them to become more aware of their emotions and thoughts and to develop a conceptual-linguistic system for expressing their emotions. They are taught to differentiate between feelings and thoughts and are given practice in verbalizing sets of rational self-statements. Older children and adolescents are taught the ABC's of RET and the difference between rational and irrational beliefs, as well as how to dispute irrational concepts and beliefs. In addition, the practitioner helps young clients to correct their perceptions of reality.

There are a myriad of cognitive, emotive, and behavioral methods that RET practitioners employ to help youngsters overcome their emotional difficulties. The most popular and the newest of these are illustrated in this book. With an eye on the cognitive-linguistic maturity of the young client, Waters (1982b) has made the following suggestions for working with young clients who have emotional problems.

1. Determine whether the client wishes to keep or give up the feeling and point out the consequences of each.
2. Have the client keep track of the frequency, location, and outcome of emotional reactions.
3. Challenge and dispute irrational beliefs, concepts, and self-statements and generate rational alternatives.
4. Discuss RET concepts of self-acceptance, demandingness, approval-seeking, catastrophizing, intolerance, and condemnation.
5. Use rational-emotive imagery to practice changing the feeling.
6. Encourage client to focus on the present and avoid focusing on the past or future.
7. Encourage client to answer the question: "Where does this negative thought get me?"
8. Brainstorm with the client about other options in handling feelings.
9. Encourage client to observe how others handle their emotions.
10. Encourage client to reward herself or himself for handling problem emotions.
11. Teach relaxation, assertion, and prosocial skills. (pp. 242–245)

In tackling practical and behavioral problems, RET employs other cognitive-behavioral approaches that are geared to helping the young client come up with ways of improving the situation (interpersonal cognitive problem solving—Spivack & Shure, 1974; self-instructional training—Meichenbaum, 1974).

RET is deemed successful when the client is successful in solving emotional and practical problems. Younger clients can be expected to solve independently a more limited range of problems than older and more capable clients. The degree of emotional responsibility that a young client is able to assume is also bound by cognitive-affective developmental limitations.

Allied Cognitive-Behavioral Approaches

In working with both the emotional and the behavioral problems of childhood, the practitioner often combines several other important cognitive-behavioral approaches with RET. In the main, they are designed to restructure cognitive processes and cognitive content in an effort to reduce the stress that is often associated with interpersonal difficulty.

SELF-INSTRUCTIONAL TRAINING

The approach that has become almost synonymous with cognitive-behavior modification (e.g., Meichenbaum & Asarnow, 1979) has been referred to as *verbal self-instruction* or *self-instructional training* (SIT). SIT is an educational procedure designed to teach clients both cognitive and behavioral skills for solving problems. Its application is based on a thorough cognitive-behavioral analysis of a task or situation that a client has not effectively dealt with and that may or may not be a source of unhappiness. There are two basic components of SIT. First, the practitioner analyzes behaviorally the performance skills that the client needs in order to demonstrate mastery of a task or a situation. Second, a cognitive-functional analysis is performed, which involves an inventory of the client's thinking (strategies, skills, and inner speech) as it relates to task performance and which seeks to answer the question: "In what psychological processes is the successfully achieving individual to engage, and in which of these is my subject failing?" (Meichenbaum, 1977). Once the task-appropriate mediators and performance skills are linked together and sequenced from simple to complex, the task of the practitioner is to instruct the client in how to employ the cognitive-behavior skills in relevant contexts.

SIT is most widely recognized for its training approach. It is based largely on the theorizing and research of the Soviet psychologists Vygotsky (1962) and Luria (1961), who have indicated that the self-control of behavior is developed from the gradual internalization of language and speech. From this perspective, external speech is seen as serving the social function of communication, whereas inner speech functions to regulate and guide human behavior. A three-stage model is proposed to describe an age-related developmental process in which (1) the child's behavior is initially guided by adult instructions; (2) the child begins to control his or her own behavior through overt self-repetitions of adult instructions, and (3) the child's external speech goes underground into inner speech and assumes the function of self-control and self-guidance. Using this model as a training guide, the SIT practitioner combines modeling, overt and covert rehearsal, prompts, feedback, and social reinforcement. The general outline for conducting think-aloud training programs for the teaching of performance-relevant skills is as follows:

(a) problem identification and definition of self-interrogation skills ("What is it I have to do?"); (b) focusing attention and response guidance, which is usually the answer to the self-inquiry ("Now carefully stop and repeat the instructions"); (c) self-reinforcement involving standard-setting and self-evaluation ("Good, I'm doing fine."); and (d) coping skills and error-correcting options ("That's okay. . . . Even if I make an error I can go slowly."). (Meichenbaum & Asarnow, 1979, p. 13)

SIT has been widely applied with school-age children. The training procedure is specifically designed to take into account and to specifically remediate the three major types of verbal mediation deficits that the child development literature has brought to light (Meichenbaum, 1977): (1) comprehension—understanding the nature of the problem, and therefore what mediators are required; (2) production—not only having the appropriate mediators in the repertoire, but producing them when needed; and (3) mediation—guidng one's behavior by means of the mediating process.

Initially developed to teach hyperactive, aggressive, and impulsive children to think reflectively (to "stop, look, and listen"), SIT is now being increasingly applied to academic tasks. SIT makes it possible "for students to do a kind of thinking they could not, or would not, otherwise do" (Meichenbaum & Asarnow, 1979, p. 18). In seeking to promote the wider use of reflective self-control thinking skills in children, Kendall and Finch (1979) have proposed that children can be taught a more "conceptual" set of self-instructions that can be applied both to a specific training task and to other tasks and in other situations. This strategy represents an effort to obtain a more general and elegant solution.

Recently, Bernard, Kratochwill, and Keefauver (in press) illustrated how RET and SIT can be combined effectively in the treatment of chronic hair-pulling in a 17-year-old girl. The initial therapy sessions made extensive use of disputational techniques in order to deal with the client's obsessional anxieties. SIT, which was introduced during the middle treatment sessions, consisted of the therapist modeling a problem-solving dialogue that the client progressively internalized. An example of the SIT dialogue that the client was to employ while she was doing her homework was as follows: (1) *problem definition:* "What am I supposed to do?"; (2) *problem approach:* "I'd better pay attention to my assignment. What is the next thing I have to do?"; (3) *coping statements:* "Oh, I'm starting to get worried about school . . . and I just pulled out a hair. I know if I just relax and focus on my work that I won't worry"; and (4) *self-reinforcement:* "Hey, that's great. I finished that bit of work. I didn't worry. And I didn't pull my hair. You knew you could do it." Reviews of SIT research (Hobbs, Moguin, Tyroler, & Lahey, 1980; Urbain & Kendall, 1980) indicate that SIT holds great promise for helping to change dysfunctional thinking-behavioral patterns in younger populations.

STRESS INOCULATION TRAINING

Although stress inoculation has been employed primarily in the treatment of adult disorders, its potential use with younger populations is becoming increasingly recognized (e.g., Cormier & Cormier, 1979). The stress inoculation approach was formulated by Meichenbaum and Cameron (1973) and has been used to help people cope with anxiety (Meichenbaum & Cameron, 1973), anger (Novaco, 1978), and pain (Turk, 1976). Thus, it can be conceived of as an approach to solving emotional problems rather than practical problems. It shares with RET the assumption that a person's thoughts and beliefs can lead to emotional difficulties and, as a consequence, behavioral problems. Additionally, stress inoculation attempts to alter emotional consequences through the altering of the client's cognitions.

The name *stress inoculation* draws on concepts borrowed from engineering and medicine. As inoculation against disease (by means of controlled exposure) provides the person with greater resistance and a "built-in" means of coping when exposed to the disease, so stress inoculation is thought to enable the person to deal with situations and events that previously prompted incapacitating emotional reactions (e.g., anxiety and anger). *Stress*, in the psychological context, is perceived as analogous to the condition of strain on a physical structure, as studied in engineering. Novaco (1978) made the useful distinction between

> *stressors* as aversive events that exert demands for adaptation, *stress* as a hypothetical state denoting a condition of imbalance between demands and responses for coping, and *stress reactions* as the adverse health and behavioral consequences of exposure to environmental demands. (p. 137)

Stress inoculation training, which involves several phases, is often taught via the self-instruction training method and frequently includes a behavioral component of relaxation training. First, the *educational phase* is designed to enable the client to understand his or her emotional reactions, to establish a language of communication between therapist and client, and to facilitate agreement about the planned therapy. Diaries or logs are often used in this phase to enable the client and the therapist to become aware of specific emotional reaction patterns. These logs may form the basis for later self-monitoring and therapy evaluation.

What follows is *"rehearsal"* or *"skill acquisition" phase*, in which coping skills specific to the client's problem are practiced. An example of a set of stress-reducing self-instructions for the regulation of anger, as provided in Novaco (1979), illustrates the sequence of stages in which the skill acquisition phase is introduced:

1. *Preparing for a provocation*
   "This could be a rough situation, but I know how to deal with it. I can work out a plan to handle this. Easy does it. Remember, stick to the issues and don't take it personally. There won't be any need for an argument. I know what to do."
2. *Impact and confrontation*
   "As long as I keep my cool, I'm in control of the situation. You don't need to prove yourself. Don't make more out of this than you have to. There is no point in getting mad. Think of what you have to do. Look for positives and don't jump to conclusions."
3. *Coping with arousal*
   "My muscles are getting tight. Relax and slow things down. Time to take a deep breath. Let's take the issue point by point. My anger is a signal of what I need to do. Time for problem solving. He probably wants me to get angry, but I'm going to deal with it constructively."
4. *Subsequent reflection*
   Conflict unresolved: "Forget about the aggravation. Thinking about it only makes you upset. Try to shake it off. Don't let it interfere with your job. Remember relaxation. It's a lot better than anger. Don't take it personally. It's probably not so serious."
   Conflict resolved: "I handled that one pretty well. That's doing a good job. I could have gotten more upset that it was worth. My pride can get me into trouble, but I'm doing better at this all the time. I actually got through that without getting angry." (p. 269)

The third phase, *application training*, provides practice in the exercise of newly acquired coping skills, in role rehearsal with the therapist, or in artificially induced stress situations.

When stress inoculation is being used within an RET framework, both the cognitive preparation phase and the rehearsal phase contain strong RET elements (e.g., understanding one's own role in triggering the maladaptive emotions by irrational self-statements; exploring the beliefs underlying the self-statements; generating new rational self-statements; and affirming one's ability to cope).

Interpersonal Cognitive-Problem Solving

An extremely popular and influential cognitive-behavioral approach that has been developed specifically for children and adolescents who have problems in social relationships is interpersonal cognitive-problem solving (ICPS) (e.g., Spivack & Shure, 1974; Spivack, Platt, & Shure, 1976), which has been developed at the Hahnemann Medical

College and Hospital in Philadelphia, Pennsylvania. Spivack and Shure (1974) define their approach in this way:

> The philosophy implicit in the program is that if one wishes to affect the behavior of people one must affect the specific (cognitive) abilities that mediate the behavior in question. The search has been, and still is, to discover the mediating cognitions intimately affecting social adjustment. (p. 131)

In their clinical work and research with younger populations, Spivack and his colleagues have identified a number of cognitive skills or types of thinking that are thought to mediate social behavior:

1. *Sensitivity or perspective taking* is the awareness that there are difficulties or "problems" in human interactions and that other people may have different thoughts and feelings from one's own.
2. *Alternative thinking* is the generation of a variety of possible ways of dealing with a problem situation. By implication, the greater the number of possible alternative solutions a person can evolve, the more likely he or she is to come up with the best possible solution.
3. *Means–ends thinking* is the conceptualization of the step-by-step means needed to reach a specific objective. Knowing a solution is of little help if one cannot devise the way to reach it.
4. *Consequential thinking* involves the "thinking through" of the likely consequences of each alternative. An alternative that may initially look promising may, on reflection, turn out to have undesirable or have uncertain consequences if carried out.
5. *Causal thinking* is the spontaneous linking of cause and effect. Awareness of the connections between events and emotional states may be a prelude to identifying elements of the problem situation and generating solutions.

These cognitive processes are not thought of as personality traits or facets of general intelligence (as measured by an IQ score) but as skills that emerge at different developmental ages and are often acquired as a result of modeling by parents and other adults in real problem situations. Spivack and his colleagues have researched the relationship between ICPS skills and general intelligence measures and claim to have demonstrated a relationship between ICPS and social adjustment that is not accounted for by general intelligence.

ICPS is used to help children and adolescents to think before they act. In a counseling-therapy context, it teaches young clients the importance of exploring alternatives for handling difficult situations, of thinking how they will go about realizing desired goals, and, equally important, of exploring the positive and negative consequences of alternatives before selecting one. In younger children (4- and 5-year-olds), alternative and consequential thinking is generally illustrated concretely; that is, the practitioner helps the child to solve a particular problem. Children in the 6- to 12-year-old age group can be taught to apply alternative and consequential thinking skills across situations, as well as how to generate step-by-step plans to reach solutions to problems (means–ends thinking). With adolescents, the practitioner is able to combine work on alternative, consequential, and means–ends thinking skills with an emphasis on increasing the ability of adolescents to understand the thoughts and feelings of other individuals in the problem situation (perspective taking).

While ICPS emphasizes the resolving of practical and behavioral problems, the ICPS skills acquired may both lead to the reduction of emotional stress and facilitate the effectiveness of RET. On the one hand, when a young client learns to overcome an interpersonal obstacle, the emotions that had previously surrounded the source of frustration abate. A more reflective problem-solving approach to life enables children to deal more effectively with situations at home and at school that had previously led (via cognition) to emotional upset. On the other hand, ICPS skills may facilitate the process of therapeutic change. For example, exercises in alternative thinking may expedite the giving up of established maladaptive thinking habits. Or to take another example, as causal thinking appears to play a role in identifying one's irrational beliefs, training in causal thinking may aid in the process of disputation.

ATTRIBUTIONAL RETRAINING

As we have indicated in our discussion of the psychological conditions that influence childhood adjustment, the explanation that children "construct" and believe concerning the causes of events in their lives may play a strong role in determining their adaptive behavior and emotional well-being. Statements such as "It was my lucky day" and "My teacher must have favored me" reflect attributional beliefs about why a child received a good grade on a test that are different from statements such as "I got to the top because I worked extra hard" or "This is my special field—I'm good at maths." Individual differences in attributional beliefs have been the target of the theoretical and research interests of workers in several different fields. Personality theorists (Weiner, 1974), social learning psychologists (Rotter, 1966), and cognitive theorists (Dweck, 1975) have all approached this area, and although they may have used slightly different linguistic labels (e.g., *causal attribution, locus of control*, or *personal causation*), the overlap is marked (for an excellent review of theory and research from the attributional perspective, see Metalsky & Abramson, 1981).

Rotter (1966) has explored two dimensions of causal attributions that influence how these beliefs influence behavior: the *stability* of the factors that the individual has identified as causes, and the *internal versus the external* origin of these factors. Stable causes are those that the individual believes persist over time. "Internal" attributions center on the individual's belief that effort is largely responsible for behavior and that he or she has control over what happens. "External" attributions are environmental factors the individual believes he or she has little control over. Four combinations that emerge from these two dimensions have been proposed to explain how a student may view his or her success and failure experiences in school: (1) stable–internal (e.g., ability); (2) unstable–internal (e.g., effort); (3) stable–external (e.g., task difficulty); and (4) unstable–external (e.g., luck). The force of these beliefs is evidenced in students' expectation of future success or failure, as well as their self-acceptance, their feelings of power or helplessness, and their achievement motivation.

Early work with attribution constructs examined the consistency with which the person holds attributions across situations and time (i.e., the construct was accorded a trait status). Continued research, however, has indicated that a person's attributional thinking varies with the situation. For example, different causal attributions may be made for success and for failure by the same individual, who may assume he or she has control over success but may ascribe failure to external factors (e.g., Crandall, Kratkovsky, & Crandall, 1965; Mischel, Zeiss, & Zeiss, 1974).

The attributions of children appear to influence both behavior and emotion. The literature on the contributions of children's attributions to "learned helplessness" (e.g., Dweck & Reppucci, 1973) suggests that children who believe that their personal failures are related to internal conditions and their successes to external factors are likely to give up in the face of failure and to feel depressed.

The procedures used to retrain attributional thinking have been of two kinds: (1) contingent feedback in conjunction with manipulation of tasks and the environment, especially success and failure (Miller, Brickman, & Bolen, 1975); and (2) self-instructional training (Hanel, 1974, cited by Meichenbaum, 1977).

Although there has been increasing interest in the role that attributional beliefs play in influencing the school performance and efforts of children, there has been little work in the cognitive-behavioral area, to our knowledge, that has looked at the effects of attributional retraining on social behavior and emotional stability. It appears that RET practitioners who are working with children and parents would do well to tap into those attributional beliefs that are at odds with reality and that appear to lead to a variety of cognitive errors (e.g., errors of insertion and errors of discounting). The detailed analysis of the attributional dimension has close links with RET, and the assessment methods that have been developed (e.g., locus of control inventories—Crandall *et al.*, 1965) can readily be utilized in conjunction with rational-emotive methods.

THE FUTURE

It is expected that the prevention and treatment of the emotional and behavioral problems of children and youth will be increasingly influenced by RET and allied cognitive-behavioral approaches. There are a number of trends we can anticipate in this area.

There is little question that the understanding of how the cognitive-affective developmental status of children relates to maladjustment will serve as a background to determining the type of cognitive intervention that is best suited to children who manifest different levels of mental and emotional maturity. We still have a way to go in understanding the world from a child's perspective.

The use of cognitively oriented preventive mental health programs will also increase with the proliferation of cognitive-behavioral interventions and with our improved understanding of cognitive-developmental limitations. School-based and community support for these sorts of programs has yet to be demonstrated.

The extent to which faulty thinking processes and the irrational beliefs of parents and teachers influence childhood maladjustment will be more fully analyzed. The role that significant others can play in correcting the maladaptive thinking patterns and beliefs of younger populations will be of increasing interest. The popularity of cognitively oriented parent and teacher education programs will grow.

The 1980s will, it is hoped, see a refinement of the assessment methodology used to evaluate cognitive programs. Two areas of greatest want are psychometrically sound instruments to assess the range of childhood emotions and fully validated scales to measure the rational beliefs of school-age children.

Behaviorally oriented cognitive practitioners will begin to recognize (assess and treat) more fully that children and their significant others have emotions that influence both behavioral dysfunctions and the potential effects of treatment. Cognitively oriented practitioners working with children in families and in classroom settings will conduct more systematic assessments of behavioral problems so that the benefits of treatment can be more fully and objectively verified.

Child-oriented research scientists will begin to study more systematically how individual differences interact with cognitive treatments. In her review of the use of cognitive self-instructional techniques in the treatment of childhood disorders, Copeland (1981) has listed the following subject characteristics as likely to influence treatment outcome: (1) age; (2) cognitive maturity; (3) language developmental level; (4) attribution of personal causality; and (5) the type and the quality of the therapist–child relationship.

There will be an increasing cross-fertilization of cognitive approaches to the problems of childhood. As the contributors to this volume attest, there is a greater acceptance within the cognitive-behavioral school of the utility of cognitive practices that have originated in different psychological theories and traditions. It is hoped that this trend will continue.

References

Adler, A. *Understanding human nature.* New York: Garden City Publishing, 1927.
Agosto, R., & Solomon, H. Unclassified. *Rational Living,* 1978, *13,* 41–42.
Albert, S. *A study to determine the effectiveness of affective education with fifth grade students.* Unpublished master's thesis, Queens College, 1972.
Bandura, A. *Principles of behavior modification.* New York: Holt, Rinehart & Winston, 1969.
Bard, J. A. *Rational-emotive therapy in practice.* Champaign, Ill.: Research Press, 1980.
Beck, A. T., Rush, A. J., Shaw, B. F., & Emery, G. *Cognitive therapy of depression.* New York: Guilford Press, 1979.
Bedford, S. *Instant replay: A method of counseling and talking to little (and other) people.* New York: Institute for Rational Living, 1974.
Bedrosian, R. C. The application of cognitive therapy techniques with adolescents. In G. Emery, S. D. Hollon, & R. C. Bedrosian (Eds.), *New directions in cognitive therapy.* New York: Guilford Press, 1981.
Bernard, M. E. *Rational-emotive group counseling in a school setting.* Paper presented at the American Educational Research Association's Annual Meeting, San Francisco, April, 1979.
Bernard, M. E. Private thought in rational-emotive psychotherapy. *Cognitive Therapy and Research,* 1981, *5,* 125–142.
Bernard, M. E., & Joyce, M. R. *Rational emotive therapy with children and adolescents: Theory, treatment strategies, preventative methods.* New York: Wiley, 1984.
Bernard, M. E., Kratochwill, T. R., & Keefauver, L. W. The effects of rational-emotive therapy and self-instructional training on chronic hair-pulling. *Cognitive Therapy and Research,* in press.
Blanco, R., & Rosenfield, J. *Case studies in clinical and school psychology,* Springfield, Ill.: Thomas, 1978.

Block, J. Effects of a rational-emotive mental health program on poorly achieving, disruptive high school students. *Journal of Counseling Psychology,* 1978, *25,* 61–65.

Bokor, S. *A study to determine the effects of a self-enhancement program in increasing self-concept in black, disadvantaged sixth-grade boys.* M.A. thesis, Queens College, 1972.

Brody, M. *The effect of the rational-emotive affective education approach on anxiety, frustration tolerance and self-esteem with fifth-grade students.* Ph.D. thesis, Temple University, 1974.

Brown, D. A. Rational success. *Art in Daily Living,* 1974, *3,* 7.

Brown, D. A. The fourth "R": A school psychologist takes RSC to school. In J. Wolfe & E. Brand (Eds.), *Twenty years of rational therapy.* New York: Institute for Rational Living, 1977.

Brown, D. A. Chad cannot be rotton. *Journal of School Health,* 1979, *19,* 503–504.

Cangelosi, A., Gressard, C. V., & Mines, R. A. The effects of a rational thinking group on self-concepts in adolescents. *The School Counselor,* 1980, *27,* 357–361.

Copeland, A. P. The relevance of subject variables in cognitive self-instructional programs for impulsive children. *Behavior Therapy,* 1981, *12,* 520–529.

Cormier, W. H., & Cormier, L. S. *Interviewing strategies for helpers.* Monterey, Calif.: Brooks/Cole, 1979.

Costello, D. R. T., & Dougherty, D. Rational behavior training in the classroom. *Rational Living,* 1977, *12,* 13–15.

Craighead, W. E. A brief clinical history of cognitive-behavior therapy with children. *The School Psychology Review,* 1982, *11,* 5–13.

Crandall, V. C., Kratovsky, W., & Crandall, V. G. Children's beliefs in their own control of reinforcers in intellectual-academic achievement situations. *Child Development,* 1965, *36,* 91–109.

Daly, S. Using reason with deprived preschool children. *Rational Living,* 1971, *5*(2), 12–19.

D'Angelo, D. C. *The effects of locus of control and a program of rational principles on fear of negative evaluation.* Ed.D. thesis, West Virginia University, 1977.

DeVoge, C. A behavioral approach to RET with children. *Rational Living,* 1974, *9*(1), 23–26.

DiGiuseppe, R. *A developmental study of the efficacy of rational-emotive education.* Ph.D. dissertation, Hofstra University, 1975. (a)

DiGiuseppe, R. The use of behavioral modification to establish rational self-statements in children. *Rational Living,* 1975, *1,* 18–20. (b)

DiGiuseppe, R. Cognitive therapy with children. In G. Emery, S. D. Hollon, & R. C. Bedrosian (Eds.), *New directions in cognitive therapy.* New York: Guilford Press, 1981.

DiGiuseppe, R., & Kassinove, H. Effects of a rational-emotive school mental health program on childrens' emotional adjustment. *Journal of Community Psychology,* 1976, *4,* 382–387.

DiGiuseppe, R., Miller N. J., & Trexler, L. D. A review of rational-emotive psychotherapy outcome studies. In A. Ellis & J. M. Whiteley (Eds.), *Theoretical and empirical foundations of rational-emotive therapy.* Monterey, Calif.: Brooks/Cole, 1979.

DiNubile, L., & Wessler, R. Lessons from the living school. *Rational Living,* 1974, *9*(1), 29–32.

Doress, I. The teacher as therapist. *Rational Living,* 1967, *2,* 27.

Dweck, C. The role of expectations and attributions in the alleviation of learned helplessness. *Journal of Personality and Social Psychology,* 1975, *31,* 674–685.

Dweck, C., & Reppucci, N. Learned helplessness and reinforcement responsibility in children. *Journal of Personality and Social Psychology,* 1973, *25,* 109–116.

D'Zurilla, T. J., & Goldfried, M. R. Problem solving and behavior modification. *Journal of Abnormal Psychology,* 1971, *78,* 107–126.

Edwards, C. RET in high school. *Rational Living,* 1977, *12*(1), 10–12.

Ellis, A. *How to live with a "neurotic."* New York: Crown, 1957. Rev. ed., New York: Crown, 1975 and North Hollywood: Wilshire, 1975.

Ellis, A. *Psychotherapy session with an eight-year-old female bedwetter.* Casette recording. New York: Institute for Rational-Emotive Therapy, 1959.

Ellis, A. *Reason and emotion in psychotherapy.* Secaucus, N.J.: Lyle Stuart and Citadel Press, 1962.

Ellis, A. Talking to adolescents about sex. *Rational Living,* 1967, 2(1), 7–12.

Ellis, A. An experiment in emotional education. *Educational Technology,* 1971, 11, 61–64. (a)

Ellis, A. *Rational-emotive therapy and its application to emotional education.* New York: Institute for Rational-Emotive Therapy, 1971. (b)

Ellis, A. The contribution of psychotherapy to school psychology. *School Psychology Digest,* 1972, 1, 6–9. (a)

Ellis, A. Emotional education in the classroom: The living school. *Journal of Child Psychology,* 1972, 1, 19–22. (b)

Ellis, A. *A demonstration with an elementary school child.* Filmed psychotherapy session. Washington: American Personnel and Guidance Association, 1973. (a)

Ellis, A. Emotional education at the living school. In M. M. Ohlsen (Ed.), *Counseling children in groups.* New York: Holt, Rinehart and Winston, 1973. (b)

Ellis, A. *Humanistic psychotherapy.* New York: McGraw-Hill, 1973. (c)

Ellis, A. *Raising an emotionally healthy, happy child.* Videotape. Austin Texas: Audio Visual Resource Center, School of Social Work, University of Texas, 1975. (a)

Ellis, A. Rational-emotive therapy and the school counselor. *School Counselor,* 1975, 22, 236–242. (b)

Ellis, A. The basic clinical theory of rational-emotive therapy. In A. Ellis & R. Grieger (Eds.), *Handbook of rational-emotive therapy.* New York: Springer, 1977.

Ellis, A. Rational-emotive therapy as a new theory of personality and therapy. In A. Ellis & J. M. Whiteley (Eds.), *Theoretical and empirical foundations of rational-emotive therapy.* Monterey, Calif.: Brooks/Cole, 1979.

Ellis, A. An overview of the clinical theory of rational-emotive therapy. In R. Grieger & J. Boyd (Eds.), *Rational-emotive therapy: A skills-based approach.* New York: Van Nostrand Reinhold, 1980. (a)

Ellis, A. The rational-emotive approach to childrens' and adolescents' sex problems. In J. M. Sampson (Ed.), *Childhood and sexuality: Proceedings of the International Symposium.* Montreal: Editions Etudes Vivantes, 1980. (b)

Ellis, A. Rational-emotive therapy and cognitive behavior therapy: Similarities and differences. *Cognitive Therapy and Research,* 1980, 4, 325–340. (c)

Ellis, A. *Rational-emotive therapy and cognitive behavior therapy.* New York: Springer, 1984.

Ellis, A., & Grieger, R. *Handbook of rational-emotive therapy.* New York: Springer, 1977.

Ellis, A., Wolfe, J. H., & Moseley, S. *How to Raise an emotionally healthy, happy child.* New York: Crown; and Hollywood: Wilshire Books, 1966.

Eschenroeder, C. How rational is rational-emotive therapy? A critical appraisal of its theoretical foundations and therapeutic methods. *Cognitive Therapy and Research,* 1982, 6, 274–282.

Forman, S. G., & Forman, B. D. A rational-emotive therapy approach to consultation. *Psychology in the Schools,* 1978, 15, 400–406.

Franks, C. *Behavior therapy: appraisal and status.* New York: McGraw Hill, 1969.

Gagné, R. M. *The conditions of learning* (3rd ed.). New York: Holt, Rinehart, & Winston, 1977.

Gerald, M., & Eyman, W. *Thinking straight and talking sense.* New York: Institute for Rational-Emotive Therapy, 1981.

Glicken, M. Counseling children: Two methods. *Rational Living*, 1967, *1*(2), 27–30.

Glicken, M. D. Rational counseling: A dynamic approach to children. *Elementary School Guidance and Counseling*, 1968, *2*, 261–267.

Grieger, R. M., & Boyd, J. D. Rational-emotive therapy. In H. T. Prout & D. T. Brown (Eds.), *Counseling and psychotherapy with children and adolescents: Theory and practice for school and clinical settings*. New York: Mariner Press, 1982.

Grieger, R. M., Anderson, K., & Canino, F. Psychotherapeutic modes. In E. Ignas & R. Corsini (Eds.), *Alternative educational systems*. Itasca, Ill.: Peacock, 1979.

Hanel, J. *Der Einfluss eines Motivanderungsprogramms auf Schulleistungschwach misserfolgsmotivierter Grundschuler der 4 Klasse*. Unpublished dissertation, Psychologische Institut der Ruhr Universität, 1974.

Harris, S. R. Rational-emotive education and the human development program: A guidance study. *Elementary School Guidance and Counseling*, 1976, *11*, 113–123.

Hauck, P. A. *The rational management of children*. New York: Libra Publishers, 1967.

Hauck, P. A. Public forum: Eleven myths of child counseling. *Rational Living*, 1974, *9*, 38–43.

Hauck, P. A. Irrational parenting styles. In A. Ellis & R. Grieger (Eds.), *Handbook of rational-emotive therapy*. New York: Springer, 1977.

Hauck, P. A. *Brief counseling with RET*. Philadelphia: Westminster Press, 1980.

Hobbs, S. A., Moguin, L. E., Tyroler, M., & Lahey, B. B. Cognitive behavior therapy with children: Has clinical utility been demonstrated? *Psychological Bulletin*, 1980, *87*, 147–165.

Horney, K. *Self-analysis*. New York: Norton, 1942.

Jacobs, E. E. *The effects of a systematic teaching program for college undergraduates based on rational-emotive concepts and techniques*. M.A. thesis, Florida State University, 1977.

Katz, S. *The effects of emotional education on locus of control and self-concept*. Unpublished doctoral dissertation, Hofstra University, 1974.

Kazdin, A. E. *History of behavior modification*. Baltimore: University Park Press, 1978.

Kelly, G. *The psychology of personal constructs*. New York: Norton, 1955.

Kendall, P. C. On the efficacious use of verbal self-instructional procedures with children. *Cognitive Therapy and Research*, 1977, *1*, 331–341.

Kendall, P. C., & Finch, A. J., Jr. A cognitive-behavioral treatment for impulse control: A case study. *Journal of Consulting and Clinical Psychology*, 1976, *44*, 852–857.

Kendall, P. C., & Finch, A. J., Jr. Developing nonimpulsive behavior in children: Cognitive-behavioral strategies fo self-control. In P. C. Kendall & S. D. Hollon (Eds.), *Cognitive-behavior interventions: Theory, research and procedures*. New York: Academic Press, 1979.

Kendall, P. C., & Hollon, S. D. Cognitive-behavioral interventions: Overview and current status. In P. C. Kendall & S. D. Hollon (Eds.), *Cognitive-behavior interventions: Theory, research and procedures*. New York: Academic Press, 1979.

Kendall, P. C., & Hollon, S. D. (Eds.). *Assessment strategies for cognitive behavioral interventions*. New York: Academic Press, 1981.

Kendler, T. S., & Kendler, H. H. Reversal and nonreversal shifts in kindergarten. *Journal of Experimental Psychology*, 1959, *58*, 56–60.

Klausmeier, H. J., Ghatala, E. S., & Frayer, D. A. *Conceptual learning and development*. New York: Academic Press, 1974.

Knaus, W., & Bokor, S. The effect of rational-emotive education on anxiety and self-concept. *Rational Living*, 1975, *10*(2), 7–10.

Knaus, W., & McKeever, C. Rational-emotive education with learning-disabled children. *Journal of Learning Disabilities*, 1977, *10*, 10–14.

Knaus, W. J. *Rational-emotive education: A manual for elementary school teachers*, New York: Institute for Rational-Emotive Therapy, 1974.
Knaus, W. J. Rational-emotive education. In A. Ellis & R. Grieger (Eds.), *Handbook of rational-emotive therapy*. New York: Springer Publishing Co., 1977.
Kovacs, M., & Beck, A. T. An empirical clinical approach towards a definition of childhood depression. In A. G. Shutterbrandt & A. Raskin (Eds.), *Depression in children: Diagnosis, treatment and conceptual models*. New York: Raven Press, 1977.
Kovacs, M., & Beck, A. T. Maladaptive cognitive structures in depression. *American Journal of Psychiatry*, 1978, *135*, 525–530.
Kranzler, C. *Emotional education exercises for children*. Eugene, Oregon: Cascade Press, 1974.
Kujoth, R. J. *The effects of teaching rational idea concepts vs. teaching insight concepts on community college students in a course in human relations*. Ed.D. dissertation, Marquette University, 1976.
Lafferty, G., Dennell, A., & Rettich, G. A creative school mental health program. *National Elementary Principal*, 1964, *43*, 28–35.
Lafferty, J. C. *Proceedings of the Eighth Inter-Institutional Seminar in Child Development*. Dearborn, Mich.: Edison Institute, 1962.
Lazarus, A. *Behavior therapy and beyond*. New York: McGraw-Hill, 1971.
Lazarus, R. *Psychological stress and the coping process*. New York: McGraw-Hill, 1966.
Luria, A. *The role of speech in the regulation of normal and abnormal behaviors*. New York: Liveright, 1961.
Maes, W., & Heinman, R. *The comparison of three approaches to the reduction of test anxiety in high school students*. Final report project 9-1-040. Washington, D.C.: Office of Education, U.S. Department of Health, Education and Welfare, October 1970.
Mahoney, M. J. *Cognitive behavior modification*. Cambridge, Mass.: Ballinger, 1974.
Mahoney, M. J. Reflections on the cognitive learning trend in psychotherapy. *American Psychologist*, 1977, *32*, 5–13.
Mahoney, M. J., & Arnkoff, D. B. Cognitive and self-control therapies. In S. L. Garfield & A. E. Bergin (Eds.), *Handbook of psychotherapy and behavior change* (2nd. ed.). New York: Wiley, 1978.
Marzillier, J. S. Cognitive therapy and behavioral practice. *Behavior Research and Therapy*, 1980, *18*, 249–258.
Maultsby, M. C., Jr. The classroom as an emotional health center. *The Educational Magazine*, 1974, *31*, 8–11.
Maultsby, M. C., Jr. Rational behavior therapy for acting-out adolescents. *Social Casework*, 1975, *56*, 35–43.
Maultsby, M. C., Knipping, P., & Carpenter, L. Teaching self-help in the classroom with rational self-counseling. *The Journal of School Health*, 1974, *44*, 445–448.
McGory, J. E. Teaching introspection in the classroom. *Rational Living*, 1967, *2*, 23–24.
McMullin, R., Asafi, I., & Chapman, S. *Straight talk to parents*. Lakewood, Colo.: Counselling Research Institute, 1978.
Meichenbaum, D. *Cognitive-behavior modification*. Morristown, N.J.: General Learning Press, 1974.
Meichenbaum, D. *Cognitive-behavior modification: An integrative approach*. New York: Plenum Press, 1977.
Meichenbaum, D., & Asarnow, J. Cognitive-behavioral modification and metacognitive development: Implications for the classroom. In P. C. Kendall & S. D. Hollon, (Eds.), *Cognitive-behavior interventions: Theory, research and procedures*. New York: Academic Press, 1979.

Meichenbaum, D., & Cameron, R. Training schizophrenics to talk to themselves: A means of developing attentional controls. *Behavior Therapy*, 1973, *4*, 515–534.

Merluzzi, T. V., Glass, C. R., & Genest, M. (Eds.). *Cognitive assessment*. New York: Guilford Press, 1981.

Metalsky, G. I., & Abramson, L. Y. Attributional styles: Towards a framework for conceptualization and assessment. In P. C. Kendall & S. D. Hollon (Eds.)., *Assessment strategies for cognitive-behavioral interventions*. New York: Academic Press, 1981.

Miller, G. A., Galanter, E., & Pribam, K. N. *Plans and the structure of behavior*. New York: Holt, Rinehart & Winston, 1960.

Miller, N. J. *Effects of behavioral rehearsal, written homework and level of intelligence on the efficacy of rational-emotive education in elementary school children*. Ph.D. dissertation, Hofstra University, 1978.

Miller, R., Brickman, P., & Bolen, D. Attribution versus persuasion as a means for modifying behavior. *Journal of Personality and Social Psychology*, 1975, *31*, 430–441.

Mischel, W. Toward a cognitive social learning reconceptualization of personality. *Psychological Review*, 1973, *80*, 252–283.

Mischel, W., Zeiss, R., & Zeiss, A. Internal-external control and persistance: Validation and implications of the Stanford Preschool Internal-External Scale. *Journal of Personality and Social Psychology*, 1974, *29*, 265–278.

Muirden, G. Violence is a school problem. *Associate News*, June 28, 1976, 12–13.

Murray, E. J., & Jacobson, L. J. Cognition and learning in traditional and behavioral therapy. In S. L. Garfield & A. E. Bergin (Eds.)., *Handbook of psychotherapy and behavior change* (2nd. ed.). New York: Wiley, 1978.

Nardi, T. J. Irrational beliefs of an adopted child. *RETwork*, 1981, *1*(1), 2–4.

Novaco, R. W. Anger and coping with stress. In J. Foreyt & D. Rathsen (Eds.), *Cognitive behavior therapy: Therapy, research and practice*. New York: Plenum Press, 1978.

Novaco, R. W. The cognitive regulation of anger and stress. In P. C. Kendall & S. D. Hollon (Eds.), *Cognitive-behavioral interventions: Theory, research and procedures*. New York: Academic Press, 1979.

Patton, P. L. The effects of rational behavior training on emotionally disturbed adolescents in an alternative school setting. *Dissertation Abstracts International*, 1978, *38*(7)A, 4013–4014.

Piaget, J. *The origins of intelligence*. New York: Norton, 1952.

Protinsky, H. Rational counseling with the adolescents. *School Counselor*, 1976, *23*, 240–246.

Rand, M. E. Rational-emotive approaches to academic underachievement. *Rational Living*, 1970, *4*(2), 16–18.

Ritchie, B. C. The effect of rational-emotive education on irrational beliefs, assertiveness and/or locus of control in fifth grade students. *Dissertation Abstracts International*, 1978, *39*(4B), 2069–2070.

Rossi, A. S. RET with children: More than child's play. *Rational Living*, 1977, *12*(2), 21–24.

Rotter, J. B. *Social learning and clinical psychology*. Englewood Cliffs, N.J.: Prentice-Hall, 1954.

Rotter, J. B. Generalized expectancies for internal versus external control of reinforcement. *Psychological Monographs*, 1966, *80*, 1–26.

Sachs, N. J. Planned emotional education: The living school. *Art in Daily Living*, 1971, *1*, 8–13.

Schacter, S. The interaction of cognitive and physiological determinants of emotional state. In C. Spielberger (Ed.), *Anxiety and behavior*. New York: Academic Press, 1966.

Seligman, M. E. P. *Helplessness.* San Francisco: W. H. Freeman, 1975.
Sharma, K. L. *The rational group therapy approach to counseling anxious underachievers.* Ph.D. thesis, University of Alberta, 1970.
Shibles, W. Emotion: *A critical analysis for children.* Whitewater, Wis.: Language Press, 1978.
Smith, G. W. *A rational-emotive counseling approach to assist junior high school students with interpersonal anxiety.* Unpublished doctoral dissertation, University of Oregon, 1979.
Solomon, H. Unclassified. *Rational Living,* 1978, *13*(2), 41–42.
Spivack, G., & Shure, M. B. *Social adjustment of young children: A cognitive approach to solving real-life problems.* San Francisco: Jossey-Bass, 1974.
Spivack, G., Platt, J., & Shure, M. *The problem-solving approach to adjustment.* San Francisco: Jossey-Bass, 1976.
Staggs, A. M. *Group counseling of learning disabled children in the intermediate grades enrolled in the public school special education program: Training in cognitive behavior modification.* Unpublished doctoral dissertation, University of Denver, 1979.
Sutton-Simon, K. Assessing belief systems: Concepts and strategies. In P. C. Kendall & S. D. Hollon (Eds.), *Assessment strategies for cognitive-behavioral interventions.* New York: Academic Press, 1981.
Sydel, A. *A study to determine the effects of emotional education on fifth grade children.* M.A. thesis, Queens College, 1972.
Taylor, M. H. A rational-emotive workshop on overcoming study blocks. *Personnel and Guidance Journal,* 1975, *53,* 458–462.
Tosi, D. J. *Youth: Toward personal growth, a rational-emotive approach.* Columbus, Ohio: Charles E. Merrill, 1974.
Turk, D. *An expanded skills training approach for the treatment of experimentally induced pain.* Unpublished doctoral dissertation, University of Waterloo, 1976.
Urbain, E. S., & Kendall, P. C. Review of social-cognitive problem-solving interactions with children. *Psychological Bulletin,* 1980, *88,* 109–143.
Vygotsky, L. *Thought and language.* New York: Wiley, 1962.
Wagner, E. E. Counseling children. *Rational Living,* 1966, *1*(2), 26, 28.
Walen, S. R., DiGiuseppe, R. A., & Wessler, R. L. *A practitioner's guide to rational-emotive therapy.* New York: Oxford University Press, 1980.
Warren, R., Deffenbach, J., & Broding, P. Rational-emotive therapy and the reduction of test anxiety in elementary school students. *Rational Living,* 1976, *11*(2), 28–29.
Waters, V. Series of pamphlets on parenting: *Accepting yourself and your child; The anger trap and how to spring it; Building frustration tolerance in you and your children; Fear interferes; Rational problem solving skills; Teaching children to light up their lives.* New York: Institute for Rational Living, 1980. (a)
Waters, V. Series of stories for children: *Cornelia Cadinal learns to cope; Fasha, Dasha and Sasha Squirrel; Flora Farber's fear of failure; Freddie Flounder; Maxwell's magnificent monster.* New York: Institute for Rational Living, 1980. (b)
Waters, V. The living school. *RETwork,* 1981, *1,* 1.
Waters, V. R.E.T. with a child client. Unpublished manuscript, New York, 1982. (a)
Waters, V. Therapies for children: Rational-emotive therapy. In C. R. Reynolds & T. B. Gutkin (Eds.), *Handbook of school psychology.* New York: Wiley, 1982. (b)
Weiner, B. (Ed.). *Achievement motivation and attribution theory.* Morristown, N.J.: General Learning Press, 1974.
Wessler, R. A., & Wessler, R. L. *The principles and practices of rational-emotive therapy.* San Francisco: Jossey-Bass, 1980.

Wolfe, J., & Staff. Emotional education in the classroom: The living school. *Rational Living,* 1970, *4,* 23–25.

Young, H. S. A framework for working with adolescents. *Rational Living,* 1974, *9,* 2–7. (a)

Young, H. S. *A rational counseling primer.* New York: Institute for Rational-Emotive Therapy, 1974. (b)

Young, H. S. Counseling strategies with working class adolescents. In J. L. Wolfe & E. Brand (Eds.), *Twenty years of rational therapy.* New York: Institute for Rational-Emotive Therapy, 1977.

Zelie, K., Stone, C., & Lehr, E. Cognitive behavior intervention in school discipline: A preliminary study. *Personnel and Guidance Journal,* 1980, *59,* 80–83.

2

Principles of Assessment and Methods of Treatment with Children
Special Considerations

RAYMOND DiGIUSEPPE AND
MICHAEL E. BERNARD

Psychology has gone cognitive, and cognitive-behavior therapy has become the zeitgeist in psychotherapy. Despite this trend, the cognitive orientation has been slow to filter down to interventions with children. The majority of practitioners working with children use behavioral or family-systems conceptualizations to plan treatment. As a result, children are often viewed as passive recipients of external influences. Although it is true that children are often dependent on others for much of their physical need, rational-emotive theory would challenge the notion that children have no influence over their own emotional reactions, and that their pathology is the result only of systemic variables or reward contingencies. Although such factors are obviously important in shaping children's psychological development, cognitions are viewed by rational-emotive theory as the mediational variable by which these external factors (family systems and behavioral contingencies) have their effect. One can change children's behavior by restructuring systems or by rearranging contingencies or, more directly and perhaps more efficiently, by attempting to change the child's cognitions directly.

RAYMOND DiGIUSEPPE • Institute for Rational-Emotive Therapy, New York, New York 10021. MICHAEL E. BERNARD • Department of Education, University of Melbourne, Victoria, 3052 Australia.

As with adults, rational-emotive theory would hypothesize that children's disturbed emotions are largely generated by their beliefs (Ellis, 1962). Irrational ideas and distortions of reality are likely to create anger, anxiety, and depression in children just as they do with adults. In fact, because children are children—immature, less sophisticated, and less educated—one might expect them to make more cognitive errors than adults and to become upset more easily.

There has been considerable research on the role of cognitions in causing emotions in adults (see Ellis, in press, for a review). However, researchers have failed to perform similar types of investigations with youngsters. Less evidence exists to support rational-emotive and cognitive-behavior hypotheses with children. Although there is a great deal of literature on the cognitive intellectual development of children, research on the role of cognitions in children's social and emotional development is small by comparison (Urbain & Kendall, 1980). However, it would be inconsistent to believe that cognitions create emotional disturbance in adults, yet to view children as externally controlled. One would have the difficult theoretical task of identifying at just what age emotional reactions go from external to internal control.

Many therapists can accept the notion that children's thoughts lead to their emotions on a theoretical level, yet they are skeptical that one can implement change by direct attempts to manipulate children's cognitions. It may be helpful here to remember Piaget's stages of cognitive development. According to Piaget, children enter the stage of concrete operations around the age of 7 or 8. The next, and final, stage of development, formal operations, occurs in adolescence. However, Piaget pointed out that many adults never reach the stage of formal operations. They remain in concrete operations for the remainder of their lives, the same stage they entered when they were 7 or 8. One is left with the startling conclusion that many an adult client is in the same Piagetian stage of cognitive development as a fourth-grader. One could argue, then, that children are capable of many of the logical processes necessary to participating in and benefiting from cognitive disputing. Children who have not yet reached the stage of concrete operations undoubtedly have a difficult time with logic and the disputing modes of cognitive therapy. However, such children can benefit from other types of cognitive interventions, such as verbal self-instruction or training in the solving of social problems, which do not require the logical manipulation of thoughts.

The remainder of this chapter deals with ways of conceptualizing children's cognitions and emotional problems, with the ways in which

RET differs with children as compared with adults, and with strategies of assessment and treatment.

Theoretical Assumptions

RET and allied cognitive-behavioral interventions share similar views concerning the role of thinking in human emotion and behavior. We briefly describe three cognitive theories of maladjustment that have direct and practical implications for the treatment of childhood disorders. The distinctions between emotional and practical problems, as well as rational and irrational beliefs, are elaborated.

RET Conceptualization of Emotional Disorders

Incidents of emotional upset are complicated psychological phenomena. Ellis (1962) has provided his now famous ABC model to help clients grasp the role of their thoughts in causing emotional disturbance. Wessler and Wessler (1980) have recently expanded the ABC model to help therapists to a fuller understanding of these complex psychological events. At the start of every emotional event, a stimulus is presented to the child:

Step 1: Stimuli are then sensed by the person's eyes, ears, sense of smell, touch, etc.

Step 2: Sensory neurons process the stimuli and transmit them to the CNS.

Step 3: Not all sensations enter consciousness. Some are filtered out and others are perceived. Perception is Step 3. Perception, however, is not an exact replication of reality. Perceptions consist of equal parts of information provided by the senses and information provided by the brain (Neisser, 1967). At this point, all information is organized, categorized, and defined. Perception is as much a peripheral as a CNS function.

Step 4: People usually do not stop thinking after they have perceived information. In most cases, they attempt to extract more information than is present in the perception, so some interpretations or inferences are likely to follow perceptions.

Step 5: Humans are not just passive processors of information. Inferences and conclusions usually have some further meaning associated with them. Conclusions and inferences may vary in their importance to an individual. Almost all inferences are evaluated either positively or negatively in relation to the person's life. This appraisal or evaluation is Step 5.

Step 6: According to rational-emotive therapy, affect or emotion follows appraisal. We feel happy or sad or mad at Step 6, after we have appraised something as being beneficial, threatening, etc.

Step 7: Emotional states are not separate psychological phenomena. Emotions have evolved as part of the flight–fight mechanism and exist primarily to motivate adaptive behavior. Therefore, emotions usually include not only the reactions of the autonomic nervous system and the phenomenological sensations, but action tendencies or behavioral response sets that are learned.

Step 8: Responses, once they are made, usually have some impact on the external world. This effect can be desirable or undesirable, and feedback of our action tendencies serves as a reward to strengthen or extinguish a response set.

Elements of the Emotional Episode:
(1) Stimulus,
(2) Sensation,
(3) Perception,
(4) Inference,
(5) Appraisal,
(6) Affect,
(7) Action tendency, and
(8) Feedback

Given this model, emotional disturbance develops because of one or two types of cognitive error: empirical distortions of reality that occur at Step 4 (inferences) and exaggerated and distorted appraisals of inferences at Step 5. According to traditional rational-emotive theory, it is primarily the appraisal that is necessary for emotional disturbance. This is the B in Ellis's ABC. Ellis has noted, however, that, many times, the appraisals are about distortions of reality. Faulty inferences usually do accompany exaggerated appraisal, but the appraisal alone is sufficient to arouse disturbed affect.

Let's take a hypothetical clinical example to explain how these two cognitions operate. George, a 10-year-old, has moved to a new neighborhood and has not met new friends. He is sitting quietly in the neighborhood playground while the other children are running about. He feels frightened, and his associated action potential is withdrawal. He sits alone leaning up against a wall, reading a book. As he sees the other children coming, George thinks, "They'll never like me, they'll think I'm not very good at these games, and they won't play with me no matter what I do." George has drawn these inferences about the other children's behavior. In fact, they are predictions about what might happen but never actually has happened. Inferences alone are not sufficient to arouse fear. Some children, although not George, might be perfectly happy to sit by themselves and read books, but George appraises this situation quite negatively and catastrophizes: "It's awful that I don't have anyone to play with"; "I must be a jerk if they won't play with me."

SOCIAL-PROBLEM-SOLVING VIEW OF MALADJUSTMENT

Wessler and Wessler's (1980) diagram of the emotional episode focuses on the presence of maladaptive, illogical, antiempirical, and irrational cognitions. Other cognitive theorists have taken a different perspective and see emotional disturbance as resulting from a deficit in the cognitions that are usually present in well-functioning children. Spivack, Platt, and Shure (1976) have identified several interpersonal cognitive problem-solving skills. Their research focused on developing psychometric measures of these skills and correlating them with psychopathology. So far, their research has been impressive, and they have identified several skills in solving social problems that consistently distinguish psychopathological from normal populations. The most important skill they have uncovered is alternative-solution thinking (i.e., the number of different solutions that a child can generate to solve a specific practical problem). The second most important skill, consequential thinking, measures children's ability to predict the social consequences or results of their actions. Once children can generate alternatives and predict sequences, the next skills that seem to be important are the ability to anticipate problems and the implementation of a solution to plan around them. Spivak and his colleagues have termed these "means–end thinking."

There is a growing body of research to suggest that attempts to teach children interpersonal, cognitive problem-solving skills can lead to reduced emotional upset and more adaptive behavior (Urbain & Kendall, 1980). Interpersonal, cognitive problem-solving skills can be effective for several reasons within the context of Wessler and Wessler's emotional episode model. Problem solving could occur after the inferences, the appraisals, or the affect. Effective problem-solvers may experience disturbed affect less often because (1) they distract themselves from the appraisal and thereby lift affect—as long as one is thinking about how to go about solving a problem, one is less likely to be entertaining catastrophizing ideas and therefore to become upset; (2) social-problem solving may bring about solutions to change the activating event and thereby eliminate the problem in the first place; and (3) thinking of alternative solutions may help one change one's appraisal of a negative event. People who believe they have options may be less likely to view events as awful or catastrophic.

BEHAVIORAL DISORDERS AS VERBAL MEDIATIONAL DEFICITS

A variety of childhood disorders (e.g., aggression, hyperactivity, and impulsivity) are being increasingly analyzed in terms of verbal mediational deficits. Inappropriate behavior (excessive or insufficient action tendencies) is seen as deriving from the child's either thinking too quickly or not thinking at all. Meichenbaum (1977, pp. 30–31) has characterized the thinking styles of these children in terms of three mediational deficiencies: (1) they may not comprehend the nature of the problem or the task and thus cannot discover what mediators to produce—what Bem (1971) called a "comprehension" deficiency; (2) they may have the correct mediators within their repertoire but may fail to produce them spontaneously and appropriately—what Flavell, Beach, and Chinsky (1966) called a "production" deficiency; and (3) the mediators that children produce may not guide their ongoing behavior—what Reese (1962) called "mediational" deficiency.

There seems to be increasing evidence that verbal self-control strategies can be utilized by children to guide their ongoing behaviour (Urbain & Kendall, 1980). Indeed, cognitive self-verbalization treatment programs are being designed to foster the acquisition both of specific skills and of more general reflective thinking strategies. By providing the child with skills that can be employed in problem situations, these programs appear to influence the inferences made (Step 4) by the child when initially faced with a difficult impersonal or interpersonal task. Equipped with a task-specific skill, the child may no longer underestimate his or her coping resources; a result would be a reduction in the affective stress that presumably would previously have been experienced (Step 6). Alternatively, adaptive task performance brings about self-perceived "need satisfaction," thereby reducing the frequency with which the child's demands are not fulfilled. It can be seen that both the interpersonal cognitive problem-solving and the verbal mediational perspectives tend to emphasize direct cognitive-behavioral solutions to childhood problems, whereas RET is very much oriented toward emotional problem solving.

Emotional- and Practical-Problem Solving

There are two types of problems that people can experience: emotional and practical. Emotional problems can be defined in terms of Step 6 of Wessler and Wessler's model (1980). Waters (1982) differentiates between these problems as follows:

> Emotional problems are generated by self and goal defeating belief systems and are characterized by extremely uncomfortable, stagnated feelings, while practical problems are realistic difficulties in the environment resulting in unsatisfactory situations, which one wishes to change. (p. 570)

In children, common emotional difficulties include anger, anxiety, and self-downing (depression), and practical problems are not having enough friends, getting into fights, being teased and not knowing what to do, etc. It is frequently but not always the case that practical problems are accompanied by emotional problems and that, indeed, emotional problems often originate in practical problems.

By way of example, let us see the variety of ways of helping George, who has no friends. There are several ways. The first would be to play camp counselor and introduce George to new friends. This would be very helpful to George and he would probably greatly appreciate it. However, it would not help George to learn to cope with fearful situations. This approach is called in RET the *practical solution.* It is usually considered inelegant and inadvisable because it in no way helps the person to develop psychological coping mechanisms for facing difficult problems in the future, as he or she most certainly will. Practical solutions change the stimuli or activating event. Although they are often effective in changing children's specific emotional episodes, they are palliative. If George were again in a strange environment, he would have the same problem and become upset once again. Stop and think of your own interventions with children and those of your colleagues. How often have you seen therapists opt for the practical solutions and miss the opportunity to teach the child how to learn coping skills. Practical-problem solving assumes that the child cannot learn to deal with the adversity on her or his own. Carried to extremes, it could become a self-fulfilling prophecy because the child would get no practice in solving *emotional problems.*

A second strategy to help George in the situation mentioned above is to reduce his anxiety. There are two primary ways that RET teaches a young client to resolve emotional difficulties. At the inferential stage in Wessler and Wessler's diagram, George believes that the other children will never like him. How does he know this to be true? He did not try to meet them. He most probably has had other friends in other places. Few kids in his past have actively disliked him. One could go on eliciting from George reasons that the other children would not like him and put these to the empirical test. If George became convinced that the other children would like him if he introduced himself, there would be no reason for him to be fearful. He might then attempt to behave differently and actively initiate social contact. We call this the *empirical solution* because it attempts to test empirically the truth of inferential thinking by collecting data. George is probably distorting reality in believing that the children would have such a negative view of him, and the therapist could show George how his thinking in this manner is untrue. Although the empirical solution deals with changing George's emotional reaction to the situation, it is considered, in RET, an inelegant solution. It is considered inelegant because it challenges the inferences and not the appraisal. George's inferences could be true—if not this time, maybe the next. Suppose that in his next move he encounters children who dislike him for his race, creed, color, or any other characteristic. No amount of empirical challenging may change his emotional devastation at being disliked if the other children's negative prejudice against him is real.

The *elegant solution* in rational-emotive theory challenges the appraisal, the evaluation, or the meaning that a person applies to the inferences and conclusions he or she draws. In this way, George can learn to reduce his anxiety in this situation and other like situations that may occur. We would help him to come to the conclusion that it is not awful if others don't like him. Even if he would rather play with them, he can go about his business, do the next most enjoyable thing, and not catastrophize. If George believes that it would not be terrible if the other children did not like him, he might also take the risk of asking them to play with him because the stakes would be lowered considerably for rejection.

RATIONAL AND IRRATIONAL BELIEFS

Underlying the appraisals that a person applies to inferences and conclusions is what Ellis has referred to as the person's "belief system," which is composed of both rational and irrational beliefs. This is as much the case with children and adolescents as it is with adults. Rational beliefs (and appraisals) tend to be consistent with objective reality, are expressed conditionally and relativistically, and lead to self-enhancing emotions and goal-directed behaviors. Irrational beliefs are generally distortions of reality, are expressed unconditionally and absolutistically, and lead to inappropriate feelings that often block goal attainment. Major categories of irrational beliefs include demandingness, awfulizing, and self-downing. The common irrational beliefs of children include (adapted from Waters, 1982):

1. It's awful if others don't like me.
2. I'm bad if I make a mistake.
3. Everything should go my way; and I should always get what I want.
4. Things should come easily to me.
5. The world should be fair and bad people should be punished.
6. I shouldn't show my feelings.
7. Adults should be perfect.
8. There's only one right answer.
9. I must win.
10. I shouldn't have to wait for anything.

Special Considerations with Children

RET was initiated, refined, and practiced on adult clients. Most of the books, research articles, clinical literature, and folklore focus almost exclusively on treating various adult populations. Working with youngsters is a relatively new step in RET. In fact, this is the first book comprehensively dealing with the use of rational-emotive therapy with children and adolescents. This section deals with some of the ways in which classical RET is practiced with children. The topics covered include defining expectations and developing rapport, language, developmental limitations, assessment, teaching critical thinking skills, and disputing strategies.

Expectations and Rapport

Few children understand what psychotherapy is about. They have some notion that a psychologist is a person who "helps" people, but outside of this, most of their notions are negative. Many children believe that our profession treats "crazy people" and therefore that being at our office is a stigma. The other model that children have for us is the school psychologist. Often, they perceive this role as a disciplinary one. What kind of children get sent to the school psychologist in your district?

Besides not knowing about the process of psychotherapy, many children arrive at our offices with no awareness of why they have come. Their parents have not discussed it with them. Children are unlikely to become collaborators in a process they don't understand. Therefore, a first job is to explain to them what a psychologist is, who we help, how we help people, and what we help people with. After such an explanation, the child should have a problem-solving set and hopefully a positive schema for the profession, as well as no negative stereotypes. The following transcript shows how this topic can be introduced to children (from DiGiuseppe, 1981, p. 54):

THERAPIST: Johnny, I'm a psychologist. Do you know what that is?
JOHNNY: Oh! No. Well a kind of doctor for crazy people?
THERAPIST: Well, that's not totally true. Psychologists are doctors who study how people learn things. And psychologists help people learn things they have been unable to learn. For example, some children have trouble learning to read. And psychologists help them learn to read better. Other children are sad or scared. They haven't learned not to be unhappy or afraid. Psychologists help them learn not to feel that way. We help children with other problems, too, like anger, bed-wetting, making friends, and lots of things they don't know how to do. Do you understand that?
JOHNNY: Yes.
THERAPIST: Well, what problem do you think I can help you with?

RAPPORT

Self-disclosure is a prerequisite for any verbal psychotherapy. Children are less likely than adults to self-disclose to therapists because they desire help. For most children a warm, accepting relationship is probably a necessity before they will honestly tell how they feel or think. With children, and especially with adolescents, rapport becomes much more important before starting traditional rational-emotive therapy. We do not mean to imply that rapport is curative in and of itself with children, but that it is more desirable to attain self-disclosure and to convince them to listen so that the therapist's interventions can have an effect.

Although reflection has been the primary strategy by which therapists develop rapport, reflection is not the only way to accomplish this end. Another strategy is honest, direct questions that communicate a commitment to help. Children are quite sensitive to dishonesty, and they generally respond well to people who are open and who trust them. Many therapists ask children questions when they already know the answer (e.g., after the mother has called to inform the therapist that $20 is missing from her pocketbook, the therapist's first inquiry is "Were there any problems at home this week?" or "Did you do anything wrong?"). Children are not stupid and are not likely to bring about rejection willingly. Therefore, they may be reluctant to disclose their misdeameanors. So they usually respond to inquiries about their misdeeds with "No, I didn't do anything," or "No there are no problems." Here the therapist has set up a situation in which the child is most likely to lie. Once the child has lied, the therapist is placed in the difficult situation of revealing a lie before it can be discussed. Exposing the child's lie impacts negatively on rapport. To avoid such situations, we think it better to confront children honestly with the facts as you know them, and then to ask for their opinion or interpretation of the events.

Another strategy to help foster rapport is to discuss with the child how therapy can achieve ends that the *child* desires, rather than focusing on the goals of the parents and teachers. Because children are not self-referred and they may not always have the goals of the significant others in their lives, it may be particularly important to show children how they can benefit from therapy before they will be willing to participate. Some goals of therapy that children desire may be (1) to lessen the degree of their parents' anger at them; (2) to develop more predictable rules within the family so that life does not seem as arbitrary; or (3) to attain some major rewards they are seeking, such as a larger allowance, staying out later, or a home video game. The therapist may then act as the child's agent in negotiating for these items when contracting for appropriate behaviors. An additional strategy is to help shift some of the responsibility for the problem and referral away from the child. A child may feel outnumbered if there is a group of adults trying to induce change. By focusing on how the parent's behavior may contribute to the child's problems or how the parents' upset exaggerates the problem, one diffuses responsibility away from the child and may form an alliance with the child.

CONSEQUENCES AND ALTERNATIVES

Disputing is the process whereby a client's irrational beliefs are challenged and attempts are made to substitute more rational alternative ways of thinking. Disputing makes sense to rational therapists because they have some prerequisite assumptions about the client and about the nature or emotional disturbance. The first assumption seems somewhat obvious. It is the idea that the client's affect or behavior is negative, disturbed, self-destructive, and better changed. The second assumption is that negative, disturbed emotions can be replaced with alternative nondisturbing, non-self-destructive, albeit unpleasant, affective states. A third is that irrational beliefs create the disturbed affect in the first place. Given these prerequisite assumptions, it logically follows that disputing one's irrational cognitions would be helpful. If these assumptions are not made, however, a client might find disputing a critical, unpleasant process and either drop out of therapy or become extremely uncooperative.

Many children do not recognize that their behaviors or emotional states have a negative impact on their lives. Nor are they necessarily aware that there are alternative ways to act or feel. Most adult clients have a head start on children in this way. Because adults are usually self-referred, they usually recognize that their actions and emotions are self-defeating and that the therapist is there to help them develop alternative ways of responding. If they did not believe this, they probably would not have come in the first place. Children are almost never self-referred. The initial stages of treatment may be exclusively devoted to an *evaluation* of children's affect and action potential and to convincing them that these bring about negative consequences that are avoidable. Focusing on the consequences of the child's present *modus operandi* is the first treatment step.

Children may have limited schemata for emotional reactions. They may conceptualize feelings as bipolar dichotomous constructs (i.e., happy–mad or glad–sad). It would be quite unlikely for a child to work with a therapist to change mad to only annoyed when her brother pulls her hair if she has no schema to incorporate the latter emotion. Schachter (1966) has demonstrated that social expectations play a large role in a person's emotional experiences. Social cues and private interpretations determine what emotions a person reports to experience when aroused by injections of adrenaline. We would argue for an extension of Schachter's theory and suggest that cognitions drawn from external cues influence not only the types of emotions but also the *intensity or degree* of emotions as well. Many disturbed children appear to believe that their intense fear or depression is either a desirable or a necessary reaction to certain events. Aggressive adolescents commonly report the desirability of becoming fighting mad at taunts by their peers in order to preserve their reputation. In many cases, children say that they have no options, that their disturbed emotions are the way they should or must feel. Children may have developed these beliefs concerning their emotional responses by either modeling or direct reinforcement from their parents or families. In many families, the parents respond in the same exaggerated ways as their children do, so that the child has never seen an alternative response. The parents may show a wider range of emotional reactions, but they may never expect this range of their children and fail to directly teach them alternatives. In summary, *before one can proceed to identifying and disputing irrational beliefs, one must first agree on a goal. Before one can agree on a goal, it might be necessary to expand the child's schema concerning emotional reactions so that the goal is within his or her frame of reference.* This expansion can be accomplished through modeling, imagery, stories, parables, and discussions of TV characters who play out different emotional reactions.

Evaluating the consequences of the child's emotional reactions, and developing a wider range of perceived, possible emotional reactions is likely to be an important and lengthy step in therapy. Once children perceive that their affect and action tendencies are self-defeating and conceptualize alternative ways of responding both emotionally and behaviorally, they will be more willing to enter into a discussion of how their thinking causes their emotions, and they will be more likely to participate in the disputing and not to see it as an attempt to be critical of them. The therapist is advised not to assume that these two initial steps in therapy will be achieved instantaneously. It may take a number of sessions to explore these issues before the child becomes convinced of them.

LANGUAGE

A common error among novice rational-emotive therapists is to use the jargon of rational-emotive therapy (e.g., *awfulizing, terrible, should, shithood, self-downing*). Children are likely to express their irrational ideas in vocabularies different from adults' or rational therapists'. Pay close attention to the child's words that represent the irrational concept. Many children express the concept of demandingness by referring to "unfairness." The concept of self-downing or self-worth may be expressed by phrases such as "He is a jerk" or a "jerk-off," or whatever word is currently in vogue in the child's subculture. It is best to avoid translating the child's vocabulary to RET jargon and, rather, to attempt to use the child's own lexicon. Children may also lack a vocabulary for expressing emotions. Even if they do possess a schema for a wide degree of emotional reactions to problems, they might not have the words to express these differences. If they do not have the wide range of alternative emotional reactions mentioned in the above sections, along with teaching the emotions themselves it is desirable to provide children with a vocabulary for easily expressing the emotions.

The lack of a vocabulary for expressing subtleties in emotional reaction may partly be a result of the structure of the English language. The common use of words to define emotion is rather vague and imprecise. People frequently use affective words in idiosyncratic ways. One child's "fear" may be another's "panic" or a third's "concern." It is also helpful to check out what the child means by emotional words behaviorally, physiologically, and phenomenologically. Setting definitions of emotional words helps to prevent confusion as the sessions progress. One helpful suggestion is to use Wolpe's (1973) SUD scale (subjective units of discomfort) to describe the child's present emotional state and to provide a numerical rating that indicates the intensity of an emotion. In this way, children learn that affects can be named along a continuum and that their own emotional states can be compared with the desired goal of the treatment. Thus, a child may talk about becoming angry at an SUD 4. If this numerical system appears undesirable to the therapist, she or he can set a specific vocabulary to try to describe the different intensities of emotional states.

Developmental Limitations

We are just beginning to take into account the child's cognitive-developmental status in selecting appropriate cognitive assessment and intervention procedures. Armed with the knowledge that basic learning processes and abilities (e.g., attention, memory, verbal mediation, and cognitive strategies) appear to develop progressively over the childhood period, child-oriented practitioners have in the past few years begun to question the role of different developmental characteristics in determining the efficacy of cognitive-behavioral intervention (e.g., Cohen & Myers, 1983). The main work in this area has been in determining whether children's level of cognitive development influences their capacity to profit from self-instructional training (Meichenbaum, 1977), which is introduced at different levels of complexity employing different teaching formats. Schleser, Meyers, and Cohen (1981) suggested that pre-concrete-operational children may not have achieved a sufficient level of metacognitive development to profit from verbal self-instruction that employs directed discovery rather than direct expository methods. The related research of Cohen and Meyers (1983) seems to indicate that preoperational children are unable to spontaneously generate cognitive self-guiding strategies.

We employ several principles and guidelines in taking into account the child's cognitive status. We know from our review of Piaget that it is only when children are in the formal operational period (approximately 12 years and older) that they are generally capable of the type of hypotheticodeductive reasoning we believe is a necessary prerequisite for the disputational examination of irrational beliefs. In line with this proposition, Bernard and Joyce (1984) have written:

> Many children do not have the cognitive capacity to (a) recognize their *general* irrational beliefs (e.g., "The world should be fair and bad people should be

punished") *when it is presented as a hypothetical proposition,* (b) rationally re-state beliefs (e.g., "The world is not a fair place to live and people who mistrust others can be helped to correct their ways"), and (c) employ their rationally re-stated belief in all situations (where they are treated unfairly).

We know from Piaget and others (e.g., Flavell, 1977) that children between the approximate ages of 7 and 11 structure their world in an empirical and inductive manner. As a consequence, basic RET attitudes, insights, concepts, and beliefs are taught to children *through intensive analyses of specific situations.* Concrete examples and teaching illustrations are the rule. Bernard and Joyce (1984) illustrated this "child orientation" as follows:

> For example, in working with aggressive and conduct disordered young boys (7–11 years of age), we find they frequently believe that people whom they perceive "doing them in" deserve to be "done in" themselves. We have achieved good success in getting this population to change their beliefs by (a) discussing a specific situation (e.g., being unfairly treated in a math class by a teacher), (b) defining the concept of "fairness" and having them empirically analyze whether the current situation is unfair or not; this step frequently involves using puppets so that the child can view the situation from another's perspective, (c) discussing the concept of "mistake making" and explaining the different reasons why a math teacher may act unfairly and make mistakes, (d) providing a set of rational self-instructions (e.g., "It's okay to make mistakes; no one's perfect; I can handle this situation; I don't have to get upset") which are modelled and role-played, (e) discussing the concepts of "fairness" and "mistake making" in the context of other problematic situations (e.g., other teachers, parents, siblings, in-class, at play, at home), (f) giving practice in applying the rational self-statements to novel situations, and (g) reinforcing the child (and getting him to self-reinforce) for using rational self-talk with the practitioner and in "real life situations."

In the section of this chapter that deals with treatment, we illustrate how disputational strategies can be modified for use with younger populations.

When we work with very young children (under 7 years old) we are especially cognizant of their difficulty in readily taking into account the perspective of others (egocentrism) as well as considering more than one relevant dimension at a time. As children during this period rely heavily on perceptual analysis rather than conceptual inference (Morris & Cohen, 1982), we deemphasize extensive discussion and analysis of irrational concepts and, instead, relying on the child's more advanced capacity for dealing with iconic representation, and employing a great many concrete and simple materials (pictures, diagrams, stories) that young children can readily learn from.

Developmental work in verbal mediation (e.g., Flavell *et al.*, 1966) indicates that children between the ages of 6 and 9 who fail to spontaneously produce functional self-guiding verbal mediators may learn to do so from instruction. Therefore, we spend a great deal of time with younger children teaching them through a variety of different techniques what to think and how to spontaneously use rational self-talk in problem situations.

RET practitioners are also aware that children, especially at the earlier developmental levels, are active learners and that knowledge acquisition is facilitated by "doing" and "seeing" as much as by "hearing." We again recommend the use of pictures and stories, which may serve as imaginal mnemonic aids and may also to enhance the experiential aspect of the learning episode.

Assessment Guidelines

A framework, rationale, and logic of RET child assessment are emerging. A number of different targets of assessment, as well as different approaches, are highlighted in this section.

The Purpose of Assessment

A cognitive-behavioral (and emotive) approach to the assessment of childhood disorders consists of two identifiable stages (Bernard & Joyce, 1984).

Problem identification involves the use of both formal and informal tests and methods to determine whether a problem does exist or whether it is solely in the mind of the parent or teacher who has referred the child. During the initial phase of assessment, the dynamics of the referral are untangled. It is not infrequently the case that parents and teachers refer a child who is exhibiting perfectly normal behavior. They may misdiagnose a problem because of ignorance of the normal patterns of child behavior, because of conflicts that they may be experiencing with the child, or as a sole consequence of their own psychological difficulties. During this phase, it is recommended that the practitioner collect information from a variety of sources to determine whether a problem exists and, if it does, whether it belongs to the child, the parents, or the teachers. A review of a child's cumulative school report, as well as interviews with a variety of people who know the referred child and the circumstances that surround the referral, is advisable. The identification of a problem as well as whether it seems to be a child problem or someone else's is a prerequisite to more thorough problem exploration and definition. The importance of determining problem ownership is revealed in the following excerpt from a case report:

> Mr. and Mrs. S. sought help about their children's behavior. Mrs. S. had been married twice before and the three children were the product of these previous unions. Mr. S. had no previous marriage and had no children. During the two years of their marriage Mr. and Mrs. S. fought frequently about the children. Mr. S. viewed them as "destructive, unkempt barbarians." He complained they talked too much, ate too much, played too roughly, and spoke too loudly. Mrs. S. felt angry at her husband and enforced rigid rules and harsh penalties to avoid his wrath.
>
> A total assessment involved a behavior analysis, psychological testing, and family and individual interviews. It revealed that the older daughter had a mild learning disability and considerable social anxiety, and that one of the sons was encopretic and had some minor school difficulties; the other son displayed no behavioral problems at all. The children's behavior at home which Mr. S. complained about most vehemently, appeared to be quite normal. The problem seemed more to lie in Mr. S.'s low frustration tolerance and low anger threshold and Mrs. S.'s unassertiveness with her husband. The therapist made attempts to change some of the children's behavior (i.e., the incopretic behavior); however, most of the interventions were aimed at the parents. (DiGiuseppe, 1981, p. 54)

Once the practitioner has established that a problem does exist and who owns it, the *problem analysis* phase of assessment is conducted. Problem analysis results in a determination of the client's dysfunctional cognitions, emotion, and behavior of concern, which then become integrated into an overall treatment plan.

It is important to emphasize that *problem analysis is an ongoing part of therapy*. That is to say, although it is possible to arrive at insights into behavioral problems and their cognitive and emotive concomitants during initial interview sessions, it is often not until more advanced levels of rapport have been achieved between the practitioner and the client that the central concerns of the client and their internal and external activating events are revealed. As new information is disclosed over the course of therapy, it is repeatedly analyzed into cognitive, emotive, and behavioral components as a prerequisite to problem solving.

As the practitioner analyzes the presenting problem, he or she is also tuned into the cognitive strengths and weaknesses of the child. Although the age of the client provides a very rough index to abstract reasoning capacities, the manner in which the young client describes problems is a direct guide how the client arrives at knowledge, the degree to which behavior is under the control of language, and the capacity of the client to distance himself or herself from the problem.

DIFFERENT TARGETS FOR COGNITIVE ASSESSMENT

After the practitioner operationally defines target behavior (including the identification of antecedent and consequent conditions) as well as ascertaining maladaptive emotions (including degree of upset), the analysis of dysfunctional cognition begins. A variety of different types of cognitions are of concern.

Irrational self-statements and beliefs that are expressed in the client's appraisal of perceived and interpreted reality (Step 5) are seen as central to emotional upset. Clients who appraise situations in self-defeating and irrational ways (demandingness, awfulizing, self- or other-downing) will very likely be referred for emotional problems and associated behavioral difficulties. As we indicated earlier, the emotional disorders of a young client can be initiated by *distorted perceptions of reality*. The practitioner attempts to discover not only a young client's antiempirical inferences and conclusions, but also the logical errors that lead to reality distortion (arbitrary inference, selective abstraction, overgeneralization).

Another area assessed is the client's *causal attributions*. If a young client tends to believe falsely that negative events in his or her life are caused by internal and stable personal characteristics (i.e., ability), whereas positive events and success experiences derive from external forces (i.e., luck), then a variety of self-defeating emotional and behavioral consequences are likely to manifest themselves.

When emotionally overwrought, clients not only upset themselves by their own negative self-talk but also suffer from an absence of *coping self-statements*. It is important for the practitioner to be able to tap into the young client's self-talk in order to determine whether appropriate cognitions are available to combat anger, anxiety, and depression.

It is often apparent that young clients who are referred for behavioral problems lack *practical-problem-solving skills and solutions*. Behavioral repertoire deficits stem from the client's being unable to conceptualize other ways of reaching a goal or resolving an interpersonal difficulty. Through a variety of direct and indirect elicitational techniques, the practitioner determines the extent to which the client is to think his or her way out of situations (alternative and consequential thinking).

An example of a cognitive assessment is revealed in the case of John, age 11, referred to the second author for fighting and disruptive classroom behavior. As is not uncommon, John's school reports indicated that he had a moderate reading difficulty. A group-administered intelligence test (OTIS) revealed a test score of 106:

> When John's parents were initially interviewed, they indicated that he had a history of noncompliant behavior at home. When he was asked to

do something, he would often get extremely angry and sometimes break something. John frequently fought both verbally and physically with his older brother, Andrew, though the intensity of the fights appeared to be moderate and the duration short-lived. John's father would become extremely angry with John when he refused to do what he was asked to do. His father would frequently slap John or use a strap on him. John's mother would attempt to get John to help around the house by being excessively nice to him. As a consequence, John appeared to have things pretty much his way—though at some cost. The therapy with parents, which was successful, involved the father's learning to control his temper largely by changing his belief that "My son must always obey me when I ask him to do something" and by teaching him to accept his son with all his imperfections. Both parents were taught to be more firm and assertive with John, and the use of logical and natural consequences as a punishment procedure proved effective in increasing compliant behavior.

John was seen for 16 sessions. A problem analysis revealed a complex set of cognitive deficiencies. John appeared to break rules and get into fights (consequent behavior) when he interpreted a situation as being "unfair" (antecedent events). At these times, his emotions were generally of anger and frequently registered above 8 on a 1–10 scale of intensity. John was quite open in discussing his thoughts and feelings. His expressive language was somewhat restricted, leading to an inference of an inadequate self-control inner-language system. Primary among his dysfunctional beliefs were (1) "Everyone should be fair to me at all times"; (2) "I should always get what I want"; (3) "I'm no good if I break a rule or make a mistake"; and (4) "I must be comfortable at all times and I can't stand the discomfort I have when I have to work hard." This last belief resulted in undesirable levels of frustration tolerance and discomfort anxiety, which, because of John's pattern of work avoidance, led to a low level of educational achievement. When John was confronted with situations with his peers in which he believed they wanted to "take the 'mickey' out of me," he could not think of any alternatives to fighting. When he believed that a teacher was saying something or requesting something that he felt was unfair, his only response was simply to refuse to comply with the teacher's instruction. Moreover, when he became aroused, he failed to consider at that moment the range of negative consequences that would result from his misdeeds. At times when he became angry, his self-talk was highly provoking, and he lacked appropriate self-statements for keeping his anger in check. Therapy was partially successful in helping John to give up his "demandingness" and was very successful in improving his self-esteem. He acquired the ability to control his temper by the use of coping self-statements and was "caught" only once for fighting during the remainder of the school year. During treatment, he became more aware of the perspective of others, began to recognize when situations were fair and when they were not, and began to realize that the world did not always have to revolve around him. He began to accept the behavior of others, understood the notion that it is unfair to get angry with people who make mistakes, and was seen by both parents and teachers as being more cooperative.

Different Methods of Assessment

In both the assessment and the treatment phases, it is most important that the practitioner be able, when necessary, to tap into the self-talk of the young client. Many children have probably never been asked to report their thoughts to someone else. Most do not have a sufficient vocabulary to describe the thoughts they experience when they are upset. Moreover, children who manifest a variety of different conduct disorders appear to very quickly subvocalize anger-producing ideas in problem situations and, as a consequence, are unaware that they are thinking anything at all. In both assessing dysfunctional cognitions and preparing the young client for the teaching of emotional-problem-solving skills, the practitioner has the tasks of (1) helping children to be more aware of their feelings and (2) enabling them to tune into and report their self-talk. A number of assessment methods, described below, have been developed to elicit feelings and thoughts from young clients; to enable them to describe their thoughts orally in a manner that will facilitate and further their self-understanding; and to provide the practitioner with the young client's conceptual outlook and verbal-linguistic repertoire, which provides the basis for cognitive restructuring (see Bernard & Joyce, 1984, for a more detailed description of assessment methods).

Emotional (feeling) scales are aids for helping to determine the degree of emotional impact that children experience. Children are given a 10-point scale and asked to describe how much of a particular emotion they are experiencing in a given situation. Clinical experience suggests that feelings of 8 or higher usually represent emotional overreactions and upsets that are likely to lead to inappropriate behavior. These scales are useful in teaching children that their emotions can vary from strong to weak and, thus, may serve to expand the emotional schema of children.

The *Subjective Units of Discomfort Scale* (Wolpe, 1973) involves children in role-playing situations in which they are asked to experience a certain degree of emotionality along a 10-point continuum.

Emotional flashcards, |emotional detective, and feeling charts (Waters, 1982) are activities that are especially good for increasing emotional awareness. The practitioner and the child can use *emotional flashcards* in a guessing game in which each, in turn, "acts out" the emotion on a chosen card and the other has to guess it, or each can take turns making up stories about each emotion. *Emotional detective* involves the practitioner's asking the child to help investigate how either the child or other people handle their emotions and to report all evidence in the next session. *Feeling charts* involve the child's describing his or her feelings according to various criteria (e.g., strong–weak, helpful–hurtful, pleasant–unpleasant, long–short).

Hand puppets can be good vehicles for helping children to gain sufficient psychological distance from themselves and, by so doing, to gain some insight into not only what they are thinking and feeling in different situations, but into what others, such as parents and teachers, are thinking and feeling.

Emotional vocabulary building (Waters, 1982) involves asking children to name all the feelings they can think of. Once a list is obtained, the practitioner asks the child to provide a situation in which she or he experienced the feeling, and if possible, what she or he was thinking of at the time. The practitioner can sensitize the child to a wider range of emotional options and may provide each emotion with its own definition.

Thought bubbles can be employed to convey the general idea that thoughts create feelings; it can also be used to elicit responses from the unforthcoming child. For example, in a series of cartoons, it is possible to illustrate different temporally related scenes that illustrate a problem that the child may be having. Empty bubbles then can appear over the child in the next scene. The emotional expressions on the faces of the characters help to dramatize the scenes, and the child is asked to fill in the bubble with what he or she thinks the child in the scene is thinking.

The sentence completion technique is employed to elicit a variety of cognitions including copying self-statements, irrational beliefs, and practical- and emotional-problem-solving skills. The practitioner develops a number of incomplete sentences that tap into the relevant content area (e.g., "When I find my math homework hard, I generally think . . .").

Think-aloud approaches (Genest & Turk, 1981) involve the practitioner's assigning the child a task to complete and requesting the child to think out loud at the same time. For example, a child who is having difficulty with his mathematics could be asked to work for 15 minutes on some difficult problems. Aside from being able to examine the child's mathematical algorithms, the practitioner can also get an idea of the affective quality of the child's self-talk, such as "This is hopeless; I'm dumb; I'll never get this done."

The TAT-like approach (Meichenbaum, 1977) is an elicitational method that may be helpful when more direct techniques are not successful. This method uses pictures of ambiguous social situations selected for their relevance to the target behaviors. The child is asked to make up a story, including the thoughts and feelings of the characters, and what they can do about the situation.

Expansion–contraction (Bernard, 1981) is a procedure that attempts to expand the abbreviated and elliptical self-talk of young clients through the use of verbal prompts. The youngster is directed to describe in his or her own words the thoughts that he or she has during a problem situation. As the youngster begins to describe these thoughts, the practitioner provides verbal instructions and questions such as "What do you mean when you say 'you thought that . . .'?" "Why do you think that . . . ?" "What did you think after that?" "Describe to me the first thing that comes into your mind when you think about . . . ?" Contraction refers to the need to be sure that therapeutic instructions and ideas are expressed in a linguistic-conceptual form that can be meaningfully and nonarbitrarily incorporated by the young person.

Peeling the onion (Bernard, 1981) can almost be viewed as a component of expansion–contraction and can be described as involving the peeling away of the layers of thought until one reaches the level that is activating emotional upset. Often, hidden behind a facade of rational thought statements are layers of thought not immediately accessible to the client. It is recommended that the practitioner not be dissuaded, fooled, or discouraged in searching for irrational thoughts and that she or he keep focusing the youngster's attention on thoughts through the use of verbal prompts.

"And," "but," and "because" (Hauck, 1980) are extremely useful words that practitioners can use to help young clients to tune into and report automatic self-talk. If the child pauses at the end of what seems to be an incomplete sentence about what he or she is thinking, the practitioner coaxes and prods the client along with words such as *but, and,* and *because*.

Instant replay (Bedford, 1974) is a therapeutic technique developed for use with parents and children. Bedford requests that each member of the family keep track of situations and events during the week that result in unpleasant emotions ("rough spots"). During the next meeting, each member of the family is requested to do a "rerun" or "instant replay" of the rough spot. Children and parents are asked to describe the feelings and thoughts that they had in relation to the problem.

Guided imagery (Meichenbaum, 1977) involves the practitioner's asking the youngster to relax and then to imagine as vividly as possible a problem situation and to focus on feelings and self-talk. The client is asked to describe the scene and is encouraged to experience and communicate the feelings and thoughts associated with the setting.

Methods of Treatment

As a reading of the current writing of Ellis, Beck, Meichenbaum, and other leading proponents of the cognitive-behavior school reveals, emotional and behavioral problem solving is often accomplished through the use of a combination of cognitive, emotive, and behavioral change methods. In this section, we review the behavioral aspects of the use of RET with children; we review the different stages and goals of comprehensive RET; we emphasize the importance of teaching critical thinking skills; we discuss basic cognitive strategies for bringing about change; and we highlight some potential problems in trying to correct a child's veridical interpretations of reality.

Behavioral Components

RET has always been a cognitive-*behavioral* therapy. Even though Ellis (1962, 1979) stressed the role of cognitions in pathology, he has frequently acknowledged that for change to be lasting, one had better get clients to start acting differently. Because children are not self-referred, are likely to be less motivated for change, and are less responsible, it is incorrect to assume that they will carry out their behavioral assignments alone. However, their parents are usually willing to cooperate and can be enlisted to help structure the behavioral components of therapy. In almost all cases, except where the parents are uncooperative, one can use a behavioral modification program to reinforce the desired target behaviors while doing RET. Whether the emotional problem is fear, depression, or anger, the parents can provide structured, systematic rewards for the nonoccurrence of the target behaviors and for behaviors that are incompatible with the target behavior, or they can provide response costs when the target behavior does occur. Behavioral programs that reward or penalize behavior may not only help children to behave better but may also help them to become more motivated to cooperate with the therapist and learn cognitive strategies to control their emotions and to internalize behavioral gains—now there will be some payoff for overcoming their fear, depression, or anger.

While remembering again that children are not self-referred, it may be helpful for us to go into a little more detail about how the construction of behavioral reinforcement systems motivates children to learn control of their emotional reactions. Self-referred adults who are anxious not only experience fear but they are also in conflict (Dollard & Miller, 1950). Let us take the example of a young man, Fred, frightened of approaching women. Fred seeks therapy because he wants to find a lover. He is in an approach–avoidance conflict. Suppose he thinks that it would be awful and terrible if women rejected him; as a result, he experiences fright and avoids women, especially those he would like to date. On the other hand, he has a great desire to meet women for sex, romance, and companionship. It is this conflict that causes discomfort and motivates Fred to seek therapy. If for some reason Fred did not desire female companionship, he might still fear rejection by women; yet, under such circumstances, he would experience little discomfort from this fear. The fear would not be stopping him from achieving any desired goals. It would be quite easy for him to avoid women altogether. His anxiety would be limited to those situations in which he was forced to be in the company of women and was unable to avoid them. If you review your own case load, you may find that most of those who are self-referred are in one of Dollard and Miller's (1950) classic conflicts: approach–avoidance, avoidance–avoidance, or approach–approach. Conflict, then, causes most of the pain. Without the conflict, a person can easily avoid the feared stimuli. Discomfort arises only when people are forced to be in the presence of the feared stimuli and cannot escape, as in Fred's case. For example, the first author has a dreadful fear of alligators. He does not wish to date them or seek their company in any way. Because he does not seek alligators and there are none in his native Long Island, the fear never strikes him, except on those rare occasions when he visits the Bronx zoo. If, however, he developed a fondness for or an erotic attachment to alligators, he might wish to be in their company. Experiencing this fear when he attempts to do so would cause him discomfort, and it is this approach–avoidance that may bring him to the therapist's office. Other types of conflicts operate in a similar way.

Children's fears often provide them no *conflict:*

> The case of Karen, a school phobic, is a good illustration. She experienced extreme panic whenever called on in class to give an answer. As a result, she did not wish to attend school. She developed stomach pains and had a few days off, and the illness seemed to linger. Her mother, realizing that the ailment was more than an upset stomach, kept Karen home and felt sorry for her daughter when she realized the extent of Karen's emotional reaction to school. Karen was allowed to stay home and experienced no response cost for this behavior. During school hours, Karen watched TV, played alone, or listened to her records. After school, she met friends and joined in their activities. Not a bad life! Karen felt no desire to attend school and was not interested in any of the rewards that this institution dispensed. Why should she want to change? She listened carefully to a discussion of how thoughts caused feelings and how her catastrophizing about making mistakes caused her to feel frightened. She

agreed. However, this is as far as we got. There was no conflict and therefore no motivation for her to overcome her fear. Disputing was out of the question. After a few sessions with Karen's mother, we succeeded in lessening her sympathy for Karen's fear. We then set out the following rules. Karen was denied access to her TV and stereo whenever absent from school. She was not allowed to join her peers unless she attended class that day. Once these rules were in effect, Karen was more willing to start disputing those irrational beliefs that she had identified earlier and was now willing to attend school and control her anxiety with the procedures we had used. Once she was inside school, there was really no reason for Karen to attempt to raise her hand and answer questions, and she continued to make excuses to avoid answering questions when called on. We had made some progress, but the lack of any continued motivation stalled treatment. At this point, a reinforcement system was provided for answering in class. The teacher sent home daily feedback on the number of questions Karen attempted to answer. For each question, she was allotted a certain degree of money. Although this reinforcement did not help Karen to overcome her problems completely and she still experienced fear, again she was more interested in discussing her irrational beliefs and in attempting to overcome them because she wanted the money.

Behavioral incentives may provide the motivation for children to attempt to search for alternative strategies to overcome their emotional reactions. Although behavioral approaches to fear have achieved some success, it has not been the total improvement that one would expect. A cognitive-behavioral program, though, may be more successful. The behavioral incentives provide the motivation to change, and the cognitive interventions help to foster that change and to reduce the fear.

Overview of Course of Therapy

There are four discernible stages in applying RET and allied cognitive-behavioral approaches with children: (1) rapport building; (2) assessment; (3) skill acquisition; and (4) practice and application. We have already alluded to the necessity of building a relationship with a young client to maximize the likelihood that the child will be open about thoughts and actions. To facilitate self-disclosure, three strategies have been recommended:

1. *Don't be all business.* If your initial expectations are too high, the child may find the sessions aversive and then just not talk to you. Allow the child some time to get acquainted with you through play and off-task conversation. Shaping can be used to develop the self-disclosure and on-task conversation required in therapy.

2. *Always be honest with the child.* Children are more cautious than adults, probably because they are more vulnerable. They appear to be sensitive to deception, which they use as a measure of a person's trustworthiness.
3. *Go easily and carefully on the questions.* Children do not trust those who try to give them "the third degree." (DiGiuseppe, 1981, p. 56)

Waters (1982) indicated that self-disclosure can be learned quite effectively if the practitioner: (1) is a good model for self-disclosure; (2) accepts whatever the child says without putting her or him down; and (3) reinforces the child for disclosing.

We have already revealed the nature of RET assessment, including its ongoing role in treatment after it has been decided whether a problem exists and what the problem is. Explicit treatment goals expressed in terms of emotional and practical problems to be resolved derive from the assessment stage.

There are two distinct sets of skills taught during skill acquisition: emotional-problem-solving skills and practical-problem-solving skills (see Waters, 1983). Teaching children to solve their own emotional problems involves their initially understanding and expressing their emotions. Techniques for building emotional awareness have been discussed in the problem assessment section. Children begin to understand that there is a difference between helpful and hurtful feelings, that feelings come from thoughts, and that their thoughts control their feelings. A second step taken in emotional problem solving is teaching the ABC's of RET. Specifically, children are made more aware of their self-talk; of the connections among behaviors, emotions, antecedent events, and their self-talk and beliefs; and, with older children, the difference between rational and irrational beliefs. Other critical thinking skills and concepts taught include (from Waters, 1982): (1) absolute versus conditional thinking; (2) consequential thinking; (3) discriminating among fact, opinion, inference, and assumption; and (4) perspective taking. The final aspect of teaching emotional-problem-solving skills is demonstrating how cognitive change can occur and how it influences emotions and behavior. With younger children, the practitioner may provide practice in coping self-statements, whereas older children are taught how to challenge and dispute irrational thinking. These cognitive strategies will be illustrated shortly.

It may be necessary to teach practical skills to children who demonstrate limitations in their knowledge of how to behave in certain situations. A practical-problem-solving approach would involve the following steps (from Waters, 1982):

1. Define the problem in concrete, behavioral terms.

2. Generate as many solutions as you can without evaluating them. Remember, quantity is more important than quality; the more solutions the better.
3. Go back and evaluate each alternative solution, giving both positive and negative consequences and eliminating absurd solutions.
4. Choose one or two of the best solutions, and plan your procedures step by step.
5. Put your plan into action and evaluate the results. (p. 575)

Indeed, interpersonal cognitive problem-solving training may be the most appropriate treatment with certain children. Some children are not severely upset when they misbehave. They do not experience disturbed affect and do not appear to have irrational beliefs. Such children may think rationally and may manifest appropriate affect but behave in a self-destructive or antisocial manner because they do not have an adequate alternative response. This repertoire deficit might exist because of poor modeling or poor training. Children who *do* have irrational beliefs at the appraisal stage and who *do* have disturbed affect may still fail to behave appropriately (once they have changed their irrational beliefs and reduced their affect) because of the same limited repertoire at the action potential level. Here, interpersonal cognitive problem-solving skills may be a very important component of a *comprehensive* treatment plan. Many disturbed children have irrational beliefs, disturbed affect, and a limited action potential with few alternative adjusted responses. Thus, the comprehensive rational-emotive therapist would be best advised to make sure that he or she teaches skills in solving both emotional and practical problems.

The final stage of RET, practice and application, involves the practitioner's helping the young client to practice his or her newly acquired skills in problem situations at home and in school. In seeking to foster generalization, the child is given a variety of homework assignments including (from Waters, 1982):

(a) monitoring feelings, (b) making a list of personal demands, (c) employing rational-emotive imagery. (The client is asked to vividly imagine a situation where they experience a hurtful feeling. While they are imagining the scene they are asked to change the feeling to a more appropriate one and to become aware of the changes in their self-talk), (d) practicing changing feelings and thoughts in a real situation, (e) taking a responsible risk, and (f) reinforcing self with positive self-talk. (p. 576)

THE IMPORTANCE OF PREREQUISITE CRITICAL THINKING SKILLS

Rational-emotive therapy is concerned primarily with epistemology, the philosophical study of knowledge. In therapy, we are constantly asking clients, "How do you know that what you are thinking is accurate?" Disputing assumes that the client and the therapist share criteria for determining the truth or falsity of a statement. Many children have failed to develop critical thinking skills. Even if they have developed critical thinking skills and logic about the objective world, they may not have transferred these logical manipulations to the intrapersonal or interpersonal realm. As a result, they may have separate epistemologies for judging objective data and psychologically interpersonal statements. Children often have quite simple personal epistemologies. They may believe that things are true, so that they think they are true. Or just because they think them. Or because Mommy or Daddy says that they are true. Or because some other people think they are true, and, for adolescents, because their peers think they are true. All of these philosophical positions can get one into trouble.

Before attempting to dispute a child's irrational beliefs, it is a good idea to check out whether he or she can tell the differences among facts, opinions, and hypotheses and to ascertain if he or she can follow logical arguments in verifying statements or in discovering illogic. If they are like most adults, children may find it easier to be logical about external matters and may find it easy to believe that all automatic negative thoughts are true because they have thought them. The idea of examining and questioning one's thoughts about private, personal issues may be new to many young clients. It may be best to start teaching these skills by modeling and parable rather than by first challenging their irrational creations. One strategy is to present the irrational ideas of other clients when one has helped and to talk about how their errors were spotted and how they learned to challenge them. It may also help to talk about the therapist's own irrationalities and how he or she tested these out and discovered that they were false.

COGNITIVE STRATEGIES

As mentioned earlier, rational therapists try to help their clients reach the elegant solution and to realize that even if life's events are bad, they need not upset themselves and can appraise these events less negatively. In working with children, this is still our goal; however, it is less often accomplished. Ellis has commented many times in supervision that not all clients reach the elegant solution, and some appear particularly resistant no matter how hard they try. Children are less likely to reach this goal because of their inability to handle the degree of abstraction necessary. When the elegant solution appears unreachable with a child, there are three alternative solutions:

1. To change the child's appraisal of the one particular activating event about which she or he is upset.

2. To change the child's inferences when distortions of reality precede negative appraisals and disturbed effect. This approach is easier than elegant disputing because the empirical solution is more concrete.

3. To settle for verbal self-instruction that guides the child toward nonupsetting emotional responses and more adaptive behavior. This approach requires no disputing of the child's cognitions, but it does require an overriding cognition that directs the child to react differently. It is likely to be successful for a single stimulus or a narrow set of stimuli.

Some case studies may help exemplify these alternatives.

> Thomas was a 13-year-old student with a history of behavioral and academic problems. Thomas reported that his teacher had a great dislike of him, and she *had* become quite disgusted with him. As therapy progressed, Thomas made changes and behaved more appropriately in school. He became less angry and less disruptive. However, empirical disputing of his thoughts that the teacher did not like him showed them to be accurate. Given the way he had been behaving, it was hard to blame her. When Thomas made some improvements or behaved well, she frequently did not acknowledge the change or still accused him of behaving inappropriately. Thomas became angry at this point and had the action potential of giving up and acting badly again. His irrational beliefs leading to this anger were somewhat along the lines that "people should be fair." My attempts to dispute this idea with Thomas got nowhere. He believed that people should be fair. After all, how would the world survive if people couldn't be trusted. Fairness was necessary for social life, so he said. Rather than trying to convince him that unfairness was a fact of life, which it is, and that there were probably millions of unfair people out there, we focused on a more narrow set of beliefs, that is, that this particular teacher had to be fair. We discussed the particular reasons that she should be unfair; the fact that we could not change her even though we thought most people should be fair; to have an ordered world, we could not demand that she be fair and, that there was no way we could force her to be so. Although Thomas was not willing to accept the fact that unfairness would survive in the universe, he was willing to concede that this particular individual would remain unfair and that he could tolerate that little degree of unfairness. Thus, although we did not reach an elegant solution in changing his appraisal to a wide span of stimuli, we did teach him to appraise this particular stimulus in a very different way. His anger was reduced, and he continued to make behavioral gains throughout the school year.

> Sara was a 9-year-old who was particularly depressed because of the infrequency with which she saw her father. Her parents had been di-

vorced for six years, and her mother and father still continued to argue. Sara had a large number of siblings, all of whom were much older than she and who felt a great deal of animosity toward the father. The father reacted by avoiding them. Our discussions revealed that Sara believed that as her father did not love or care for her mother or her siblings, he could not really care for her. Empirical disputing of this inference revealed quite the opposite. While the father made little attempt to see the siblings and continued to argue with the mother whenever he came to visit Sara, he came to visit Sara quite regularly. Although he was not the most demonstrative person, he was much more dedicated to this child than to any of his other children and spent a considerable amount of time visiting her, calling her, and taking her places. Sara's upset was caused, first, by her inference that her father's behavior toward other members of the family indicated that he felt the same way toward her and, second, by her appraisal that, if he did not care for her, that would be catastrophic. Sara was quite unwilling even to discuss this last possibility. Challenging the idea that it would not be terrible if her father did not care for her led to silence and withdrawal. However, the empirical solution here interested her in collecting data to verify her inferences. She was pleased with the results. This strategy was acceptable because of the therapist's inference that the father really did care for Sara. If the empirical disputing had not led in the direction that it did, a more elegant approach would have been necessary. But here, it was acceptable to limit ourselves to the empirical solution.

Greg was a 9-year-old who was referred by his parents for temper tantrums, pouting, and noncooperative behavior. Greg had a family history of extreme noncontingent reward. During most of his life, his parents had pampered him and he had been allowed to do what he pleased. Although this behavior had been cute when he was younger, with maturity it became more unacceptable. Greg's parents attempted to have him follow rules and to behave appropriately. They punished him whenever he did not complete chores or show age-appropriate behaviors. Greg believed that this meant that they no longer cared for him. He also thought that it was terribly unfair that he should have to do such mundane things as clean his room and put his dirty clothes in the hamper. These things were just too difficult. Greg was a nonverbal child with low average intelligence, and he had difficulty following many of the disputing strategies. However, he was able to role-play these situations with the therapist. During these role plays, the therapist modeled verbal self-instructions such as "My parents care for me, they are only trying to do their job and help me grow up," and "I don't have to feel upset about these things because I can do them." Through practicing these self-statements and through reinforcement for appropriate behavior, Greg slowly learned to stop pouting, and this reaction provided the impetus for more mature, independent behaviors.

Correct Inferences: A Cautionary Note

As noted above, the empirical solution to emotional problems is often the easiest for children to grasp. Because of this ease, it is the strategy taken for many child therapists. A caveat is in order. A serious problem can arise in using the empirical solution when the child gets upset about the behavior of significant other adults, as children so frequently do. Children are apt to become upset when they believe that important adults in their lives do not love them, behave unfairly, or display serious personality disturbances. I have noticed a disturbing tendency on the part of child therapists to assume that the child incorrectly perceives such events. Rather than assuming that the child may be correct ("Let's suppose you're right, but why is that so awful?" as Albert Ellis so often says) and pursuing the elegant solution, the therapist sticks to the empirical disputing even when the data indicate that the child is correct. Many therapists do this because *they believe* that the realization that their parents are uncaring, unfair, or disturbed may be too much for the child to bear. Such a realization, they believe, would present an insurmountable obstacle to the child's emotional health.

Suppose children do confront situations in which a parent really does not care for them, or in which a parent does love another sibling more than the identified patient, or in which a teacher or parent is grossly unfair toward the child, or in which a parent is severely disturbed. When such situations are reality, the empirical solution is unwarranted and could cause iatrogenic damage. If a child is not cared for by a parent and we try to reduce that child's depression by (1) relabeling the parent's behavior as caring, (2) attempting to find good in this parent and to deny the uncaring behaviors, or (3) convincing the child that the parent really does care, are we not creating a disturbed perception of love and caring in that child? If a parent does behave unfairly and we pursue an empirical strategy to reduce the child's upset by presenting the parent as possibly fair, are we not also creating a distorted idea of fairness if we succeed? In the above two situations, the therapist may choose to avoid the issue and may choose not to corroborate the child's perceptions one way or the other. If this strategy is pursued, are we not sending the child a nonverbal message that this is a topic not to be talked about and that one cannot criticize parents or recognize their faults? Who knows what other solutions or conclusions the child may draw and how healthy they may be? Thus, not to comment on the child's perceptions may lead to unknown conclusions on the part of the child and unknown iatrogenic side effects.

Some children correctly perceive that they have verifiable adversity in their lives. Uncaring, capricious, and disturbed parents exist. They are not only characters in Grimms' fairy tales. Therapists are often unwilling to pursue the elegant solution in such cases because they believe that it must be awful to live in such a situation. Empirical solutions for the children of these parents are unlikely to help and are likely at best to lead to reduced rapport because the child will know that the therapist cannot or will not help. At the worst, the therapist may succeed and leave the child feeling temporarily better, but with some distortions about love, fairness, and authority. Another therapeutic intervention often tried in such cases is to provide the child with a supportive relationship, again, temporarily making the child feel better. According to rational-emotive therapy, this strategy is merely palliative and leads to no permanent resolution.

When children's adversity is verified by the therapist, it may be best largely to seek the elegant solution. Children may be more resilient than we believe, and at least, we may do them no harm. Two case summaries may illustrate this point:

> Mike, a 12-year-old, was referred because of depression. The school feared that he was suicidal. Mike's dad, a recovered alcoholic, experienced chronic episodes of depression. His mother felt particularly angered by these events because they greatly imposed on her life as well. The father's depression usually resulted in periods of parental arguing. Previous therapists had attempted to help Mike by focusing on the marriage and the resolution of its fights or the father's depression. But all sorts of marital therapy, family therapy, individual therapy, and chemotherapy had failed to lift the father's depression or resolve the parents' arguing. Mike was stuck with a depressed father and a mother who was angered by the depressive episodes.
>
> The initial interview with Mike revealed that he believed it was best not to acknowledge his father's mistakes or personality failures and not to acknowledge his mother's anger. Once he did talk of these things, it was discovered that Mike believed he was destined to be depressed if his father was, that one had to be unhappy if his parents fought, and that it was awful to have both a depressed father and a fighting mother. Direct disputing of these irrational beliefs proved quite successful in a short period of time. In order to succeed, I had to agree with Mike that his dad was depressed and that his parents did fight bitterly. But he already knew that. He did not realize that fathers do not have to be perfect and are allowed to have serious problems, and that despite their serious problems they can still be nice and one can still love them. Mike learned to forgive his dad for his depression and his mom for her arguing. He also learned how to focus

more on the positive aspects of both parents and how not to get upset when they put their worst foot forward.

Jack, a 9-year-old, was also depressed. His father worked long hours at a very successful practice. Jack believed that his father did not love him. My initial intervention was to help Jack to make an operational definition of loving behaviors and then to see how many of these behaviors his father performed and how frequently. After a few sessions of defining the list and empirically verifying his father's responses, we unfortunately came to the conclusion that Jack's father did not fare too well on this empirical test. Although he performed most of the behaviors on the caring list, he did so at a very low frequency.

Did the father love Jack? That was the next question that Jack struggled with. How many loving behaviors does one have to perform toward another to demonstrate love? How frequently does one have to perform loving behaviors toward a person to receive that person's love? I tried to convince Jack that any decision we made about a cutoff score of frequency of loving behaviors and types of loving behaviors was arbitrary. My cutoff score might be different from his. Someone else's might be different altogether. Love is what one person defines it to be. Any definition that we made of love would be just that, our definition, and might not represent a universal reality. We could not define whether or not Jack's father loved him, and we also did not know how Jack's father *felt*. Although we could infer his affective state toward Jack from his behavior, the result would be just that, an inference. I used lots of examples to show how Jack very often felt quite differently from the way he acted. Jack was still left with one real adversity. He experienced fewer loving behaviors from his father than he wanted. It was evident that Jack's father demonstrated caring behaviors much less frequently than the fathers of Jack's peers. So Jack's lack of received affection was real. The important issue I pointed out to Jack was not whether his father loved him, but how miserable he was going to make himself over the way his father reacted. I challenged the ultimate irrational belief that one has to experience love and loving behaviors from one's parents in order to be worthwhile and even to be happy. Jack's father might never change; he might always prefer work to family involvement, but Jack learned to be less upset about this fact and to enjoy other things in his life.

In these two cases, several aspects seem clinically important. Children often have negative perceptions about their parents that are emotionally charged. Unless the therapist shows a willingness to entertain these ideas and acceptance of the child for thinking them and speaking about them, it is unlikely that the child will be open with the therapist. Some therapists may feel frightened about confirming the child's ideas about the parent, or they may feel that discussing the parents' behavior when the child is referred is risky. Other therapists have often told me that the discussion of such situations would be too traumatic for a child to face. I maintain that an openness and willingness to discuss such issues will get to the true irrational beliefs that are often upsetting children and to the true evaluations that they make.

Case Illustration

The following is a transcript of an interview conducted by the first author with an 8-year-old girl was was referred for therapy just after her parents' separation. She had become very hostile and had started to act out. Her concerns were highlighted when her parents started dating other people. During this first session, she was helped to understand what her beliefs were and how they were leading to her fears:

T: How many times have your seen your father this week?
C: Not too many.
T: Well, when did you see him?
C: Sunday, he took us to Cape May.
T: Sunday? He took you to Cape May?
C: Yeah, that's where I was born.
T: You were born at Cape May?
C: Yeah?
T: Cape May is pretty far. How long did it take you to get there?
C: It took three hours.
T: Did you stay overnight?
C: No.
T: You just drove down for the day?
C: Yeah.
T: Who went with you?
C: My brother, my father . . . that's all.
T: Did you have a good time?
C: Yep.
T: What did you do in Cape May?
C: Well, um . . . we stopped for some gas and a soda. And after we finished, my father got us some candy bars. And then we took off.
T: So you had a good time?
C: And we picked up two hitchhikers.
T: You did?
C: Yep.
T: Girls? Gee, did your daddy like the girls?
C: Yes.

T: Were they pretty girls?
C: I don't know.
T: Did your daddy want to go out with them?
C: No!
T: What do you mean, no?
C: Of course not.
T: Why not?
C: They were too young.
T: Oh, they were too young. What if they were older?
C: Like, daddy's age?
T: Yeah, what if they were daddy's age?
C: Well, I don't think if he . . . he would.
T: He would what?
C: Go out with them.
T: What do you mean? Why not?
C: I don't want him to.
T: I know you don't want him to, but—why don't you turn around and look at me? Don't talk to the wall.

T: All right? So you said your daddy wouldn't go out with these girls because they were too young, huh?
C: Right.
T: What if they were older and closer to your daddy's age? Then would he like to?
C: I think he would.
T: You think he would? Why would he?
C: Don't ask me.
T: Well?
C: I don't know everything.
T: That's true. You don't know everything, but maybe you'd know why he'd want to go out with them.
C: No.
T: No? You don't like that idea at all, do you?
C: No.
T: No way.
C: Got a ruler?
T: Got a ruler? I don't know. Let me see if I have a ruler in here.
C: Here. I want it.
T: I'll get it. Hold on.
C: I got it. I want to make the lines perfect . . .
T: O.K. Now we were talking about if your daddy would date other women, right?
C: Yeah.
T: You don't think he would?
C: Right.
T: Do you?

C: I don't think he will. He wouldn't do such a thing.
T: Well, you make it sound like it would be a really bad thing if he did it.
C: It isn't bad, but I just don't want Dad to do it.
T: How would you feel if he did date other women?
C: I would kill 'em.
T: Now wait a sec. That's what you'd do—how does it feel?
C: Sad.
T: Well, why would you feel sad if your daddy dated other women?
C: Because he might get married to 'em.
T: Well, what if he did get married to another woman?
C: I would hate it.
T: You would hate who?
C: The other girl.
T: Why would you hate her?
C: For being there when Mummy and Daddy weren't—aren't married anymore. He—he—he'll still be my father.
T: Well, even if he married another woman, wouldn't he still be your father then?
C: Yeah.
T: So he'd still be your father.
C: I don't know . . .
T: Would you be afraid that he might have other children by this lady.
C: Yes!
T: You would. What if he did?
C: I'd kill the kids.
T: You would kill the kids. Why would you kill the kids?
C: Because I wouldn't like them.
T: Why wouldn't you? They didn't do anything to you.
C: But they took my father away.
T: No. They didn't take your father away.
C: Then, how come they took my father away?
T: Your father would have them. The kids wouldn't be taking him away from you.
C: I don't want the other lady.
T: I don't want the other lady to what?
C: I don't want . . . I just don't want it.
T: But there is no other lady yet.
C: Right. And I'll make sure it will stay that way.
T: You will? How will you make sure it stays that way?
C: I will foul up my . . . my father's marriage.
T: How will you foul up your father's marriage?
C: After I'm invited to her wedding, I'll mess it all up.
T: Will you mess it up before he gets a chance to marry?
C: Yes. And the the ladies will hate him.
T: They'll hate him?
C: Right.

ASSESSMENT AND METHODS OF CHILDHOOD TREATMENT

T: So that's what you have to do, to have all the women he dates hate him so they don't marry him.
C: Right.
T: Why would you want to do something like that?
C: I don't know.
T: Doesn't seem to be a very nice thing to do, does it?
C: No.
T: What are you looking for?
C: A gray pen.
T: I don't have a gray pen; there's a crayon there.
C: Not that one.
T: What if your mom met a man and wanted to marry him?
C: I wouldn't let her go out with him.
T: Why not?
C: I just wouldn't let her.
T: Well, how could you stop her?
C: I don't know.
T: Could you stop them?
C: Yeah.
T: How?
C: Don't know.
T: Let's pretend that your mom and dad got the divorce all right. OK? They really won't get it till the summer, but let's just pretend that they did.
C: Yeah.
T: And let's suppose your mom came home and said, "Saturday night, I've got a date with some guy and I am going to go out with him." What would you—
C: Then I'll sneak in the back seat and watch what they would do and listen to what they say.
T: Why would you do that?
C: Cause I've got to see what—if he—um—asks her to go anywhere.
T: What if he did? What if he dated her five or six times and then asked her to stay. How would you feel about that?
C: He wouldn't see me. I'd be under a rock.
T: You would be under a rock? What would you do under a rock?
C: I would crawl under a rock and . . . close to her.
T: Why?
C: Well . . . I don't know.
T: How would you feel if they got married? If your mom got married again?
C: Don't even say such a thing.
T: Don't say such a thing? Sounds to me like you'd be pretty sad about that.
C: Hey.
T: Hey what?
C: I would.
T: You would? Well why would you be so sad about it. 'Cause why?
C: 'Cause I wouldn't like it.
T: You wouldn't, huh?

C: 'Cause I wouldn't like to have another father.
T: What would it mean to you if you had another father?
C: Well, I wouldn't. I just wouldn't like it.
T: Would you be afraid that you'd lose your other father?
C: Right.
T: Right, huh? But wait a second. How do you know you'd lose your other father?
C: I don't know.
T: Well let's think about it. What makes you think you would lose your other father.
C: It would be different; it wouldn't be the same.
T: That's right, it would be different; it wouldn't be the same as it is now.
C: And the guy might charge more rent.
T: Charge more rent? What do you mean he might charge more rent: Who, what guy?
C: Um, my . . . if my mother gets married again, 'cause, then . . . and he might charge more rent to us.
T: And then what?
C: Well, then we would move out; then we would get an extra room.
T: Then you would get what?
C: Then we would get an extra room.
T: So this guy that your mother marries might charge more rent on the apartment upstairs. Is that what you're afraid of?
C: Yeah.
T: And if he did, who would move out? Huh?
C: Me!
T: Why would you move out? You really don't like the idea of your mother getting married again.
C: No I . . . anyway she couldn't get married right now.
T: No, that's true, but you'd be pretty upset if she did, huh?
C: Yeah.
T: What makes you get so upset?
C: I don't know.
T: Well, think about it. Do you know anybody else whose parents got divorced?
C: Yeah, my friend Emily.
T: Your friend Emily? Did her mother get remarried?
C: No.
T: Do you think there are people—
C: 'Cause her father walked out on her mother when she was only one year old. That was nine years ago, she's ten right now.
T: How would Emily feel if her mother remarried?
C: I don't know . . .
T: Huh?
C: I don't know.
T: You don't know what she wants. Do you think everybody would feel as upset as you if their mother remarried?
C: Probably.

ASSESSMENT AND METHODS OF CHILDHOOD TREATMENT

T: Probably? Well, wait a second. Check that out. How do you know that?
C: I don't know.
T: That's right, you don't know. As a matter of fact, some kids are very happy when their mom remarries.
C: Happy?
T: Some of them are real happy about it.
C: They've got to be nuts.
T: No, they don't have to be nuts. Some of them like the idea, so it really can't be the fact that your mom may remarry that makes you sad, could it?
C: Yes. It does.
T: That's a really nice picture. Can I keep that?
C: Yeah.
T: Well, thank you.
C: Now I'm going to draw a picture for my mother.
T: What picture are you going to draw for her?
C: You'll find out.
T: What do you think would make you so upset if your mom remarried and other people not upset?
C: Well, they wouldn't be upset.
T: And you see what makes people upset—it's the way they think about things. If you thought differently about it, you wouldn't feel sad about it. Do you know that?
C: No.
T: Well, it's true. You think that it would be a pretty terrible thing, don't you?
C: No.
T: No? What do you think about it?
C: Well, I just think I wouldn't like it.
T: You just think you would not. But you don't know for sure, do you?
C: Right.
T: That's like if somebody says, "Why don't you try these peas?" if you have never had peas before, and you say, "No I'm not going to try it—I don't think I'd like peas. I can tell by the way they look." But you really don't know whether or not you like peas do you?
C: I don't like them.
T: But if you never had any before, you wouldn't know until you tried them. Right?
C: Right, but I just don't like peas anyway.
T: Yeah. Well, OK, if somebody gave you asparagus. You know asparagus?
C: No.
T: Well, if somebody gave you asparagus, and you said, "I don't think I'd like that"—well, how do you know?
C: I don't know.
T: So you don't know—you might like asparagus a lot. Right?
C: How do I like asparagus if I don't even know what it is?
T: Well you might like it. Same thing if your mommy married. You couldn't say, "I don't think I would like it"—you really can't tell until you try it.
C: I know that.

T: Also you think that if your mom remarried that would mean that you wouldn't have your father anymore. Right?
C: Right. And if my father got remarried—
T: That means he wouldn't want to see you anymore. Is that what you think?
C: Right.
T: Well, let's check that out. I think both of those thoughts are not true.
C: They aren't?
T: No. I don't think they're true at all. Why would your father, who loves you very much, not want to see you if he married someone else?
C: He wants—he likes to see me. He took me to Cape May last Sunday.
T: That's right.
C: He wanted to see us.
T: That's true.
C: He let us sleep over on Saturday.
T: That's right. And if he got remarried—if he married another woman—he would still want to see you. Just as much as he does now.
C: I know that.
T: I don't think you know that. I think that you think the opposite at times.
C: Do I think the opposite?
T: That's right, and you would be a little jealous that he might have other children by this woman—
C: Yeah—
T: And then he would love them more than you?
C: No, he wouldn't.
T: But aren't you afraid of that?
C: Yeah.
T: Yeah. But you don't want him to get married so he won't have other children.
C: Right.
T: But you see, there's no reason to believe he would love them more than you. He would love them a lot and he would have to help them, but he would love them just as much as he loves you. And he would still want to see you just as much.
C: . . . He loves me just as much as he loves . . .
T: He would love the other children just as much as he loves you, and he would never stop loving you.
C: But what if he forgot all about me?
T: Now, wait a minute. How are we going to forget all about a nice little girl like you? Answer me that?
C: . . .
T: How is he going to forget about you? Huh?
C: I don't know.
T: Has he forgotten about you yet?
C: No.
T: Tell me, how long has it been that he's been out of the house?
C: I don't know.
T: Has it been two months, three months, a year?

C: He hasn't been out for a year, out of our house for a year.
T: Has it been a couple of months?
C: I don't know.
T: Has he forgotten about you yet?
C: No.
T: No, he hasn't. What makes you think that he might?
C: Who said I thought he might?
T: You did. You said if he got remarried and married someone else and had children by them, by her, he might forget about you with other children and another wife. Isn't that you said?
C: Yeah, kind of.
T: Kind of? But that seems pretty unlikely to me—that your father would forget about you. Some people think that you can only love one family at a time; for example, you might think that if he married another woman and had children by her that he could only love those children and that wife and would have to forget about you and wouldn't be able to love you. But that's not true. He could love you just as much, and want to see you just as much, and could see you just as much.
C: But what if his wife was mean and wouldn't let him see us?
T: Well, then he would have to just demand that he see you. She can't stop him from seeing you.
C: I'd give her a bloody nose.
T: That's right. But do you really think that your father would marry somebody like that? That would be that mean?
C: No.
T: You see, so it's unlikely that he is going to marry anybody as mean as that.
C: Right.
T: So you see if he remarried, it's nothing to be afraid of is it?
C: No.
T: Nothin' bad going to happen from it.

T: You want to stick to your real father. And I guess if your mom makes love and junk to another man, marries him, there's no chance that your real father will ever come home.
C: Right.
T: And that means that it's really over between your mom and dad.
C: This is the third time he moved out.
T: It is, I know. But if she gets married again, that means that it's for good. Right?
C: No.
T: No?
C: They might not get along.
T: Who might not get along?
C: My mother and the man she might marry.
T: And then what would happen?
C: They'd get divorced again.

T: And then what might happen?
C: I don't know.
T: Then your real father could come home?
C: Right.
T: Right. That's really clever of you. Huh? But you know it's not so terrible if he doesn't.
C: Oh, yes, it is.
T: Oh, yes, it is. Why is it so terrible?
C: 'Cause I want him to stay with us.
T: Yeah but you . . . that doesn't make it terrible.
C: Yes, it does.
T: What does terrible really mean?
C: Awful.
T: Awful. What does awful mean?
C: Terrible.
T: Well, wait a second. It's like saying red means blue and blue means red, because red means blue doesn't make sense. What does it mean to be terrible or awful?
C: I don't know.
T: Well, isn't it—doesn't it mean a catastrophe?
C: No.
T: Really 110% bad?
C: Yeah.
T: Yeah, huh? Well, why is it 110% bad and a catastrophe if your father doesn't come home? And if they stay separated?
C: I don't know.
T: Well, you think it is.
C: No, I don't.
T: Yes, you do. You just said before that it was terrible if he doesn't come home.
C: Yeah, it is terrible.
T: Well, wait a second. Why is it, why is it terrible?
C: Because I would miss him.
T: Yeah, but you see that's why it would be bad, but that doesn't mean that it's terrible.
C: Yes, it does.
T: No, it doesn't.
C: Yes.
T: There are lots of things in the world that are bad that aren't terrible. They're just a little bad. Or they may be a lot bad, but they're still not terrible. Do you think there's just one kind of bad and that's awful?
C: No, I don't.
T: What do you think?
C: I think it's—it's crummy.
T: It's crummy. That's right—it's just crummy. It's too bad that your father's not ever going to live at home again, isn't that unfortunate? And tough? But it certainly isn't terrible. It's not going to kill you if he doesn't come home, is it?

C: No.
T: You're not going to die?
C: No. I'll die of old age.
T: You'll die of old age, right. You're not going to turn into some kind of bad person because your father's not going to come home, are you?
C: No.
T: So it doesn't seem like it is such a catastrophe, if he . . .
C: It isn't.

This example reveals the use of empirical disputation to "check out" and correct the young girl's antiempirical assumptions concerning the consequences of her parents' divorce. Persistent and directed questioning elicited a variety of beliefs and feelings appeared to be responsible for the client's state of unhappiness and misbehavior. Even within the initial session, it can be seen that it was possible to identify and begin to challenge irrational concepts such as the "catastrophic" effects of possible remarriage.

References

Beford, S. *Instant replay: A method of counseling and talking to little (and other) people.* New York: Institute for Rational Living, 1974.

Bem, S. The role of comprehension in children's problem solving. *Developmental Psychology,* 1971, *2,* 351–359.

Bernard, M. E. Private thought in rational-emotive psychotherapy. *Cognitive Therapy and Research,* 1981, *5,* 125–142.

Bernard, M. E., & Joyce, M. R. *Rational-emotive therapy with children and adolescents.* New York: Wiley, 1984.

Cohen, R., & Meyers, A. W. Cognitive development and self-instruction interventions. In B. Gholson & T. L. Rosenthal (Eds.), *Applications of cognitive development theory.* New York: Academic Press, 1983.

DiGiuseppe, R. A. Cognitive therapy with children. In G. Emery, S. D. Hollon, & R. C. Bedrosian (Eds.), *New directions in cognitive therapy.* New York: Guilford Press, 1981.

Dollard, J., & Miller, N. E. *Personality and psychotherapy.* New York: McGraw-Hill, 1950.

Ellis, A. *Reason and emotion in psychotherapy.* New York: Lyle Stuart, 1962.

Ellis, A. The theory of rational-emotive therapy. In A. Ellis & J. M. Whiteley (Eds.), *Theoretical and empirical foundations of rational-emotive therapy.* Monterey, Calif.: Brooks/Cole, 1979.

Ellis, A. *Rational-emotive therapy and cognitive behavior therapy.* New York: Springer, in press.

Flavel, J. H. *Cognitive development.* Englewood-Cliffs, N.J.: Prentice-Hall, 1977.

Flavell, J., Beach, D., & Chinsky, J. Spontaneous verbal rehearsal in a memory task as a function of age. *Child Development,* 1966, *37,* 283–299.

Genest, M., & Turk, D. C. Think-aloud approaches to cognitive assessment. In T. V. Merluzzi, C. R. Glass, & M. Genest (Eds.), *Cognitive assessment.* New York: Guilford Press, 1981.

Meichenbaum, D. *Cognitive-behavior modification: An integrative approach.* New York: Plenum Press, 1977.

Morris, C. W., & Cohen, R. Cognitive considerations in cognitive behavior modification. *School Psychological Review,* 1982, *11,* 14–20.

Neisser, U. *Cognitive psychology.* New York: Appleton-Century-Crofts, 1967.

Reese, H. Verbal meditation as a function of age. *Psychological Bulletin,* 1962, *59,* 502–509.

Schacter, S. The interaction of cognitive and physiological determinants of emotional state. In C. D. Spielberger (Ed.), *Anxiety and behavior.* New York: Academic Press, 1966.

Schleser, R., Meyers, A., & Cohen, R. Generalization of self-instructions: Effects of general versus specific content, active rehearsal, and cognitive level. *Child Development,* 1981, *52,* 335–340.

Spivack, G., Platt, J., & Shure, M. *The problem-solving approach to adjustment.* San Francisco: Jossey-Bass, 1976.

Urbain, E. S., & Kendall, P. C. Review of social-cognitive problem-solving interactions with children. *Psychological Bulletin,* 1980, *88,* 109–143.

Waters, V. Therapies for children: Rational-emotive therapy. In C. R. Reynolds & T. B. Gutkin (Eds.), *Handbook of school psychology.* New York: Wiley, 1982.

Wessler, R. A., & Wessler, R. L. *The principles and practice of rational-emotive therapy.* San Francisco: Jossey-Bass, 1980.

Wolpe, J. *The practice of behavior therapy.* New York: Pergamon Press, 1973.

3

Principles of Assessment and Methods of Treatment with Adolescents
Special Considerations

HOWARD S. YOUNG

Historical and clinical evidence is replete with innumerable instances in which adolescents have habitually, rather than merely occasionally or sporadically, acted in the most maladaptive and self-defeating ways imaginable (Ellis, 1971). Various explanations have been offered for this phenomenon, ranging from the hormonal changes of puberty to the psychosocial pressures of growing up. My observations, however, suggest that the self-defeating behavior so common to adolescence is primarily the result of the young person's evaluation and appraisal of his or her life experiences rather than being the result of any particular set of biological, social, or environmental circumstances. This conclusion flows from an ongoing exposure to the beliefs and value systems of countless teenagers, who consistently reveal thinking patterns grounded in ignorance, misconception, and, quite often, utter nonsense.

Let me point out that practically every adolescent client I have worked with has managed to distort, exaggerate, and misinterpret, reality and to suffer accordingly. Adolescents seem to find it incredibly easy to turn disappointments into disasters; desires into demands; wants into necessities; difficulties into impossibilities; and failure and criticism into proof that they are subhuman creatures. Although they do so unwittingly, adolescents *think* themselves into their social and emotional problems.

HOWARD S. YOUNG • Hibbard Psychiatric Clinic, Huntington, West Virginia, 25701.

When faced with the teenager as a client, therefore, the counselor would ideally direct therapeutic endeavors at changing attitudes—persuading the young person to think in logical, sensible, and scientific ways. Unfortunately, this is not an easy task. Not only do adolescents possess the normal human inclination to resist change, but they are frequently rebellious and contrary, sometimes to the point of sabotaging their own best interests. Add these attitudes to what appears to be a universal distrust of adults and adult values, and the resulting situation is one that is hardly conducive to a therapeutic exchange.

In spite of their well-earned status as difficult clients, however, adolescents can be helped to overcome their emotional and behavioral conflicts through psychotherapy. The approach I have found most effective is based on the theoretical principles of rational-emotive psychotherapy (Bard, 1980; Ellis, 1962, 1974; Ellis & Harper, 1975; Walen, DiGiuseppe, & Wessler, 1980; Wessler & Wessler, 1980). This approach structures the counseling process according to the following considerations:

- Relationship building
- Problem defining
- Problem intervention
- Problem solving

Although each area usually requires attention, one need not hold to this particular order, and it is understood that there is overlapping. For instance, one could be developing a relationship while defining a problem, and vice versa. The therapist might also want to concentrate more on one area than on another. Regardless of how it is managed, I have found reliance on this framework is productive in maintaining a therapeutic direction with the adolescent client.

Relationship Building

The purpose of relationship development in RET is to create an atmosphere in which the client can feel free to talk about personal problems and difficulties. This usually involves the sharing of one's thoughts, fantasies, feelings, and the like. Unfortunately, the average adolescent is usually unaccustomed to discussing such private concerns with an adult. Because this kind of disclosure is essential to cognitive analysis and intervention and is best encouraged by the well-known virtues of empathy, warmth, nonjudgmental regard, and the like, relationship building is a primary consideration when attempting to counsel young people. I do emphasize, however, that the relationship is not the therapy. It is, rather, the means by which a problem-facing and problem-solving format can be established on behalf of the client. Some of the approaches I have found helpful in fostering a trusting and accepting alliance with the adolescent are the following:

1. *Allowing long periods of uninterrupted listening.* This is, perhaps, a departure from the more active, interventional approach usually employed in RET. However, I have found that many adolescents have not had the opportunity to "tell their story" without some kind of admonishment or interruption. As a result, I tend sometimes to allow chatting or rapping in the interest of encouraging ease and comfort in the therapeutic situation.

I also try to avoid silences with teenagers. With the exception of a client who is pausing to collect his or her thoughts or to frame an answer to a question, every attempt is made to keep the conversation going without breaks. I find that most teenagers feel very uncomfortable and self-conscious when silences are deliberately allowed to last.

2. *Accepting the client's reality perspective regardless of how distorted or limited it may be.* If, for example, a young client decides that his parents are always on his back or that a probation officer is out to get him, I usually accept such convictions at face value, even though I may know that they are untrue. Often, this acceptance indicates that I am an ally rather than an opponent and accordingly decreases the client's defensiveness. This is an especially useful technique with adolescents considered delinquent or antiestablishment.

3. *Discussing openly my own opinions and attitudes.* I try to answer all personal questions casually and directly, including questions about my marriage, my political preferences, religious issues, and personal problems. I have found that I tend to be asked questions of a more personal nature by teenagers; this is understandable, because many of them are trying to find out what adulthood is really all about. They usually do not have such an opportunity to question other adults—parents or teachers, for example, who often hide in moral or idealistic roles.

4. *Allowing a companion to sit in on a session.* Quite often, permitting a young person to bring along a friend seems to ease the situation and pave the way for future progress. In fact, I sometimes use the companion to make a point or two. On more than one occasion, I have found that the companion has perceived a message quite clearly and has been able to repeat it to the primary client, thus facilitating the therapy. I have also used this approach with good results by allowing a pet to join us for a session or two. Encounters have been shared with dogs, hamsters, cats, mice, turtles, and birds, although I did turn down a pony.

5. *Giving the adolescent priority.* When a teenager is brought in by parents who are registering a complaint and asking for therapy, I very frequently see the teenager first. Thus, I can sometimes give the impression that I am willing to listen to her or him and to respect her or his point of view, and it can help lessen her or his concern that I am in collaboration with the parents.

6. *Extracting from the parents an initial concession.* I sometimes try to have especially strict or overprotective parents give in on some of their demands or restrictions. Increasing the amount of an allowance, extending a curfew, or reducing a yard-work commitment are good examples. This approach sometimes gives the teenager the idea that I have influence over the parents, a concept not previously considered, and it often paves the way to a more responsive relationship.

Problem Defining

The purpose of problem defining in RET is to obtain a diagnostic assessment of the client's reality-based and psychologically induced complaints. Although this might seem an obvious step with any client, it deserves special attention with the adolescent. It is not unusual for young people to be vague, general, and downright hostile when asked why they have come in for counseling. Furthermore, adolescents seem to wander into tangents easily, to get wrapped up in the details of their volatile life experiences, or to get lost in meaningless philosophy-of-life excursions. Sometimes, I permit such meanderings in the interest of relationship building, but usually, I make an effort to encourage the young person to be problem-focused. Some of the tactics I have used to introduce a problem-facing format are:

1. *Defining the problem for the adolescent.* In many cases, young people who come to my attention are initially referred by parents, schools, or police. Usually, I have some knowledge of their difficulties beforehand; a simple statement like "I understand you are here because you ran away from home" leads to a lively problem-focused discussion.

Sometimes, however, the client denies the problem suggested by the referral agent. For instance, a probation officer might see dropping out of school as the reason for counseling, whereas the client might see difficulties with a boy or girl friend as the problem area. Faced with this kind of dilemma, I usually offer help on the problem identified by the adolescent with the hope that I can get to other concerns later.

On other occasions, the client flatly denies problems. Often, this denial is best handled by suggesting that the referral agent is the problem. If, for example, a teenager is referred by her parents for school underachievement and the young person vehemently insists that neither this nor anything else is troubling her, I try to gain her cooperation by suggesting that I can help her deal with her parents who are trying to run her life. In other words, I suggest that she has problem parents who could be the subjects of counseling endeavors. This tactic is sometimes useful with teenagers who come to therapy against their wishes.

2. *Simplifying the definition of a problem.* Many times a young client is afraid to reveal a problem because he thinks he has to tell his innermost secrets or that anyone with a problem is crazy. In order to overcome this obstacle, I will sometimes oversimplify, describing a problem that deserves counseling as hurt feelings, hassles with others, or doubts about the future. A problem-facing discussion often ensues, because most adolescents usually admit to concerns in one of these areas.

3. *Using a representative example from the life of another young person.* By discussing another teenager's problem, I am sometimes able to illustrate what I am looking for. This approach not only provides the client with a sense of "At least I'm not the only one with problems," but it also offers a concrete example of the kind of subject matter discussed in counseling.

4. *Offering a problem example out of my own life.* This tactic is especially effective if it deals with criticism, rejection, and failure—all areas about which adolescents are frequently overly concerned. Not only do such admissions humanize the therapist, but they also help the young person to discover that such problems are inherent in life, no matter what the person's age.

5. *Using visual aids.* I have found the most effective approach with the evasive or "problem-free" client is to use wall posters illustrating irrational ideas and their corollaries. I ask the young person to look at this list and see if she or he holds any of the ideas. This is a quick way to get a diagnostic impression of the client's thinking, and it can serve as a stepping-stone to identifying a specific problem area.

6. *Unraveling the problem from a rambling dialogue.* Some teenagers come in for counseling and admit that they have problems but remain unable to pinpoint an issue. With this group, I merely ask questions about school, family, friends, love life, and so on. Before long, I usually perceive a problem that could use counseling assistance. I then suggest this area to the client with a brief explanation of how I could help. For example, one teenager, referred by her mother, admitted that she wanted counseling but was unable to identify with any of the problem examples I suggested. I let her give me a rundown of her life experiences on a typical day. After a few minutes, it was evident that she was extremely upset with a younger sister who was always borrowing her clothes. I

asked if she wanted to know how to feel less angry about the situation and perhaps learn how to stand up to her sister without getting in trouble with her mother. She agreed and we were in business.

Problem Intervention

Problem intervention in RET is the place in which the so-called work of therapy occurs. Ideally, this involves helping clients learn to recognize, challenge, and correct the irrational attitudes that cause emotional distress and generate self-defeating behavior. Even when I have his or her undivided attention, this is often an arduous task with the average teenaged client. Perhaps this difficulty might be explained by the likelihood that adolescents are only beginners when it comes to manipulating thought and understanding abstract concepts (Piaget & Inhelder, 1969). Most likely, too, they have had scant training in or encouragement of the capacity for logical or sensible thinking. I have therefore found it best to keep things *simple, visual,* and *brief.* The following suggestions follow this framework and have been generally effective in imparting rational insights to adolescent clients:

1. *Teaching or not teaching the relationship between thinking, feelings, and actions.* Usually, I make an initial effort to teach the role of cognitions in causing emotions and behavior. I rely on the ABC model, sometimes introducing it verbally and other times using cartoon drawings or some other kind of illustrations. I explain the ABC's to adolescents as a formula that can be used for understanding their problems more clearly, and I rarely devote more than five minutes to the task.

Most of the time, however, I avoid teaching this principle as such. Experience has shown that many teenagers do not want to learn "psychology" or have too much difficulty fitting their problems into an ABC format to make this approach feasible. In most cases, I am lucky if they remember my name, so I figure it is unlikely that they are going to spend much time learning a process. With this group, probably the majority of my adolescent clients, I discuss problems in terms of their thinking, but I am not concerned with their understanding or with applying the theory behind what we are doing.

2. *Confronting and confuting "awfuls," "terribles," and "horribles."* According to RET theory (Wessler & Wessler, 1980), irrational thinking is most often characterized by "catastrophizing": mentally converting hassles into outright horrors. Once this ideational pattern is detected, every effort is expended to make the adolescent client aware that he or she is

"awfulizing," why such thinking is unrealistic, and what a more sensible outlook might be. This goal is usually achieved in the following way:

a. Substituting the words *disaster, catastrophe,* or *tragedy* for *awful, terrible,* or *horrible*. The words *awful, terrible,* or *horrible* are so much a part of the average adolescent's working vocabulary that I have found it difficult to convince the adolescent that the meaning behind such words is the cause of his or her suffering. The emotionally distressed adolescent who insists that his or her problem is awful is asked, "Was it a disaster?" or "Was it really a tragedy?" These words have a more precise meaning and can be subjected to question and reason more easily than *awful*.

b. Using the phrase "end of the world" to show the client that he or she is awfulizing. Again, I find that asking, "Would it be the end of the world?" usually elicits an eye-rolling "Of course not" from most adolescents and permits the next question, "Then exactly what would it be?" The answer, almost always in the realm of realistic disadvantage, begins to persuade the client to correct his or her exaggerated evaluation of the problem.

c. Using the phrase "a fate worse than death." Once more the use of a familiar but obviously magnified term sometimes helps adolescents to begin to understand that their excessive, disturbing feelings come from exaggerated, unrealistic ideas in their minds.

d. Asking, "Could it be any worse?" Often young clients exaggerate, considering a situation totally bad. Encouraging them to conjure something that could make their problem even worse sometimes enables them to see that it is highly unlikely that any disadvantage (especially their own) is 100% bad. This tactic can sometimes be used in a humorous way by adding all kinds of ridiculous dimensions to the problem situation. I find that this approach helps clients to realize that problems are not always as bad as they think they are; by viewing situations in less exaggerated and more realistic terms, they learn to feel much less distressed.

e. Asking, "What's the worst that could actually happen?" I show anxiety-ridden teenagers they are catastrophizing their complaints by encouraging them to focus on the most realistic but worst outcome they can imagine. This forces them to stay away from possibilities and to concentrate on actualities. In essence, they are learning to deal with the hassle and not with the horror of their problem.

3. *Confronting and confuting "shoulds," "oughts," and "musts."* Another, equally significant aspect of irrational thinking is the tendency of clients to treat their wants and desires as if they were Jehovah's commandments. Adolescents typically believe that they must have their way simply because it is deserved, earned, right, fair, just, or whatever. A good many of my efforts, therefore, go to sensitizing teenagers to their personal imperatives and helping them to understand why absolutistic thinking usually results in emotional and social conflict. The most useful tactics for accomplishing this end include:

a. Using *must* in place of *should*. Teenagers use the word *should* so frequently and indiscriminately that sometimes just getting them to change the word to *must* gets the imperative quality across. Once this is established, they can begin to learn how to live without absolutes.

   b. Using *gotta* in place of *should*. "I should get an A" makes sense to a lot of teenagers, but "I gotta get an A" often encourages them to see the error of their ways.

   c. Changing *should* to *no right*. Another method of getting across the absolutistic meaning of *should*, especially with angry teenagers, is to exchange "He shouldn't do that" for "He's got no right to do that." The irrationality of "He's got no right" is often easy for teenagers to understand.

   d. Using the want–need concept. Another way of getting teenagers to recognize and challenge absolutes is to teach them the difference between wanting and needing. I have found that some of the most resistant and stubborn young people, especially those involved in behavioral excesses, are capable of understanding the critical distinction between desires and necessities and of using this insight productively.

   e. Teaching *should* equals "unbreakable law." I sometimes get somewhere with young clients who have difficulty understanding the absolutistic meaning of *should*'s and *must*'s by suggesting that they are upset because their self-proclaimed laws have been broken. "Debbie's Commandments have been violated" or "It was Tom's turn to be God, and he got upset because someone broke one of His rules" are examples of this approach. Once the adolescents understand what it means to be unrealistically demanding, I proceed to show them that they do not run the universe, so they had better expect things to go wrong.

4. *Challenging the "can't stand" philosophy.* Probably the main source of teenagers' low frustration tolerance is their persistent conviction that they can withstand no inconvenience or discomfort. This kind of irrational thinking, which seems endemic to this age group, generates a variety of neurotic behaviors, ranging from school underachievement to drug abuse. My experience shows that adolescents seem able to grasp the irrationality of "can't stand" thinking more easily than other RET concepts. If I do run into problems, though, I find the following usually get results:

   a. Substituting "unbearable" for "can't stand." Often, I can help a young client realize how pernicious the "can't stand" concept is by equating it with the term *unbearable*. Hearing things put this way, many teenagers conclude, "Well, it's not *that* bad. I mean I can *bear* it."

   b. Explaining *difficult* versus *impossible*. Often, the "can't stand" concept can be better understood by investigating whether a particular problem situation is impossible or is merely difficult to tolerate. Even some of the most resistant teenagers, grasping this point, can realize that just because something is a pain in the neck does not mean that it cannot be lived with.

   c. Substituting *won't* for *can't*. Frequently, when I hear the word *can't*, I quickly substitute *won't*. This is an effective way of showing that the situation is governed by one's attitude, which is under the individual's control. It is the attitude, not the situation, that is overwhelming.

   d. Suggesting to the client that he or she *is* tolerating the conflict in question. Despite complaints and protests, I remind the client, he or she *is* enduring the problem. This tactic is especially useful with clients experiencing long-running problems with parents, teachers, or siblings. For example, the teenager who threatens to quit school in his senior year because he claims he can no longer stomach the bullshit is advised that he is, in fact, stomaching things. He may be miserable, but he has nevertheless been putting up with school for twelve years, and this qualifies him as an outstanding stomacher of bullshit!

e. Explaining that a genuine "can't stand" situation would either end the client's life or render her unconscious. I frequently suggest that if her problem were truly impossible to bear, it would either cost her life or she would very likely pass out from the overwhelming agony involved. Up to that point, I suggest, the client is standing the adversity or discomfort; she may not like it, but she is standing it.

5. *Teaching the principle of self-acceptance.* When low self-esteem is responsible for adolescent distress, I make every effort to show the client how to avoid global ratings of oneself (or others). I find that self-acceptance is one of the most difficult RET principles to get across to teenagers, perhaps because comprehension requires a sophisticated level of understanding; what's more, teenagers are geared to judging their self-image solely on the basis of peer opinion. Usually, however, I get somewhere with the following maneuvers:

a. Using a visual aid. I draw a circle and label it *self*. Next I draw a series of smaller circles inside the "self" circle. These represent the various traits, characteristics, and performances of the individual client. I try to demonstrate that rating one trait or feature as bad does not make all the other circles bad. In essence, I try to show adolescents that they are a collection of qualities, some good and some bad, none of which equal the whole self.

b. Using an analogy. Although many examples can illustrate the illogicality of overgeneralizing from act to personhood, I have found that the flat tire example works best with teenagers. I ask if they would junk a whole car because it had a flat tire. The key word is *junk*. Once clients pick up on this word image, I use it thereafter when they overgeneralize about mistakes or criticism. "There you go again," I tell them, "junking yourself because you did such and such."

c. Helping the client understand that although one is responsible for what one does, one is not the *same* as one does. This is sometimes tricky for adolescents to understand. They frequently argue that if they do something bad, they, too, are bad. I counter by suggesting, "If you went around mooing like a cow, would that make you a cow?" I usually receive a negative answer. Then I say, "But you are the one doing it. How come it doesn't turn you into a cow?" A few more examples like this one, and clients usually begin to separate what they do from who they are.

d. Explaining the difference between a person-with-less and less-of-a-person. Young clients suffering from feelings of shame, embarrassment, or inferiority have usually fallen victim to downing or degrading themselves. To the client who gets criticized or makes mistakes, I point out that such problems only prove that he is a person with less of what he wants (success or approval), rather than being less of a person. Sometimes I illustrate this principle by taking something from him (a shoe, a watch, etc.) and then asking, "What are you now? Are you less of a person or just a person with less of what you want?"

e. *Showing that blaming oneself is like being punished twice for the same crime.* With those adolescents who damn themselves and feel excessively guilty, I usually try to illustrate that mistakes and failings have built-in penalties. Whenever we err, I point out, we not only disappoint ourselves and fail to live up to our own standards, but we very likely endure some kind of adverse consequence. Through examples, I help clients to see that just living with the disappointments or consequences of their actions is punishment enough. Adding to these by damning oneself only adds insult to injury and makes matters worse than they need be.

6. *Correcting misperceptions of reality.* In addition to the disputation of irrational thinking, another area of congitive intervention with teenagers involves reality misperception. Teenagers are especially prone to inaccurate descriptions and conclusions about their reality experiences, particularly those involving peer relationships. Such errors in thinking, identified and discussed in detail by Beck (1976, 1979), sometimes lend themselves to more understandable analysis and effective remedy with adolescents than do the dialectics involved in correcting irrational thinking.

For example, a teenager reported feeling quite upset because a boyfriend had ignored her flirtations in history class that day. She had decided that he hated her and would never speak to her again, even though earlier in the day he had arranged a date with her for the weekend. Encouraged to offer proof of her conclusions, she eventually decided that the young man hadn't really rejected her and that it was highly unlikely that he hated her and would never speak to her again.

No attempt was made to get at the irrational ideas behind the client's upset, because she was able to correct her misperceptions and come to the conclusion that she really was not facing the loss of a boyfriend. If, however, her observations had actually been correct (or had she demonstrated a chronic overconcern about rejection), efforts would have been made to help her realize that her distress was the result not of poor reality testing but of a grossly distorted evaluation of that reality.

I will note that the correction of misperceptions and the disputation of irrational thinking in the problem intervention phase of counseling adolescents is not an either-or proposition; in actual practice, the two approaches are often used together. RET, however, places primary emphasis on the disputation of irrational beliefs because the highly evaluative, absolutistic quality of such thinking is considered the controlling dynamic in emotional and psychological disorders.

Problem Solving

Problem solving, the basic goal of RET, is usually accomplished by persuading clients to put the knowledge gained in therapy into practice in concrete and specific life situations. This usually requires conscious effort and hard work, traits that unfortunately are not high on the list of adolescent virtues. Young people are notoriously reluctant to apply themselves to any task that does not promise immediate results.

It is important, therefore, not to harbor unrealistic expectations about counseling adolescents. Clinical experience has shown that teenagers usually do not undergo sweeping or dramatic personality changes, living happily ever after as a result of their therapy endeavors. Most come in for relatively few interviews; if these clients are handled skillfully along the lines I have suggested, they generally make moderate improvement. The following tactics usually encourage rational problem-solving by helping teenagers understand what therapy is about, what to expect from their efforts, and how to put insight into action:

1. *Explaining psychological and emotional problems as habits.* Sometimes I can encourage effort by adolescents through labeling their problems as habits. This labeling often takes the mystery out of how psychotherapy is supposed to work and puts the clients' roles in the change process in a framework that they can understand and accept. What I usually do is ask in each session about progress. When a reported lack of improvement can be traced to a client's failure to put into practice what we have been discussing, I suggest that the client's problem, no matter how complicated or painful, is merely a habit. After some explaining and clarifying, I point out that the client can expect improvement if she or he puts in the necessary work to change that habit.

2. *Checking out the client's expectations about therapy.* Often adolescents have the wrong idea about what to expect from counseling. They usually believe that therapy will leave them either carefree and happy or uncaring and unemotional about their problems. Unless these misconceptions are corrected, clients will very likely lose faith in therapy because it will not give them what they want.

To those who expect to feel good all the time in spite of their problems, I point out that I follow the principles I am trying to teach them, and that I have yet to enjoy disappointments. If I can't feel cheerful about disappointments, how do they expect to do so? I also note that those who smile or feel cheerful in the face of adversity or hardship are usually not termed well adjusted or normal. They are usually called crazy!

To those who believe that rational thinking will rob them of their emotions, I suggest that our goal is to make them feel unhappy instead of miserable. Sometimes, I use a continuum illustration to get the concept across, showing the client that he or she belongs somewhere in the middle of the continuum between "calm" and "upset." At other times, I suggest that rational thinking about disappointments will only help him or her to feel *less* upset—less angry, less anxious, less embarrassed, and so on. The point that I try to emphasize is that our efforts will not eliminate emotions; they will only lessen the intensity, frequency, and duration of their distress.

3. *Writing out an ABC homework for them*. Although I am frequently successful in helping adolescents to understand why their thinking is irrational, I find it difficult to get them to practice challenging and correcting their irrational ideas outside of therapy sessions. With this group, the hard work involved in changing cognitions begins and ends in the office. For this reason, I try to outline their problems on a blackboard or a sheet of paper, using the ABC model. At each session, I try to take the client through the model, and I also suggest that she or he take my writing efforts home and look at them if the problem comes up during the week.

4. *Sticking to accepted insights*. Once a particular insight has been presented, understood, and accepted by a teenager, I strongly suggest that this information be repeated without significant change. In other words, stick to what seems to impress the client as the cognitive source of his or her distress and use the same words, analogies, visual examples, and the like to reinforce the message. Putting clarifications and interpretations into different words or using other but similar analogies may prove stimulating and creative to the therapist but confusing and bewildering to most adolescents. Although such repetition may be monotonous at times, it usually proves effective in helping young clients to understand and accept rational concepts.

5. *Telling the adolescent what to think*. I have found that, despite heroic efforts, some adolescents are not going to learn how to reason things out according to prescribed RET dogma. In such cases, I simply give them the correct sentences to think. I am not concerned with whether they understand the logic behind the statements, just so they will repeat the ideas during a time of distress. This kind of approach is usually recommended for young children, but I have found that it works equally well with certain teenagers. For instance, I might tell a client, "Next time someone calls you an asshole, tell yourself, 'If they called me a finger, it wouldn't make me a finger, so why get so upset over being called an asshole?'"

6. *Arranging homework assignments.* I usually try to design some kind of appropriate homework assignment for the client between sessions. This is probably the most efficacious way to encourage the client to put therapeutic insights to the test. It is also the best way for the therapist to check on the client. For instance, I might help a shy adolescent understand the cognitive source of his shyness, but I also want to get him to do something assertive, such as going to a party, asking a girl out, or maybe saying no to someone he usually accommodates with a yes. I have found that young people are more likely to accept the ideas of rational thinking after they have tried them out in emotionally provoking situations.

For the most part, these homework tasks are activity-oriented as opposed to being reading or writing assignments. I have not been particularly successful in persuading adolescents to read the RET literature or to write out ABC forms or their equivalent. No doubt, reading and writing chores are too closely associated with unpleasant school duties; although I sometimes suggest such assignments, I do not become concerned about lack of interest in these areas. I usually figure it's unlikely that adolescents will extend themselves much beyond appearing for their sessions. For this reason, I frequently put more effort into those sessions than I would with adult clients.

Other Methods

Finally, I would like to mention some problem-solving tactics that do not necessarily rely on direct cognitive intervention. Although I usually make a determined effort to help adolescent clients through philosophical methods, experience has shown that this approach is not always feasible. Sometimes, less elegant and more practical methods are better used. With some adolescents, it is advisable to take what we can get as long as it relieves suffering and does not create further difficulties. This approach can be put into practice in the following way:

1. *Telling clients what to do.* Some adolescents do not respond to direct efforts to change their thinking, no matter what method I use or how simple I make things. In cases like this, I concentrate on telling them how to do things in such a way as to still enjoy themselves and yet keep out of trouble. For instance, I advised a teenaged girl on parole to cry in front of her parole officer. She was the type who consistently broke the rules of parole and was on the verge of returning to a correctional school. Her parole officer did not like the girl, because she was defiant and did not respect his authority. The girl did cry, and although

she continued to break the rules, she was not incarcerated because she had gained the good graces of her parole officer, who now thought he had "broken" her.

2. *Teaching verbal assertiveness techniques.* Many teenagers believe themselves to be trapped in oppressive relationships. Those viewed as holding them in bondage include parents, teachers, or other adults charged with their keeping. In some cases the adolescents' complaints are valid, but often these clients have created oppressive situations through their own defiance or rebellion. Although I make an effort to get at the cognitive source of the problem ("I must have what I want" or "I can't stand being deprived"), I usually find that adolescents in this category are best helped by teaching them verbal assertiveness behaviors such as fogging and negative assertion. Those teenagers who learn such methods usually report good results.

3. *Getting a reduction rather than an elimination.* Sometimes, I am able to modify the behavior of certain adolescents by getting them to cut down rather than cut out. In other words, I try to convince them to pass just one of four subjects they are failing or to smoke only outside their homes. Sometimes, such a minor alteration in behavior alleviates parental or school pressures. I emphasize that this tactic will not work with the abuse of drugs or alcohol.

4. *Making use of the relationship to encourage change.* I find that, at least initially, some young people change because they want to please me. This motivation may keep them working until they can experience the rewards of their own efforts, rewards that thereafter can replace the relationship as a motivating factor. As I mentioned earlier, relationship development with adolescents is an integral part of RET and is often a significant factor influencing positive outcome. Although I could list a number of ways to use "friendship power" to encourage problem solving, I am not above telling some clients, "Do it for me!" Others I sometimes advise, "My job depends on your changing." I do this half kiddingly but still I try to get the message across that their lack of progress could have serious implications for me.

5. *Making use of parental involvement.* Often, adolescent problems are best resolved by including the parents in the counseling process. This inclusion could be in the form of family interviews or sessions with one or both parents. Sometimes, especially in those cases in which the adolescent refuses to participate in the counseling, the parents become the clients and are helped to cope more rationally with the situation. The same could be said for those occasions when the teenager is discovered to have fairly normal problems to which the parents are overreacting and thereby putting unnecessary pressure on the adolescent. On the

other hand, there are times, as with issues involving subjects such as sex and drugs, when it is wise to leave parents out of the therapy. There are no hard-and-fast rules governing when to involve parents in counseling teenagers. It depends on the teenager, the problem, the parents, the laws governing the treatment of adolescents in one's community, and the skill and judgment of the counselor.

6. *Referring to a more appropriate resource.* With some adolescents, the most effective tactic is referral to a more appropriate service. Some teenagers, in spite of what appears to be an obvious need for counseling, do not respond no matter how ingenious the approach. For example, a teacher referred a bright 14-year-old boy with extremely low self-esteem. The client was overcompensating for feelings of inferiority by acting out and casting himself in the role of class clown. He possessed a number of well-entrenched irrational ideas about self-worth and a need for the approval of others. Unfortunately, after a few sessions, it was apparent he would be unable to benefit from therapy no matter how I put things. I suggested to the school that he be referred to a Big Brother program. It was my hope that a friendship-oriented experience with an adult would bolster his self-image and reduce his attention-getting behavior in school. Although hardly an elegant solution, it was, under the circumstances, the only viable alternative if the young man was to receive any help at all.

Case Illustration

The following condensed and edited interview illustrates some of the techniques suggested in this chapter. Dave, a 17-year-old, was referred by his parents in a telephone conversation. Their main concern was school truancy, but they mentioned, rather casually, that Dave's "horrible temper" had frequently got him into trouble. Dave showed up for his first interview alone, insulted the receptionist, and announced to the office staff that this was his first and last interview with a shrink.

THERAPIST (T): What brings you to see a counselor?
CLIENT (C) (*sarcastically*): My car!
T: Clever! You mean you have a car problem? If so, you're in the wrong place. You need a mechanic, not a head shrinker. I help people with mental and emotional problems.
C (*even more sarcastically*): Then I don't belong here, because I'm not mental. I'm not crazy.
T: I agree. You certainly don't seem crazy to me. Who told you to come here for help?

C: My asshole parents!

T: What reason did they give you for sending you to a counselor?

C: I don't know. Why don't you ask them?

T: I can't. They're not here now. But I think I know what your problem is.

C (*very defiantly*): What?

T: You've got problem parents. You've got parents that think they know everything. They plan your life for you, and if you don't like it, they figure there's something wrong with *you*, not them!

T: You're goddamned right! My parents are all fucked up! They're all over my case.

T: Then you're in the right place.

C: What do you mean?

T: I specialize in problem parents. I can help you learn to manage your parents better.

C: I don't need your help!

T: Sure you do! You're getting nowhere doing things your way. In fact, that's what got you in here, isn't it? Do you like being here?

C: No!

T: I'll bet coming here isn't the only hassle you've had to endure because of your parents.

C: Yeah. They won't allow me to drive the car, and no one's allowed to come over to the house.

T: The more you fight them, the worse it gets. And you're telling me you don't need help with your parents.

C: What kind of help?

T: First, help in controlling your temper. I've talked to you just a little while, but it seems that your temper is a problem. Second, I can show you how to talk to your parents so you don't always end up in trouble.

C: Yeah, I got a temper. My friends are all afraid of me when I get mad. They think I'm crazy.

T: Okay, then, let's start with your temper. Give me an example of the last time you got really mad and lost your cool.

C: That's easy. An hour ago, when they told me I had to see you.

T: Okay, now let me ask this: What do you think made you so mad?

C: I told you: my parents' making me see you.

T: I'd like you to consider another possibility: maybe *you're* the one who made you feel angry.

C: Me? I didn't make myself come in here! *They* did!

T: No, no, Dave. I'm suggesting it's your attitude about your parents' making you come in that did the damage and got you so upset. Sure, they told you what to do, but it was your brain that turned a pain in the ass into a major crime! Here, let me show you what I mean. Take this. (*I hand him a rubber hammer.*) Now, suppose you were to hit yourself over the head with it. Whose fault would that be? Whom would you blame?

C: Me!

T: Even if I was the one who gave the hammer to you?

C: You just handed it to me. It would be my fault if I hit myself over the head with it.
T: Dave, it's the same with your parents' making you come in here. (*Dave looks inquisitive.*) They hand you the crap and you hit yourself over the head with it. They tell you what to do, and you make a big deal, a major crime out of it. (*Dave nods attentively.*) So, it's not what they do, but what you do in your mind that's probably causing your anger. You're blaming your parents for something you're doing to yourself. They keep handing you the hammer, and you keep hitting yourself over the head with it. You put all your energy into blaming them instead of working on a way to stop giving yourself a hard time.
C: You mean my parents have nothing to do with it? I make it all up?
T: That's a good question, Dave, because that's not what I mean. Your parents contribute—they dish it out. But it's the way you take it, the way you blow it up in your mind, that's the real cause of your anger. Your parents play a part—they're not innocent bystanders—but you're the one that's mentally making a big deal out of things. (*There's a pause of a few minutes while Dave considers what I've been saying.*)
C: It makes sense, I guess. I never thought about it that way.
T: Would you like to learn what kind of thinking makes you so angry? (*Dave shrugs his shoulders in resigned agreement.*) Okay, let's use an illustration. I'm not an artist, but maybe this cartoon will help you understand better. (*I draw a face that looks angry and put a thought bubble next to it. I leave the bubble blank.*) You notice I left the idea part blank, because I want you to help me fill it in. What went through your mind right after your parents told you that you had to come in and see me?
C: Oh, shit! Here we go again! I'm fed up with all this shit! Enough's enough! (*I write in the thought bubble, "I can't stand it anymore!"*)
T: Anything else?
C: Who do they think they are? Why can't they get off my back. They're fucking up my life! (*I add to the thought bubble, "They've got no right telling me what to do!" and hold it up for Dave to see.*) Is this it? Is this what went through your mind when your parents told you that you had to see me?
C (*showing surprise*): That's what I was trying to say. Especially that last one. I think that all the time.
T: These two ideas not only get *you* angry, but they probably would get anyone just as upset. In fact, these are two of the nuttiest ideas people think. Would you like to learn how to change these ideas, feel less angry, stop blaming your parents, and get a grip on your temper? Or maybe you want to keep having temper tantrums.
C: No, the anger gets me into trouble. I got kicked out of school one time because of a stupid fight.
T: Okay. Here's how we do it. First, we see if the ideas make any sense or if they're just bullshit. We'll tackle that "I can't stand it anymore" idea. Do you really believe that you can't stand it when your parents tell you what to do and try to run your life?
C: It seems as though I can't, as though it's too much. Sometimes it's . . .

T: It's what you make of it. "It" doesn't have any power over you at all. For example, is your parents' interference in your life difficult to handle or is it impossible to handle? Which is it? Difficult or impossible?
C: Well, difficult, I guess.
T: Why isn't it impossible? (*A blank look crosses Dave's face.*) If it were impossible to put up with your parents, you would've been killed off by now, but you're still alive. In other words, no matter how much of a pain in the ass your parents give you, you've survived, haven't you?
C: Yeah.
T: Suppose that the next time your parents tell you to do something stupid, such as coming in to see me, you tell yourself, "Here we go again. Sure, it's the same old bullshit, but it won't kill me. I can stand it, even though I don't like it." How do you think you'd feel?
C: If I could think like that? (*I nod.*) A lot less angry.
T: Okay, let's take a look at that other anger-producing idea. (*I point to the cartoon and to "They've got no right telling me what to do!"*)
C: Well, they don't have a right. I've got my rights . . .
T: Okay, wait a minute. Let me agree with you on one thing. It's wrong for your parents to order you around and tell you what to do. Your parents are wrong, okay?
C: You're goddamned right!
T: Are your parents human? Be serious.
C: Yeah.
T: Do humans make mistakes?
C: Yeah.
T: Do your parents have a right to make mistakes, such as bossing you around?
C: Not when it comes to me. They ought to know . . .
T: Are your parents human? Do humans make mistakes? Isn't it human nature to do wrong things?
C: Yeah.
T: Do your parents have a right to be wrong? Even when they're bossing you around and trying to run your life?
C: Yeah, I guess so, when you put it that way.
T: Suppose the next time they tell you what to do, the next time they make you do something you don't like, you say to yourself, "It's wrong, but they have a right to be wrong. After all they're just fucked-up humans like everyone else!" How angry do you think you'd feel if you thought things out like that?
C: If I could think that way, it wouldn't bother me so much.

In addition to cognitive intervention, I suggested some verbal assertiveness techniques that Dave could use when he felt pressured by his parents. Subsequent sessions revealed that Dave's anger with his friends was the result of low self-esteem; this issue was handled in much the same style. After the third session, I encouraged Dave to have his girlfriend join us. She exercised a profound influence over him, made sure he kept appointments, and assisted my efforts by repeating rational insights to Dave between sessions. He proved quite receptive to RET philosophy, showed marked improvement, and was able to work on a number of issues in addition to his temper, including his school attendance.

REFERENCES

Bard, J. *Rational emotive therapy in practice.* Champaign, Ill.: Research Press, 1980.
Beck, A. *Cognitive therapy and the emotional disorders.* New York: International Universities Press, 1976.
Beck, A., Rush, A., Shaw, B., & Emery, G. *Cognitive therapy of depression.* New York: Guilford Press, 1979.
Ellis, A. *Reason and emotion in psychotherapy.* Secaucus, N.J.: Lyle Stuart, 1962.
Ellis, A. Sexual problems of the young adult. *Rational Living,* 1971, 5(2), 2–11.
Ellis, A. *Humanistic psychotherapy.* New York: McGraw-Hill, 1974.
Ellis, A. & Harper, R. A. *A new guide to rational living.* Englewood Cliffs, N.J.: Prentice-Hall, 1975.
Piaget, J., & Inhelder, B. *The psychology of the child.* New York: Basic Books, 1969.
Walen, S., DiGiuseppe, R., & Wessler, R. *A practitioner's guide to rational-emotive therapy.* New York: Oxford University Press, 1980.
Wessler, R., & Wessler, R. *The principles and practice of rational-emotive therapy.* San Francisco: Jossey-Bass, 1980.

II

Problems of Childhood

The chapters in this section are written so that the practitioner may readily (1) define the problem; (2) recognize the dysfunctional cognitive elements that underlie the problem; (3) assess and treat the problem; and (4) recognize the difficulties inherent in employing cognitive approaches with younger populations.

Raymond DiGiuseppe outlines a cognitive-behavioral treatment program for overcoming conduct disorders in Chapter 4. A distinctive contribution of his chapter is the identification of both the irrational beliefs that are held by the parents of conduct-disordered children and the effects of their beliefs on feelings and on their behaviors toward their children. Also noteworthy is his detailing of a combined treatment program for use with parents and children, which includes (1) behavioral management programs carried out by parents; (2) cognitive restructuring of parents' beliefs to facilitate compliance with behavioral homework assignments; (3) disputation of the child's beliefs that lead to anger and anxiety; (4) social-problem-solving skills that are taught to children; and (5) self-instructional training to teach cognitive rehearsal and linguistic elements to direct adaptive behavior.

In Chapter 5, William J. Knaus, one of the founders of rational emotive education, provides an insightful analysis of the cognitive components of low frustration tolerance. He illustrates how procrastination and task avoidance can be related to a child's sensitivity to discomfort and tendency to self-down or to blame others. Case illustrations reveal how the discomfort-dodging self- and other-doubting cycle, which underlies a variety of childhood disorders (e.g., phobias and underachievement), can be broken.

Philip C. Kendall and Gary L. Fischler provide detailed documentation in Chapter 6 about the effectiveness of a cognitive-behavioral approach to the treatment of lack of control and impulsivity in children. Their discussion of a treatment approach that relies heavily on self-instructional training and response cost procedures is supplemented by an indication of the most effective and efficient way to bring about change in younger populations. Similarities and differences between their cognitive-behavioral approach and RET are considered.

James A. Bard and Harold R. Fisher combine in Chapter 7 to elaborate basic irrational beliefs and assumptions that can be seen to lead to educational underachievement in older children and adolescents. The pernicious influence of peer-group pressure is persuasively documented. Details of the family background factors, the student characteristics, and the treatment approach particular to each irrational belief are included.

The cognitive etiology of children's fears, phobias, and anxieties is presented by Russell M. Grieger and John D. Boyd in Chapter 8. These authors provide a comprehensive detailing of the variety of parental cognitive distortions and irrational beliefs as well as disturbed parenting styles, which frequently lead to children's acquiring anxiety-evoking ideation. The chapter includes an extensive discussion of the different anxiety-related problems of children in terms of dysfunctional irrational ideas, emotions, and behaviors.

In Chapter 9, W. Kim Halford presents an in-depth analysis of the role of cognition in social isolation in children. The increasingly well-developed assessment methodology in this area is reviewed, and the methods for employing rational self-statements with a younger client are elaborated. A case history illustrates how cognitive and behavioral skills can be successfully taught together in remediating this problem.

John P. Foreyt and Albert T. Kondo, in Chapter 10, indicate the extreme difficulties encountered in treating childhood and adolescent obesity. The importance of the young obese client's context in the selection of assessment and treatment methods is apparent. These authors emphasize the significant role that the family plays in both supporting and resolving the problem. The behavioral basis of a treatment program and the role of cognitive interventions are presented.

Chapter 11, by Susan R. Walen and Gloria K. Vanderhorst, emphasizes how the problems of childhood sexuality are often rooted in cold, nonaccepting, and judgmental attitudes about sex held by adults. They indicate that if healthy sex attitudes are to be communicated to children by educators and therapists, then the "grown-ups" had better have their heads on straight. They therefore review basic background facts concerning childhood sexuality. According to these authors, the treatment of sexual problems in younger clients is, in principle, no different from the treatment of other childhood problems: The problem is defined, its ownership is clarified, the affective stress is acknowledged, and cognitive distortions are challenged cognitively and behaviorally.

4

Rational-Emotive Therapy and Conduct Disorders

RAYMOND DiGIUSEPPE

Children are referred to mental health practitioners not because they are disturbed but because they are disturbing. Conduct disorders represent the largest category of referrals to clinical services. Children with conduct disorders are more likely to develop psychological adjustment problems as adults than any other diagnostic category of child psychopathology (Quay & Werry, 1979). The clinical lore is full of antidotes for and complaints about the resistance of these children to treatment and the resistance of many therapists to treating them. For these reasons, conduct disorders represent one of the greatest challenges to clinical child psychology. Before we discuss how RET and other cognitive strategies can be used in treating this disorder, it would be helpful to briefly develop some theoretical perspective on the problem.

DIAGNOSIS

Conduct disorder children are best diagnosed by what they *do*, not by their thoughts, feelings, or family lineage. Two categories of behaviors are important: behavioral excesses and behavioral deficits. Behavioral excesses may include teasing, temper tantrums, hitting, stealing, or verbal aggression. Behavioral deficits usually include noncompliance with parental instructions, for example, requests to do chores, to keep appropriate hours, or to complete homework or study. Generally, these

---

RAYMOND DiGIUSEPPE • Institute for Rational-Emotive Therapy, New York, New York 10021.

children are annoying to adults because of the aversiveness of their behavior or because of the difficulty caused by the child's noncompliance.

Behavioral and cognitive impulsivity appear to be frequent characteristics of conduct disorder children. They often respond to a situation quickly with inappropriate behavior without first assesing the consequences of their behavior. Such impulsivity and behavioral hyperactivity are frequently labeled as being organic, and the child is diagnosed as minimally brain damaged. In Great Britain and other European countries, these problems are more likely to be labeled as conduct disorders, and organic etiology is less often inferred than in the United States.

It is important to note that although misconduct is the key to the diagnosis, not all children who misbehave are diagnosed as misbehaving. All children engage in some temper tantrums and behavioral excesses and fail to comply with some parental requests. Behaviors of children have to be examined in terms of such dimensions as frequency, intensity, duration, and severity. The exact point where one makes the diagnosis of conduct disorder is not written in any textbook and will not appear here. It is a judgment that is left to the wisdom and the experience of the clinician. The clinician's judgment about whether a behavior is a problem may differ from that of the referring adult. Possessing different definitions is an important consideration that will affect treatment. Parents may have different standards from society and may believe that their children's behavior falls within acceptable limits, whereas the school, the courts, or the neighbors do not. Treating such families is difficult, because one must first convince the parents that the child's behavior is a problem before they will cooperate in therapy. If this fails, the parents will either reinforce or tolerate the behavior. Continued treatment may be difficult if not impossible.

On the other hand, a child may be well behaved but may still be referred for conduct problems because of the demanding standards of parents or teachers. In these cases, a diagnosis of conduct disorder is not made, and family therapy aimed at changing parental expectations is most appropriate. The practical implication for the clinician, then, is always to assess the standards of conduct in the minds of all the significant others in the child's life and to determine how these standards interact with the problem.

As with all psychopathology, the way one conceptualizes conduct disorders dictates the hypothetical constructs one looks for in the child and the therapy that follows. The behaviors displayed by children with conduct disorders have long been referred to as *acting-out* behaviors. This term is so widely used by mental health workers that for many it is synonymous with aggressive behavioral excesses. This term presents serious problems because it communicates a subtle yet strong connotation of etiology and underlying mechanisms. *Acting out* refers to the belief that the misbehavior is a symbolic representation of some unconscious emotional conflict. Some analytic thinkers postulate more specifically that acting-out behavior represents hostility directed toward the parents because of too little affection. The use of the term *acting out*, then, focuses the therapist on the child's affect and unconscious needs for affection. This type of conceptualization can be misleading. The child's misbehavior may not represent anything symbolically and may not derive from deficits in parental affection.

I do not mean to imply that emotions are never involved in conduct disorders or that a child's misbehavior can never be associated with hostility toward the parents because the parents are unaffectionate. It is, however, an error to make such an assumption before making an assessment.

The emotional disturbance in conduct disorder children is more likely to be elicited by frustration, and they define most limit-setting as awful. My own clinical experience has suggested that the majority of children do not misbehave as a result of a lack of parental affection, but as a result of poorly arranged rewards and punishments. In this way, the children fail to learn self-control and delay of gratification, and also, they never learn to outgrow the demandingness of infancy. Many parents love their misbehaving children dearly and show this love in providing noncontingent rewards and in demonstrating guilt over punishing their children.

Conduct disorder children almost never identify their emotions as the problems. In fact, they may be quite unaware of them. Often, their misbehavior is so effective in getting what they want that they are hardly frustrated. When they are frustrated, their cognitions are of such a nature that these children define the problem as others' not acquiescing to their demands. Children with conduct disorders may believe that their parents are uncaring whenever their parents set limits or deny some reward. However, this belief represents a distortion of reality. Many of these children believe that parental love means giving the child all that he or she wants. By definition, all else is rejection.

Although unconscious motivation or symbols appear to be unnecessary in the conceptualization of conduct disorders, a considerable literature has appeared that examines the relationship of various familial and parental variables with conduct disorders. Quay and Werry (1979) provided a good review of these studies and cited the following parental strategies as being correlated with conduct problems: extremes of restrictive and permissive discipline; extreme use of physical punishment; permissiveness of aggression; and parental inconsistency. One is left with the clear impression that conduct disorders result from both family problems and a learned pattern of behavior. The pattern seems to develop from one or more of the following factors: (1) from direct modeling of parental behaviors; (2) from a failure of the parents to teach socially acceptable behaviors; (3) as a strategy to deal with verbal attacks from family members; and (4) from indirect reinforcement and tolerance by the family of inappropriate behavior. This view appears to be consistent with the social learning literature in childhood aggression (Bandura, 1973), which focuses on the role of modeling and social reinforcement in the experimental shaping of aggressive behavior.

The theoretical basis chosen for the remainder of this chapter is that conduct disorders most often result from social learning principles. Aggressive and noncompliant behaviors appear to be modeled, learned, or reinforced directly or indirectly. Children may fail to learn appropriate behaviors either because they are not reinforced for such behaviors or because the behavior is not required for reinforcement. The emotional component of conduct disorders includes anger at limits, rules, and frustration, and it results from a failure to learn frustration tolerance and the modulation of emotion because of poor child-management strategies. Parents may reinforce or model excessive emotional outbursts. In addition, they may fail to teach the child strategies to control emotions.

The third edition of *The Diagnostic and Statistical Manual* (DSM-III—American Psychiatric Association, 1980) lists four types of conduct disorders: undersocialized aggressive; undersocialized nonaggressive; socialized aggressive; and socialized nonaggressive. The *undersocialized* types show a failure to form social attachments to others. There is a lack of affection and empathy in their relationships. Egocentrism is demonstrated by their willingness to exploit and manipulate others. Guilt or remorse about misbehavior is generally absent. The *socialized* types form social attachments; however, they often appear callous and unempathetic to persons to whom they have no attachment.

The *aggressive* types are characterized by frequent antisocial and aggressive acts, such as theft, mugging, assault, and extortion. The *nonaggressive* types do not demonstrate physical assaults and thefts, but there is a pattern of conflict with parents over rules concerning age-appropriate behavior. Chronic violations of rules at home and school are the norm.

There are no data to suggest which types of conduct disorder are the most difficult to treat or which have the best prognosis. Treatment varies, however, depending on the diagnosis, because different problems prevail.

Behavioral Approaches

The behavioral view of conduct disorders is probably best exemplified by the work of Patterson and his colleagues (Patterson & Fleischman, 1979; Patterson, Reid, Jones, & Conger, 1975). Patterson believes that the parents of conduct disorder children have failed to learn skills of child management such as defining specific behaviors, behavior monitoring, extinction of inappropriate behavior, and reinforcement of desired behavior (Patterson, 1974). Patterson's more recent work goes beyond the strictly operant model. He now believes that much of the child's aggressive behavior may be caused by aggressive attacks by other family members and that the child's aggressive behavior is negatively reinforced by the termination of these attacks (Patterson & Fleischman, 1979).

The behavioral treatment designed by Patterson (Patterson et al., 1975) focuses on building certain child-rearing skills in the parent. These skills include active monitoring of the child's behavior, setting appropriate expectations of compliant behavior, providing rewards contingent on appropriate behavior, and applying response costs to the occurrence of inappropriate behavior. These programs have been well researched, and considerable clinical success has been demonstrated.

Readers may be puzzled here. They probably know about the ABC's of rational-emotive therapy (RET): people cause their own disturbances by thinking. Also, readers know that rational therapists usually do not take a historical view of the problem or hold parents responsible for emotional disturbance in their children; and so far, this chapter has focused on the role of parental disciplines in conduct disorders. Can this be RET? Yes, for RET can be integrated successfully with the behavioral treatments that hold so much promise.

Ellis (1980a) has made the distinction between preferential or specialized RET and general RET. According to his view, preferential RET focus on the philosophical disputing of irrational beliefs with the primary focus on "antimustabatory thinking." General RET includes all or most cognitive-behavioral techniques and may employ less elegant empirical disputing, social-problem solving, verbal self-instruction, and behavior assignments. This chapter, then, focuses on the use of general RET as well as preferential RET.

For several reasons, it is recommended that behavioral treatments form the basis of therapy for conduct disorders:

1. Children with conduct disorders are almost never self-referred. Why should they be? They usually have learned to get what they want by being aggressive and noncompliant, and generally, they possess more power than other family members.

2. When these children do recognize the desirability of change, they usually have not developed the cognitive skills to stop and think through ways of solving their problems.

3. The emotional excess in conduct disorders is usually anger, and the child is usually not willing to change the anger because it is a righteous emotion.

4. RET was primarily devised for treating clients with emotional excesses who volunteer for treatment.

5. Behavior therapy and parent-training procedures have been well researched and appear to be the treatment of choice if empirical results are a criteria.

6. With a few exceptions, therapy outcome studies have failed to demonstrate that cognitive interventions change behavior when used alone (Abikoff, 1979), the exceptions being studies by Block (1978) and Kendall (1981).

RET has always been a cognitive-*behavioral* approach and Ellis (1980a) has defined general RET as including cognitive, emotive, and behavioral methods. RET and cognitive procedures can be combined with behavioral approaches in the treatment of conduct disorders in children to (1) augment gains and foster the generalization of behavior change; (2) help to reduce the anger in children once they realize that their anger is not going to be reinforced; (3) help the parents to get over the emotional problems that prevent them from adhering to behavioral treaments; and (4) teach children to be less impulsive and to think through behaviors before acting.

Cognitive Approaches

Behavioral theory research, and practice, has greatly expanded our knowledge concerning the role of social learning influences (e.g., inconsistent style of parental discipline; ineffectual reinforcement contingencies) in causing conduct disorders in children. These influences may at the same time foster and teach certain maladaptive cognitive styles and particular irrational beliefs in children.

Several cognitive models can be used to explain the irrational thinking that may underlie conduct disorders: RET, interpersonal cognitive problem-solving, and self-instructional training. Each of these is discussed here briefly. These models fall into two categories: they may focus on problems resulting from the presence of disruptive cognitions, or they may focus more on the absence of appropriate thinking processes.

RET

Although parental reinforcement contingencies play a large role in shaping conduct disorders, these children do experience some disturbed emotions that coincide with or help to motivate their behavior. Clinical experience suggests that two cognitive-affective clusters predominate in these children. Infants and toddlers usually have temper tantrums when their desires are frustrated or when pressure is brought to bear on them to complete chores and assignments. The youngsters may believe that they must have their way. When the temper tantrum leads to parental recapitulation, the parents reinforce not only the behavior but the irrational beliefs as well.

Like adults, children usually get angry when they demand that the world be the way they want it to be (Ellis, 1977). Significant others in the lives of children may very early treat them as if they are special and should have unlimited rewards. Children are not hard to convince that they should always have their way. The children's disturbance comes from the belief that because their parents believe that they should always have what they want, the rest of the world should do the same.

The second emotional-cognitive state that appears in children who manifest disorders in their conduct is discomfort anxiety and the corresponding irrational beliefs associated with low frustration tolerance. Ellis (1980b) has discussed the clinical syndrome of discomfort anxiety and two beliefs related to it. These are, first, that any discomfort, pain, or anxiety is terrible, awful, and intolerable, and, second, that denial of a desire is unbearable and intolerable. According to Ellis, people with discomfort anxiety and low frustration tolerance believe that much gratification must be immediate and that the discomfort of denial or delay is awful.

These cognitive-affective clusters (demandingness–anger and "I can't stand-it"–discomfort anxiety) may be difficult for the child or the clinician to spot. These children usually engage in impulsive aggressive behaviors that quickly terminate the activating events that subsequently elicit clusters of irrational beliefs and upsetting emotions. This negative reinforcement can be so immediate that the behaviors occur before the affect or the cognitions ever reach awareness. Given this state of affairs, these children may have difficulty understanding the role of their thoughts or feelings in their behavior.

Clinical experience with extremely disruptive institutionalized children has presented a third cognitive-affective cluster that underlies conduct disorders in children. Some antisocial children behave aggressively because of a combination of depression and anger that is connected to the belief that they are worthless and will never be able to succeed in life. These children are usually seen in residential centers for adolescents and usually have a history of parental abandonment or obvious and sustained parental rejection. They have had a history of relaxed controls and thus, like other children who misbehave, have failed to learn many appropriate behaviors and cognitive control skills. In addition, they condemn themselves for being unlovable. These children appear to experience no fear or negative consequences for their misbehavior and to have no concern for the negative impact that misbehavior will have on their lives. There is an absence of hope and a sense of helplessness. All the bad things have already happened. Some view life as externally controlled and all the payoffs as negative, so they might as well do as they please.

In the clusters described above, irrational beliefs lead to disturbing emotions, which lead to antisocial behavior. From the RET perspective, it is the presence of the maladaptive irrational ideas that leads to the problem.

SOCIAL-PROBLEM SOLVING

After interviewing children with conduct problems, one is usually struck by the speed with which they respond to events. Often, the cognitively oriented therapist's probe of "What were you telling yourself?" elicits blank stares and the ubiquitous retorts, "I don't know," "I didn't think anything," "I just did it." Many therapists refuse to accept these answers and hypothesize complicated unconscious dynamics or defense mechanisms to explain the behavior. (Perhaps the children have good clinical insight, and they really do not think before they act.)

Researchers are only beginning to investigate what cognitive skills need to be developed to ensure adequate social adjustment. Spivack, Platt, and Shure (1976) have outlined several hierarchically related social-problem-solving skills that have been negatively correlated with adjustment. The ability to notice social conflict or the presence of a social problem is the first such skill. Alternative-solution thinking appears to account for a great deal of behavior and involves the overall number of solutions that children can generate for a particular problem. After solutions are generated, well-adjusted youngsters usually make some judgment about the effectiveness or quality of the solution. These judgments, of course, may vary in accuracy. The more accurately the judgments match reality, the more likely the child will be to avoid problems. Spivack, Platt, and Shure (1976) termed this skill "consequential thinking." After children generate alternative solutions, judge their consequences, and choose a solution, they develop a specific plan to implement the solution. Spivack *et al.* (1976) call the ability to predict and solve problems in implementing solutions "means–ends thinking."

Socially appropriate behavior, delay of gratification, inhibition of impulses, frustration tolerance, and social-problem-solving skills are all influenced by the current repertoire of cognitive skills and strategies acquired through learning. Most young infants and toddlers do not possess these skills. They cry and scream to get what they want until their desires are met. Somewhere along the line, most children learn to control their emotional impulses and to acquire the social-problem-solving skills that allow them to function in society.

Many theorists and clinicians who work with this population have focused on the role of disturbing emotions resulting from parental and family neglect in creating conduct disorders. However, an alternative explanation is that parents who are inconsistent, permissive, tolerant of aggression, and unaffectionate are poor models and poor teachers. Such parents fail to teach the child the cognitive skills necessary for appropriate problem-solving. Even if the child were upset about the parent's behavior, any therapy—whether it be RET or psychoanalytic—aimed at the emotional upset may not be sufficient to correct the behavior if the child has failed to develop appropriate self-control skills. Thus, this type of maladaptive behavior may develop because of the presence of irrational beliefs that cause disturbing emotions, or because of a lack of the cognitive self-control skills, *or both*. Given the nature of the parenting of many children with conduct disorders, it is most likely that cognitive self-control skills are not learned.

Spivak *et al.* (1976) presented convincing evidence that children and adolescents with various clinical problems differ from normals in their social-problem-solving abilities. Specific therapy manuals have been developed to teach children interpersonal cognitive-problem-solving skills. Although these lessons were designed initially for preventive purposes, they serve very well in therapy for conduct-disoriented children and are discussed below.

The ability of children to *recognize* appropriate alternative solutions and consequences is *not* related to behavior. Rather, it is their ability to *generate* these cognitions that is associated with adjustment. In evaluating children, it is not very helpful to know that they recognize an alternative strategy to a problem when it is suggested by the therapist. A more valid evaluation would be to present children with hypothetical or actual problems and then to ask them to suggest alternatives and their consequences. In treatment, teaching the child to generate these ideas, not to recognize them, leads to change. Social-problem-solving skills appear to be unrelated to intelligence, academic skills, or even the ability to solve objective problems, so that there is no need to assume that any child is too dull or too immature to learn them.

Verbal Self-Instruction

A third cognitive approach that holds promise for the treatment of conduct disorders is self-instructional training. VSI or SIT is also based on the notion that conduct problems develop because of the absence of appropriate thought and verbal mediational control. This theory is primarily based on the work of Vygotsky and Luria and has been integrated into clinical practice in the United States by Meichenbaum (1977). Vygotsky's (1962) theory suggests that thought, as expressed in one's inner speech, serves a self-guiding and problem-solving function. That is, as people are either thinking about or actually engaging in some activity or task, they are controlling and directing their ongoing behavior by what they are saying to themselves. Luria (1961) has proposed a three-step sequence to describe the manner in which children acquire control over their own behaviors through the use of verbal self-instructions. He indicated that the behavior of very young children is controlled by the instructions provided by their parents, which tell them what to do. As children grow older, they begin to regulate their own behavior by repeating aloud the instructions previously heard from their parents. The final stage of verbal self-control is attained when children instruct themselves silently. These covert self-statements are viewed as the major way in which children exercise control over their own behavior.

Most of the literature in self-instructional training has included outcome studies of various treatment packages with clinical populations (Urbain & Kendall, 1980). Few studies have attempted to discriminate clinical and normal populations on measures of cognitive self-instructional skills. Camp (1980) did show that hyperaggressive youngsters did more poorly than normal children on a number of measures of verbal mediation of behavior. This study, however, used measures that appear to be related much more to academic functioning than to social functioning. In any case, more research is needed to corroborate Camp's findings and to assess the nature of self-instructional deficits in clinical populations. It would also be helpful to know how adaptive self-instruction develops in normal children.

The self-instructional model has been shown to be quite successful in helping adults to control anger (Novaco, 1975). Sackles (1980) reported encouraging corroboration that this procedure can be helpful in teaching young adolescents to control anger. Because anger is often present in conduct-disordered children, self-instructional training can be a helpful strategy in a comprehensive treatment plan.

In summary, a comprehensive cognitive-behavioral treatment of conduct-disordered children may include the following:

1. Behavioral management programs carried out by the parent.
2. Cognitive restructuring of the parent's beliefs to facilitate compliance with the behavioral assignments.
3. Disputation of the child's irrational beliefs that lead to anger and discomfort anxiety.
4. Social-problem-solving skills that teach the child how to conceptualize appropriate behavior in difficult situations.
5. Self-instructional training to teach the child cognitive rehearsal and linguistic elements to direct adaptive behavior.

Effective, long-lasting treatment is likely to involve all of these areas. A different emphasis on each strategy may result in any one case, depending on the particulars of that case.

Children who are less emotionally disturbed and experience little anger but whose parents consistently reinforce for their misbehavior may need more of a behavioral program with less emphasis on cognitive intervention. Others, who have been less influenced by direct reinforcement but lack social sophistication, may benefit more from treatment focused on training in social-problem solving. When the emotional component is strong and exaggerated, elegant disputing of irrational ideas and stress innoculation training are more advisable.

Steps in Treatment

The treatment of conduct disorder children is a complex and often prolonged task. It may be helpful for the therapist to follow an outline or flowchart in planning treatment so that all of the areas mentioned above are included. *My* order of preference for covering these topics is as follows:

1. Assessment of behavioral and emotional targets, and assessment of behavioral contingencies.
2. Development of rapport with the child.
3. Assessment of the parents' child management skills, their emotions toward the child and the misbehavior, and their philosophies of child rearing.
4. Cognitive-behavioral interventions to change disturbed parental emotions.
5. Cognitive interventions aimed at child's cognitions and emotions.

The remainder of this section discusses the first three stages of treatment.

ASSESSMENT

The first few sessions with children referred for problems of conduct are most helpful if the child and *both* parents are present. During these sessions I advise the therapist to achieve several goals:

1. The first order of business is to get the parents and the child to define the target behaviors or emotions as objectively and clearly as possible. The importance of specificity in problem identification cannot be overemphasized. This may require persistent refocusing and questioning by the therapist (e.g., "He doesn't do well in school" is refined to failing math and reading and minimally passing the rest of the major subjects; rarely doing his homework is refined to "He completes homework on the average of two to three times a week"; "He misbehaves in school" is refined into "He gets into fights in school on an average of two to three times a week"; "He gets angry when I ask him to do something" is refined to "He grits his teeth, turns red, and storms off to his room"). The more specifically the problems are stated, the easier it is to define the intervention and to assess the family's attitudes and emotions toward the target behaviors.

2. After the target behaviors are defined, the therapist moves on to assess the contingencies and consequences of these behaviors. What happens when the child behaves this way? Do the parents do anything? Do they lecture? Is there a penalty or punishment? How consistent are the parents in their approach? Do the parents have similar strategies or do they differ in their reactions to the problem? How long have the parents responded to the child in the present manner? All of these

questions are important to putting the behavior in context. It is possible that the child possesses no cognitive deficits or irrationalities at all. The troublesome behavior can be positively reinforced by parental attention or other rewards. More likely, one will uncover in families of "conduct-disordered" children parents whose child-rearing strategies are inconsistent, permissive, or at least tolerant of the child's misconduct. Regardless of what the parents may say about the child's behavior in the consulting room, it is what they *do* that counts.

The children may provide a more valid indication of what the parents do than the parents themselves. Therefore, it is helpful to direct many of the questions concerning contingencies toward the child. Most parents of "conduct-disordered" children do not provide appropriate contingencies to shape adequately compliant behavior. Usually, they are too soft, and limits are unclear or poorly reinforced. A full knowledge of behavior management principles for child behavior problems (Ross, 1981) is helpful before a therapist uses a cognitive-behavioral intervention.

3. Parental behavior is partly controlled by each parent's theories of child rearing and child development. The therapist had better know what the parent thinks about how he or she is parenting before suggesting alternative strategies. Thus, it is important not only to find out what the parent does but also to find out the rationale behind the parents' behavior.

Rapport

The use of rapport may be questioned by the reader at this point. After all, most books on psychotherapy with children stress the importance of trust and rapport in building a therapeutic relationship. How realistic is it to expect children to open up and self-disclose when the therapist checks up on their misbehavior and makes sure that the parents follow their contract to penalize or deny rewards for such misbehavior?

The groundwork for developing rapport with the child has been set in the previous stages of therapy. In setting the goals of therapy, the parents and the therapist often discuss what the long-term fears of the parents are: "How will she ever finish high school?" "How will he ever cope with a job if he can't cope with school now?" "How will she ever keep friends or earn a living when she can't even get up on time and get along with us?" It is made clear from the outset that both the therapist and the parents have the child's long-term interests in mind even if the child does not appear to agree. While setting up the behavioral management system, the therapist constructs not only a system of response costs but also a system of *rewards*. In addition, the response costs system is organized and specific. The child knows exactly what to expect. This consistency may be perceived as a lot less aversive than the inconsistent, arbitrary, and capricious punishment that the parents may have been using. The behavioral management system also results in a reduction of the verbal assault and nagging incidents between parents and child. The therapist has thus led the way to a more positive parent–child interaction. The therapist has also corrected many of the parents' misconceptions and challenged their irrational beliefs. This procedure communicates that the child is not the only one who contributes to the problem. For reasons such as these, rapport develops.

Occasionally, rapport appears to wither and children remain silent during the therapy sessions. Perhaps only unpleasant words are directed at the therapist. Although such occurrences are rare, they do take place. At this point, several decisions are required. Is therapy more likely to succeed if meetings with the parents are stopped and the behavioral management component is abandoned? Perhaps, meeting with the children alone and waiting for a trusting relationship to grow will result in their willingness to discuss their problems and to seek help. I think not! The outcome literature on traditional nondirective therapy with conduct-disordered children is poor and scarce. If I had to choose, I would rather that the child remain silent or even express dissatisfaction about coming, but that the parents stick to the behavioral components. Numerous clinical failures with traditional approaches have suggested this strategy.

It is helpful for children who refuse to talk or cooperate to remain in treatment and for the behavioral components to be continued for the following reasons:

1. The response costs that are used now to shape their behavior are much less severe and more short-term than those that would naturally occur if the target behaviors remained unchecked.

2. Extinguishing the child's behavior is also a good behavioral homework assignment in frustration tolerance.

3. Extinction procedures communicate from the parents and the therapist that they believe the child is able to change and to stand the frustration provided—it is an affirmation of faith in the child.

4. The child may just be stonewalling: "If I don't cooperate and even act worse, I'll convince my parents that this therapist can't help, my parents will give up, and I can have my way again." The child may just be playing on the parents' low frustration tolerance.

5. The parents' new behavior in setting limits for the child is a more

rational, self-controlled, appropriate model to show the child. Over time, this model may have a positive effect by itself.

Assessing the Parents

Parents may fail to provide an adequate structure for their children for two reasons: they may be ignorant, or they may be disturbed. It is more parsimonious to assume ignorance until one has evidence of disturbance. Many therapists do the reverse. They act on the parental disturbance hypothesis before they have made a full assessment. I am usually amazed at the frequency with which I hear my peers blaming parents for the conduct of their children. I am somewhat disturbed by the elaborate hypotheses that therapists devise to make the parents look sick. Such a therapeutic attitude can be a grave error that will either send the therapy on needless tangents or unnecessarily alienate the parents. Parental personality problems, marital problems, or transient emotional difficulties frequently interfere with the parents' good judgment and result in poor child management. However, no parenting courses are required in high school or college, and the manufacturer fails to send operating instructions with the infant. It is not surprising, then, that some parents fail to know what to do with their children. A good working assumption is that most parents are well meaning and would like to do the best by their child.

George Kelly (1955) postulated that humans behave like scientists and develop theories to explain their environment and the behavior of others. Each of us has implicit personality theories that influence the explanations we give concerning the causes of others' behaviors. These attributions influence our behavior toward others. Most parents have, in addition to implicit personality theories, implicit theories of personality development on which they base their child-rearing strategies. Parents who believe "Spare the rod and spoil the child" may seem hard, angry, and aggressive to some therapists. They may be very loving and may be behaving only as they think best for their child. Their behavior follows from their informal theories of child development. How often have you heard parents say, "If I only could get my child to understand . . ." Such parents are really functioning as cognitive therapists and believe that understanding always comes first and automatically leads to behavior change. As a result, they may reject punishment; they lecture instead. Other parents, following more progressive lines, believe that their children will automatically do the right thing when they are ready.

Although parental theories of child development abound, it appears that the last two decades have fostered permissive child-rearing strategies in this country. Open classrooms, students' rights, and relevant curricula all contribute to a reducing of discipline. Many parents today believe that children should not be frustrated, that all punishment is wrong, and that children should always be free to express themselves. Regardless of the influences that have shaped these permissive attitudes, it appears that they represent the source of many parental difficulties. It is difficult to raise children without denying them some reward, or without limiting their behavior in some way, or without punishing some behavior. I would argue that it is not enough for therapists to teach parents behavioral child-management skills. It is also important to convince the parents of a philosophy of child rearing that emphasizes the desirability of teaching frustration tolerance, the importance of setting limits, and the advantages of inculcating appropriate social skills in compliance with the demands of others.

Some parents do have disturbed emotions that interfere with their parenting, and many of these parents are ignorant as well. Parents may not be willing to reveal their problems and emotions. They have sought professional help for their child and may be insulted, angered, defensive, or alienated if their problems are immediately put on the agenda. Blaming the parents may only lead to quick termination. Convincing parents to work on their own emotional problems is a particularly delicate matter. A collaborative relationship with the parents designed to explore the causes of their child's problems and collectively to investigate solutions is a good first step in developing rapport.

Strategies for assessing the parents' emotional disturbance and for helping them to become aware of their role in the child's problems can be found. It may be helpful to explain to the parents that the therapist's impact on a child is minimal. A 45-minute-per-week session cannot have the effect of the parents' love and attention. Rather than treating the child, then, therapists explain that they will teach the parent to manage the child. The parents are then instructed that, for some time, they will meet with the child and the therapist as a group and that strategies for changing the child's behavior will be discussed. The parents will be the ones who actually implement the behavior change strategies. It is important to make the parents feel important and helpful in the therapy process.

The parents' disturbed emotions can then be assessed by two strategies. The first occurs when the therapist elicits information about the eliciting stimuli or consequences of the target behaviors in the first assessment phase of treatment. Does the child behave inappropriately more when one parent is around? Is the child's behavior related to the parent's own upsetness? Does the parent get angry when the target behavior occurs? How do both parents feel when their child misbehaves? What do they think when their child misbehaves?

The second strategy can be implemented after the therapist has constructed a behavioral management program and sent the family home to implement it. Failure to stick to the behavioral regime is often due to parental problems such as dysfunctional thoughts and feelings, which can be assessed: "What stopped you from punishing Jack?" "How did you feel when Julie didn't have enough points to go skating?" "What stopped you from giving Kim her rewards when her homework was completed?" "What feelings did you have when those temper tantrums started?" "How do you feel when you notice that Dean has not done his chores?" "What kinds of feelings do you have about having to check up on Scott to make sure his homework is done?" Such questioning naturally leads the parents to see that their emotional reactions have prevented them from successfully using the prescribed interventions. In this way, they may develop some "insight" into the dynamics of their family and how their emotions influence the way they interact with their children. It has been my clinical experience that the two above strategies are more helpful in getting the parents to see the complicated involvement of the whole family in the child's problems than lecturing parents on the role of family systems or the importance of everyone's taking responsibility for the child's behavior.

As I have indicated, when parents do become upset, their upset interferes with child rearing. Parental emotional disturbance may occur because they are (1) upset about the child or (2) upset about outside issues, such as their marriage, their work, or themselves. It does not appear necessary that parents resolve all of their personal or marital problems before they can learn to use effective child-management strategies. The parents need not be sent off to individual therapy to work on themselves or their marriage before attempting to change the child. Neither does the entire family structure need to be changed. Rather, the parents are asked to change their emotions in limited situations with their children, even if they do not wish to work on the other major issues in their lives. Again, clinical experience suggests that parents are often able to learn rational modes of thinking in this arena. They can control their emotional upset about dealing with their children, while they stubbornly refuse to control their emotional upset about other activating events in their lives.

Changing Dysfunctional Feelings of Parents

The emotions of anger, guilt, and discomfort anxiety are most likely to surface when the parents are upset about their children. The following are some of the emotions, as well as the irrational ideas that elicit them, that make parents upset about their children.

Guilt

When guilt is involved, the parents are most likely blaming themselves for the child's behavior problems and condemning themselves for being to blame. Such blame does not derive only from the parent's inability to handle the child. In addition, it flows from frustrating and unpleasant events that may have befallen the child. Single parents may believe that their inability to remain married has unfairly inflicted a divorce and the loss of one parent on their child. A loss, the parent believes, is catastrophic for the child. Parents of sick children (even if the illness occurred years ago), learning-disabled children, retarded children, and handicapped children may believe that they are partly responsible for their child's misfortune. Perhaps, there was something they could have done to prevent the child's problem. Even if the parent does not feel a guilty responsibility for the child's problems, she or he may feel guilt for having been unable to prevent the problem, or for being unable to ameliorate or remove the problem immediately.

Many guilty parents think that their child has been frustrated or wronged and that the child does not deserve and cannot bear other misfortunes and frustrations. Their child *needs special* consideration to make up for past inequities. The child is seen as unable to stand up to normal parental discipline. Certainly, it would be cruel and unjust punishment to have Janet miss TV because she has not completed her homework. Even such small, inconsequential activating events or frustrating events inflicted in normal child-rearing are seen as too catastrophic for the child to stand. These parental attitudes about a particular child may account for the finding that, in some families, one child presents a conduct disorder whereas the siblings may be normally behaved.

> John N., a 13-year-old learning-disabled child with mild cerebral palsy, had a long history of academic difficulties despite his superior IQ. Over the years, he had developed a number of conduct problems and in particular had long, loud shouting matches with his parents. Family life focused almost entirely on John's schoolwork and chores. Yelling and confusion were a family style. His mother felt particularly guilty about John's neurological problems. She tried in every way to make up for his deficits. She sat for long hours with him, literally doing his homework, doing his chores, and becoming his friend. As a result of her overinvolvement, John had never learned social and study skills. Whenever she was instructed to

let John handle his own affairs, she became upset and nervous. "It hurts me to see him struggle," she would say. As a result of her upset, John's mother blamed herself for his illness and blamed his father for not doing enouth. Whenever John did fail or make a mistake, she would also blame him and become enraged. Each task had taken on so much importance because her worth and her husband's rested on John's doing well. With such high stakes, it was no wonder she was so upset about his failure. Despite all of the irrationality and upset concerning John, Mr. and Mrs. N. behaved quite differently toward their other children. Even more suprising, when John was away at camp or visiting relatives overnight, the normal, hectic, yelling family life calmed down considerably. Rather than changing the family system, I focused on changing Mrs. N.'s attitude toward her son's disability, specifically her beliefs that she was to blame, that John shouldn't have to struggle, and that her upset was related to his school success.

In disputing guilt-causing cognitions, several important points can be emphasized. First, the parent erroneously assumes that he or she is the sole cause of the child's past problems, or the sole possible protecting force. Such parents can be reminded that they can never be so omnipotent as to prevent a learning disability or diabetes. It is healthful to list specifically the many other factors that may have caused the child's actual problems. A second key irrationality imbedded in these parents' guilty thinking is the notion that some past or present adversity is so unpleasant and awful that their child cannot be expected to live normally and that restitution must be made for this activating event. This clearly is an antecedent event–consequence causal statement concerning the child. Examples abound of children with similar problems who have adjusted well and who live normal lives. A therapist can recount such stories and convince the parents of their irrationality. It is also helpful to dispute their idea that the adversity suffered by their child inevitably weakens all children.

The most destructive aspect of guilty-producing parental thinking, however, is the idea that children are too labile to tolerate frustration. Such is the stuff of self-fulfilling prophecies. Parents believe that their children cannot handle frustration and therefore give them reduced practice in developing frustration tolerance and reinforce the child's catastrophizing. Appropriate skills in frustration tolerance and coping are thus not learned. Frequently, the parent uses present behavior problems as evidence that the past activating event devastated the child (i.e., "I can tell Jack's illness had a terrible effect on him; he still gets upset when I ask him to do something"). It is most important here to stress the resilience of children and to show repeatedly the function that the parents' guilt serves in maintaining the present problem. It is also helpful to ask the parents how long they expect to live and care for their child. Because the parents believe that their offspring cannot cope, do they believe that their child will require constant care? If the parents do expect the child to develop frustration tolerance someday, how do they expect this to happen? Coping skills do not develop magically when a child reaches maturity. If the future is constantly referred to, perhaps the parents can be persuaded that training in frustration tolerance can be initiated gradually under the watchful eye of the therapist.

The type of guilt that is most resistant to change usually occurs when the parents blame their parenting skills for producing the aberrant behavior of their child. Here again, the guilt leads to short-term restitution in the form of relaxed discipline. The parental logic usually is "I'm a lousy parent, ergo I'm a lousy person." All the disputes suggested by Ellis against such self-worth and self-rating beliefs apply here. However, clinical experience has suggested that self-downing about failure as a parent, especially among women, is a pernicious irrational belief. If philosophical disputation does not produce a satisfactory solution, and the parents insist on blaming themselves, empirical disputes may be more helpful. As indicated, parents are never solely responsible for their child's behavior and personality. Genetic, physiological, cultural, educational, and peer factors all have an influence in shaping a child. Minimizing the parents' exaggerated sense of responsibility can be achieved by a detailed discussion of the many factors that shape the child into an adult.

Anger

Parental anger is the second most frequent emotion that the therapist encounters in parents of children with conduct disorders. Anger is always a difficult problem to deal with, especially within these families. Parents usually view their anger as functional. They yell, scream, or lecture at their children. They often perceive this behavior as punishing the child, and the punishment is assumed to suppress the behavior that they got angry about in the first place. Not only is the anger initiated by the parents' irrational beliefs, but the expectation that the anger will be an effective child-managing tool reinforces both the irrationality and the emotional state.

The first step in changing the anger is to convince parents that this emotion will not help them or their children. Many parents punish their children solely by angry outbursts of yelling. However, the verbal anger of the parents is usually not considered aversive enough by the children to suppress the inappropriate behavior. They can do as they please and have to suffer only the moderate irritation of ten minutes of yelling. Parents often feel better after yelling and also delude themselves into thinking that they have done something about the problem. Talk is cheap and so is yelling. Response cost and extinction procedures seem to be more effective ways of controlling children's behavior than yelling. Another problem with anger, besides its ineffectiveness, is that it usually begets more anger. Children are more likely to become more emotionally upset about their parents' verbal aggression than they are about standard, basic behavior-management techniques. Increased upset on the part of the children only exacerbates their problem and decreases the likelihood that the parents will prevent the behavior from happening in the future. Among other reasons, yelling is more personally insulting and degrading.

Many parents equate discipline and limit setting with anger. They do not take action until they are mad. These parents use their emotional arousal level as a cue to discipline the child. Here, the child's behavior is initially ignored, but not long enough to be extinguished. As the behavior increases in force or persists across time, so does the parents' irrational thinking. Ultimately, the parents' emotion reaches a threshold of anger, and they react aggressively to stop the child's behavior. The parents again leave the interaction confident that they have had an impact on the child. Things look different from the child's view. The parent has tolerated their misbehavior over repeated occurrences and for a specific period of time. For example, children learn that they can tease their siblings eight times, but that the ninth time will probably bring parental retribution. Or they learn that they can ignore the parent's request to do a chore for twenty minutes, but that a thirty minute delay will cause a response. Parents are generally unaware of the ineffectiveness of their child-management strategies, and little change is likely to occur until they understand that their own behavior tends to intensify the behavior that they wish to change in the child. What is necessary to teach parents this rule is to provide the parents with specific behavioral criteria for identifying undesirable behavior before they react to the problem and not to their own momentary emotional upset over the behavior.

Once the parents understand that anger at their children will not change their children, they may be more willing to look at their own irrational beliefs, which get them angry. According to Ellis (1977), anger usually comes from demanding rather than desiring philosophies. Parents' anger at the children is no exception. They can demand all they want that their child behave nicely, but obviously, there is no objective rationale (law of the universe) for insisting that what they wish to happen must occur. Children are, after all, children. They are all mischievous, ignorant, and partly unsocialized—because they are still children. It is helpful to point out to angry parents that they were also unruly children. Only through learning, supervision, and parental controls did they learn to behave less obstreperously. Their children will require the same effort. Magic elixirs for good children are unreliable and have not yet been approved by the Food and Drug Administration. Child rearing takes work and time. Once the parents accept the fact that children will be children and this entails much undesirable behavior and that parenting requires a great deal of effort and work, they will start accepting the fact that only through appropriate structure are the children likely to learn and change.

Discomfort Anxiety

Much of parents' upset at their child will, on closer examination, turn out to be discomfort anxiety or low frustration tolerance (Ellis, 1980b). Most parents seem to have a rather romantic notion about offspring and child rearing. Although the rewards of procreation are many, the frustrations, hardships, and hassles are at least equivalent. Possibly, the most trying hassle of child rearing is its omnipresence. Although there are regular vacations from work and even a few from one's spouse, children usually take 20 years to grow up. Parents may believe that they are overwhelmed by the constant stressors provided by their children. At such times, it is quite easy for them to give their little darlings just what they desire so that they will keep quiet and leave their parents alone. Children, being as resourceful as they are, are ever quick to exploit the parents' weakness. A pattern can easily develop whereby the parents give in to childish requests to escape the torture of the child's persistent nagging. Here, too, parents are unlikely to recognize the role of their irrational beliefs in getting them upset until they understand that the entire pattern of behavior is self-defeating. The parent finds the child's behavior annoying. The adult then gives in to the child's demands to immediately terminate the child's annoying. The result is relief! However, the rewards provided to the child ensure that he or she will behave similarly the next time around. Discomfort anxiety and low frustration tolerance can be dealt with inelegantly by stressing that the short-term pain of listening to the child's whining will get long-term gains by helping the parent to extinguish the child's behavior. The result is that both parents and child experience better rapport because the parents spend less time dealing with the child's whining and more time engaging in positive interactions.

Parents with discomfort anxiety often start following behavioral contracts but quickly give up if change is not immediately forthcoming. Their children usually know this about them. Response cost or extinction procedures are likely to cause an extinction burst before the child changes positively: "If I behave bad now, Mom will give up." "I'll convince Dad that this time out stuff won't work; then I'll have no problems doing what I want to." It is important to prepare the parents for these extinction bursts and to help them realize their child may be purposely manipulating them and trying to get them to succumb to their low frustation tolerance by behaving more obnoxiously. Very often, it becomes a battle of wills between the parents and the child. Will they give up first or will the child? It is helpful to have the parents stand next to the child and ask them who they think is going to be in control and who is going to have psychological strength.

Phillosophical disputes that focus on the parents' low frustration tolerance can deal with the obvious strengths that parents have shown in many previous child-rearing situations. Especially relevant is convincing them that they can tolerate frustration and that it is not imperative for them to be cool, calm, and collected at all times. Regardless of what disputational strategies the therapist chooses, the reduction of low frustration tolerance is likely to be a crucial step in getting the parents to adhere to behavioral contracts.

Cognitive-Behavioral Interventions with Children

Once the parents adhere to the behavioral strategies, the child has some motivation to talk privately with the therapist. The cognitive strategies that the therapist teaches now have some meaning and purpose for the child. The child may wish to avoid response costs or to seek additional rewards. In a sense, the child has been placed in a conflict; conflict is uncomfortable, and discomfort very often motivates the child to look for change.

At this stage of therapy, I usually meet with the parents and the child at the beginning of each session. We discuss the child's progress on the target behaviors, the parents' adherence to the behavioral regime, and any changes that are required in the behavioral contract to progressively shape the child's behavior to the ultimate goal (e.g., requiring a higher percentage of homework completed). This review of progress, then, becomes the "meat" of the session with the child. By knowing that Johnny did not finish his homework two nights and had three fights in school, the therapist focuses on the emotions and cognitions that could have prevented the target behavior from occurring.

Cognitive Change

Disputing and challenging the irrational aspects of the thinking of children with conduct disorders can be somewhat more difficult than dealing with middle-aged neurotics. As with all children (DiGiuseppe, 1981), it is important to make sure that they have a schema and a vocabulary for the emotions that you would like them to develop. I would put forth the hypothesis that people can not experience an emotion for which they do not possess a schema. Emotions not only are caused by cognitions but to some extent are cognitions. That is, emotions are a mixture of the experienced sensations from physiological arousal plus the interpretation and evaluation of that arousal. The evaluation has either a positive or a negative valence. The same degree of arousal may be judged either good or bad (e.g., excitement or fear). In addition, one makes an assessment of the appropriateness of an emotional experience, given social mores (Schacter, 1964). For example, guilt may be considered the label we give depression about wrongdoing. Jealousy is the label we give the fear of losing something we have to another. The label one gives the emotion is taken from social cues and circumstances. People carry around expectations about both the type and the degree of the emotion that they consider appropriate for specific situations. Children often have limited schemata concerning emotional reactions to events. They may have either a limited repertoire or a fixed notion of the appropriateness of an emotion for a specific event.

A clinical example may be used to make this point more clear:

> A 10-year-child, John, was referred for conduct problems including fighting at home and at school. In one session he presented the problem of getting in trouble because of fighting with his brother, who had broken one of John's toys. John eagerly admitted to thinking, "It is awful that my brother broke my toy and he should not have done that." When I attempted to dispute these ideas, John shockingly retorted, "What is the matter with you! You want me to be happy about it."
>
> This child's reasoning went as follows: If thoughts do cause feelings and the therapist wants me to change my thoughts, he obviously wants me to change my feelings. If the therapist wants me to change my feelings, he believes that some other emotional response is appropriate. John searched his mind for a reasonable alternative. When the only alternative seemed foolish to him, he rejected me and my disputing. Further discussion with John revealed that he had a bipolar schema of emotion for this event: happy/mad. Because I had demonstrated by my disputing that mad was wrong, he assumed that I was suggesting happy, truly an inappropriate affect.
>
> Before John and I could work collaboratively on challenging the be-

liefs that lead to his anger, we had to agree on a goal acceptable to him. Before he could reach such a goal, he had to expand his schema of emotional reactions to include more alternatives. After we discussed different ways that people could feel in such situations, and how each of these helped or hindered a person, John was able to choose a goal. Then, finally, we could move on to the next phase of analyzing the thought that elicited his anger.

Building schemata of emotions and evaluating their usefulness are often-neglected steps in treatment. Many therapists assume that if they treat the underlying problem, the behavior will change. If the therapist sticks to the original hypothesis that children who misbehave are often ignorant of and untrained in many normal reactions, this error can be avoided.

Because of the nature of conduct disorders, the work of disputing is more the construction of new, rational cognitions than the restructuring of old, irrational ones. Although anger is a frequent problem, the anger literature in cognitive therapy is sparse. The most helpful model for our young clients, in my opinion, is Novaco's (1975) stress innoculation procedures, which he initiated and applied with adults. Some preliminary research suggests that this model can be adapted successfully to "conduct disorder" children of preadolescence and early adolescence (Sackles, 1980; Schlichter & Horan, 1981). The children are first taught the appropriate use of anger, as well as the role of irrational beliefs and thinking styles in generating and maintaining anger. However, because these children are impulsive, they usually do not recognize their irrational beliefs and dispute them *in vivo*. Self-instructional training is used to get them to stop and think more rationally before they behave.

The importance of self-instructional training in stopping and promoting thoughts cannot be overemphasized for this population. Anger and impulsivity do not lend themselves to reflective disputing. Consider the case of a socially anxious adult or child and the sequence of events and cognitions and how they differ from those for a client displaying impulsive behavior. When presented with a social situation, the anxious client catastrophizes about the outcome and experiences anxiety. The anxiety then inhibits the person's behavior and she or he does nothing. After a while, our anxious client may start to dispute, and after a little longer, the disputing starts to reduce the anxiety. When the anxiety is sufficiently reduced, the inhibiting effect is lost and the client can act. This experience has shown the client that she or he can cope. Angry clients, on the other hand, may not have such an easy time of it. When confronting a difficult situation, they start demanding. This approach leads to anger. Anger is more likely to motivate quick action than anxiety and to lead to physically or verbally aggressive behavior. In a short period of time, the entire incident is over. The angry client has not tried any disputing and has not experienced any success in coping.

Disputing takes time and practice. Because of the nature of angry behavior, the conduct disorder child does not take the time to think. Some latency-extending or response-delaying strategy is necessary to slow the client up, so that disputing can start before the coping trial is complete.

At this point, I would like to emphasize that all of the cognitive and emotive issues reviewed in this chapter are incorporated into the individual therapy with the child or adolescent. The ideal therapy, then, includes the following elements:

1. The activating events to be discussed should be drawn from actual situations in which the children have experienced the emotional or behavioral problem.

2. The emotional vocabulary of the children should be expanded. The therapist reviews the hedonic value of various emotional reactions. This review is aimed at motivating the children to see the desirability of changing their emotional consequences.

3. The irrational beliefs causing the disturbed emotions are identified and disputed.

4. Specific self-instructional statements are taught to inhibit immediate responding, to focus on cognitive disputing, and to guide appropriate behavior.

5. Social-problem-solving skills (i.e., alternative solutions and consequential thinking) are taught to encourage the child to avoid problem situations in the future.

The material presented in this chapter is meant to provide a model for working with this difficult group of youngsters. Although an attempt has been made to expand the model so that it is as comprehensive as possible, no doctrine is implied. It is hoped that this bare-bones discussion will be a jumping-off point for readers to expand on.

REFERENCES

Abikoff, H. Cognitive training interventions in children: A review of a new approach. *Journal of Learning Disabilities*, 1979, *12*(2), 123–135.

American Psychiatric Association. *Diagnostic and statistical manual* (3rd ed.). Washington, D.C.: Author, 1980.

Bandura, A. *Aggression: A social learning analysis.* Englewood Cliffs, N.J.: Prentice-Hall, 1973.

Block, J. Effects of a rational-emotive mental health program on poor achieving, disruptive high school students. *Journal of Counseling Psychology*, 1978, *25*, 61–65.

Camp, B. Two psychoeducational treatment programs for young boys. In C. Whalen & B. Henler (Eds.), *Hyperactive children: The social ecology of identification and treatment.* New York: Academic Press, 1980.
DiGiuseppe, R. A. Cognitive therapy with children. In G. Emery, S. D. Hollon, & R. C. Bedrosian (Eds.), *New directions in cognitive therapy.* New York: Guilford Press, 1981.
Ellis, A. *How to live with and without anger.* New York: Reader's Digest Press, 1977.
Ellis, A. Rational-emotive therapy and cognitive behavior therapy: Similarities and differences. *Cognitive Therapy and Research,* 1980, *4,* 305–340. (a)
Ellis, A. Discomfort anxiety: A new cognitive behavioral construct. *Rational Living,* 1980, *15*(1), 25–30. (b)
Kelly, G. *Psychology of personal constructs* (Vols. 1 and 2). New York: Norton, 1955.
Kendall, P. One year followup of concrete versus conceptual cognitive-behavioral self control training. *Journal of Consulting and Clinical Psychology,* 1981, *49,* 748–749.
Luria, A. *The role of speech in the regulation of normal and abnormal behavior.* New York: Liveright, 1961.
Meichenbaum, D. *Cognitive-behavior modification.* New York: Plenum Press, 1977.
Novaco, R. *Anger control.* Lexington, Mass.: D. C. Heath–Lexington Books, 1975.
Patterson, G. Interventions for boys with conduct problems: Multiple settings, treatment and criteria. *Journal of Consulting and Clinical Psychology,* 1974, *42,* 471–481.
Patterson, G., & Fleischman, M. Maintenance of treatment efforts: Some considerations concerning family systems and follow-up data. *Behavior Therapy,* 1979, *10,* 168–185.
Patterson, G., Reid, J., Jones, S., & Conger, R. *A social learning approach to family intervention: Families with aggressive children.* Eugene Ore.: Castalia Press, 1975.
Quay, H., & Werry, J. *Psychopathological disorders of childhood* (2nd ed.). New York: Wiley, 1979.
Ross, A. *Psychological disorders of children: A behavioral approach to theory, research and therapy.* New York: McGraw-Hill, 1981.
Sackles, J. *Three treatment programs for anger control in young adolescents.* Unpublished doctoral dissertation: Hofstra University, 1980.
Schachter, S. The interaction of cognitive and physiological determinants of emotional states. In L. Berkowitz (Ed.), *Advances in experimental social psychology.* New York: Academic Press, 1964.
Schlichter, K., & Horan, J. Effects of stress inoculation on the anger and aggression management skills of institutional juvenile delinquents. *Cognitive Therapy and Research,* 1981, *5*(4), 359–366.
Spivack, G., Platt, J., & Shure, M. *The social problem solving approach to adjustment.* San Francisco: Jossey-Bass, 1976.
Urbain, E., & Kendall, P. Review of social-cognitive problem solving interventions with children. *Psychological Bulletin,* 1980, *88,* 109–143.
Vygotsky, V. *Thought and language.* New York: Wiley, 1962.

5

Children and Low Frustration Tolerance

WILLIAM J. KNAUS

Children exhibiting low frustration tolerance and weak frustration management skills may go through life inconsistently responding to challenge, having problems in organizing, demonstrating impatience, inhibiting competencies, giving up easily, procrastinating, and agitating themselves about their frustrations. The greater the deviation from age-expectant behavior toward low frustration tolerance, the greater the child's vulnerability.

Because frustrations are so much a part of daily life, one of our greatest challenges is to help children acquire effective frustration mastery skills so that they might build upon them throughout childhood and their adult lives.

In this chapter I will point out why I think teaching children frustration mastery principles is of prime importance. Initially, I will discuss frustration, low frustration tolerance, and frustration disturbances as a prelude to the discussion of specific strategies for helping children master their frustrations and overcome low frustration tolerance.

FRUSTRATION: A COMPLEX PROCESS

In studying the relationship between frustrating conditions and children's frustration responses, scientists originally thought that frustration led to aggression. Thus, managing frustrations would be a matter

---

WILLIAM J. KNAUS • Psychologist in Private Practice, 113 Arlington Road, Longmeadow, Massachusetts 01106.

of learning to modulate aggressive responses. One of the classic frustration-aggression studies was conducted by Barker, Dembo, and Lewin (1941) using kindergarten children. In the experiment, the children initially played with a mixture of toys with missing pieces: the ironing board had no iron, the water toys had no water. At first, the children disregarded the missing pieces and made imaginative use of the toys. Later, the experimenters exposed the children to superior and complete toys, and blocked the children from using these new toys. When the children returned to play with the old toys, the fun ceased. Now frustrated and disgruntled, the children squabbled among themselves, behaved poorly toward the experimenters, and destroyed some of the toys. With raised expectations, the children found little satisfaction with inferior toys.

Berkowitz (1969) saw the frustration–aggression model as both too sweeping and too simple. He proposed that we need to focus on other considerations to understand the relationship between frustration and aggression. These include:

1. Motives the aggressor ascribes toward others.
2. The person's attitude toward the problem area.
3. Past learning.
4. The person's interpretation of his own emotional, reaction to the frustration conditions.

Berkowitz's views on frustration and aggression support the rational-emotive position that we feel the way we think (Ellis & Greiger, 1977). In effect, we cause our own frustrations because of what and how we think about our impediments.

There are several classical views concerning frustration. Psychologists Dollard, Doobs, Miller, Mower, and Sears (1938) define frustration as a condition that exists when a goal "suffers interference." Heider (Benesh & Weiner, 1982) pointed out that frustration occurs when we *believe* that a desired goal is unattainable. Maier (1948, 1954) points out that frustration gets confused with goal directed behavior. He sees frustrated behavior as undirected, stereotypic, rigid, destructive, compulsive, and growth retarding. Frustration researcher, Bull (1957), proposes that frustration is a complex emotional state that erupts when we face an impediment. Each of these positions has merit.

For purposes of this chapter, I will use a taxonomic definition. Frustrations erupt when we face an impediment. They exist when our wants, wishes, and desires get thwarted or interrupted. Frustration begins with a feeling of discomfort and ranges from imperceptable to powerful. If sufficiently intense, frustration can disrupt memory functions and result in disorganized thinking and behaving. At moderate levels, frustration can motivate problem-solving behaviors. Frustration overlaps with threat, conflict, stress, annoyance, and irritations—each condition reflects a disparity between *what is wanted* and *what is* (Knaus, 1983).

In our encounters with frustration, there is opportunity to gain, to learn, and to advance. There is opportunity to construct and to create. This opportunity is echoed in the Muslim bible, the Koran: "Do you think that you can pass through the portals of the immortals without having done that which those before you have done?" This same message is suggested in Campbell's (1968) *The Hero of a Thousand Faces* (i.e., trials, tribulations, and frustrations are part of the human condition). How one meets these challenges is what tells the tale.

Strong frustration provides a powerful incentive for change. It is the *intolerance* for frustration–tension (or the fear of any strong negative or positive emotion) that proves self-defeating. Indeed, tension fears are central to most psychological disturbances. For example, if people were not afraid of tension, other than real danger, what else would there be to fear (Knaus, 1979, 1983)?

The Effects of Frustration on Performance

Most children are adaptable and improve their frustration management skills as they grow older. Others display a marked adversion for frustrating circumstances and either try to shelter themselves or try to expediently remove the source of tension. Their reaction patterns might conform with Dollard and Miller's (1950) frustration–aggression hypothesis, McDougall's (1926) view that the response may be overt or imperceptible, and Rosenzweig's (1944) theory that frustration responses are directional (i.e., extropunitive, blaming others; intropunitive, blaming self; or impunitive, blaming no one). Such patterns that prove self-defeating in childhood can continue throughout life adding stress and distress to a person's existence. Chronically frustrated youngsters are often labeled troubled, behavior problem, inhibited, or *burnt-out*.

The school experience can be an on-going frustration for children and contribute to schoolage burnout. For example, about 25% of school-age youngsters disturb themselves because they view the school learning process as something they cannot control (Knaus & Eldridge, 1982). Like adults who fall victim to occupational stresses and burnout, these youngsters may burnout at school due to heightened school-learning stresses. For example, children who are required to persistently work on tasks which seem uninteresting, unattractive, and unrewarding, are prime burnout candidates.

B. F. Skinner (1965), in an article entitled "Why Teachers Fail," noted that the school environment can be adversive when it elicits tensions that cause students to work at escaping and avoiding rather than learning. He reports that those who do poorly in their studies are likely to stay away from school, suffer from mental fatigue, daydream, or counterattack.

The avoidance behaviors that Skinner described result from chronic frustrations and are symptomatic of burnout. I might add that the highest risk candidates are those with low frustration tolerance who rush their school work, miss detail, have to relearn material, and are at risk of falling behind and of failing.

Coopersmith (1967) has noted that there is a positive relationship between self-concept and academic achievement. Thus, the low achieving child tends to view himself as less adequate than his higher-achieving peers. Under such conditions, it is reasonable to assume that substandard school performance may contribute to a negative self-concept. Conversely, children who develop a sense of pride in the quality of their work will probably think better of their abilities and of themselves.

It is quite unusual to find a youngster whose tolerance for frustration is low and who does not also suffer from some form of self-concept disturbance. There are, of course, exceptions. The infant who howls at the slightest discomfort probably is not thinking he or she is a bad person. The individual with a frustrating itch will probably not view himself or herself in derogatory terms.

Because low frustration tolerance seems implicated in performance deficiencies, a look at what low frustration means and more about how this process surfaces is needed.

Classical Signs and Symptoms of Low Frustration Tolerance

Low frustration tolerance, a strong urge to throw off discomfort, occurs with little forethought and frequently involves the following process:

1. The child views certain situations as frustrating when he or she cannot do what he or she wants to do.
2. The child exaggerates the importance of avoiding discomfort and predicts the situation will be *too* uncomfortable.
3. The prediction takes place in a "twinkling of an eye" and the child's response is impulsive or inhibited.

4. The individual exhibits a low frustration tolerance language system. This system includes expletives, avoidance phrases ("I don't want to," or "I can't do it"), extropunitive phrases ("he, she, or it is causing all the trouble"), distress phrases ("I feel overwhelmed"), intolerance phrases ("I can't stand it"); and reference phrases ("I hate myself," or "I feel odd"). This language system develops in the context of daily living.
5. The low frustration language system intensifies visceral sensations and cognitive disorganization. Because of the interactive links between low frustration tolerance language and visceral sensations, unpleasant feelings can stimulate low frustration tolerance self-talk.
6. This visceral language reciprocal process distracts from the child's ability to cope and consequently feeds into the development and maintenance of a self concept disturbance.
7. The individual discovers and develops self-protective diversionary methods that prove temporarily palliative but reinforce self-concept and frustration disturbances.

Low frustration tolerance has been implicated as a factor in emotional disturbance by clinicians of various theoretical persuasion such as Freud (1955), Overstreet (1925), Low (1950), Hybl and Stagner (1952), Cattell (1962), Ellis (1982), and Ainslie (1975). Although each theorist employs a different label, (primary process thinking, comfort cult, effort stress, specious reward, or discomfort anxiety), they describe the same dynamic.

Frustration disturbances are self-created. For example, some youngsters (and adults) are afraid of almost any negative sensation. When frustrated, these sensation sensitive youngsters try to squelch the feeling rather than confront the problem. And as Proust has said, it is "that fear of suffering in the immediate present which condemns us to perpetual suffering" (Painter, 1965).

Low frustration tolerance takes many forms among school children—importunity; day-dreaming; refusing to discharge responsibilities; procrastinating; whining and complaining; arguing and fussing; fabricating to cover minor mistakes; focusing on "unfairnesses" and demanding that they cease; cursing when personal rules are violated; quivering in terror at the thought of talking in front of the class; shyness; compulsive eating; copying other children's homework; poor spelling due to failure to look up words; inattentiveness; disrupting the class; blaming others; impatience; and withdrawal.

Children's behavioral problems are normally classified according to symptom: eating problem, impulse disorder, compulsive disorder, avoidant disorder of childhood, temper tantrum, anxiety disorder, depression, conduct problem, and so forth. Each of these classifications have as a common factor, *low frustration tolerance*. For example, obese children with eating problems have significant difficulty resisting the tempting morsels they wish to ravenously gulp down. Eating problems, like other compulsive disorders, result when the child thinks he or she cannot stand the tension from not doing what he or she has an urge to do. In avoidance disorders the child restricts his or her actions out of fear of appearing inept, wrong, or foolish. Children with conduct problems such as fighting, stealing, or truancy often react on the basis of impulse.

While most childhood behavior problems can be organized around an intolerance to frustration model, this is typically not done. For example, the new *Diagnostic and Statistical Manual Of Mental Disorders* (DSM-III, 1980) contains little reference to frustration intolerance as underpinning major symptoms, such as eating disorders. Thus the DSM-III system falls short of specifying low frustration tolerance correlates that are common to the various psychological symptom classifications.

Low frustration tolerance is often neglected in books on childhood psychopathology. For example, in Wolman's (1972), *Manual Of Childhood Psychopathology*, low frustration tolerance (LFT) was not mentioned in the index even though many of the problem descriptions seem to correlate with LFT.

Schaefer and Milman (1977) are among the few clinical writers who discuss treating children who display impulse disorders or low frustration tolerance problems. Others include Pollack (1968), Knaus (1977), Meichenbaum and Goodman (1971), and Kagan (1971).

Factors Contributing To Low Frustration Tolerance Disturbances

The following factors contribute to the development of a low frustration tolerance disturbance process. Following each hypothesized factor are general frustration management strategies.

1. *Inadequate expressive language skills*. The child does not have an adaptive emotive vocabulary to accurately define or express desires or discontents. He may use a short hand method of self-expression that reflects a restrictive language system (Bernstein, 1961). Sometimes however, children with exceptionally good language skill are highly intolerant toward frustration. In such cases, the child will tend to use his verbal ability to defend against discomfort. We can help the child to reverse either pat-

tern by helping him or her develop an understanding of and practice expressing what he or she honestly thinks and feels.
2. *Poor modeling.* A child reared in an environment with people who display low frustration tolerance, will tend to imitate this same response pattern. To alter this trend, we expose the child to effective models and provide him or her with opportunities to practice the effective new behaviors he or she observes.
3. *Social conditioning.* There are conditionable and conflicting ideas common to Western Society: Get ahead and achieve if you can; avoid tension if you can. Not uncommonly a child comes to believe that achievement should be tension free. If a child comes to that conclusion, he or she is likely to frustrate himself or herself when he or she tries to effortlessly do excellent work. We can help the child alter this dysfunctional viewpoint by helping him or her to develop a clear perspective on the relationship between planning, effort, and results.
4. *Poor coping skills.* The child with poor coping skills is likely to stress and frustrate herself. She or he is likely to poorly organize her or his efforts, lack a functional sense of timing and pacing, and too frequently experience the disorganizing effects of intense frustration or anxiety. To help her or him change this pattern, we start by helping her or him learn ways to defuse her or his distress and to develop organizing skills.
5. *Reward for delay.* The child discovers that when he or she puts something off, makes up excuses, lies, or engages in other expedient actions, he or she is intermittently rewarded for this behavior. We can help to reverse this trend by helping the child examine the impact of his or her delaying actions on his or her emotional security and accomplishments.
6. *Misreading the signal.* The child misinterprets the meaning of frustration. Instead of using the feeling as an impetus for purposeful action, she or he interprets the feeling as a signal to avoid the provocative stimulus. By helping the child learn to view the frustrating condition as a challenge, the frustration avoidance bias can be changed to a problem-solving bias.
7. *Constitutional predisposition.* Some children are genetically equipped with advantageous tendencies such as athletic prowess, musical ability, and frustration tolerance. Others are predisposed toward undesirable qualities such as low frustration tolerance, perceptual distortions, anxiety, or depression. Tendencies, of course, need not be actualized. The person with musical talent need not learn to play music. The person who is

inclined toward obesity need not get fat. The person primed for intolerance toward frustration can learn to be tolerant. (The following section describes how this is to be accomplished.)

Action Strategies

How a child responds to frustration avoidance urges may prove either beneficial or dysfunctional. For example, low frustration tolerance fueled by a vague negative attitude can promote a sense of intolerance and lead to dysfunctional responses.

Frustration tolerance is pivotal to mastering challenges and effective coping. It is the capacity to (1) delay gratification (when required) and (2) face problems.

Can children learn to master their frustrations? To one degree or another, they can learn to tolerate frustrations and master frustration evoking problems. Indeed, *frustration tolerance training* is readily teachable and involves (1) frustration problem recognition, (2) frustration problem analysis, (3) development of frustration management skills, (4) application of frustration management strategies, and (5) utilization of feedback to improve coping skills.

In the remainder of this section I will discuss frustration tolerance training strategies. To begin, I will describe the theory and practice of rational-emotive education. Next I will introduce the self-doubt discomfort-dodging model as a conceptual method for diagnosing children's frustration and behavioral problems. This model leads into a discussion of frustration management applications of the rational-emotive education (REE) model. Finally, I will conclude with a case description of the treatment of a battered child which illustrates some of the rational-emotive education principles put into practice with a five-year-old polysymptomatic child.

Rational-Emotive Education

Rational-emotive education (REE) is an approach I developed to help children identify, clarify, and cope with their problems. REE has been gaining prominence since I wrote *Rational Emotive Education: A Manual For Elementary School Teachers* (Knaus, 1974). It has been the subject of doctoral dissertations (Brody, 1974; Casper, 1981; Katz, 1974; Krenitsky, 1978; Miller, 1977) as well as reviewed in various studies and reports (Albert, 1972; Block, 1978; DeVoge, 1974; DiGiuseppe, 1975; DiGiuseppe & Kassinove, 1976; Knaus, 1970, 1975, 1977a, 1977b, 1979, 1980; Knaus & Bokor, 1975; Knaus & Eyman, 1974; Knaus & McKeever, 1977).

The REE system is philosophically related to rational-emotive therapy (RET) and consistent with RET concepts as described by Ellis (1962, 1979). The system can be effective as a school mental health program with classes of "normal" children or adolescents. The model and concepts can be highly effective in both group and individual psychotherapy with emotionally and behaviorally disturbed children, especially those with low frustration tolerance and self-concept disturbances.

The system was built upon five basic assumptions.

1. Children who learn and use coping and problem solving skills will more appropriately and effectively handle their daily problems and advance their interests than youngsters who have not been taught these principles.
2. Children cannot relate or apply what they do not know and so they first need to learn basic rational psychological principles prior to applying them. Once learned, the concepts can be employed to prevent problems or employed as a benign intervention by a knowledgeable adult interested in helping the child apply what he already has practiced.
3. Most normal and disturbed youngsters can profit from learning how to competently deal with a variety of life stresses because they are, or will be, faced with a wide range of stresses throughout their lives. A positive mental health program that provides opportunities to learn multiple strategies is, therefore, likely to prove more effective than a single-intervention method. A multiple-intervention system can use music, literature, stories, television shows, personal examples, the school curriculum—anything to complement the basic program and help the child understand and use positive mental health concept(s). Admittedly, however, a single-tested intervention technique, if accurately applied, may prove effective in countering a target problem behavior.
4. Multiple applications of a single intervention may be necessary to alter a self-defeating cognitive-behavioral pattern such as intolerance of frustration.
5. The REE system is an organic process subject to modification and change based on both experience and experiment. This experimental attitude is conveyed to the children who are testing the system.

The original REE program (Knaus, 1974) consisted of a series of *rational-emotive education lessons* developed to aid children in identifying and understanding their feelings; to understand from where those feelings came; to develop an objective perspective; to problem-solve; to build self confidence; and to develop tolerance for frustration. The lessons were designed so that they could be taught by both teachers and school counselors. Occasionally, parents worked with their children, playing some of the games outlined in the REE manual. Thus, counselors, parents, and teachers played collaborative roles to help young children develop a problem-solving frame of reference.

A central principle underlying the REE program is that the positive mental health concepts that the children learn could be effectively employed in a psychotherapeutic setting. In that setting, the therapist helps the child apply principles he or she has been taught and teaches new problem solving concepts that will help the child solve his or her problem. The system seems especially applicable to frustration tolerance training because it emphasizes problem recognition and problem solving methods designed to help youngsters develop frustration management skills.

The following section discusses low frustration tolerance and negative self-concept factors that can be uprooted through the REE approach.

The Self-Doubt and Discomfort-Dodging Model

The Self-Doubt and Discomfort-Dodging model describes the relationships between self-concept disturbances, intolerance for frustration, and self-defeating behaviors such as procrastination (Knaus, 1973, 1979, 1982a, 1982b). According to the model, both children and adults disturb themselves when they lock into a negative self-concept and low frustration tolerance process and tend to be free of disturbance once outside of this process.

The self-doubt dimension of the model describes what happens when a child comes to doubt herself or himself (see Figure 1). For example, if the child perfectionistically questions her or his capabilities, the child is likely to second guess herself or himself and hesitate. Not uncommonly, the child will down herself or himself for presumed weaknesses by defining herself or himself as stupid or no good, and come to think of herself or himself as peculiar or different from others. This conclusion will result in more self-doubts because if she or he thinks she or he is a "peculiar" or "odd" person, she or he will have trouble accepting herself or himself and trusting her or his judgments.

The second phase of the model describes intolerance toward frustration. A person who is intolerant toward frustration tends to be sensa-

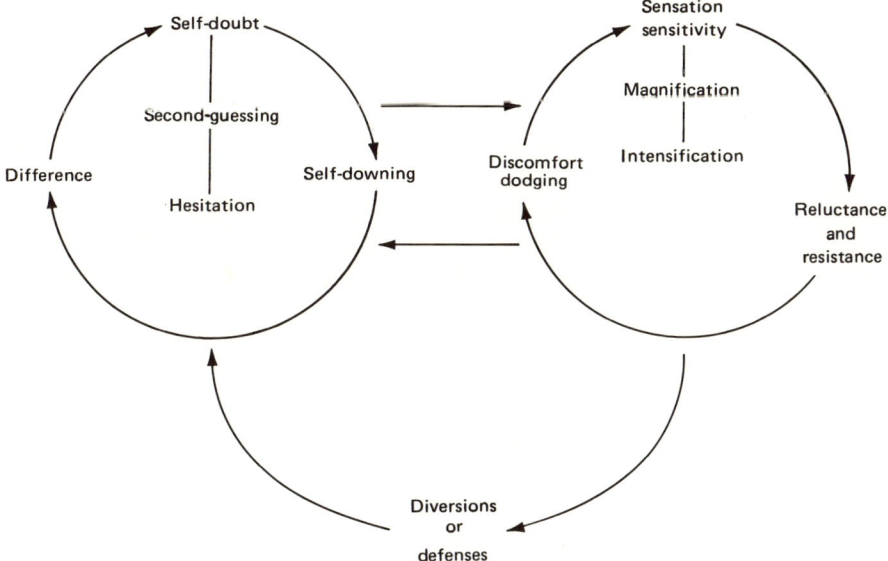

FIGURE 1. The self-doubt tension-intolerance model: A schematic representation.

tion sensitive and is likely to focus on tensions, magnify and intensify them, and try to escape them.

Once a child is entangled in this whirlpool of mental-physical innervation he is primed to get emotionally drenched in a "cognitive storm" where self doubts fuel frustration-tensions which disrupts reasoning, discharges short term memory, and adds more self-doubt fuel to the affective fires. For example, while encapsulated in this cognitive and emotive interactional matrix the child who believes he cannot manage his tensions will frequently escalate self-doubts, perceive of himself or herself as helpless, and intensify emotional stress. Under such innervating conditions, he or she will be prone to abort the process by adapting various dysfunctional self-protective defenses to become insulated from fears, tensions, and sense of helplessness.

The third phase of the model describes the defensive escape hatch. The individual diverts himself from this vicious cycle through various self-protective avenues. In the process, he fails to cope adaptively with the precipitating conditions, procrastinates, loses opportunity to gain practice in developing problem-solving skills, and tends to maintain a distorted view toward self and circumstances (Knaus, 1982a,b).

The Self-Doubt and Discomfort Dodging model was designed to be flexible. Its' modular format makes it easy to modify. For example, the child who doubts others and blames them for misfortunes may not seem on the surface as if he or she were second-guessing himself or herself and hesitating. Nevertheless, his thoughts and reactions take different form from those of the child who is immobilized by indecision. So, we would have to adapt the model to reflect what we observe. For example, we change "self-doubts" to "doubts others." The punitive child who doubts others is likely to overfocus obstinately on what he or she sees as their untrustworthy qualities. His or her style is likely to be that of externalizing blame when frustrated and of condemning those whom he or she faults. The child is likely to be intolerant of the tension his or her blaming and condemning promotes as he or she are trapped in a labyrinth of painful emotional constraints. Figure 2 pictorially describes this modification of the Self-Doubt and Discomfort-Dodging model.

Naturally, the model can get too flexible and lose its value. However, the intent of the model is to describe self-concept and frustration tolerance disturbances and their relationship.

The model provides a conceptual map that can be followed in treatment planning. It describes intervention points where these disturbance

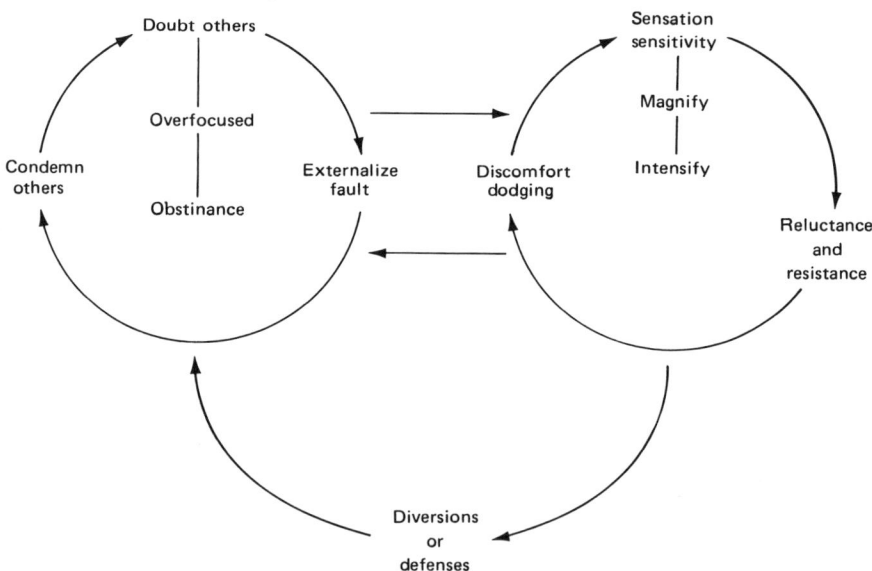

FIGURE 2. The doubt-others discomfort-dodging model: A schematic representation.

processes can be disrupted and replaced with a beneficial and realistic growth process. For example, the counselor can help the child build self-confidence by teaching him or her to challenge erroneous self-doubts and self-downing self-talk. The counselor could help the child defuse a tendency to dodge discomfort by helping the child accept tension, reduce tension through relaxation training, and learn rational-emotive strategies to master frustrations.

Constructive changes in one phase of the Self-Doubt and Discomfort Dodging process weakens the other links. For example, self-downing can be isolated and a child who downs himself or herself can learn how to build self-confidence through recognizing and successfully challenging erroneous beliefs. When the child feels self-confident, the other mental components in this vicious circle are more readily challenged.

Specific strategies can be employed to change self-defeating self-doubts. Rational self-questioning may serve as a key strategy the therapist employs to reduce self-doubts (Ellis & Knaus, 1979). RET and REE systems can be particularly effective if, for example, the child believes he or she cannot tolerate delay because he or she believes the feeling of frustration that is associated with delay is unbearable. Carefully targeted psychological homework assignments prompting the child to act on the basis of alternative methods that demonstrate the benefits of orderly actions can help. For example, the child might try to think of three alternative actions to take each time he or she felt frustrated and implement the one he or she predicts would provide the best long term result.

Thoughtful action often tips the balance in favor of better mental health. Thus the child who engages in problem solving activities is likely to practice positive coping skills that add up to a positive mental outlook and tolerance for frustration.

REE frustration tolerance training further illustrates the utility of this model.

Application Of REE To Low Frustration Tolerance Problems

Rational-emotive education is both an intervention and preventative approach that embraces the philosophy that children at risk of frustration disturbances and related dysfunctional states would best be identified early as a first step toward the prevention of later and possibly more serious disorder. As noted by Weissberg, Cowen, Lotyczewski, and Gesten (1983), childhood mental disturbances can be detected early and treated effectively. Thus, it is important to develop a comprehensive cognitive-behavioral diagnosis of the child's disturbance in order to determine if the child is on a pathway of increasing distress that exceeds age-expectant variations in the complex, undulating, developmental process. The following outlines the diagnostic process employed as part of the REE approach.

Step 1: Identify determinants of behavior: what, how, where, when, and to what extent. Define exceptions to pattern. Determine what has previously proven helpful in alleviating the problem. Find out what has served to aggravate the problem.

Step 2: Determine the extent to which the described problem represents pathological deviancy through analysis of age-expectant behavior, cultural and sub-cultural norms, socioeconomic expectancies, problem intensity, and problem persistence. When appropriate, use psychometric evaluation, observation, and special problem simulation techniques to make the diagnosis.

Step 3: Make a *conceptual diagnosis* concerning beliefs the child holds about self, problem situation(s), and feeling sensations. This phase of the diagnostic process is designed to reveal the quality and extent of the child's emotive vocabulary, quality of self-expression, as well as low frustration tolerance language system. It includes a description of the degree, and frequency of self-downing statements, as well as other self-defeating beliefs.

Step 4: Use the Self-Doubt and Discomfort-Dodging framework to help decide on the interventions you will use and how, where, and when to apply them.

Step 5: Set the stage by guiding the child through a sequence of REE lessons designed to provide him or her with a problem solving frame of reference and basic psychological coping tools. This step can include: teaching an emotive vocabulary; showing that the way one thinks influences how one feels and behaves. Experientially involve the child in this process so that he or she can learn directly from experience.

Step 6: In session problem simulation. The child is given the opportunity to apply what he has learned to solve the frustration problem(s) under simulated conditions such as role playing, acting out the problem solution, and so forth.

Step 7: Behavioral assignment. The child tests and practices the frustration management strategy(s) under *in vivo* problem conditions.

In REE-oriented therapy, diagnosis and skill building are part of the on-going therapy. The therapist's interventions are often created in the session as well as pre-planned. They are geared to help the child develop awareness of misconceptions as well as learn clear thinking and effective behavior skills. As Flavell (1979) has pointed out, children are surprisingly weak in their ability to detect errors of ommissions and obscurities and do relatively little monitoring of their memory and other cognitive processes. The REE system is geared to help the child develop problem awareness and take sensible frustration mastery steps.

A process description of how REE principles can be put to practice to promote problem awareness can be elucidating. The following example of a child who makes "a lot out of a little" is instructive.

Sometimes a simple exercise, such as having the child look through a rolled up telescope-shaped paper, can help her or him realize what is meant by blowing problems out of proportion. The rolled paper provides an example of tunnel vision: The child can only see what is at the open end of the paper. If that was all the child believed was in the room, then she or he would be "making a mountain out of a molehill" and frustrating herself or himself because of her or his misperception.

The "Chicken Little" story can set the stage for the same lesson. To use the story to teach coping skills, the child can play "Detective Chicken Little". How would Detective Little deal with the falling sky problem? The child, if he or she follows this approach, can start to develop reflective thinking skills important to changing low frustration tolerance patterns.

Through multiple interventions like the molehill and Chicken Little scenarios, the child has been exposed to a concept that is likely to be remembered. And it will be far easier for her or him to understand how a person can make a lot out of a little and to change that pattern if she or he has a highly memorable set of experiences that serve as a coping frame of reference.

While the REE process is simple and straight forward, it is not a quick fix system. Indeed, it may take an average of three to eighteen months to help a child develop and *maintain* positive behavior changes.

Case Application: REE With a Battered Child

The following case example illustrates the use of the REE frustration tolerance training method with a polysymptomatic child with low frustration tolerance.

> Kathy was a 5-year-old child with five older siblings. At the time she entered therapy, she was temporarily living in a foster home and was scheduled to return to her natural mother within three months. Prior to her removal from her natural parents, she had been routinely battered by

her mother. On occassion she had been burned with a hot iron. Significantly, Kathy was the only one among her siblings who was battered.

From court records, the foster mother's description, and the child's own report, Kathy experienced considerable difficulty containing her impulses. If she had an impulse to do something, she would. For example, she unraveled a sweater her foster mother was knitting. She pulled up the foster mother's prize flowers from the garden. She threw groceries from the shelves when she went shopping with her foster mother. She jumped up and down in a moving auto yelling and laughing and directly disrupting the driver. She routinely broke glasses and dishes. She also had a habit of doing the opposite of what she was told to do. In addition, the child had a short attention span and was enuretic.

At least part of the child's problem was low frustration tolerance characterized by poor impulse control. Her poor impulse control also served as an expedient way of attracting negative attention.

I assumed that Kathy's natural mother was irrationally exasperated by the child's impulse behavior. And since the mother had not beaten her other children, it made sense to try to teach the child how to deal with her impulses and to get attention in a less destructive manner. Since part of her beatings were associated with her enuresis, this became the second behavior targeted for extinction. The natural mother was uncooperative, so the program commenced without her help.

To reduce Kathy's impulse control problem, two behaviors were initially targeted for extinction—jumping in the car and throwing groceries off shelves in grocery stores. To reduce these behaviors, it was important first to get Kathy to think before she acted. By developing reflective thinking skills, many youngsters learn to manage low frustration tolerance urges. The method I used to teach Kathy reflective thinking skills was the "if you want something, you do something" method. The purpose of the method is to teach cause, effect, and accountability. The method breaks down to demonstrating the principle, simulated practice of the principle, and direct problem solving application.

The first step was to demonstrate the principle. Initially, I discussed the grocery throwing problem with Kathy. I told her that if we were going to make a movie and I was going to play her part, I would need her to help me learn my part. Once I understood how to play the part, I asked her to watch me to see if I knew how she acted in the grocery store. Then I pretended to skip down a grocery store isle pushing a shopping cart, and feigned throwing groceries out of the cart and pushing them off the shelves. As I dramatized her role I shouted, "Oh boy, I'm having such fun! I'm going to get mommy mad at me so I can get a spanking. What fun!" After acting this part with the child laughing at my antics we got back to being serious again. It seemed I got the right idea except that Kathy was not looking forward to the outcome—receiving a spanking. Then we went back to the grocery throwing act but this time we had a new twist: She acted out her own part and as she did, we made up a song called the "If You Want To Get Spanked You Have To Throw The Groceries Song." As she pretended to go down the isle throwing groceries we sang the song. She quickly caught on to the concept: If she wanted to get in trouble there were ways she could succeed.

Kathy liked to ride in the car and go shopping and watch her favorite television shows. These "privileges" had been regularly taken away from her. So it was clear that if she wanted to miss her television shows and get into trouble, then she could do something to make that happen. But since she did not, she could also "do something to get something" that she wanted.

In the following week, she made a 180 degree turn in her behavior. She stopped breaking dishes, she stopped jumping up and down in the auto, and she went grocery shopping and helped put the groceries in the cart. Over the next few weeks, this new pattern dominated. Only a few relapses were reported.

Next, we tackled her enuresis pattern. While she was still too young to be classified as an enuretic, the behavior was a conflict point. Thus, it was important to deal with this problem prior to her return home, as there was no guarantee that her natural mother would prove flexible in coping with daily bedsheet changes until the child gained night control.

Over the next several sessions, it became clear that she did have considerable control over her bed-wetting. It was also determined that she was very desirous of visiting a local amusement park. So we made a deal. She wanted to go to the amusement park. Her foster parents wanted her to stop bed-wetting. She thought she could succeed if she got to go to the amusement park. The procedure was that she would eat supper early and would not drink any liquids after supper. She would go to the bathroom just before she went to bed. She would get out of bed and go to the bathroom if she had to urinate during the night. If she succeeded for five nights (the child could count to five) she would go to the amusement park. If she wet her bed before the five days were up, she would have to start from scratch.

During the next three weeks, the child kept a dry bed for four successive nights and wet it on the fifth. She demonstrated she could maintain constance. She knew the "if you want something you have to do something" principle. She could count to five. Why would she not stay dry on the fifth night?

By this time it was clear that she did not want to return home. With a little prodding I found out that she believed that if she was too good, she would have to go home right away. She didn't want to do that. Staying where she was was more important than the amusement park. If she misbehaved she could not do some of the things she liked to do, like go shopping, watch television, or go out to play. The solution was to be *almost* good enough. After this point, the tone of the session changed to one of great seriousness. I explained to her that whether she behaved or misbehaved she would have to return to her home at the end of the summer. In this process I used analogies, stories, and description of natural phenomenon to show that there are some things you can control and some things you cannot control. She cried but understood.

Two weeks later she went to the amusement park because she succeeded in overcoming bedwetting. Following that, she spent several weekends with her natural family prior to her return home. During those visits she kept trying the "if you want something you have to do something" method. She succeeded in her attempts to maintain control. Fortunately, the beatings stopped.

The child attributed the cessation of the beatings to the "want something do something" idea. At that time, she learned that even if you act well, you may not always get what you want but you may be able to avoid what you don't want.

In the remaining sessions, we worked on how she felt about herself and why she was not a bad person even if she acted poorly. In this phase of Kathy's therapy the Self-Concept PinWheel technique (Knaus, 1974) proved helpful in combination with the "want something–do something" idea. The "want something–do something" idea proved versatile and valuable as it was applicable to showing her that if she had "bad" thoughts about herself she would feel badly; if she concentrated on helping herself get what she wanted, she would tend to feel better. The Self-Concept Pinwheel method showed her that she was a person with many attributes and consequently could not be totally good or bad. She could, however, have "poor habits" that were in need of change.

Kathy left therapy with a few new coping tools and a whole life ahead to practice them.

References

Ainslie, G. Specious reward: A behavioral theory of impulsiveness and impulse control. *Psychological Bulletin*, 1975, 82, 463–496.

Albert, S. *A study to determine the effectiveness of affective education with fifth grade students.* Unpublished master's thesis, Queens College, 1972.

Barker, R. G., Dembo, T., & Lewin, K. Frustration and regression: An experiment with young children. *University of Iowa Studies in Child Welfare*, 1941, *18*(Whole No. 386).

Benesh, M., & Weiner, B. On emotion and motivation: From the notes of Fritz Heider. *American Psychologist*, 1982, *37*(8), 887–895.

Berkowitz, L. Control of aggression. In B. M. Caldwell & H. Ricciuti (Eds.), *Review of Child Development Research*, 1969.

Bernstein, B. Social structure, language, and learning. *Educational Research*, 1961, *3*, 163–176.

Block, J. Effects of a rational emotive mental health program on poorly achieving, disruptive, high school students. *Journal of Counseling Psychology*, 1978, *25*(1), 61–65.

Brody, M. The effect of the rational-emotive affective approach in anxiety, frustration tolerance, and self esteem with fifth grade students. Unpublished doctoral dissertation, Temple University, 1974.

Bull, N. Emotion and frustrational behavior. *Journal of Nervous and Mental Disease*, 1957, *125*(4), 622–628.

Campbell, J. *The hero of a thousand faces*. Princeton, N.J.: Princeton University Press, 1968.

Casper, E. *A study to determine the effectiveness of rational-emotive education upon the academic achievement of sixth grade children*. Unpublished doctoral dissertation, University of Virginia, August, 1981.

Cattell, R. Advances in the measurement of neuroticism and anxiety in a conceptual framework of a unitary trait theory. *Annals of the New York Academy of Sciences*, 1962, *93*(20), 813–856.

Coopersmith, S. *The antecedents of self esteem*. San Francisco: W. H. Freeman, 1967.

DeVoge, C. A. A behavioral approach to RET with children. *Rational Living*, 1974, *9*(1), 23–26.

Diagnostic and statistical manual of mental disorders (3rd ed.). Washington, D.C.: American Psychiatric Association, 1980.

DiGiuseppe, R. The use of behavior modification to establish rational self-statements in children. *Rational Living*, 1975, *10*(2), 18–20.

DiGiuseppe, R., & Kassinove, H. Effects of rational-emotive school mental health program on children's emotional adjustment. *Journal of Community Psychology*, 1976, *4*(4), 382–387.

Dollard, J., & Miller, N. *Personality and psychopathology*. New York: McGraw-Hill, 1950.

Dollard, J., Doob, L., Miller, N., Mower, O. H., & Sears, R. *Frustration and aggression*. New Haven, Conn.: Yale University Press, 1938.

Ellis, A. *Reason and emotion in psychotherapy*. Secaucus, N.J.: Lyle Stuart, 1962.

Ellis, A. *Theoretical and empirical foundations of rational-emotive psychotherapy*. Monteray, Calif.: Brooks/Cole, 1979.

Ellis, A. Psychoneurosis and anxiety problems. In R. Greiger & I. Greiger (Eds.). *Cognition and emotional disturbance*. New York: Human Sciences Press, 1982.

Ellis, A., & Knaus, W. *Overcoming procrastination*. New York: New American Library, 1979.

Ellis, A., & Greiger, R. *Handbook of rational-emotive therapy*. New York: Springer, 1977.

Flavell, J. Metacognition and cognitive monitoring: A new area of cognitive-developmental inquiry. *American Psychologist*, 1979, *34*(10), 906–911.

Freud, S. *Beyond the pleasure principle* (Standard ed.). London: Hogarth, 1955.

Hybl, A. R., & Stagner, R. Frustration tolerance in relation to diagnosis and therapy. *Journal of Consulting Psychology*, 1952, *16*(3), 163–170.

Kagan, J. *Understanding children: Behavior, motives, thought*. New York: Harcourt Brace Javanovich, 1971.

Katz, S. *The effects of emotional education on locus of control and self concept*. Unpublished doctoral dissertation, Hofstra University, 1974.

Knaus, W. J. *Innovative use of parents and teachers as behavior modifiers.* Paper presented at the seventh annual School Psychologists Conference, Queens College, January 1970.
Knaus, W. J. Overcoming procrastination. *Rational Living*, 1973, *8*, 2–7.
Knaus, W. J. *Rational emotive education: A manual for elementary school teachers.* New York: Institute for Rational Living, 1974.
Knaus, W. J. Rational-emotive education. In A. Ellis & R. Grieger (Eds.), *Handbook of rational emotive therapy.* New York: Springer, 1977. (a)
Knaus, W. J. Rational-emotive education. *Theory into Practice*, 1977, *14*(4), 251–255. (b)
Knaus, W. J. *Do it now: How to stop procrastinating.* Englewood Cliffs, N.J.: Prentice-Hall, 1979.
Knaus, W. J. *Getting exceptional children to accept and understand themselves, using a modified rational-emotive approach.* Paper presented at the Conference on Social Skills Training for Special Children, Ontario Psychological Association, Toronto, May 1980.
Knaus, W. J. *How to get out of a rut.* Englewood Cliffs, N.J.: Prentice-Hall, 1982. (a)
Knaus, W. J. The parameters of procrastination. In R. Greiger & I. Greiger (eds.), *Cognition and emotional disturbance.* New York: Human Science Press, 1982. (b)
Knaus, W. J. *How to conquer your frustrations.* Englewood Cliffs, N.J.: Prentice Hall, 1983.
Knaus, W. J., & Bokor, S. The effects of rational-emotive education lessons on anxiety and self-concept in sixth grade students. *Rational Living*, 1975, *11*(2), 25–28.
Knaus, W. J., & Eldridge, F. *The prevention and treatment of school age burnout.* Unpublished report, Leslie Schools, Boston, Mass., 1982.
Knaus, W. J., & Eyman, W. Progress in rational-emotive education. *Rational Living*, 1974, *9*(2), 27–29.
Knaus, W. J., & McKeever, C. Rational-emotive education with learning disabled children. *Journal of Learning Disabilities*, 1977, *10*(1), 10–14.
Krenitsky, D. L. *The relationship of age and verbal intelligence to the efficacy of rational-emotive education with older adults.* Unpublished doctoral dissertation, Hofstra University, 1978.
Low, A. A., *Mental health through will training.* Boston: Christopher Publishing, 1950.
Maier, N. R. F. Experimentally induced abnormal behavior. *The Scientific Monthly*, 1948, September, 210–216.
Maier, N. R. F. Reasoning in humans: The mechanisms of equivocal stimuli and of reasoning. *Journal of Experimental Psychology*, 1954, *34*, 349–360.
McDougall, W. *An introduction to social psychology* (Rev. ed.). Boston: Luce, 1926.
Meichenbaum, D., & Goodman, J. Training impulsive children to talk to themselves. *Journal of Abnormal Psychology*, 1971 *77*(2), 115–126.
Miller, N. J. *Effects of behavior rehearsal, written homework assignments, and level of intelligence on the efficacy of rational-emotive education in elementary school children.* Unpublished doctoral dissertation, Hofstra University, 1977.
Overstreet, O. H. *Influencing human behavior.* New York: Norton, 1925.
Painter, G. D. *Proust, the later years* (Vol. 2). Boston: Little Brown, 1965.
Pollack, C. A conditioning approach to frustration reaction in minimally brain injured children. *Journal of Learning Disabilities*, 1968, *1*, 691–688.
Rosenzweig, S. An outline of frustration theory. In J. Hunt (Ed.), *Personality and the behavior disorders.* New York: Roland Press, 1944.
Schaefer, C. E., & Milman, H. L. *Therapies for children.* San Francisco: Jossey Bass, 1977.
Skinner, B. F. Why teachers fail. *Saturday Review*, October 16, 1965, pp. 80–82, 90–103.
Weissberg, R. P., Cowen, E. I., Lotyczewski, B. S., & Gesten, E. I. The primary health project: Seven consecutive years of program outcome research. *Journal of Consulting and Clinical Psychology*, 1983, *51*(1), 100–107.
Wolman, B. *Manual of child psychopathology.* New York: McGraw-Hill, 1972.

6

Teaching Rational Self-Talk to Impulsive Children

PHILIP C. KENDALL AND GARY L. FISCHLER

The problem of impulsive/hyperactive behavior in children is of major concern to a substantial number of parents, teachers, and mental health professionals. Such problems are among the most common brought to guidance counselors, school psychologists, and other mental health professionals. Although the children themselves do not typically seek help with these difficulties, the behaviors that are often exhibited, such as restlessness, distractibility, failure to complete school assignments, and disruptive or aggressive acting-out, are quite troublesome to those individuals who have care-taking and/or educational responsibilities for these children.

This chapter has several aims. First, we seek to briefly describe the problem of impulsivity and lack of self-control. Second, a cognitive-behavioral treatment approach is outlined, and specific "how to" guidelines are delineated. In this section, we will specifically define the targets of therapeutic endeavors and the most effective and efficient way to pursue their change. Third, this chapter briefly reviews the therapy

---

Portions of this chapter were adapted from P. C. Kendall, "Cognitive-Behavioral Interventions with Children," in B. B. Lahey & A. E. Kazdin (Eds.), *Advances in Clinical Child Psychology* (Vol. 4). New York: Plenum Press, 1981, and P. C. Kendall & E. S. Urbain, "Cognitive Behavioral Intervention with a Hyperactive Girl: Evaluation via Observations and Cognitive Performance," *Behavioral Assessment*, 1981, 3, 345–357.

PHILIP C. KENDALL AND GARY L. FISCHLER • Department of Psychology, University of Minnesota, Minneapolis, Minnesota 55455. We wish to thank the National Institute of Mental Health (Grant No. 1 RO MH 34623-01) and the Graduate School of the University of Minnesota for their support of our research, some of which is discussed in the present manuscript.

outcome literature that has accumulated and evaluates the conclusions that have been drawn. In so doing, we highlight the most effective cognitive-behavioral components of treatment that seem consistent across studies.

Lastly, we discuss the philosophical issues that bear directly on how we, as therapists, choose to work with impulsive children. In this section, we consider what similarities and differences there are between our cognitive-behavioral approach and rational-emotive therapy (RET), and how the therapeutic approaches might be modified to accommodate clients of different developmental levels, types of psychopathology, and skill deficits. Our goal here is to raise more questions than we can answer, in order to stimulate thoughtful research and practice in dealing with a heterogeneous population of clients whose problems others have labeled as impulsivity, hyperactivity, or lack of self-control.

Definition of the Problem

Cognitive-Behavioral Perspective

That internal (i.e., cognitive) and external (i.e., reinforcement-contingency) factors operate reciprocally has recently been put forward as an important part of social learning theory (e.g., Bandura, 1977). Similarly, the cognitive-behavioral view of impulsive behavior posits that the cognitive acts *both* of considering different problem-solving alternatives and of choosing to execute or to inhibit the execution of a particular alternative are essential components, neither alone being sufficient to account for impulsive behavioral problems (Kendall & Williams, 1982). Kendall and Wilcox (1979) defined impulsivity by proposing that it

> involves two components of children's self-control: cognitive (legislative) and behavioral (executive). Deliberation, problem-solving, planning and evaluation are the active cognitive factors. In this regard a self-controlled child is seen as nonimpulsive. Behaviorally, a self-controlled child has the ability, following the deliberation, to execute the behavior that is chosen or inhibit the behaviors that we cognitively discarded. (p. 1021)

From this perspective, then, the impulsive child shows (1) deficits in cognitive processing and planning capabilities and (2) an inability to adequately inhibit inappropriate responses. This notion is consistent with some behavioral models such as Kanfer and Karoly's (1972), inasmuch as self-monitoring and self-evaluation clearly have cognitive components (such as recognizing the problem, analyzing the situation, and remembering to self-monitor and evaluate) in addition to the obvious behavioral components. Furthermore, the self-reinforcement process also has an influence on both the child's cognitive processes and his or her ability to inhibit inappropriate responses.

In order to assess the degree to which a child exhibits these cognitive and behavioral determinants of self-control, Kendall and Wilcox (1979) developed the Self-Control Rating Scale (SCRS). This measure, which has high internal consistency (.98), test–retest reliability (.84), convergent validity (with the Matching Familiar Figures test and the Porteus mazes), and discriminant validity (from IQ and mental age), has also been shown to be sensitive to treatment-induced behavioral changes (e.g., Kendall & Zupan, 1981). Kendall, Zupan, and Braswell (1981) correlated teacher ratings of the SCRS with second-grade through fifth-grade children's task persistence, ability to delay gratification, social-perspective taking, means–ends problem-solving, and a measure of the internalization–externalization dimension of maladjustment. In addition, classroom observation provided the data for comparisons between the SCRS and the observed behavior. The results indicated that lack of self-control as measured by the SCRS was significantly related to externalizing (i.e., acting out) behavioral problems, overall maladjustment, and deficits in social-perspective taking, but that it was not related to the persistence measure, the delay-of-gratification measure, or means–end problem-solving (MEPS) (which were also not correlated with each other). The behavioral observational data, in general, and the off-task behaviors, specifically, evidenced significant relationships with self-control, thus highlighting the distractible/uncontrolled quality of non-self-controlled children. Based on these findings, Kendall *et al.* concluded that children who lack self-control exhibit more off-task disruptive behavior, display acting-out (as opposed to internalized) behavioral problems, and are deficient in social-perspective taking.

EARLY INFLUENCES

Cognitive Deficit

The degree to which children consider alternative solutions to a problem may be a critical factor in how impulsively they behave, and how quickly or how accurately they solve everyday problems. It is not difficult to imagine that without thoughtful consideration of problem-solving solutions, a child is disadvantaged in his or her ability to cope successfully with assignments or interpersonal conflicts; the results may be lowered frustration tolerance, increased frequency of acting out, or heightened distractibility. Kagan (1966) described the cognitive dimension of reflection-impulsivity: a reflective child delays a problem-solving response until all alternative solutions have been carefully considered, and an impulsive child responds quickly, making many errors. The type of cognitive deficit described here is not an intellectual one, in that the impulsive child is thought to have the ability to eventually produce the correct solution. Rather it is one of cognitive tempo; the impulsive child simply responds too quickly.

The instrument that has been traditionally used to measure the reflection–impulsivity dimension is the Matching Familiar Figures (MFF) test (Kagan, Rosman, Day, Albert, & Phillips, 1964). This test asks subjects to correctly match-to-sample a picture of a familiar object with an identical picture that is illustrated among six variants. Both the latency of the first response and an error score are derived, and children with short latencies and high error scores are identified as impulsive. The MFF, however, is not without problems. Although the test–retest and internal consistency reliabilities have been generally statistically significant, they have been low to moderate in magnitude (e.g., Egeland & Weinberg, 1976). More recently, Cairns and Cammock (1978) have developed a longer, more reliable version of the MFF (for use with children) consisting of 20 items (MFF-20); however, therapy-outcome researchers have not yet utilized it.

Behavioral Correlates

Impulsivity may also be seen as the choice of obtaining one (specious) reward when another, larger reward may be available but delayed. Ainslie (1975) and Mischel (1974) have proposed such a behavioral theory of impulsivity, which explains impulsive behavior as a function of delay of reward. That is, although the attractiveness of a larger reward should decrease as a function of delay, this function is accelerated for impulsive children. Thus, impulsive children are more likely to take the first reward to come along, whether or not a bigger, delayed reward is a possibility. Although Burns and Powers (1975) found no evidence for this model, their sample consisted of only two children.

Kanfer and Karoly (1972) have described the process of behavioral self-regulation, in which impulsive children are thought to be deficient. This process includes self-monitoring (noting instances of impulsive behavior), self-evaluation (judging whether this behavior has met previously set standards), and self-reward or -punishment contingent on the prior evaluation. Consistent with other behavioral theorists (e.g., Mahoney & Thoresen, 1974; Skinner, 1953), Kanfer and Karoly see the reinforcement of self-controlling behaviors as a critical factor (see also Karoly & Kanfer, 1982).

Psychiatric Classification

In order to place our work within the context of current psychiatric diagnostic thinking, it is important to mention how such a classification may be used and what criteria are of importance when diagnosing non-self-controlled children. Users of the current *Diagnostic and Statistical Manual* of the American Psychiatric Association (DSM-III—1980) would be likely to classify children with impulsive or hyperactive behavior as having an "Attention Deficit Disorder with Hyperactivity." Such children are described as having restless or excessive motor activity, as well as attentional difficulties. Teachers report that these children are easily distractible, fail to follow through on school assignments, are disorganized and inattentive, and disrupt others' work and play activities. Parents often describe these children as "running like a motor" and as having difficulty sitting still. According to DSM-III, the quality of such activity is also important: overactivity is characteristically unplanned and disorganized, lacking a clear goal. DSM-III specifies that the condition must persist for one full year in order for the diagnosis to be made. Not all children with one or more of these symptoms would be diagnosed as having this disorder. Related diagnoses, such as "Attention Deficit Disorder without Hyperactivity" or "Conduct Disorders" may be more appropriate. Moreover, not all children who exhibit impulsive, non-self-controlled behavior should be psychiatrically diagnosed.

Treatment Approaches

Description of Clinical Procedures

After our overview of the problem of impulsivity and our delineation of the concomitant deficits and correlates, we now turn our attention to the methods of clinical intervention that have been developed for this group of children. In so doing, we highlight each deficit and its implications in the choice of intervention.

Cognitive Approaches

To the extent that impulsivity and attentional difficulties arise from faulty or deficient thinking strategies, training programs that teach children how to—or at what tempo to—think about problem solutions may be effective. Verbal self-instructional training has been one such method that has been employed with impulsive children. Originally developed by Meichenbaum and his colleagues (Meichenbaum, 1975, 1977; Meichenbaum & Goodman, 1971), self-instructional training seeks to instill self-talk in children as an effective regulator of behavior. Theoretically, self-instructions are effective through assisting the child to develop an internalization of verbal commands. The impulsive child's voluntary control of his or her behavior is facilitated in much the same way that this process is said to develop normally (e.g., Luria, 1961; Vygotsky, 1962). The approach does not seek to treat *dysfunctional* cognitions; instead, it seeks to *induce* cognitions that appear to be lacking (Kendall, 1981). In this way, children are taught to stop and think before responding.

Training in verbal self-instruction involves several sequential procedures that are implemented while the child and the therapist interact around a training task, typically for 40–60 minutes. The tasks used in this procedure vary considerably, but they most typically begin with some type of psychoeducational task (e.g., Porteus mazes, sequential recognition, or the block design subtest of the WISC-R). Later, they involve interpersonal games and role plays. The relative efficacy of various training materials is an important issue requiring further investigation (Kendall, 1977).

The actual content of the self-instruction may vary from child to child and from task to task. Typically, however, the content includes a reference to problem definition, problem approach, focusing of attention, coping statements, and self-reinforcement. These components are illustrated, with maze performance as an example, in Table 1. The self-statements are modeled by the therapist and then rehearsed and practiced by the child in the following sequence. First, the therapist performs the task while talking out loud to himself or herself and modeling appropriate behaviors (e.g., attending to the task, holding the pencil while visually scanning the maze). The client is then asked to attempt the same task while talking out loud. The self-instructions are then faded through the therapist (and then the child) talking progressively more softly until they become more like whispers. Finally, the child performs the task alone while using covert instructions.

One of the strengths of the self-instructional procedures is that both the content and the sequence can be tailored to different training tasks (or behavioral problems) and to different verbal styles. Clinically, it is important that the therapist work to ensure that the child will not simply repeat the self-statements by rote but fully understands them so that

TABLE 1. Content of Self-Instructional Procedures with Impulsive Children

Problem definition
"Let's see, what am I supposed to do?"
Problem approach
"Well, I should look this over and try to figure out how to get to the center of the maze."
Focusing of attention
"I'd better look ahead so I don't get trapped."
Coping statements
"Oh, that path isn't right. If I go that way, I'll get stuck. I'll just go back here and try another way."
Self-reinforcement
"Hey, not bad. I really did a good job!"

Note. Adapted from Kendall (1977); Kendall and Finch (1978); Meichenbaum (1975, 1977); and Meichenbaum and Goodman (1971).

they are meaningful to him or her. For example, at the beginning or end of each treatment session, the therapist might ask if the child can recall the self-instructions. It is preferable that the child recall them in his or her own words in a manner which suggests a genuine comprehension of the material rather than repeating the instructions verbatim. To maximize generalization to nontraining situations, the therapist should encourage the child to use self-statements outside therapy and may engage the child in discussion about such a situation and how the child could use (or did use) the self-instructions.

Information Processing

What is often referred to as *search-and-scan behavior* may be defined as the efficiency with which attention is deployed over a visual display. Some of the studies in this area have measured eye movements during tasks in which children scan a visual display for task-relevant information in an attempt to infer such attentional deployment (e.g., Day, 1975). The actual number of eye movements and eye fixations and the amount of viewing time in both impulsive and reflective children's approaches to the MFF have been monitored in several studies in both the United States (Drake, 1970; Siegelman, 1969) and Japan (Usui, 1975). In summarizing this literature, Messer (1976) concluded that impulsives spend less time viewing the stimuli, base their decisions on less information, and gather this information less systematically than do reflectives.

Egeland, Wozniak, and Schrimpf (1976) have provided evidence that the information-processing deficits exhibited by impulsives can be corrected through training. Their training program consists of teaching children three distinct but interrelated abilities: (1) the identification of part–whole hierarchical concepts; (2) organization of the deployment of attention across the surface of a visual display through scanning systematically and exhaustively, and (3) identification of the dimensions of difference among various objects, such as form, size, spatial organization, and number. The child is taught how to describe these differences, how to encode them mnemonically using an imagery procedure, and how to employ feature analysis in combination with systematic attentional deployment in hierarchical analysis to solve match-to-sample and recall problems. In general, the program stresses the child's mastery of "terms" that represent concepts in order to facilitate further use and generalization of these concepts, as well as an emphasis on the child's learning to describe what it is that he or she is going to do. The children are also encouraged to use these concepts and strategies in the classroom, at home, and in the community, thus working to further the treatment effects.

The results of the Egeland *et al.* study indicated that on measures of both visual processing (including the MFF) and academic achievement, the children who participated in the program performed better than control children. Moreover, the academic progress made by these children was particularly noteworthy as it represented a true generalization of treatment effects (these skills were not taught directly in the program). Although MFF latency scores improved (i.e., lengthened after training), error scores did not improve. Thus, it seems likely that training in visual processing may favorably affect information-processing skills, but that its effect on actual problem-solving ability (as measured by the MFF) is more equivocal.

Behavioral Treatments

Inasmuch as impulsive children are seen as unable to delay gratification, some programs designed to modify impulsive behavior have focused on imposing an extended delay period before allowing the child to respond. Research by Kagan, Pearson, and Welsh (1966), Heider (1971), and Finch, Wilkinson, Nelson, and Montgomery (1975) suggests that although imposed delay interventions may favorably affect latencies on the MFF, it may not reduce response errors.

The modeling of appropriate delay of responses as well as search-and-scan strategies has been shown to be of value as an intervention technique. That the acquisition of new, therapeutically desirable response patterns may be obtained in this way is certainly not a new concept (Bandura, 1969). Using teachers, who naturally modeled impulsive or reflective styles (as determined by the MFF), Yando and Kagan (1968) found that impulsive children's latencies, but not errors, were improved following school-year exposure to reflective teachers. Similar results in support of modeling were obtained by Debus (1970) and Denny (1972), using trained reflective and impulsive sixth-grade models.

More encouraging results were obtained by Ridberg, Parke, and Hetherington (1971). They used filmed models who either displayed appropriate scanning of the materials or verbalized a scanning method, or a combination of the two. Furthermore, by splitting the group on the basis of IQ, it was found that although high-IQ children in all treatment groups improved on both latency and error rate, low-IQ children improved on both measures in the combined verbal cuing and scanning condition only.

By using fourth- and sixth-grade male peer models who also *verbalized* their task strategy, Cohen and Przybycien (1974) demonstrated significant changes in subjects for both latency and error measures on the MFF. Thus, the results of these treatment-outcome studies suggest the importance of *verbal cues* in addition to modeling appropriate scanning behavior in achieving both desirable latency and accuracy-of-responding changes in impulsive children.

One reason that impulsive children fail to delay their responses in order to obtain more accurate and/or more rewarding consequences may be that there are response contingencies in favor of immediate responding. Manipulations of reward contingencies have been widely accepted and often highly useful with many types of childhood behavioral problems (e.g., O'Leary & O'Leary, 1977). However, several different forms of response contingencies (i.e., reward, punishment, and response cost) exist and have been shown to have different effects on the behavior of impulsive children. In general, it has been found that the effectiveness of a reward contingency alone in the modification of impulsiveness in children is questionable, and punishment appears to be somewhat more effective (e.g., Hemry, 1973; Massarri & Schack, 1972).

Response-cost contingencies, however, appear to be much more promising. Such a contingency initially requires giving the child a number of rewards (e.g., tokens or coins) with subsequent removal for each occurrence of an incorrect behavior or response. The effectiveness of response-cost contingencies has been demonstrated in studies by Errickson, Wyne, and Routh (1973) and by Nelson, Finch, and Hooke (1975). Using latency and error measures from the MFF, both studies showed that impulsive children who had tokens taken away from them for inaccurate responses improved on both measures. Furthermore, the Nelson *et al.* (1975) study compared response cost with reinforcement, as it is conceivable that performance improved as a function of having tokens left after the task was completed (i.e., reinforcement). The results were quite interesting: for impulsive children, reinforcement was not as effective as response cost; however, for nonimpulsive children, reward was more effective in reducing errors. Firestone and Douglas (1975) suggested that the performance of impulsive children is more disrupted than that of normal children by partial and noncontingent reinforcement. Furthermore, positive reinforcement attracts the attention of hyperactive children, distracts them from their task, and orients them toward the rewarding adult.

Kendall and Finch (1979) also pointed out that when presented with a choice of alternative answers, impulsive children sometimes answer correctly, conceivably obtaining the right answer by chance, or because the problem is too easy. Moreover, the child may first answer incorrectly (impulsively) and then change to a correct response. If the child is rewarded only for correct answers, which may be a matter of luck, fast guessing, or multiple guessing (until the correct answer is obtained), then one is in effect spuriously rewarding the child for being impulsive. Based on the available data, Kendall and Finch (1979) concluded that "impulsive children appear to respond less quickly and more accurately when they are subjected to conditions under which they incur a loss for inappropriate responding" (p. 53).

COGNITIVE-BEHAVIORAL INTERVENTIONS

In the hope of developing a multifaceted training program to address both cognitive and behavioral deficits, Kendall and Finch (1976) combined several different components in their clinical intervention program. The program has been used extensively by Kendall and his colleagues (Kendall, 1981; Kendall & Braswell, 1982; Kendall & Finch, 1978; Kendall & Urbain, 1981; Kendall & Wilcox, 1980; Kendall & Zupan, 1981). The original treatment components included verbal self-instructions, modeling, and response-cost contingencies, and it focused on psychoeducational tasks. However, the program has evolved in recent years to also include solving interpersonal problems in a nonimpulsive manner, primarily through role playing difficult interpersonal situations in addition to the other components of impersonal problem-solving training. There is also an increased emphasis on self-evaluation, more enactive role-plays, and greater use of social praise.

The program consists of a variety of tasks around which the child's behavior and cognitive processes are gradually "shaped." First, the therapist teaches the use of self-instructions on simple academic tasks, then on more challenging impersonal tasks, and finally on real personal and interpersonal problem situations. As the difficulty of the tasks increases, so does the degree to which they are emotionally charged. The primary goal of the training is to facilitate the child's habitual use of self-instruction. As the child's understanding and experiencing of the procedure deepens he or she becomes better able to deal with real-life problems without "freezing" when asked to think out loud about emotionally laden material. Sample tasks are presented in Table 2.

Verbal self-instructions are a central component of this program. An additional component of the cognitive training, however, is the frequent use of cue cards. For example, separate cue cards might state: "Stop," "Look and listen," and "Think before responding." If the child is having particular difficulty remembering self-statements, the cue cards may simply list the self-statements to be remembered. The therapist and the child can construct the cue cards together, and the child can put the self-instructions in his or her own words as long as the meaning is preserved.

The program also utilizes therapist modeling of appropriate behaviors for nonimpulsive responding, thereby attempting to minimize direct orders or instructions to the child. The therapist does not tell the child what to do but works with the child, demonstrating alternative ways of thinking through problems. Thus, the therapist serves as a *coping* model. Distinctions have been drawn between mastery and coping models (e.g., Kazdin, 1974; Meichenbaum, 1971; Sarason, 1975): the former performs the task perfectly, demonstrating ideal performance, whereas the latter makes mistakes occasionally and shares with the child the difficulties that were encountered in solving the problem. A mastery model completes the therapy tasks without difficulty or making mistakes, whereas the coping model demonstrates effective coping strategies for dealing with these difficulties and mistakes. For children who may be somewhat anxious about failing, and who answer impulsively merely to "get off the hook," a coping modeling strategy may be particularly helpful.

In accordance with what at this time appears to be the most effective response contingency, this cognitive-behavioral intervention utilizes response-cost contingencies in order to encourage nonimpulsive responding. Using this strategy, the child is given a number of tokens (e.g., 20) to start with and loses a token each time he or she either makes a mistake (answers incorrectly) or misuses (or forgets) any of the self-

TABLE 2. Description of the Tasks and Highlights of the 12-Session Cognitive-Behavioral Program for Self-Control

Session	Task	Highlights
1	"Which one comes next?"	Introduction to self-instructions, response-cost contingency, self-evaluation and bonus-chip systems, and reward menu; overt verbal self-instruction (VSI); concrete labeling or response cost; assign homework project.
2	"Following directions"	Review self-instructions and homework project; overt VSI for majority of session; begin fading process to whispered VSI with final 2–3 tasks; concrete labeling.
3	"Specific skills series"	Review self-instructions (especially coping statements) and homework assignment; encourage rephrasing of VSI to curb rote memorization; continue fading process with whispered VSI, some overt; begin conceptual labeling with final 1–2 errors.
4	"The little professor math skills"	Encourage rephrasing of VSI and note additional steps possible with a new task; whispered VSI; conceptual labeling; child begins self-evaluation.
5	"The little professor math games"	First interpersonal task; homework project reviewed: example of when the child actually used the 5 steps outside therapy; whispered VSI; begin fading to covert VSI; conceptual labeling.
6	"Tangram puzzles"	Continue fading from whispered to covert VSI; conceptual labeling; emphasis on coping model. Coping statements during difficult tasks.
7	Checkers	Covert, occasionally whispered, VSI; conceptual labeling; inquiry into specific classroom and home problems.
8	"Cat and mouse"	Last of interpersonal play sessions; homework assignment for next time; example of using VSI in social and interpersonal situation; covert, occasionally whispered, VSI; conceptual labeling.
9	Identifying emotions	First session related directly to interpersonal-problem solving; mixture of VSI (i.e., overt-covert); modification of steps; probing by therapist when necessary; conceptual labeling.
10	Hypothetical situations: "What would happen if?"	Rephrasing and adjustment of VSI for new problem-solving situation; mixture of VSI; conceptual labeling.
11	Role playing: Hypothetical situations	Role-playing of social situations, both "created" and "real"; mixture of VSI; conceptual labeling.
12	Role playing: Real-life situations	Role playing of child's real problems; mixture of VSI; conceptual labeling; child pretends to teach therapy procedures to another child.

Note. From the manual *Developing Self-Control in Children: A Manual of Cognitive-Behavioral Strategies*, by W. J. Padaver, B. A. Zupan, and P. C. Kendall. Available from P. C. Kendall, Department of Psychology, University of Minnesota, Minneapolis, Minnesota 55455.

statements. In this way, not only is nonimpulsive *behavior* reinforced, but nonimpulsive *cognition* is reinforced as well.

Following a response cost, the therapist again models completion of the task using overt self-instruction. This takes place even if the child has previously demonstrated competence in overt self-instruction and is now at the covert self-instructional stage.

When the therapist takes away a token, it is important that she or he label and explain the child's mistake so that the child can understand what was done wrong and how to avoid the same mistake in the future. Two labeling approaches are involved: *concrete labeling* and *conceptual labeling*. In concrete labeling, the child's mistake is explained very specifically (e.g., "You lose one chip because you didn't say the step 'I have to look ahead so I don't get trapped,'" or "You lose a chip because you entered into a blind alley instead of getting all of the way out"). In contrast, conceptual labeling involves telling the child what he or she did wrong in general terms. For examples, "You lose a chip for not going through all the steps," or "You lose one chip for not taking your time and not getting the correct answer." Over the course of the therapy sessions, the therapist fades from concrete to conceptual labeling, until, at the end of training, most of the labeling (as well as the self-instructions themselves) may be described as conceptual. Support for the effectiveness of conceptual labeling over concrete labeling has been demonstrated (Kendall & Wilcox, 1980; see also Schleser, Meyers, & Cohen, 1981). Throughout the training, the therapist attempts to be matter-of-fact, rather than punitive, in explaining mistakes. Moreover, the therapist uses smiles and positive comments such as "fine" and "good" or any of the other generally socially rewarding messages with the child. In addition, a self-reward statement for a correct response is one of the actual self-statements taught. Therefore, the child is specifically told to use it as a reward. Thus, the response-cost procedure is not the only contingency to be employed, and it is not seen as a punitive control. It is simply designed to help the child to stop and think before responding so that he or she can minimize errors, reduce the rapidity of responding, and increase the use of the self-statements.

The child can also earn bonus chips as rewards. For example, the child is typically encouraged to use self-instructions in the classroom. He or she may earn a bonus chip by describing to the therapist an instance in which he or she could have used (or, in later sessions, actually did use) self-statements to deal more effectively with a problem. Accurate self-evaluation, described below, also earns extra chips. Two additional important strategies in this program include role-playing the use of problem-solving self-instructions in real and hypothetical interpersonal situations and the use of self-evaluation during the sessions.

Role playing attempts to provide a performance base for the child's problem-solving skills. For example, when the child is trying to identify emotions or the consequences of problem-solving alternatives, the child and his or her therapist act out situations and stop at the critical moment to concentrate on the problem-solving steps. The therapist might use a stop sign, drawn on cardboard, to signal to the child the appropriate time to "Stop and think."

Role playing is also critical during the later sessions when real and hypothetical problem situations are the treatment tasks. For example, the therapist may begin one of these sessions by randomly selecting an index card on which is described a "problem situation." The card might read, "You are waiting in line to buy lunch at the cafeteria. The people in front of you are pushing and another boy (girl) cuts in front of you." The child and the therapist then pretend to be in that situation (i.e., in line) and practice using the self-instructional steps to identify the problem, to think of alternatives and their consequences, to select an option, and to provide a self-reward for thinking the problem through.

The "How I did today" chart is used to teach youngsters self-evaluation. The chart describes levels of performance from 1 to 5 (i.e., 1 = not so good; 2 = OK; 3 = good; 4 = very good; and 5 = super extraspecial), and the child's task is to rate his or her own behavior during the session. If accurate (within 1 point of the therapist's rating), the child earns extra chips. Here is a closer look at this procedure. At the end of the first session, the therapist rates the child's performance using the chart and also explains the rating. For example, the therapist might tell the child, "You did pretty well today; you did the problems carefully and made very few mistakes. Also, you remembered the self-instructions. I think I would rate your performance a 4—'very good.' If you had made many errors, gone too fast, or forgotten the five steps, I would probably rate you 1—'not so good.' If you had done even better, by not making any mistakes, I probably would rate you a 5—'super extraspecial.'" Later on, the child is asked to self-evaluate, that is, to use the chart to evaluate his or her own performance.

A test of the clinical utility of the cognitive component of this treatment package was performed by Kendall and Braswell (1982). Twenty-seven children who were identified as lacking self-control were randomly assigned to one of three conditions: (1) a *behavioral* treatment group in which response-cost contingencies as well as therapist modeling of task-appropriate behavior were utilized; (2) a *cognitive-behavioral* group that included these behavioral components supplemented with self-instructions, cognitive modeling, and training in self-control; and (3) an attention control group. Twelve sessions, with individual therapist contact, were received by each child in all groups. In addition, all children engaged in psychoeducational play, as well as interpersonal role-play situations that served as the vehicle for training. At the conclusion of treatment, only the cognitive-behavioral group evidenced improvements in teacher ratings of self-control or on self-report measures of self-concept. Both active treatment groups improved in teachers' ratings of hyperactivity as well as cognitive style and academic-achievement performance-measures, although the two groups did not differ from each other. The results of the teachers' blind ratings are presented in Figure 1. As can be seen, the desired changes were maintained at 10-week follow-up. Classroom observational measures of both verbal and physical off-task behavior suggested improvement in both active treatment groups. Parents' reports evidenced improvement across all treatment conditions. Finally, the significant differences across conditions were no longer evident at one-year follow-up (data not included in Figure 1). Although the interpretations of these results need to be tempered by the lack of generalization to the home as well as lack of mainte-

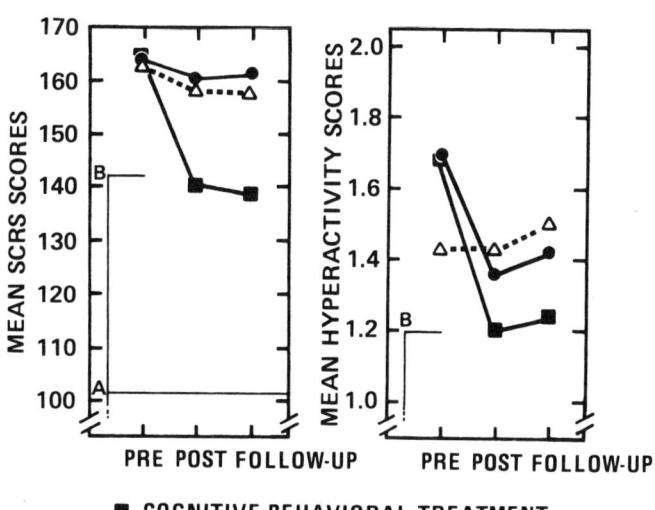

FIGURE 1. Mean Self-Control Rating Scale (SCRS) and hyperactivity ratings for the cognitive-behavioral condition, the behavioral condition, and the attention–control condition across the assessment periods. The "A" in the illustration represents the mean for 105 randomly selected nondisturbed children for that measure; the B represents one standard deviation from that mean. (Adapted from Kendall & Braswell, 1982.)

nance at one-year follow-up, the data provide some support for the efficacy of cognitive-behavioral treatment, as well as for some more specific advantages when the cognitive component is included in the treatment program. The authors speculated that longer treatment periods with more emphasis on in-class intervention and home situations may be necessary for the attainment of more positive treatment outcomes.

A Clinical Case Example

In order to describe and illustrate the intervention procedures further, we examine here the case of a hyperactive and impulsive 7-year-old (Kendall & Urbain, 1981). The child, Rosanne (not her real name), was described by her parents and teachers as distractible, as having a short attention span, as being generally noncompliant, and as having unsatisfactory peer relationships because of verbal aggressiveness.

The intervention in this clinical case employed several strategies to foster the development of self-control.[1] These strategies included self-instructional training on psychoeducational tasks and self-instructions with special cue cards for affect recognition, perspective taking, and interpersonal cognitive-problem solving. The treatment also employed and emphasized a series of behavioral contingencies involving reward and response cost that, with the use of chips, allowed Rosanne to earn rewards at the end of each session.

The self-instructional procedures began with the therapist modeling task performance and verbalizing the task analysis and performance strategies out loud. For example, the therapist might try to find the "hidden picture" by stating, "Let's see, what am I supposed to do? I need to look ahead and check all the possible places, and pay attention to what I'm doing." More specifically, the therapist verbalized a problem definition, a problem approach, a focusing-of-attention statement, and a statement of self-reward on successful performance ("I did a good job!"). The child and the therapist then took turns practicing self-instruction on various psychoeducational tasks. No behavioral reinforcement contingencies were used in this initial phase of self-instructions. It should be noted that these self-instructions were *task-related* and were not directly related to the target behaviors that were being observed and recorded. Thus, it was possible to examine changes in the target behaviors in terms of response generalization.

The next phase of the intervention utilized self-instructional training

---

[1] One-hour therapy sessions were conducted, approximately weekly for a period of 12 months, followed by bi-monthly sessions for a 3-month period.

in conjunction with a response-cost contingency. During this phase, Rosanne and the therapist continued to rehearse the use of self-statements on psychoeducational task materials. Response costs (removal of tokens) were exacted for incorrect task performance or for failing to utilize the self-statements. Lost tokens could be earned back by appropriate performance.

The next phase of the intervention continued to employ self-instructions and behavioral contingencies in a variety of activities designed to foster affect recognition, role taking, and social-problem-solving skills. During these sessions, self-instructional cue cards were introduced. These cue cards stated: (1) "STOP AND THINK (I need to Stop and Think!)," (2) "THINK AHEAD (What might happen next if I do that?)," and (3) "PLAN (I need to think of lots of *different* things I could do to solve the problem!)." Two additional cards were employed to assist Rosanne in self-reward and in coping with frustration: (1) "GOOD! (I did a good job!)," and (2) "OOPS—I GOOFED! (I made a mistake. Try again!)."

In order to assist Rosanne in applying self-instructions to interpersonal situations, the cue cards were first used in behavioral role-play situations during which Rosanne would help the *therapist* to "Stop and Think." For example, the therapist might create a situation in which Rosanne was playing with her favorite toy and then might role-play a potentially interfering child. Rosanne would be instructed to hold up the cue cards to help the child (played by the therapist) to learn when to stop and think. Also a part of these sessions was the use of four pictures of emotional faces (sad, happy, scared, and angry) and one picture of a crowd of children expressing diverse emotions. Following the role playing of a social situation in which Rosanne had "cued" the therapist as to when to stop and think, the therapist might then ask Rosanne how the child might have felt if each of several different outcomes had occurred. Rosanne would then have to identify the appropriate emotion by selecting the correct face.

Once Rosanne was fairly familiar with the meaning of the cue cards, the following general procedure was employed. First, the therapist presented a situation involving some form of interpersonal conflict, and Rosanne and the therapist role-played an impulsive response to the situation. Second, the therapist modeled the use of the cue cards in a spoken self-instructional sequence aimed at solving the problem in a reflective fashion. Rosanne was then encouraged to "try it on her own," with the therapist presenting the cue cards as prompts to assist Rosanne in self-verbalization. The "plan" generated through self-instruction was then enacted in a role play, followed by a discussion of how well the plan had worked. Often several alternative courses of action might be role-played, with the therapist emphasizing to Rosanne the difference between the initial, impulsive way of responding and these more reflective ways of handling the situation.

At the end of each session after Session 7, Rosanne was instructed to use the "stop-and-think" method outside therapy. The therapist also stated that he would use "stop and think" and tell about it at the next session. At the start of the subsequent sessions, Rosanne could paste a gold star reward on a chart and earn an extra chip or two for reporting on the use of self-instructions to stop and think outside the therapy sessions.

After three months of intervention, more intensive efforts to facilitate a generalization of Rosanne's use of the self-instructions were begun. In the thirteenth session, the target behaviors being observed were incorporated into the training as explicit "rules" for in-therapy behavior. These rules included staying in her seat, listening or paying attention, and not interrupting. The rules were printed on a stop sign, and the response-cost contingency was applied to infractions.

A self-evaluation procedure was added at this time. In this procedure, Rosanne assigned herself extra "bonus points" at the end of each session. At the time of self-evaluation, the therapist also inquired, "What were the neat things you did today?" and "What are some things you still need to work on to do better?" The therapist helped Rosanne in learning to evaluate her behavior in a highly specific and realistic way. If the therapist and Rosanne disagreed on the number of "bonus points" she deserved for the day, the matter was discussed and a fair solution was negotiated.

Subsequent reports from Rosanne's mother indicated that Rosanne at times rehearsed the self-instructions out loud at home, but her impulsive behavior was still quite a problem around the house. At this point, the mother was included in two conjoint sessions in which Rosanne demonstrated the use of the cue cards, the star chart, and the role plays. Greater effort was made to incorporate real-life versus hypothetical problem situations into the role play, and a second set of cue cards was prepared for Rosanne to post in her room. In addition, the mother devised a time-out, "stop-and-think" chair in which Rosanne would be required to sit for one or two minutes at home when impulsive behavior was observed.

The results of this study in terms of the frequency of target behaviors are presented in Figure 2. A decrease in inappropriate, impulsive behavior can be seen, with the bulk of these results apparently due to the implementation of self-instruction and response-cost contingencies during the psychoeducational tasks and during the targeting of in-therapy behavior as the rules (rather than training in dealing with hypothetical interpersonal problems or social-perspective taking). Unlike the time-limited treatments employed in therapy outcome comparisons with moderately disturbed children, this case illustrates the more extended duration of treatment required for more severe clinical cases.

Philosophical Issues

The therapist's philosophy regarding both the phenomenology and the treatment of impulsive disorders plays a critical role in the way that that treatment is conceptualized and implemented. Thus, it is important

TEACHING RATIONAL SELF-TALK TO IMPULSIVE CHILDREN 177

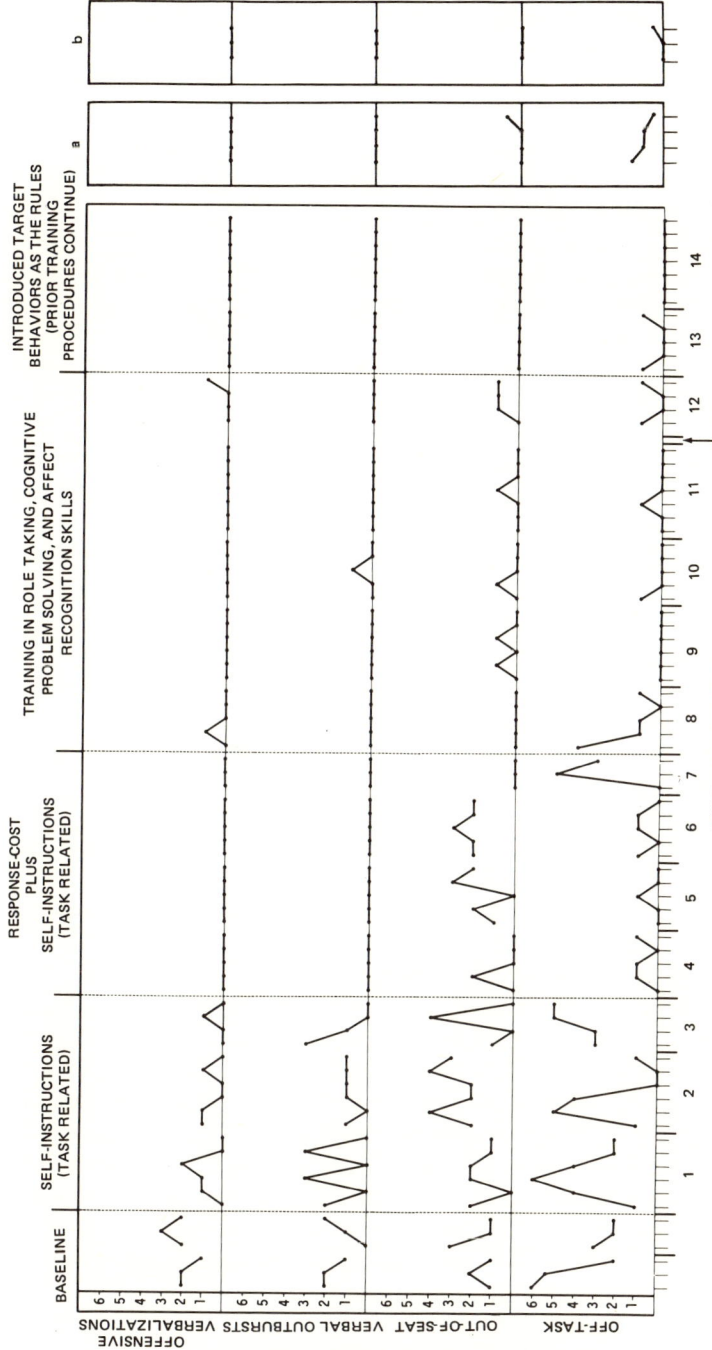

FIGURE 2. Frequency of offensive verbalizations, verbal outbursts, out-of-seat instances, and off-task behaviors across five-minute segments of the therapy sessions as a function of different treatment components: (a) six-month data are the averages of 27 five-minute observational units gathered over four therapy sessions; (b) one-year data are the averages of 16 five-minute observational units gathered over three therapy sessions.

to identify and address these philosophical issues, any differences that may occur between therapists, and exactly what the subsequent implications may be for treatment. In this section, we consider several of these issues. More specifically, our focus is on rational-emotive therapy (RET) techniques as they compare with other cognitive-behavioral strategies. In addition, we consider how certain characteristics such as developmental level, psychopathological classification, and presence or absence of certain cognitive and behavioral component skills may affect the treatment process. Finally, we discuss issues regarding how research methods may affect the clinician's ability to extract viable treatment strategies from the research literature.

Comparisons between Approaches

Cognitive-behavioral approaches seem to share the therapeutic goal of seeking to alter the client's thinking and behavioral patterns so that they are more consistent with objective reality. Where the approaches typically differ, however, is in the emphasis each places on different aspects of reality. Verbal self-instruction and related approaches focus on teaching the child the realities of the problem-solving situation, such as how to define the problem, analyze the most effective problem-solving strategy, and understand the importance of adequate attention focusing, and on giving him or her a yardstick by which to measure the effectiveness of the solution (i.e., self-monitoring, evaluation-reinforcement skills). The aim of self-instructional training is to help the child to gain a more accurate means of assessing social, behavioral, and emotional realities, and to gain the necessary skills to consider behavioral alternatives based on these realities.

On the other hand, RET-based approaches, in addition to encouraging an accurate appraisal of the problem situation (although the approach to this end is less structured than ours), realistically appraises the philosophy with which the young client interprets the emotional meaning of the problem situation. In this way, it may be said, RET and related approaches (e.g., DeVoge, 1974; DiGiuseppe, 1975; Ellis, 1962) emphasize a hypothesized link between impulsive behavior and emotionality. More specifically, RET theory hypothesizes that the more a child experiences anger, low frustration tolerance, and lowered self-esteem, the more likely he or she is to act impulsively and/or antisocially. Given this model, the therapeutic task becomes one of changing the beliefs or philosophies that the child may possess about the world. For example, the child is taught that an insult directed at him or her is neither terrible nor factually based and that he or she can, in fact, stand to be called names. Thus, feelings of anger, frustration, or hurt (lowered self-esteem) are less likely, and the child has less of a need to act inappropriately. When less intense feelings are experienced, it is assumed, the child finds it easier to stop and think about alternative solutions to problems rather than behaving impulsively.

Early versions of current training programs (e.g., Kendall & Finch, 1976; Meichenbaum, 1971) essentially ignored the child's emotional responses (Bernard, 1981) in favor of attempting to influence behavior via cognitive-behavioral and behavioral contingency links. Moreover, although social-cognitive programs include techniques aimed at increasing the child's ability to recognize the emotional states of others (e.g., Kendall & Urbain, 1981; Robin, Schnieder, & Dolnick, 1976; Spivack & Shure, 1974), few programs to date have attempted to train impulsive youngsters to become better monitors of their own emotional state and subsequently to use rational self-talk methods to dealing with these emotions and thus to prevent impulsive acting-out behavior. The design and implementation of such a program would be of substantial theoretical and practical value and would potentially add empirical support to RET-based programs. As later discussed, however, the ability of the child to think in abstract terms is a critical determinant of his or her ability to recognize and deal with these emotional responses. Such a program would therefore need to be sensitive to developmental issues.

The distinction between altering behavior via direct cognitive-behavioral change and altering through emotional change has direct bearing on the theoretical and practical issues involved in cognitive interventions. If behavior is thought to be changed via teaching children to be more effective problem-solvers or information-processors, then, in effect, therapists are identifying the absence of cognitive skills in their clients and teaching the skills that help to remediate these problems. On the other hand, if behavior is thought to be changed via ameliorating disturbing emotions (such as anger), then it becomes important to change the underlying philosophies that are operating to distract the child. In this latter case, cognitive *errors* are usually associated with these disturbing emotions and should be corrected to achieve therapeutic results. Whereas self-instructions and related approaches assume the position of teaching cognitive skills where none are thought to exist, RET-based approaches seek to correct the cognitive errors underlying erroneous personal philosophies. These different approaches may be entirely desirable, as each may be effective for different child behavior problems.

The use of reinforcement contingencies to augment cognitive therapy strategies appears to be of paramount importance when dealing with impulsive children. However, not all programs emphasize this use. For example, Spivack and Shure (1974) made no mention of using contingencies *per se* in their Interpersonal Cognitive Problem-Solving (ICPS) training program. The assumption appears to be that the effective use of the ICPS skills attained brings about higher levels of adjustment, the consequences of which are reinforcing enough in and of themselves to maintain the newly learned behavior. Similarly, RET, although often emphasizing the importance of some behavioral components of therapy (e.g., behavioral homework assignments), focuses primarily on *behavior as it affects thought* (see Ellis, 1973, 1980, for his view on the relatedness of RET to other cognitive-behavioral interventions). In contrast, we view reinforcement contingencies as important (see also Kendall, 1977, 1981) in their own right in directly modifying impulsive behavior as well as in indirectly affecting behavior through the reinforcement of appropriate self-verbalizations. However, this gap may be gradually narrowing, as RET theorists (such as DiGuiseppe, 1975) have suggested the importance of reinforcing rational self-talk, thus treating these cognitions as a special class of behaviors that are subject to the same behavioral principles as other behaviors.

Dispelling the "Patient Uniformity Myth"

Kiesler (1966) described the "patient uniformity myth" as a fallacy that occurs when researchers assume that all types of patients with similar disorders will respond to the same type of therapy in the same way. This issue is especially salient with children as, in addition to all the other possible differences among them, they may differ in developmental level even if they are of the same chronological age.

Developmental differences among children may affect the usefulness of different therapeutic approaches in at least two ways. First, the child's ability to understand the therapeutic strategies themselves may be limited. As would be consistent with Piagetian theory (1926), abstract concepts, such as rational philosophies, may not be understood by children prior to the cognitive developmental stage of concrete, or even formal, operations (which occur in most children at approximately ages 7 and 11, respectively). Thus, the forceful confrontation of irrational beliefs that is often a highly useful technique with adult neurotics may well be interpreted by the child as a scolding. The analysis of belief systems, both as to whether they are rational or irrational and as to what effects these beliefs might have on their feelings and behaviors, is likely to go "over" rather than "into" the heads of young children. This is not to say that rational versus irrational thinking may not be a worthwhile goal. Rather, it is important to recognize the child's limitations and to modify the RET approach so that children can be taught rational thinking, not only as an approach to immediate problems, but in an effort to prevent them from becoming irrational, disturbed adults (cf. Knaus, 1977). However, in treating impulsivity, behavioral techniques such as modeling, reinforcement contingencies, and a more structured approach to problem solving and information processing would seem to be necessary.

Second, the child's ability to conceptualize the treatment process itself, to monitor how effectively he or she is using the self-instructions, and subsequently to apply these principles to future situations that were not covered in therapy (i.e., generalization of treatment effects) is intricately related to how well the child is able to think about the thinking process itself. This metacognitive ability (see Meichenbaum & Asarnow, 1979) is a central part of the therapy process, without which improvement by way of cognitive therapy techniques becomes difficult at best.

A thoughtful analysis of the role of children's cognitive stage of development in the generalization of treatment effects has been given by Meyers and Cohen (1984). The experiments that have been conducted by these researchers and their colleagues (Schleser *et al.*, 1981; Cohen, Meyers, Schleser, & Rodnick, 1980; Nichol, 1981) suggest that the child's cognitive level of development, as defined in Piagetian terms, mediates the ability of both the content and the process of the self-instructional strategy to produce generalization to other, nontherapy tasks.

In these experiments, first- and second-grade children were screened for Piagetian level and were subsequently placed in either a preoperational or a concrete operational group (with chronological age remaining statistically similar). Both the training content and the training procedures were systematically varied within each developmental group. The training content varied in the specificity of the target of the interventions: *specific* content applied to only the training task at hand (the MFF), whereas *general* content was intended to provide the child with a more general problem-solving strategy. This distinction parallels the concrete versus conceptual contrast reported by Kendall and Wilcox (1979). The training procedures consisted of either the traditional *fading-rehearsal* self-statement intervention (after Meichenbaum, 1975) or a *"directed-discovery"* procedure in which the child was led to "discover" the same set of self-instructions via a semiprogrammed question-and-answer interchange with the experimenter. The purpose behind the latter strategy was to increase the child's active cognitive involvement with the new learning. All the children generalized from the training following a general-content, faded-rehearsal intervention. However, only concrete operational children showed significant generalization following either specific or general content when the directed-discovery intervention was used.

That general problem-solving statements rather than self-statements specific to the task at hand enhance generalization replicates the earlier work of Kendall and Wilcox (1980). What is of equal importance here is that developmental cognitive level seems to interact with the degree of abstraction inherent in a particular technique, to produce different levels of generalization. Meyers and Cohen (1983) hypothesized that the directed-discovery procedure, in which the process of integrating the responses to the experimenter's queries into a general problem-solving approach is taught, is extremely difficult for the preoperational child's level of metacognitive development. As these authors stated, "The concrete operational child can comprehend the nature of the procedure: the purpose and potential of the process as well as the content. The preoperational child has no difficulty participating in the process but this child focuses on the content, not the process or form of the training" (p. 15). Within the context of cognitive therapy, it makes sense for the therapist to make some kind of an assessment of the child's level of metacognitive development and subsequently to tailor both the intervention content and the intervention process to that child's level. Furthermore, RET strategies, which often use forensic methods to convince clients of their irrational philosophies seem to be closer to the directed-discovery approach and therefore may be unsuitable for preoperational children.

Differences in Psychopathology

A "myth" that may too often prevail is that all impulsive children have identical psychopathological problems. Although it is true that at least most of the children who are labeled as impulsive do display symptoms that are concomitant with that designation, not all children within this category display an identical combination or severity of symptoms. In fact, as stated in the beginning of this chapter, there are a wide variety of symptoms that may lead to a child's being classified as impulsive or as lacking in self-control. Thus, different cognitive-behavioral programs may be expected to have different effects, contingent on the particular constellation of problems presented by an individual. For example, an impulsive child whose primary difficulty is school achievement may improve most with a program consisting of techniques for improved attentional information-processing and problem-solving skills. Alternatively, a child who has difficulty functioning in class because he or she cannot get along with the teacher or with his or her peers may benefit most from a program that includes recognition-of-limitations and social-problem-solving skills training. In another example, a child who appears to be chronically hostile and tries to find reasons to fight with her or his peers may find the greatest change through the rational restructuring of the belief systems that lead to anger and frustration.

Children may also differ in the types of emotional problems that they have in addition to the problem of impulsivity. Interventions whose primary focus is on instilling rational philosophies in children may have better results, for example, with impulsive children who are also anxious or depressed than with those who display no or limited signs of subjective distress. Just as RET appears to work better with introverts than with extraverts (DiLoreto, 1971), it may also work better with children whose primary style of dealing with problems is to "internalize" rather than to "externalize" conflict (Achenbach, 1979). Because impulsive children do, in general, seem to externalize conflict to a greater extent than do reflectives (e.g., Kendall et al., 1981; Montgomery & Finch, 1975) and appear to respond more positively when response contingencies are added to rational self-talk (Kendall & Finch, 1979), it may be hypothesized that an RET cognitive approach, although somewhat efficacious for some impulsive youngsters, is more effective alone with internalizers and needs "help" from response-contingency treatment components with externalizers. In general, more accurate and refined assessments of psychopathological factors, as well as the subsequent study of these variables as they bear on therapeutic effectiveness, should allow therapists in the future to fine-tune their approach to each of their young clients.

Analyses of Component Skills

Task analyses of a behavior of interest are performed in order to identify those components of one's behavioral or cognitive repertoire that, when lacking or in error, make it difficult to perform that behavior adequately. Task analyses that have been undertaken in the areas of assertiveness (Schwartz & Gottman, 1976) and heterosocial response (Cacioppo, Glass, & Merluzzi, 1979) have been aimed at a better understanding of the topography of competent responding. In the Schwartz and Gottman (1976) study, for example, nonassertive behavior was found to be the product not of skill deficits (the subjects knew what were the appropriate assertive responses) but of self-perceived anxiety and an "internal dialogue of conflict" in which negative self-statements prevailed. Applying such a study to impulsive behavior would yield important information about the deficit(s) that needs to be treated. Furthermore, it is likely that different children have different behavioral and cognitive deficits. Even a crude assessment of whether the child has the requisite skills to produce a nonimpulsive response would be most helpful in planning the treatment strategy. For example, an intervention strategy that emphasizes skills training would be inappropriate for a child who possesses the requisite problem-solving skills, but who, because of some emotional reaction within the problem-solving situation (e.g., anger or anxiety), is unable to use them.

THE PROBLEM OF GENERALIZATION

Generalization of treatment effects, a problem in psychotherapy research in general, is a problem of equal magnitude in the treatment of children. Just as many of the studies cited throughout this chapter call attention to a lack of generalization to other tasks and/or situations (see Meichenbaum & Asarnow, 1979, for a thorough review of this issue), the therapist working with a child may become falsely encouraged by any improvement that occurs during therapy.

As previously discussed, generalization may be optimized through the therapist's assessing the child's cognitive level, structuring the therapy process and content to fit this level, and providing therapeutic tasks that consist of a wide variety of social/interpersonal, academic, and psychological tasks.

Another possible avenue for optimizing generalization might be the training of "natural change agents," such as teachers and parents, in providing cognitive-behavioral interventions for impulsive children in natural settings. Glenwick and Barocas (1979) undertook such an investigation, but unfortunately, they found only modest support for the usefulness of such an approach. Specifically, although achievement gains in reading and arithemetic were noted, no generalization was evident in either home or nonacademic classroom behavior. However, it is possible that more encouraging results might be obtained with somewhat different procedures. Glenwick and Barocas taught parents and teachers how to use Meichenbaum's (1975) self-instructional procedure, but they never actually observed its use. Thus, it is possible that the procedure was not executed properly. Just as professional therapists need supervised training in order to achieve optimal results, so, probably, do paraprofessionals! In addition, the children were trained *either* by a professional therapist, a teacher, a parent, or a teacher and a parent. In no case was a client trained by a therapist with adjunctive support by a parent or a teacher. We would hypothesize that such a training regimen, with the addition of behavioral contingencies, would optimize both therapeutic effect and the generalization to natural settings.

The Problem of Generalizing from Research Findings

Some practicing clinicians have complained that psychotherapy research is of marginal usefulness in their daily routine. It is our concern, too, that research have relevance to treatment as it is typically implemented. For the most part, we are comfortable with the assertion that the components of cognitive-behavioral therapy that have been purported to be effective by the research data—such as direct instructions to the child, modeling, reinforcements, response-cost contingencies, role playing (behavioral rehearsal), self-instruction, self-rehearsal, feedback, and interpersonal/social applications—can be assets to the therapist who deals with impulsive youngsters. However, we have not discussed the methodological issues that concern us when we attempt to draw conclusions from any specific psychotherapy study. We have not covered this subject because of our attempt to limit the scope of this chapter to its primary aims: descriptive and practical.

References

Achenbach, T. M. The Child Behavior Profile: An empirically based system for assessing children's behavioral problems and competencies. *International Journal of Mental Health*, 1979, 47, 223–233.
Ainslie, G. Specious reward: A behavioral theory of impulsiveness and impulse control. *Psychological Bulletin*, 1975, 82, 463–496.
American Psychiatric Association. *Diagnostic and statistical manual of mental disorders* (3rd ed.). Washington, D.C.: Author, 1980.
Bandura, A. Self-efficacy: Toward a unifying theory of behavioral change. *Psychological Review*, 1977, 84, 191–215.
Bandura, A. *Principles of behavior modification*. New York: Holt, Rinehart, & Winston, 1969.
Bernard, M. E. Private thought in rational-emotive psychotherapy. *Cognitive Therapy and Research*, 1981, 5, 125–142.
Burns, D. J., & Powers, R. B. Choice and self-control in children: A test of Racklin's model. *Bulletin of the Psychonomic Society*, 1975, 5, 156–158.
Cacioppo, J. T., Glass, C. R., & Merluzzi, T. V. Self-statements and self-evaluations: A cognitive-response analysis of heterosocial anxiety. *Cognitive Therapy and Research*, 1979, 3, 249–262.
Cairns, E., & Cammock, T. The development of a more reliable version of the Matching Familiar Figures Test. *Developmental Psychology*, 1978, 14, 555–560.
Cohen, S., & Przybycien, C. A. Some effects of sociometrically selected peer models on the cognitive styles of impulsive children. *Journal of Genetic Psychology*, 1974, 124, 213–220.

Cohen, R., Meyers, A., Schleser, R., & Rodnick, J. D. *Generalization of self-instruction: Effects of cognitive level and training procedures.* Paper presented at the biennial meeting of the Southeastern Conference on Human Development, Alexandria, Virginia, April 1980.

Day, M. Developmental trends in visual scanning. In H. W. Reese (Ed.), *Advances in child development and behavior* (Vol. 10). New York: Academic Press, 1975.

Debus, R. L. Effects of brief observation of model behavior on conceptual tempo of impulsive children. *Developmental Psychology,* 1970, *2,* 22–32.

Denny, D. R. Modeling effects upon conceptual style and cognitive tempo. *Child Development,* 1972, *43,* 105–119.

DeVoge, C. A behavioral approach to RET with children. *Rational Living,* 1974, *9,* 23–26.

DiGiuseppe, R. A. The use of behavior modification to establish rational self-statements in children. *Rational Living,* 1975, *10,* 18–19.

DiLoreto, A. O. *Comparative psychotherapy: An experimental analysis.* Chicago: Aldine-Atherton, 1971.

Drake, D. M. Perceptual correlates of impulsive and reflective behavior. *Developmental Psychology,* 1970, *2,* 202–214.

Egeland, B., & Weinberg, R. A. The Matching Familiar Figures Test: A look at its psychometric credibility. *Child Development,* 1976, *47,* 483–491.

Egeland, B., Wozniak, R., Schrimpf, V. *Visual information processing: Evaluation of a training program for children with learning disabilities.* Paper presented at the Twenty-First International Congress of Psychology, Paris, France, 1976.

Ellis, A. *Reason and emotion in psychotherapy.* Secaucus, N.J.: Lyle Stuart, 1962.

Ellis, A. Are cognitive behavior therapy and rational therapy synonymous? *Rational Living,* 1973, *8,* 8–11.

Ellis, A. Rational-emotive therapy and cognitive behavior therapy: Similarities and differences. *Cognitive Therapy and Research,* 1980, *4,* 325–340.

Errickson, E. A., Wyne, M. D., & Routh, D. K. A response-cost procedure for reduction of impulsive behavior of academically handicapped children. *Journal of Abnormal Child Psychology,* 1973, *1,* 350–357.

Finch, A. J., Jr., Wilkinson, M. D., Nelson, W. M., & Montgomery, L. E. Modification of an impulsive tempo in emotionally disturbed boys. *Journal of Abnormal Child Psychology,* 1975, *3,* 47–51.

Firestone, P., & Douglas, V. I. The effects of reward and punishment on reaction times and autonomic activity in hyperactive and normal children. *Journal of Abnormal Child Psychology,* 1975, *3,* 201–216.

Glenwick, D. S., & Barocas, R. Training impulsive children in verbal self-control by use of natural change agents. *Journal of Special Education,* 1979, *13,* 387–398.

Heider, E. R. Information processing and the modification of an "impulsive cognitive tempo." *Child Development,* 1971, *42,* 1276–1281.

Hemry, F. P. Effect of reinforcement conditions on a discriminative learning task for impulsive vs. reflective children. *Child Development,* 1973, *44,* 657–660.

Kagan, J. Reflection-impulsivity: The generality and dynamics of cognitive tempo. *Journal of Abnormal Psychology,* 1966, *71,* 17–24.

Kagan, J., Rosman, B. L., Day, D., Albert, J., & Philips, W. Information processing in the child. Significance of analytic and reflective attitudes. *Psychological Monographs,* 1964, *78*(Whole No. 578).

Kagan, J., Pearson, L., & Welsh, L. Modifiability of an impulsive tempo. *Journal of Educational Psychology,* 1966, *57,* 359–365.

Kanfer, F. H., & Karoly, P. Self-control: A behavioristic exursion into the lion's den. *Behavior Therapy,* 1972, *3,* 398–416.

Karoly, P., & Kanfer, F. (Eds.). *Self-management and behavior change: From theory to practice.* New York: Pergamon Press, 1982.
Kazdin, A. E. Covert modeling, model similarity, and reduction of avoidance behavior. *Behavior Therapy,* 1974, *5,* 325–340.
Kendall, P. C. On the efficacious use of verbal self-instructional procedures with children. *Cognitive Therapy and Research,* 1977, *1,* 331–341.
Kendall, P. C. Cognitive-behavioral interventions with children. In B. Lahey & A. E. Kazdin (Eds.), *Advances in child clinical psychology* (Vol. 4). New York: Plenum Press, 1981.
Kendall, P. C., & Braswell, L. Cognitive-behavioral self-control therapy for children: A components analysis. *Journal of Consulting and Clinical Psychology,* 1982, *50,* 672–689.
Kendall, P. C., & Finch, A. J., Jr. A cognitive-behavioral treatment for impulsive control: A case study. *Journal of Consulting and Clinical Psychology,* 1976, *44,* 852–857.
Kendall, P. C., & Finch, A. J., Jr. A cognitive-behavioral treatment for impulsivity: A group comparison study. *Journal of Consulting and Clinical Psychology,* 1978, *46,* 110–118.
Kendall, P. C., & Finch, A. J., Jr. Developing nonimpulsive behavior in children: Cognitive-behavioral strategies for self-control. In P. C. Kendall & S. D. Hollon (Eds.), *Cognitive-behavioral interventions: Theory, research and procedures.* New York: Academic Press, 1979.
Kendall, P. C., & Urbain, E. S. Cognitive-behavioral intervention with a hyperactive girl: Evaluation via observations and cognitive performance. *Behavioral Assessment,* 1981, *3,* 345–357.
Kendall, P. C., & Wilcox, L. E. Self-control in children: Development of a rating scale. *Journal of Consulting and Clinical Psychology,* 1979, *47,* 1020–1029.
Kendall, P. C., & Wilcox, L. E. A cognitive-behavioral treatment for impulsivity: Concrete versus conceptual treatment in non-self controlled problem children. *Journal of Consulting and Clinical Psychology,* 1980, *48,* 50–91.
Kendall, P. C., & Williams, C. L. Assessing the cognitive and behavioral components of children's self-management. In P. Karoly & F. Kanfer (Eds.), *Self-management and behavior change: From theory to practice.* New York: Pergamon Press, 1982.
Kendall, P. C., & Zupan, B. A. Individual versus group application of cognitive-behavioral self-control procedures with children. *Behavior Therapy,* 1981, *12,* 344–359.
Kendall, P. C., Zupan, B. A., & Braswell, L. Self-control in children: Further analyses of the Self-Control Rating Scale. *Behavior Therapy,* 1981, *12,* 667–681.
Kiesler, D. J. Some myths of psychotherapy research and the search for a paradigm. *Psychological Bulletin,* 1966, *67,* 110–136.
Knaus, W. J. Rational-emotive education. In A. Ellis & R. Grieger (Eds.), *Handbook of rational-emotive therapy.* New York: Springer, 1977.
Luria, A. R. *The role of speech in the regulation of normal and abnormal behavior.* New York: Liveright, 1961.
Mahoney, M. J., & Thoresen, C. E. *Self-control: Power to the person.* Belmont, Calif.: Brooks/Cole, 1974.
Massari, D. J., & Schack, M. L. Discrimination learning by reflective and impulsive children in a function of reinforcement schedule. *Developmental Psychology,* 1972, *6,* 183.
Meichenbaum, D. Examination of model characteristics in reducing avoidance behavior. *Journal of Personality and Social Psychology,* 1971, *17,* 298–307.
Meichenbaum, D. H. Self-instructional methods. In F. Kanfer & A. Goldstein (Eds.), *Helping people change.* New York: Pergamon Press, 1975.
Meichenbaum, D. H. *Cognitive-behavior modification: An integrative approach.* New York: Plenum Press, 1977.

Meichenbaum, D., & Asarnow, J. Cognitive behavior modification and metacognitive development: Implications for the classroom. In P. C. Kendall & S. D. Hollon (Eds.), *Cognitive-behavioral interventions: Theory, research, and procedures*. New York: Academic Press, 1979.

Meichenbaum, D. H., & Goodman, J. Training impulsive children to talk to themselves: A means of developing self-control. *Journal of Abnormal Psychology*, 1971, 77, 115–126.

Messer, S. B. Reflection-impulsivity: A review. *Psychological Bulletin*. 1976, 83, 1026–1052.

Meyers, A. W., & Cohen, R. Cognitive behavioral interventions in educational settings. In P. C. Kendall (Ed.), *Advances in cognitive-behavioral research and therapy* (Vol. 3). New York: Academic Press, 1984.

Mischel, W. Processes in delay of gratification. In L. Berkowitz (Ed.), *Advances in experimental Social Psychology* (Vol. 7). New York: Academic Press, 1974.

Montgomery, L. E., & Finch, A. J., Jr. Reflection-impulsivity and locus of conflict in emotionally deprived children. *Journal of Genetic Psychology*, 1975, 126, 89–91.

Nelson, W. M., Finch, A. J., Jr., & Hooke, J. F. Effects of reinforcement and response-cost on cognitive style in emotionally disturbed boys. *Journal of Abnormal Psychology*, 1975, 84, 426–428.

Nichol, G. *Generalization of self-instruction training as a function of cognitive level, content of instruction and delivery procedure*. Unpublished master's thesis, Memphis State University, 1981.

O'Leary, K. D., & O'Leary, S. G. *Classroom management: The successful use of behavior modification* (2nd ed.). New York: Pergamon Press, 1977.

Piaget, J. *The language and thought of the child*. New York: Harcourt, Brace, 1926.

Ridberg, H. E., Parke, R. D., & Hetherington, E. M. Modification of impulsive and reflective cognitive styles through observation of film mediated models. *Developmental Psychology*, 1971, 5, 369–377.

Robin, A., Schneider, M., & Dolnick, M. The turtle technique: An extended case study of self-control in the classroom. *Psychology in the Schools*, 1976, 13, 449–453.

Sarason, I. G. Test anxiety and the self-disclosing coping model. *Journal of Consulting and Clinical Psychology*, 1975, 43, 148–153.

Schleser, R., Meyers, A., & Cohen, R. Generalization of self-instructions: Effects of general versus specific content, active rehearsal, and cognitive level. *Child Development*, 1981, 52, 335–340.

Schwartz, P. M., & Gottman, J. M. Toward a task analysis of assertive behavior. *Journal of Consulting and Clinical Psychology*, 1976, 44, 910–920.

Siegelman, E. Reflective and impulsive observing behavior. *Child Development*, 1969, 40, 1213–1222.

Skinner, B. F. *Science and human behavior*. New York: Macmillan, 1953.

Spivack, G., & Shure, M. B. *Social adjustment of young children*. San Francisco: Jossey-Bass, 1974.

Usui, H. Psychological study of cognitive style (reflection-impulsivity): Analysis of visual search strategies of reflective and impulsive children. *Japanese Journal of Educational Psychology*, 1975, 23, 20–25.

Vygotsky, L. S. *Thought and language*. New York: Wiley, 1962.

Yando, R. M., & Kagan, J. The effect of teacher tempo on the child. *Child Development*, 1968, 39, 27–34.

7

A Rational-Emotive Approach to Academic Underachievement

JAMES A. BARD AND HAROLD R. FISHER

In this presentation we hope to establish some definitional guidelines that may serve to reduce some of the ambiguity and confusion that plague the study and treatment of academic underachievement. In addition, we intend to provide a conceptual framework that may help to focus and direct the efforts of practitioners and researchers in their respective approaches to the problem.

DEFINING ACADEMIC UNDERACHIEVEMENT

With respect to definitional guidelines, we pose the following questions: First, by what criteria is it determined that a problem exists; that is, how does one decide if a student is actually underachieving? Or how does one describe any such condition so that other observers can and will agree? Second, given that the first question has been settled and some students have been "identified" as underachievers, what is "wrong" with them? What is the nature of the conditions that cause them to underachieve? Or how does one account for and explain whatever has been described, with any claim of validity?

So far as diagnostic (descriptive) criteria are concerned, it seems that

---

JAMES A. BARD • Department of Psychology, Cleveland State University, Cleveland, Ohio 44102. HAROLD R. FISHER • Clinical Psychologist in Private Practice, Cleveland Institute for Rational Living, Beachwood, Ohio 44122.

the concept of academic underachievement has been defined quite differently at different times by different people. In a fairly comprehensive review, Arndt (1971) mentioned several definitions of the underachiever, including one by Peterson (1962): "a student who has the ability to achieve a level of academic success significantly above that which he actually attains" (p. 379). Arndt hastened to caution that "these definitions are deceptive . . . because when put into operational terms, different students can be identified as 'underachievers,' depending on the method use, with little overlap" (p. 1). He cited several studies that document the point rather convincingly. We do not interpret this documentation to mean that the concept of underachievement is to be abandoned, only that researchers had better acknowledge these problems in the study of a serious educational problem that nearly everyone agrees does exist.

If some agreement on diagnostic criteria can be achieved so that practitioners and researchers are considering the same client population, we believe that the prospects for future progress will be greatly improved. To this end, we call attention to a method first suggested by Thorndike (1963). He proposed that actual achievement level be predicted on the basis of the "regression of intelligence on achievement." A substantially lower level of achievement than that predicted would be considered underachievement. According to Behrens and Vernon (1978), this criterion has been widely used in classifying students as underachievers in recent years. Along this same line, McLeod (1979) has developed a more advanced formula, which provides an even more precise measure for selecting research samples to be used in the study of underachievement.

We mention these references for the benefit of those whose primary interest is research. We view the problem as practitioners whose impressions have been gleaned from years of working with underachieving students, one at a time. We decided, a long time ago, that before making any therapeutic effort to improve the student-client's school performance, we had better garner compelling evidence that such improvement was possible, that is, that we define a criterion of underachievement that we could depend on. We settled on past performance; that is, any student whose grades declined sharply from one period to another, in the same school system, might be considered an underachiever. In our sample, there is one subset that does not meet this criterion. We shall discuss it last. Obviously, the criterion we propose will probably lose some students who may legitimately be considered underachievers by practitioners who employ a different yardstick. In defense of our view, we submit that it is better (more productive in the long run) to begin study with a sample of students whom nearly all practitioners and researchers would agree on. We expect that our criterion will satisfy minimum requirements for most.

Explaining Academic Underachievement

Turning now to our second question of how to explain their underachievement, we intend to show that what is wrong with many underachievers is mainly a matter of cognitive distortion. Before proceeding, however, we want to mention some other formulations that, to a greater or lesser extent, resemble our own. Although most of these views are not firmly rooted theoretically, they do attempt to explain underachieving, and we believe that they deserve mention.

Psychopathology

We were interested to note that, in spite of the considerable journal literature on the subject of underachievement as a clinical problem, we could find only one of several current textbooks in the field of childhood psychopathology (Erikson, 1978) that lists the word *underachievement* in the index. Unfortunately, this particular text provides no specific references, nor does it offer any definitional help. This seems especially puzzling to us in view of the fact that so many of those who write on the topic of underachievement conceptualize it in terms of "pathology." For example, Arndt (1971) referred to a paper by Kowitz (1961) that discerned three dominant approaches to underachievement in literature: (1) an illness involving the personality . . . (2) a problem resulting from inadequate motivation, and (3) a problem stemming from poor educational administration or organization. Another writer, Goodstein (1979) views underachievement as a symptom that relates to psychopathology and suggested that there are three distinct patterns: (1) neurosis; (2) the nonachievement syndrome (NAS); and (3) the adolescent reaction. And still another, Kisch (1967), classified college sophomore underachievers in terms of the specific pathology presumed to be involved: (1) overcompensating for feelings of social inadequacy by adopting an extraverted stance; (2) highly motivated but socially isolated, angry, and alienated; (3) well adjusted socially, but having weak academic interests; and (4) authoritarian, conformist, nonintellectual, and therefore poorly fitted for majoring in this particular program. So, it is clear that underachievement and psychopathology are very much related in the minds of many.

The Antiachiever

Some other writers (e.g., Hoefel, 1978; Sherman, Zuckerman, & Sostek, 1975) have suggested that *antiachiever* might be a better designation that *underachiever*. Sherman *et al.* offered a classification of the antiachiever which is based on what they consider the preeminent goals of the students. One of these goals is to maintain immature, dependent relationships with their families and avoid the risks of independent action as well as the consequent responsibility. A second goal is to be extraordinary, which is linked to a low sense of self-worth fostered by adverse reaction to the school environment. Finally, a third type of antiachiever, in order to avoid any possible failure, makes no effort to succeed academically.

We mention these several classifications because each one in the above sequence gets closer to our own scheme, which is based on the cognitive theoretical system of rational-emotive therapy. Thus, we would hypothesize that Sherman's third type of antiachiever (perhaps more aptly labeled the *antiattempter*) suffers from the irrational (false) belief that failure is catastrophic and/or degrading and therefore is to be avoided at all costs.

Factor-analytic Findings

Before getting into the particulars of our own system, there is one other classification that, though considering a larger clinical population, comes very close to our approach and therefore may help set the stage for our proposal. Using factor-analytic methods, Quay (1972) delineated several subtypes of childhood behaviour disorders, which he chose to label "conduct disorder," "socialized delinquent," and "Personality Disorder" (these same patterns have been assigned different labels in the recent revision of Quay and Werry, 1979). The feature of this study that we find especially interesting is the responses that juveniles gave to a questionnaire designed to sample their attitudes. Although the subjects had been differentiated mainly on the basis of behavioral data, it seems to us that their attitudinal differences set them apart just as distinctly. Those labeled "conduct disorder" endorsed such ideas as "I do what I want to whether anybody likes it or not" and "I'm too tough to get along with most kids." In contrast, the "socialized delinquent" said, "It is very important to have enough friends and social life" and "Before I do something I try to consider how my friends will react to it." And the "personality disorder" (almost predictably) said, "I often feel as though

I have done something wrong or wicked" and "I have more than my share of things to worry about."

In what may be a striking oversight, Quay discussed the learning and performance correlates of the behavioral deviations, the physiological correlates, and other personality correlates. There is no discussion of the cognitive correlates (i.e., the attitudes mentioned above), which seem to us so compelling. Whatever the weakness of such an analysis, it certainly serves to set the stage for our own proposal, and so we shall proceed with our own cognitive analysis of the problems of underachievers, describe several distinguishable patterns and what makes them different, and finally, describe those remedial approaches that we have found to be most effective.

RET and Underachievement

Our work with students whom we have diagnosed as underachievers (i.e., showing a sharp decline in performance quality for no apparent reason) has lead us to conclude that these students define their goals and objectives differently from their parents and the "system." To make matters worse, their definitions of what is good for them (i.e., their beliefs, values, etc.), are not only different from the conventional, they are antithetical. With these considerations in mind, we propose that academic underachievement be defined (i.e., described or explained) as very poor academic performance resulting mainly from students' beliefs that are false and incompatible with the objectives of the system. Now, let us see if we can process this idea so as to make it useful.

First, there is the matter of determining that academic performance is indeed very poor. Traditionally, the two most widely accepted measures of performance quality are school grades (assigned by teachers) and scores attained on standardized achievements tests. We strongly recommend that, before any judgement of underachievement is made, it be determined that these two measures (and any others that may have been obtained) are consistent. It does happen sometimes that students are assigned very low grades only to astound their critics later by scoring much higher on the standardized tests. One example of this mysterious phenomenon is the student who cannot *afford* to get good grades because of negative peer pressure, and so learning must go on secretly. This is not underachievement. It may be more aptly labeled *undercover achievement*. It also happens that grades may be high and achievement scores low. A discrepancy in this direction can mean several things. We would suspect poor classroom assessment as one likely possibility. Our point is that the judgment of underachievement is ill advised unless the measures of achievement agree.

Then there is the matter of the incompatibility between students' beliefs and the objectives of the system. We believe that students who could be achieving the objectives of the system at a much higher level, but are not, simply do not have those same objectives. They have their own beliefs about what is good for them and what is not, and when these beliefs conflict with the objectives of the system, academic effort may simply stop.

Undoubtably one of the reasons for the confusion and ambiguity in the study of this tricky subject is the fact that, in any given school system, it is theoretically possible that every single student who is underachieving may be doing so for a different reason (i.e., because of a different false belief). Thus, the individualized approach recommended by many may have considerable merit.

Conceptual Distinctions

Before moving on, we might offer some comments aimed at resolving any confusion that might arise from the terminology we have introduced. Some have proposed that underachievement is essentially a problem of motivation and that we only muddy the waters by talking "philosophically." We hope not. We and other cognitive practitioners (Ellis, 1966, 1977) like to think that we are helping to clarify this and other thorny clinical problems by recasting certain constructs (e.g., motivation and emotion) along more cognitive lines. As one example, we regard the aim and direction of much human motivational energy as being largely determined by what the individual *believes* to be worthwhile. With respect to the emotional aspects of experience, we believe that "the qualitative differentiation of one emotion from another is essentially a matter of differences in cognitive content" (Bard, 1980, p. 21).

As we have seen, a great many students who would be labeled underachievers by some practitioners would not be so labeled by others. We repeat, it is our hope to establish some definitional guidelines that may serve to resolve some of the confusion. Our definition limits the concept of underachievement to only those students who perform poorly because some of their beliefs conflict with the expectations of the system. All other children who perform poorly for other reasons (e.g., brain damage) we suggest be labeled differently. There are those children who strive to achieve the objectives set for them by the system but fail for reasons that we are unable to discern. Our assessment instruments are not yet sufficiently refined to detect all real disabilities. Some other youngsters are demonstrably neurologically handicapped and therefore unable to achieve certain objectives that otherwise might be possible. And there are those students who perform poorly because they are handicapped by emotional problems (e.g., anxiety, which impairs concentration). One example would be the student who is generally so perfectionistic that any attempt to accomplish anything that may be evaluated is demoralized by intense anxiety. Another example would be the student who is so completedly convinced that he or she can never succeed at anything as to be depressed to the point of inertia. The likelihood is that these students will do very poorly in their schoolwork and will achieve so little as to fit any reasonable definition of underachievement. And it is just as likely that psychotherapy holds the best promise of help for them. We expect that problems of anxiety and depression, which are primary symptoms, are dealt with elsewhere, and therefore, we do not consider them here.

The Rational-Emotive Approach

As we review our own clinical records and experience with underachieving students, we find that certain cognitive patterns occur with sufficient frequency to be memorable. Although agreeing wholeheartedly with the many writers who urge an individualized approach to treatment, we believe that a relatively small number of antiempirical and nonconforming beliefs (which are the targets of treatment) can account for the overwhelming majority of underachievers.

A Cognitive Analysis of Underachievement

We have been able to identify five beliefs of adolescents that we have observed to underlie the type of underachievement that we have been discussing (i.e., achievement that is *not* primarily related to other, more pervasive emotional disorders):

1. "Things will turn out OK whether I work or not."
2. "Everything should be entertaining and/or enjoyable, and there should be no unpleasantness whatsoever."
3. "To do well in school would betray the relationships I have with my friends."
4. "It is demeaning, dishonorable, and destructive of my personal integrity to cooperate with authority in any way."
5. "Nothing I do at school will ever benefit me."

We trust it will be understood that we have worded and phrased each of the above ideas so as to represent or capture the essence of a great many other statements that we consider variations on a single theme.

Although we have a sizable sample gathered over a period of many years, we are mindful of certain biases based on referral sources, etc., and therefore, we are reluctant to make any judgments about the frequency of these various patterns in the population at large. We are not encumbered by the problems of the criteria of underachievement as the overwhelming majority of our clients were judged to be underachieving because they had demonstrated so much higher achievement in their earlier years in the same school system. As indicated earlier, we consider this a very reliable criterion.

General Treatment Considerations

Before proceeding with discussions of the several patterns of thinking that we have enumerated above, it may be useful to take note of some general considerations.

First, our format for discussion follows the outline of our clinical approach to these problems. We begin by talking with parents, seeking to determine (1) which of their attitudes and practices may be *supporting*, even reinforcing, the erroneous beliefs of the student and (2) how much help or cooperation can be reasonably expected from them. Then we move to the student, seeking to determine (1) which belief or combination of beliefs is responsible for the underachievement and (2) what kind of approach may be most likely to engage the student's interest and cooperation in some therapeutic work. Finally, there is the therapeutic process itself, which, in most cases, moves from an initial phase through one or more phases to a more-or-less successful resolution.

Second, we underscore the phrase "supporting . . . the erroneous beliefs" so as to minimize the danger that readers will assume from our discussion of parents and their particular foibles that we believe that their attitudes and actions have been the cause of the student's distortions. It so frequently happens that, because certain child behaviors tend to be associated with certain parental attitudes, people assume that the behaviors must have resulted from these attitudes. We make no claim to understand precisely what caused any human belief to be established in the first place. Thus, we simply refuse to say that parents caused the problem. Questions of cause and effect are to be answered through rigorous research, not clinical speculation. We do believe that beliefs are sustained by supportive influences and, if so, that any significant change will require some modification of those influences. We assume that parents may be at least unwittingly involved, and so we explore those possibilities from the beginning, through the course of therapy.

Another matter of general importance is the fact that underachieving students have numerous authority-subordinate relationships, any one of which may be pivotal in the determination of the therapeutic outcome. Not only does the student have to deal with the requirements and constraints imposed by parents, there is the math teacher, the English teacher, the counselor, the principal, etc. The point we wish to establish is that, indeed, any practitioner who works with children had better be prepared to deal with a host of other people. This means that time will be spent on the telephone in direct communication with each one or, hopefully, with only one very reliable liaison person. If there is any failure of communication (e.g., if the math teacher is not informed that a therapeutic program is in effect), the whole program may collapse. It is extremely important to the success of therapy with underachievers that everyone involved know what everyone else is doing and agree, at least tentatively, that it is worth trying.

Finally, let us emphasize again that the patterns we are about to discuss represent *some* of the common beliefs underlying underachievement. Ours is not an exhaustive list. As we noted earlier, it is theoretically possible for each underachieving student to have a unique distortion underlying his or her poor performance. So we recommend an open-minded approach that will admit exceptions and thus broaden the practitioner's range of effectiveness. In this same vein, we want to emphasize that our analyses and the suggestions that they afford are just that, suggestions. They are not prescriptions to be applied rigidly. The state of the art is not yet finalized, and we would be dismayed if anyone regarded our suggestions as sacred.

Modifying Underachievement

Having set the stage with these considerations, we can now proceed with discussions of the underachieving students we have seen. Our discussion of how rational-emotive therapy (RET) can be employed to resolve academic underachievement will be in terms of the five different beliefs that underlie the problem, and which have differential treatment implications.

"Everything Will Turn Out OK Whether I Work or Not"

Family. At first glance, it might seem that such a belief would result from the experience of being overindulged. And, in some cases, overindulgence is apparent. However, we have noticed some other aspects that we believe to be more salient or more likely to be supportive of this unrealistic belief. For one thing, it seems that the fathers of these (mostly male) students tend to put the cart before the horse when it comes to rewarding effort. Instead of promising and then delivering a reward when the work is completed, they deliver the reward first and then expect the task to be done thereafter. What to make of this fact is, of course, a matter of interpretation. We find it very tempting to infer that such a policy or practice tends to support the belief that "Everything will turn out OK, etc." That temptation is further encouraged by the fact that many experimental studies of animal learning (Maier & Seligman, 1976) have shown that reward before effort is not only not productive but may be counterproductive. Many laboratory animals have responded to that "reward-before-effort" sequence with such "indifference" as to inspire investigators to coin the phrase "learned laziness" (Engeberg, Hansen, Welker, & Thomas, 1972). So, fathers who reward before the effort may actually be discouraging the effort. The reasons for such a twist are not clear, but there is some reason to think that these fathers are applying at home the same philosophy they use at work. For example, many of the individuals we have seen work as manufacturers' representatives or lucrative franchise operators and are extremely fortunate in the sense that they make a lot of money for seemingly very little effort. In these arenas, tokens and favors frequently are given "up front," and so it may be simply an extension of that same approach to buy junior a 10-speed bike before he ever cracks a book.

We have the impression that these individuals are product-oriented, and so they press for grades without much attendant interest in curriculum or substantive content. So, it may well be that their objectives are different from those of the system, and perhaps also incompatible.

In general, the mothers of these underachieving students tend to be inconspicuous, apparently following the lead of the father in most respects. Although they may express concern about the child's poor academic performance and, in some instances, even disagree with the father's methods, there is very little open conflict. In fact, the mother usually is more troubled about the student's failure to complete household tasks.

Students. We are dealing with an individual who believes that "Everything will turn out OK whether I work or not" (we are reminded of a characterization by Whyte, 1977: "students tend to depend on . . . luck, chance or Kismet for academic performance.") With that in mind, the pattern of the student's behavior is fairly easily understood. The one most outstanding aspect of that pattern is the remarkable facility of the students to "dodge the bullet." Deadlines are extended; makeup exams are arranged; homework assignments are negotiated; and all the while the student manages to get along fairly well with the teachers. It is extremely important to realize that these shenanigans are not the product of any premeditated malice, nor do they represent any conspiracy. They are simply the skillful exercise of delay and avoidance tactics, which are entirely justified at the moment, because "Everything will turn out OK." If, in any given case, there is evidence of some other motive (e.g., hostility), then the practitioner is dealing with a different, perhaps more complex, belief system. The most likely possibility is that the student believes that "Everything will turn out OK" *and* that "Everything should be enjoyable, and there should be no unpleasantness." The addition of this latter idea changes the complexion of the pattern dramatically, as will be shown in later discussion. For the time being, suffice it to say that such a combination complicates the practitioner's task enormously, and so it is very important to note any evidence that might be suggestive. Hostility would be a prime example of the kind of evidence we refer to. Our happy-go-lucky underachiever is not hostile. He may be dismayed by the pressure and exasperation of the persons who nag him, but he simply cannot understand all the fuss, because "Everything will turn out OK."

Therapy. Unlike some young underachievers, these students are generally quite willing to attend therapy sessions and seem quite affable from the beginning. They are not so willing to engage in serious discussion about their undone homework and other academic "sins." So the first phase in therapy with these individuals is devoted to establishing a reliable communication network with family and school to provide the evidence that the therapist will need in order to effectively dispute the evasive response (e.g., "Oh, things are much better . . . yeah, things are OK"). Again, we want to emphasize that these evasions are not designed to frustrate the therapist or for that matter to deceive anyone. Rather, they simply serve to stall for time, because, in the end, "Everything will turn out OK."

The therapeutic aim in the second phase is to turn the chitchat into serious and meaningful discussion of the problem so that remedial work can begin. The ultimate objective is to improve academic achievement, but that will happen only when the student acknowledges his belief that things will turn out OK and begins to realize that such a notion is very dubious and probably false. This process requires the cooperation of all parties concerned, so that on all fronts the evidence is unmistakable (i.e., Everything is not OK). An "F" means failing, which in turn means repeating the course or the whole year. That is not OK. The 10-speed bike will not be forthcoming. That is not OK. It is extremely important for the therapist to have the evidence available, to calmly and supportively keep attention focused on that evidence, and to move in to help the student to develop a new approach to this important area of his life.

This brings us to the third stage of the therapeutic process, which we might call *reconstruction*. There are various ways to help students in this sometimes painful work, but we have found it helpful to start with a kind of "values clarification." Once the student sees that his philosophy will not work, we ask, "What would *you* really like . . . what do *you* want?" Very frequently these students come up with some surprising answers (e.g., they would like to feel better about themselves and *really* be liked by their teachers, or perhaps one teacher in particular). Once these hopes have been expressed, the therapist can proceed to encourage and assist in the formulation of appropriate plans that seem to have a good chance of succeeding.

"Everything Should Be Entertaining and/or Enjoyable and There Should Be No Unpleasantness Whatsoever"

As we indicated earlier, this belief may exist in combination with the first belief. It may also stand by itself. In either case, the practitioner had better be prepared for an uphill effort, because we consider this to be the most difficult of the patterns we are describing.

Family. These families usually have no more than two children, and the socioeconomic level is definitely above average. The features that we consider supportive of the student's philosophy include "doting" and marital conflict. By *doting*, we mean that someone or several members of the family, including grandparents sometimes, have singled out this one child for special favors and/or extraordinary treatment, which tends to minimize the unpleasant consequences that ordinarily follow certain behaviors. A common example, which includes the element of marital conflict, has the father setting very strict standards that are not only not enforced by the mother but are subverted instead. In addition, this mother may cater to whims as a way of compensating the favored one for even having to listen to the father's anger. Whether this arrangement is the cause of the effect of the marital conflict is very hard to tell, and in the final analysis, it doesn't matter that much. As long as it continues, the supports for the student's philosophy remain. Although it might seem that the father could put his foot down and force some change, the skill of the mother in making excuses and covering for the student is more than ample buffering. The potential force of the father is effectively blunted. This is one example of a pattern that can involve family members in different roles. Thus, it may be a very strong-willed and influential grandparent who controls the situation. The question of who does what is important in therapy planning, but the results are pretty much the same regardless (i.e., the student's beliefs go unchallenged, and so the schoolwork may or may not be satisfactory).

Student. Some of these students frequently perform quite well some of the time. This might seem to put them in a different classification category than underachievement. Depending on how one chooses to classify the problems of children and young people, a different label might be appropriate. We see the commotion and uproar centered on poor academic performance, in the early years, and so we include these students under the heading of academic underachievement. The performance of these students is erratic, ranging from very good to very poor. The mystery of these ups and downs unravels rather quickly when we consider the underlying belief that "there must be no unpleasantness." If this student, who, incidentally, is just as likely to be female as male, has a teacher who "dotes" or is studying a subject that seems very intriguing, the work may be very satisfactory, even excellent. It is only when the student encounters something or someone who is not entertaining or enjoyable that the work stops. So we may see this condition at a much younger age than some of the others. One of the outstanding features of this pattern is the ability of the student to adopt an attitude of "I don't care" and really mean it. Ordinarily, when young people assume that attitude, it is just a pose designed to deflect or discourage harassment. With these underachievers, not so. We have the distinct impression that they can turn off caring or turn it on, at will. If such an impression sounds implausible and/or outlandish, it may be. On the other hand, it may be that certain features of the student's mentality are outlandish. We agree that the idea of a "switch-on-and-off" caring seems incredible, if not bizarre. And we strongly suspect that some of these students are "psychotic" or at least on the borderline. Thus, their likes and dislikes, their patterns of caring and hating, may be incomprehensible to conventional wisdom. As might be expected, there may be other negative features associated, which overshadow the academic shortcomings. As these students get older, there is an increasing probability of drug and alcohol abuse and a pattern of sexual promiscuity.

Therapy. Naturally, these students are uninterested in and/or opposed to therapy, although they may be willing to attend one or more sessions with a practitioner. We believe that there is some chance (though admittedly slim) of a successful therapeutic outcome, if the therapist can keep the student willing to return for additional conversations. As long as the student continues to meet with the therapist and talk about anything, there is the possibility that he or she may begin to care about the therapist and/or what the therapist thinks of him or her. The probability of such a turn of events is low, but it may improve significantly if the therapist can muster some genuine sentiment in favor of the student's long-range future. This is a big *if*, because (1) practitioners are usually subject to the human tendency to rate those persons who operate with a different philosophy as somehow or other inferior and, therefore, in need of "salvation," and (2) these same practitioners, like some of their clients, demand good results, in a hurry. If the practitioner can maintain some degree of objectivity with these very difficult customers, it may be possible to do some believable "doting" that encourages the student to return and pay attention. If the therapist succeeds in changing family attitudes and practices for the better (i.e., backing off so as to allow consequences in the real world to have their effect), the chances of improvement are sometimes greatly enhanced. We regret to say that we have not been very successful in this regard, and so our attitude is essentially pessimistic.

"To Do Well in School Would Betray the Relationships I Have with My Friends"

One might wonder why any student would join forces with a group of other students who are so devoted to the ideal of academic failure that they would ostracize the "achiever" in their midst. As far as we can tell, it is not the "anti-academic-achievement" ideal that attracts this type of underachiever. It is the general philosophy—a kind of "let it all hang out"—that has the appeal because it is the opposite of the dogma to which they have been subjected for so long. We believe that these students have been "turned off" and alienated by the policies and practices of their parents and are ready to be "turned on" by another set of principles, especially those that diverge from the family tradition.

Family. The parents of this group of underachievers tend to be very conservative, with much emphasis on the "proper" customs and on rigid adherence to conventional codes. These are the folks who live by the "shoulds," with no particular rhyme nor reason to be offered as explanation or rationale. They may represent a broad range of the socioeconomic spectrum, but most of the families we have seen were not particularly affluent. To what extent the "working-class" orientation sponsors these rather narrow and proprietary ideas is not clear to us. The parents' views seem to be supported by the company they keep, but there is very little evidence of their "closeness" to anyone. Our impression is that they operate by rule rather than by sentiment, thus making their social relations more "proper" than "friendly." In a word, they don't seem to have much fun, and as far as we can tell, they never did. We suspect these individuals, as children, were cowed by their parents into accepting arbitrary traditional ideals. Alternative views were considered dangerous, and there probably was some "gruesome evidence" presented in support of that attitude. Whatever may have been the origins of this philosophy, the influence it exerts on some students results in a kind of alienation; the recalcitrants see no common ground on which to share common concerns, and their perceptions may be on target. Not all children react negatively to such traditional-proprietary policies and practices. In many cases, only one of several children in the family rebels, the others apparently being content to abide by the rules as specified and enforced.

Students. These students seem to be the victims of a kind of blindness, in that they have stumbled into an allegiance to ideals that inhibit their own personal growth (i.e., developing skills and/or knowledge of some of the alternatives to their own point of view). Even more regrettable are those instances in which the student fails academically, so as to meet a group standard that does not exist (i.e., the other members of the group really don't mind if some one of them gets good grades!). The point of these observations is that the young people who fit our characterization of this category are not antiachievers. They are progroup individuals whose primary allegiance is to the other members, and beyond that, they may be very cordial and friendly in any context that is not threatening to the integrity of the group. They may be fiercely loyal to one another and may therefore go to great lengths to assist or "rescue" one of the friends.

Therapy. The first order of business in working with these students is to establish credibility as an impartial and reasonable adult, in the view of the student. Sometimes, this can be accomplished in short order, especially if the student is seen together with the parents. We recall numerous instances in which the student was visibly shocked to hear one adult (the therapist) question the wisdom of the parents' policy—to their faces! We hasten to underscore the word *question,* which we differentiate from *challenge* or *contradict.* We mean that we do question parents, literally, about their reasons for the rules they impose. And, as might be expected, they rarely have any better answer than "Well, that's the way our parents did it, and I think we turned out pretty well." If the therapist has his or her own children, there may be a lot of therapeutic mileage in certain personal disclosures (e.g., "I know. That's what I thought too. But I discovered, the hard way, that times have changed").

Once credibility has been established, we move on with the student to talk about the group: What do the members like to do? What problems do they have? And, most important, what benefits are perceived to be derived from membership in the group and interaction with the other members? Very early, we check the possibility that the group does not disapprove of academic achievement, and in cases where that is true, positive results are achieved almost automatically—as long as the therapist makes it clear that resuming homework activity does not represent a victory for the parents. In short, we believe that the idea that relationships with friends would be betrayed by schoolwork is destroyed with a single blow. In other cases, the group really does hold academic achievement in contempt, and so there may be some degree of real risk. In such a case, it becomes the task of the therapist to engage the student in cost accounting (i.e., "What will this allegiance and its immediate benefits cost, in the long run?"). If the therapist has been successful in establishing credibility as a caring, concerned person, there is a very good chance that the student will come around to a different and more constructive philosophy.

"It Is Demeaning, Dishonorable, and Destructive of My Personal Integrity to Cooperate with Authority in Any Way"

Clearly this is an antiauthority philosophy. Whether such a position is antisocial is another matter. The difference is semantic (i.e., the words may be defined differently and, in fact, are defined differently). We do not intend to enter the arena of debate about which of several definitions is best. We mention the distinction because it seems to us that some of the underachievers who hold this particular belief are more amenable to nonauthority influence than some other young people who hate, indiscriminately. These underachievers do not seem to harbor the same hostile attitudes toward everything and everybody with no particular reason. If our observations are correct, these antiauthority underachievers may be somewhat more accessible to therapeutic influence than would otherwise be the case.

Family. The families of this group of underachievers seem to have only one thing in common, namely, parental helplessness. We have seen families from practically all rungs of the socioeconomic ladder, families of all sizes, of all religious persuasions and ethnic backgrounds. This is not to say that certain backgrounds are not as likely to be involved as others; rather, it is to say that the pattern is not limited to any one or several groups. Again, the common feature is ineffectual parenting (i.e., a helplessness in enforcing any and all rules or policies that might be specified). Such a feature is different from the family that seems to be indifferent to what the children are doing and/or where they might be. Such indifference might seem like ineffectual parenting, and in some respects, it is. However, when the child of such "indifferent" parents behaves so as to annoy or inconvenience the parents, the consequences are swift and painful. There is little room for doubt or misinterpretation. Indifference and helplessness are different conditions, as far as our evaluation of family philosophies is concerned.

We believe the fact of parental helplessness serves to support the idea that "No one can make me do anything I don't want to do," which is another way of saying, "It is demeaning . . . to cooperate with authority." Naturally, we are very concerned about the capacities of these parents (i.e., their potential to strengthen their influence on the student), but the assessment of that potential is very tenuous. There are no reliable guidelines. When and if the practitioner has decided that parental potential is limited, it may be that clinical judgment is best served by calling on other resources (e.g., agents of the juvenile court) in order to stabilize a bad situation.

Student. Like those who believe that they do not have to tolerate any unpleasantness, these individuals go their own way, apart from any group affiliations. They seem to be extremely self-centered and uninterested in socializing in the usual ways. If they are involved with others, it tends to be coincidentally (i.e., they just happen to be in the same place at the same time, doing the same thing). They can be explosive in their refusal to accept regulation, and the practitioner is well advised to be alert to any signs of restiveness or irritation. These are signs that the student perceives regulation "coming down," whether it is or not, and because the perceptions of such students are frequently distorted (i.e., they "read in" regulation or constraint out of their own paranoid frame of reference), their behavior can be very unpredictable. In short, they are to be considered dangerous. We suspect that some of these individuals are psychotic or borderline psychotic, and so they may go off on a destructive tangent to demonstrate their ability to resist regulation and to demonstrate further that no one can do anything about it.

Therapy. Obviously, these students are difficult customers, and it goes without saying that the prospects of significant improvement are not good. As we indicated above, it is extremely important to form some impression regarding parental potential as soon as possible, because if that potential is limited or non-existent, then other forces may have to be mobilized. Of prime importance is preventing an outburst that will result in a penal sentence to be served in a reformatory or some other correctional institution that offers little or no remedial services. One way to prevent such an outcome is to persuade the parents to cooperate in a plan that involves an agent of the juvenile court (e.g., a probation officer), thus providing some leverage to induce the student to consult with the practitioner. If this can be arranged, it may be possible to convince the student that there may be some advantage in cooperating, if the therapist can stay clean of any taint of authority.

One of our most effective ploys (although we do not claim a high success rate) is to play the role of legal counsel (i.e., we are preparing a defense for the accused). If that role can be established, the door is opened slightly to the possibility of therapeutic influence. Thus, we might say, "Judge Jones? Oh shit, that mother fucker is impossible. Once he makes up his mind, nobody can change it. We'll have to work around him somehow." If the student goes for this, the cooperation that he or she has been refusing to give is a *fait accompli,* even though the student may not realize it at the time. Later on, it may be shown that cooperating was not so painful after all-certainly not demeaning—and this realization may open the door to further therapeutic work. We try to show these antiauthority underachievers that they are subject to the laws of nature (e.g., gravity) and that really isn't demeaning or disgraceful. Eventually, we hope to get them to see the difference between stupid, indiscriminate rebellion and determined self-interest. When this is accomplished, the outcome is very good. Unfortunately, the prospects of achieving that outcome are not very good.

"Nothing I Do at School Will Ever Benefit Me"

If these students were only saying, "Nothing I do at my present school will benefit me," they might be right. There is no question that some schools are so out of touch with the needs and interests of the families they serve that they have very little to offer the students. In such cases, our analysis of underachievement would still hold, but the detriment associated with the philosophical differences would be mainly due to flaws in the system rather than flaws in the student's belief system. Having noted this possibility, let us assume that the school is doing a fairly good job and that the student is still not performing well because of the belief that "Nothing I do at school will ever benefit me." This is the exception mentioned above (i.e., the one subset of underachievers who have no prior record of higher achievement). It seems that these youngsters enter the system expecting nothing and then are bewildered to find that some academic achievement is expected of them.

Family. When this condition exists, we expect to find certain attitudes and practices prevailing in the family group. As might be expected, we are talking about families that represent the lower socioeconomic levels. They tend to be large families and they have less of everything. There is less space, less money, and less of all the things that money can buy, (e.g., clothes, toys, and entertainment). Permeating the family mood and expectation is often an attitude of resignation that may be expressed in terms of "Yeah, I expect I'll be working in the mill someday" or "down in the mine." There is no hope of anything different, let alone better, that might provide the inspiration and energy to make a greater effort to achieve. These are not angry folks, simply resigned. They do sometimes take a kind of pride in their position at the bottom of the heap, and so they may become resentful of anything that smacks of "pushing them around." Otherwise, they clearly support the notion that school offers no benefit and that it is to be escaped from as soon as the law allows.

Student. These students are not so easily identified as the others we have been describing because they may do poorly from the very beginning. Furthermore, the level of environmental stimulation and enrichment in these homes is such that one would expect scholastic aptitude to be somewhat depressed. These children usually go unnoticed because it is assumed that they are doing as well as can be expected. It isn't until later, when they get into trouble of one kind or another, that the question of underachievement may arise. When it does, it may be that the practitioner suspects underachievement and after administering a standardized intelligence test notices a discrepancy between low verbal and high performance scores. This discrepancy would certainly justify some suspicion that the student is more intelligent than was previously believed and that this same student has been getting shortchanged all along.

Therapy. Obviously, conventional psychotherapy cannot be expected to have much impact on the belief that inhibits the motivation and energies of these students. To explain to them that there may be some benefit to be gained from hard work put forth in a different school situation is roughly equivalent to talking to a tree. What is needed is cooperative demonstration, including parents and school, tangible evidence that the school can provide useful information and training. This, of course, means counseling and/or educating parents to whatever extent they will allow. If they resist any and all such plans or programs, then it may be necessary to broaden the base of community education or, in some cases, to remove the child from the home and arrange placement in a better environment.

PREVENTION

We have argued elsewhere (Bard, 1980) that rational-emotive *therapy* proceeds with little or no study of the history of the person's presenting problem or how that problem originated. That is not to say that RET practitioners have no interest in learning more about the conditions and events that encourage the development of irrational beliefs and modes of thinking. Quite the contrary. Many RET practitioners are keenly interested in any new data or hypotheses that might lead to better prevention. In this regard, we believe that an ounce of prevention is worth years of human achievement that bring satisfaction, and so we wish to close with some comments and suggestions that may be of particular interest to those practitioners who hold positions of some influence within school systems (e.g., school psychologists). We do not share the despair of those who think that most school systems and programs have degenerated beyond all hope. We do believe that all systems probably could improve their programs and thus do a better job of preparing young people for whatever future they might choose for themselves. And so we submit the following:

First, there is the matter of objectives, which we consider vital to the success of any enterprise. It we are not clear about what we hope to accomplish with our curricula, classroom activities, homework, exams, and extracurricular programs, then we may have great difficulty determining how well we are doing, and we may, in fact, turn out to be "underachieving" ourselves. More important, do we and the students share the same objectives? If we do not share them, why not? The American system was founded in large part on the principle of home rule, and we adhere to that principle in education—to having local school systems run by members of the community who have been elected by the people of the community. To some extent, school board members are elected on the basis of the objectives they espouse. To what extent the children of voting citizens have any influence on parental decisions is another question, and the answer is probably "very slight"—except perhaps on very specific issues involving tax increases versus no football, etc. We urge that, whatever the particular decision-making procedure, students be involved in it. We believe that any participation by students in the formulation of objectives will tend to reduce the risk of incompatibility between student and system objectives, thus reducing the risk of underachievement. Developing computational skills seems to us to be a worthwhile objective, but we wonder if that objective seems as worthy to elementary-school students. We are not advocating that local school boards invite elementary children to discuss objectives (although, come to think about it, why not?) What we are recommending is that student input into the decision-making process be encouraged in whatever ways may be most realistic and appropriate—at all levels.

Second, we believe that it is possible to enhance the prospects of academic achievement as well as the general pursuit of happiness by incorporating the essential philosophical features of RET into classroom programs. This is sometimes referred to as rational-emotive education (REE), and the guidelines of such a plan have been systematically outlined elsewhere (Knaus, 1974, 1977). If children can learn to focus their attention and thinking on the reasons that they make the errors and how to improve, rather than focusing on how worthless they are for making the errors, their chances of success in the short and the long run may be enhanced greatly. That is the ultimate aim of the RET philosophy.

References

Arndt, J. R. Underachievement: A general overview. Recorded in *Educational Resources Information Center* (ERIC), ED 132 482; CG 010 957, 1971.
Bard, J. A. *Rational emotive therapy in practice.* Champaign, Ill.: Research Press, 1980.
Behrens, L. T., & Vernon, P. E. Personality correlates of overachievement and underachievement. *British Journal of Educational Psychology,* 1978, *48,* 290–297.
Ellis, A. The basic clinical theory of rational emotive therapy. In A. Ellis & R. Grieger (Eds.), *Handbook of rational emotive therapy.* New York: Springer, 1977.
Ellis, A., with S. Moseley & J. Wolfe. *How to raise an emotionally healthy happy child.* North Hollywood: Wilshire Books, 1966.
Engeberg, L. A., Hansen, G. A., Welker, R. L., & Thomas, D. R. Acquisition of keypecking via autoshaping as a function of prior experience. *Science,* 1972, *178,* 1002–1004.
Erikson, M. T. *Child Psychopathology.* Englewood Cliffs, N.J.: Prentice-Hall, 1978.
Goodstein, M. *The diagnosis and treatment of underachievement.* Paper presented at the B'Nai Brith Career and Counselling Services Staff Conference, 1979.
Hoefel, E. C. *The antiachieving adolescent.* Unpublished doctoral dissertation, Boston University, 1978.
Kisch, J. M. *A comparative study of patterns of underachieving male college students.* Unpublished doctoral dissertation, University of Michigan, 1967.
Knaus, W. J. *Rational emotive education: A manual for elementary teachers.* New York: Institute for Rational Living, 1974.
Knaus, W. J. Rational emotive education. In A. Ellis & R. Grieger (Eds.), *Handbook of rational emotive therapy.* New York: Springer, 1977.
Kowitz, G. T. An analysis of underachievement. In M. Kornrich (Ed.), *Underachievement.* Springfield, Ill.: Charles C Thomas, 1965.
Maier, S. F., & Seligman, M. E. P. Learned helplessness: Theory and evidence. *Journal of Experimental Psychology: General,* 1976, *105,* 3–46.
McLeod, J. Educational underachievement: Towards a defensible definition. *Journal of Learning Disabilities,* 1979, *12*(5), 327–330.
Peterson, J. The researcher and the underachiever: Never the twain shall meet. *Phi Delta Kappan,* 1963, *44,* 379–381.
Quay, H. Patterns of aggression, withdrawal and immaturity. In H. Quay & J. Werry (Eds.), *Psychopathological disorders of childhood.* New York: Wiley, 1972.
Quay, H., & Werry, J. (Eds.). *Psychopathological disorders of childhood* (2nd ed.). New York: Wiley, 1979.

Sherman, S., Zuckerman, D., & Sostek, A. Antiachiever: Rebel without a future. *School Counselor*, 1975, 22(5), 311–324.

Thorndike, R. L. *The Concepts of over and under-achievement.* New York: Columbia University, Teachers College, 1963.

Whyte, C. B. High risk college freshmen and locus of control. *Humanist Educator*, 1977, 16(1), 2–5.

8

Childhood Anxieties, Fears, and Phobias
A Cognitive-Behavioral-Psychosituational Approach

Russell M. Grieger and John D. Boyd

It is perhaps unfortunate that in the field of childhood psychopathology and psychotherapy the old models are no longer sufficient. In some ways, it was easy to view the referred child as "owning" a problem and then simply go about "fixing" it for him or her.

A good many recent developments, however, have shown this "child-oriented" approach to be woefully inadequate and, indeed, very often wrong. The development of systems models of family therapy; factor-analytic studies of aberrant childhood behavior in which the child's impact on the environment is integral to problem definition; the emergence of the behavioral and cognitive-behavioral movements in psychotherapy; and the legal advances *vis-à-vis* children's rights—these are just a few of the things that argue for a model of childhood pathology and therapy that incorporates the interplay between the child and his or her significant environment as coperpetrators of childhood clinical problems and their solution (Bersoff & Grieger, 1971; Grieger & Abidin, 1972; Mischel, 1968, 1973a,b; Peterson, 1968). Indeed, those who work clinically with children testify to the frustrations inherent in being limited only to direct work with a "disturbed" child.

Reflecting on these developments, this chapter describes a cogni-

---

Russell M. Grieger • Clinical Psychologist in Private Practice, and Institute of Clinical Psychology, University of Virginia, Charlottesville, Virginia 22903. John D. Boyd • Institute of Clinical Psychology, University of Virginia, Charlottesville, Virginia 22903.

tive-behavioral-psychosituational model (Bersoff & Grieger, 1971; Grieger and Abidin, 1972) for understanding and treating anxiety problems in children. It focuses on both the child and his or her significant others as "causes" of these problems and their cures. It first distinguishes among fears, anxieties, and phobias. Then, after describing the psychosituational model as it pertains to emotional and behavioral problems in general, it emphasizes the cognitive factors in creating children's anxiety problems in *both* the child *and* the child's significant others. The chapter then addresses methods and issues in cognitive-behavioral-psychosituational assessment and treatment of these types of problems, with a particular emphasis on cognitive change or restructuring.

Definition of the Problem

Fears have traditionally been differentiated from anxieties and phobias on the basis of objectivity. That is, if something can be objectively proved to be dangerous, such as a physically abusive parent or a live electrical wire, then the aversion to that object is considered reasonable and the reaction would be labeled a fear; on the other hand, if some object or situation is not objectively dangerous, and the person still responds fearfully, then the reaction is considered unreasonable and labeled an anxiety or a phobia.

Although this may be a reasonable distinction when applied to adults, it is a dubious one with children. Very simply, children often find it difficult to distinguish real from imaginary dangers because of their limited cognitive development, and hence, they respond anxiously to safe or neutral objects. Their thinking is characterized by animism (e.g., giving life to inanimate objects); egocentrism (e.g., confusing their own motivations and feelings with those of others); concreteness (or giving literal interpretations to experiences); and limitations in concepts of size, time, and distance. It is little wonder, then, that all children develop a certain number of unreasonable fears, often at particular ages (Kessler, 1966). Indeed, research shows that precocious intelligence accelerates the emergence and decline of age-related fears.

One way out of the definitional dilemma rests with the concepts of reactions and overreactions. The "normal" child reacts appropriately (i.e., within reasonable limits, although perhaps in a frightened manner) to both real and sometimes fictional dangers; the anxious or phobic child overreacts to real or fictional danger. That is, the disturbed child more frequently, habitually, and intensely reacts with apprehension for longer durations, and with more debilitating behavioral, social, and physical side effects, than the "normal" youngster of the same age and intelligence.

Thus, we might define fear, anxieties, and phobias as follows:

A *fear* is an apprehensive reaction to an external event or situation that is (1) objectively dangerous or (2) objectively safe but typically feared by a child of a given age and intelligence. The fear neither debilitates the child nor significantly interferes in his or her life. Therapeutic intervention in these instances, if necessary at all, would consist of reassuring the parents—and perhaps the child—that her or his fears are "normal."

A *phobia* is an apprehensive overreaction (including an obsessive avoidance) to some external event or situation that is neither developmentally appropriate nor objectively dangerous. It can also be an apprehensive overreaction to some external event that is truly aversive or dangerous. In both instances, there is a belief that because the event is dangerous, it is horrible to experience, and that one should be deathly afraid of it. With these beliefs, the response is marked by its abnormal intensity, duration, and frequency. Social phobias and phobias to specific objects like dogs are examples.

An *anxiety* is an apprehensive overreation to the possible consequences of some external event rather than to the event itself. For example, the child dreading taking a test is usually anxious about what will happen to him or her if the test is failed, such as being rejected by peers, feeling depressed, or being scolded by parents. Most typically, the dreaded consequence includes a strong, aversive feeling state (e.g., anxiety, depression, or feelings of worthlessness) that the youngster believes to be too horrible to experience. More is said about this subject later. In any event, the intensity, duration, and frequency again signify the anxiety. We may indeed offer reassurances in cases of phobia or anxiety, but it is generally agreed that some form of psychotherapeutic intervention is called for.

A COGNITIVE-BEHAVIORAL-PSYCHOSITUATIONAL MODEL OF CHILDHOOD PSYCHOPATHOLOGY

Before focusing on the cognitive distortions in children's anxieties and phobias, it is important to describe a general model of childhood psychopathology. The psychosituational model contrasts with a view that sees human behavior as resulting predominantly from the "press of basic needs or cardinal personality structures" (Wallace, 1966, p. 123). In this view, behavior is seen to occur independently of the situations in

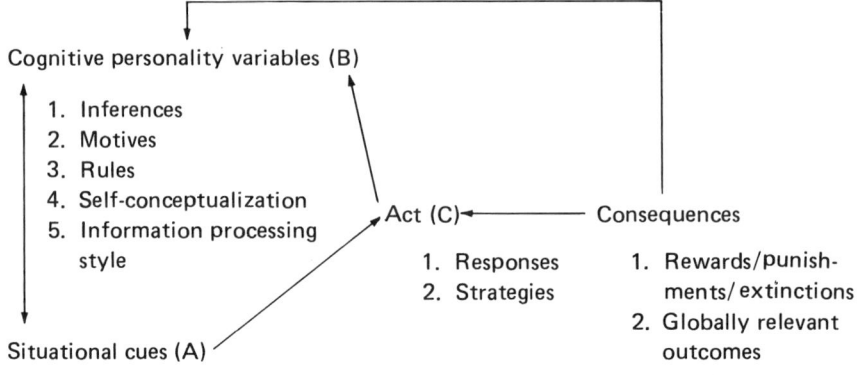

FIGURE 1. A schematic representation of a psychosituational model of behavior and psychopathology.

which the person operates, so that the stimulus for action is primarily self-generated. Behavioral or emotional disorders develop and reside within the child, and the thrust is to "fix" him or her.

The psychosituational model is consistent with both social learning theory (Bandura & Walters, 1963; Mischel, 1968, 1973a,b; Rotter, 1954) and cognitive-behavioral therapy (Beck, 1976; Beck, Rush, Shaw, & Emery, 1979; Ellis, 1962, 1971, 1973; Meichenbaum, 1977) in regarding "personality as sets of abilities . . . which, with regard to acquisition, maintenance, and modification share much in common with other abilities" (Wallace, 1966, p. 132). Rather than assuming that human behavior results solely from internal traits destined to emerge, this model believes that a person's response patterns develop and are maintained through the interplay of situational presses and developing internal capabilities. In effect, this viewpoint eschews a conception of human motivations as unidirectional and holds a basic premise taught to all beginning psychology students: Behavior (and deviant behavior) is a function of the interaction between personality and environment.

The psychosituational model of childhood behavior is illustrated in Figure 1.[1] The center of the model is an *act* (or the C of rational-emotive therapy's ABC theory). *Act* is broadly defined as referring both to a simple response to some internal or external stimuli (e.g., hitting another child or leaving one's desk) and to more complex behavioral strategies that are purposeful (i.e., motivated by personal values and by

---

[1]The model is developed from Peterson (1968).

situational appraisals) and multifaceted (i.e., containing emotional, behavioral, and attitudinal components).

Within this model, acts are seen to be influenced by three variables, the first two of which recognize the power of the child's significant others, particularly the parents, in motivating actions. The first of these variables, the *consequences* following a child's behavior, acknowledges the empirical law of effect. As Carson (1969, p. 68) noted, "With few exceptions, behavior tends in the direction of maximizing pleasure and minimizing displeasure." So, what others *do* to encourage or discourage, teach or suppress, is exceptionally important in forming children's response and strategy patterns. We hasten to caution the reader, however, against a reductionistic conceptualization of consequences. Although it is true that youngsters' actions are shaped directly by immediate and single rewards an punishments, it is also true that children observe the consequences of their actions, come to value some and disvalue others, learn to make predictions about the probability of their delivery, and adopt attitudes about themselves and their parents through the process. They therefore come to instrumentally plan and strategize, based on their experiences, to obtain complex, global, hedonically relevant outcomes (e.g., love, power, and recognition) and to avoid other, more aversive ones (e.g., rejection and pain). Through both simple and complex action–consequence sequences, both action patterns and various personality traits develop.

One more note about consequences. The consequences that parents provide are in part stimulated by the child's actions, but equally powerful are the various attitudes and feelings that the parents hold about themselves, their children, and child rearing in general. This subject is addressed more fully in the next section, where the irrational attitudes of parents that prompt anxiety problems in children are detailed.

The second parental ingredient influencing acts is the immediate *situational cue* (or the A in the ABC theory). Again, rather than taking a mechanistic view, the authors agree with Rotter (1954), Mischel (1968, 1973a,b), Kelly (1955), and others in holding that the most relevant unit of study is the interaction of the child and his or her meaningful environment. That is, out of the array of situational cues, the individual will most likely select and attend to those that are most meaningful. In particular, the presence or absence of significant others, along with the personal and task rules they impose, and the child's inferences about their motivations, demands, and affections for the child, will be most relevant.

By far the most significant influence on children's actions are the *personality variables* learned over time through experience in the child's consequential world and carried from situation to situation. They are defined cognitively (the B's of the ABC theory) and serve to flavor perceptions of and inferences about situational cues; they may also influence predictions about the consequences of actions and affect the child's personal experience of the consequences of her or his actions. They include at least the following:

1. *Inferences* are either some specific, situationally relevant perceptions or more habitual patterns of expectations, predictions, or conclusions (e.g., "No one likes me"). Inferences can be drawn about virtually anything, but they frequently fall into three categories: (a) stimulus–outcome inferences, in which a prediction is made about the likelihood of something's occurring if some other event occurs (Mischel, 1973b); (b) behavior-outcome inferences, in which a prediction is made about the likelihood of some consequence if a particular action is taken (Mischel, 1973b); and (c) locus-of-control inferences, in which outcomes are consistently attributed to one's personal power or to chance (Rotter, 1954). The more stable the expectations, the more predictable is the youngster's behavior.

2. *Motives* in the broadest sense refer to "an internal stimulus which is effective in the initiation of behavior" (Peterson, 1968, p. 70). Rather than viewing motives as "senseless" drives, however, the psychosituational model interprets motives in terms of cognitively held values. That is, children learn to value positively certain outcomes or circumstances and to value negatively certain others; and, all things being equal, they tend to act to acquire the positive and to avoid the negative states of affairs, often after an *assessment* of the current situation and with a *prediction* of outcome. Children often "awfulize" themselves into emotional distress by exaggerating the negative values during their assessment and prediction, and when this becomes characterological, it is called *low frustration tolerance*.

3. *Rules* are guidelines for correct behavior for oneself, for others, and for the correct ordering of the conditions of the world. Rules may be defined in terms of guidelines or preferences, and they lead the child to act reasonably in the appropriate direction; or they may be cast in absolute, all-or-none ways when held as absolutes (I should . . . ; you should . . .; the world should . . .). Rational-emotive therapists refer to these latter rules as "irrational demands," which prompt the child to act desperately; they constitute the nucleus of most neurotic conditions.

4. *Self-conceptualizations* are the evaluative ideas that the child holds about herself or himself. Self-conceptualizations are learned and may be

of a rating or an accepting kind. A self-rating view generally uses external criteria (usually success in some act or skill, or approval by another) to rate oneself as either good or bad; a self-acceptance view makes no generalization about the goodness or badness of the self at all and assumes either that the self is innately worthy or realizes that such a rating is simply an impossible chore. Most children are taught a self-rating view; that is, they learn to demand certain things of themselves and thereby act to succeed in those things; they then rate themselves as either good or bad, depending on their perception of their success in this endeavor. The criteria they hold to determine their self-rating is highly motivating, as is the general goal of viewing oneself as good.

5. The *information-processing style* is the child's typical manner of processing information. Distorted styles include selective attending to certain data while ignoring others; arbitrarily drawing conclusions without sufficient evidence; unjustifiably overgeneralizing from one circumstance to another; magnifying the significance of something beyond its true importance; and thinking in all-or-none, black-and-white terms (Beck, 1976). Processing information via these styles leads the child to ignore relevant information from the environment, to draw false conclusions, to overreact falsely to events, and the like. The rub is that young children developmentally think in these ways.

Psychopathology

To sum, the cognitive-behavioral-psychosituational model conceptualizes children's actions as resulting from the interplay of both situational variables (most notably the cues and consequences from significant others as generated in large part by their own attitudes and beliefs) *and* personality factors (particularly cognitive variables). With regard to reported or suspected child pathology, this model refuses to make an *a priori* judgment that a referred child is the sole owner or even the central figure in a problem. Instead, it takes the position that a child can be disturbed only in the context of a disturbed situation. It therefore advocates a systematic exploration of all elements of the problem situation. In the last analysis, the child may indeed "own" a behavioral or emotional problem; or she or he may have a problem that coexists with and may even result from problems that others in the situation "own"; or the child may be totally free of problems whereas one or several other situational elements have a problem; or no problem may actually exist except for the referring adult's faulty perception that there is one.

Beyond these generalities, where might emotional and/or behavioral problems arise in the child or in his or her psychosituational world? For one thing, the child may act inappropriately because he or she is deficient in an ability to receive, perceive, organize, or appreciate the relevance of information and behavior in certain situations. Indeed, the abnormality of many children lies in the fact that they do not have the skills to comprehend, know, or do what is expected. For another, the child may act inappropriately (i.e., overreact emotionally and/or behaviorally) because he or she has learned from the consequential environment that such behavior will pay off. That is, the child's inappropriate actions may have been learned and maintained because of an accurate expectation that it will lead to some valued consequence or avoid some aversive consequence. And finally, the child may act inappropriately (i.e., overreact) because of the acquisition of faulty inferences, rules, self-evaluations, and cognitive process styles that directly prompt the actions and that constitute a problem in and of themselves.

As for the situation itself, the significant others in the situation (e.g., the parents or teachers) may themselves act to provide cues and consequences for the child that directly "create" inappropriate actions in the child. These responses may be due to ignorance, to faulty expectations about what are appropriate child actions, or to irrational ideas about themselves and the child. Finally, the task demands and/or role demands of a particular situation (e.g., a third-grade class) may be so totally out of line in terms of what is reasonable or may be so conflicting and confusing that appropriate actions on the child's part may be impossible.

Cognitive Distortions in Children's Anxiety Problems

The relationship between anxiety problems and cognitions is basically the same in children and in adults. Like adults, children develop and maintain anxieties and phobias when they draw inferences and/or hold attitudes that logically lead to these emotional and related behavioral states.

Yet children, typically with limited logical thinking powers, are extremely vulnerable to faulty thinking in response to both the sensible and the not-so-sensible actions of their parents and other significant adults. Therefore, it behooves us to examine the cognitive distortions in children, or the personality variables of the psychosituational model, that constitute anxiety problems, but it is also important to examine those ideas and behaviors of parents that make it easy for children to adopt and maintain their anxiety-evoking ideation.

Cognitive Distortions in Parents

Faulty Inferences about Child Behavior

A growing body of literature indicates that children referred for psychological care are members of a highly select group (Ross, 1974). They are select in that what prompts their parents to seek treatment for them are behaviors that are often highly prevalent in unselected samples of children (Connors, 1970; LaPouse & Monk, 1972; Miller, 1967a,b; Miller, Hempe, Barrett, & Noble, 1971; Werry & Quay, 1971).

In this regard, Ross (1974) has raised a number of interesting questions about the validity of the judgments, if not the motivations, of the significant people in the child's psychosituational world. Why are some children referred and others with the same behaviors not? When is a child's "problem" a problem? When is a problem attributed to the child really an adult's problem? In many cases, it is a powerful adult (a teacher or parent) who arbitrarily determines whether a child's actions are deemed a problem. The fact may be, however, that the actual problem may reside not in the child but in the adult's eyes.

Two major cognitive distortions often prompt parents (and sometimes teachers) to mistakenly view a child as having a problem. One is ignorance; that is, parents often mistake fairly appropriate child behavior for a problem. They do this because they know no better or have simply learned faulty expectations. They may then respond with some formal action (i.e., a referral) and/or react to the child as if there is indeed a problem, perhaps prompting the child to hold a similar idea.

A more serious psychosituational problem exists when parents hold cognitive distortions that constitute low frustration tolerance *vis-à-vis* their children (Ellis, 1978, 1982). Low frustration tolerance is characterized by people's holding the irrational ideas that others or outside events can and do upset them; that it is horrible, awful, or terrible when things go wrong or hassles arise; and that it is catastrophic to be frustrated. Holding these attitudes, the parents then easily upset themselves about the disturbed and not-so-disturbed behavior of their child (Ellis, Wolfe, & Moseley, 1966; DiGiuseppe, 1981; Ross, 1974); they easily label their child's behavior as disturbed and act accordingly. If they are overreacting to fairly appropriate child behavior, then it is solely the parents who own a problem, one that would be best treated quickly and thoroughly before they become the source of a problem in their child. If they are overreacting to a problem that the child truly owns, then two problems exist, one of the child's and one of the parents. In either case, the danger is that the child will label himself or herself as having a problem and/or will develop anxiety problems or other emotional problems about all this.

Disturbed Parenting Styles

Probably the most important time to include parents in treatment is when they are themselves disturbed and behave in ways that create, maintain, or exacerbate emotional-behavioral problems in their children. It is when they hold inappropriate expectations for their child and/or hold irrational attitudes themselves that debilitating parental practices flourish.

Although there is a vast variety of parenting behavior, the following six faulty parenting styles seem to be most closely associated with the development of childhood anxiety problems.

The criticism trap (Becker, 1971) is the most frequently found pattern of poor parenting. Associated with fears of failure and disapproval, anxious withdrawal, low self-esteem, and a whole host of related childhood-anxiety difficulties, it is a style characterized by a high frequency of subtle and not-so-subtle criticizing behaviors: nagging, correcting, moralizing, reminding, blaming, and even ridiculing and directly putting down the child. The key to this style is that the parents, rather than noticing desirable behaviors and acknowledging them, catch the child being bad and then respond in one or more of the ways mentioned above.

The parents who fall into this trap are usually fairly angry, demanding, and punitive people in general. They typically hold one or more of the following irrational attitudes: (1) children *should* always and unequivocally do well (e.g., be motivated and achieve) and behave correctly (e.g., be kind, considerate, and interested); (2) parents *are* always correct, or at least the authority in a situation, and therefore children *must* never question or disagree with them; (3) it is *horrible, terrible,* and *awful* when children do not do well, misbehave, or question or disobey their parents; (4) doing bad things *must* be punished because punishment, blame, and guilt are effective methods of child management; (5) because a child should do well, praise and rewards are unnecessary and spoil the child; and (6) a child and her or his behavior are the same, and thus children who act badly or err *are bad* (Hauck, 1967; Grieger & Boyd, 1982).

The perfectionism trap is also highly associated with childhood anxiety problems. Typically very demanding of themselves, parents who fall into this trap also act out their demandingness on their children. As with themselves, they take the attitude that the child *must* do well and succeed in most endeavors, and they hold that the child's value or worth, as well as their own, is dependent on superb performance. As a consequence, they habitually criticize and even reject the child for doing poorly, become angry at the child for less than sterling performance, and regularly let the child know that even good effects could have been better. They are relentless in the pressure they place on the child, and they communicate that the child is valuable and loved only if she or he does well.

Not surprisingly, it is easy for children who are exposed to the perfectionism trap to adopt the perfectionistic attitudes for themselves. In the process, they learn to fear disapproval and even abandonment if they do not do well; to become very anxious in the face of performance tasks like homework, tests, or athletic competition; and to illogically equate their self-worth with doing well and getting approval. As a dramatic example, the senior author once had a highly anxious sixth-grader tell him that he most feared being "orphaned" by his dad if he did not do well in school. Emotionally and behaviorally, anxiously perfectionistic children either strive mightily to succeed (and are anxious all the time) or they phobically tend to withdraw and avoid risks.

In the *scared-rabbit trap,* the parent is highly afraid of his or her own shadow. He or she chronically models both timid behaviors and fearful attitudes, including the attitudes that (1) dangers abound *everywhere,* and one *must* be constantly on the alert lest something harmful take one by surprise; (2) if something is painful or frustrating, it *must* be avoided at all costs; (3) bad things that happen are *awful, horrible,* and *terrible;* (4) one *cannot stand it* if something bad or painful happens; (5) one *has to get upset* when things go wrong; and (6) one *must* have a guarantee that things will go well or else one cannot survive. Clearly, the child who observes these attitudes and endorses them will likewise be fearful, timid, overcautious, and compulsively safety-seeking.

The *false positive* and the *guilt traps* most often lead to the egocentric, selfish, spoiled child with low frustration tolerance. Yet, these parental styles sometimes contribute to anxiety problems in children as well. For when the child leaves the protective and indulgent world of the parent, she or he often encounters unexpected responses of others of which she or he has had little experience; other children reject, punish, and in general turn her or his expectations upside down. At these times, it is difficult for the child to predict how to act, and the child begins to awfulize about the consequences of wrong actions and to doubt her or his self-worth. In both these faulty parenting styles, the parents lavish a great deal of positive affection on the child, but excessively and indiscriminately. The youngster receives praise not only for appropriate behavior, but for inappropriate acts as well; and the parents attempt to remove all frustrations from his or her life. Although often couched in a great deal of love, these two parental styles are often motivated by rather neurotic attitudes: (1) "It is *awful* for my child to suffer, and I *must* therefore prevent it at all costs"; (2) "I *must* always do right by my child"; (3) "I *must* always be loved and approved of by my child"; and (4) "My *self-worth* is tied to how I do as a parent, so I had better not make mistakes." The result is that the child has few if any limits and can easily conclude that anything and everything he or she does is OK.

A final disturbed parenting style might be called the *inconsistency trap*. In one variation of this tyle, parents essentially have no consistent way of dealing with the child, haphazardly rewarding and punishing the child by whim or mood. A second variation is strongly criticizing the child for errors while setting no rules or guidelines. Either way, the typical cognitive distortions include the following: (1) "Whatever feels right is right"; and (2) "I'm too weak and helpless to know what is the right thing to do, so I'll leave it up to the moment." The result is that the child has no predictability or certainty, not knowing how to act or exactly what the consequences of his or her actions will be. Punishment, disapproval, and even catastrophe are ever-present possibilities.

Cognitive Distortions in Children

Clearly, parental attitudes and actions are significant in the genesis of childhood anxiety problems. Yet, children develop anxiety problems only when the cognitive dimensions of personality described earlier become illogical, distorted, or exaggerated. The cognitive-behavioral-psychosituational model, following Beck (1976) and Ellis (1962, 1971, 1973, 1982), recognizes that children, like adults, make two types of cognitive errors that cause themselves to be fearful, anxious, or phobic: (1) errors of inference about what has occurred or will occur and (2) errors of evaluation (i.e., irrational attitudes, ideas, or beliefs) about what has occurred or will occur. Although either type of error may occur alone and cause anxiety problems, it is probable that a child who has anxiety problems has both in his or her thinking.

Errors of Inference

Inferential errors are predictions or conclusions that falsely represent reality (DiGiuseppe, 1981). A child who consistently distorts reality probably does so through one or more of several illogical processes such as arbitrary inferencing, overgeneralizing, selectively abstracting, minimizing, and maximizing about what they experience (Beck, 1976).

A case in point is the highly school-anxious sixth-grader mentioned above. He found it virtually impossible to remain calm when taking tests, sitting through classes in which there was a chance he might be called on to respond, or even doing schoolwork at home. He gauged his anxiety as rising to an 8 or 9 on a scale of 1–10 at these times. When asked to tell what went through his head, he said he thought or predicted that, if he failed or did poorly, his parents would "orphan" him and his friends would reject him. Of course, he also engaged in evaluative errors (e.g., it would be *terrible* for his friends to reject him), but his inferences made his academic enterprises apocalyptic and fed into the evaluative errors (discussed below).

The important elements in most children's lives include the home, the school, friends and play, and their abilities and skills. The cognitive-behavioral-psychosituational clinician would do well to be alert for evidence of erroneous inferences that youngsters might draw about these arenas when it comes to anxiety problems, particularly predictions about loss of love and approval, abandonment, rejection, harm, and incompetence.

Errors of Evaluation

The cataloging of evaluative errors or irrational attitudes in children's anxiety disorders has, to date, been sparse and is limited to only two attempts. Years ago Ellis *et al.* (1966) distinguished between children's fears of external things and fear of their own inadequacy. Shortly thereafter, Hauck (1967) discussed separately fears of people, fears of failure, fears of injury, and fears of rejection and ridicule.

More recently, Ellis (1982) has outlined two kinds of anxieties, each of which is prompted by its own set of cognitive distortions. In our experience, they are both relevant to understanding children's anxiety disorders. *Ego anxiety*, as its name implies, is "anxiety about one's self, one's being, one's essence" (Ellis, 1982, p. 25). It results from a child's holding the belief that she or he must do well and be approved for doing well, or else she or he is a bad and unworthy person whom no one could ever care for again. With so much at stake (i.e., one's value and lovability), anxiety is a highly predictable outcome.

A good many typical childhood emotional and behavioral problems can be easily understood as manifestations of ego anxiety. Most of the more prominent ones are presented in Table 1.

TABLE 1. Ego Anxiety Problems of Childhood

Anxiety problem	Accompanying manifestations		Typical irrational ideas
	Behavioral	Emotional	
Avoidance/withdrawal from people	Shrinking from peers and strangers Dependency on family Labored communication Timidity Lack of assertion	Generalized anxiety Self-doubt Feelings of inferiority Depression (secondarily)	"I must do well and be lovable in all respects or I will be rejected." "Others not liking me makes me nothing." "If I do not do well and/or if I am not lovable, then I will be worthless. I must therefore avoid trying and getting noticed at all costs." "As long as I can be left alone, and nothing is demanded of me, my worthlessness will not be obvious, and I won't feel worthless."
Attention seeking	Model child—cute, charming Class clown—show-off, pest Apparently shy, helpless child	Anxiety Self-doubt Feelings of insecurity Sense of pleasure when efforts pay off	"I must be noticed at all costs or else I am lost and worthless." "I must be loved and approved at all times or else I am worthless."

Avoidance/withdrawal from tasks	Expressions of concern about competence and/or difficulty of task Complaints about physical ailments Passive in classroom—never volunteers Homework undone or sloppily done Procrastination	Generalized anxiety Worries about impending deadlines Feelings of inferiority Self-doubt	"I must do well and be approved for doing well or else I will be a terrible person whom no one could love." "Since I will be proved to be worthless for doing poorly, it is better to try nothing at all." "As long as I try nothing, my worthlessness will not be obvious and I won't feel worthless." "If others saw my inadequacies, they would reject me, and that would make me worthless."
Perfectionism	Compulsive Overachieving Overdriven	Sense of pleasure when succeeds Generalized anxiety Heightened anxiety before performance Depression, guilt, self-downing when fails Worries about deadlines Obsessional self-doubt	"I must do well or else I will be rejected, lost, and worthless." "I must always do my best." "My performance at school and everywhere else must always be competent." "If I don't totally and always do well, then I am totally and always a failure."

In *discomfort anxiety*, the child may or may not begin a cognitive distortion with a faulty inference, such as, "Because the neighbor kid was pushed down on the school playground, I'll be hurt if I go to school." Regardless, discomfort anxiety always has a number of irrational evaluations at its core. The philosophical set is that it is *horrible, terrible,* and *awful* when things go wrong or when something difficult or dangerous is confronted (Grieger & Boyd, 1979). The child who makes a faulty inference but does not have discomfort anxiety will be afraid; the child with only discomfort anxiety will be highly fearful; and children with both are usually terrified of many things, and their terror prompts them to continually create more faulty inferences and irrational evaluations.

The catastrophizing of discomfort anxiety comes from the following kinds of attitudes: "I *cannot stand* troublesome events or emotional and physical pain; I *must* be certain that nothing bad will ever happen to me; I *must* be able to protect myself totally from dangerous or obnoxious conditions; I *cannot stand* to feel distress; if something is difficult, I *must* be terribly upset by it." In a nutshell, children with discomfort anxiety feel that their comfort is threatened and that it's *awful* to feel discomfort. Moreover, they grandiosely and demandingly believe that they *should* always get what they want, easily and quickly, and *should* never get what they don't want (Ellis, 1979, 1982).

The diagnosis of discomfort anxiety is difficult because the disorder is so easily disguised and overshadowed by other forms of irrational distortion (e.g., ego anxiety); likewise, other disturbing emotions may underlie discomfort anxiety. Four diagnostic guidelines are therefore offered here to help the clinician identify discomfort anxiety:

1. Children often make a faulty inference or receive incorrect information that leads them to expect discomfort in an upcoming situation; then they awfulize about the anticipated discomfort and create discomfort anxiety. Look for these inferences and faulty premises.

2. Unwanted and discomforting situations and tasks are a realistic part of life, but youngsters (particularly pampered and sheltered children) are known for exaggerating the pain involved, thereby creating a primary problem of discomfort anxiety. It is well to remember that low frustration tolerance is endemic to children, and that a child can become very anxious about what seems to be an ordinary responsibility.

3. Through various irrational thought processes, children can create ego anxiety, anger, depression, and other forms of emotional distress, and these unpleasantnesses then become the antecedents of secondary discomfort anxiety. Children are frequently afraid of the pain of their own distressful emotions.

4. Discomfort anxiety easily leads to other forms of emotional disturbance. Children can angrily damn others and the world for causing their discomfort, can pity themselves into dysphoria, or can adopt a hopeless and helpless attitude of depression. These emotions can mask a primary problem of discomfort anxiety.

Many childhood anxiety disorders have discomfort anxiety as the primary or secondary dynamic, and in Table 2, some of these are presented. When reading this table, it is important to remember that the philosophy and attitudes of discomfort anxiety are rarely articulated in consciously, and that an infinite variety of derivatives are possible. Though covert, this kind of ideation is, however, a driving mediational force that produces phobias, obsessions, compulsions, and various forms of anxiety-induced symptoms.

Cognitive-Behavioral-Psychosituational Assessment

The cognitive-behavioral-psychosituational (CBP) model emphasizes the interactive nature of the person (child) and the environment (particularly the parents) in the genesis and maintenance of anxiety problems. That is, individuals bring their own phenomenological perspective (i.e., patterns of thinking and behaving) to other family members and thereby play the major role in their own emotional and behavioral dysfunctioning; yet, children are tremendously vulnerable to the actions of their significant others and thus highly susceptible to the irrational thinking and behaving of those significant others.

Within the framework of the CBP model, then, it is crucial to sort out problem ownership, determining to what extent the child's problems really belong to the child (i.e., come from his or her aberrant actions) and to what extent the child's problems really belong to or are caused by the behaviors, feelings, perceptions, and attitudes of the parents.

In dealing with children's anxiety problems, we strongly recommend starting with a cognitive-behavioral-psychosituational assessment strategy (Bersoff & Grieger, 1971; Grieger & Abidin, 1972). The overall structure of this strategy focuses the clinician on the total psychosituational picture, not just on the referred child, and pays special attention to the mutual influences of both the parents and the child. It includes a detailed analysis of the child's alleged problem behaviors, including his or her feelings and attitudes, as elicited and maintained by the behaviors and attitudes of the relevant people in his or her life. It is comprised of three steps.

TABLE 2. Discomfort Anxiety Problems of Childhood

Anxiety problem	Accompanying manifestations			Typical irrational ideas
	Behavioral	Emotional		
School phobia	Refusal to attend school Avoidance of children who attend school Clinging to mother	Acute anxiety in the morning Nightmares and/or insomnia Psychosomatic symptoms Secondary ego anxiety, anger, depression		"Because a neighbor child got hurt at school, it means I will get hurt if I go. I might even be killed!" and/or "Bad things might happen at school and I couldn't stand that. I must have protection." "I must never leave Mother and the comfort and security of home; it would be horrible to give them up even for a few hours; I couldn't survive." "Because I'm nervous, I'll make mistakes and the other children will not like me; this will show that I'm no good." "My feelings of anxiety are horrible, and they will increase if I go to school; I'll completely fall apart and look foolish." "They shouldn't make me do what I don't want to; they deserve to be punished."
Procrastination on schoolwork and home chores	Forgetfulness Avoids contact with requesting adults Feigns ignorance, ineptitude Dawdles, daydreams, incomplete work	Diffuse anxiety Insecurity, inferiority Tiredness, laziness Psychosomatic symptoms Secondary anger Guilt about procrastination Anxiety about adults' disapproval		"Life should be easy and comfortable, and I should get everything I want and nothing I don't want." "When life is not this way, it's horrible, awful. I can't stand the pain and fatigue of doing what I don't want to do." "Because doing what I can't stand is so horrible, I must find ways to put it off. Somehow, maybe it will go away if I avoid it." "Difficult tasks are impossible; work should be easy."

Disorder	Behaviors/Symptoms	Beliefs/Self-Statements
		"I can't do difficult things. I'll fail if I try and show how inept and worthless I am." "They should not make me do these painful things. They are awful people." "I am a bad person for not doing what I was told to do."
Obsessive worrying about an event or activity	Preoccupied with preparations Lack of spontaneity, too serious Intrusive thoughts Irritable behavior Continual tension and anxiety Nausea and other psychosomatic symptoms Absence of laughter, controlled affect Acute anxiety before target event Secondary anger	"This event may be terribly horrible and aversive, so painful it's beyond description." "I can't stand aversion and pain; it's more than I can bear." "I shouldn't have to bear discomfort; I am entitled to a happy life without discomfort." "I must be absolutely sure nothing will happen to cause me discomfort. I must use all my energies to plan and avoid potential pain. I must not relax until the danger is over." "People who cause me discomfort are bad and I hate them." "The world is rotten because it put me in this spot."
Childhood obesity	Continuous eating Timid, nonassertive Overweight Lethargic Socially withdrawn Sedentary activities Affectively constricted Insecure Low self-esteem Nervous most of the time Sometimes is irritable and has anger outbursts Shame over appearance Guilt about eating habits	"I must have the approval of others and do well in my performances; otherwise, I'm a worthless nothing" (ego anxiety problem). "I can't stand the discomfort of anxiety, loneliness, and boredom; it is too painful, and it reminds me of how worthless and miserable I am." "I must have food to make me feel better; I need it to be less miserable." "Because of my fatness and eating, I am a slob. I should be a better person than I am, but there's nothing I can do. I can't stop eating." "Others have it easy and that's not fair. They shouldn't be happy if I can't be, damn them."

Step 1: Cognitive-Behavioral-Psychosituational Parent Interview. The goals of this initial step are several: (1) to gather relevant information about the child, his or her problem, and the parents' perception of his or her problem; (2) to gather information about the role that the parents play in creating and/or maintaining the "problem"; (3) to ferret out perceptual distortions, irrational attitudes, and maladaptive behaviors in the parents; and (4) to begin to educate the parents to a psychosituational and cognitive definition of the problem and its eventual alleviation. The parent interview includes the following aspects, all of which have a significant cognitive focus:

1. An explicit, behavioral detailing of the parents' concerns or complaints about the child, including their frequency, intensity, and duration. This serves to reconstruct vague, interpretive, and/or blaming perceptions with objective units that lend themselves to problem solving, to perception checking about their "awfulness," and to the diffusion of overt or covert anger and hostility.

2. An explication of the specific situations or circumstances in which the "problem" behavior occurs. Particularly open to inquiry here are the expectations or rules (i.e., "shoulds") that the parents have about the child's behavior in these situations.

3. An identification of the immediate consequences following the child's behavior, including specifically what the parents think, feel, and do when the child behaves as she or he does at these times. The interview is particularly attentive at this point to the attitudes and behaviors that may serve to promote inappropriate and inhibit appropriate child behavior; concurrently, the interviewer is on the alert for evidences of the faulty parenting styles described previously as they impact on the child in relation to the "problem" behavior and in a more general sense.

4. A definition of goals for the child, again stated as explicitly and behaviorally as possible. This helps the interviewer to set appropriate goals; equally important, it provides another opportunity for both the clinician and the parents to reflect on the appropriateness of the expectations for the child and the rules or demands in the parents' cognitive schema.

5. An exploration of the more general, ongoing patterns of interaction between the parents and the child, including the perceived ratio of positive to negative interactions, the kind and quality of both positive and negative interactions, the methods and frequency of punishments, and the kind and quality of communication.

Step 2: Cognitive-Behavioral-Psychosituational Child Interview. The theoretical framework for interviewing the child is the same as that for parents. That is, acts are seen as resulting from the interaction of the child with his or her significant environment. Within the psychosituational framework, an attempt is therefore made to assess the child's personality variables, and also the elements of his or her perceived prior and consequential environment. As with the parents, this interview step has several components:

1. An explication of who the practitioner is (e.g., a psychologist), what she or he does (e.g., "My job is to teach people to get along better and be happy. . ."), and what information she or he already has. We cannot agree too much with DiGiuseppe (1981) in emphasizing how helpful such an open approach is in fostering communication that is honest, direct, and nondefensive. At the same time, it leads naturally to the rest of the interview content.

2. A detailing of the child's perception of the problems. The child may indeed perceive the problem exactly as the parents do; yet, she or he might see the parents as "owning" the problem. Nevertheless, the interviewer takes each concern of the parents in turn and determines how the child views it. Not to be overlooked are complaints that the child has about the parents as well.

3. An explication of the specific situations in which the "problem" behaviors take place. What we have found particularly helpful at this point is to ask the child what she or he thinks causes the problem behavior to occur. This question not only serves to elicit beliefs about problem ownership but also often serves to reveal blaming or angry attitudes in the child, as well as the child's perception of the motivations, feelings, and attitudes of the parents toward him or her. Such a question might be answered with something like "My dad just doesn't like me." Follow-up questions like "What does he do to lead you to think this?" give details about the consequences that the child receives from the parents and may indeed prompt some cognitive restructuring as well.

4. A determination of the situational consequences of his or her action as perceived by the child. What exactly do the parents do when he or she misbehaves? How does he or she think the parents feel when they respond in these ways? What are their attitudes? Again, the answers reveal significant information about what the child experiences as a consequence of his or her actions, and they also serve as a check on the accuracy of the parents' reports about what they do at these times.

5. A functional cognitive analysis of the thoughts, attitudes or evaluations, and logical processes that the child goes through when acting in the identified ways. What are his or her thoughts? Does he or she awfulize or catastrophize when the parents criticize? What are the opinions that he or she holds about the self—are they accepting or rating-oriented? Are there coping statements in stressful or provoking situations, or is there an absence of these? In general, an attempt is made to ascertain the B's that the child has when confronted with stimulating situations, when acting, and when receiving parental consequences.

6. Finally, an articulation by the child of her or his goals. As before, the interviewer notes whether the goals are realistic and whether they are aimed at the child, the parent, or both. The interviewer can often act directly as a change agent at this point by helping the child to formulate realistic goals for himself or herself and others.

Step 3: Psychodiagnosis and Goal Setting. The verbal or written description of the results of the assessment procedure is called a *psychodiagnosis proper*. It is a general statement of the role that each party plays in the situational dilemma and may be delivered individually or in a family setting. It is highly behavioral and cognitive in nature. The purpose is to help each family member to see the complexity of the problem, to accept responsibility for his or her own actions as contributions to the problem, and to see what he or she can do to contribute to individual and family well-being.

COGNITIVE-BEHAVIORAL-PSYCHOSITUATIONAL THERAPY OF ANXIETY DISORDERS

Cognitive-behavioral-psychosituational therapy (CBPT) of children's anxiety disorders most appropriately includes both the parents and the child. Although it may be wise to assemble all family members together in one room, we often find it more helpful to see the child and the parents separately, perhaps bringing them together at various times during the course of therapy as clinical needs dictate. Our reasons for seeing parents and child separately are several: (1) to remove the child from the parental pressures and to provide him or her a safe haven for change; (2) to communicate the pyschosituational nature of the problem to the parents; (3) to give the parents a safe forum for acknowledging their respective roles in the child's problems; and (4) to give ourselves the "space" to make statements to the child without risking alienating the parents.

Even when separating the parents from the child in treatment, however, cognitive-behavioral-psychosituational intervention for both follows the orderly process described previously by us (Grieger & Boyd, 1980, 1983) in our skills-based model of rational-emotive therapy. This model sees cognitive-behavioral therapy as flowing through three overlapping yet distinct stages, as follows.

COGNITIVE-BEHAVIORAL INSIGHT

The first task of therapy proper is to facilitate in both the parents and the child the insights necessary to making change possible. For the parents, these insights entail an awareness that (1) their actions have significantly negative consequences for their child's adjustment in general and for his or her anxiety problem in particular; (2) their own attitudes, ideas, and beliefs, not the behaviors of the child, are in large measure responsible for their actions toward the child (note: this is the ABC theory of RET); (3) certain particular attitudes that they hold about themselves and/or their child (e.g., shoulds, awfuls) prompt them to behave toward the child as they do; (4) these attitudes may be conceptually illogical and empirically unsupportable, as well as consequentially untenable, and that they can be analyzed to determine whether this is so or not; (5) the adoption of more rational attitudes and behaviors on their part will have markedly positive effects on the child's performance and adjustment; and (6) they can indeed give up their child- and self-defeating attitudes and adopt more constructive ones if they are willing to devote time and energy to doing so. To establish these insights, the therapist uses the typical techniques with adult clients in general (Grieger & Boyd, 1980, 1983).

In outlining these insights, we do not suggest that they can be taught in only one session. Indeed, several may be needed, and the clinicians had better take pains to convey these points persuasively and gently to many parents, lest they become resistant. For instance, it has been our experience that parents caught in the criticism and/or perfectionism traps can easily conclude that the therapist is too soft on their child, and they worry that changing their attitudes and behaviors will give the youngster license to misbehave or act in a lazy, goalless fashion. Because of these and other pitfalls, we generally take great pains to initially empathize with their concerns. We let them know that we share their goals for their child, but that we fear that their strategies (supported by evidence) actually thwart rather than facilitate what *we all* want.

Because children are not as intellectually and emotionally developed as adults, the establishment of basic insights is more difficult and more fundamental for them than for adults. Probably, the most basic insight for children is the awareness that there are alternative ways that they can act and feel about their typical problems of responding (DiGiuseppe, 1981). This insight helps them to know that other responses exist and that change is possible, a revelation to a good many youngsters. In teaching this insight, we have found it helpful to draw a "feeling/behaving" graph, or thermometer, in which different emotional levels of responses are marked at various points. For example, I (R.G.) drew a "mad thermometer" for 12-year-old Jeff showing cool (0°), warm (25°), hot (50°), very hot (75°), and boiling (100°) points. Then, through example, self-disclosure, and especially role playing, the child is asked to imagine or act out (i.e., experience) different responses along the continuum.

Once children see that different responses exist and are possible to acquire, they are ready to explore the negative consequences of their disturbed feelings and behaviors and the positives that alternative responses could provide. This insight is designed to motivate them to put energy into changing. Virtually any technique is acceptable within the cognitive-behavioral-psychosituational framework, including making lists, observing other children, playing with puppets, using games and stories, and role playing. Figure 2 shows the way Jeff and I (R.G.) arrived at these two insights.

The key insight for children, of course, is that their own thoughts are the bad guys that cause their anxiety. For older children, a minilecture, backed by examples, often works to teach the ABC's. For younger ones, however, the use of role playing and drawings is advisable, so that they can both experience and see how their thoughts lead to their reactions, and how different thoughts can lead to different reactions. For instance, 8-year-old Bobby was taught to label as "nervous thoughts" certain of his thoughts that led to his tantrums and to label as "cool thoughts" the ones that led to certain appropriate and rewarding responses (see Figure 3).

COGNITIVE-BEHAVIORAL-PSYCHOSITUATIONAL WORKING THROUGH

Once family members gain the insights, they are ready for CBP working through. For parents, this involves the use of the cognitive,

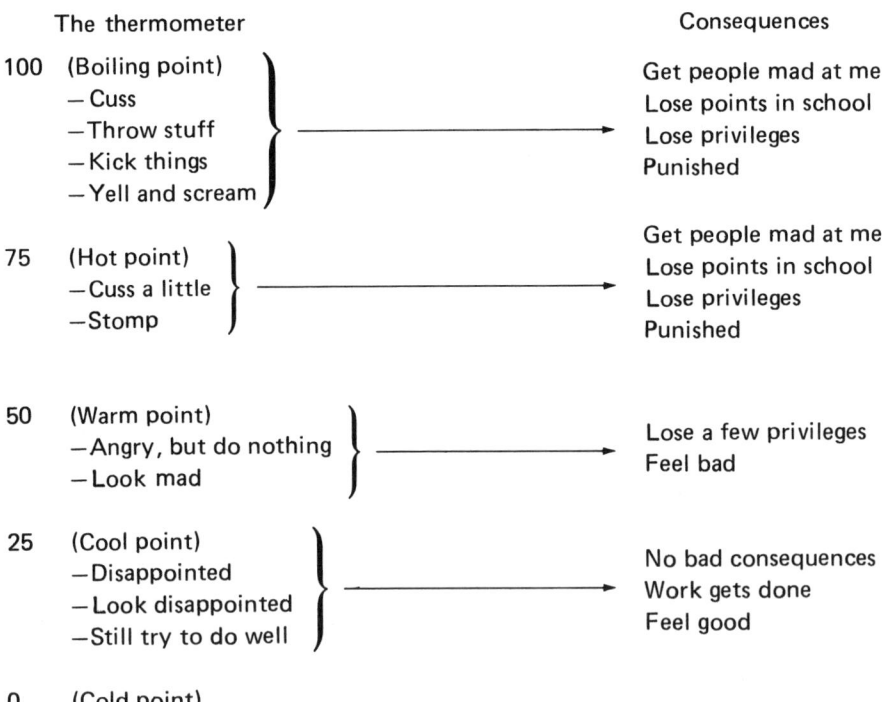

FIGURE 2. Jeff's "mad thermometer."

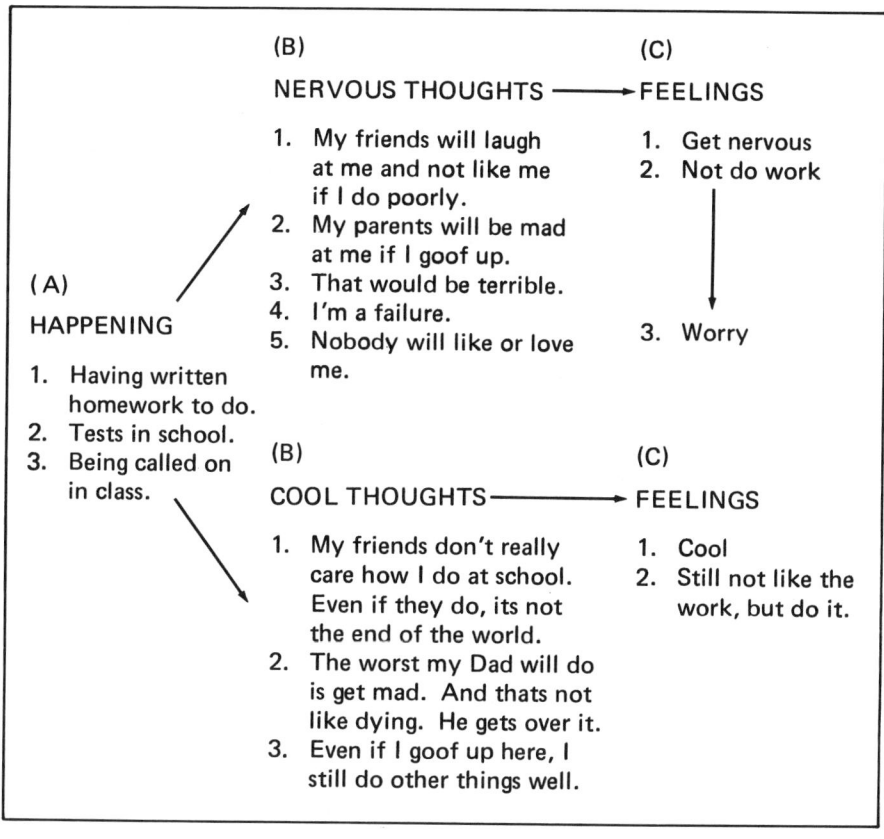

FIGURE 3. Bobby's thought-reaction drawing.

imaginal, emotive, and behavioral challenging or disputation techniques of RET and other forms of cognitive-behavioral therapy (Beck, Rush, Shaw, & Emery, 1980; Ellis, 1962, 1974, 1977, 1979; Grieger & Boyd, 1980; Walen, DiGiuseppe, & Wessler, 1980; Wessler & Wessler, 1980). The goal is a profound understanding of the illogic of, the lack of empirical support for, and the self-defeating and child-defeating nature of their basic beliefs, as well as an awareness of more plausible and constructive alternatives.

As opposed to adults, however, children rarely appreciate the importance of logicoempirical disputation; most often have no idea how to do it; and, particularly in the case of children below 7 or 8, often are incapable of doing it. For some older children, then, the therapist may find it more appropriate to teach critical thinking skills prior to a working-through process (DiGiuseppe, 1981). In this case, the therapist first instructs and then practices the youngster in empirical and conceptual disputations.

More typically, however, the therapist wants to construct a sequence of appropriate rational attitudes, positive emotional responses, and constructive behaviors with which to rehearse and train the child to think rationally (Grieger & Boyd, 1982). Central to this approach is the method of rational self-instruction and coping. It consists simply of constructing a rational self-talk dialogue that the child can practice at various times and can use when confronted with problem situations. The rational beliefs are put in the child's language and are practiced through imagery, role playing with the therapist, and rehearsal with adults, among other methods, with immediate and strong rewards for putting energy into this skill practice. This practice is most effective if it follows Meichenbaum's (1977) guidelines for teaching verbal self-instruction.

One final note here! We do not mean to imply that only cognitive strategies are used. On the contrary, this is the stage where the therapist attempts to "drown out" the child's habits of irrational thinking, feeling, and behaving through as many techniques as possible. They might include structured homework assignments (e.g., to tell a friend that you got a "D" on a test and see what happens), written homework, rational-emotive imagery, problem-solving training, and the like.

Generalized Learning and Skill Training

Success in the working-through stage means that the clients are doing well with those situation-specific problems on which therapy is focused. For older children and adults, an effort is made to generalize by helping them to adopt rational beliefs or philosophies that apply across situations. For these individuals, this stage of CBP treatment is best focused on the learning of specific skills in effective living. There are two sets of skills that are the most relevant for parents whose child suffers from anxiety disorders: behavior modification techniques and empathetic listening techniques. The focus in both should be positive, supportive behaviors that help the child to feel accepted by the parents and acceptable to themselves as people.

For younger children, whose generalization ability is slim, a final stage in the CBP process is to generalize the therapeutic learning beyond the few specific situations in question to similar problems in other situations. This generalization would involve repeating the prior intervention steps in one or two new arenas at a time, until the child gradually chips away his or her irrational, anxiety-prompting cognitions across the board.

To sum up, the cognitive-behavioral-psychosituational therapy of children's anxiety disorders typically incorporates the treating of the family. This treatment can be given either in family sessions or, more likely, in separate sessions for the child and the parents. Regardless of the format, CBP therapy follows an orderly process, from a psychodiagnosis through insight, working through, and generalized learning and skill training. At each stage, the emphasis is on the irrational cognitions that prompt the anxiety problems: on the parents' part, the ideas that cause them to behave in anxiety-inducing ways, and on the child's part, the irrational inferences and evaluations that directly cause her or his own anxiety reactions.

Conclusion

In this chapter, we have described and explained a comprehensive model for diagnosing and psychotherapeutically treating the anxieties, fears, and phobias of youngsters. The CBP model considers those intrapersonal and ecological variables that theory and research have shown to be particularly keen influences on human behavior. We believe this approach to be the most clinically practical and effective schema that we have discovered in our years of study and practice. It would be grandiose to say that the CBP model is the single best available model for dealing with children's anxious disorders, but we feel justified in encouraging clinicians to consider it and to base their diagnosis and treatment on this type of comprehensive view.

References

Bandura, A., & Walters, R. *Social learning and personality development.* New York: Holt, Rinehart & Winston, 1963.

Beck, A. *Cognitive therapy and the emotional disorders.* New York: International Universities Press, 1976.

Beck, A. T., Rush, A. J., Shaw, B. F., & Emery, G. *Cognitive therapy of depression: A treatment manual.* New York: Guilford Press, 1980.

Becker, W. *Parents are teachers.* New York: Human Services Press, 1971.

Bersoff, D. N., & Grieger, R. M. An interview model for the psychosituational assessment of children's behavior. *American Journal of Orthopsychiatry,* 1971, *41,* 483-493.

Carson, R. C. *Interaction concepts of personality.* Chicago: Aldine, 1969.

Connors, C. K. Symptom patterns in hyperkinetic, neurotic, and normal children. *Child Development,* 1970, *41,* 667-682.

DiGiuseppe, R. A. Cognitive therapy with children. In G. Emery, S. D. Hollon, & R. C. Bedrosian (Eds.), *New directions in cognitive therapy.* New York: Guilford Press, 1981.

Ellis, A. *Reason and emotion in psychotherapy*. Secaucus, N.J.: Lyle Stuart, 1962.
Ellis, A. *Growth through reason*. Palo Alto, Calif.: Science and Behavior Books, 1971.
Ellis, A. *Humanistic psychology: The rational-emotive approach*. New York: Crown, 1973.
Ellis, A. *Growth through reason*. Hollywood, Calif.: Wilshire Books, 1974.
Ellis, A. Elegant and inelegant RET. *Counseling Psychologist*, 1977, 7, 73–82.
Ellis, A. *Discomfort anxiety: A new cognitive-behavioral construct*. Invited address to the Association for Advancement of Behavior Therapy Annual Meeting, November 17, 1978. New York, BMA Audio Cassettes, 1978.
Ellis, A. Rational-emotive therapy. In R. J. Corsini's (Ed.), *Current psychotherapies* (rev. ed.). Itasco, Ill.: Peacock, 1979.
Ellis, A. Psychoneurosis and anxiety problems. In R. Grieger & I. Grieger's (Eds.), *Cognition and emotional disturbance*. New York: Human Sciences Press, 1982.
Ellis, A., Wolfe, J. L., & Moseley, S. *How to prevent your child from becoming a neurotic adult*. New York: Crown Publishers, 1966.
Grieger, R. M., & Abidin, R. Psychosocial assessment: A model for the school community psychologist. *Psychology in the Schools*, 1972, 9, 112–119.
Grieger, R., & Boyd, J. *Rational-emotive therapy: A skills-based approach*. New York: Van Nostrand Reinhold, 1980.
Grieger, R. M., & Boyd, J. D. Rational-emotive therapy. In H. T. Prout & D. T. Brown's (Eds.), *Counseling and psychotherapy with children and adolescents: Theory and practice for school and clinic settings*. New York: Mariner Press, 1983.
Hauck, P. A. *The rational management of children*. New York: Libra Publishers, 1967.
Kelly, G. A. *The psychology of personal constructs* (2 vols.). New York: W. W. Norton, 1955.
Kessler, J. *Psychopathology of childhood*. Englewood Cliffs, N.J.: Prentice-Hall, 1966.
LaPouse, R., & Monk, M. An epidemiological study of behavioral characteristics of children. *American Journal of Public Health*, 1972, 48, 1134–1144.
McFarlan, J. L., Allen, L., & Honzik, M. P. *A developmental study of the behavior problems of normal children between 21 months and 14 years*. Berkeley: University of California Press, 1957.
Meichenbaum, D. *Cognitive-behavior modification: An integrative approach*. New York: Plenum Press, 1977.
Miller, L. C. Dimensions of psychopathology in middle childhood. *Psychological Reports*, 1967, 21, 897–903. (a)
Miller, L. C. Louisville Behavior Checklist for males, 6–12 years of age. *Psychological Reports*, 1967, 21, 885–886. (b)
Miller, L. C., Hempe, E., Barrett, C. L., & Noble, H. Children's deviant behavior within the general population. *Journal of Consulting and Clinical Psychology*, 1971, 37, 16–22.
Mischel, W. *Personality and assessment*. New York: Wiley, 1968.
Mischel, W. On the emperical dilemmas of psychodynamic approaches: Issues and alternatives. *Journal of Abnormal Psychology*, 1973, 82, 335–344. (a)
Mischel, W. Toward a cognitive social learning reconceptualization of personality. *Psychological Review*, 1973, 80, 252–283. (b)
Peterson, D. *The clinical study of social behavior*. New York: Appleton-Century-Crofts, 1968.
Ross, A. O. *Psychological disorders of children: A behavioral approach to theory, research and therapy*. New York: McGraw-Hill, 1974.
Rotter, J. B. *Social learning and clinical psychology*. Englewood Cliffs, N.J.: Prentice-Hall, 1954.
Walen, S. R., DiGiuseppe, R., & Wessler, R. L. *A practitioner's guide to rational-emotive therapy*. New York: Oxford University Press, 1980.

Wallace, J. An abilities conception of personality: Some implications for personality measurement. *American Psychologist*, 1966, *21*, 132–138.
Werry, J. S., & Quay, H. C. The prevalence of behavior symptoms in younger elementary school children. *American Journal of Orthopsychiatry*, 1971, *41*, 136–143.
Wessler, R. A., & Wessler, R. L. *The principles and practice of rational-emotive therapy.* San Francisco: Jossey-Bass, 1980.

9

Teaching Rational Self-Talk to Help Socially Isolated Children and Youth

W. KIM HALFORD

This chapter is a review of how rational-emotive therapy (RET) and other cognitive-behavioral interventions can be used to help socially isolated and withdrawn children and youths. The basic premise of the chapter is that how young people think affects how they feel and react toward others, and that changing how they think can help overcome difficulties in social interaction with others. The review presented consists of five sections: (1) the significance and definition of social withdrawal in children and youths; (2) a description of a model of the cognitive steps postulated as being involved in social withdrawal; (3) a review of the clinical methods of assessment of social withdrawal; (4) a description and evaluation of cognitive treatment methods; and (5) special considerations in applications of the described cognitive methods with children and adolescents.

THE SIGNIFICANCE OF SOCIAL ISOLATION IN CHILDREN AND YOUTH

THE FREQUENCY AND IMPACT OF THE PROBLEM

Interacting with, and relating to, other people is a very important aspect of all our lives. Yet social interaction is something that many of us

---

W. KIM HALFORD • Department of Psychology, Brisbane College of Advanced Education, Queensland, 4055 Australia.

find difficult, at least some of the time. Bryant and Trower (1974) found that all respondents in a survey of Oxford undergraduates ($n = 233$) reported that they experienced "some difficulty" in, or tried to avoid, at least 1 of 30 everyday social situations. Zimbardo, Pilkonis, and Norwood (1974) found that 42% of a sample of high school and university students rated themselves as dispositionally "shy persons." Of these shy persons, 63% rated their shyness as a "real problem." In a survey of third- to sixth-grade children, Gronlund (1959) found that nearly 6% of the children had no friends in their classroom, and an additional 12% had only one friend. In adults, difficulty in coping with social interaction and social isolation is an important component of a range of severe behavioral and psychiatric disorders. For example, surveys and clinical impressions of psychiatric outpatients indicate that there is a high incidence of social anxiety and isolation in this group (Argyle, Bryant, & Trower, 1974; Trower, Bryant, & Argyle, 1978). Anxiety and inadequacy in social interaction are also characteristic of alcoholics and drug abusers (Kraft, 1971; Miller & Eisler, 1977) and people suffering from depression (Libet & Lewinsohn, 1973; Lewinsohn, 1975). Furthermore, across almost all diagnostic categories, psychiatric inpatients who are socially isolated and unskilled tend to stay longer in psychiatric hospitals, and have poorer posthospital adjustment, than other patients (Curran, Miller, Zwick, Monti, & Stout, 1980).[1]

Many of the problems in adulthood described above, may have their origin in social isolation and difficulty in childhood. As O'Conner (1969) pointed out:

> A child who is grossly deficient in social skills will be severely handicapped in acquiring many of the complex behavioral repertoires necessary for effective social functioning. . . . Such negative experiences would be expected to reinforce social avoidance which, in turn, further impedes the development of competencies which are socially mediated. (p. 15)

[1]The relationship between severe social difficulties and other behavioral problems is often not clear. It is possible that social difficulty is a primary causal factor that may generate other problems. For example, anxiety in hetrosexual dating situations may lead, via social isolation, to a range of abnormal behaviors (Annon, 1975). On the other hand, there may be a more generalized disturbance, which affects social behavior and many other areas of behavior. For example, psychotic hallucinations may induce fear and anxiety that can deleteriously affect many areas of functioning, including social behavior.

Regardless of whether social anxiety is a primary cause of a disorder or is a symptom of a broader disturbance, it is likely to be a source of stress to the person concerned. Overcoming this stress may lead to an improvement in the functioning of the individual. For example, Miller, Hersen, Eisler, and Hilsman (1974) found that stress in social situations increased the rate of drinking of alcoholics. Whatever the original cause of alcoholism in these people, a reduction in their social anxiety might well alleviate their alcoholism.

Support for this contention is provided by the finding that socially isolated, unpopular children are disproportionately represented later in life in psychiatric populations (Cowen, Pederson, Babigan, Izzo, & Trost, 1973). It has been found that many maladaptive social behaviors in childhood (e.g., interpersonal anxiety, ease of anger arousal, and aggressiveness) persist through to adulthood (Kagen & Moss, 1962; Patterson, 1976).

Additional evidence of the likely long-term consequences of social isolation in childhood are found in the association of isolation with a high rate of juvenile delinquency (Rolf, Sell, & Golden, 1972); dropping out of school (Ullman, 1957); and poor academic performance at school (Cartledge & Milburn, 1978; Green, Forehand, Beck, & Vosk, 1980.)

The importance of adequate social interaction skills may be particularly pronounced in children with disabilities. In an extensive review of the literature, Gresham (1981) demonstrated that children with physical and/or mental disabilities are often poorly accepted by their nondisabled peers. Furthermore, he established a strong case that specific training in social interaction skills may be necessary to promote greater levels of acceptance and to reduce social isolation.

DEFINITION OF SOCIAL ISOLATION

In this section, there is an attempt to define the nature of social isolation in children and youths. In the relevant literature, there have been a number of conceptualizations of this problem. O'Conner (1972) viewed social isolation as a low frequency of peer interactions. Others have seen the problem as poor peer acceptance, as indicated by sociometric measures (e.g., Gottmann, Gonso, & Rasmussen, 1975). In a third perspective, social isolation has been conceptualized as an excess of certain negative social behaviors (such as aggression or abuse) or deficits of positive behaviors (such as assertiveness and friendliness—e.g., Minkin, Braukmann, Minkin, Timbers, Timbers, Fixsen, Phillips, & Wolf, 1976; Whitehill, Hersen, & Bellack, 1980). A fourth possible view of social isolation is in terms of subjective anxiety in social interaction and avoidance of social situations. Social difficulty has been conceptualized in these terms in adult groups (e.g., Trower *et al.*, 1978; Watson & Friend, 1969), but subjective feelings have received scant attention in the relevant literature on children's social difficulties.

There is overlap between some of the above theoretical frameworks, but there are some important distinctions to be made. It is primarily measures of peer acceptance that are associated with indications of current adjustment, and that are predictive of future behavior (Foster &

Richey, 1979). Consequently, this is probably the most important of the conceptualizations. Low frequencies of peer interaction have been shown to be unrelated to peer acceptance (Gottmann, 1977), and hence, *simple frequency counts of peer interactions are not useful indicators of social isolation.*

There are behavioral differences between popular and unpopular children. For example, unpopular children exhibit lower frequencies of certain positive behaviors, such as giving attention and/or approval to others, than other children (Gottman *et al.*, 1975; Hartup, Glazer, & Charlesworth, 1967). However peer acceptance is associated with a range of factors other than overt behavior, factors such as physical attactiveness, body type, and a child's special skills (Foster & Richey, 1979). Consequently, a distinction must be drawn between unpopularity and lack of social skill. *Social isolation cannot be defined in terms of the frequency of particular social behaviors alone, though these may contribute to social isolation.*

In adults, individuals who report subjective feelings of anxiety and/or a desire to avoid certain social situations tend to behave in a less socially skillful manner in those situations (e.g., Curran, Little, & Gilbert, 1976; Halford & Foddy, 1982; Pilkonis, 1977b; Twentyman & McFall, 1975). Furthermore, they are viewed less positively by others on dimensions such as desirability as a date (Arkowitz, Lichenstein, McGovern, & Hines, 1975) and degree of friendliness (Pilkonis, 1977a). The relationships among subjective states in children, their overt behavior, and the reactions they elicit from stress have not been studied systematically. Hence, the *relationship between subjective emotional states and social isolation in children is unknown.*

In addition to the above considerations, two further factors must be taken into account when defining social isolation. First, peer acceptance varies from one situation to another. For example, children often nominate different members of their peer group as their favorite persons to play a certain game with, as distinct from those whom they chose to do schoolwork with (Oden & Asher, 1977). Second, there appear to be two groups of children who are low in peer acceptance: children who are actively disliked by their peers and children who are simply overlooked and ignored by their peers (Foster & Richey, 1979). There may well be important behavioral differences between these groups. For example, it is possible that the disliked group engage in aggressive or abusive behaviors and that the ignored group simply lack certain friendly behaviors that would make their company reinforcing to their peers. Clearly, such differences have important implications for interventions designed to overcome this isolation.

Based on the above discussion, *social isolation* is defined as "active rejection, or being ignored, by peers in one or more important social situations." This isolation may be associated, but not necessarily, with excesses or deficits of certain social behaviors and/or subjective states of anxiety.

THE ROLE OF COGNITIONS IN SOCIAL ISOLATION

Argyle and Kendon (1967) have proposed a social skill model of social interaction, which provides a very useful framework within which to conceptualize the role of cognitions in social isolation. This model is represented schematically in Figure 1.

In the social skill model, it is proposed that social interaction is analogous to any serial motor skill. External stimuli are perceived by the individual and are cognitively translated into goals to be achieved in the situation, and a response is made that is designed to achieve those goals. The effect of this response on the environment feeds back and

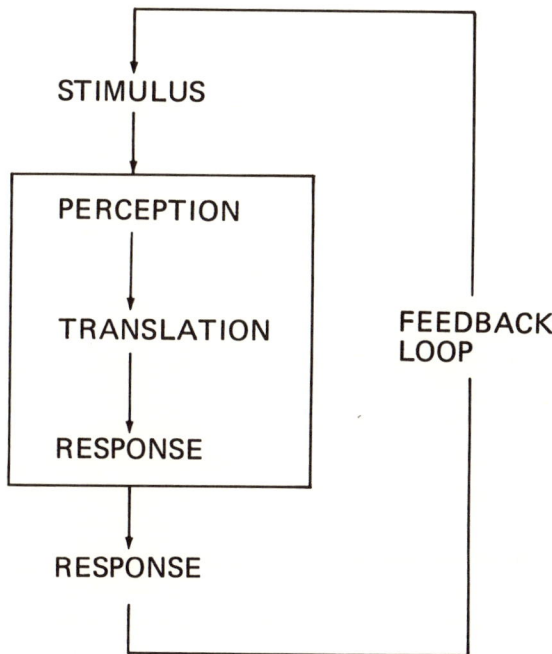

FIGURE 1. Schematic representation of the social skill model. (From Argyle & Kendon, 1967.)

influences the next response. For example, a child might look around a school classroom, see a group of other children who seem to be having fun (perception), decide to try and join in their game (translation), and walk up to the group and ask to take part in the game (response). The reactions of the group to this approach will influence the child's next response (feedback).

In this section we review evidence of the influence on social isolation of the cognitive factors in these processes of perception, translation, and responding. Unfortunately, the research on children and youths is sparse. Consequently, the relevant evidence on adults is considered here, and an attempt is made to highlight the relevance of these findings to children and youth.

PERCEPTION OF SOCIAL SITUATIONS AND SOCIAL ISOLATION

There is considerable evidence that adults who have difficulty in social interaction have systematic biases in their perception of social situations. Clarke and Arkowitz (1975) and Curran, Wallander, and Fischetti (1977) have found that socially anxious adults tend to underestimate (in comparison to judges' ratings) the level of skill with which they respond to social situations. Halford (1979) and Smith and Sarason (1975) showed that highly socially anxious persons also tend to perceive the same feedback from others as more negative than low-anxious persons. Furthermore, O'Banien and Arkowitz (1977) found that highly socially anxious persons selectively remember a higher proportion of negative interpersonal feedback than low-anxious persons. Thus, highly socially anxious adults show a consistent bias toward appraising their own social behavior, and the reactions of others to them, overly negatively.

There is no directly equivalent evidence to that cited above for children or youths, though this author's clinical observations suggest that such a negative bias in social perception is evident in socially isolated youths. There is some research indicating that socially isolated children perceive social situations differently from other children, particularly with respect to their interpretations of why others behave as they do. Unpopular, isolated children perform more poorly at referential communication tasks, which require being able to view the situation from the perspective of another, than other children (Gottmann *et al.*, 1975). They also perform more poorly on role-taking tests (Gottmann, 1977). Goetz and Dweck (1980) found that there is an association between peer unpopularity in children and a general tendency to attribute social rejection to personal incompetence (e.g., "I was rejected because I find it hard to make friends") or incompatibility with others (e.g., "I was rejected because of the way I am"). In that study, attributions of personal incompetence as the cause of social rejection were associated with higher frequencies of getting upset and withdrawing following rejection and fewer attempts to overcome that rejection.

Cognitive Translation of Social Situations

Having perceived a given social situation (e.g., "I am being rejected" or "That group of children is having fun"), an individual must cognitively translate this perception into an appropriate response. This cognitive translation process can usefully be viewed as a decision-making process constituted of three steps: (1) the generation of response alternatives; (2) an assessment of the probabilities of various outcomes resulting from the different possible responses; and (3) an evaluation of the subjective utilities attached to those outcomes. There is considerable evidence that socially isolated individuals are idiosyncratic in each of these three steps.

Butler and Meichenbaum (1981) reviewed a considerable body of evidence that indicates that socially maladjusted children and adolescents are able to generate fewer alternative responses to interpersonal problem situations than adjusted children. For example, Spivack and associates have found that children and adolescents rated by teachers as socially maladjusted perform more poorly than other children on standardized tests in which they are asked to generate alternative means of responding to interpersonal conflict situations (Shure, Spivack, & Jaeger, 1971; Shure & Spivack, 1972). Similarly Stein and Goldman (1981) and Asher and Renshaw (1981) have reviewed evidence that children without friends generate fewer positive responses than other children to hypothetical social situations. Related research has shown an association between the performance of psychiatric patients on similar tests and premorbid social competence (Platt & Spivack, 1972). Training in interpersonal-problem solving has been shown to result in the generation of more response alternatives to standard interpersonal problems in both adults (D'Zurilla & Nezu, 1980) and children (Shure & Spivack, 1974). Furthermore, such training programs result in improvements of global ratings of social adjustment (Coche & Douglas, 1977; Spivack, Platt, & Shure, 1976).

In a recent study, Bruch (1981) found that young adults who were divided into high-, moderate-, and low-assertive subjects on the basis of a self-report inventory were different in several respects in their knowledge of responses to social situations. Low-assertive subjects were poorer than other subjects in discriminating between different styles of responses (assertive versus aggressive versus passive) to various social situations. Furthermore, when asked to demonstrate what constituted assertive responses to various situations, they performed more poorly. Given the generally recognized association between social isolation or difficulty and unassertiveness (see Bellack & Hersen, 1979; Halford, 1979), this poor performance is further evidence that socially withdrawn persons are able to conceive of less response alternatives to problem social situations than other people.

Adults with difficulty in social interaction have been shown to perceive negative outcomes (e.g., rejection and disapproval) as more probable in social interactions than other people. For example, Eisler, Fredricksen, and Peterson (1978) reported that unassertive subjects rate rejection or disapproval as more likely to occur to them in given situations than assertive subjects. Similarly, Halford (1979) found that socially anxious persons viewed rejections from and misunderstandings with others as generally more likely to occur than nonanxious persons. My clinical observations suggest to me that there are at least two possible sources of this estimation of the probability of rejection. Sometimes, individuals simply cannot think of an appropriate response to a problem situation. For example, they may be able to think only of aggressive ways of refusing an unreasonable request. In this instance, they often quite reasonably conclude that the interaction is likely to have a negative outcome. However, sometimes, they do think of a reasonable response (e.g., a firm and assertive but polite refusal) but erroneously attach to it a high probability of a negative outcome. For example, I have worked with several clients who have persistently agreed to dates with others, when they did not really want to go, because they believed that a refusal would, in all probability, be devastating to the other person. This unrealistic view was disconfirmed when they did eventually say no.

There are a number of studies that have shown an association between excessive, irrational fear of rejection or disapproval and anxiety in, and withdrawal from, social situations in adults (e.g., Gormally, Sipps, Raphael, Edwin, & Varvil-Weld, 1981; Richardson & Tasto, 1976; Sutton-Simon & Goldfried, 1979; Watson & Friend, 1969). Again, equivalent studies have not been conducted with children.

The influence of concern about rejection or disapproval on social behavior is reflected in individuals' self-statements. A number of studies have shown that socially anxious, isolated, and unskilled adults have a higher frequency of certain negative self-statements both in anticipation of and during social interaction (Bruch, 1981; Cacioppio, Glass, & Merluzzi, 1979; Halford & Foddy, 1982; Schwartz & Gottmann, 1976). Most of these negative self-statements are concerned with rejection or disapproval from others (e.g., "What will I do if I run out of things to say?" and "If I say no, they might get really upset"). When people are asked to deliberately concentrate on and make such negative self-statements prior to an encounter with others, they become less likely to initiate conversations with those others and are more likely to break off the conversation early if they do initiate an interaction (Mandel & Shrauger, 1980). They also report greater subjective feelings of anxiety and other negative affect, and fewer feelings of cheerfulness or happiness. Mandel and Shrauger's (1980) findings support the idea that cognitions have a causal effect on affect and behavior in social interaction.

No equivalent studies on the self-statements of children or youth during social interaction, like those cited above with adults, have been undertaken. However, the reported clinical impressions of some authors suggest that socially isolated children may make similar negative self-statements (DeVoge, 1977; Halford, 1980).

In summary, socially anxious, withdrawn adults tend to have a negative bias in the way that they cognitively process and react to social situations. They perceive their own behavior, and others' reactions to it, overly negatively. High probabilities are attached to disapproval or rejection in social interaction, and a high utility is attached to the avoidance of such rejection. The moment-to-moment self-statements of these people reflect this preoccupation with the possibility of negative outcomes from social interaction. Equivalent research into the cognitions of children and youth is extremely sparse, but what exists is consistent with the findings in adults.

Overt Responses and Social Isolation

The overt behavior of socially anxious or isolated persons in initiating social interaction is different from that of nonisolated persons. In young adults (college students), it has been found that socially anxious persons are less likely to initiate interactions with others, even when those others give nonverbal cues indicating approachability and friendliness (Curran et al., Gilbert, 1976; Twentyman & McFall, 1975). Similar avoidance of interaction has been noted in children. Gottmann (1977) has identified a number of what he calls "hovering behaviors" in socially isolated children (defined on the basis of both a low frequency of peer interactions and low peer acceptance). These behaviors are exhibited by children who locate themselves in close proximity to, but do not actually interact with, other children. Examples of such behaviors include pouting, lip chewing, fixated gaze, sucking digits, shrugging, crouching, whining, talking "like a baby," and sidling. These same children spend more time in "switched-off," noninteractive behavior (such as daydreaming and engaging in off-task and lone behavior) in the classroom than other children (Gottmann, 1977; Gottmann et al., 1975).

Socially isolated individuals behave in recognizably different ways from others while actually in social interaction. Differences in the global ratings of social behavior by observers on dimensions such as assertiveness, skill, and friendliness have been found to discriminate between adults dichotomized into high- and low-social-anxiety/skill groups on the basis of self-report inventories of social anxiety (Daly, 1978; Halford & Foddy, 1982; Pilkonis, 1977a; self- and other-ratings of assertiveness (e.g., Bruch, 1981; Eisler, Miller, & Hersen, 1973; Schwartz & Gottman, 1976); dating frequency and comfort (e.g., Arkowitz, Lichenstein, McGovern, & Hines, 1975; Glasgow & Arkowitz, 1973); and clinical judgments of social competence (e.g., Gillingham, Griffiths, & Care, 1977; Trower, 1980). For children, less evidence is available. Gottmann et al. (1975) found that isolated, unpopular children were less skilled than other children when asked to role-play starting a friendship. In this same study, it was also found that socially isolated children responded positively to others less often than other children, which replicated a similar finding by Hartup et al. (1967). Eisler and Fredriksen (1980) described a number of global prosocial behaviors that they believe to be deficient in some socially isolated children, including sharing behaviors, conversation initiations, praising and complimenting others, expressing affection, and asking for help from others. However, those behaviors have not been demonstrated empirically as being associated with social isolation, though there is a considerable intuitive appeal to this notion.

The traditional view of the cause of the behavioral differences described above is that there is a response repertoire deficit. That is, it has been hypothesized that certain persons either have never learned or have forgotten appropriate modes of responding to critical social situations. Treatment, within this conceptual framework, consists of a range of skill-training procedures. It is assumed that, once these new skills are learned, they will be maintained by reinforcement from the natural social environment (Goldsmith & McFall, 1975).

The available evidence leads to the conclusion that an adequate response repertoire may be necessary, but is not sufficient, to change social behavior and to influence social isolation and difficulty. Schwartz and Gottman (1976) identified young adults with socially skilled responses in their behavioral repertoire who failed to use those responses in social situations. Similarly, Kazdin, Matson, and Esveldt-Dawson

(1981) found that children in an assessment situation did not always show their maximum social-skill levels, their performance being improved by feedback and incentives. Evaluations of social-skills-training programs have shown that individuals who use certain social skills in one situation sometimes fail to use those responses in very similar situations after training (Kirschner, 1976; Twentyman & Zimmering, 1979). It has been shown that a subjective assessment of the likely outcomes of making a particular response, and the utility of those outcomes, affects the choice of what response an individual selects to use in a given social situation (Fiedler & Beach, 1978). These findings are consistent with the view expressed in earlier sections that cognitive factors mediate the selection of responses to social situations. Furthermore, it shows that overt behavior is a function of more than just behavioral repertoire.

CLINICAL IMPLICATIONS

From the evidence I have reviewed above, a picture of the socially withdrawn child and adolescent emerges. Such individuals tend to be able to think of fewer alternative ways to deal with social situations. They think about the negative aspects of social interaction much more frequently than others. Concern about rejection or disapproval by others is very influential in determining their behavior; they have a bias toward viewing social situations negatively, see negative reactions as more probable than others do, and attach great importance to avoiding such negative reactions. Rejection or disapproval can occur in almost any social situation: a child asking someone to play with him or her allows the possibility of rejection; an assertive statement may offend someone; initiating a conversation with a stranger could result in not being accepted. Consequently, the socially isolated or withdrawn person often behaves in ways to minimize the risk: avoiding initiating interactions, breaking off conversations, and avoiding assertive and opinion-giving statements. Unfortunately, this strategy reduces the possibility of attaining positive outcomes from social interaction, outcomes such as forming friends, having one's opinions taken into account, or getting things to turn out the way one might like them to.

The implications of the above for clinicians are that there is a need to identify the particular cognitions of any given individual that influence her or his social withdrawal by means of the model described as a guide, and then to use appropriate intervention strategies to modify those cognitions.

Appropriate assessment procedures are the topic of the next section, and treatment methods are considered in the section after that.

Assessment of Social Withdrawal

The assessment of social withdrawal usually involves two phases: (1) an initial screening phase, in which a determination is made about whether social isolation is a problem for a particular individual; and (2) a more detailed, cognitive-behavioral analysis designed to identify the likely etiology of the problem. This latter phase is intended to define specific change objectives and to generate hypotheses about the intervention(s) most likely to be efficacious in assisting a given individual. Consideration is given in this section to the suitability of the assessment methods reviewed for achieving both these purposes. The methods reviewed below are (1) sociometrics and peer ratings; (2) self-report inventories; (3) observations and role-play tests; and (4) other assessment methods.

Sociometrics and Peer Rating

A variety of sociometric measures have been used to assess children's social isolation, the most widely used of which are (1) peer nominations; (2) peer ratings; and (3) teachers' ratings. All these measures assess global acceptance of children within a given context, but they differ in their psychometric characteristics.

In the peer nomination method, children are asked to nominate a number of children from a given group whom they would most like to be with, or to do a particular activity with, or like the most. (With younger children, a "point-to-the-picture" system is often used to obtain nominations.) A sociometric score is then calculated based on the number of nominations a child receives. Peer ratings are similar, except that each child in an assessment group is rated on a scale (usually a 3- or 5-point Likert-type scale) by every other child. Again, pictures or drawings can be used to simplify the process for young children. For example, children can be asked to say how they feel about another child by pointing to a smiling, frowning, or neutral face. In a third general method, teachers have been asked to rate on scales, or rank, students on dimensions such as peer popularity, frequency of peer interaction, and social skill (e.g., Greenwood, Walker, Todd, & Hopps, 1979).

Each of the above methods seems to be influenced by the exact phrasing of the questions on which nominations, ratings, or rankings are based. For example, children differentiate between others they like to work with and others they like to play with, in both their peer nominations and their ratings (Gottmann et al., 1975; Oden & Asher, 1977). Consequently, it is important for clinicians to define in precisely which situations they wish to assess social isolation, and to reflect definition in the wording of the questions used.

Teachers' ratings and rankings seem to have better test–retest reliability than peer nominations (Greenwood et al., 1979), which, in turn, seem generally more reliable than peer ratings (Kane & Lawler, 1978). However, it should be noted that there has been considerable variation in the reported reliabilities from one study to another. For example, although most others have reported at least moderate test–retest reliability for peer nominations (e.g., Dunnington, 1957; McCandless & Marshall, 1957), Greenwood et al. (1979) reported a very low reliability. Reliability should be assessed rather than presumed when using any of these measures.

The concurrent validity of teacher rankings and observed interaction preferences is high (Greenwood et al. 1979). However, there is little association between peer nominations and rankings, and interaction preferences and frequency (Gottmann et al., 1975; Greenwood et al., 1979). The one study on predictive validity, which was described earlier, indicated a strong prediction of later social adjustment by peer nominations (Cowen et al., 1973). Further research is required before any definite conclusions can be drawn on the validity of the sociometric and rating measures of social isolation.

Regardless of how reliable or valid the above measures may turn out to be, all of them, at best, provide only a global indicator of social isolation. None of the measures provides indicators of specific cognitive or behavioral targets for change within an intervention program. Consequently, such measures can be used only as an initial screening device in assessing social isolation.

Self-Report Inventories

There are a very large number of self-report and other inventories designed to assess social isolation, difficulty, and related variables in adult populations. Scales have been developed to assess adult affective responses to social situations, that is, scales such as the Social Avoidance and Distress Scale by Watson and Friend (1969) and the Stanford Shyness Scale by Zimbardo (1977). There are numerous self-report assertiveness and social-skill scales, such as the Rathus Assertiveness Schedule (Rathus, 1973) and the College Self-Expression Scale (Gay, Hollandsworth, & Galassi, 1975) for adult populations. There are also a number of scales that in themselves, as subscales thereof, measure cognitive factors relevant to social isolation in adults. For example, Watson and Friend (1969) have developed a Fear of Negative Evaluation Scale, and the Irrational Beliefs Test by Jones (1968) contains subscales assessing "excessive need for approval" and "dire fear of rejection." Unfortunately there are very few self-report inventories designed to measure equivalent variables for children or adolescents. Although some of the above-mentioned scales might be used with young adults and adolescents in their mid-teens, most have language and item contents that are inappropriate for use with young teenagers or children. One self-report inventory has been developed by Deluty (1979) that is designed to measure responses to interpersonal conflict situations in 7- to 10-year-old children. This inventory consists of 39 items on which children are asked to make a forced choice of which of two alternative responses they would make to a range of interpersonal conflict situations. Both the situations and the response alternatives presented were developed by a careful behavior-analytic approach, so that the items have good face validity. The inventory yields three scores: aggressiveness, assertiveness, and submissiveness. The split-half reliability of the scales is moderate (r's ranging from .63 to .77); significant convergent validity with peer and teacher ratings has been established; and the scales have been shown to discriminate between clinically hyperaggressive children and normal children (Deluty, 1979). Test–retest reliability over a four-month period was significant but low (r's between .48 and .60).

The scale developed by Deluty (1979) illustrates some of both the limitations and the potential advantages of the use of self-report inventories to assess social isolation in children. Like all self-report inventories, Deluty's scale asks respondents to make cross-situational generalizations about their behavior for each item (e.g., "What would you *usually* do in this sort of situation?"). These individual items are then combined to give scale scores. This process obscures individual differences. It also reduces the situational specificity of the data collected, which is so necessary for cognitive-behavioral interventions. On the other hand, Deluty has demonstrated that scores provided by such inventories can be reliable and valid measures of global social adjustment. Consequently, such inventories have the potential to be very useful general screening measures for social isolation. The development of self-report inventories to assess social isolation in children and youth should be a priority research area. In particular, it would be very useful to have scales that measure the levels of anxiety in social situations and the degree of concern about rejection or disapproval by others.

Observations and Role-Play Tests

Direct observation has been used widely to assess children's social behavior. Usually, the data have been collected in terms of the frequency and duration of all interactions (e.g., O'Conner, 1972) or of particular sorts of interactions, such as receiving or giving positive comments (e.g., Gottmann et al., 1975). Usually, such methods are used to assess overt behavior, though spontaneous verbalizations have been suggested as an indicator of cognitive behavior (Kendall & Hollon, 1981). Although this approach has maximum ecological validity for assessing overt behaviors, there are a number of practical difficulties in the approach. Often, reliable ratings of behavior can be obtained only after considerable training of raters. Even then, a range of factors such as rater expectations, the reactivity of the observational process, and reliability decay make the obtaining of reliable, valid results difficult (see Kent & Foster, 1977). Van Hasselt, Hersen, Whitehill, and Bellack (1979) recommended that considerable attention be paid to ensuring unobstrusive sampling methods are used, to carrying out appropriate reliability checks, and to scoring from audio or video- recordings, rather then live observation. All these steps can be time-consuming for the practitioner, but it is ultimately the aim of all cognitive-behavioral interventions to modify behavior in the problem situation(s), and hence, it is vital that *in vivo* assessment occur. However, in my view, the value of observing spontaneous verbalizations is questionable, as it is difficult to know the significance of an absence of such verbalizations. Does it mean that no cognitive self-statements are occurring or that they are just not being verbalized? *In vivo* self-monitoring of cognitions and behavior can be a very useful clinical tool in assessing social isolation. In Figure 2, a self-monitoring form that I have used with adolescents is depicted, and some typical responses are included. As can be seen, the form provides information on behavior, self-statements, affect, and environmental consequences, all of which are very useful for planning interventions. Furthermore, the results often provide both the clinician and the client with insights into the links between these factors.

Self-monitoring does have some methodological drawbacks, such as its reactivity (particularly with negatively valued targets like aggression), and its inaccuracy if clients are asked to monitor complex targets such as nonverbal behavior frequency (see review by Kendall & Hollon, 1981). These limitations probably make it unwise to rely on this method as the sole means of evaluating treatment outcome. The task of self-monitoring is generally too complex, and consequently often unsuitable, for younger children.

Role-play tests often have been used as a substitute for *in vivo* observation in the assessment of the social behavior of adults (e.g., Eisler, Hersen, Miller, & Blanchard, 1975; Halford and Foddy, 1982), and there have been some tests developed for use with children (e.g., Bornstein, Bellack, & Hersen, 1977; Kazdin et al., 1981). All these tests have the

SITUATION	SELF-TALK	BEHAVIOR	FEELINGS	CONSEQUENCES
(Place, time, people, what's happening)		(what I did)	(how I felt)	(What happened as a result of your behavior)
At home, want to ring up Sally and ask for a date	I feel too edgy tonight, she'll probably say 'no' anyway, what's the point?	Nothing	A bit down	Nothing much, I'll probably stay home on Saturday night
My mates were "hanging it on me"	Why don't they leave me alone? Hell, they always pick on me.	I got mad and left	Felt stupid	Felt dumb later when I saw them again.

FIGURE 2. A self-monitoring form for assessing cognitions and behavior in socially isolated adolescents.

same basic format: a series of social situations is presented to the person being assessed (usually by being described by a narrator); a prompt is delivered by a confederate for each situation, which is supposed to occur within the content of that situation; and the subject responds to the prompt as if he or she were in the situation. For example, Kazdin *et al.* (1981) described a typical situation in their role-play test for children as follows: "The child would be on the floor pretending to play a game. (Narrator) 'Imagine you are playing a game and another child comes up and threatens to hit you.' He (role model prompt) walks over and says: 'I am going to punch you'" (p. 147).

Overt responses to scenes such as the above can be scored immediately, or the role play can be audio- or video-recorded for subsequent coding. There are a number of methods by which cognitions can be assessed from such role-play tests. After the role-play, clients can be presented with a "thought-listing" form, as described by Cacioppo *et al.* (1979), in which the client is asked to list all the thoughts occurring to her or him during the role play. (Thought listing can, of course, also be used after an *in vivo* experience). Alternatively, one can present clients with a series of self-statements and ask them to indicate which thoughts occurred to them. This latter approach has the advantage that the task required of the client is simpler, making it more suitable for younger children. It also excludes the many self-statements generated in thought listing that are essentially irrelevant to social isolation. A third method is to replay an audio- or videotape of an interaction, stopping the tape at intervals, and asking the client what her or his self-talk is at that point. The self-statements that result from any of the above methods can be coded into appropriate categories to give a general description of a client's thought processes. There are several category systems that have been used, but I find that a dichotomous positive/negative categorization is best. Such a system is simple, can be reliably scored, and is usually adequate for clinical applications. Definitions of positive and negative self-statements, and some representative examples of each, are presented in Table 1. These definitions are derived from the model of cognitions influencing social isolation described earlier.

The reliability and validity of role-play tests has been a subject of controversy in recently published literature. The available research indicates that there is little association between scores on the frequency and duration of specific behavior (e.g., eye contact and response latency) in role plays and *in vivo* observations, a finding that has been interpreted as reflecting low ecological validity for the tests, (e.g., Bellack, Hersen, & Turner, 1978, 1979). However, significant correlations have been observed between ratings on global measures of behavior, such as social

TABLE 1. Characteristics and Representative Examples of Positive and Negative Self-Statements Used by Children and Youths in Social Interaction

	Characteristic content	Example
Negative self-statements	Overestimating likelihood of negative outcomes	"I always say something dumb." "Everybody will hate me."
	Underestimating likelihood of positive outcomes	"No one will want to talk to me."
	Catastrophization (exaggerating the importance of negative outcomes)	"I can't stand it when they rubbish me."
	Self-effacement	"I'm too stupid." "They don't really think I did it well."
	Anxiety-inducing, goal-irrelevant ideas	"Everybody's staring at me." "I never know what to say." "Hell, I feel nervous."
Positive self-statements	Realistic estimation of likelihood of outcomes	"It may work out, it might not." "He's probably looking for someone to talk to as well."
	Realistic assessment of the importance of outcomes	"I would rather he said yes—but I guess I can ask someone else if he says no."
	Goal-relevant self-instruction	"What do I have to do first?" "I'll never know if I don't try; I'll ask them."
	Coping self-instruction for negative feelings or outcomes	"I'm uptight—just take a deep breath and relax." "Damn!—Still, I'll get by."

skills and assertiveness, in role-played and *in vivo* situations (Wessburg, Mariotto, Conger, Farrell, & Conger, 1979). Furthermore, such global ratings of role-play performance discriminate between groups dichotomized into high/low social isolation and high/low social anxiety on the basis of self-ratings and significant-other ratings (e.g., Arkowitz *et al.*, 1975; Gottmann *et al.*, 1975; Halford & Foddy, 1982). Thus, it would seem that role-played behavior can be a useful indicator of global social behavior, but that the frequency and duration of specific behaviors in such role plays is unreliable.

The reliability and validity of measures of cognition obtained from the role-playing methods described previously has not been researched much at all. Evidence reviewed by Kendall and Hollon (1981) indicates that it is possible to develop coding systems with good interrater reliability for classifying the self-statements generated. The test–retest reliability and ecological validity of such measures has not been investigated. However, the observed group differences in self-statement scores during role-play tests between high and low socially anxious or unassertive subjects (Bruch, 1981; Halford & Foddy, 1982) provide preliminary evidence of the method's validity.

Other Assessment Methods

Storytelling and game playing are both useful clinical cognitive-behavioral assessment methods with children. Stein and Goodman (1981) have used storytelling by children about making friendships as a means of assessing children's cognitive conceptualization of social interaction processes. This approach can often provide insights into the appropriate content for self-instructional training. For example, if a child fails to consider the impact of her or his behavior on another, as revealed in the child's storytelling, instruction can be given in using self-statements such as "How will _____ feel if I do that?" Similarly, children can be asked to act out various social situations using puppets or similar props. Unfortunately, there is no evidence of the reliability or validity of such assessment methods.

Another assessment strategy is the behavioral interview. Particularly with older children, simply asking what they do and what they think in specific situations can often provide useful information on the nature of social withdrawal. However, it is necessary to be aware of the evidence, which was reviewed previously, that there are biases in socially withdrawn persons' perceptions of social interaction. Such biases limit the value of information gained via interview.

Treatment Methods

The cognitive treatment of social withdrawal can usefully be viewed as being made up of three steps: (1) the acquisition of rational self-statements; (2) the practice of rational self-statements; and (3) the generalization of the use of rational self-statements. This process is almost always combined with an overt response-skills training program. In this section, the three cognitive steps are described, and brief mention is made of overt skills training. (Detailed reviewsthis latter aspect of treating social withdrawal can be found in Eisler & Fredericksen, 1980; Halford, 1980; or Van Hasselt *et al.* 1979.)

Acquiring Rational Self-Statements

Methods of Acquisition

Acquiring rational self-statements involves providing clients with the appropriate self-statements to meet their needs, as identified in the cognitive-behavioral assessment. In what Ellis (1977) has described as "elegant R-E-T," the clinician attempts to teach the client a general belief system. The clinician usually begins by prescribing set reading (e.g., *A New Guide to Rational Living,* Ellis & Harper, 1975) and homework tasks of assessing one's beliefs, followed up by verbal disputation of irrational beliefs. Although this process may generate a generalized positive result in adults, in my experience few adolescents and almost no children are cognitively sophisticated enough to follow this process. I attempt to teach more specific cognitions for more specific problem situations in almost all instances of working with children and adolescents.

The modeling of positive self-statements is a good means of teaching specific cognitions to clients. A range of methods of modeling can be used. Films and videotapes can be used to illustrate self-statements by the dubbing of self-talk, as has been done by Jabichuk and Smeriglio (1976). In a group training situation, fellow group members generate and can demonstrate appropriate self-statements "out loud" in role plays. For younger children, use can be made of games involving puppets, dolls, cartoons, etc., to model self-talk. Story reading is another method of modeling useful with children. For adolescents who are reasonably sophisticated cognitively, use can be made of guided reading to illustrate appropriate self-statements.

Whatever the specific nature of the modeling, it is important to keep in mind three general principles. First, modeling is more effective when the model and the client are similar (Bandura, 1977). Thus, models of the same age, sex, race, and verbal skills as the client are preferable. Second, models demonstrating coping, rather than mastery, levels of skills are most effective (Bandura, 1977). Consequently, models should show evidence of having difficulty, feeling anxious, etc., in target social situations and should show how to cope with such difficulties and anxieties. Finally, different cognitive strategies seem to work for different people (Jaremko, 1979). Therefore, it is preferable to offer clients a range of models and allow them to select what works best for them.

An important cognitive skill reviewed previously in the second section of this chapter is the ability of individuals to conceptualize and generate alternative responses to social situations. Toward this end, I have found that introducing participants to the assertive/ aggressive/ passive typology, described by authors such as Alberti and Emmons (1974) and Lange and Jakubowski (1976), is invaluable. For verbally skilled youths, prescribing books such as Alberti and Emmons (1974) can be useful. Lecturettes, modeling of different styles of responding, group discussion of the effects of different styles on the recipient and the person behaving, and paper-and-pencil tests on discrimination of response styles are all good methods of teaching this typology, and each can be used with less cognitively sophisticated clients.

Practicing Rational Self-Statements

Having been exposed to appropriate rational self-statements, it is necessary for the client to practice using these self-statements. A common method used is to role-play the situations using the method of training self-statements described by Meichenbaum (1977). Clients first role-play the situation saying the self-statements out loud, then repeat the role play just moving their lips, and finally role-play simply saying the statements to themselves covertly. Rehearsal via guided imagery is a useful supplement: clients are asked to imagine themselves being in the situations and using appropriate self-statements. For younger children, this procedure can be incorporated into play, by getting them to use dolls and similar props to act out scenes using positive self-statements. (All these methods have the advantage that training overt behaviors can be incorporated into this same process.)

It is important to get clients to practice their self-statements in the target *in vivo* situation, and hence, it is desirable to make use of appropriate homework assignments (e.g., "OK, Jenny, next time you want to say something in class and feel scared, what if you *do* tell yourself 'I want to say it, nothing too bad can happen, I will say it.' Then put your hand up. Will you do that?"). The use of prompts can facilitate this process. These can involve the use of cards, reminder pins, and verbal/nonverbal prompts from others such as peers or teachers to establish the behavior. Such antecedent prompts can be faded once the behavior is established.

The reinforcement of the appropriate use of self-statements is important in establishing cognitive-behavior change. In training situations, extensive use of verbal praise from the trainer is desirable. In group training situations, positive feedback on successes from peers should be encouraged. Self-monitoring of cognitions in *in vivo* situations via forms such as the one depicted in Figure 2 can be used as the basis of monitoring and rewarding behavior.

GENERALIZING RATIONAL SELF-STATEMENTS

The generalization of the use of rational self-statements across situations and persistence in this use over time are clearly vital if therapy is to have its optimal impact for the socially withdrawn child or adolescent. Previous reviews have noted that the generalization of overt behavior following social skills training is limited and that results can dissipate over time (e.g., Van Hasselt *et al.*, 1979; Whitehill *et al.*, 1980). No directly relevant evidence is available about the cross-situational generalization or persistence of the use of rational self-statements relevant to social withdrawal. However, my clinical observations suggest that generalization may be limited. Below, I describe some clinical strategies that may enhance generalization. Clearly, more systematic research into their efficacy is highly desirable.

One clinical procedure that has been used to enhance generalization is "booster sessions." That is, the client is encouraged to return to the clinician intermittently to practice the use of the cognitive self-statements in new social situations as they arise. Another possibility is to maximize, within practical bounds, the ranges of situations within which the client acquires and rehearses rational self-statements in the initial training phase. A third option is to attempt to ensure that the use of self-statements will be prompted and reinforced across a range of naturalistic situations. For example, teachers or parents can be asked to get clients to continue to monitor the use of rational self-statements, and to reinforce that use, after the termination of therapy.

It has been my experience that clients who are able to follow through on the steps of analyzing self-statements or beliefs, as described by Ellis (1977), generalize their therapeutic gains more than those who simply role-learn specific self-statements for specific situations. However, most young children, and many youths and adults, find this process very cognitively complex. Therefore, I attempt to teach RET-type principles where possible, to enhance generalization, but I recognize their limited applicability.

Finally, and perhaps most important, the ultimate determinant of the persistence and generalization of rational cognitive self-statements is whether their use is reinforced. That is, it is dependent on the extent to which such self-statements can reduce negative affect, increase positive affect, facilitate the use of overt behaviors that are reinforced, and reduce the frequency of negative, punished behaviors in the target situation(s).

OVERT RESPONSE TRAINING

The term *social skills training* has been used most frequently to describe training in specific overt responses such as eye contact, short response latencies, assertive verbal content, and appropriate voice volume and modulation. A range of combinations of procedures has been used in social skills training; however, all of these can be conceptualized as falling into three general categories: response acquisition procedures, response practice procedures, and response generalization procedures. Among the procedures designed to help clients to acquire new responses have been instructions; and models presented by peers and therapist, audiovisually, or in the imagination (e.g., Bornstein *et al.*, 1977; Whitehill *et al.*, 1980). The response practice procedure most commonly used has been behavior rehearsal, combined with various forms of selective performance feedback (Van Hasselt *et al.*, 1979). Response generalization has generally been attempted by the use of instructional sets to use role-play-acquired responses and/or extending training across a range of situations (e.g., Whitehill *et al.*, 1980).

One of the difficulties in social skills training has been to specify target behaviors that are adaptive for children to use in target situations. Some people have gone to considerable trouble to validate the adaptiveness of behaviors (e.g., Minkin *et al.*, 1976). However, as was noted by Freedman, Rosenthal, Donahue, Schlundt, and McFall (1978), large-scale social-skills-training programs often have been embarked on without an appropriate assessment of behavioral deficits. It is noteworthy that there is little evidence that assertive children are better accepted by peers, are better adjusted, are less likely to solicit aggression from others, or are happier than unassertive children. Yet there are a considerable number of studies attempting to train children to be more assertive.

AN ILLUSTRATIVE CASE HISTORY: ALLEN

> Allen was a 15-year-old referred to me by a welfare agency for the long-term unemployed. He was described by the referral source as "totally socially isolated, unable to make friends, and far too shy to be able to get a job." As an illustration of the material covered above, I describe here the work that Allen and I did together on his presentation at job interviews. This work began after Allen had seen me four times on a weekly basis, and we had jointly selected job interviewee skills as a first target for change.

Allen's main ambition was to be a cabinetmaker's apprentice, but he indicated to me that he would take any job he was offered. We worked out that he had gone for approximately 65–70 job interviews in the preceeding four months without receiving a job offer. In order to assess how Allen currently behaved in job interviews, we role-played an interview, which was videotaped. We then viewed the videotape together, with me stopping the tape and asking him to describe his self-statements at various points (as in the procedure described previously in this chapter). In addition, I gave him a guided imagery of being in a job interview and again asked him to describe his thoughts during the imagery. Finally, I set him a task of going to an interview during the next week and, immediately afterward, listing all the thoughts that occurred to him during that interview and how he thought he had performed.

During that week, I contacted three cabinetmakers selected at random from the telephone book and asked them to describe what they would want to see in a candidate for an apprenticeship in an interview. The common elements in the answers offered were a willingness to work hard, a sense of enthusiasm about the job, and evidence of a sense of responsibility about matters such as punctuality and workmanship.

The results of the assessment of Allan's self-statements across the three assessment modalities (role play, guided imagery, and *in vivo*) were reviewed in the next session and generally were consistent. Allen persistently used highly self-critical, goal-irrelevant, negative self-statements, such as "What's the use? I'll never get a job"; "Don't know what to say"; "This guy probably wants someone older"; and "I'm too dumb to get a job."

An examination of the videotape of the role-played interview by Allen and me indicated that Allen gave very short answers to the questions asked (e.g., "Yeah"; "Guess so"; and "Dunno"), had minimal eye contact with the interviewer, and used almost no hand or facial gestures. These behaviors were contrasted with the attributes that the potential employers had described, and a general behavioral goal was mutually agreed to of communicating those three attributes of willingness to work, enthusiasm, and responsbility.

Allen and I role-played brief segments of an interview several times while he deliberately used as many negative self-statements as possible. (This is an example of the procedure described by Meichenbaum (1977) as "negative practice.") He became quite distressed in this process, and we then discussed the effect on him of these self-statements. We then brainstormed together on the many positive self-statements that he might use instead. Further role playing ensued, rehearsing these self-statements. Some of the thoughts that were practiced were "I want this job, so show him I want it"; "I'm trying to learn to be better at interviews, and even if I blow this one, it's all good practice"; "Just keep calm and think about what to say"; and "Make sure I show my willingness to work." The contrast in Allen's feelings using these positive self-statements and his earlier reactions during negative practice was obvious to him and to me. We then did a guided imagery of Allen going to an interview and using these positive self-statements. I asked him to rehearse this imagery and to role-play being an interviewee in front of a mirror, over the next week.

The following week Allen and I role-played two more mock interviews. Then, a colleague, experienced in job interviewing, interviewed Allen while he again concentrated on using positive self-statements. Prior to this interview, we made a "self-instruction card," which he read just before entering the interview. This consisted of a card with three sentences in it: "Breath deep, relax, relax. Remember: I want work, I'm enthusiastic, I'll do it well. I'll be positive." The videotape of this latest interview was vastly different to the first role play that Allen did with me, and we jointly decided that Allen should seek out more job interviews over the next week. Again, I asked Allen to record his self-statements and feelings immediately after any interview he had.

In the ensuing week, Allen went to four interviews and was offered a job as a storeman as the result of one of these interviews. He accepted this job. We did a lot more work together over the next eight weeks, working on improving his ability to cope in a range of social situations, including asking girls on dates, chatting with work colleagues, and talking with authority figures (e.g., bosses). The instructions were essentially of the same character as that described above.

On termination of therapy, Allen rated his shyness as "greatly reduced." Allen filled in Watson and Friend's (1969) Social Avoidance and Distress Scale at the end of therapy, as he had in his first session with me. His score decreased from 24 out of a possible 28 on the scale at the initial session, to 11 in the final session, a score decrease of over two standard deviations based on Halford's (1979) normative data for that scale.

Special Considerations in Applications of Cognitive Procedures with Children and Youth

As I have attempted to demonstrate throughout this review, most of the research on cognitive approaches to social withdrawal has involved adult subjects. Consequently, much of what I have suggested for working with children and youths has been an adaptation of procedures developed for adults. Further research into the role of cognitions in social withdrawal in children and youths is urgently needed. In the interim, clinicians must attempt to ensure, via careful behavioral analysis, that both the overt and the cognitive responses that they teach their young clients really will be adaptive within the social situations with which those young clients have difficulty.

It is necessary to adjust the clinical approach to an appropriate level of cognitive complexity for young clients. The younger and the less cognitively sophisticated the client, the more the treatment needs to focus on teaching specific skills for specific problem situations. Older, more sophisticated clients can be taught more generalizable, less specific cognitive strategies for dealing with social situations.

REFERENCES

Alberti, R. E., & Emmons, M. L. *Your perfect right* (2nd ed.). San Luis Obispo, Calif.: Impact, 1974.
Annon, J. S. *The behavioral treatment of sexual problems* (Vol. 2): *Intensive therapy.* Honolulu: Enabling Systems, 1975.
Argyle, M., & Kendon, D. The experimental analysis of social performance. *Advances in Experimental Social Psychology,* 1967, *3,* 55–98.
Argyle, M., Bryant, B., & Trower, D. Social skills training and psychotherapy: A comparative study. *Psychological Medicine,* 1974, *4,* 435–443.
Arkowitz, H., Lichenstein, E., McGovern, K., & Hines, P. The behavioral assessment of social competence in males. *Behavior Therapy,* 1975, *6,* 3–13.
Asher, S. R., & Renshaw, P. D. Children without friends: Social knowledge and social skills training. In S. R. Asher & J. M. Gottmann (Eds.), *The development of children's friendships.* New York: Cambridge University Press, 1981.
Bandura, A. *Social learning theory.* Englewood Cliffs, N.J.: Prentice-Hall, 1977.
Bellack, A. S., Hersen, M., & Turner, S. M. Role-play tests for assessing social skills: Are they valid? *Behavior Therapy,* 1978, *9,* 448–461.
Bellack, A. S., Hersen, M., & Turner, S. M. Relationship of role-playing and knowledge of appropriate behavior to assertion in the natural environment. *Journal of Consulting and Clinical Psychology,* 1979, *47,* 670–678.
Bornstein, M. R., Bellack, A. S., & Hersen, M. Social skills training for unassertive children: A multiple baseline analysis. *Journal of Applied Behavior Analysis,* 1977, *10,* 183–195.
Bruch, M. A. A task analysis of assertive behavior revisited: Replication and extension. *Behavior Therapy,* 1981, *78,* 217–230.
Bryant, B., & Trower, P. E. Social difficulty in a student sample. *British Journal of Educational Psychology,* 1974, *44,* 13–21.
Butler, L., & Meichenbaum, D. The assessment of interpersonal problem-solving skills. In P. C. Kendall & S. D. Hollon (Eds.), *Assessment strategies for cognitive-behavioral interventions.* New York: Academic Press, 1981.
Cacioppo, J. T., Glass, C. R., & Merluzzi, T. V. Self-statements and self-evaluations: A cognitive-response analysis of heterosocial anxiety. *Cognitive Therapy and Research,* 1979, *3,* 249–262.
Clarke, J. V., & Arkowitz, H. Social anxiety and self-evaluation of interpersonal performance. *Psychological Reports,* 1975, *36,* 211–221.
Coche, E., & Douglas, A. A. Therapeutic effects of problem-solving training and play-reading groups. *Journal of Clinical Psychology,* 1977, *30,* 820–827.
Cowen, E. L., Pederson, A., Babigan, H., Izzo, D., & Trost, H. A. Long-term follow-up of early detected vulnerable children. *Journal of Consulting and Clinical Psychology,* 1973, *41,* 483–486.

Curran, J. P., Little, L. M., & Gilbert, F. S. *Response of high and low heterosexual dating anxious males to female approach cues.* Unpublished manuscript, Purdue University, 1976.

Curran, J. P., Wallander, J. R., & Fischetti, M. *The role of behavioral and cognitive factors in the maintenance of heterosexual-social anxiety.* Paper presented at the Midwestern Psychological Convention, Chicago, May 1977.

Daly, S. Behavioral correlates of social anxiety. *British Journal of Social and Clinical Psychology,* 1978, *17,* 117–120.

Deluty, R. H. Children's action tendency scale: A self-report measure of aggressiveness, assertiveness and submissiveness in children. *Journal of Consulting and Clinical Psychology,* 1979, *47,* 1061–1071.

DeVoge, C. A behavioral approach to RET with children. In A. Ellis & R. Grieger (Eds.), *Handbook of rational-emotive therapy.* New York: Springer, 1977.

Dunnington, M. J. Behavioral differences of sociometric status groups in a nursery school. *Child Development,* 1957, *28,* 103–111.

D'Zurilla, T. J., & Nezu, A. A study of the generation-of-alternatives process in social problem solving. *Cognitive Therapy and Research,* 1980, *4,* 67–72.

Eisler, R. M., & Fredriksen, L. W. *Perfecting social skills: A guide to interpersonal behavior development.* New York: Plenum Press, 1980.

Eisler, R. M., Miller, P. M., & Hersen, M. Components of assertive behavior. *Journal of Clinical Psychology,* 1973, *29,* 295–299.

Eisler, R. M., Hersen, M., Miller, P. M., & Blanchard, E. B. Situational determinants of assertive behaviors. *Journal of Consulting and Clinical Psychology,* 1975, *43,* 330–340.

Eisler, R. M., Fredericksen, L. W., & Peterson, G. L. The relationship of cognitive variables to the expression of assertiveness. *Behavior Therapy,* 1978, *9,* 419–427.

Ellis, A. The basic clinical theory of rational-emotive therapy. In A. Ellis & R. Grieger (Eds.), *Handbook of rational-emotive therapy.* New York: Springer, 1977.

Ellis, A., & Harper, R. A. *A new guide to rational living.* Hollywood, Calif.: Wilshire, 1975.

Fiedler, D., & Beach, L. R. On the decision to be assertive. *Journal of Consulting and Clinical Psychology,* 1978, *46,* 537–546.

Foster, S. L., & Richey, W. L. Issues in the assessment of social competence in children. *Journal of Applied Behavior Analysis,,* 1979, *12,* 625–638.

Gay, M. L., Hollandsworth, J. G. Jr., & Galassi, J. P. An assertiveness inventory for adults. *Journal of Counseling Psychology,* 1975, *22,* 340–344.

Gillingham, P. R., Griffiths, R. D. P., & Case, D. Direct assessment of social behavior from video-tape recordings. *British Journal of Social and Clinical Psychology,* 1977, *16,* 181–187.

Glasgow, R. E., & Arkowitz, H. The behavioral assessment of male and female social competence in dyadic heterosexual situations. *Behavior Therapy,* 1975, *6,* 488–498.

Goetz, T. C., & Dweck, C. S. Learned helplessness in social situations. *Journal of Personality and Social Psychology,* 1980, *39,* 246–255.

Goldsmith, J. B., & McFall, R. M. Development and evaluation of an interpersonal skill-training program for psychiatric patients. *Journal of Abnormal Psychology,* 1975, *84,* 51–58.

Gormally, J., Sipps, G., Raphael, R., Edwin, D., & Varvil-Weld, P. The relationship between maladaptive cognitions and social anxiety. *Journal of Consulting and Clinical Psychology,* 1981, *49,* 300–301.

Gottmann, J., Gonso, J., & Rasmussen, B. Social interaction, social competence and friendship in children. *Child Development,* 1975, *46,* 709–718.

Gottman, J. M. Toward a definition of social isolation in children. *Child Development,* 1977, *48,* 513–517.

Green, K. D., Forehand, R., Beck, S. J., & Vosk, B. An assessment of the relationship among measures of children's social competence and children's academic achievement. *Child Development*, 1980, *51*, 1149–1156.

Greenwood, C. R., Walker, H. M., Todd, N. M., & Hops, H. Selecting a cost-effective screening measure for the assessment of preschool social withdrawal. *Journal of Applied Behavior Analysis*, 1979, *12*, 639–652.

Gresham, F. M. Social skills training with handicapped children: A review. *Review of Educational Research*, 1981, *51*, 139–176.

Gronlund, N. E. *Sociometry in the classroom*. New York: Harper, 1959.

Halford, W. K. *Cognitive and social skill variables in social anxiety*. Unpublished doctoral dissertation, La Trobe University, Bundoora, Australia, 1979.

Halford, W. K. Social skills training for children. In A. Hudson & M. Griffin (Eds.), *Behavior analysis and problems of childhood*. Bundoora, Australia: PIT Press, 1980.

Halford, W. K., & Foddy, M. Cognitive and social skills correlates of social anxiety. *British Journal of Clinical Psychology*, 1982, *21*, 1–12.

Hartup, W. W., Glazer, J. A., & Charlesworth, R. Peer reinforcement and sociometric status. *Child Development*, 1967, *38*, 1017–1024.

Jabichuk, Z., & Smeriglio, V. L. The influence of symbolic modeling on the social behavior of preschool children with low levels of social responsiveness. *Child Development*, 1976, *47*, 838–841.

Jaremko, M. E. A component analysis of stress innoculation: Review and prospectus. *Cognitive Therapy and Research*, 1979, *3*, 35–48.

Jones, R. A. *Factured measure of Ellis' irrational belief system*. Unpublished doctoral dissertation, Texas Technological College, 1968.

Kagen, J., & Moss, H. A. *Birth to maturity: A study in psychological development*. New York: Wiley, 1962.

Kane, J. W., & Lawler, E. E. Methods of peer assessment. *Psychological Bulletin*, 1978, *85*, 555–586.

Kazdin, A. E., Matson, J. L., & Esveldt-Dawson, K. Social skill performance among normal and psychiatric inpatient children as a function of assessment conditions. *Behavior Research and Therapy*, 1981, *19*, 145–152.

Kendall, P. C., & Hollon, S. D. Assessing self-referent speech: Methods in the measurement of self-statements. In P. C. Kendall & S. D. Hollon (Eds.), *Assessment strategies for cognitive-behavioral interventions*. New York: Academic Press, 1981.

Kent, R. N., & Foster, S. L. Direct observational procedures: Methodological issues in applied settings. In A. R. Cininero, K. S. Calhoun, & H. F. Adams (Eds.), *Handbook of behavioral assessment*. New York: Wiley, 1977.

Kirschner, N. M. Generalization of behaviorally orientated assertive training. *The Psychological Record*, 1976, *26*, 117–125.

Kraft, T. Social anxiety model of alcoholism. *Perceptual Motor Skills*, 1971, *33*, 797–798.

Lange, A. J., & Jakubowski, P. *Responsible assertive behavior: Cognitive-behavioral procedures for trainers*. Champaign, Ill.: Research, 1976.

Lewinsohn, P. M. The behavioral study and treatment of depression. *Advances in Behavior Modification*, 1975, *1*, 19–64.

Libet, J. M., & Lewinsohn, P. M. Concept of social skill with special reference to the behavior of depressed persons. *Journal of Consulting and Clinical Psychology*, 1973, *40*, 304–312.

Mandel, N. M., & Shrauger, J. S. The effects of self-evaluative statements on heterosocial approach in shy and non-shy males. *Cognitive Therapy and Research*, 1980, *4*, 369–381.

McCandless, M. R., & Marshall, H. R. A picture-sociometric technique for preschool children and its relation to teacher judgements of friendship. *Child Development*, 1957, *28*, 139–149.

Meichenbaum, D. M. *Cognitive-behavior modification: An integrative approach.* New York: Plenum Press, 1977.
Miller, P., & Eisler, R. Assertive behavior of alcoholics: A descriptive analysis. *Behavior Therapy,* 1977, *8,* 146–149.
Miller, P., Hersen, M., Eisler, R., & Hilsman, E. Effects of social stress on operant drinking of alcoholics and social drinkers. *Behavior Research and Therapy,* 1974, *12,* 67–72.
Minkin, N., Braukmann, C. J., Minkin, B. L., Timbers, G. D., Timbers, B. J., Fixsen, D. L., Phillips, D. L., & Wolf, M. M. The social validation and training of conversational skills. *Journal of Applied Behavior Analysis,* 1976, *9,* 127–139.
O'Banien, K., & Arkowitz, H. Social anxiety and selective memory for affective information about the self. *Journal of Consulting and Clinical Psychology,* 1977, *45,* 717–718.
O'Conner, R. D. Modification of social withdrawal through symbolic modeling. *Journal of Applied Behavior Analysis,* 1969, *2,* 15–22.
O'Conner, R. D. Relative efficacy of modelling, shaping and the combined procedures for modification of social withdrawal. *Journal of Abnormal Psychology,* 1972, *79,* 327–334.
Oden, S., & Asher, S. R. Coaching children in social skills for friendship making. *Child Development,* 1977, *48,* 495–506.
Patterson, G. R. The aggressive child: Victim and architect of a coercive system. In E. J. Mash, L. A. Hamerlynck, & L. C. Hardy (Eds.), *Behavior modification and families.* New York: Brunner/Mazel, 1976.
Pilkonis, P. A. The behavioral consequences of shyness. *Journal of Personality,* 1977, *45,* 596–611. (a)
Pilkonis, P. A. Shyness, public and private, and its relationship to other measures of social behavior. *Journal of Personality,* 1977, *45,* 585– 595. (b)
Platt, J. J., & Spivack, G. Problem-solving thinking of psychiatric patients. *Journal of Consulting and Clinical Psychology,* 1972, *39,* 148–151.
Rathus, S. A. A 30 item schedule for assessing assertive behavior. *Behavior Therapy,* 1973, *4,* 398–406.
Richardson, F. C., & Tasto, D. L. Development and factor analysis of a social anxiety inventory. *Behavior Therapy,* 1976, *7,* 453–462.
Rolf, M., Sells, B., & Golden, M. N. *Social adjustment and personality development in children.* Minneapolis: University of Minnesota Press, 1972.
Schwartz, R. M., & Gottmann, J. M. Toward a task analysis of assertive behavior. *Journal of Consulting and Clinical Psychology,* 1976, *44,* 910–920.
Shure, M. B., & Spivack, G. Means-end thinking, adjustment and social class among elementary school-aged children. *Journal of Consulting and Clinical Psychology,* 1972, *38,* 348–353.
Shure, M. B., & Spivack, G. *Preschool Interpersonal Problem Solving (PIPS) Test: Manual.* Philadelphia: Hahnemann Community Mental Health/Mental Retardation Centre, 1974.
Shure, M. B., Spivack, G., & Jaegar, M. A. Problem-solving thinking and adjustment among disadvantaged preschool children. *Child Development,* 1971, *42,* 1791–1803.
Smith, R. E., & Sarason, I. G. Social anxiety and the evaluation of negative interpersonal feedback. *Journal of Consulting and Clinical Psychology,* 1975, *43,* 429.
Spivack, G., Platt, J. J., & Shure, M. B. *The problem-solving approach to adjustment.* San Francisco: Jossey-Bass, 1976.
Stein, N. L., & Goldman, S. R. Children's knowledge about social situations: From causes to consequences. In S. Asher & J. Gottmann (Eds.), *The development of children's friendships.* New York: Cambridge University Press, 1981.
Sutton-Simon, K., & Goldfried, M. R. Faulty thinking patterns in two types of anxiety. *Cognitive Therapy and Research,* 1979, *3,* 193–203.

Trower, P. Situational analysis of the components and processes of behavior of socially unskilled and skilled patients. *Journal of Consulting and Clinical Psychology,* 1980, *48,* 327–339.

Trower, P., Bryant, B., & Argyle, M. *Social skills and mental health.* London: Methuen, 1978.

Twentyman, C. T., & McFall, R. M. Behavioral training of social skills in shy males. *Journal of Consulting and Clinical Psychology,* 1975, *43,* 384–395.

Twentyman, C. T., & Zimmering, R. T. Behavioral training of social skills: A critical review. In M. Hersen, R. M. Eisler, & P. M. Miller (Eds.), *Progress in behavior modification* (Vol. 7) New York: Academic Press, 1979.

Ullmann, C. A. Teachers, peers, and tests as predictors of adjustment. *Journal of Educational Psychology,* 1957, *48,* 257–267.

Van Hasselt, V. B., Hersen, M., Whitehill, M. B., & Bellack, A. S. Social skill assessment and training for children: An evaluative review. *Behavior Research and Therapy,* 1979, *17,* 413–437.

Watson, D., & Friend, R. Measurement of social-evaluative anxiety. *Journal of Consulting and Clinical Psychology,* 1969, *33,* 448–457.

Wessburg, H. W., Mariotto, M. J., Conger, A. J., Farrell, A. D., & Conger, J. C. Ecological validity of role plays for assessing heterosocial anxiety and skill of male college students. *Journal of Consulting and Clinical Psychology,* 1979, *47,* 525–535.

Whitehill, M. B., Hersen, M., & Bellack, A. S. Conversation skills for socially isolated children. *Behavior Research and Therapy,* 1980, *18,* 217–225.

Zimbardo, P. G. *Shyness: What it is, what to do about it.* Reading, Mass.: Addison-Wesley, 1977.

Zimbardo, P. G., Pilkonis, P. A., & Norwood, R. M. *The silent prison of shyness.* (ONR Tech. Rep. 2-17). Stanford, Calif.: Stanford University, November 1974.

10

Cognitive-Behavioral Treatment of Childhood and Adolescent Obesity

JOHN P. FOREYT AND ALBERT T. KONDO

DEFINITION AND PROBLEM

Obesity is the state of having an excess of adipose tissue. Although this definition may seem straightforward and to the point, considerable confusion and misuse occur in its practical application. For example, *obesity* is frequently used as a synonym for *overweight* (i.e., weight in excess of the ideal for individuals of a particular sex, age, and height). Although overweight often suggests the presence of obesity, this relationship does not always hold. An individual may be overweight because of factors other than the presence of excessive fat tissue (e.g., a high relative level of muscularity). This point was illustrated in the often-quoted case of the Green Bay Packers football team. When several members of the Packers underwent their physical examinations prior to possible induction into the armed services, a majority of them were found to be ineligible because of their overweight! However, it is doubtful if even the most casual observer would have accused any of them of being obese. Later in this chapter, the determination of obesity and its associated complexities will be discussed.

JOHN P. FOREYT • Department of Medicine, Baylor College of Medicine, Houston, Texas 77030.   ALBERT T. KONDO • Department of Psychology, University of Houston, Houston, Texas 77004. This research is supported by Grant No. HL17269 from the National Heart, Lung, and Blood Institute, National Institutes of Health, Bethesda, Md. Dr. Kondo is a research Fellow in Behavioral Medicine at the University of Houston, supported by the National Heart, Lung, and Blood Vessel Institute Grant No. 1 T32 HL07258-01A1.

The problems accompanying the presence of obesity in a child or an adolescent are numerous. Obese children are at a higher risk for a number of health problems as well as difficulties in psychological and social adjustment. With respect to health, childhood obesity has been shown to contribute to the occurrence of shortness of breath, orthopedic difficulties, inadequate circulatory adjustment to exercise, and general clumsiness (Mayer, 1970; Mobbs, 1970). The presence of obesity in children also appears to enhance their probability of demonstrating selected cardiovascular disease risk factors. In comparison to their normal-weight peers, obese children have been found to have higher levels of serum cholesterol and triglycerides (Clark, Menow, Morse, & Keyser, 1970; Laver, Conner, Leaverton, Reiter, & Clarke, 1975) and a tendency to evidence hypertension (Laver et al., 1975; Londe, Bourgoignie, Robson, & Goldring, 1971).

The health risks associated with early-onset obesity may not be confined to the childhood years. Substantial evidence suggests that obese children tend to become obese adults (Weil, 1977). Thus, the health risks attendant on obesity in adulthood, including cerebrovascular accidents and maturity-onset diabetes mellitus (Mann, 1974), appear to be the legacy of the obese child.

Although overweight in childhood may be the precursor of a number of health hazards, the most difficult problems faced by the child are likely to be those associated with self-concept and social acceptance. The contemporary American culture values slimness to an almost inordinate degree. The images of attractiveness, youth, strength, and even intelligence, as portrayed by the mass media, are frequently bound to pencil-thin silhouettes. With such emphasis on thinness, it is no wonder that social acceptability has an association with the attainment or maintenance of this state. To be overweight is to be unacceptable. To be overweight is to face the barbs of social isolation, overt prejudice, and diminished opportunity (Allon, 1975; Millman, 1980). Although most, if not all, of the obese suffer from the consequences of such negative societal attitudes, children and adolescents are particularly vulnerable (Dwyer & Mayer, 1975). Their vulnerability is undoubtedly related to a myriad of factors, including their strong need for peer acceptance, the heightened self-consciousness attendant on their age, and their still underdeveloped capabilities of psychological rationalization and defense.

The nature of the prejudice toward the overweight child has been demonstrated in previous research. In a survey of children's attitudes toward others, Lerner (1973) found that children indicated a desire to maintain a greater personal distance from their overweight counterparts than from those of normal weight. Staffieri (1967), in his study of 6- to

10-year-olds, revealed a tendency to assign the most negative character adjectives to silhouettes of the obese and the very thin. As if the barbs of prejudice received by overweight children from their age peers weren't enough, investigations have uncovered similar attitudes in adults (including health professionals!) toward this much-maligned group (Goodman, Dornbusch, Richardson, & Hastorf, 1963; Maddox, Back, & Liederman, 1968).

The social and psychological problems associated with childhood obesity do not end with the coming of adolescence; if anything, they seem to get worse. Adolescence is a time when personal appearance becomes a substantial preoccupation. Any deviation from the "norm" of appearance often causes concern and self-consciousness. Their realization of being different and the social-cultural schema that accentuates the difference appear to have a significant influence on the way obese adolescents view themselves. Monello and Mayer (1963), for example, found that obese adolescent girls exhibited personality characteristics similar to those of racial minorities. The girls demonstrated such characteristics as excessive passivity, withdrawal, concern about their status, and an acceptance of the dominant value system, which promulgates a negative view of the obese.

Among some adolescents, primarily females, the need or perhaps the obsession to appear thin becomes perverted into a mania. This disturbance can result in either of two conditions: anorexia nervosa or bulimarexia. Anorexia nervosa has become so widespread that the term has entered into the vocabulary of many Americans—and authorities fear that its incidence is steeply on the rise (Wooley, Wooley, & Dyrenforth, 1979). Somewhat less known than anorexia nervosa is the condition of bulimarexia. Bulimarexia, or the gorge–purge syndrome, as coined by Boskind-Lodahl and Sirlin (1977), is a condition in which the individual eats well in excess of her physical needs and shortly thereafter goes through a ritual of purging—usually through vomiting. The repeated practice of this behavior frequently results in serious health consequences, including ulcers, hernias, dental problems, and a disturbance of the body's chemical balance. That bulimarexia and anorexia nervosa tend to be afflictions of young adolescent girls suggests the intensity of pressure experienced by this population for slenderness.

Etiology

It is widely held that most obesity is caused by an imbalance between energy intake and energy expenditure. Obese persons have either (1) consumed too much food in relation to their needs; (2) expended too little energy in relation to their intake; or (3) both. Although this equation of obesity causation is immutable, numerous intervening factors make this matter more complex than it first appears.

The trait of obesity in humans appears to be caused by the complex interactions of "nature and nurture" (Weil, 1975). That is, some of us appear to have a genetic propensity toward overweight that may or may not appear, depending on the environmental influences to which we are exposed.

The possible avenues by which heredity may predispose individuals to overweight have been studied by several investigators. Beller (1977) suggested that the tendency toward overweight by some may be an adaptive characteristic passed on from their earliest ancestors. For those of European heritage, she theorized that primitive ancestors may have evolved in a manner that adapted to the cold climates and intermittent food supplies characteristic of their environment. This adaptation translated into a facile tendency to accumulate adipose tissue for purposes of insulation and energy storage. Mayer (1975) found that individual body type (or somatype) appears to influence tendencies toward fatness or thinness. For example, the dominant ectomorph (i.e., individuals characterized by elongated skeletal structures) is rarely found to be overweight. On the other hand, overweight is more likely among those whose somatype predisposes its occurrence, that is, those who have short limbs and barrel chests. Mayer's (1975) investigation of infants and the factors associated with their weight showed substantial differences between fat and thin babies: fat babies were generally inactive and placid and gained weight on moderate intakes of food, whereas thin babies were active and tense and consumed even more food than their heavier counterparts. Mayer concluded that tendencies toward inactivity and placidity are characteristics of birth for some and predisposes them to the overweight condition.

Although controversy exists about the extent to which heredity influences the propensity to accumulate adipose tissue, it obviously plays at least *some* role. The manner and extent to which a genetic predisposition is expressed, however, is dependent on the influences of one's social and physical environment. A number of environmental factors can influence infant weight: maternal weight, weight gained during pregnancy, nervous system damage, breast versus bottle feeding, infection, social status, customs, and parental attitudes (Weil, 1975). Hirsch (1975) proposed that there are two major periods for the numerical growth of adipose cells: during the perinatal period and in adolescence. For the remainder of one's life, fat cells have the capability to change in size but not in number. Presumably, a large number of fat cells increases the tendency toward general adiposity. The validity of this hypothesis, however, has been questioned in recent research (Coates & Thoresen, 1978; Jung, Gurr, Robinson, & James, 1978). Jung *et al.* (1978) contradicted the fat cell theory through an investigation of biopsy samples taken from adult subjects. These samples, taken from subcutaneous and intra-abdominal locations, demonstrated no relationship between fat cell number and early-onset obesity.

Environment influences the factors regulating weight and adiposity throughout one's life. The dietary customs and habits of the parents are likely to affect the feeding of their offspring. If parents eat excessively and inappropriately, it is probable that they will feed their children in a similar manner, with obesity as a frequent by-product. A self-perpetuating cycle seems to exist in many families: obese parents tend to have obese children (Charney, Goodman, McBride, Lyon, & Pratt, 1976). Mayer's (1975) findings indicated that if neither parent is obese, the probability of their children's being obese is 7%. If, however, one parent is obese, this probability increases to 40%, and if both parents share this condition, the probability leaps to 80%. It may be argued that such findings are attributable completely to genetic factors. This viewpoint has been countered by several researchers (Garn, Cole, & Baily, 1976; Hartz, Giefer, & Rimm, 1977; Shenker, Fisichelli, & Lang, 1974) in their investigations of adoptive and foster homes. Their findings indicated that foster and adopted children tend to emulate their caretakers with respect to matters of weight. That is, overweight among the caretakers appeared to enhance the probabilities for the accumulation of adipose tissue among their charges.

The combined influences of "nature and nurture" appear not only to predispose some children to overweight, but they may also help to keep them that way. In a study of 366 infants born between 1945 and 1955, Charney *et al.* (1976) found that infants whose weight exceeded the 90th percentile during the first six months of life had a 2.6 times greater probability of being overweight as an adult than those whose weight was below the 90th percentile. If the overweight infant develops into an overweight child, the likelihood of obesity in adulthood appears to be substantial. Miller, Billewicz, and Thompson (1972) found a high correlation between the weight for height ratios for individuals at ages 5 and 22 years. In their study of overweight children between the ages of 10 and 13 years, Abraham and Nordsieck (1960) found that 80% of them were still overweight on reaching 26–35 years of age. Thus, it appears that overweight parents tend to have overweight children, who themselves are likely to carry this characteristic into their adult years.

Obesity Assessment

In most cases, the assessment of obesity in a child poses little difficulty. At the beginning of treatment, visual inspection or self-report is sufficient to determine the child's need for help. As the therapy progresses, these indicators may continue to be of use as evidence of treatment efficacy. In addition to these subjective methods of assessment, however, an objective means is also necessary. The ultimate purpose of treatment is to reduce accumulated body fat; thus, a technique for its measurement is required.

Weight is the most common indirect means of assessing the presence of excessive body fat. This criterion, however, must be used with some care. A child's weight is dependent on a number of factors: sex, age, height, and body build. The mean weight norms for children and adolescents can be found in most pediatric manuals. Because the norms do not usually take body build into account, they must be used with discretion. For example, a muscular, mesomorphic, adolescent boy may be overweight according to the height and weight tables but may not be overfat. Conversely, an adolescent of the ectomorphic body type can be underweight and have excessive adipose tissue. Assessment of body fat is only crudely determined by weight; a more accurate determination requires more direct measurement techniques.

Perhaps the most common technique utilized to estimate body fat is skinfold measures. This technique involves the measurement of skinfold thickness taken at any of several locations on the body (e.g., triceps, upper back, abdomen, and pectorals). The measurement thus taken can then be translated into an estimated figure for body fat by means of the appropriate conversion tables.

Two regions commonly used for skinfold measurements and for which procedural standards have been published are the triceps and the scapula (Tanner & Whitehouse, 1975). The most easily accessible site for skinfold measurement is the triceps region. Standards have been developed for children (Seltzer & Mayer, 1965). Such standards are useful as guidelines for the presence of excessive adiposity in children.

It should be noted that skinfold measurements are subject to considerable variability. Error in the location of the skinfold, for example, gives misleading results. Greater degrees of obesity cause increased measurement error. Despite these disadvantages, however, it is a very useful technique, and its use is supported by a number of researchers (Franzini & Grimes, 1976; Weil, 1977).

For the therapist, the problems associated with skinfold measurements may be somewhat counteracted through assiduous care in using the technique and interpreting the results. With regard to the latter point, the result of most concern is generally the change in adiposity, for which the skinfold technique is an exceptionally useful measurement.

One of the most accurate means of determining body fat content is through the use of densiometry. The bases of this technique is the knowledge that fat has a density of .90 (90% as dense as water) and that lean body mass has a density of 1.10 (Bray, 1976). The technique involves a complete submersion of the child in water to determine whole body volume. The weight is then divided by body volume to determine density. From this information and the appropriate calculations, the percentage of body fat is approximated. Because of the elaborate equipment required, this procedure is impractical for most behavioral practitioners.

A Model of Treatment

Innumerable factors, including degree of cognitive development, depth of interaction, and level of parental involvement, make the treatment of obesity in children substantially different from that of adolescents. Despite these differences, the structural bases for cognitive-behavioral treatment are the same for both groups. A model of treatment intended for use by practitioners is presented below.

Table 1 outlines the elements of a treatment approach applicable to both children and adolescents. Each major aspect of the treatment is discussed in brief.

Assessment

Assessment of the child's problems is the initiating point of treatment, where baseline information regarding physical, psychological, and social health is obtained and examined. This information serves to formulate several factors associated with the treatment, including goals, approach, length, and limitations.

The presenting problem for most children (though not necessarily all of them) is excessive adiposity. The extent to which fatness exists should be determined through the use of skinfold calipers (or densiometry, if available). A medical history and examination are encouraged so that underlying physical causes for the condition are effectively ruled out. The medical history and a conversation with the physician can provide vital information concerning the child's experiences with overweight. For example, if overweight has been present since birth and has

TABLE 1. A Model for Treatment

Assessment

  Physical
    Medical history
      Particular physical factors causing or exacerbating the condition
      Time of obesity onset
      Fluctuations in weight
    Physical dimensions
      Height and weight
      Percentage of fat
    Physical characteristics of parents
  Psychological and social characteristics
    Psychological
      Level of self-esteem?
      Introverted or extraverted?
      Withdrawn? Shy?
    Social
      Does the patient have close friends? Are they overweight?
      Does the patient participate in group activities with others of his or her age?
      Is the patient at approximately the same level of maturity as his or her age peers?
      How does the patient perceive himself or herself *vis-à-vis* his or her peers?
      How is the patient's weight and how is *he* or *she* received by his or her family?
      Do the patient's parents appear overprotective—or do they allow a reasonable degree of independence?
      How do the parents and other family members perceive the child with regard to physical, social, and intellectual capabilities in comparison to others of the same age?
  Family/parents
    Is obesity evident in either or both parents? Do any of the other children in the family demonstrate signs of excess fat?
    How does the family eat? Do they eat in a nutritionally sound manner?
    Is food often used to reward or punish?
    Who wants the child to lose weight—the parents or the child?

Goals

  Weight
  Eating behaviors
  Family eating behaviors
  Perceptions of self
  Interactions with family and others

Treatment characteristics

  Treatment format
  Family context
  Behavioral methodologies
  Examination of the energy balance: energy intake versus energy expenditures
    Nutrition awareness
    Exercise activity
  Self-esteem
  Social interaction

Evaluation

progressed steadily since that time, it may have both genetic and familial lifestyle origins. If, on the other hand, the child's weight has fluctuated widely over the years, investigation is required to determine the events associated with the periods of weight gain and loss.

Physical assessment of the child is not complete without a similar, though much less intensive, assessment of the parents. In particular, a determination should be made of the existence and the extent of overweight in both parents. If overweight is present in both, then it may be suspected that the child has a physical and environmentally derived tendency toward the condition. In this case, the child and the parents need to understand the presence of the familial tendency and the difficulty of the task that lies before them.

As described earlier, overweight children are the recipients of substantial prejudice in our society. They are often ridiculed, excluded, and taunted with pejorative stereotypes. It can be expected that with this climate, most overweight children reflect such treatment in psychological symptomatology (Israel & Stolmaker, 1980). Part of the initial assessment should be used to examine the psychological status of the child. Especially important in this regard is a determination of the child's self-esteem, personal capabilities, physical image, and social attractiveness. In addition, a parental report concerning the child's behavior at school, in the home, and with friends may be used to develop a total "picture." For example, if the child spends considerable time alone, social ostracism and a bad effect on the child's self-esteem and self-image can be suspected.

In conjunction with a psychological assessment, the child's social life and social interactions should be examined. Three phases of life provide the structural bases for this effort: (1) school; (2) family; and (3) all other situations. The purpose of this assessment is to develop an understanding of the child within the context of daily social interactions. The manner in which children, as social beings, are treated by the people in their milieu may have a substantial impact on all phases of their lives. Recurring messages of their unacceptability will undoubtedly have an effect on their sense of self-worth and self-esteem. Table 1 provides an outline of basic questions that can serve as the foundation for an exploration of the child's social life.

A final area of assessment is the family of the child. The practitioner needs a reasonable understanding of the family's overall functioning. This investigation may range from such nuts-and-bolts issues as the kind and quantity of foods served in the household to the messages that the parents give their children regarding their overweight. With respect to the latter point, it is important to determine *who* is most desirous of weight loss, the child or the parents. If interviews reveal that the primary motivation behind the child's endeavor to lose weight is the parents', the practitioner may structure a portion of the treatment to explore this matter.

Another particularly important matter for the therapist is to determine if the obesity is a trait shared by all members of the family, some members, or the child alone. If the child is the only one overweight, less understanding and empathy may exist among family members than if they all experience this condition. A lack of empathy among family members may compound the feelings of isolation and diminished self-worth that the child may already experience from the social milieu. A family that shares the overweight condition may be able to provide sympathy and understanding so that the home life serves the child as a respite from the travails of the outside world.

Goals

Weight loss is the usual goal of most obesity treatment programs. Although this goal has obvious utility for an overweight person, its application to a child must be accomplished with care. If the child is in a linear phase of growth, weight gain is a natural by-product of the process. In such cases, and most others as well, goals directed toward the reduction of body fat, as opposed to absolute weight, may be more appropriate. As noted earlier, the measurement of body fat may be estimated with relative ease through the use of skinfold calipers.

Weil (1977) recommended two standards for goal setting while the child is growing and over the age of 5 years: (1) caloric restriction limited to no more than 20%–25% and (2) weight reduction to range from stability to no more than one-half pound per week. Needless to say, caloric restriction for children under the age of 5 years should be done with great care. Reductions should be focused in areas of obvious excess, such as high-calorie snacks, excess fat on meat and fowl, or the use of deep fat frying when other means may be used, so that the nutritional requirements of the child are not compromised.

A particularly important reason for limiting weight-loss or body-fat-reduction goals to modest amounts is to make them achievable by the child. Many obese children come into treatment with feelings of low self-esteem, some of them created by past failures to lose weight (Coates & Thoresen, 1978). Goals should be set that are well within the capabilities of the child, so that the probabilities of success are enhanced.

Behavioral goals of treatment are even more important than those directed toward the reduction of adipose tissue. Many overweight children have food-related behaviors that exacerbate their condition. Some of them eat beyond physical satiation, at the sight of environmental cues, as a response to anxiety and stress, and while standing or on the run. Many tend to be highly efficient machines, exerting as little effort as possible in their daily lives and participating infrequently in the active play of their normal-weight counterparts (Mayer, 1975). Because many children (especially very young ones) have yet to "overlearn" these maladaptive behaviors, a unique opportunity is present to alter and shape them in a more adaptive direction before these behaviors become fixed in adult life.

Behavioral goals are set after the assessment in each of the problem areas requiring resolution. For each problem designated, an ideal goal is set that is to be the ultimate end point of a series of intermediate steps. Generally speaking, the time frame for the achievement of each intermediate goal should be flexible and should be negotiated with the parent and child. The monitoring of the process will depend on the age of the child. For very young children, recordings by the parents based on their observations, as well as the children's reports, are suggested. The practitioner should warn parents of the need for discretion in this process, lest their children have the feeling of being constantly watched and evaluated. Most preadolescents and adolescents are able to monitor and record their own behaviors, thus removing the need for parental involvement. A clinical example of behavioral goal-setting illustrates this process:

> Blake is 10 years old, and although he is overweight, he is not excessively so. He is a fairly active youngster, playing at sports and other games frequently after school. However, his activity is more than compensated for by his hearty appetite at meals and his frequent between-meal snacks. His snacks generally include high-calorie items, such as candy bars, cakes, and ice cream. Following assessment, we felt that change in his snacking behaviors would be one of the logical areas of intervention. In conference with Blake and his mother, we decided that a reasonable goal would be for Blake to reduce his high-calorie snacking to once per day. We also decided that other snacks might be included during the day but that they would be limited to those of a low-calorie nature, such as fruits or vegetables. These snacks were included because of his activity and frequent hunger, and to help him develop a taste and liking for these foods. Progression toward this goal occurred through intermediate steps. During the first week, Blake replaced two of his usual five snacks per day with low-calorie items. This goal remained until he developed mastery in this pattern and was ready for further substitution. It took Blake five weeks to achieve this goal.

Besides adipose tissue loss and behavioral change, three other areas are suggested for inclusion in the treatment process: (1) family eating behaviors; (2) self-perceptions; and (3) interactions with family and others. Although these areas often receive only cursory attention in many programs, they are of paramount importance. Goal setting in these areas may be of a less formal nature than those related to adipose tissue loss and behavior change. Descriptions of these treatment areas are given later in this chapter.

Treatment Characteristics

The treatment program suggested for the obese child has several components. The goals of treatment are directed not only toward the children themselves but toward their social and family life as well.

Treatment Format

Most behaviorally based weight-control programs function in a group format. Presumably, this approach has gained popularity for a number of reasons, including efficiency in the use of time and resources, the availability of programs designed for presentation in this format, and the positive characteristics (e.g., group support) associated with its use. Although the group format has demonstrated that it can yield positive results, it has its limitations. Group formats do not always address the unique needs of the individual, and they sometimes seem to offer an atmosphere of acceptance rather than providing pressure to change. Wilson and Brownell (1980) lauded groups for the support they provide but suggested that assessment of problems would best be conducted individually. The most effective treatment format would perhaps utilize both the individual and the group approaches, taking the most beneficial elements of each in the development of a final package.

Two treatment formats are suggested. Each combines the group and individual modalities into an overall program. The first approach (Foreyt & Goodrick, 1981a) begins with an intensive initial assessment of the child, including background, medical history, psychosocial status, family life (i.e., interactions and dietary habits), weight loss aspirations, motivation, and barriers to success. Following this assessment, an overview of the basic techniques integral to behavioral treatment is presented in a group setting. This group is generally conducted once a week for 8–10 weeks. With the completion of the group phase, an intensive individual treatment phase directed toward resolving the specific weight-control problems of each child is begun. This portion of treatment not only addresses the matter of weight but also seeks to explore the child's difficulties with self-image, self-esteem, social interaction, and family life. Because of the extensive nature of such treatment, this phase requires a year or more of active involvement.

A second treatment format that attempts to combine the best qualities of the individual and group approaches is the small-group approach (Wooley et al., 1979). By limiting group size to from three to five, a substantial amount of attention may be given to individual problems while maintaining the efficiencies and support functions of a group setting. Assessment, however, is still best accomplished on an individual basis.

Family Context and Family Involvement

Environmental influences contribute substantially to the etiology of overweight. For children, the environment of largest influence is the family. The younger the child, the greater the impact.

Inappropriate eating habits practiced by children are frequently paralleled by similar habits practiced by the entire family. To expect children to change their behaviors while the remainder of the family continue theirs is more than can be expected of anyone. Families not only need to support their children in their efforts but also to provide models of correct behavior. As many overweight children come from families in which some or all of the members have similar difficulties, all can benefit from such involvement.

Food plays an important part in the daily lives of most families. Food, from its purchase to its disposal, is often the basis for many of the family's interactions. In this regard, parents sometimes use food for many purposes outside its usual function of providing sustenance. It can be withheld when children misbehave (sending children to their room without dinner) or used as a reward when they act in "appropriate" ways. In some families, eating heartily and thoroughly becomes symbolic of love demonstrated for the mother. On the other hand, not eating thoroughly may be perceived as waste or ingratitude, and as a source of conflict and tension (Foreyt & Goodrick, 1981a). Such uses can make food and eating a confusing matter for children. Beyond its intended function of satisfying hunger, it may become associated with an entire range of emotional states, including loneliness, boredom, guilt, sadness, and happiness (Millman, 1980; Orbach, 1977). An exploration of the familial use of food needs to be conducted to determine if it is being used inappropriately. If so, treatment should be aimed at correcting the problems.

The attitude of family members toward obese children while in the program is another issue that requires close consideration. During the period when they are involved in the weight control effort, it is best if all family members treat them in a normal, but empathetic, manner. They will need frequent support and encouragement for any improvements that they make and understanding when they falter and become discouraged. Families can also serve the important function of helping these children to improve their self-image and self-esteem. With their cooperation and encouragement, children can develop in areas that will form the foundation for personal growth and confidence. These latter considerations are perhaps as important to their personal development as the primary concern with weight.

The awareness and skills required of family members to function in this manner need to be provided in a systematic fashion. Generally, the "education" of the family occurs through contact with one parent during the treatment process. For adolescents, the parents should receive training separate from the treatment of their child. With younger children, both child and parent may be seen together (Brownell & Stunkard, 1980). Periodic sessions with the entire family are considered highly beneficial for a number of reasons: (1) they convey information to the entire family; (2) they determine the extent to which the family is learning and practicing the new behaviors and insights; (3) they develop a "feel" for the family's dynamics and structures; and (4) they uncover problems or barriers that serve to impede progress. If practical, these sessions are most beneficial if conducted in the family home. When interviews and observations are done in this context, the possibilities of the occurrence of more natural behaviors and interactions are enhanced. Additionally, the therapist may ask to join the family in a meal in order to observe *in situ* eating behaviors. These observations can provide the bases for suggested remedial interventions where judged necessary. Of course, some families may not desire such high levels of involvement, though they may be supportive of their child's efforts.

Behavioral Methodologies

Four elements form the structure of most behavioral approaches: (1) self-monitoring; (2) stimulus control; (3) eating management; and (4) contingency management. An explanation of each of these techniques is given later in this chapter and may also be found elsewhere (Ferguson, 1976; Stuart & Davis, 1972).

Although most behaviorally oriented programs present a standard package of techniques for all children to follow, this may not be the most effective approach. Coates and Thoresen (1981) speculated that the poor compliance shown by many participants in behaviorally based weight-control programs could be caused by the lack of relationship between the myriad of activities asked of them and their problem of overweight. Brownell (1979) punctuated this point by noting, "Subjects might be displaying more wisdom in not following our advice than we display in giving it." Behavioral techniques should be based on the problems determined through the initial and subsequent assessments.

Examination of the Energy Balance: Energy Intake versus Energy Expenditures

Along with behavioral methodologies to control adiposity, substantial attention must be given to the child's daily energy balance, or energy intake versus energy expenditures. Interestingly, most behaviorally oriented programs for children place the greater emphases on reducing caloric inputs rather than on increasing caloric expenditures (Foreyt & Goodrick, 1981a). This emphasis appears to be misplaced, as studies have suggested that many obese children eat no more than their normal-weight counterparts (Dwyer, Feldman, & Mayer, 1967; Huenemann, 1972, 1974). The difference between the two groups may lie in the extent to which they utilize their energies. Consideration of the energy balance for these populations requires a strong emphasis on the utilization of energy as well as its consumption (Mayer, 1975).

Assessment of caloric intake is most frequently accomplished through a daily food diary in which individuals are asked to write down everything that they eat each day. The maintenance of food records may be conducted with relative ease by adolescents without parental assistance, although younger children require substantial parental involvement in this task. With younger children, observations and reports given by them serve as the informational sources for the food records.

Besides providing a mechanism for calculating daily caloric intake, food records may be used to determine the nutritional adequacy of the diet. When these records show nutritional deficiencies, a few suggestions for substitutions can result in a more sound diet while yielding fewer calories on a daily basis.

Changing the child's diet to one that is nutritious and lower in calories is required in the treatment of most overweight children. This process requires varying degrees of parental involvement. In the case of the very young child, the involvement is almost total, as the parent has considerable control over the child's intake. Adolescents are more able to select their own food items, so that parental control is more limited. Parents may assist in improving their children's selections through modeling, teaching, or encouraging good nutritional habits. Parental modeling of good nutritional habits has a powerful influence on most children. The therapist should emphasize this point to parents and work with them in making personal improvements where obvious and necessary.

Increased physical activity is integral to any treatment of obesity in children. However, this increase may be difficult for some because of an inherent tendency toward placidity and quiet (Mayer, 1975) and a self-consciousness about their bodies. Encouraging exercise among these populations must be approached with creativity, patience, and sensitivity.

Encouraging exercise in children should begin with a discussion directed toward helping them understand its benefits. This presentation may be incorporated into a general discussion covering energy balance and nutrition. Subsequently, they should be probed concerning their current activities and those in which they may desire to participate. In both instances, increased activity is the ultimate objective.

As many overweight children are self-conscious about how they look when they move, it may be best if they begin with rather unobtrusive activities. This may be done by a gradual daily increase of the frequency of energy expenditures. For example, if they live within a reasonable distance from school, they might walk or ride a bike instead of taking a bus or riding in a car. Or they may be encouraged to assist with the daily household chores, such as running errands, cleaning the furniture, or cutting the grass.

Physical activity may also be increased through participation and encouragement given at school. Typically, most schools' physical education programs are not designed to instill in children a desire to achieve physical fitness and maintain activity throughout their lifetime. Their emphases seem to be on games and sports, with only the best athletes monopolizing participation (Nelson, 1978). In such settings, it can be assumed that obese children receive little physical benefit. Parents may act to improve matters through communication with physical education instructors. Such communication should be aimed at helping the instructor to become aware of the child's needs and devising mutually agreeable means for achieving them.

Family participation in exercise, sports, and other activities is another means by which physical activity in the overweight child may be encouraged and maintained (Brownell & Stunkard, 1980). By making such activities as walking, biking, jogging, and swimming a regular part of family life, children will increase their activity levels in a manner that may be perceived as natural and part of life. The social support and skills developed in this setting may provide the confidence for engagement in activities outside the home.

Self-Esteem

Many overweight children have difficulties with their self-image and self-esteem (Dwyer & Mayer, 1975; Mayer, 1975). Improving their perceptions of themselves is considered a vital part of treatment. The necessity of this effort is underscored by the relatively discouraging long-term prognosis of obesity treatment (Coates & Thoresen, 1978). Helping the child with low self-esteem is exceedingly complex and requires time and multimodal techniques of treatment. The bases of the approach suggested is a cognitive one and is discussed later in this chapter.

Social Interaction

Overweight children are often subject to considerable stigmatization and prejudice. The consequences of these negative communications often include poor self-image, low self-esteem, passivity, and an expectation of rejection (Neumann, 1977; Weil, 1977). This psychological climate can lead to a social withdrawal in which food becomes both a source of gratification and a solace for negative feelings (Neumann, 1977). When food and eating are repeatedly used in this manner, the initial problem of excessive adiposity may be futher exacerbated and the likelihood of continued ridicule is enhanced.

Because the child's difficulties with social interaction may serve to worsen the problem of obesity, it is incumbent on the therapist to assist in this matter. Treatment of this problem differs with the age of the child. However, certain goals are applicable to all ages:

1. Improve self-acceptance and self-esteem.
2. Develop or improve assertiveness skills.
3. Develop or improve social skills.
4. Develop areas of personal competence valued by the peer group (e.g., intellectual capabilities, musical talent, or knowledge of interesting hobbies).
5. Develop physical skills within the child's capabilities and interests.

Evaluation

Evaluation of the child during the course of treatment is integral to the process. It is the means by which progress may be assessed and necessary alterations in the treatment strategy may be determined.

Evaluation should occur in two ways: (1) as an ongoing process without formality and (2) in a formal, comprehensive fashion. The former occurs as a natural process of treatment. Its conduct is dependent on the therapist's skill in developing a relationship of mutual trust and open communication with the child. Within this context, the therapist may stay abreast of the child's progress and problems through verbal processes. Additionally, sensitivity to and familiarity with the child may allow the therapist to receive nonverbal forms of communication. Such communication may express concerns that are difficult or embarrassing for the child to state openly. When information received through these methods indicates that changes are required, they may be instituted as a natural process of treatment.

Periodically, formal evaluation is desired, for both the therapist and the child. The content of the evaluation should be similar to the initial assessment as its purpose is to compare change with baseline status. Measurements of weight, fat content, psychological status, and social skills are needed. The information derived will help determine the effectiveness of the treatment strategies utilized. If areas of ineffectiveness are found, the therapist needs to work collaboratively with the child to find the possible reasons and the subsequent solutions.

Behavioral Bases of Treatment

Review of Previous Work

Recent reviews (Coates & Thoresen, 1978; Israel & Stolmaker, 1980; Weil, 1977) have indicated that the traditional methods of treating childhood obesity, including diets, hormones, fasting, and anorectic drugs, have been relatively ineffective. The primary drawbacks of these approaches have been their limited, short-range effects and, in some cases, the potential dangers involved in their use. Because of these disadvantages, behaviorally oriented treatments have arisen as an alternative and have gained widespread acceptance and use. Although these approaches have been shown to be more effective than a variety of alternatives in treating mild obesity in adults (Abramson, 1977; Leon, 1976; Stunkard & Mahoney, 1976), treatment outcomes have been modest. In one review of behavioral-treatment outcome-studies in which posttreatment results were provided, the mean weight loss one year following treatment was 6.1 kg (Foreyt, Goodrick, & Gotto, 1981). In another review of long-term, controlled outcome-studies, participants lost an average of 4.7 kg at the end of treatment (Wilson & Brownell, 1980). These losses were generally maintained at one-year follow-up. Needless to say, the losses achieved by most subjects in behavioral treatment are modest, and very few achieve their goal weight. The limited success of this approach has been attributed to a number of possible factors (Foreyt et al., 1981):

- The time-limited nature (i.e., usually 8–12 weeks) of the treatment.
- The difficulty that participants have in maintaining their newly learned eating behaviors.
- The recent doubts concerning the effectiveness of various components of the standard behavioral-treatment package.
- The dissatisfaction among many participants at the slow rates of weight loss.

Although many studies exist on the use of behavioral approaches in the treatment of adult obesity, substantially fewer studies are currently available on children and adolescents. In the studies that have been conducted, the results have been modest at best (Brownell & Stunkard, 1980; Coates & Thoresen, 1978; Israel & Stolmaker). However, several researchers (Brownell & Stunkard, 1980; Jordan & Levitz, 1975; Weil, 1977) feel that this relatively new direction in treating overweight among children and adolescents holds great promise, especially when compared with the dismal performances of the more traditional methodologies.

Behavioral treatments, originally developed for use with adults, require considerable modfication and reemphasis when applied to children. Special emphases should be placed on family involvement, problem solving, and the use of more structured and intensive treatments (Coates & Thoresen, 1978). Treatments need to be tailored to the particular child. Instead of exposing each child to an array of behavioral techniques, of which only a few may be effective, an assessment should be conducted to determine those that prove to be most helpful. Increased activity should also be a major goal.

A major innovation in the behavioral treatment of childhood obesity is the use of cognitive-behavior modification. Cognitive-behavior modification can be used in a number of forms to assist obese children. Its utility ranges from helping to bolster self-esteem to enhancing compliance through self-control. Its use should be a major part of behavioral treatment (Brownell & Stunkard, 1980; Foreyt *et al.*, 1981).

The behavioral treatment of childhood obesity is in its formative stages of development. It has met with numerous difficulties in transferring its technologies from adults to a youthful population. Additionally, particular problems arise in the application of this treatment to children because consideration must be given to their high level of physical and psychological dependency, their stage of cognitive development, and their social-environmental influences, including parental attitudes. Despite these problems, the future for the behavioral treatment of overweight among our youth appears to be promising, especially when compared with the limited effectiveness of the more traditional techniques.

STRUCTURE OF BEHAVIORAL TREATMENT

The ultimate goal of the behavioral treatment for overweight is to change the child's maladaptive eating behaviors to ones that are more adaptive. This process involves the how and why of one's eating behaviors more than the *what*. Treatment frequently focuses on changing such maladaptive factors as eating too rapidly, having a household filled with high-calorie foods, eating while standing, or eating in an unconscious manner. Behavioral treatment seeks to impart more adaptive approaches to food by teaching self-control methodologies that are intended to become an important part of the child's life. The methodologies used most frequently in treatment programs include (1) self-monitoring; (2) stimulus control; (3) eating management; and (4) contingency contracting.

Self-Monitoring

This is an important aspect of most treatment programs. In practice, the child is asked to record the numerous factors surrounding daily eating occurrences. Typical factors recorded include the quantity and the nature of the food, the time of ingestion, who shared the meal, where eating occurred, and the mood or feeling associated with the event. Such information can be used as a diagnostic tool whereby the therapist, in conjunction with the child, may analyze the data to determine the presence of inappropriate eating patterns and related causative factors. With this information, a systematic approach to treatment may be designed and conducted.

During treatment, self-monitoring serves the important function of providing a means of assessing behavioral changes. That is, at any time during treatment, the child's eating behaviors may be compared with those of the pretreatment period to determine the extent to which improvement has occurred.

Stimulus Control

Stimulus control is the modification of factors that appear to serve as the cues leading to inappropriate eating. These cues can vary widely, depending on the individual involved, but generally speaking, the following are common sources of difficulty: (1) handling food frequently; (2) having high-calorie snacks in the household; (3) having food located throughout the house; and (4) eating while watching television, doing homework, or reading. The particular stimuli causing difficulty may be determined through the child's personal assessment of the matter as well as through an examination of eating records. Following this examination, alterations in the child's environment or life patterns are suggested so that the influence of the troublesome stimuli are effectively negated. This technique is exemplified by the adolescent who finds that certain high-calorie foods in the home are the source of much of her or his difficulty. The resolution of this problem can take one of two directions: the child can (1) ask the parents to refrain from purchasing the foods or (2) help them place the foods in places or containers that reduce their visual impact and, hopefully, their temptation.

By taking either of the above actions, the child controls the stimuli that have led to prior inappropriate eating.

Eating Management

This technique is applied to the actual act of eating. For some children, eating occurs so rapidly that insufficient time is provided for satiation to reach cognitive awareness. The treatment of this pattern involves techniques that slow the child's usual rate of eating; such as chewing slowly and thoroughly, laying down one's fork or spoon frequently, and taking an extended pause during the meal. An added advantage of this approach is that children often find that their enjoyment of food is increased. Some even find that the enhanced pleasure diminishes the previous desire to overeat.

Contingency Management

In many behavioral treatment programs, the performance of appropriate behaviors is rewarded and inappropriate ones are "punished";

this process is referred to as *contingency management*. The theory for this approach derives from operant conditioning. Operant conditioning suggests that behaviors that receive consequent rewards are likely to strengthen, whereas those that are punished are likely to extinguish. This theory is applied to treatment programs to enhance the probability of desired eating behaviors while reducing those that are less desirable. The consequences of performing or not performing the behaviors may be administered by the patient, friends, family, or therapist.

Contingency management has been applied in several areas of behaviorally based weight-control programs. For example, the completion of eating records on a daily basis may be negotiated so that a punishment is imposed for lapses in this behavior. Or the person may have determined that eating while standing at the refrigerator door is a recurring and difficult problem. In this regard, he or she may decide to reward himself or herself for each week when the occurrences of such behavior are limited to a specified number.

In some programs of weight control, contingency contracts are drawn on the child's ability to lose a specified amount of weight in a given period of time. Although this approach has been shown to be effective as a weight loss technique in several investigations (e.g., Dinoff, Rickard, & Colwick, 1972; Mann, 1972), deleterious possibilities exist in its use. Rewarding or punishing children contingent on achieving particular weight-loss goals may motivate them to use physically abusive techniques in order to demonstrate "success." They may use laxatives, diuretics, self-induced vomiting, or short-term fasting. As behavioral treatment seeks to inculcate adaptive eating behaviors, weight loss obtained in these ways is patently inappropriate. Extreme care must be taken by the therapist in using this approach so that the goals may be achieved without abuse.

Cognitive Interventions

Cognitive interventions have been suggested by several researchers (Brownell & Stunkard, 1980; Coates & Thoresen, 1978; Foreyt & Goodrick, 1981b; Price & Geronilla, 1981) for use in behaviorally oriented weight-control programs directed toward children and adolescents. Their uses in such programs are numerous, ranging from aiding children in managing their eating behaviors to improving their self-image. These objectives are accomplished by therapeutic processes aimed at changing maladaptive thoughts, attitudes, and beliefs to ones that are more adaptive.

For children, the source of many maladaptive attitudes, habits, and beliefs regarding food and eating is the family. As a primary source of pleasure, food can be used as more than a means of providing bodily sustenance. It can also be used by parents to control "uncooperative" children through reward and punishment. Repeated use of food as reward and punishment undoubtedly leads to various distortions regarding its role and function. Price and Geronilla (1981) suggested some of the ways in which food can be used inappropriately because of predisposing psychological factors:

> Eating may be used to soothe tensions, calm anxiety, and to compensate for frustrations. Symbolically, food can become a substitute for love between a parent and child, a chosen means to express love they find difficult to express in any other way. (p. 193)

Eating can serve the child as a defense mechanism, a means of relieving stress, and a way of coping with loneliness and boredom.

Inappropriate use of food by children can frequently result from its "normal" inappropriate use in the family. For example, some parents exhort their children to clean their plates thoroughly (after filling them to overflowing) so as not to cause waste. There may be a reference made to the starving children in China or India who are not as lucky as they and will to go sleep hungry. Somewhere in this quagmire of reasoning, the child is made to feel indirectly responsible for the world food problem; the result can be a clean plate, an overfull stomach, and a growing disassociation between food and its use to fulfill bodily hunger. Other inappropriate uses of food may be adopted by children by modeling them from their parents. In families where both parents work and maintain active lifestyles, time pressures may result in a number of behaviorally inappropriate eating patterns. Children may take note of their father's daily pattern of eating breakfast: a cup of coffee, a doughnut, and involvement with the sports page. Or they may feel that the rapid consumption of food during mealtimes in their household is normal and therefore appropriate. These habits, as well as the inappropriate cognitions associated with food, may be treated systematically through cognitive-behavior-modification interventions.

Because of the high level of interaction of the dysfunctional eating styles of the parents and of the child, treatment must be directed to all involved. Resolution of children's inappropriate thoughts and behaviors with respect to food will be extremely difficult if they reside in an environment that is not supportive (through attitudes and actions) of the changes being made. Thus, the therapist should aim the treatment toward the family with the child as its focus. This approach was shown to be very effective in the treatment of obesity among preadolescents (Epstein, Wing, Koeske, Andrasik, & Ossip, 1981).

Treatment of the family is usually conducted through the parent, generally the mother accompanying the child. In order to assess the existing problems, the therapist explores the full range of family eating behaviors, attitudes, and beliefs with this parent. The therapist must also determine how the child is treated in the family milieu *vis-à-vis* eating habits and weight, and as an individual. Through such analyses, the therapist may develop an understanding of the constellation of family problems present and how they may impact on the child. From the information thus derived, a treatment program, with prioritized intervention points, may be developed.

In order to carry on family-based treatment, cognitive interventions and training are frequently required of all members involved, with special attention placed on the accompanying parent. Family interventions and training may be conducted through periodic sessions in the therapist's office or, preferably, in the family household. The latter approach provides a more natural setting for family interaction to occur as well as giving the therapist an *in situ* view of their food-handling and eating practices. Coates and Thoresen (1981) developed the Eating Analyses and Treatment Schedule (EATS) to systematically record information on households with respect to food-related environmental data (e.g., the caloric value of the food in the refrigerator) and eating behaviors. This schedule is very helpful for systematically recording and evaluating the food-related behaviors and milieu of a family.

Cognitive interventions with the family often require the utilization of several methodologies (Foreyt & Goodrick, 1981b; Mahoney & Arnkoff, 1978). For example, if a parent is extremely concerned about the child's physical appearance and therefore places inordinate pressure on the child to lose weight, the therapist might use rational restructuring (Ellis, 1962, 1979) to assist in the development of a more adaptive viewpoint. Or if the family recognizes certain problem behaviors regarding their eating habits, they may be taught a generalized problem-solving technique (Mahoney, 1977) to aid in their resolution. In the discussion that follows, the cognitive interventions described focus on the specific problems of children and adolescents.

CHILDREN

It is the general view of cognitive behavior therapists that the critical processes in therapy are cognitively mediated (Foreyt & Goodrick, 1981b). Thus, the demonstration of maladaptive behavior is thought to be grounded in cognitions that are also maladaptive. With this framework, the job of the therapist is to alter the child's cognitions to ones that are more adaptive.

In treating overweight children, three areas of maladaptive cognitions must be considered: those related to (1) food and eating; (2) self-image and self-esteem; and (3) social interaction. These factors assuredly interact, often resulting in an exacerbation of the presenting problem of obesity. For example, poor self-esteem and social isolation may cause the child to resort to food for companionship and as an alternative to boredom (Price & Geronilla, 1981). Thus, a comprehensive treatment of the child requires multiple interventions and perhaps a goal more broadly defined than the reduction of adipose tissue alone. Dwyer and Mayer (1975) presented such a goal when they stated:

> The ultimate goal of obesity treatment is to inculcate habits which bring about fat reduction and eventually maintenance of fatness at more normal levels than previously. All of this must be accomplished while helping the patient to retain (or gain) a positive as well as realistic body image and sense of worth as a person, regardless of the outcome of treatment. (p. 108)

The particular cognitive strategy used with children may or may not be effective, depending on their cognitive stage of development (Cole & Kazdin, 1980). Thus, the various cognitive interventions must be applied with flexibility. If the therapist finds that a particular tactic is not yielding the desired results, another approach more suitable to the child's level of cognitive development may be considered. For example, Denney (1975) found that 8- and 10-year-old children improved their problem-solving capabilities after viewing a self-instructing model, but not when they applied the self-verbalization technique. As knowledge of the appropriateness of the various cognitive interventions at different stages of cognitive development is in its infancy, the therapist must use judgment and experimentation to determine the best intervention for a particular child. Guidelines for this selection may be obtained through an examination of the literature. In this regard, the recent review by Kendall (1981) of work completed in the area of cognitive-behavioral interventions with children provides an excellent bibliographic resource.

Modeling (e.g., Bandura, 1971) and a variation of self-instructional training (Meichenbaum, 1977) have been combined to form an effective generalized approach to the treatment of weight control problems in children. This technique relies heavily on the involvement of the child's family in communicating the desired behaviors as well as modeling them. The behaviors are taught to the parent and the child by the therapist in the office. In addition, the parent is given instructions concerning the methods of self-instructional training and modeling. For the very young child, the instructions may be given with the child present; for the older child, it is advisable that they be given to the parent alone.

After it has been determined that the parent and the child have a good understanding of the new behaviors and how they are to be applied, they are encouraged to utilize them within the home. Preferably, the implementation of the behaviors is conducted within the family context as a family project. The purpose of taking this approach is twofold: (1) having all members of the family model the new behaviors should increase the probability of their adoption by the child; and (2) in a family project where all are involved in the change process, the child is less likely to feel "different" or " odd." In families where several members are overweight, this approach will undoubtedly benefit each of them.

The "teaching" and modeling of new eating behaviors should be accomplished in the family setting in a natural and relaxed manner. They should be seen and practiced as part of life. New approaches to eating may be practiced at meals and snacks as a major part of the family process. The task of learning the new habits should be enjoyable. Games, stories, and play are possible mechanisms by which this objective may be accomplished. For example, we use the "inverse race" game, which teaches children to eat slowly and thoroughly. This game may be conducted at family meals with all members as participants. The objective of the inverse race is to see who finishes eating last. Of course, a time limitation is required, lest the game last too long! An added benefit of this game is that the periods of not eating may be filled with conversation, a pasttime languishing in many families. A variation of this game can also be played covertly by the overweight child. While eating with unknowing peers, the objective is to eat at a pace that will allow the child to win the secret game, to finish last.

A case study of the modeling and self-instructional approach is given below:

> From the report given by 6-year-old Todd's mother, he tended to bolt down his food at mealtimes. The rapidity of his eating invariably led to his being first in completing the meal and in asking for an after-dinner snack. It was obvious that slowing Todd's eating pace should be integral to the program to improve his overall eating patterns. Self-instructional training was the primary technique used to achieve this objective. Todd was instructed to "think aloud" to himself before he began to eat a meal or a snack, as well as several times while he was eating. The content of his internal "self-talk" was as follows: "I'm going to eat slowly and thoroughly. Tasting food happens in my mouth so I need to keep it there a long time if I want to enjoy it. Also, I'm going to put my fork down every third bite so that I can rest." In addition to Todd's training, his mother received instructions that would be supportive of his efforts.
>
> Prior to starting family meals, we encouraged Todd's parents to ask

one of the members (including themselves) how they should eat. Although the focus of this activity was Todd, it was carried out so that he did not feel as if he were the target of the activity. Each member of the family participated in the eating behavior and therefore served as a model for Todd. Gamelike activities were introduced to help him learn and support the establishment of the new behaviors. One of them we call "tasting the ingredients and textures." This eating activity involves a conscious exploration of the food that is consumed. Members of the family are asked what spices made up the sauce or to describe the texture of the cooked broccoli. A variation of this activity is to have the family eat a portion of the meal with their eyes closed, removing that sensory distraction. A discussion of the experience often occurs after its completion. Frequently, we used such discussions during mid-meal eating breaks, thereby supporting an atmosphere of leisurely and relaxed mealtimes.

Eating slowly was further reinforced by Todd's mother during snack times. On these occasions, she used a Socratic dialogue with Todd to determine the existence of the appropriate "self-talk":

MOTHER: Todd, how should Mommy eat this apple?
TODD: You take small bites, chew it real well and eat it slowly.
MOTHER: Good! Now how are you going to eat yours?
TODD: The same way.

Another problem area in which this approach can be used is in helping the child to learn the feeling of satiation and to stop eating when it occurs. Overweight children often eat and overeat for reasons other than their biological needs (Israel & Stolmaker, 1980; Price & Geronilla, 1981; Weil, 1977). Because this problem is usually associated with multiple factors (e.g., anxiety, frustration, and boredom), its treatment requires multiple interventions. A key intervention in this treatment is having the child become more sensitive to biological "signals" and respond to them. With the use of modeling and self-instructional training, the child is taught to recognize the internal sensations associated with eating, from hunger to fullness.

Having the child learn biological signals is best conducted in a context that is natural and pleasant, usually within the home as an activity that may be perceived as play. A game we use to accomplish this purpose involves making a cutout in the shape of the stomach on a piece of cardboard or other stiff material. Another piece of cardboard of a different color is used to demonstrate different degrees of fullness. This latter piece is used behind the cutout and is moved to different levels to show everything from an empty to a full stomach. An informal family game using the "fullness board" (FB) is suggested to help the child become more aware of internal sensations. For example, at mealtimes, the parent asks the child how her or his stomach feels. The child may respond, "It feels about three-quarters full." The parent then represents this state of fullness on the FB. This visual feedback assists in an understanding of the concept as well as making the process of satiation a more concrete one. The parents model the desired behavior and associated self-talk to further concretize the process. At a meal, the parent may vocalize internal self-talk in the following manner:

> I'm beginning to feel real full now. I'm almost to the top of my stomach [showing this state on the FB]. My next bite will put me to the top and I'm going to stop right there.

In carrying out this process, it is important that the parent sometimes leave a little food on the plate when satiation occurs. By so doing, the parent teaches the child (and the rest of the family) that it should be the state of stomach fullness that dictates the cessation of eating and not the amount of food on the plate.

This game may be carried on with the child during the course of the day when the occasion is appropriate. For example, during a mid-morning snack, the child may be asked by the mother about her or his state of satiation. By so doing, the mother is encouraging the practice of her child's self-vocalizations as well as demonstrating an interest in the child's progress.

In addition to treating eating behaviors, cognitive methodologies may also be used in helping the child with problems of self-esteem and social interaction. These problem areas should be approached in a comprehensive fashion, with cognitive techniques serving as an important part of the intervention strategy. For example, obese children with low self-esteem may attempt to improve this characteristic through work in several areas of their lives: (1) noting their physical attributes; (2) recognizing talents they may possess; (3) developing skills in socially desirable interest areas (e.g., playing a musical instrument); and (4) acknowledging to themselves that they are worthwhile and likable human beings. These interventions should be supported and paralleled by others whose purpose is to inculcate within them an *internalized belief* that they are worthwhile and lovable persons (Ellis, Wolfe, & Moseley, 1966).

To assist them in establishing this perspective, the therapist may ask these children to list their qualities on a piece of paper, highlighting those that they feel are particularly outstanding. With this list, the children often find that their attributes exceed their prior estimation of themselves. Convincing themselves of their worthwhileness involves practicing self-talk supportive of this objective. They are encouraged to practice self-statements of the following kind: "I like myself for who I am. I like my nose, hair, teeth, and skin. I am a good student, play the piano, and have three good friends. I am a worthwhile and good person." Such statements are practiced throughout the day, with support given to this effort by the parents and other members of the family. Parents, for example, may ask their children what they like about themselves. Or as a variation, they may ask, "Tell me at least one way in which you felt good about yourself today." In addition to helping them with their self-vocalizations, the family members play an important role by recognizing and acknowledging improvements in developing skills and attributes. They can also help to soften the impact of the sadness and despair the children may feel because of unkind treatment received from peers.

The cognitive interventions presented represent only a few of the possibilities that may prove effective for particular children. Other techniques that may be considered are imagery, problem-solving techniques, and various coping skills. The application of these and other methodologies with children may be found in various published works (e.g., Fagen, Long, & Stevens, 1975; Palmer, 1978; Spivack & Shure, 1974; Wrenn & Schwarzock, 1970). As noted earlier, a high level of flexibility is needed in their utilization, as their effectiveness depends considerably on the particular personality of the child, his or her level of cognitive development, the therapist's comfort and skill with the technique, and the applicability of the technique to the problem. Thus, if a technique does not prove to be helpful after a reasonable period of time, the therapist is encouraged to try another.

Creativity in the therapy format is important in working with children. For example, the determination and treatment of the child's psychological and social problems are most effectively conducted in formats where the child feels comfortable and expressive. Storytelling, play, and games are media that may be used for this purpose. These media often elicit responses from the child concerning difficulties with self-image and social interaction that cannot be obtained with the more traditional approach. After the problems are determined, they can additionally serve as the media by which the treatment may be communicated. Thus, a story may be told of how an obese child learned to use assertive behavior and coping self-statements in handling the teasing of schoolmates. Using dolls or puppets in a similar manner can be especially effective, as it concretizes the interplay to an even greater extent than does a story. The techniques used need be restricted only by the imagination of the therapist and the child's response to it.

Treating obese children for their problems must be done with considerable sensitivity. Many of them are subject to considerable ridicule and ostracism in their daily lives. They often have poor self-esteem and substantial doubt concerning their capabilities, especially those in the realm of weight control. The self-doubts of some regarding weight are based on a history of attempts to lose weight, all of them ending in eventual failure. The therapist needs to be aware of any doubt, despair, or even trepidation that these children may carry with them. If these things do exist, the children need to be assured that this experience is not going to be a judgmental one, in which reward and punishment are received according to the single criterion of weight loss. These children need to feel that the therapist, the parent, and the rest of the family are on their side and that this experience is a learning process from which they may learn new and better ways of eating. They need to feel that it is the learning and trying from day to day that are important and not the tyrannical numbers of the scale. And above all, they need to learn to feel that they are acceptable and worthwhile persons as they are, regardless of weight loss.

Adolescents

The treatment of adolescent obesity using cognitive-behavior-modification techniques is similar in methodology and philosophy to that used with children. However, the adolescent's higher level of cognitive development and maturity allows for greater sophistication in the techniques utilized as well as the introduction of several inappropriate for a child. Often, this group may be treated similarly to adults.

In comparison to children, adolescents usually have a greater level of autonomy and independence, especially regarding the control of their eating behaviors. They usually have free access to the food sources in the household as well as the capability of requesting the purchase of favorite items. In some families, they may be able to participate in the planning of family menus, having a voice in the selection of food. As many adolescents receive an allowance or have other sources of funds (e.g., an after-school job), their consumption of food is not confined to the selection available within the household. Overweight adolescents need to learn a level of self-control in their eating behavior that is greater than that required for children.

As with children, the treatment of overweight adolescents should also include the matter of self-image and self-esteem. Adolescence is frequently a time when similarity to one's peers is of overriding importance. To be overweight and therefore atypical can be very difficult to accept. To be overweight as an adolescent is often accompanied by a negative self-image and feelings of guilt and lack of willpower (Dwyer & Mayer, 1975). The negative self-assessments made during this critical period can have long-lasting consequences, often influencing individual self-perceptions as an adult (Heald, 1975). It is therefore important for the therapist to explore this matter thoroughly with the adolescent and to institute a comprehensive program of treatment.

In treating adolescents, it is recommended that the therapist use group therapy in conjunction with the individual format. A group can provide both a "mirror" by which adolescents may better understand themselves and a "window" into the hearts and minds of others who share the same difficulty. This sharing can have a substantial impact, for it derives from the peers who are so important to them during this period of life (Erikson, 1968). For many adolescents, just finding others who share the same feelings makes the group and their participation in it worthwhile. It can also serve as the basis on which friendships are formed, a very important occurrence for many who find themselves socially isolated.

The use of cognitive interventions in behaviorally based weight-control programs for adolescents has many applications; Table 2 provides examples of several. The problems exhibited in Table 2 may be approached with a variety of cognitive techniques. Self-instructional training (Meichenbaum, 1977), cognitive restructuring (Ellis, 1962,

TABLE 2. Possible Areas for Cognitive Interventions

Eating behaviors

    Eating too rapidly
    Eating while standing (e.g., at the refrigerator or in the pantry)
    Excessive snacking
    Unconscious eating
    Anxiety-induced eating
    Binging

Interpersonal problems

    Family
    Adults, other than parents
    Peers

Self-perception

    Self-image
    Self-esteem

1979), problem solving (D'Zurilla & Goldfried, 1971; Mahoney & Mahoney, 1976), and imagery (Homme, 1965) are just a few. Other techniques and their applications may be found elsewhere (Foreyt & Goodrick, 1981b; Mahoney & Arnkoff, 1978; Meichenbaum, 1977; Kendall & Hollon, 1979).

The development of the ability to determine and resolve specific problems is considered an important part of working with adolescents and their difficulties with weight. Such capabilities may serve as the bases for confronting a myriad of weight-related problems both during treatment and after. Additionally, the ability to solve problems in one's own life can serve to improve feelings of self-efficacy (Bandura, 1977), which are lacking in many adolescents. Mahoney and Mahoney (1976) devised a systematic approach to problem solving that is highly applicable to many weight control problems (and other areas, as well). The components of their methodology may be remembered through use of the acronym *SCIENCE:*

*S*pecify the general problem area.
*C*ollect data.
*I*dentify regularities (patterns) and possible problem sources.
*E*xamine the various options and possible solutions.
*N*arrow the options and experiment.
*C*ompare your current data with your previous data.
*E*xtend, revise, or replace.

We recently used this technique with a 15-year-old overweight ninth-grade student:

> Melissa identified her problem as excessive late afternoon snacking. Her daily monitoring forms clearly demonstrated the recurring pattern of this behavior and the extent to which it added to her daily caloric totals. The options she considered in resolving this problem included:
>
> - Joining the YWCA and exercising after school.
> - Using that time to work on homework at the library.
> - Getting a part-time job.
> - Asking her mother to refrain from buying her favorite munchies.

After considering the above options, she decided that using the time for homework at the library made the most sense. This choice seemed to have more merit than the others for several reasons: (1) her schoolwork was lagging and a concentrated effort was needed; (2) the library got her away from the temptations at home; and (3) the walk to and from the library provided additional exercise. This solution was helpful as she succeeded in controlling her snacking problem, as well as in losing weight.

Although the solution appeared satisfactory, her later insights suggested that it was only of a temporary nature. She recognized that the basic issue surrounding her late afternoon snacking was the use of food as a means of quelling the feelings of loneliness and boredom during that time of day. Having gained this insight, we revised her problem definition and proceeded, once again, through the SCIENCE sequence.

Besides the management of eating behaviors, problem-solving methodologies can be used for personal and interpersonal difficulties as well. A great deal of the development in this area can be credited to Spivack and his colleagues (e.g., Shure & Spivack, 1972; Shure, Spivack, & Jaeger, 1971; Spivack, Platt, & Shure, 1976), and the reader is referred to one of their works (Spivack & Shure, 1974) for further exploration of this area.

The interpersonal problems confronting obese adolescents are often most effectively handled in a group setting. Besides providing a forum for commiseration among kindred souls, the group serves as the basis for exploring and practicing interpersonal-problem-solving techniques. Modeling and role playing are recommended for use in this setting (Fagen, Long, & Stevens, 1975).

An acute problem of many obese adolescents is poor self-image. This negative self-image often influences their personal assessment at several levels, from negative feelings concerning their physical appearance to a diminished evaluation of their self-worth. Overweight adolescents having this perspective should be treated for this problem as well as for the presenting problem of excess weight.

One approach used to help adolescents with their self-image and their efforts to lose weight is a program of self-talk referred to as *cognitive ecology* (Mahoney & Mahoney, 1976). Cognitive ecology is a technique by which individuals "clean up" what they say to themselves. The negative, maladaptive internal monologues are replaced by those that are more realistic and positive. Mahoney and Mahoney (1976) suggest that appropriate behavior and feelings are accompaniments of the process.

In order to conduct a systematic program of cognitive ecology, an inventory of thoughts should be taken throughout the day. Thus, when individuals are feeling tempted by food, anxious, or depressed, they are instructed to inspect the adaptiveness of their thoughts. Cognitive ecology can be used for other cognitions as well. It can assist obese adolescents in their negative self-assessments regarding their physical appearance, capabilities, and self-worth. Adolescents can be taught to make coping self-statements whenever they recognize that they are in the midst of a negative monologue. Examples of how this technique may be used include:

> *Negative monologue:* Kim didn't invite me to her party. It's probably because I'm so fat and ugly that she probably thought I would be an embarrassment to her. I guess I can't blame her. I wouldn't want somebody like me around either.
>
> *Adaptive monologue:* Well, Kim didn't invite me to her party. Maybe she forgot about me with all of her preparations. Well, whatever the reason, I'm not going to brood about it. I wonder if Sandi would like to go to a movie?
>
> *Negative monologue:* I'm getting awfully tired of being turned down for dates. It's probably because I'm fat; they want the slim Robert Redford type, not somebody who is short and dumpy like me.
>
> *Adaptive monologue:* Being turned down for dates is really disappointing but it's not the end of the world. Those girls probably didn't see all of my qualities. I'd rather date someone who will accept me for who I am.

Modeling and role playing can be used to assist adolescents in learning the methodologies of cognitive ecology. These techniques are especially useful in helping them to devise appropriate self-statements to substitute for those that are inappropriate.

A cognitive technique that can have considerable utility in treating overweight adolescents is covert modeling. It can be used to assist in rectifying problems of eating behavior, as well as those of a personal and an interpersonal nature. For example, unconscious eating, or eating without conscious control, occurs among some overweight adolescents when they are under the influence of certain affective states (e.g., boredom, anxiety, or loneliness). Covert modeling (Cautela, 1971) can assist an individual with this problem through a rehearsal of coping thoughts and behaviors prior to the incident. The rehearsal occurs through the use of mental images.

In practice, adolescents are asked to replicate the problem eating situation in a highly vivid manner. They reproduce, as best they can, the feelings, thoughts, and settings that accompany a typical occurrence. During this imagined sequence, they find that they are able to cope with the situation through the utilization of previously learned skills (e.g., adaptive self-talk, relaxation techniques, or the substitution of an alternate activity). The success achieved through coping is rewarded at the covert level with positive feelings and a sense that it can be done again.

For "unconscious" eating, the covert modeling approach is especially useful. The rehearsal utilized in this technique makes many adolescents sensitive to and aware of the problem situation. Thus, when the "real-life" incident occurs, some obtain a feeling of *déjà vu*, a recognition of the scene and the situation. In this manner, the unconscious behavior is brought to consciousness.

The above examples are only representative of the many ways in which cognitive interventions can be used in helping adolescents with the problem of obesity. These interventions can be used with adolescents in a manner similar to their use with adults. Most adolescents have the cognitive development and intellectual capacity to perform the necessary procedures. However, they often need assistance, flexibility, and understanding to a degree not required by most adults. Overweight adolescents who have gone through a succession of weight control groups and diets are likely to have a feeling of low self-efficacy in this area. This feeling, added to a negative self-image, frequently yields an individual who is hopeful, but who has little optimism. It is important to work not only on their negative outlook, but also on the equally basic issue of self-image.

During treatment, the therapist needs to "listen" for problems unexpressed by the overweight adolescent. Obese adolescents tend to demonstrate a higher degree of shyness, passivity, and withdrawal than their normal-weight peers (Monello & Mayer, 1963). Because of such characteristics, many of them may not express their problems and feelings to the extent that is desirable. The therapist may facilitate this expression by developing a relationship based on mutual trust, confidentiality, and sincerity.

Summary

The cognitive-behavioral treatment of childhood and adolescent obesity is a particularly challenging area. To date, traditional behavioral techniques have not been very successful with this difficult population. The addition of cognitive strategies, within the context of the family setting, may significantly improve weight loss results. We hope that clinicians and researchers will begin to incorporate cognitive techniques into their treatment programs. The potential of such programs is extremely encouraging.

References

Abraham, S., & Nordsieck, M. Relationship of excess weight in children and adults. *Public Health Reports*, 1960, 75, 263–273.

Abramson, E. E. Behavioral approaches to weight control: An updated review. *Behaviour Research and Therapy*, 1977, 15, 355–363.

Allon, N. The stigma of overweight in everyday life. In G. A. Bray (Ed.), *Obesity in perspective* (Vol. 2, Part 2). (DHEW Publication No. 75-708, National Institutes of Health). Washington, D.C.: U.S. Government Printing Office, 1975.

Bandura, A. Psychotherapy based on modeling principles. In A. E. Bergin and S. L. Garfield (Eds.), *Handbook of psychotherapy and behavior change: An empirical analysis.* New York: Wiley, 1971.

Bandura, A. Self efficacy: Toward a unifying theory of behavior change. *Psychological Review*, 1977, *84*, 191–215.

Beller, A. S. *Fat and thin: A natural history of obesity.* New York: Farrar, Straus, and Giroux, 1977.

Boskind-Lodahl, M., & Sirlin, J. The gorging-purging syndrome. *Psychology Today*, 1977, *10*, 51–52, 82–83.

Bray, G. A. *The obese patient.* Philadelphia: Saunders, 1976.

Brownell, K. D. Personal communication, May 24, 1979. Cited in T. J. Coates & C. E. Thoresen, Behavior and weight changes in three obese adolescents. *Behavior Therapy*, 1981, *12*, 383–399.

Brownell, K. D., & Stunkard, A. J. Behavioral treatment for obese children and adolescents. In A. J. Stunkard (Ed.), *Obesity.* Philadelphia: Saunders, 1980.

Cautela, J. R. Covert conditioning. In A. Jacobs & L. B. Sachs (Eds.), *The psychology of private events: Perspectives on covert response systems.* New York: Academic Press, 1971.

Charney, E., Goodman, H. C., McBride, M., Lyon, B., & Pratt, R. Childhood antecedents of adult obesity. *New England Journal of Medicine*, 1976, *295*, 6–9.

Clark, R. P., Menow, S. B., Morse, E. U., & Keyser, D. E. Interrelationships between plasma lipids, physical measurements, and body fatness of adolescents in Burlington, Vermont. *American Journal of Clinical Nutrition*, 1970, *23*, 754–763.

Coates, T. J., & Thoresen, C. E. Treating obesity in children and adolescents: A review. *American Journal of Public Health*, 1978, *68*, 143–151.

Coates, T. J., & Thoresen, C. E. Behavior and weight changes in three obese adolescents. *Behavior Therapy*, 1981, *12*, 383–399.

Cole, P. M., & Kazdin, A. E. Critical issues in self instruction training with children. *Child Behavior Therapy*, 1980, *2*, 1–21.

Denney, D. The effects of exemplary and cognitive models and self rehearsal on children's interrogative strategies. *Journal of Experimental Child Psychology*, 1975, *19*, 476–488.

Dinoff, M., Rickard, H. C., & Colwick, J. Weight reduction through successive contracts. *American Journal of Orthopsychiatry*, 1972, *42*, 110–113.

Dwyer, J., & Mayer, J. The dismal condition: Problems faced by obese adolescent girls in American society. In G. A. Bray (Ed.), *Obesity in perspective* (Vol. 2, Part 2). (DHEW Publication No. 75-708, National Institutes of Health). Washington, D.C.: U.S. Government Printing Office, 1975.

Dwyer, J., Feldman, J. J., & Mayer, J. Adolescent dieters: Who are they? Physical characteristics, attitudes, and dieting practices of adolescent girls. *American Journal of Clinical Nutrition*, 1967, *20*, 1045–1056.

D'Zurilla, T., & Goldfried, M. Problem solving and behavior modification. *Journal of Abnormal Psychology*, 1971, *78*, 107–126.

Ellis, A. *Reason and emotion in psychotherapy.* Secaucus, N.J.: Lyle Stuart, 1962.

Ellis, A. Rational emotive therapy. In R. J. Corsini (Ed.), *Current psychotherapies* (2nd ed.). Itasca, Ill.: Peacock, 1979.

Ellis, A., Wolfe, J. L., & Moseley, S. *How to raise an emotionally healthy, happy child.* Hollywood, Calif.: Wilshire Books, 1966.

Epstein, L. H., Wing, R. R., Koeske, R., Andrasik, F., & Ossip, D. J. Child and parent

weight loss in family based behavior modification programs. *Journal of Consulting and Clinical Psychology*, 1981, *49*, 674–685.
Erikson, E. H. *Identity, youth and crisis.* New York: W. W. Norton, 1968.
Fagen, S. A., Long, N. J., & Stevens, D. J. *Teaching children self control: Preventing emotional and learning problems in the elementary school.* Columbus: Charles E. Merrill, 1975.
Ferguson, J. M. *Habits, not diets: The real way to weight control.* Palo Alto, Calif.: Bull Publishing, 1976.
Foreyt, J. P., & Goodrick, G. K. Childhood obesity. In E. J. Mash & L. G. Terdal (Eds.), *Behavioral assessment of childhood disorders.* New York: Guilford Press, 1981. (a)
Foreyt, J. P., & Goodrick, G. K. Cognitive behavior therapy. In R. J. Corsini (Ed.), *Handbook of innovative psychotherapies.* New York: Wiley, 1981. (b)
Foreyt, J. P., Goodrick, G. K., & Gotto, A. M. Limitations of behavioral treatment of obesity: Review and analysis. *Journal of Behavioral Medicine*, 1981, *4*, 159–174.
Foreyt, J. P., Mitchell, R. E., Garner, D. T., Gee, M., Scott, L. W., & Gotto, A. M. Behavioral treatment of obesity: Results and limitations. *Behavior Therapy*, 1982, *13*, 153–161.
Franzini, L. R., & Grimes, W. B. Skinfold measures as the criterion of change in weight control studies. *Behavior Therapy*, 1976, *7*, 256–260.
Garn, S., Cole, P. E., & Baily, S. M. Effect of parental fatness levels on the fatness of biological and adoptive children. *Ecology of Food and Nutrition*, 1976, *6*, 1–34.
Goodman, N., Dornbusch, S. M., Richardson, S. A., & Hastorf, A. H. Variant reactions to physical disabilities. *American Sociological Review*, 1963, *28*, 429–435.
Hartz, A., Giefer, E., & Rimm, A. A. Relative importance of the effect of family environment and heredity on obesity. *Annals of Human Genetics*, 1977, *41*, 185–193.
Heald, F. P. Juvenile obesity. In M. Winick (Ed.), *Childhood obesity.* New York: Wiley, 1975.
Hirsch, J. Cell number and size as a determinant of subsequent obesity. In M. Winick (Ed.), *Childhood obesity.* New York: Wiley, 1975.
Homme, L. E. Perspectives in psychology: XXIV. Control of coverants, the operants of the mind. *Psychological Record*, 1965, *15*, 501–511.
Huenemann, R. L. Food habits of obese and nonobese adolescents. *Postgraduate Medicine*, 1972, *51*, 99–105.
Huenemann, R. L. Environmental factors associated with preschool obesity. *Journal of the American Dietetic Association*, 1974, *64*, 480–487.
Israel, A. C., & Stolmaker, L. Behavioral treatment of obesity in children and adolescents. In M. Hersen, R. M. Eisler, & P. M. Miller (Eds.), *Progress in behavior modification* (Vol. 10). New York: Academic Press, 1980.
Jordan, H. A., & Levitz, L. S. Behavior modification in treatment of childhood obesity. In M. Winick (Ed.), *Childhood obesity.* New York: Wiley, 1975.
Jung, R. T., Gurr, M. I., Robinson, M. P., & James, W. P. Does adipocyte hypercellularity in obesity exist? *British Medical Journal*, 1978, *2*, 319–321.
Kendall, P. C. Cognitive behavioral interventions with children. In B. Lahey & A. Kazdin (Eds.), *Advances in clinical child psychology.* New York: Plenum Press, 1981.
Kendall, P. C., & Hollon, S. D. (Eds.) *Cognitive behavioral interventions: Theory, research, and procedures.* New York: Academic Press, 1979.
Lauer, R. M., Conner, W. E., Leaverton, P. E., Reiter, M. A., & Clarke, W. R. Coronary heart disease risk factors in school children: The Muscatine Study. *The Journal of Pediatrics*, 1975, *86*, 697–706.
Leon, G. R. Current directions in the treatment of obesity. *Psychological Bulletin*, 1976, *83*, 557–578.

Lerner, R. M. The development of personal space schemata toward body build. *The Journal of Psychology*, 1973, *84*, 229–235.
Londe, S., Bourgoignie, J. J., Robson, A. M., & Goldring, D. Hypertension in apparently normal children. *Journal of Pediatrics*, 1971, *78*, 569–577.
Maddox, G. L., Back, K. W., & Liederman, V. R. Overweight as social deviance and disability. *Journal of Health and Social Behavior*, 1968, *9*, 287–298.
Mahoney, M. J. Personal science: A cognitive learning therapy. In A. Ellis & R. Greiger (Eds.), *Handbook of rational emotive therapy*. New York: Springer, 1977.
Mahoney, M. J., & Arnkoff, D. B. Cognitive and self control therapies. In S. L. Garfield & A. E. Bergin (Eds.), *Handbook of psychotherapy and behavior change: An empirical analysis* (2nd ed.). New York: Wiley, 1978.
Mahoney, M. J., & Mahoney, K. *Permanent weight control: A total solution to the dieter's dilemma*. New York: W. W. Norton, 1976.
Mann, G. V. The influence of obesity in health. *New England Journal of Medicine*, 1974, *291*, 178–185, 226–232.
Mann, R. A. The behavior therapeutic use of contingency contracting to control an adult behavior problem: Weight control. *Journal of Applied Behavior Analysis*, 1972, *5*, 99–109.
Mayer, J. Some aspects of the problem of regulating food intake and obesity. *International Psychiatry Clinics*, 1970, *7*, 255–334.
Mayer, J. Obesity during childhood. In M. Winick (Ed.), *Childhood obesity*. New York: Wiley, 1975.
Meichenbaum, D. *Cognitive behavior modification*. New York: Plenum Press, 1977.
Miller, F. J., Billewicz, W. Z., & Thompson, A. M. Growth from birth to adult life of 442 Newcastle Upon Tyne children. *British Journal of Preventive and Social Medicine*, 1972, *26*, 224–230.
Millman, M. *Such a pretty face*. New York: Berkeley, 1980.
Mobbs, J. Childhood obesity. *International Journal of Nursing Studies*, 1970, *7*, 3–18.
Monello, L. F., & Mayer, J. Obese adolescent girls: An unrecognized "minority" group? *American Journal of Clinical Nutrition*, 1963, *13*, 35–39.
Nelson, R. A. Exercise in the treatment of obesity. In G. A. Bray (Ed.), *Recent advances in obesity research* (Vol. 2). Westport, Conn.: Food and Nutrition Press, 1978.
Neumann, C. G. Obesity in pediatric practice: Obesity in the preschool and school age child. *Pediatric Clinics of North America*, 1977, *24*, 117–122.
Orbach, S. *Fat is a feminist issue*. London: Paddington Press, 1977.
Palmer, P. *Liking myself*. San Luis Obispo, Calif.: Impact Publishers, 1978.
Price, J. H., & Geronilla, L. A. Childhood obesity: A review. *Health Values: Achieving High Level Wellness*, 1981, *5*, 192–198.
Seltzer, C. C., & Mayer, J. A simple criterion of obesity. *Postgraduate Medicine*, 1965, *38*, A101–107.
Shenker, I. R., Fisichelli, V., & Lang, J. Weight difference between foster infants and overweight and non overweight foster mothers. *Journal of Pediatrics*, 1974, *84*, 715–719.
Shure, M. B., & Spivack, G. Means-ends thinking, adjustment and social class among elementary school-aged children. *Journal of Consulting and Clinical Psychology*, 1972, *38*, 348–353.
Shure, M. B., Spivack, G., & Jaeger, M. Problem solving thinking and adjustment among disadvantaged preschool children. *Child Development*, 1971, *42*, 1791–1803.
Spivack, G., & Shure, M. B. *Social adjustment of young children: A cognitive approach to solving real life problems*. San Francisco: Jossey-Bass, 1974.
Spivack, G., Platt, J. J., & Shure, M. B. *The problem solving approach to adjustment*. San Francisco: Jossey-Bass, 1976.

Staffieri, J. R. A study of social stereotype of body image in children. *Journal of Personality and Social Psychology*, 1967, *7*, 101–104.
Stuart, R. B., & Davis, B. *Slim chance in a fat world*. Champaign, Ill.: Research Press, 1972.
Stunkard, A. J., & Mahoney, M. J. Behavioral treatment of eating disorders. In H. Leitenberg (Ed.), *The handbook of behavior modification and behavior therapy*. Englewood Cliffs, N.J.: Prentice Hall, 1976.
Tanner, J. M., & Whitehouse, R. H. Revised standards for triceps and subscapular skinfolds in British children. *Archives of Diseases in Childhood*, 1975, *50*, 142–145.
Weil, W. B. Infantile obesity. In M. Winick (Ed.), *Childhood obesity*. New York: Wiley, 1975.
Weil, W. B. Current controversies in childhood obesity. *Journal of Pediatrics*, 1977, *91*, 175–187.
Wilson, G. T., & Brownell, K. D. Behavior therapy for obesity: An evaluation of treatment outcome. *Advances in Behaviour Research and Therapy*, 1980, *3*, 49–86.
Wooley, S. C., Wooley, O. W., & Dyrenforth, S. R. Theoretical, practical and social issues in behavioral treatments of obesity. *Journal of Applied Behavior Analysis*, 1979, *12*, 3–25.
Wrenn, G., & Schwarzock, S. *The coping books*. Circle Pines, Minn.: American Guidance Service, 1970.

11

A Rational-Emotive Approach to Childhood Sexuality

SUSAN R. WALEN AND
GLORIA K. VANDERHORST

Sex. Such a simple word. Such a short word. Such an emotionally charged word. Notice the title of this chapter: "Childhood Sexuality." Do we really mean to imply that children are sexual? And what do we mean by children? It is time, obviously, to stop and define our terms.

The children we discuss in this chapter range from pretoddlers to late adolescents. We address the whole gamut, leaving out perhaps the neonate with her or his still-developing neural pathways, although we know from research studies that infants *in utero* display genital signs of arousal (Wolman, 1980).

And sex. How shall we define this word. Definitions typically reflect cultural values and orientations. Thus, before we commit ourselves to a definition, it is appropriate to let you know that our values are necessarily relativistic, a reflection, in part, of the era in which we live and the social milieu in which we work. The views expressed here are therefore a combination of these contemporary issues as they are presented to us in clinical practice when we work with parents and children and of our personal experiences as children and parents. With these considerations in mind, we choose to define sex in a very broad way, including all of the following concepts (and more): body awareness and

---

SUSAN R. WALEN • Department of Psychology, Towson State University, Towson, Maryland 21204.   GLORIA K. VANDERHORST • Psychologist in Private Practice, Baltimore, Maryland 21210.

sensuality, pleasure seeking, love and caring, sex role and gender identification, and genital arousal, intercourse, and orgasm. If all of these considerations are part of our sexuality, there can be no doubt that we are sexual creatures from the cradle to the grave. Sex is a normal integral part of the human life-span, as basic as any other biological system.

We satisfy our children's most basic biological needs when we prepare meals for them. We teach them how to eat. We guide them in what to eat. We encourage them to try new foods. We talk often about food. We share our pleasure in good meals with others. But sexuality? No, that we do not discuss. There is very little—shockingly little—in the way of teaching, guiding, encouraging, and pleasure sharing here. Sex, you see, is supposed to be "natural."

WHEN DOES SEX EDUCATION BEGIN?

Although sex *is* perfectly natural, it is rarely naturally perfect. Therein lies some evidence that sexuality involves a great deal of learning. Sexuality is a complex business, including not only a set of behaviors, but also a set of beliefs and values. These, like other values, do need to be taught.

Most sex education goes on in the home, and it begins from the earliest days of an infant's life. Most of this education, however, is unplanned, has no formal curriculum, and goes on without the awareness of the educator or the learner. Messages are transmitted in very subtle ways, but their impact on the child is not subtle.

Some parents do not want to educate their children about sex; they do not want to discuss it at all. Many times, when sexually troubled adults come for sex therapy, we ask them about the messages they got from their parents about sex. Frequently, such patients disclaim this factor, saying, "I never got any negative messages about sex at home . . . why we never even talked about it!" No communication is not the absence of a message. In fact, it is probably the strongest message of all. Parents discuss eating, playing, sleeping, toileting, and many other topics with their children. What kinds of topics are the ones to be avoided? Why, the really taboo ones, of course. The message is "That's so distasteful a subject that we won't even talk about it."

Some parents teach by nonverbal messages. One working mother described an elegant example of nonverbal learning. She picked her 18-month-old daughter up from the baby-sitter's house one day, brought the baby home, and decided to change her diaper. As soon as the diaper was removed, the child reached for her genitals, but she looked up at her mother with a playful, "testing" look. After a few such incidents, this attentive mother decided to ask the baby-sitter how she handled diaper rituals, and if she punished the child for touching herself. "Why, no," exclaimed the kind and matronly sitter, "I'd never punish her. I just whisk away her hand and pull up the clean diaper very quickly." Teaching? Of course. The message is "That's something we don't do; we don't touch electric outlets, the pretty decorative knickknacks, or our genitals." The outcome of this vignette was more positive. Mom discussed her values with the baby-sitter and requested that the sitter behave consistently with those values. And at home, when the baby was being undressed and she reached for her genitals, Mom cooed at her, "Feels good, doesn't it, honey? Mommy likes to do that, too."

Some parents, like the enlightened mother above, want to teach their children about sex. Often, their stated objective is to provide their children with a better sex education and more positive sex messages than they themselves received. If their own training was negative and if they're still working through their own negative values, however, these parents can be confusing teachers. One such mother gave her daughter a very upbeat and informative lecture about sexual intercourse but was overheard to say, as she summarized, "And so, darling, when sex rears its ugly head . . ." These messages are heard, too.

In the two-parent household, the teaching of sex may be further complicated by conflicting messages from Mom and Dad. One parent may discuss sexual issues openly and honestly, while the other remains silent or contributes only through humor that is caustic and derogatory. In therapy, we can be attuned to these differences and can work to develop more consistent, complementary messages.

One major study on parents as sex educators (Roberts, Kline, & Gagnon, 1979) pointed out in detail how poorly the job is being done. A representative sample of 1,400 parents was interviewed about how they discussed sexual topics with their 3- to 11-year-old children. Most, quite simply, were silent. For example, less than half of the parents of 11-year-old children had even mentioned intercourse to their children. Among girls approaching the age of menarche, almost 40% had never heard of the topic from a parent. Less than 2% of the fathers had discussed wet dreams with their sons. In fact, many of these parents stated that they did not even display physical affection toward one another in front of their children. Presumably, the notion was that what they don't see, they won't ask about. Apparently, the message was received: by the age of 9 or 10, questions on sexually related topics had virtually ceased.

Why were these sampled parents so uncomfortable? The researchers concluded that their hesitation stemmed from a "fundamental ambiguity about their own attitudes and the applicability of these values for their children's lives." Although most young people say they would like to hear about sex from their parents, most parents (71% in one study) favor sex education in the schools. How do the schools fare as sex educators?

According to recent estimates, only 10% of young people receive anything approximating an adequate sex education in the school setting (Gordon, 1981). Many sex-education courses consist of a presentation on reproductive anatomy (the "plumbing"), with a bit of physiology, and may constitute one hour in a year-long curriculum. Our own state is one that has chosen to mandate sex education in the schools, but the quality of instruction can vary widely within a narrow geographical range. One third-grade teacher informed us that she was required to teach sexuality, but had been given no curriculum guide nor even a list of the topics to be tackled. In a neighboring school district, fifth-grade teachers have a 100-page manual to work from that lists resource materials, discussion exercises, and so forth. Even in a sophisticated curriculum, however, important topics are often omitted. A colleague who has reviewed the curriculum in New York City, for example, reported no mention of the female sex organ, the clitoris, nor of masturbation, nor of the role of love and caring.

Although the vast majority of parents and educators would like to see high-quality sex education in the schools, they face strong—and vocal—opposition. The opponents apparently believe that if we do not talk about sex, then children and adolescents will not engage in it. Ignorance is not bliss, however, as attested to by more than one million unwanted teenage pregnancies each year, as well as the rampancy of venereal disease in this country.

Children need to be taught, and a wise teacher assesses the learners' capabilities, organizing the teaching around the students' interests and cognitive abilities. Therapists, particularly those who use rational-emotive therapy (RET), are educators, too. What do we know about the interests and cognitive abilities of children at various stages of growth?

How Do Children and Adults Think about Sexuality?

To answer this question, we turn to the theory and research of Jean Piaget (1950, 1951, 1952). Piaget defined thought as a biological process of adapting to and organizing information. The child uses hereditary physical systems to interact with the environment, thereby building psychological structures or thought processes. The hereditary physical systems set broad limits on the child's cognitive abilities. For example, the afferent-efferent nervous system limits the speed and the amount of sensory information that can be transmitted at one time. All of our sensory systems permit us to handle certain types of information while prohibiting others. We hear and see stimuli within certain wavelengths and not others. The sex organs are responsive to certain forms of touch and pressure and not others.

In interacting with the environment, the child begins to organize behaviors into higher order systems. For example, eye–hand movements represent coordination between scanning and grasping. The coherently ordered action of sighting an object in space, reaching for the object, and grasping it is neurologically a complex activity. Piaget inferred that such activity is guided by a psychological scheme, which is somewhat like an organized set of self-instructions. Such schemata underlie all complex behavior. The specific action may vary from one instance to the next, and the scheme represents an abstraction of the common features of these actions. The schemata used by the individual become more varied and elaborate as the individual gets older. Once a schema is developed, there is a tendency to exercise and apply that schema throughout development, although the type of exercise or application varies from one stage of development to the next.

In order to understand childhood sexuality, we must examine the nature of the sensual schema at each stage of development. In the following section, we suggest examples of cognitive schemata that may be helpful in understanding childhood sexuality, without attempting to present an exhaustive study of children's thought processes. We refer the reader who is interested in a more thorough presentation of the developmental stages in cognitive psychology to the work of Furth (1969).

The physical systems of sexuality are obviously present at birth. During the first months of life, the child's behavior is dominated by reflex actions. Genital pleasures and orgasm are reflexes just like sucking and sneezing, frequently providing just as much or more relief and pleasure. The infant has a natural tendency to explore its body, repeating actions that are interesting or pleasurable. Genital play and masturbation are actions involving eye–hand coordination guided by the same schema or set of self-instructions that would be involved in shaking a rattle, grabbing a toy, or eating a cookie. It is as if a child were saying, "If I put my hand where my eye is focused, and I move it around a bit, something nice will happen."

Most new parents are honestly surprised by the frequency with which their babies reach for their genitals. The message from the child is clearly that sexual pleasure is a natural part of daily life. The parents can send important messages to the child by the way in which they respond to masturbation, nudity, and sensual play such as hugging, kissing, and tickling their babies.

The parents' behavior in the above situations is important because a child's understanding of events is developed not through the logical reasoning processes of deduction or induction with which we are most familiar, but through a form of irrational association called *transductive reasoning*, which depends on the temporal or spatial contiguity of events. Transductive reasoning means that young children, perhaps through 7 or 8 years of age, reason from one specific event to another specific event when there is no logical connection between them. Think back to the example of the baby-sitter who would whisk the baby's hand away from the genitals and then rapidly pin up the diaper. To the adult, this sequence of events did not appear to be logically connected with masturbation. The temporal association of her action with the child's action, however, presented a clear message that the *child* could understand without any difficulty.

As therapists, we need to attend to the sequence of events that the adult describes in order to predict the irrational associations that the child can build, associations that the child frequently is not able to report to us. We can also teach the parents how the principle of contiguity may build up false associations in the child, thus helping the parents to understand and predict their children's conceptualizations.

Children can apply transductive reasoning not only to actions, but to labels and to thoughts about those labels. As the child develops language, an insatiable appetite for labels develops. Anything that can be seen, heard, touched, or smelled demands labeling. The words we choose to teach our children for sexual organs and behaviors are important sources of healthy attitudes; they also open up numerous possibilities for building irrational beliefs. One mother referred to her little girl's genital area as a bunny. Can you imagine the association developed by this child through transductive reasoning? The cute little pictures in the Beatrix Potter books, the animals hopping through the yard in spring, were somehow attached to her body right between her legs. If she disturbed it, it might jump up and hop away, leaving her sexless. No wonder she stopped touching herself there.

It is at this stage that the child begins to associate the word *dirty* with sexuality; this irrational association could be built up as follows: Every time little Johnny goes into the bathroom, Mom asks, "Did you wash your hands? Did you wash *with soap?*" Clearly, the message that the child may understand is that touching one's lower body makes one unclean, when, in fact, urine is usually sterile, and Johnny would probably be engaging in a more sensible act if he washed his hands *before* he touched his penis. His hands are most likely grimy, whereas his penis has been under wraps and is clean.

As preschoolers, children begin to experiment in a wide variety of ways. They experiment with words, actions, people young and old, male and female, and they begin to question or challenge. This is the time of the eternal string of "why's" that please and frustrate parents. When Johnny asks why grass is green, Father is delighted to phrase a simple answer. When he asks, "Why do you have a furry butt?" Father ignores the question, changes the subject, or sends Johnny out of the room. This reaction inevitably gives the question more value in Johnny's mind. In Piaget's terms, a disequilibrium has been created. The child will now work hard to create equilibrium. Parents could do a great service by responding to questions about sex in the same simplistic way that they respond to "Why is grass green?" "Why do you have a furry butt?" Because I'm grown up and all grown-ups have furry butts.

Sometime around 6 to 8 years of age, the child's thinking takes on a new dimension. *Concrete reasoning* emerges, freeing the child from the limitations of transductive reasoning, although this form of thought may never be completely abandoned. (As adults, some of our beliefs may still be based on this type of association.) Now the child operates something in the way a scientist does. Data are collected and conclusions are drawn from them. The child can reorder data, abandon irrelevant information, and recombine data. However, the child cannot contemplate possibilities, only realities—things that are immediately available to the senses. The child is not skilled at imagining transformations of data and then operating on these transformations. Another characteristic of this stage is frequently described by parents as stubbornness, but it is actually the child's assertion that his or her solution is the only accurate one. After arriving at a conclusion, considering any other would require entertaining possibilities. The young elementary-aged child is not ready to do this. In conducting therapy with children, or advising parents on coping with their children, an understanding of the above notion is helpful.

To reason properly, the child needs accurate data that are as concrete as possible. In a recent report of a major cross-national study (Goldman & Goldman, 1982), American children were shown to be significantly retarded in the area of sexual thinking when compared with Australian, British, and Swedish children. On a test of cognitive levels of thinking, however, American children scored as well as the others (in fact, higher, although this trend was not statistically significant). What we can conclude from these facts is that, although the level of logic and reasoning abilities reflects earlier social maturation in the United States, these same children are woefully deprived of *facts*. For example, the correct physiological terms for the sex organs were often described as *dirty*, and euphemisms abounded. When the latter were tabulated as a measure of sexual language inhibition, North American children were the most handicapped.

The following example illustrates how the child uses facts and how important accuracy is. This exchange between father and son takes place after the boy spots a condom in Dad's dresser drawer. "What's that, Dad?" "Oh, nothing. It's just a balloon, see?" Dad blows up the condom as best he can. The son leaves and a few hours later asks his mother about the "funny thing" he saw in Dad's dresser drawer. Mother, being a bit more enlightened, says, "You leave those things alone. Your father and I use those because we don't want to make any more babies." Now, the little scientist retreats to contemplate these data. Of course, he already knows that babies are somehow made in mother's tummy. Conclusion: mothers who don't want babies swallow balloons.

As the child matures, approaching puberty, the same principles of thought continue to operate. Data about the changing body are sought, and new sensations and interests are discovered. Erotic publications are sneaked under the covers, and the data collection about the opposite sex takes on new meaning and appetite. The parent is soon confronted with two forms of reasoning that will provide hours of frustrations if not properly understood. The adolescent is now capable of contemplating possibilities and hypotheses as well as realities. This contemplating, however, sometimes works overtime in the form of what David Elkind has called the imaginary audience and the personal fable (1967).

The *imaginary audience* describes adolescents' tendency to believe that all others make the same judgments of them as they make of themselves. Their thoughts are magnified as though a large audience were shouting in unison, carrying common beliefs. The adolescent female who wails to her mother that her breasts are too small and that no one will ever love her is responding to the imaginary audience. Mother's calm reassurance is one small voice that has little chance of being heard in the crowd.

The *personal fable* is a belief in uniqueness and immortality. Adolescents reason that no one else has ever had the same feelings as they and that the natural consequences that accrue to others will not be visited on them. In essence, they are exempt from the laws of nature. This belief is particularly important when considering the decision-making process in sexual issues. Even when a teen is well informed about the risks of pregnancy, she often may fail to take precautions because she believes that she is special or different and that it won't happen to her.

Of course, all of the above modes of thinking are not abandoned with the onset of adulthood or parenthood. All of us continue to use the above thought processes at some point in time. As adults, we also acquire two other important illusions that are helpful in understanding some parents' behaviors: the generational illusion and the immediacy illusion (Elkind, 1967). These beliefs further complicate the communication process between parent and child.

The *generational illusion* is an irrational belief that the younger generation of today is drastically different from the younger generation of yesterday. Research does not bear this idea out; certainly, some things change, but the basic struggles and milestones remain the same. The generational illusion serves only to create distance between parent and child.

The *immediacy illusion* involves a sense of urgency about present problems; solutions must come quickly, and the implication is that they are or should be obvious and absolute. This belief system, in part, accounts for the parents' intolerance of adolescent experimentation in sexuality. Many parents are surprised to learn that their adolescent has had homosexual encounters. They may demand instant termination of the relationship without recognizing that it is a common experiment for adolescents.

These characteristics of adult thought may make it difficult for many parents to be good listeners and counselors with respect to sexual issues. As reviewed in Table 1, both parent and child are handicapped by a set of irrational beliefs that invite conflict, friction, and misunderstanding. With some good RET work that challenges these beliefs, however, many parents can learn to be more comfortable with their own sexuality and with that of their child. An honest, caring attitude that says, "I'm an askable parent" will prove to be an invaluable tool for both parent and child.

Sexuality in Therapy

It's easy to overlook sexual issues in therapy. Often the problems will not be brought up boldly and are merely alluded to or mentioned in passing.

In interviewing parents, we frequently ask questions about the child's physical health, developmental milestones, academic achievement, peer relations, and sibling relations. When discussing physical

TABLE 1. Irrational Belief Sets in Children and Adults

Some irrational beliefs of childhood

Transductive reasoning:	"Things that happen close together in time or space are causally or logically linked."
Concrete reasoning:	"My conclusion is the only accurate one."
Imaginary audience:	"Everyone believes what I believe."
Personal fable:	"I'm different from others. No one else has ever had the same feelings or experiences. Negative consequences happen to others, but not to me; I'm different."

Some irrational beliefs of adulthood
(The above remain with us but in less intense form.)

Generational illusion:	"Kids today are different from when I was a kid."
Immediacy illusion:	"This problem must be solved now!"

health, the addition of a few questions about sexuality lets the parents know that we are willing and able to discuss a topic that other therapists and the family pediatrician may have avoided. Consider adding the following questions to your list of initial interview data:

- What are the family labels for the child's genitals?
- How far along is your child in pubertal development?
- Has she started to menstruate?
- Are there signs of breast development?
- Have his testicles descended?
- Does he or she have pubic hair?
- Have you discussed conception with your child?
- How about contraception?
- How frequently? What data have you given him or her?
- What are the family rules about nudity?
- Is masturbation discussed or alluded to?
- Are you openly affectionate with each other?
- With the children?
- What are the family rules about locking doors on bedrooms and bathrooms?
- Do your kids take baths or showers together?
- With parents?
- Are erotic books and materials hidden away or easily available?
- What messages did you get from your own parents about sex?

This list is not exhaustive; hopefully, it will generate more questions in your mind that can be added to the list.

In working with children and adolescents, it is important to take time with the parents to learn about their values, and to alert them to the fact that sexual issues may come up in therapy with their child. Gaining the parents' cooperation will help to prevent misunderstandings later, and many times parents are relieved to learn that they have a skilled professional serving as a resource in this "difficult" area.

In interviewing children and adolescents, questions about sexuality are frequently met with giggles and squirming. The therapist can respond to this discomfort by trying to disinhibit the child by using slang words and flooding them with sexual language, or by ignoring the giggles and maintaining a pleasant, professional demeanor while continuing to probe for information using formal sexual language. In our experience, the latter is more productive in individual therapy, and the former may be an effective desensitization technique when working with groups of adolescents or adults. The following questions may be helpful in opening these discussions with younger children:

- What words did your parents teach you for the private parts of your body?
- What words did they teach you for going to the bathroom?
- What's the difference between girls and boys?
- Did your parents teach you how babies get made? Tell me how.

With older children and adolescents, these questions can be modified to fit their more sophisticated vocabulary. Questions such as these may be good starting points for discussing a variety of sexual issues and establishing the therapist's interest in and comfort with the topic, leading to an open climate for future discussions.

If the therapist is uncomfortable with sexuality issues, is unsure of her or his information base, or has strong moralistic sexual standards, these questions may create discomfort. However, they are no less disquieting than the questions many parents receive from their children. Consider the following list of questions actually posed by fifth-graders to their teacher in a unit on health issues:

- Can you get pregnant before you menstruate?
- How does a boy know when his sperm has developed?
- What is a contraceptive?
- Do birth control pills kill babies?
- Why do mothers act a little funny when they have their period?
- How do babies get out?

- Will you say something about masturbation?
- How does the baby get food when it's in the stomach?
- Can a man have an abortion so he can't be a father?
- How does milk get into the breasts?

Know your limitations; it's all right to have limitations. If sexual issues are not easy for you to discuss openly and freely, if sexual language "hurts your ears" or gets "stuck in your throat," if you really believe that there are "right" and "wrong" ways to be sexual, these are your limitations. Refer your client to another therapist for help in the sexual arena. Then, if you wish, enhance your training; special courses in human sexuality or SAR (sexual attitude reassessment) workshops are offered at many universities.

Who Presents the Problem: Whose Problem Is It?

Occasionally, a child directly initiates a discussion about a sexual concern. Somewhat more commonly, the therapist may become aware that there are sexual issues by means of observations made during play therapy or by visits to the child's home or school. Most often, however, childhood sexual problems are presented by the adults in the child's life. For example, a father came in worried about his son, who seemed to be more interested in playing with dolls than with his football. A distraught mother wanted to make an appointment for her daughter because she had found contraceptives in the teenager's purse. A teacher suggested psychotherapy for a first-grade girl because of the child's "compulsive masturbation." In each of these instances, important questions arose: "Does this "problem" have more to do with the adult's sexual hang-ups than with the child's behavior? Do both parties need sexual counseling? Obviously, a careful diagnostic assessment is necessary.

Consider the little boy who prefers dolls to footballs. A combination of interview and observations indicated that he did indeed have a problem: headaches. He was under a great deal of stress at home. Almost daily, his dad would insist that they go out and play football, Dad nearly knocking the little fellow down with the force of his throws. Dad teased him and taunted him about being a sissy, didn't like it when he hung around in the kitchen when Mom was cooking, and worried if he saw the boy engaged in quiet, solitary activities. In fact, the child engaged in many sex-role-appropriate behaviors, was well liked in school, and was basically self-accepting. Dad had the problem; he didn't understand that the world has lots of room for nurturant, gentle men.

The teenager with contraceptives was another story. After a number of interviews with her, the issues became clearer. The problem, of course, was not that she was sexually active; the problem was why she was sexually active. She had recently entered a new school and had brought to this situation a bookbag laden with heavy burdens: painful shyness, a desperate need to be quickly accepted, and an extremely poor self-image. Providing sexual favors seemed to be one way to gain social admittance, but predictably, the effect backfired; she failed to get the acceptance she thought she needed, and she accepted herself less and less as a consequence. She was caught in a nasty cycle; she had a problem.

Cognitive Therapy and Sexuality

One essential dependent variable in therapy is emotional distress; it is this that sends patients to our offices, and it is reduction in distress that lets us know we have begun to be effective in treatment. There are four major categories of distress common to patients in therapy: anger, depression, guilt, and fears or anxieties. In dealing with children's sexual concerns, the latter two seem to predominate: fear and guilt.

The cognitive therapist works from the assumption that the emotional distress stems largely from distressing thoughts, which are characterized by misconceptions, distortion, exaggeration, and horrific evaluation. Among children, the idiosyncratic nature of these thoughts and the illogical connections between them can be staggering. Brief case vignettes may best illustrate the nature of such thinking.

> Bernie was an 8-year-old who had a very big worry on his mind: he was afraid of the operation. Here is the background of this worry. From the age of 3 to 6, Bernie would go to his friend David's house each day; their mothers worked, and a joint-baby-sitter arrangement had been in effect. Sometimes, Bernie and David would get out some of David's mother's clothes and would dress up in them and play sexy games. Since that time, Bernie had occasionally tried on his mother's pantyhose or her silky underwear. Often, he would get an erection and masturbate with sexy thoughts. Bernie had never told anyone about these activities, but he worried about them. He decided that they meant that he was really a girl. If he was really a girl, he couldn't have a penis, so naturally, it would have to be removed. He was really getting scared because, as he said, "I'm too young to have an operation like that!"

> Carl was 16 and in love. He and Nancy spent hours together, snuggling and talking and beginning to explore their sexuality. Step by step, they tried out new things—french kissing, removing articles of clothing,

stroking and fondling each others' bodies. One day they had the house to themselves for a few hours, so they spent the time in Carl's bedroom. "Today," he thought, "I will kiss her down there." He helped Nancy remove her jeans and panties and began to kiss her tummy and thighs. As he got closer to her genitals, however, he began to feel strange sensations: his heart began to race, he felt short of breath, and his legs began to shake. He retreated and tried again a few minutes later, only to find the same scary feelings recurring, this time accompanied by a twinge of nausea. "Good lord," he thought, "maybe I'm allergic to girls' genitals. I can't even get near Nancy's without feeling sick. I must be gay! Oh, my God!" It never occurred to him that what he was experiencing were merely the symptoms of anxiety.

As Ellis has repeatedly taught us, the RET or cognitive therapist knows that there are usually two problems for the price of one: a presenting symptom and the distress that the patient feels about this symptom (Ellis & Harper, 1975; Ellis, 1975, 1980). This secondary problem has been referred to as *symptom stress* (Walen, DiGiuseppe, & Wessler, 1980) and is typically the first order of business therapeutically. In the example above, 16-year-old Carl had the same set of performance demands that plague more mature males in the sexual arena and that had resulted in a case of performance anxiety. What happened next was even more devastating, however. Carl misinterpreted his sensations ("I'm allergic"), leapt to an incorrect diagnosis ("I must be gay"), and evaluated this assumed reality as a horror (inferred from his cry, "Oh, my God!"). Carl's first task, therefore, was to understand and make peace with his anxiety. Once this step was accomplished, he could then methodically and unanxiously set about dismantling his self-inflicted performance demands.

Correcting Misconceptions

Much of the work of sexual counseling with children (and their parents) consists of sexual education. Much of this education consists of providing accurate information in order to dispel myths and misconceptions. Bernie, the 8-year-old, and Carl, the 16-year-old, were greatly relieved to learn that their fears were groundless, and that what they were doing and experiencing were quite normal events that many people experience. Bernie was told that many little boys like to feel soft textures of clothes and that lots of boys try on their mom's or sister's clothes and find them sexy. That doesn't mean that they are girls, and no one ever operates to remove a boy's penis. Bernie's dad and older brother were encouraged to involve Bernie in more of their activities, such as weight lifting and bike riding. Some months later, when we checked with Bernie about his worries, he informed us that he didn't have them any more; he knew he was a boy. Carl, similarly was encouraged to reexamine his interpretation of his experience and to uncover more thoughts that would better explain why he was so anxious in sex play. Much of his concern resembled the concern we hear in adult male patients: performance anxiety. Carl was worried about "doing it right," about pleasing his partner without any communication training between them, and about "going as far" as his friends had claimed to have gone. On reflection, Carl decided that these were silly thoughts, and he determined to go only as far as he felt like going in each encounter with Nancy, and to focus on the nice feelings he was having and on the closeness between them.

Some of the work of counseling entails clarifying values. Many children and adolescents are caught in the bind of conflicting messages given by our sexually oriented culture and the prohibitive messages given by parents and church. They can become victims of peer pressure and often are not given the opportunity to think things out for themselves in a rational, thoughtful way. The teenaged girl described earlier, who was using her sexuality to obtain social acceptance, eventually learned to be quite articulate and clear about when, how, and for what reasons she wished to be sexual. She learned to say "no" when she sensed she was going into a sexual relationship for the wrong reasons. She also began to work with her therapist on her need for approval, her tendency toward negative self-evaluations, and her social skills.

Sometimes, the therapist works on all fronts: school, home, and in individual consultation. Such a multipronged approach may be desirable even in dealing with fairly common problems, such as evidenced in the case of Penny.

> Penny was 6 years old and a first-grader, when her mother was called in to school to discuss her problems with the principal. Penny's teacher had noticed that Penny was not completing class assignments and often was inattentive to classroom presentations. The child frequently spent her time rocking back and forth on the edge of her chair and staring blankly into space. Then, she would often put her head down on her desk and doze. The teacher, feeling very uncomfortable, went to the principal and described Penny's inattention, her missing work, and her rocking and staring behavior. The word *masturbation* was never mentioned, but clearly, the two school professionals felt that they were dealing with a very "delicate" matter. When Penny's mother came to the meeting at the school, it was suggested to her that Penny might be seriously disturbed. Perhaps,

the child did not even belong in that school and should be placed elsewhere. In any case, clearly a complete psychological evaluation was needed, and Penny's mom was given the names of two psychologists with whom she was advised to consult immediately.

Penny's mom was understandably shaken by this news and phoned to speak to the first doctor on her list. Dr. X was a psychoanalytically trained therapist and made an appointment to interview her. During this consultation, Dr. X was quite direct in questioning the mother on issues relating to sexuality. She reported that she had been separated from her husband for two years. The children saw her nude at bath times, and the daughter frequently bathed with her brother, who was one year younger. Sometimes, the children slept together in the brother's room, though not in the same bed. In the mornings, both children would climb in bed with Mom and snuggle for a few minutes before getting up. The girl had been rubbing herself on furniture and toys since infancy. This had not concerned the mother because it generally did not interfere with other activities.

At the end of the consultation, Dr. X announced that there was no apparent physiological cause for Penny's behavior. The problem was in the way Mom was raising her. He advised the mother to stop appearing nude in front of her children. Furthermore, brothers and sisters should never bathe or sleep together. At night, the mother's bedroom door should be locked, making her room off limits for both children. The mother was told that her daughter was "overstimulated" and that the objectionable behavior would stop when the mother followed the above prescription.

By now, Penny's mom was really upset. The little girl she had thought was so bright and happy was really so disturbed that she might need to go to a "special school," and it was all the mother's fault. She'd somehow been sexually promiscuous with her children and "overstimulated" them. What should she do? She decided to consult with the second psychologist on her list, a cognitive therapist.

She arrived at the psychologist's office quite distressed, and hurriedly recounted the events leading up to the appointment. After listening carefully, the second psychologist allowed that the first psychologist's view was a highly regarded interpretation in many mental-health circles, but not necessarily the only possible one. A few questions uncovered the fact that none of the adults in question had ever spoken to Penny about her behavior. A discussion of the language used by the family to describe genitalia, secondary sex characteristics, and bathroom behavior followed. The mother was given some literature on childhood sexuality to educate herself on the normal course of childhood sexual behaviors (see "Suggested Readings"). She was also encouraged to view her child's masturbation from a sociological view; that is, Penny didn't have a problem because she masturbated, but the social context in which the behavior occurred created a problem, in part because the adults around her had trouble dealing with her behavior. A role play was enacted in which the mother spoke to the child frankly about masturbation as a pleasant but private matter. Mom rehearsed asking Penny to go to her room, the bathroom, or some other private place when she felt like masturbating. Essentially, the mother was encouraged to treat the issue in the same context as teaching her child not to pick her nose in public (which she had accomplished successfully).

A consultation between the psychologist and Penny's teacher was arranged. The teacher was instructed to stop the child whenever she began to masturbate and to remind her that the classroom was not the appropriate place. The teacher was asked to use the language of the family and to allow the child to leave the class and go to the bathroom when she requested.

A meeting with Penny indicated that she was of average intelligence, emotionally healthy but baffled by everyone's concern. She stated that she rubbed herself because it felt good. She didn't know that her teacher was upset. She agreed to follow the privacy rules established by her mother.

A follow-up indicated that Penny had stopped masturbating in class and was now excelling academically. No signs of distress were evident in the classroom or at home. The family was still enjoying morning snuggles. The mother now knew what sexual behavior to expect from her children and was committed to more open communication about sexuality.

In summary, how the cognitive therapist deals with issues of childhood sexuality is, in principle, no different from how she or he tackles other childhood problems. The problem is defined, its ownership is clarified, the affective distress is acknowledged, and the attendant cognitive distortions are challenged both cognitively and behaviorally.

The one unique aspect of these childhood problems is the effect that they seem to have on grown-ups. Adults, unfortunately including some educators and therapists, too often do not have their own heads on straight in the area of sexuality and are uncomfortable with the topic. Our clinical admonition, therefore, is to assess the grown-ups—including yourself—to see if healthy sexual attitudes are present and are being communicated. Above all, we want to have "askable" adults in the child's life, adults who can project a warm, accepting, and nonjudgmental attitude about sex. Quite simply, the more we can talk about sex, the more natural—and trouble-free—it can become.

Suggested Readings

Books for Young Children

Growing Up Feeling Good: A Child's Introduction to Sexuality by S. Waxman (1979). Available from:

Panjandrum/Aris Books
11321 Iowa Ave.
Los Angeles, Calif. 90025

A simple introduction to many important concepts about human sexuality, presented with dignity.

The Body Book by C. Rayner (1980). Available from:
Barron's Educational Series
113 Crossways Park Drive
Woodbury, N.J. 11797

For parents to read with their young ones, about the anatomy and function of body parts.

Did the Sun Shine before You Were Born? by S. and J. Gordon (1977). Available from:
Ed-U Press
P.O. Box 583
Fayetteville, N.Y. 13066

For children aged 3–6. Deals with many questions about family life, including the age-old one: "Where do babies come from?"

The Kids' Own XYZ of Love and Sex by S. Widerberg (1972). Available from:
Stein and Day
Scarborough House
Briarcliff Manor, N.Y. 10510

Written in question-and-answer format.

What's Happening to Me? by P. Mayle (1975). Available from:
Lyle Stuart
120 Enterprise Ave.
Secaucus, N.J. 07094

A straight-shooting guide to puberty for preadolescent children.

Books for Early Teens

Changes: You and Your Body by Choice (1978). Available from:
Choice
1501 Cherry St.
Philadelphia, Pa. 19102

Easy-to-read pamphlet prepared with input from a panel of teens.

Facts about Sex for Today's Youth by S. Gordon (1979). Available from:
Ed-U Press
P.O. Box 583
Fayetteville, N.Y. 13066

A delightful and well-illustrated book, including a section answering the 10 most frequently asked questions.

Facts about VD for Today's Youth by S. Gordon (1979). Available from Ed-U Press (see above).

Simple, clear, and informative, with a stress on VD prevention.

Sex with Love: A Guide for Young People by E. Hamilton (1978). Available from:
>Beacon Press
>25 Beacon St.
>Boston, Mass. 02108

Deals with dating, affection, and sexual expression.

Books for Later Teens

Changing Bodies, Changing Lives by R. Bell et al. (1980). Available from:
>Random House
>201 E. 50th St.
>New York, N.Y. 10022

Highly recommended.

Learning about Sex: A Contemporary Guide for Young Adults by G. F. Kelly (1977). Available from:
>Barron's Educational Series
>113 Crossways Park Drive
>Woodbury, N.J. 11797

A highly recommended book that presents facts, attitudes, and sexual decision-making.

Parenting: A Guide for Young People by S. Gordon and M. Wollin (1975). Available from:
>Wm. H. Sadlier, Inc.
>117 Park Place
>New York, N.Y. 10007

A guide that prepares potential parents for mature parenting roles.

Sex and Birth Control: A Guide for the Young by E. J. Lieberman and E. Peck (1981). Available from:
>Harper & Row, Inc.
>10 E. 53rd St.
>New York, N.Y. 10022

A book not only about birth control, but about developing a thoughtful approach to values by which young people can live sexual lives.

References

Elkind, D. Egocentrism in adolescence. *Child Development*, 1967, *38,* 1025–1034.

Ellis, A. The rational-emotive approach to sex therapy. *Counseling Psychologist*, 1975, *5,* 14–21.

Ellis, A. The rational-emotive approach to children's and adolescents' sex problems. In Jean-Marc Sampson (Ed.), *Childhood and sexuality: Proceedings of the International Symposium.* Montreal: Éditions Études Vivantes, 1980.

Ellis, A., & Harper, R. A. *A new guide to rational living.* Englewood Cliffs, N.J.: Prentice-Hall; Hollywood: Wilshire Books, 1975.

Furth, H. G. *Piaget and knowledge: Theoretical foundations.* Englewood Cliffs, N.J.: Prentice-Hall, 1969.

Goldman, R., & Goldman, J. Children's sexual thinking: Report of a cross-national study. *SIECUS Report*, 1982, *10*(3).
Gordon, S. The case for a moral sex education in the schools. *Journal of School Health*, 1981, *51*, 214–218.
Piaget, J. *The psychology of adolescence*. London: Routledge and Kegan Paul, 1950.
Piaget, J. *Judgment and reasoning in the child*. London: Routledge and Kegan Paul, 1951.
Piaget, J. *The origins of intelligence in children*. New York: International Universities Press, 1952.
Roberts, E., Kline, D., & Gagnon, J. Parents' sexual silence. *Psychology Today*, 1979 (Jan.), 14–15.
Walen, S. R., DiGiuseppe, R., & Wessler, R. *A practitioner's guide to rational-emotive therapy*. New York: Oxford University Press, 1980.
Wolman, B. B. (Ed.). *Handbook of human sexuality*. Englewood Cliffs, N.J.: Prentice-Hall, 1980.

Applications

As the chapters in this section reveal, there are a number of different ways that the ideas, principles, and procedures discussed in the first two sections of this book can be applied by a child's significant others as well as in contexts outside the practitioner's office to resolve emotional and behavioral difficulties of the childhood period. The authors represented in this section are innovators in their respective areas of interest.

Paul A. Hauck has written over the past 15 years concerning the role of irrational beliefs and parenting styles in childhood maladjustment. In Chapter 12, he updates his theorizing and knowledge in this area and, in particular, sensitizes the reader to the importance of differentiating between manipulative and nonmanipulative behavior.

Nina Woulff (Chapter 13) presents an informative analysis of how rational-emotive therapy (RET) can be integrated and practiced within a family, structural-strategic therapeutic framework. Her discussion of family members' irrational assumptions about themselves and each other that contribute to hierarchical incongruities and inappropriate power boundaries within a family is illuminating. A model of rational-emotive family therapy that includes the stages of assessment, problem hypothesizing, defining goals, implementing the treatment plan, and terminating therapy is provided.

In Chapter 14, John F. McInerney presents material and ideas that he has developed for and employed with the parents and teachers of exceptional children. In departing from a tradition that examines emotional reactions to the birth of an exceptional child in terms of different stages of "coming to terms with the problem," McInerney provides an RET analysis of the common emotions (fear, anger, and guilt) and themes (denial) of parents and teachers. The consequences of inappropriate and irrational cognitive-emotive parental and teacher states as expressed in dysfunctional adult–child interaction patterns is extremely apparent and poignant.

A rational-emotive approach to helping teachers cope with stress is presented in Chapter 15 by Michael E. Bernard, Marie R. Joyce, and Pamela M. Rosewarne. The approach taken in this chapter is that, from a RET point of view, teacher stress can be equated with emotional arousal and behavioral consequences that derive from a teacher's interpretation and appraisal of external events as demanding and threatening. An inventory of the irrational beliefs of teachers is a distinctive feature of the analysis. Practical methods for introducing rational-emotive education ideas to teachers in an initial teacher-training or in-service workshop setting is the principle focus of this chapter.

During the past 15 years, basic principles and ideas of rational-emotive theory have been directly introduced to children in school settings in the form of a preventive mental-health program referred to as *rational-emotive education* (REE). REE comprises sets of curriculum units that can be employed in the classroom with primary and secondary students. In Chapter 16, Ann Vernon discusses basic REE assumptions and concepts. Her extensive use of REE in schools makes her comments concerning how to implement REE as well as the limitations of REE especially valuable.

Allen Elkin's presentation in Chapter 17 of how to introduce RET to groups of children significantly advances the practice of RET. For although rational-emotive group therapy with adults has a long and impressive history, its deployment with children has suffered from a lack of understanding of the RET group methods that can be employed with younger populations. Allen Elkin demonstrates effectively how a variety of RET and cognitive-behavioral therapy methods can be simplified and modified for use with groups of children. We believe that this chapter represents an exciting new direction in the field of child therapy.

In Chapter 18, Karen Sutton-Simon has accomplished the onerous task of identifying the different areas of research that are open to child-oriented cognitive-behavioral practitioners. Her encouragement of science in practice is qualified by her realistic awareness of the drawbacks and the difficulties in conducting applied clinical research. Her chapter should be read carefully by both neophyte and experienced scientist-practitioners who are interested in conducting investigations of cognitive approaches to child therapy.

12

Working with Parents

PAUL A. HAUCK

Some 18 years ago, when I earned my Ph.D. and began practicing as a clinical psychologist, I practiced a style of therapy involving children and parents that is very different from what it is today. For one thing, the degree of fragmentation then was considerable when judged by present-day methods. One or both parents were usually seen by the social worker, for example; the child would be seen by the clinic's psychiatrist; and if psychological testing was needed, the psychologist would be called into the picture. The parents were consulted for a history of the problem, and they were advised of what progress the child might have made. Knowing when the parents had to become an integral part of the child's therapy did not emerge until years later—probably not until we therapists began solo practices and simply could not follow the old and wasteful models set up in the post–World War II days.

What has evolved in my own career is a method that I have found very helpful and quite efficient. Parents like it because they are brought into the therapeutic process in an active way. They are constantly informed, advised, and counseled along with the child.

In writing this chapter, I hope to achieve two goals. The first is to explain the cognitive principles that parents had better know if they are to be effective in raising their children. I focus especially on the four major behavioral or affective disturbances that all adults and guardians of children want to know about if they are to help rear the children as well as possible. They are depression, anger, fear, and procrastination. I include the major and minor irrational ideas that create these disturbing feelings, and I present explanations of why these irrational ideas are, in fact, unworthy of being taken as the truth.

PAUL A. HAUCK • Clinical Psychologist in Private Practice, Rock Island, Illinois 61201.

My second goal is to present to the reader insights that have been dawning on me gradually over the past years and that have made me increasingly aware of the role of manipulative behavior, its status as a special category of behavior in children, and its requirement of different handling by the therapist and the parent from nonmanipulative behavior. I place great emphasis on the role of the parents in creating and maintaining (through reinforcement methods) the objectional behavior, which they do not realize they create and so often want to erradicate.

The Rationale for Working with Parents

Unfortunately, most people who counsel families do not understand the most significant reason for working with parents. The education of the parents in regard to the nature of the emotional disturbance of the child is generally thought to be the primary reason for bringing the parents into the therapeutic process. I too feel that this is a most important reason. However, an even more important reason for dealing with the parents is to make them more stable so that they can *then* work more effectively with the children. Some years ago, when I wrote *The Rational Management of Children* (1967), I made this point, and I make it just as firmly today. The lesson that I have learned is that when a parent encounters an emotional problem with a child, it is not wise to put the child's emotional problem first and to calm the parent later. It is much wiser for the parents to exercise whatever cognitive strategies they can to calm themselves first over the child's behavior and then to work toward calming the child.

Parents are just as human as children, and when they get upset and angry over a child's temper tantrum, they are behaving no differently from the child. Regarding the child as the major focus of one's therapeutic endeavors is being prejudiced against children, because the parents openly admit to you that they also get quite angry. How can we then ignore them as our clients and focus only on the children? Is the child's anger somehow very different from the adult's?

Parents, whether they have well-behaved children or not, are generally in need of at least some further education and counseling regarding the whole psychology of emotions. Unless they are professors of psychology, they are probably quite ignorant of the facts of life regarding emotional disturbances, and they are therefore all grist to the counselor's mill in getting them to behave more rationally.

The Rational-Emotive Approach

In this section, I present basic rational-emotive therapy (RET) concepts, insights, and practice that the practitioner had better know about in order to work with parents effectively. I initially present the basic irrational beliefs that underlie the major forms of emotional disturbance. The important distinction between manipulative and nonmanipulative behavior is then discussed. A description of the conduct of initial RET sessions then leads to a discussion of how RET works to bring about change.

General Irrational Beliefs

Every practitioner of RET and every adult, whether a parent or not, would do well to study the following list of irrational ideas, which can all cause us enormous emotional stress, and to become so familiar with them that when painful emotion arises, the irrational ideas creating that feeling can be immediately identified (Ellis, 1962; Ellis & Harper, 1975).

I will not attempt to repeat these dozen irrational ideas in their more formal language because that has already been done numerous times throughout RET literature. I find it much more useful to express these ideas in less academic terms and to make them more to the point.

- *(Irrational Idea 1)* If you are not loved or approved of by the important people in your life, you are worthless. Rejection is painful and almost devastating, and you cannot avoid being upset when rejected.
- *(Irrational Idea 2)* If you are not outstanding, gifted, and almost perfect in practically everything you do, you again are worthless. To make a mistake is not just a human quality, it is a disaster.
- *(Irrational Idea 3)* There are bad and wicked people in the world, and the only way to make bad people into good people is by being very severe with them, beating them, torturing them, and telling them how worthless they are.
- *(Irrational Idea 4)* When you don't get what you think is right or what you deserve, you are experiencing a horrible and catastrophic event. The world should be fair, and if you deserve justice, you should get it.
- *(Irrational Idea 5)* We can be pained not only by physical things but by psychological acts as well. Words can hurt, gestures are painful, and a host of behaviors, even though not affecting us physically, certainly have to hurt us emotionally.

- (*Irrational Idea 6*) If something bad and dangerous can happen to you, it makes sense to worry about it, focus on it, and dwell on it constantly because that is one of the best ways to prevent the dreaded act from happening.
- (*Irrational Idea 7*) Difficult issues in life are best handled by being avoided as long as possible. This is the best way to get instant gratification, and that benefit is always greater than the benefit you might get if you did not procrastinate and faced your problem immediately.
- (*Irrational Idea 8*) The best way to get through life is not to depend on yourself but to lean on people who are stronger than you. Don't worry about building your own skills as long as you associate with people who can do all the things you can't.
- (*Irrational Idea 9*) If you have had a habit for a long time, you will naturally have to be affected by it all of your life. Behavior cannot be changed any more than a zebra can change its stripes.
- (*Irrational Idea 10*) It is only natural and decent to become upset over other people's problems and misfortunes. Simply dealing with people in a calm and undisturbed way is not sufficient to show you care for them. You have to become upset to the point where you are almost as disturbed as the people you are trying to help.
- (*Irrational Idea 11*) If you aren't sure that a decision you want to make is right or not, then do not make it at all. Wait until you are certain that you are right, and then act. Do not take risks. Make a decision only when you are sure that you are correct.
- (*Irrational Idea 12*) Beliefs held by society, government, and all of its respected institutions must be correct and should not be questioned.

Manipulative versus Nonmanipulative Behavior

Before proceeding with therapy, whether during the first or the following sessions, it is vital that we determine whether the child's behavior is manipulative or nonmanipulative. We should actively engage the parents in the therapeutic process regardless of which type of behavior the child demonstrates. However, if we are dealing with manipulative symptoms, our assignment with parents and children is very different from when the behavior is nonmanipulative. I previously referred to these problems (Hauck, 1980) as misbehavior versus neurotic behavior. Changing the terminology to manipulative versus nonmanipulative behavior is simply more accurate, and I therefore prefer the alteration.

Nonmanipulative behavior is shown by children who would show their symptoms if they were alone on a desert island. The behavior has no ulterior purpose; it comes solely from within the interaction of the child with himself or herself over some event in his or her life. Such behavior is not meant to impress, to control, or to influence anyone at all. It is simply a reaction to the irrational thoughts that the child has expressed, and because they are irrational, they have unfortunate consequences.

An example of true nonmanipulative behavior is a boy's failing to make as many baskets in a tournament game as his teammates. He unwisely believes that he is inferior, and as a result, he becomes quite depressed. The boy has unwittingly been self-defeating and neurotic in his handling of his poor playing, and he needs counseling to teach him how to accept himself even though he dislikes his performance. Obviously, the counseling has to teach him what not to do in order to experience less psychological pain.

We could, of course, ask the parents to come in with him so that they might also use the same rational arguments that we do whenever he gets depressed and wants to be perfectionistic. Their inclusion might help them to become more lenient, understanding, and patient with this child, with their other children, and even with themselves. If the parents have been somewhat pushy for higher standards from the boy, then seeing them alone or with the child would certainly get them to understand how blaming the child for his shortcomings only creates severe emotional stress. But even if they did no such thing and the child only adopted these irrational notions from society at large (from friends, from teachers, or from movies), it is still important to have them involved as listeners who note how we talk to the child and teach him to be a more rational person. They learn to become more rational as they listen to us teach their child.

When a child develops a symptom and uses it for secondary gain, we call such behavior manipulative. Depression may exist in order to get sympathy. Anger may gain in intensity because a child hopes to scare the parents into acquiescing to her or his desires. If the child becomes nervous, perhaps his or her mother will let him or her stay home from school. Or the child who will not do chores on time, or complete homework, may be doing this for revenge against a frustrating parent.

I determine that behavior is manipulative if it seems goal-oriented. In this case, counseling is directed at teaching parents to stop being manipulated. More is said about manipulative behavior in a following section.

INTERVIEWING PARENTS AND THEIR CHILDREN

When a family is referred to me, one child is usually considered the client, and it is for this person that the appointment is made. One or both parents usually bring the child with them, and whether it is for 30 or 60 minutes, I always prefer to see the parent or parents first. At this point, I try to interview for approximately one-third of the session that we have available and try to understand the nature of the complaint. I make no interpretations at this point; I simply try to comprehend what the situation is that brings them to me, what the nature of the problem is, and what my role in helping the family might be. In a half-hour session I try to gather this information in about 10 minutes, and in a full hour session, I do the same in about 20 minutes. The longer session, incidentally, is not necessarily more productive than the shorter one. The reason that I would schedule a half-hour session rather than an hour session is determined by the openings in my schedule or the financial concerns of the client.

After I see the parents, I ask to see the child alone. At this point, I try to determine if there is any great discrepancy between the presenting complaint as given by the parents and as given by the child. I ask questions, try to determine what irrational ideas may be causing their difficulty, and try to get a clear understanding of who or what is causing the frustration. But most important, I decide whether the child's behavior is manipulative or nonmanipulative, or a combination of both. The role that the parents will be assigned from now on is determined in great degree by this decision. Finally, I bring the parents back into the room by themselves so that they can hear my impressions. I tell them what I think is causing the difficulty and what might be done to bring things around to a more stable condition. If psychological testing is recommended, I present that option to them and have it done then or have it scheduled at their convenience, but hopefully before the next session.

During this first session, I may have been perfectly able to comprehend the nature of the child's difficulty. If so, I do not hesitate to proceed with active therapy at the first visit. Whenever this is possible, in fact, I urge others to do the same. Parents are enormously relieved when they realize that the counselor is taking over. The child has already been seen, and they, too, have been advised about new ways in which to proceed with their problem child. How could they not feel relieved in view of all these corrective measures? Delaying these efforts, as we did years ago, only leaves the family on its nonlimited resources for a week or more, during which time the suffering can get worse. If not, and a spontaneous recovery happens, the outcome is not much better, because the parents and child feel enough relief so that they cancel their next appointment or terminate therapy entirely in the belief that the problem is solved.

In my experience, the problem is usually anything but solved. All that has happened in such instances is that certain temporary accommodations between parents and child have been made that put all parties at ease. The irrational philosophies that created the stress in the first instance, however, are still not detected, explained, understood, or practiced on by anyone in the family. And because no education has taken place, the likelihood of long-lasting changes resulting from their own coping strategies is limited.

How Rational-Emotive Therapy Works

The technique for getting people to change their irrational beliefs is a straightforward one and appears to be quite simple. It is. However, it is important not to make the mistake of believing that because the steps to raising children healthily and to becoming a well-functioning adult are simple, the process itself is necessarily easy. If you are careful to make the distinction between simplicity and ease, parents can more readily accept the proposition that reeducating themselves need not necessarily be complicated, although it might be difficult.

One of the first observations a parent will want to make is to determine the emotional reaction a child is having. For example, if a child is angry and the parents want to help the child over that anger, they can do one of two things: they can work hard toward removing the frustration that is indirectly related to the anger, or they can teach the child how to talk himself or herself out of the anger even if the frustration is not removed. To do the second, however, they have to be familiar with the irrational ideas that create anger in the first place. In the following pages, the most disturbing emotions are dealt with, and I list those irrational ideas that are generally connected with each of those emotions.

Once the parent has in mind which of the irrational ideas the child is using to create disturbing feelings, a process of education had better take place to instruct the child that these irrational beliefs are, in fact, incorrect and that they can be replaced by saner philosophies. Therefore, education, either by simple instruction in rational philosophy or by the disruption of an irrational philosophy, can assist the child in giving up negative philosophies in favor of positive ones. Thus, for example, the angry child can be debated with over the issue of whether or not the world owes him or her justice, whether or not the child has to have everything he or she wants, and whether or not the person or thing that is denying the child the satisfaction is in fact an evil and wicked person or thing and should be severely punished.

All parents should become conversant with the irrational idea and *why* they are irrational. Unless they know what makes an irrational ideal irrational they are not going to be in a position to debate and discuss it convincingly with their children. RET, therefore, in essence, is a debate between a believer in rational ideas and a believer in irrational ideas.

I emphasize later in this chapter the idea that, in many instances, children will not change until their parents do. This idea applies especially to living with rational beliefs. Until the therapist can get the parents to believe that they are upsetting themselves with their own irrational beliefs and can encourage them to change those beliefs, they are obviously not going to be very convincing in getting their children to change. Training for the child cannot progress very far until the parent has made some progress. The therapist will therefore want to assess parental attitudes toward RET and emotional disturbances and to attempt to remove all resistance to this viewpoint. Many adults find our views incredible and wonder about our sanity, much less that of the child. When we maintain that others cannot upset us, or that rejection is painless, or that there are no evil people in the world, we usually see raised eyebrows and doubts about our sincerity.

Nonmanipulative Behavior

If you have taken your history carefully and you decide that the symptoms presented to you by a child and/or the parents is nonmanipulative, then I suggest you save a lot of time by attempting to determine which of the four major emotional patterns the child is exhibiting. Once you have determined that, then it is a fairly expeditious matter to teach the child and the parents how to deal with that troublesome emotion. The four emotional disturbances that I have encountered the vast majority of times in my own practice over the years are depression, anger, fear, and procrastination (self-discipline). Any counselor who is skilled in teaching adult and child clients the management of these troublesome feelings will be prepared to handle a large percentage of her or his cases without much difficulty.

Talking to parents about their children's nonmanipulative emotions requires giving them enough instruction to be surrogate therapists while not overburdening them with confusing intricacies.

I have sailed carefully between these two banks for years and have consistently been rewarded. To do this, the therapist must have mastery of those salient bits of information that make the parents' job easier. Parents do not need to become skilled child psychologists to raise healthy kids. But they had better have some sound views and a fundamental understanding of the major disturbances, or they will seem helpless when help is needed. Therefore, I give them the essentials of counseling. I teach them *simplified* counseling, and I try to make *amateur* psychologists out of them *for the problems that they currently cannot handle.*

What follows is an analysis of the irrational beliefs that underlies the four basic emotional disorders of children, that is, information that parents can use to help their children overcome emotional problems and nonmanipulative behavior, as well as techniques that the practitioner can use directly with the child.

DEPRESSION

Practitioners have to be on the alert for the three different forms of depression so that they can help parents to alleviate not only their own depression but also depressive symptoms in their children. I have found that people are psychologically depressed for one or more of the following three reasons: self-blame, self-pity, and other-pity (Hauck, 1973).

Depression from Self-Blame

The irrational ideas that account for self-blame are as follows:

- (*Irrational Idea 1*) If you are not loved or approved by important people in your life, you are worthless. Rejection is painful and almost devastating, and you cannot avoid being upset when rejected.
- (*Irrational Idea 2*) If you are not outstanding, gifted, and almost perfect in practically everything you do, you are again worthless. To make a mistake is not just a human quality, it is a disaster.

Other related irrational ideas that also contribute to the creation of self-blame are the following:

- (*Irrational Idea 4*) When you don't get what you think is right or what you deserve, you are experiencing a horrible and catastrophic event. The world should be fair, and if you deserve justice, you should get it.

- (*Irrational Idea 5*) We can be pained not only by physical things but by psychological acts as well. Words can hurt, gestures are painful, and a host of behaviors, even though not affecting us physically, certainly have to affect us emotionally.

Self-blame results from our insisting that we have to be perfect, that our behavior and ourselves as human beings are one and the same, and that they cannot be separated. This misunderstanding is created through the irrational belief that one must be all-competent and achieving in order to be worthwhile. Parents the world over have been taught this by their parents and by their societies. As their counselor, it is essential that you teach both the child and the parents never to blame themselves for anything and never to feel guilty for anything. We behave badly for three understandable and excusable reasons. The first is *deficiency* (not having the intrinsic skills, talents, or intelligence ever to learn a particular skill). The second is *ignorance.* How can we hold others blameworthy when they did not know how to perform something properly in the first place? And the third reason for modifying responsibility is *disturbance.* Although people may be capable of performing without fault and may have been trained to perform without fault, they may still behave very wrong because they are so disturbed that they cannot use their talents or their knowledge. The parents are therefore advised never to hate the child, only to disapprove of the child's objectionable actions.

The RET literature has numerous books and tapes that are well suited to teaching the parents on their own to assimilate this material more fully. The therapist can recommend books if they are willing readers or tapes, if not. This is, after all, an educational process, and the more the parents are taught to be rational, the quicker things will change.

The New Guide to Rational Living by Ellis and Harper (1975) is certainly an excellent book to start parents off with if they have a good high-school and possibly a college education. *How to Raise an Emotionally Healthy, Happy Child* (1966) by Ellis, Wolfe, and Moseley is also an excellent book to recommend to parents. Maultsby's *Help Yourself to Happiness* (1975) can also be recommended for the adult reader.

My own series of self-help books have found a generous acceptance by the reading public, and I do not hesitate to recommend them as well. I especially focus on *Overcoming Depression, Overcoming Frustration and Anger, Overcoming Worry and Fear, How to Do What You Want to Do: The Art of Self-Discipline, How to Stand Up for Yourself, Marriage Is a Loving Business,* and *Overcoming Jealousy and Possessiveness.*

Depression from Self-Pity

The major irrational ideas that account for self-pity are the following:

- (*Irrational Idea 4*) When you don't get what you think is right or what you deserve, you are experiencing a horrible and catastrophic event. The world should be fair and if you deserve justice you should get it.
- (*Irrational Idea 5*) We can be pained not only by physical things but by psychological acts as well. Words can hurt, gestures are painful, and a host of behaviors, even though not affecting us physically, certainly have to affect us emotionally.

Other related irrational ideas that also contribute to the creation of self-pity are the following:

- (*Irrational Idea 6*) If something bad and dangerous can happen to you, it makes sense to worry about it, focus on it, and dwell on it constantly because that is one of the best ways to prevent the dreaded act from happening.

Feeling sorry for ourselves is a very common mistake that all of us make, and it is brought about by the irrational notion that it is terrible and awful if we do not get what we want.

Children learn self-pity, probably in part, because they are genetically or biologically predisposed to think irrationally but also because such behavior has been modeled by their parents. We therefore want to teach the adults not to pity themselves so as to discourage this practice from being copied by the children.

Telling the parents to tell their children that life is unfair; that one is usually better off than one thinks; that one should think of one's blessings; and that life does not owe us a thing—and to repeat these views whenever the child becomes depressed by self-pity—can eventually have a very healthy effect on the developing youngster.

Parents who pity themselves are often creating worse problems in their children because the children develop intense guilt feelings over the misery that the parents have actually created themselves. The ABC theory of emotions (Ellis, 1962) could be explained to the parents to help them over the notion that it is the children who have upset them so badly. Once they accept the fact that it is they, the parents, who are making themselves so miserable, they will make greater strides in not trying to manipulate their children with their own self-pity.

Children who use self-pity, even for nonmanipulative purposes, may have that effect reinforced if the parents are too solicitous when they see their children crying or moping around the house. Being indifferent to such behavior or distracting them from it can often bring a reasonably quick end to that particular episode.

Depression by Other-Pity

The major irrational idea that accounts for other-pity is the following:

- (*Irrational Idea 10*) It is only natural and decent to become upset over other people's problems and misfortunes. Simply dealing with people in a calm and undisturbed way is not sufficient to show that you care for them. You have to become upset to the point where you are almost as disturbed as the people you are trying to help.

Other related irrational ideas that also contribute to the creation of other-pity are the following:

- (*Irrational Idea 4*) When you don't get what you think is right or what you deserve, you are experiencing a horrible and catastrophic event. The world should be fair, and if you deserve justice, you should get it.
- (*Irrational Idea 5*) We can be pained not only by physical things but by psychological acts as well. Words can hurt, gestures are painful, and a host of behaviors, even though not affecting us physically, certainly have to affect us emotionally.

Parents who pity their children usually encourage the children to be self-pitiers. Again, teaching the parents to be a bit hard-nosed about the "great misfortunes" that the children are experiencing can be very salubrious. I often encourage parents to question just how miserable the children need to be because they can't go to a dance, or because they don't get to watch their favorite TV show, and so on. Giving the parents some perspective of what one is reasonably entitled to in life can help them get some balance in terms of determining what sort of frustration one needs to pay attention to and what to ignore.

Self-blame and other-pity are two behaviors of parents that have enormous effects on their children for the worse. The more effective we are as counselors in teaching parents to desist from such practices, the more healthy the children will be and the more quickly the therapy will proceed.

Anger

The major ideas that account for anger are the following:

- *(Irrational Idea 3)* There are bad and wicked people in the world, and the way to make bad people into good people is by being very severe with them, beating them, torturing them, and telling them how worthless they are.
- *(Irrational Idea 4)* When you don't get what you think is right or what you deserve, you are experiencing a horrible and catastrophic event. The world should be fair, and if you deserve justice, you should get it.

Other related irrational ideas that also contribute to the creation of anger are the following:

- *(Irrational Idea 2)* If you are not outstanding, gifted, and almost perfect in practically everything you do, you are again worthless. To make a mistake is not just a human quality, it is a disaster.
- *(Irrational Idea 10)* It is only natural and decent to become upset over other people's problems and misfortunes. Simply dealing with people in a calm and undisturbed way is not sufficient to show that you care for them. You have to become upset to the point where you are almost as disturbed as the people you are trying to help.
- *(Irrational Idea 11)* If you aren't sure that a decision you want to make is right or not, then do not make it at all. Wait until you are certain that you are right, and then act. Do not take risks. Make a decision only when you are sure that you are correct.

For my tastes, too many parents think anger is so natural and so normal that to do something about controlling it to the point of near extinction is almost unthinkable. In children, it is, of course, a very common and natural emotion and one that we do not want to suppress, lest the usual consequences show up, which we, as clinicians, are all well acquainted with from our classes in psychopathology. However, one of the reasons that parents do not do a great deal about getting their children to be more calm is that the parents themselves don't know how to talk themselves out of anger and therefore cannot teach their children how to overcome their anger.

Anger is simply the conversion of a desire into a demand (Ellis, 1962; Hauck, 1974). It makes no difference what the frustration is, the unwitting transformation of thinking that, because you *want* something, you *have* to have it will result in the development of an angry feeling. I point out to parents that when anger is clearly the result of a life frustration rather than of some kind of physical or chemical change, it can be compared to a child's having a temper tantrum. All anger, whether in children or in adults, is a temper tantrum of the same type that the child has whenever he or she does not get a lollipop or an ice-cream cone. I try to emphasize to parents that if they do not teach their children to overcome anger, they will have temper tantrums as adults. That's what the adults are actually doing when they get angry, and if they want their children to grow up spoiled, and childish, and immature, then that is their choice. But if they want to raise children who are mature, then they had better start educating their children not to act as though the world were coming to an end because they didn't get something that they felt was very important.

I further point out that anger in parents is basically no different from anger in children, with one exception. Children get angry over not being able to watch their favorite TV shows, or over going to bed early, or over not having a piece of candy. Adults don't usually get angry over these sorts of frustrations. They get angry over not getting promotions, over having someone cut ahead of them in traffic, or over some huge social injustice. It makes no difference. Both parties are telling themselves that they have to have what they want, that it is unbearable not to have everything they want, and that they are entitled to kick and scream and yell and holler and have a tantrum. Once you emphasize to the parents that their own angers bring them down to the emotional level of a 4-year-old *every time,* and that there are no exceptions, you may begin to train parents to watch their own emotional development a bit more and to want to teach this control to their children.

The rebuttal that their angers are usually justified and righteous carries no weight at all with you if you understand that every psychologically caused anger possessed by any person, at any time, is always a righteous anger. One does not have anger unless one thinks that one is absolutely correct and deserving and that the other party is absolutely incorrect and undeserving.

One of the best ways to deal with angry children is simply to remove them and put them in a time-out situation—5 or 10 minutes, at first, for small children, and a half hour or an hour for older children. If they do not learn to control their tempers because they're not getting their way, then the time should gradually be increased each time the penalty is applied. With adolescents, such a penalty may very well get up to several hours or sometimes the entire day in one's room. The point to make is that anger will not be tolerated, that the children can have a fit if they want one, but that they will have sufficient opportunity to reflect on the foolishness of that behavior. And if they want to get out of their rooms, they will have to clean up their act and grow up.

The most important piece of advice to give parents in this connection when they are disciplining children is not to discipline with anger. I have counseled numerous parents who were doing everything seemingly correctly but were not getting the results that one would have anticipated. Careful study revealed that the parents were identifying the neurotic emotion carefully, that they were penalizing the child for that improper behavior, and that they were trying to educate the child on how not to get angry, and still this program did not work. On closer inspection, it turned out that the parents were frequently angry in their explanations while dealing with the whole anger problem. Once they got angry and put the child down, and they lost control of themselves, they unwittingly developed a spiteful reaction in the child (who could have learned very nicely had the parents done the penalizing and explaining without anger). It is the parental anger and the parental put-down that cancel out the entire effort, which might have been 95% sensible and efficient. But once the parents begin to yell at the child in an angry way, then too much animosity is generated within the child and the desire not to cooperate is also generated.

I usually refer my book *Overcoming Frustration and Anger* (1974) to the parents so that they will learn how to overcome anger first and then be in a better position to teach their children how to do the same thing. I also find that several sessions at least are necessary to get them to begin to understand how to proceed with this emotion.

FEAR

The major irrational ideas that account for fear are the following:

- (*Irrational Idea 4*) When you don't get what you think is right or what you deserve, you are experiencing a horrible and catastrophic event. The world should be fair, and if you deserve justice, you should get it.
- (*Irrational Idea 6*) If something bad and dangerous can happen to you, it makes sense to worry about it, focus on it, and to dwell on it constantly because that is one of the best ways to prevent the dreaded act from happening.

Other related irrational ideas that also contribute to the creation of fear are the following:

- (*Irrational Idea 7*) Difficult issues in life are handled best by being avoided as long as possible. This is the way to get instant gratifica-

tion, and that benefit is always greater than the benefit you might get if you did not procrastinate and faced your problem immediately.
- (*Irrational Idea 8*) The best way to get through life is not to depend on yourself but to lean on people who are stronger than you. Don't worry about building your own skills as long as you associate with people who can do all those things you can't.
- (*Irrational Idea 9*) If you have had a habit for a long time, you will naturally have to be affected by it all of your life. Behavior cannot be changed any more than a zebra can change its stripes.

No child is raised without being something of a worrier or without having some fears. Children learn this from their older peers, their parents, and from life itself. The world is simply not so stable that security needs are not frustrated. They are denied in the lives of all children to the extent that love, recognition, and self-actualization are also denied.

Worry, nervousness, and apprehension are all different degrees of fear (Hauck, 1975). Children and parents alike suffer frequently from these states. To teach youngsters not to be anxious, it is important to talk to them and to educate them directly. However, additional gains are possible if we can teach the parents not to foster neurotic techniques in their kids.

To this end, I make the same point to the parents that I give the children, except that the intellectual load in the parental presentation is obviously higher and more sophisticated.

A briefer version than that offered at the start of this heading can focus on only two irrational ideas: the first is that it is a catastrophe not to have things as one would like them. The second idea is that if something bad might happen, it makes sense to think of it at all times, to focus on it endlessly, and never to let the issue out of your concentration lest the problem get out of hand.

The first idea causes tension to mount instantly. If not followed by the second idea, the tension would subside the moment the danger passed, or the moment the subject was distracted.

If the catastrophizing thinking is followed by the idea that a dangerous event must be focused on, then the event turns into worry for as long as fatigue does not intervene or a distraction does not end the focusing.

To decatastrophize is therefore critical because it brings the whole fear cycle to a screeching halt. Worry cannot even begin if we do not have an event to worry about. I therefore spend a lot of time teaching the child that things he or she is afraid of are really not as serious as believed. By vigorously debating their false notions that earning a few poor grades will destroy their futures, that being rejected by their loved ones will be a fate worse than death, or that doing something a bit risky is bound to kill them, I get children to be less frightened of these events. It is not only the rational element but often the emotive one in this instance that is effective.

I can recall one instance of a young girl who had frequent night terrors and who was referred to me because nothing worked. How quickly she settled down when I learned that her playmate was frightening her about the spooks that were coming out of the graves from the cemetery across the street from her house! I spared no adjective in assuring her that her playmate was teasing her, that it was absolutely stupid and ignorant to believe in ghosts because no one had ever seen them, that the girl was having a lot of fun at her expense, and so on. In a single session, she received considerable relief, and in two following sessions, the problem was totally controlled. (For a fuller discussion of this case see *The Rational Management of Children,* Hauck, 1967.)

Children who have actually suffered anxiety attacks can be dealt with in roughly the same way. They can be shown that it is not a catastrophe to have another anxiety attack because it can usually be easily demonstrated that the child has already had a number of such episodes and that these previous ones have not destroyed the child. And if, in addition, we point out to the youngster that these attacks last only a short while, then there is even less cause for alarm. I ask my clients to make a deliberate note of checking the time when an anxiety attack appears to be emerging and to make a note of exactly how long such an episode lasts. This procedure enables this individual to reassure himself or herself as the next anxiety attack appears to be developing that (1) the coming episode is only one of many that have never actually destroyed the child and that, therefore, there is little reason to be grossly concerned, and (2) in any event it will last on the average only a certain number of minutes or hours.

These two techniques are quite successful in giving the child the reassurance needed to calm down and to realize that what is happening is not as dreadful as was suspected.

In the case of shyness, the fear of being laughed at or rejected is, of course, terribly important to attack. Getting the child to respect himself or herself, regardless of who else does it, is of critical importance. But urging the child to develop social skills by practicing them is perhaps equally important. Shy children simply avoid the most critical experience they need in order to learn not to be shy. They avoid talking with people, and therefore, they do not learn how to be socially smart. It is critical that we give them frequent homework assignments to desensitize themselves to feared situations. A hierachy of fears can be drawn up from the least dreadful, which the child can then follow and actually practice *in vivo*.

One additional distracting technique that I have found helpful for some clients is the thought-stopping technique. Thought stopping was first suggested by Alexander Bain (1928) and was revisited by Taylor (1963) and Wolpe and Lazarus (1966). A subject is instructed to say, "Stop," the moment troublesome thoughts arise. The person is then instructed to think of something beautiful, which will act as a distraction from the distressing thoughts that the individual is currently suffering from. I usually suggest to the youngster that these distracting thoughts can be either beautiful memories, beautiful scenes, or beautiful fantasies. Anxiety feelings are difficult to sustain if one is successfully practicing a rewarding distraction technique. It is not as easy to be upset if one is thinking about relaxing and pleasant thoughts. I try to get the child to describe one type of thought in each of these categories, and I send the youngster home with instructions to implement this program whenever a fearsome thought begins to intrude on her or his equanimity.

Teaching these strategies to the parents helps them deal with their children at home as they practice their roles as social therapists.

Procrastination (Self-Discipline)

The major irrational ideas that lead to procrastination are the following:

- (*Irrational Idea 1*) Difficult issues in life are handled best by being avoided as long as possible. This is the way to get instant gratification, and that benefit is always greater than the benefit you might get if you did not procrastinate and faced your problem immediately.
- (*Irrational Idea 2*) If you are not outstanding, gifted, and almost perfect in practically everything you do, you are again worthless. To make a mistake is not just a human quality, it is a disaster.

Other related irrational ideas that also contribute to problems in self-discipline are the following:

- (*Irrational Idea 9*) If you have had a habit for a long time, you will naturally have to be affected by it all of your life. Behavior cannot be changed any more than a zebra can change its stripes.

- (*Irrational Idea 11*) If you aren't sure that a decision you want to make is right or not, then do not make it at all. Wait until you are certain that you are right, and then act. Do not take risks. Make a decision only when you are sure that you are correct.

We now come to what I regard as probably one of the most important of all the lessons a parent can teach a child. It makes no difference how gifted a child is or how much he or she may want to accomplish certain goals, none of this is usually attainable unless the child has also learned good self-discipline. This means that one's actions and drives are under the control of the person possessing those desires. And to achieve that control, it is essential that one have long experience in avoiding temptation and in delaying gratification—in most instances, for a greater reward later.

I find that it is rather difficult to teach children to overcome procrastination if they already have a problem with it. First of all, they are sent to the counselor because they don't know how to apply themselves, as they always avoid difficult tasks and do only what they enjoy. Unfortunately, psychotherapy simply becomes another onerous task to them, and they treat it in the same way they treat their homework. It is always something to be avoided and to put off for later. The irony of the whole situation, of course, is that these goof-off kids, by learning how to avoid responsible behavior, use the same escapist techniques against psychotherapy as they do against any other unpleasant task. One can easily understand why if we consider the fact that we adults, with our prescriptions for self-denial, delay of gratification, frustration toleration, and so on, are competing against instant gratification, fun on demand, and a life that, for the moment, is filled with nothing but good times. How can we compete against such a lifestyle in the mind of an immature person? It is precisely for this reason that the parents play such a valuable part in the remedy of this situation.

It is only the parents who can apply the necessary pressure to make the child endure frustration often enough, until he or she begins to see the benefits from temporary self-denial. The therapist cannot do this; she or he can only advise. Parents, however, can easily refuse to give the child a bike, or to go to a movie, or to a dance, and so on, until a particular task is done. They can withhold rewards in numerous ways until the child has earned the reward.

Therefore, instructing the parents on the fundamentals of self-discipline is crucial because you will be asking them to put pressure on their children and not to let them goof off unless they have first completed whatever assignment they were given. Such common tasks involve not being able to go out until the room is cleaned, not being allowed to watch the television until the homework is done, not being permitted to go to the football game until the garage is swept out. More long-range goals can be dealt with in the same way. If they have the resolve, the parents can withhold the family car from the child until the grades come up to an acceptable level. This may mean weeks and weeks of denying the teenager the use of the family car, but this is precisely how self-discipline is taught. The lesson we want to convey is that after self-denial and long labors, there is very often a nice reward awaiting us. And the parent is the one who can prove that to the child by seeing to it that a fine reward does, in fact, exist at the end of tasks.

Unfortunately, parents, being the truly loving people they often are, do not feel comfortable frustrating their children for their own good. We have gotten away from the notion that suffering can be good, that growth can come through pain, and that strength comes through self-denial. It is important to bear the Stoic philosophy in mind in all of our counseling and to remind ourselves always that the strong people are those who have learned how to endure frustration and adversity and who have come through as winners nevertheless. It is therefore important to get parents not to feel guilty about putting pressures on their children and denying them certain rewards until they earn them. Other-pity is the great culprit in this instance. The more sorry parents feel for their children, the sorrier the children feel for themselves. The truly practical and wise parent recognizes that life can be tough and that unless we teach children how to handle the unfairness and the hard knocks of life, they will indeed be ill-prepared for an independent existence. To teach the parent, therefore, to be rather hard-nosed at times—to hold the resolve that a reward shall not be forthcoming until it is deserved—is troublesome. Parents do not enjoy seeing their children disappointed, hurt, or depressed. However, as long as what the parent is asking for is truly not unusual and is truly meant to eventually help the child, then we had better encourage them to stick to their guns and make the children a little bit uncomfortable at this time rather than spoiling them and letting them suffer more serious frustrations when they get out into life.

The various points I try to make to parents about self-discipline come down to several rules that I have found to be sufficient in bringing about some changes (Ellis & Knaus, 1977; Hauck, 1976). First, I try to get the child and the parents to realize that it is easier to face a difficult task than it is to avoid it. Second, I try to teach that it is more important to do something than to do it well. I even phrase it more dramatically by saying that it is better to do badly than to do nothing. Third, I suggest that they always do a postmortem on the task. If a child has been unsuccessful, let him or her learn where the performance was incorrect, and, armed with this information, encourage the child to try again, thereby improving his or her performance. If this procedure is used each time, the child will eventually find out where the major mistakes are and will become more and more polished and skilled at the particular task. Only a postmortem, however, done critically and objectively, can give the child this information. It is the feedback we are looking for which tells us how we are doing and what we need to do to improve. Fourth, teach the child to give herself or himself constant praise. No matter how badly a task is done, one can always find something about one's trial to praise, even if it is nothing more than the fact that one has continued to try. With enough practice, and enough analysis of our mistakes, we eventually begin to move forward again, and it is this internal reward system that defeats negative self-statements. Fifth, always encourage the child to do a complicated task in small segments. There is no sense in being overwhelmed by a task and then being defeated because one simply does not have the strength or the patience to handle something that looms before him or her like a monster or a mountain. Instead, any huge task can be broken into smaller parts that can be digested more easily.

If the parent continually reminds the child of these five important steps toward self-discipline, you may be gratified to see more improvement than you have in the past.

Manipulative Behavior

Rudolf Dreikurs and the Adlerian school (Dreikurs & Soltz, 1964) have given us an excellent understanding of manipulative behavior. Dreikurs maintained that children misbehave for any one of four reasons, or some combination thereof. These are attention-getting, power, revenge, and to prove that one is disabled. Any counselor of children had better know these four categories intimately and how to counsel expertly on each of these conditions. For example, parents or teachers can be advised that a child who always interrupts and wants attention at inappropriate times can best be handled by simply being ignored. If the child has a temper tantrum, it is smart simply to step over him or her when he or she is having a fit on the floor. If such behavior is intolerable because company is present, then we ignore such behavior by removing the child to a room where the child is kept in isolation for an uncomfortable number of minutes or hours.

The power struggle is a very common form of misbehavior and is initiated by the child who insists that he or she must demonstrate that the child is more powerful than the parent. Unfortunately, the parent also makes the same judgment, at which point the two parties lock horns to prove who is the more powerful. It may come as a shock to a parent to be told by the counselor that it is the child who is the more powerful, because children are so headstrong and foolish in their desire to prove their superiority over the adult at any cost. It is this reckless need to put down the parent that gives the child the power to win the power struggle. A wise adult does not do something stupid that will get him fired from the job he values just to prove that he can have his way. A child frequently does precisely that. A girl can bring on a marriage that her parents forbid by allowing herself to get pregnant. And a boy can very easily get thrown out of a school that he does not want to complete by simply setting fire to it. The fact that these unwise moves will have enormous and long-lasting effects on the future of the child is of complete indifference to these immature creatures, and that is precisely why they are so invincible. After all, if they don't care what happens to them, how can they be hurt?

If it can be determined that the behavior is manipulative, then we can readily realize why talking to the child without including the parents in the therapeutic process will not work. Because the behavior is being performed in the first place to manipulate the parents, they are crucial to the outcome of counseling because they need to learn how not to accept the manipulation. To try to reason with the child that the behavior he or she is exhibiting is self-defeating may sometimes work, in which case the parents do not have to be brought into the counseling process. However, imagine how difficult it is for a child not to continue a rewarding bit of behavior when the parents, ignorant of what she or he is doing, repeatedly reinforce these irritating actions.

For example, if a girl refuses to clean up her room and she seems to be doing this simply to protest the domination of her mother, it is entirely possible to see her alone and to try to appeal to her by telling her that she will run into a great deal of flak in the near future if she does not get the room cleaned, that it is a good thing to be disciplined and neat in any event, and that such habits lead to good self-discipline, which she can use for the rest of her life. If we can appeal to her with such reasoning, the girl may, in fact, change because we have made some excellent points that she accepts. But most of the time, this is not the way that counseling with children runs. They are, after all, fully human. They are great suckers for temptation, and given a hand, they usually take an arm. Therefore, although we may make excellent sense in the office, it is simply too tempting for the girl to go home and leave the room in a shambles again if she is looking for some way to strike back at the mother over some irritating remark five minutes after she entered the house.

STRATEGIES FOR HELPING PARENTS MODIFY MANIPULATIVE BEHAVIOR

Once it is clear to you that you are dealing with manipulative behavior, then it is critical that you involve the parents as the primary clients and the child as the secondary client. Nothing serious is going to happen with the child until you alter the techniques of one or both parents. There are several important insights that both you and the parents had better accept, or change will not occur.

Insight 1: Behavior exists because it is reinforced (Mark, 1970; Patterson & Gullion, 1971).

This assertion follows the simple principles of operant conditioning, which all psychologists are thoroughly familiar with these days. Someone is reinforcing a child's behavior, if it is there at all. If it were not being reinforced, it would be extinguished through lack of satisfaction. This may be a baffling insight for parents to accept because they will declare vociferously that they have done anything but reinforce the child's objectionable behavior. What they may fail to realize, of course, is that they *have* done it in very subtle ways.

If a mother picks up a child when the child cries, the generous act of picking the child up is actually a reinforcement to the child and teaches the child to cry whenever she or he wants to be picked up. Unwittingly, the mother has trained the child to become a whiner. If the father calls his children to dinner and does so three or four times before going after them angrily, he trains them not to pay attention to him until he goes after them angrily. Or take the very common experience of a parent trying to show a child how to perform a skill and the child, being inexperienced, does poorly. The father becomes impatient, takes the tools out of the child's hand, and winds up finishing the task. Again, unwittingly, such parents have trained their children to distrust themselves, as well as to expect that when things go badly, the parents will assume the responsibility and do the job themselves.

It takes no great stretch of the imagination to figure out how, in future behaviors, the child is going to use these inadvertent learnings to manipulate the parents when a situation looks as if these techniques would benefit the child.

One of our first tasks, therefore, in counseling the family would be to alert the parents to the fact that if the behavior exists, it is because it is being rewarded.

Insight 2: Parents are usually the people most frequently involved in rewarding the behaviors of their children.

There can be little question on this point unless, of course, the child is being raised by a relative, a friend, or an institution. Otherwise, it is reasonably safe to confront the parents in your office with some certainty that they are the ones who have indirectly created most of the problems that they are now struggling to correct. It will be your task to show them how they involuntarily and unwittingly actually reinforce behavior that they strongly disapprove of.

Insight 3: When parents change their training methods, children change their behavior.

All of us have been confronted with a disappointed parent who came to our office and made the flat statement that he or she had done precisely as we had suggested but nothing had worked. The implication was that it was our responsibility now to come up with other pieces of wisdom because the first was inadequate. I am happy to say that those days for me are gone forever. I will not assume responsibility for what my clients do not do when he or she leaves my office. If I advise them to handle their children in certain ways and they do not do so, I am more than inclined to believe that they did not work very seriously on their problem or they did not know how to do it well in the first place. I therefore ask them to tell me what they did and how they handled situations at home so that I can understand why no change took place. More often than not, of course, I am able to detect serious flaws in the management techniques of the parent, and then I can advise them about what to do during the following week if they want to bring about greater changes. And somewhere along the line, I also have to remind them that we saw no improvement in the child because the parents essentially have tolerated the same old behavior. I put it in words such as, "When you stop tolerating the kid's behavior, he'll change, too. The reason we haven't seen any progress this week is because you haven't made any progress either. When you change, the child will change."

The parent can usually see the wisdom of this statement fairly easily. One would think that mothers and fathers would be rather defensive on this point, but I find that not to be the case. If the proper groundwork has been laid in teaching the parents why behavior exists in the first place, then it follows that, if they were partially responsible for their children's misbehavior, they must certainly be partially responsible for any lack of improvement in the future. I do not blame them for this, and I use the word *blame* in the RET sense, meaning that I may hold them *responsible* for making parental mistakes, but I do not personally *damn* them as human beings.

This is a crucial point to get across in your counseling. Until you make the parents responsible for what they are *not* doing, they are going to look to you as the one who has to talk to the child to straighten him or her out. And this is the time for you to remind them that children will do whatever they get away with and that no matter how many times you talk to the children about studying or cleaning up their rooms, if the parents do not reinforce proper behavior at home or do not penalize negative behavior, then no change is likely to come about despite your efforts.

We therefore talk over what needs to be done in the following days, and I do not hesitate to urge the parents to become parents in the true sense, to do the changing that is necessary, and to put pressure on the children so that we get the kinds of changes we are striving for. They seldom come back a second or third time and want to make me responsible for what they have not done. And I'm grateful to Insight 3 for accomplishing this end.

Insight 4: Actions speak louder than words.

How are the parent supposed to go home and get their child to straighten up? In all likelihood, talk is needless at this point. Most parents have given their offspring countless sermons on the same point. They have lectured until they are blue in the face, and the children are bored silly. Further talks simply feed the attention needs of the children or irritate them into a state of rebelliousness. I therefore urge the parents to stop all the sermonizing and to *do* something about the problem. By doing I mean committing an action. I frequently remind parents that when talk does not work, we have to get people to listen with their eyes rather than their ears. It is what they see that they believe, not what they hear: the old saying "Seeing is believing" is quite appropriate in this connection. So I proceed to teach parents to be assertive without being angry.

The concept of logical consequences as propounded by Dreikurs is particularly effective and is relevant to this problem. Instead of ordering children, I advise the parents to give the children a choice when it appears that they will not listen to reason. If they will listen to reason, there is no necessity of going into fancy and technical psychological strategies in order to control their behavior. A simple order gets the job done, so why complicate it with other behaviors?

However, if the child is resistant to reasoning, we want not to order the child to do something that he or she is not going to do anyway, but to give the child a choice. We might say, for example, that if the girl does not want to do the dishes, she will not get to eat dinner. If she wants a home-cooked meal, she has to clean the dishes. It is as simple as that.

That sounds like a perfectly logical proposition and can be used to reassure the child that we are not angry or spiteful against the child but are actually quite fair and indifferent as to what choice she makes. If she wants to eat a nicely cooked meal, that's fine. If she does not want a home-cooked meal, then she can make a peanut-butter sandwich for herself.

Instruct the parent that he or she had better take this advice quite literally and not care much which choice the child makes. In all likelihood, she will prefer sandwiches for days or weeks on end, but if that is her choice, so be it. By being indifferent, we teach the child that we are not going to be manipulated and that nothing the child can do in this regard is going to trouble us particularly. Therefore, if the child is unhappy with the choice, it is the child's responsibility to change that choice. She can always wash the dishes if she wants a home-cooked meal. The choice is hers. We, the parents, don't particularly care much one way or the other. That is the way we convert all of our sermonizing into actions. One act is worth a thousand words.

The same might happen with another common problem: a child's spending his money unwisely. He is given his allowance on Monday and by Tuesday he is broke. When he comes asking for more money, the parents give him a long lecture about how he must save his money and then perhaps give him money to carry him over or give him nothing to teach him a lesson. In all likelihood, neither method will work very effectively. If the child is given money when he was told to be cautious with it, he will learn only not to take us seriously and that with a little complaining or crying he can get a loan on his next allowance.

If he is given a lecture about how foolish he was and what he must do, and he is not given advance money, this approach may not be very effective again simply because of the angry statements that were made to him and the long sermon he got when he was told that he was foolish for spending his money rapidly. That act of anger will have to be revenged by the child by spitefully not profiting by the experience.

In this instance, the best thing to do is simply to calmly agree with the child that it is unfortunate that he spent his money unwisely but that he can bear the frustration and perhaps be more frugal next time. No money is to be advanced to him. But we can sympathize with the situation that he got himself into. However, sympathy does not mean bailing him out. If we merely let him *suffer the consequences* of his foolish behavior, he may eventually learn that he is his own worst enemy and that unless *he* cleans up his act, he is going to suffer again shortly in the future. And best of all, he will have to agree that he cannot blame his parents for the mess he got himself into because they gave him a choice, and he made the wrong choice.

This is what I mean by acting instead of reasoning. Reasoning works only when a person is receptive to the reasoning to some degree. It will not work when a person is convinced that he can have his own way without suffering unpleasant consequences. If we, the parents, are so right in our sermons about how bad something is going to be for a child and the child does not agree with us, there is no point in getting ridiculously repetitive about the rightness of our claims. If we are so right, we can simply let the child go his way, make his mistake, and suffer with the error as we are sure that he will. If he won't believe us, let him believe reality.

Insight 5: Guilt and other-pity prevent implementing this program (Hauck, 1979).

What are the chief obstacles in teaching parents to be objective and to allow their children to make choices that they may hurt themselves with? There are two emotional consequences that parents want to avoid at all costs and that interfere with their being sound disciplinarians. The first is guilt and the second is other-pity.

As I have shown in my book *Overcoming Depression,* one of the most frequent forms of depression is caused by self-blame, and some of the other consequences of self-blame are either inferiority feelings or guilt. It is to avoid feelings of guilt that we often back off from our children and do not become as firm as we might otherwise be. We feel we are being considerate when we let the child have the car even if he or she has not earned the proper grades to deserve the car. It is important that we teach our clients never to blame themselves for the depression that the child might have because he has to use his bicycle or she has to call up her friends for transportation. Always remind your clients that they are not responsible for the emotional disturbances of their children because they cannot upset anyone except themselves. The children upset themselves and the parents upset themselves. One cannot do this to someone else, only to oneself.

Teaching this to a parent is a routine RET task in which the notion that one has to be perfect in order to be worthwhile needs to be questioned. The other irrational idea (that other people can upset us) also deserves to be questioned.

Conscientious and loving parents may understand this from an intellectual point of view fairly easily. But getting them to change their behavior and not feel guilty when they see their children upset as a result of parental restrictions is entirely another matter. Nonetheless, it had better be encouraged over and over again, and the reasons for not feeling guilty can be reiterated from time to time.

More important than guilt as a reason for parents' being soft on their children is other-pity. We tend to feel sorry for our children because of the messes they get themselves into, and we are loathe to let them go through the pain of discovering what they did wrong. I cannot emphasize enough the necessity of letting people live with their errors once they have made an unwise decision. The more we let our offspring go through the pain of a bad choice, the sooner that choice may be rejected in the future.

I, of course, recommend that a parent help out a child when the pain would be unbearable or have a lasting effect. No parents in their right minds would simply warn an adolescent boy not to play Russian roulette. It would be absolutely foolhardy for them to say, "Well, I did advise you not to do that, son, but if you want to, you know you'll have to bear the consequences." Consequences such as these are just too serious and irreversible to tolerate if one can do something about them. In that instance, one would try to wrest the gun out of the boy's hand, knock him out if necessary, or do any number of other things to prevent such a ridiculous risk.

Fortunately, most of the consequences that children suffer as a result of their stupid choices are not irreversible and are not very dangerous. Therefore, we must encourage our parent-client to let the children suffer for their errors until they begin to understand how unwise they have been and that another course of behavior would work better the next time.

Parent Case Conference

I saw a 13-year-old youngster at the request of his parents, who reported that he was an underachiever (getting "D" grades), was incapable of succeeding, would not compete, and obviously had poor self-discipline. He was described by his parents as being a very nice boy, gentle, and full of feeling, but he had lately committed a couple of minor antisocial acts, which began to concern them.

I saw the boy for approximately 15 minutes, and he denied having any of the problems that his parents talked about. As a matter of fact, he was not even troubled by the list of complaints that his folks had given me. He readily admitted that he liked to have fun riding a bike and watching television, but in the main, was rather guarded throughout the interview. He was silent at times and was reluctant to talk about his problems, and from all I was able to determine, he suffered from a severe case of poor

WORKING WITH PARENTS 361

self-discipline. After 15 minutes, I excused him and had the following conversations with his parents.

COUNSELOR: I find that your boy has, as I said, very poor self-discipline, and I think that unless he learns how to put his work first and play second, he's going to have an increasingly bad experience in school, he may not learn skills he is capable of mastering, and he will not develop a good self-concept because he'll be accomplished at very, very few things. He talks about liking to ride horses and, if he had a horse, he might compete. But he doesn't have one, so that leaves that out. The question is, how can we teach him to be more self-disciplined?

First, I can talk to him and perhaps slowly get him to see what a sad situation he's in and how he'd better do something about it. However, the other part of this rests on you folks. I want you to start treating him differently. He is poorly disciplined because, frankly, he gets away with it at home. Now, can you tell me in what ways he's getting away with this, being a goof-off?

MOTHER: Well, he tends to whine a lot. And he knows that if he carries on with the whining, we'll give in to him and he'll get his own way. A lot of the times, it's just easier to do that than to listen to him throw a temper tantrum.

COUNSELOR: How bad do his temper tantrums get?

MOTHER: He has quite a temper. And he's big enough now so that when he gets mad, I'm afraid of him. I try to work around his temper. I try to avoid making him angry.

COUNSELOR: Does he do that with you too, sir?

FATHER: Not recently. But I think that he could. I have intervened in several of his temper tantrums down through the years. I'm thinking of one, for instance, that happened last summer across the street. He blew his cool while playing with some other children. I became very angry and frustrated with him because he was telling me to butt out of his business. He was about to knock somebody's block off and hit the neighbor. I was supposed to go back home and be a good dad. At that time, I just literally threw him down on the ground because I was so frustrated, disgusted, and mad, and it's a wonder that I didn't kill the kid.

COUNSELOR: What have you been doing so that he thinks he doesn't have to study, or to clean up his room, or help around the house, and so on? What have you done, or what had you better do from now on?

FATHER: I've seen Alma do some things, like she mentioned the other day that she was going grocery shopping and Jimmy hadn't taken his bath yet and she went up and told him, "You have not bathed. You're not going with me to get the groceries." Period. But she's not often that consistent. Recently, she gave each one of the three children an assignment. One sets the table, one clears the table, and one takes the garbage out. And very flagrantly, Jimmy doesn't have to clear the table anymore, but the other two still have to. She does that herself, and I begrudgingly help her.

COUNSELOR: Do you see it that way, Alma?

MOTHER: Yes, I do.
COUNSELOR: Why does that happen?
MOTHER: I guess it's easier for me to do it than have a fight with him and make him do it.
COUNSELOR: Do you see why, if he gets away with being cantakerous, whining, or threatening, if you give in on that, don't you see how you actually are making the habit stronger? He's going to do it more and more because it works so well.
MOTHER: Right.
COUNSELOR: So, in a sense, you have created the problem. Can you see that?
MOTHER: Right, that's what I've told him.
COUNSELOR: Now, what you want to do is to train him not to do this anymore, by not doing what you just did. In other words, I don't want you giving in to his complaints. I don't want you giving in to his threats. I want you to tell him what he has to do if it's fair, all right? Then if he doesn't do it, you have to come up with a consequence. You can be ready to say, "Look, if you don't want to do that, then this is what will happen." And then you have to enforce a penalty or some kind of ugly or uncomfortable consequence that he will regret, and somebody's got to be able to enforce it. If you can't, then when your husband comes home, he'll have to. For example, if he's supposed to clean up the table, what are you going to do if he doesn't do it?
MOTHER: That's a good question.
COUNSELOR: OK, don't cook for him. You know, the logic being that if he doesn't want to help clean the dishes, and so on, he shouldn't eat off them. You shouldn't have to cook for someone who doesn't want to help with the dishes. Let him go into the refrigerator and make something for himself if he wants to, but you will not feed him at the table. It's that simple. Would that work?
MOTHER: It should.
COUNSELOR: Or would he rebel and eat sandwiches for five months?
FATHER AND MOTHER: He might (*laughing*).
COUNSELOR: Okay, let him! Then there is no problem as long as he does his dishes. Now, if he doesn't do his dishes, when he makes his own sandwiches, then we've got another problem, haven't we? What are you going to do about that? I want you to take his dishes, then, and put them up in his room. Put them on his bed. Say, "You forgot these." Are you ready for the showdown? Don't you see how you've got to make him uncomfortable? You're going to have to say to him, "Listen , . . ."
MOTHER: I think he'd just put them under his bed.
FATHER: We might even have to go buy some more dishes (*laughing*).
COUNSELOR: Well, it may not work, I'm not so sure. But if he began to get tired of it, he might take them down and start doing them. You've got to stop playing into his behavior, into his pattern.
MOTHER: We just went through this with hamsters.
COUNSELOR: What about them?
MOTHER: Well, the family room was a mess, and I had told them if they didn't

pick up the mess (this was both boys, not just the one), that the hamsters would go out. Well, it didn't get picked up, and for two days I let it go, and finally I went downstairs and I shut off the TV and picked up the hamster cage, and there were two sets of eyes about bugged out of their heads. And I set their hamsters outside. "But they'll get a chill," they complained. "Then you better hurry and get that cleaned," I said. And they hurried.

COUNSELOR: Now, did it cure them?

MOTHER: I don't know. It's been cleaned up since then. It hasn't returned to the same mess.

COUNSELOR: OK, now suppose they begin to backslide?

MOTHER: The hamsters will go back out.

COUNSELOR: Why don't you get rid of them?

MOTHER: I'd love to.

COUNSELOR: Give them away.

FATHER: Absolutely, 100%!

COUNSELOR: Don't give them this song and dance, "Well, I'm going to give you another chance." You see how easy you are? They know when you're getting serious after five warnings because you start yelling. Don't do that. Set the rules. Say, "If you don't want the hamsters, that's fine. I'll know when you don't want them because you don't want to clean them. So if you don't clean the cage, it will be gone one day, and that will be the end of it." Boom. Just like that, okay? You say you want your boy to change. *You have to change first.* But you're very loving, gentle, and giving parents. You don't want a lot of hassle. You don't want to upset people, and so on. And so what you've done, really, is give too much. You've been too easy on the boy. Do you realize what trouble he's in? Do you realize that at 13 years of age he thinks he's slaving away doing a half hour of homework? I bet he doesn't even do that much.

FATHER: No.

MOTHER: I'm sure he doesn't.

COUNSELOR: No! I mean this guy is in trouble! He can't sit down straight for one half hour and deny himself television. Now, there's a big weapon for you. If he doesn't bring his grades up, what's going to happen to the TV?

FATHER: It should get cut off.

COUNSELOR: For him!

FATHER: Absolutely!

COUNSELOR: Yes. He can't come into the room where the TV is and watch it. Not until the grades come up. I don't care if it takes nine months! No more TV at all! Are you ready for that? Now, can you stand all the flak you are going to get from this kid? If you love him, you better. Follow me?

FATHER: Um-hum.

COUNSELOR: Am I making sense?

BOTH FATHER AND MOTHER: Yes, you are.

COUNSELOR: Where else do you see poor self-discipline? If you tell him to do a job, can he do it or does he goof off on that?

MOTHER: He goofs off on that, too.

COUNSELOR: Mow the lawn, wipe the windows, whatever, right?
FATHER: Um-hum.
COUNSELOR: Why is he goofing off?
MOTHER: He procrastinates. He puts off forever and ever.
COUNSELOR: And what is the consequence of that?
FATHER: Nothing.
COUNSELOR: You see, there it is again. If you say, do the lawn, let him put it off. But *everything* else gets put off after that. He *must* do the lawn before he gets his next favor.
FATHER: Absolutely.
COUNSELOR: You follow me?
FATHER: Absolutely.
COUNSELOR: Don't yell at him. Don't beat him. Don't put him down. Just make him regret goofing off, the procrastination. Make him regret it. Because that means he can't go out. He can't leave the yard. He hasn't done his lawn yet. He can't ride the bike. He hasn't done his lawn yet. He can't watch the television. Come on. First things first. You want to teach somebody to be disciplined? Then, when they're supposed to do something, they had better do it. *Now.* Follow me?
FATHER: Um-hum.
COUNSELOR: You see how you've spoiled the boy? You've been nice, you've been generous, and you've done a lot of yelling and all that kind of stuff. But when it comes right down to it, he never really had to do what he had to do. He could get away with being a goof-off. You've let him. And this is what you've got to change, OK?

SUMMARY

The methods I have explained above work. They are a combination of cognitive-behavioral techniques that have been validated empirically hundreds of times and are finding increasing support in the literature. The most important ideas to keep in mind in counseling parents and children are to distinguish between manipulative and nonmanipulative behavior, to make the parent the primary client when the child is manipulative, and then to teach the parents cognitive and behavioral methods that they can use on themselves first in order to bring about changes in the child second.

I have great confidence that those counselors who will follow this program will be handsomely rewarded by observing much more frequent and more lasting progress in their clients than they have observed thus far.

References

Bain, J. A. *Thought control in everyday life*. New York: Funk & Wagnalls, 1928.
Dreikurs, R., & Soltz, V. *Children: The challenge*. New York: Meredith Press, 1964.
Ellis, A. *Reason and emotion in psychotherapy*. Secaucus, N.J.: Lyle Stuart and Citadel Books, 1962.
Ellis, A., & Harper, R. *A new guide to rational living*. Hollywood, Calif.: Wilshire Books, 1975.
Ellis, A., & Knaus, W. *Overcoming procrastination*. New York: Institute for Rational-Emotive Therapy, 1977.
Ellis, A., Wolfe, J., & Moseley, S. *How to raise an emotionally healthy, happy child*. Hollywood, Calif.: Wilshire Books, 1966.
Hauck, P. *The rational management of children*. New York: Libra Publishers, 1967.
Hauck, P. *Overcoming depression*. Philadelphia: Westminster Press, 1973.
Hauck, P. *Overcoming frustration and anger*. Philadelphia: Westminster Press, 1974.
Hauck, P. *Overcoming worry and fear*. Philadelphia: Westminster Press, 1975.
Hauck, P. *How to do what you want to do*. Philadelphia: Westminster Press, 1976.
Hauck, P. *Brief counseling with RET*. Philadelphia: Westminster Press, 1980.
Mark, M. *Learning: Interactions*. New York: Macmillan, 1970.
Maultsby, M. *Help yourself to happiness*. New York: Institute for Rational Living, 1975.
Patterson, G., & Gullion, M. *Living with children* (rev. ed.). Champaign, Ill.: Research Press, 1971.
Taylor, J. G. A behavioral interpretation of obsessive-compulsive neuroses. *Behavior research and therapy*. 1963, *1*, 237–244.
Wolpe, J., & Lazarus, A. *Behavior therapy techniques*. New York: Pergamon Press, 1966.

13

Involving the Family in the Treatment of the Child
A Model for Rational-Emotive Therapists

NINA WOULFF

The ideas in this chapter arise from a desire to develop a model of rational-emotive therapy for children that accounts for the family's contribution to the child's problem and suggests a rationale and techniques for incorporating the family in the treatment of the child. Working primarily in a child guidance setting, where the referred client is always a child, I noticed that changes in presenting problems were most efficiently accomplished when the child's family was involved in assessment and treatment. However, I found no rigorous model in either the rational-emotive therapy (RET) or the family therapy literature that demonstrated how the two therapy approaches may be successfully integrated. Having been trained in both RET and structural-strategic family therapy, and believing strongly in the efficacy of both, I felt challenged to see whether the two theories were capable of mating to produce effective and successful results.

Rational-emotive therapy primarily addresses the issue of changing the client's irrational beliefs. This therapy focuses on the internal events of the problem bearer and deemphasizes the context of the problem or the client. This focus has been helpful in demonstrating the idiosyncratic manner in which clients contribute to, create, and maintain their misery.

NINA WOULFF • Dartmouth Branch of the Atlantic Child Guidance Centre, Dartmouth, Nova Scotia, and Division of Family Medicine and Department of Psychiatry, Dalhousie University, Halifax, Nova Scotia.

RET literature only rarely discusses the manner in which humans living in groups influence and affect one another (Protinsky, 1977; McClellan & Stieper, 1977; Young, 1979; Ellis, 1978, 1979, 1982).

When the client is a child, it becomes crucial that the therapist acknowledge the effect of the child's human environment because children are extremely dependent upon adults for meeting needs and learning the ways and means of relating and functioning in this world. Structural-strategic therapy (Haley, 1976, 1980; Papp, 1977; Selvini, 1978; Andolfi, 1979; Madanes, 1981) demonstrates how this human environment—specifically how the interaction between people in groups—is crucial to problem creation and maintenance.

The model of therapy proposed in this chapter is a hybrid of rational-emotive therapy and structural-strategic therapy and shall henceforth be described as rational-emotive family therapy, or REFT.

Rationale for REFT

There are several reasons that REFT is preferable to individual RET with referred children. When parents refer their child to a mental health clinic, it is not unusual that the parents are more distressed than the child. Thus, to work individually with the child in these situations is often not productive because the child is not particularly motivated to change. Even if the child is motivated to change, the therapist has relatively little influence compared with the influence of the parents. Parental reinforcement is extremely powerful, and it is highly unlikely that a child who has learned rational thinking with her or his individual therapist will continue to maintain this change when her or his parents and other family members still strongly reinforce the old irrational beliefs and consequent behavior. This problem is exemplified in the case below:

> Several years ago, I worked with a 10-year-old boy who exhibited persistent behavior problems at school and home. His parents insisted that he needed individual therapy and that they could meet with me only sporadically because of their busy schedules. Being a relatively young and unassertive therapist at the time, I agreed to their conditions. The young boy happily came to his individual sessions, during which we engaged in games and discussion aimed at correcting many misperceptions he had about his "badness." The boy was the only adopted child in his family and also had diabetes, which was controlled by medication. He had interpreted these unique characteristics as meaning that he was completely unlovable and that nothing he could do would change how adults thought about him and acted toward him. The boy was quite bright and within

several sessions was able to develop a more rational outlook about himself and plan how to change his behavior in order to get into less trouble. However, when I periodically spoke with the child's teacher or parents I would hear that his behavior had remained virtually unchanged except for brief and fleeting "good spells." I was quite perplexed but continued working with the boy. Some time later, during a session with the parents, some interesting factors emerged. Although there had been little progress in the therapy, the mother insisted that the boy continue because she believed that he had a very pathological personality and was the cause of most of the other problems in the family. She said that the fact that this boy was the only family member going for therapy proved this point. The father disagreed with the mother's manner of disciplining the boy and would give him special attention whenever the mother attempted to be firm with him. The father's justification was "but he is such a pathetic little chap—he does not need to be disciplined on top of everything else he has to deal with in life—with problems like his he can't help himself." It thus became obvious to me that the parents were actively reinforcing the boy's irrational beliefs about his innate "badness" and his misbehavior. The parents were very committed to their attitudes; they became quite irritated when I attempted to challenge their beliefs and argued that I should limit my therapeutic efforts to changing their son. I saw the boy for several additional sessions and then told the parents that I would not continue unless the whole family would attend regularly. They refused and I closed the case.

I believe much time was wasted in working with this boy and that, in effect, my agreeing to work with him individually was interpreted by the parents as further evidence that he was really bad and helpless. The above case demonstrates some of the hazards of not working with families when a child is referred. In addition, it suggests the need for several important skills when doing rational-emotive family therapy. Specifically, the therapist needs to have a conceptual model of the problems that includes the interaction among family members, do a thorough assessment, be able to overcome resistance to family treatment, and motivate family members to follow through on tasks.

Conceptual Schemata for REFT

The REFT therapist conceptualizes well-functioning families as groups of people who are able to accomplish the task of aiding the personality and social development of their offspring. This difficult task is hampered when the system has unclear or inappropriate rules, boundaries, and/or hierarchy. In an effective family system, the parents comprise a cooperative working team that operates as the "executive" unit of the system, and the children are a subsystem of clearly secondary power and status. The tasks of the parental subsystem are to work cooperatively in socializing the children and to be able to modify rules and expectations as children grow older. The task of the sibling system is to offer its members the opportunity to learn how to negotiate, cooperate, share, compete, and make friends with peers.

In order for each subsystem to carry out its specific functions, the boundaries between subsystems must be clear. The term *boundaries* refers to the intensity of interaction between people and to how responsibilities are delegated. When boundaries are enmeshed between subsystems or individuals, family members experience little sense of separateness. This lack of separateness contributes to difficulties in the development of independent activities and thinking, and in problem solving. When boundaries are disengaged, there is little helpful communication between members, and this lack can hamper the development of the capacity for living interdependently with others.

When a family presents with a problem child, the REFT therapist investigates the possibility of hierarchical incongruities and inappropriate boundaries within a family. Examples of such problems are: a parent is relating to his child as a peer; a child is closely enmeshed with one parent, and the other parent is relatively distant; an older child makes most of the decisions for a family; or all members of a family relate to each other as equals in status.

The REFT therapist believes that these organizational and relationship problems are primarily created and maintained by individual family members' irrational assumptions about themselves and each other. Thus, although the REFT therapist may have structural reorganization as the objective goal for the family with a symptomatic child, the means by which this goal is achieved is the altering of irrational assumptions. To accomplish this task, the REFT therapist utilizes a wide repertoire of RET techniques, including direct cognitive disputation, imagery and behavioral disputation, jokes and parables, paradoxical prescriptions, and problem transformation (Bergner, 1979).

Stages of REFT

It is suggested that the REFT therapist follow specific stages in working toward goals. The case of Michael P. will be used to demonstrate the crucial stages in REFT therapy:

Michael P., age 11, was brought to the clinic by his mother and father. There was one younger sister in the family, who was seemingly problem-free. Mr. and Mrs. P. were concerned about Michael because he was sleeping and eating poorly, was very antagonistic toward his father, stated that he was very miserable, and expressed intense disgust and anxiety about the idea of his parents' having sexual relations. Michael's father was concerned about his lack of friends, although Mrs. P. did not agree with this. His behavior and performance in school were not a problem. Michael had a history of problems similar to these. His parents had taken a course in parenting skills and had been in family therapy before. At the assessment session, they staunchly maintained that Michael should be seen in individual therapy because they feared that talking about their concerns in front of him would hurt him. They also said that they were dissatisfied with their previous therapy because the therapist focused almost exclusively on their marriage and the problems with the boy did not go away.

Assessing the Problem

At this point, the REFT therapist will want to obtain certain information that will reveal structural anomalies in this group of people and that will help to identify the irrational beliefs that are maintaining the symptoms and the dysfunctional structure. In order to do this, the therapist should ask herself or himself the following questions:

- Are the parents united in the way in which they attempt to solve the problem?
- How may the attempted solutions be actually reinforcing the child's problem rather than solving it?
- Does the problem child have an inappropriate amount of power and influence in the family?
- Do the parents behave assertively with their child?
- Do the family members have any practical problems that could be contributing to the presenting problem (e.g., lack of child management or negotiation skills, financial problems, communication problems with the school, physical or neurological handicaps)?
- What irrational assumptions could be influencing the way in which each member of this family reacts to the problem and to the other members of the family?
- How do the family members irrationally blame themselves or others for the problem?
- How do the child's beliefs maintain his or her symptoms?

The REFT therapist elicits the answer to the above questions by direct questioning, by observing the nonverbal behavior of individuals in the family and interactions between family members, and by assigning homework. Questions that the therapist can ask the family directly might include:

- Do you (the parents) discuss this problem? What happens when you discuss it?
- Specifically, what does each person in the family do when the problem occurs? What has been done in the past?
- What does each family member think is the cause of the problem?
- What does each family member think is needed in order to solve the problem?
- What do these problems mean about the child (e.g., is he sick, bad, stupid, evil)?
- What does each family member feel and think when the problem occurs?
- What is happening around you and what are you thinking about when you experience your problems? (Asked of the child.)
- What does each family member want from therapy?

In observing nonverbal behaviors during the session, the therapist listens for irrational emotions and for incongruities between what a person says and how he or she behaves. In addition, the therapist observes the interaction of the family members for clues about family structure and irrational beliefs. While observing, the therapist keeps the following questions in mind:

- Who answers questions first?
- Does one parent seem more involved with the symptomatic child?
- Do the parents seem intimidated by the child or vice versa?
- Who talks to whom in the family?
- What tone of voice is used when the family members address each other?
- How are the family members seated and how do they look at each other?

Finally, in giving homework assignments, the therapist is attempting to elicit cognitive and behavioral data that will further help in providing the information that is needed in order to make a hypothesis about what is creating and maintaining the problem. This information is not all gathered at once. The REFT therapist must be prepared to revise his or her understanding of the problem throughout the duration of therapy. As the therapist gives directives and as family members change, irrational beliefs are activated that the therapist must be prepared to reassess and to deal with. The information-gathering scheme outlined above was used in the assessment of Michael P. and his family.

> Both parents were spending a great deal of time with their son when he experienced his problems. The mother spent hours talking to Michael about his various anxieties, and she reported that he was very dissatisfied with his father. The father would invite Michael to participate in activities with him, but Michael would refuse. At night, when Michael entered the parents' bedroom and accused them of having sexual relations, they would both reassure him that they were only sleeping and allow him to sleep in their room for the rest of the night. At mealtime, both the mother and the father would gently coax Michael to eat his food. Both parents expressed great concern that their child was emotionally disturbed and possibly suicidal. The mother thought that the cause of the problem was that he was fearful of his father and that he had a very "sensitive" personality like hers. The father thought that Michael was too close to his mother and stayed in the house too much. Both parents discussed their son's problems *ad nauseum*, but they could not decide on an effective solution. They seemed to be rather confused about practical child-management techniques.
> When Michael was home, he was almost always in a bad mood, and there seemed to be no clearly identifiable precipitating factors. He said that when he walked home from school, he began to feel depressed as he approached his home. He said that he was aware of thinking that his father was mean and unfair and that his mother was worried and upset. He said that he also thought it was terrible to have these problems and to be coming to a child guidance clinic. The mother said that she vacillated between feeling intensely worried about her son, annoyed at him for being such a problem, and then guilty and depressed. The father said that he often felt guilty, helpless, and occasionally angry at his son. The parents said that their son needed individual therapy, and Michael said that he didn't know that would help him. Both parents stated that their goal in coming to therapy was to free their son of his problems.
> In observing the family's nonverbal behavior, I noticed several interesting patterns. The mother tended to answer questions before anyone else did, and her body was turned toward her son. Whenever she spoke to him, her voice sounded pleading and childlike. Although the boy stated that he was quite miserable, he sounded very assertive and would correct his parents when they were telling me about the problem. The parents did not get annoyed at the boy when he did this but would meekly defend themselves to him. The boy frequently rolled his eyes and sighed.

Formulating a Hypothesis about the Problem

With this information, I formulated a hypothesis about the problem. In terms of the structure of the family, it appeared that the boy had a great deal of power and influence over his parents. Thus, the hierarchy was reversed because the child seemed to influence his parents, rather than vice versa. He determined where he slept, what they did in their bedroom, and how they spent much of their time. In addition, the boundary between mother and son seemed enmeshed, in that they shared common problems and worries and did not solve problems on their own. The boundary between son and father seemed disengaged, because they had little interaction with each other. In their attempted solutions, the parents were inadvertently reinforcing the problem because the boy was obtaining much special time and attention from his mother. He was treated as though he were king.

In understanding how this dysfunctional structure is maintained, the REFT therapist looks to the misconceptions of individuals within the family system. It seemed apparent that each member of the family had irrational beliefs that were creating distressing feelings and causing them to behave in ways that reinforced the symptom. The mother had irrational fears and expectations of herself and her son. At times, she believed, "I must worry about my son all the time and help him overcome his problems; when I don't, I am a complete failure," and "The poor boy—he cannot help his problems; I am terrible to be so annoyed at him." The husband believed, "I am a worthless father because my son has so many problems," "I must not do anything that would upset my son," and "My son shouldn't be so difficult to help." The son believed, "I cannot stand it if my father doesn't act exactly as I want him to act," "I can't help myself—I am hopeless," "It is terrible for my mother to be so upset," and "I am a bad, evil person because I have all these problems." In addition, the boy had a very low frustration tolerance and believed, "I cannot stand to be worried and anxious—my mother must calm me immediately." In addition, all family members shared the irrational belief that the source and the solution of their problems was in each other and that they each had little ability to control the unhappiness they were experiencing. Families who come to a mental health clinic frequently blame each other, teachers, principals, neighborhoods, early history, baby-sitters, and even the weather for their problems. Although these factors may, in fact, be influential in activating a difficulty, I have usually found that there are a good number of irrational beliefs operating in families with a problem child.

In analyzing the irrational beliefs of the individuals in the family, the reasons for the dysfunctional structure become apparent. When parents are depressing themselves by irrational self-downing they are unlikely to behave in ways syntonic with an effective parental subsystem. If their child has low frustration tolerance and is quite demanding and if the parents believe that their self-worth rests in producing a happy child, they will probably give in to many of the child's demands. In a sense, these parents live in fear of their own child as a result of the connotations they place on her or his behavior. Thus, the child becomes the "boss" and the parents become the "child."

In the family of Michael P., the symptoms were maintained by a cycle of interactions in which the more Michael complained of his difficulties, the more his parents got upset and doted on him, and the more this happened, the more the boy acted up. The parents kept themselves indecisive and overinvolved with him by being caught in their own cycles of internal thinking, in which they would depreciate themselves for getting annoyed and angry with their son. In analyzing a family's problem, it is helpful for the REFT therapist to look for repetitive cycles of thinking in the minds of individuals and repetative cycles of behavior between individuals.

In addition, it is helpful for the REFT therapist to be cognizant of constellations of irrational beliefs that occur in families with certain structural dysfunctions. For example, in most families where boundaries are enmeshed, the therapist will find that at least two family members share several of the following irrational beliefs:

- "It is terrible to be different from other people in my family. I must not think, behave, or feel differently from the way they do."
- "It is awful to fight or to be annoyed or angry with someone in my family."
- "I must be able to change people in my family."
- "I can't stand it if someone in my family has a problem."
- "It would be horrible if a member of my family left. We all *need* each other."

Careful identification of irrational beliefs will assist the therapist in planning the focus of treatment.

DEFINING GOALS

My goals for the family of Michael P. were that the parents become an effective and assertive team in dealing with their son and that Michael learn how to solve many of his emotional problems. In order to accomplish this, I had to help the family members identify, challenge, and replace the irrational beliefs that were creating their emotional problems and preventing them from solving the practical problems of effective child management. The goals sound fairly clear and straightforward. However, in order to reach these goals, the REFT therapist must be somewhat creative in introducing the family to the notion of therapy and change.

MOTIVATING THE FAMILY FOR TREATMENT AND DEALING WITH RESISTANCE

Parents who bring their children for treatment often state, as in the example of Michael P., that they want their child changed. At the beginning of treatment, the parents are usually very reluctant to admit that they need treatment themselves and often become early treatment dropouts if the therapist prematurely attempts to demonstrate to the parents how they are irrationally upsetting themselves. Family therapy literature contains several rather exotic theories and methodologies for dealing with families' resistance to treatment (Hoffman, 1976; Papp, 1977; Selvini, 1978; Watzlawick, 1978). For example, Andolfi (1979) wrote:

> The therapist is thereby drawn into a *game* in which every effort on his part to act as an agent of change is nullified by the family group. In systemic terms, these apparently contradictory attitudes derive from the dynamic equilibrium existing between opposite and interacting forces: the tendency toward change, which is implicit in the request for help, and the preponderant tendency toward homeostasis, which leads the family to repeat its habitual behavioral sequences. (p. 123)

Suggested techniques for dealing with this problem include using a team of therapists and prescribing paradoxes and counterparadoxes.

From an RET viewpoint, resistance can be understood as a cluster of irrational beliefs that are activated when family members perceive the therapist as suggesting that the entire family participate in the change process.

Resistance can occur at the beginning of family therapy when the therapist attempts to involve the parents and throughout the therapy when the therapist gives the family specific tasks. When parents resist becoming involved in therapy, there are several irrational beliefs that commonly occur. Sometimes, these beliefs are easy to uncover, and the therapist can then challenge them directly. However, resistance, by its very nature, tends to be difficult to deal with directly, and the reasons for initial resistance often are not disclosed until later in therapy. The therapist must then infer the underlying irrational beliefs. In the case of

Michael P., both parents wanted only individual therapy for their son. When asked about this, the parents gave the following reason: "When Michael hears us discussing these problems, he becomes more upset, and we cannot bear it when he is upset." In addition, the mother indicated that the idea of coming to sessions made her feel depressed. When I asked her what she was telling herself about coming to therapy, she said, "I guess then I would think that the problems were all my fault and responsibility." Mrs. P.'s response leaves out the evaluative component of her self-statement, which later emerged as being "and that would prove I am a terrible mother." This irrational belief is not uncommon among parents of referred children. The irrational beliefs of parents that contribute to resistance to family treatment include:

- "It is a sign of complete failure to have to come for help on family matters."
- "The therapist might ask us to talk about other problems we have, and that would be disastrous."

Children in families can also be resistant to treatment, and some of their common irrational beliefs are:

- "If anyone knew I was coming to this place, I would die."
- "If my family comes here for therapy, then that is absolute proof that I am a bad person."
- "I don't want anything to change because things could get worse, and I couldn't stand that."

The therapist has at least two ways of dealing with this resistance to treatment. One way is to directly challenge the irrational inferences and evaluations. The therapist can also choose to "sidestep" the resistance. For example, the therapist can tell the parents that their involvement in the therapy is crucial because they are the most significant people in their child's life and because they, more than anyone else in the world, are best equipped to help their child. When parents hear this, they tend to think of coming to therapy as an honor rather than as a curse. In addition, I suggest that the therapist state that the goals of therapy are to help the child become free of his or her problems and that the therapist will assist the parents in helping their child. By stating the goals of treatment in this way, the therapist is likely to engage the cooperation of the parents in the therapy process. There will be many opportunities later in therapy to teach the family members how to identify and rigorously challenge their irrational evaluations.

IMPLEMENTING THE TREATMENT PLAN

Once the family has agreed to treatment, the therapist is advised to follow these steps: (1) negotiate the treatment form and frequency; (2) transform the presenting problem when necessary; (3) give behavioral homework; (4) deal with resistance to homework; and (5) help the referred child to develop strategies for independent problem-solving.

Negotiate Treatment Form and Frequency

It is not necessary, nor is it always advisable, to see all family members conjointly when doing REFT. In determining the form of treatment, the therapist should ask himself or herself the following questions:

- Through what means will the goals of therapy be most efficiently and effectively achieved?
- What form of treatment is the family likely to agree to?

With the family of Michael P., I decided on a "mixed" form of treatment. I gave the family a 1½ hour appointment every two weeks. During the first half hour, I saw Michael individually, then met with the parents for the next 45 minutes, and saw all three for the remaining 15 minutes. This decision was based on my assumptions that (1) it would be easier to encourage Michael to develop independent thinking and problem solving if I saw him alone; (2) initially, the parents would be more likely to express their own feelings and thoughts if they were free from the influence of their powerful son; (3) the last 15 minutes would give the parents the opportunity to rehearse dealing effectively with their son; and (4) the parents would be likely to accept this format.

Transform the Presenting Problem

Bergner (1979) wisely pointed out that it is important for therapists to be aware that clients can have very destructive definitions of their problems, which lead to depression and ineffective solutions. In these cases, Bergner suggested that the therapist attempt to replace these destructive problem definitions with more constructive ones. This approach is similar to reframing (Watzlawick, 1974, 1978) and positive connotation (Selvini, 1978). In REFT, the therapist will want to transform a problem definition if she or he believes that the family members will be more likely to carry out new solutions to their problem if they think about it in a new way.

With the family of Michael P., I thought it important to change the parents' inference that their son was emotionally disturbed, suicidal, and overly sensitive, because this way of perceiving the problem resulted in the parents' overprotecting him. I told the parents, that, based on the evidence, it seemed clear that their son was suffering from "separation anxiety which was precipitated by approaching adolescence" and that the only way he would overcome this problem was if his parents were "willing and able to wean him away from them." I assured the parents that this would not be an easy process. In transforming the problem this way, I created a new path for the family to follow—a path that would hopefully lead them away from the self-defeating cycle of attempted solutions in which they were stuck.

Give Behavioral Homework

The overall goal of behavioral homework is to reverse incongruent hierarchies and to eliminate the reinforcers that are maintaining the symptom. The therapist should keep the homework tasks as simple, as clear, and as inexpensive as possible.

Deal with Resistance to Homework

Therapists should not become discouraged when parents resist or sabotage homework directives. In REFT, it is this very resistance that is the royal road to the irrational beliefs that are perpetuating the cycle of interactions around the symptom. Also, the REFT therapist should be prepared to help family members solve the emotional and practical problems that may surface when the presenting problem improves.

> In the family of Michael P., I directed the parents to stop allowing their son to sleep in their bedroom; to cease sympathizing, cajoling, and encouraging him; and to apply positive consequences if he ate his meals. In addition, the father was instructed to firmly discipline his son when the boy was rude. These tasks were relatively simple and straightforward. However, it took more than a dozen sessions before the parents could comfortably and effectively carry out these new solutions. At the beginning of therapy, Mrs. P. resisted the directive that her husband take firm control of her son because she claimed it would result in a wider rift between father and son. It was necessary to identify and challenge her irrational belief: "It is terrible if a child does not love his father all the time." In addition, the father was rather fearful of disciplining his son, claiming that he thought he would lose control of himself and beat the

boy. It was necessary to teach the father the difference between irrational anger and rational annoyance and to suggest some practical child-management techniques.

Although at first it seemed as though Mrs. P. was following the directive to become less involved with her son, it soon became clear that this was not the case. Mrs. P. was talking less to her son about eating, sleeping, and sex problems. However, Michael was a rather clever boy and developed new problems, such as fighting with his sister and his grandmother, and Mrs. P. would fall back into her old ways of dealing with him. It thus became clear that something was preventing Mrs. P. from generalizing effective solutions. It emerged that Mrs. P. harbored the beliefs: "If I don't attend to all my son's problems, I will be a bad mother and that is devastating," and "I must be the opposite of my own mother, who was neglectful and awful." In challenging these beliefs and arriving at more rational alternatives, Mrs. P. was able to be more appropriately involved with her son in a variety of situations.

In working with these parents, a curious phenomenon developed. As Michael's problems became less severe, his parents became mildly depressed and claimed that "the situation was just hopeless." Because the parents kept an objective record of Michael's behavior, I knew that their response was triggered by something other than Michael's behavior. In questioning the parents about their thoughts regarding their situation, it became evident that they were evaluating themselves as failures because their child was not 100% problem-free! It emerged that the parents were both perfectionists and needed help in defining rational goals for themselves and their son.

In addition, Mrs. P. complained that her husband emphasized her difficulties in dealing with her son and never recognized her successes. In investigating this problem, I found that Mrs. P. had an irrational need for approval from her husband. However, in addition, Mr. P. was very frightened of his wife's anger and disapproval. Mr. P. was worried that as she became tougher with her son, she would also become tougher with him, not need him as much, and possibly leave him. It was necessary to help both parents challenge these beliefs before they could work cooperatively, supportively, and authoritatively in helping their son.

At the beginning of therapy with these parents, I was quite specific in my directives. However during later sessions, I encouraged the parents to generate their own solutions to specific difficulties. As the parents became free of their incapacitating irrational beliefs, they began negotiating with each other in developing plans to deal with their son's behavior. For example, during one of the last sessions, the father and the mother developed their own plan for dealing with the problem of the son's avoidance of peer contact.

Help the Referred Child to Develop Strategies for Independent Problem-Solving

When working individually with the referred child in REFT, the therapist must help the child to identify her or his faulty emotional- and practical-problem-solving techniques and must be aware that the child may experience new difficulties when the transactions in the family change:

> In working with Michael P., I discovered that he was quite a "pro" at irrational thinking. Although his parents' reactions had certainly helped him maintain his irrational thinking and behavior, it seemed clear that Michael was very adept at helping himself remain miserable. My first job was to show Michael how to overcome downing himself for seeing a therapist. Michael believed that he had the devil inside him because he felt so angry at times. Slowly Michael learned that it was not the devil, but irrational thoughts over which had control, that produced his anger. In addition, Michael also believed, as did his parents, that it was awful to not love his father. Paradoxically, as Michael learned to dispute this belief, he reported a greater number of positive interactions with his father. As his mother became more authoritative, Michael became angry and depressed. He learned how to challenge his demandingness and awfulizing related to this change in his relationship with his mother. He also came to realize that he could solve many of his problems without her help. One of Michael's most persistent problems was his lack of friends. Although he seemed to want to spend more time playing with peers he took little action to rectify the problem. After spending considerable time making direct suggestions and attempting to challenge his low frustration tolerance, I decided to transform the problem. I told him that it seemed to me that he had a much more serious problem than I had thought. Based on the evidence, it appeared that he had a deep-seated fear of fun. His reaction to this problem transformation was quite dramatic: he became very annoyed with me and at his next visit returned with several examples of enjoyable experiences with friends.

TERMINATING REFT

Termination of REFT occurs when the presenting problems have decreased and when the therapist is convinced that the family members have made significant changes in their thinking. I suggest that the REFT therapist delineate an end stage of therapy. This need not be more than two sessions, and the goals are to reinforce the changes that family members have made and to avoid future reactivation of symptoms. At this stage, it is very helpful for therapists to ask families the following questions:

- How do you explain the changes that have occurred?
- How could you slip back into your old patterns? Specifically, how would you each have to think and react to each other in order to get back into the old rut?

In responding to these questions, family members demonstrate their ability to understand how they have contributed to the problem and whether they have developed a more internal locus of control. If family members respond to the first question by saying that their child has changed because the weather is better or the teacher is nicer, then the therapist knows that her or his job is not over. At the end of REFT, parents sometimes request help with individual difficulties that are not directly related to the problem with their child. It is suggested that, if the therapist agrees to continue working with this parent, a new therapeutic contract be established.

Characteristics of REFT Therapists

Training in RET theoretically equips therapists with many of the skills that are needed to conduct effective family-therapy sessions. Family therapists need to be directive and focused in leading sessions; to plan sessions; to challenge realities that family members accept; to be persistent in encouraging people to change; to focus on present methods of coping and problem solving and not be sidetracked by the intricacies of past history; to be clearly goal-oriented; to creatively design homework assignments; and to make a flexible use of themselves in order to engage and motivate the family members (Minuchin, 1974; Haley, 1976; Watzlawick, 1974; Minuchin & Fishman, 1981). These are all skills that are basic to the repertoire of the RET therapist (Ellis & Grieger, 1977; Grieger & Boyd, 1980; Walen, DiGiuseppe, & Wessler, 1980; Wessler & Wessler, 1980). A family therapist must be able not to get distracted by the morass of content that family members present during a session. Because RET therapists are trained to look for the "B" underlying the "A," they are less likely to get absorbed by the details of a problem.

The importance of the therapist's taking a nonblaming stance is frequently emphasized in family therapy literature (Selvini, 1978; Andolfi, 1979; Minuchin & Fishman, 1981). Stanton (1981) wrote: "Blaming, criticizing and negative terms tend to mobilize resistance, as family members muster their energies to disown the pejorative label. Such negative or depressive maneuvers by the family can render the therapist impotent" (p. 376). RET therapists are unlikely to fall into the trap of perceiving some family members as "victims" and others as "bullies," because they understand all dysfunctional human behavior as stemming from irrational cognitions. Thus, the RET therapist would tend to perceive family members as all "victims" of their individual irrational ideologies.

Hazards and Pitfalls of REFT

Despite the skills that a RET therapist brings to working with families, he or she still faces several potential hazards and pitfalls.

One of the most common problems is underdiagnosing the extent of irrational thinking in family members. This is a particular problem in families in which one family member—often the mother—flagrantly expresses irrational emotions and ideas while the other family members appear quite rational in comparison. I once worked with a family in which the mother was clearly self-downing and irrationally angry in relation to her difficult 4-year-old. The father appeared to be quite rational and reasonable relative to the mother. I spent considerable time and energy in helping the mother become more self-accepting, less depressed and angry, and more effective in child management techniques. However, the management strategies never lasted very long, and the old dysfunctional patterns of coping would quickly reemerge. When I took a second look at the problem, I discovered that this seemingly reasonable husband was undermining the strategies because he had a good number of misconceptions about his child's vulnerability and irrational expectations of his wife.

Another problem with which family therapists contend is the tendency to become "inducted" into the family if the therapist tends to agree with the family's perception and definition of its problem and to do the parents' job. In other words, the therapist becomes susceptible to the group pressure exerted by the family. For example, she or he may take over the role of leader of the family in establishing rules or may fall into the unfortunate trap of acting as judge for the family in deciding what is "fair" or who is "right" or "wrong." The RET therapist who remembers the basic values and goals of RET will be somewhat protected from this pitfall. RET therapists are trained to assume that clients' statements about their problems, themselves, and others are rarely purely descriptive; rather, they are colored by inferences and evaluations. The therapists are thus unlikely to accept these statements as "truth" and to agree with family's perception and definition of their problem. Also, because RET therapists believe that the goal of therapy is to teach clients to own the responsibility for emotions and behavior, they do not run in and try to "fix" clients' problems for them.

Another problem that occasionally occurs is that one parent denigrates the other for having irrational beliefs by inferring that to have these beliefs is "weak," "bad," or "crazy." The therapist must be able to identify and interrupt this interaction quickly, because it can lead to therapy failure or a worsening of the situation. The therapist can interrupt this interaction by deawfulizing the concept of irrational thinking and by looking for the issues underlying this one-upmanship game. The therapist will often find that the "superior" mate secretly has a horde of irrational fears and expectations.

Summary

Although it seems at times a complicated and arduous task to conduct REFT effectively, there are many benefits to working in this mode. In terms of dealing with child-related problems, the family therapy approach can be very time-efficient. Many of the advantages of doing RET in groups apply to working with families: several family members can learn RET at one time, family members can reinforce their own learning by challenging each other's beliefs, and family therapy sessions can function as a live laboratory in which family members experiment with new interactions. In addition, by having family members interact together, certain emotions can be activated during the session so that the therapist can deal with them directly.

By working with the whole family, family members develop a much stronger belief in their ability to function competently and to solve their own problems. It is arguable that a therapist who works solely with children inadvertently reinforces the parents' belief that the solution to their problems rest with an outside agent—the therapist—thereby discouraging the development of an internal locus of control.

This model offers a means by which the therapist can unravel the tangled web of irrational beliefs and interactions that surround symptoms, and it suggests a direction for therapy. It is recommended that the therapist be able to assess both the functional attributes of the family as a human system and the individual cognitive and emotional makeup of its members. By changing the irrational beliefs that sustain dysfunctional organizations and destructive cycles of interaction, the therapist will be able to efficiently and effectively help families overcome their presenting problems and develop the skills necessary to maintain such changes.

References

Andolfi, M. *Family therapy: An interactional approach.* New York: Plenum Press, 1979.
Bergner, R. M. Transforming presenting problems. *Rational Living,* 1979, *14*(1), 13–16.
Ellis, A. A rational-emotive approach to family therapy: I. *Rational Living,* 1978, *13*(2), 15–19.
Ellis, A. A rational-emotive approach to family therapy: II. *Rational Living,* 1979, *14*(1), 23–27.
Ellis, A. Rational-emotive family therapy. In A. M. Horne & M. M. Ohlsen (Eds.), *Family counseling and therapy.* Itasca, Ill.: Peacock, 1982.
Grieger, R., & Boyd, J. *Rational-emotive therapy: A skills-based approach.* New York: Van Nostrand Reinhold, 1980.
Haley, J. *Problem-solving therapy.* San Francisco: Jossey-Bass, 1976.
Haley, J. *Leaving home.* New York: McGraw-Hill, 1980.
Hoffman, L. Breaking the homeostatic cycle. In P. J. Guerin (Ed.), *Family therapy: Theory and practice.* New York: Gardner Press, 1976.
McClellan, T. A., & Stieper, D. R. A structured approach to group marriage counselling. In A. Ellis & R. Grieger (Eds.), *Handbook of rational-emotive therapy.* New York: Springer, 1977.
Minuchin, S. *Families and family therapy.* Cambridge, Mass.: Harvard University Press, 1974.
Minuchin, S., & Fishman, H. C. *Family therapy techniques.* Cambridge, Mass.: Harvard University Press, 1981.
Papp, P. The family who had all the answers. In P. Papp (Ed.), *Family therapy: Full length case studies.* New York: Gardner Press, 1977.
Protinsky, H. Marriage and family therapy: Cognitive and behavioral approaches within a systems framework. *Family Therapy,* 1977, *4*(1), 85–91.
Selvini Palazzoli, M., Boscola, L., Cecchin, G., & Prata, G. *Paradox and counterparadox.* New York: Jason Aronson, 1978.
Stanton, M. D. Strategic approaches to family therapy. In A. S. Gurman & D. P. Kniskern (Eds.), *Handbook of family therapy.* New York: Brunner/Mazel, 1981.
Walen, S., DiGiuseppe, R., & Wessler, R. *A Practitioner's Guide to Rational-Emotive Therapy.* New York: Oxford University Press, 1980.
Watzlawick, P. *Change.* New York: W. W. Norton & Company, 1974.
Wessler, R., & Wessler, R. *The Principles and Practices of Rational-Emotive Therapy.* San Francisco: Jossey-Bass Inc., 1980
Young, H. S. "Is it RET?" *Rational Living,* 1979, 14 (2), 9–17.

14

Working with the Parents and Teachers of Exceptional Children

JOHN F. MCINERNEY

INTRODUCTION

Recent trends in the education of exceptional children, best exemplified in the United States by the Education of all Handicapped Children Act of 1975 (PL94-142), have created special challenges for both parents and teachers. PL94-142 among other things, emphasizes the importance of early intervention for the development of full potential in exceptional children and requires parental participation in all aspects of special education. The literature on early intervention (Hayden & McGinness, 1977; Cunningham & Sloper, 1980) emphasizes the role as change agent played by the parent of the exceptional child. Most early intervention programs include supportive parent-counseling services in recognition of the emotional demands of this role. It is the central contention of this chapter that the basic techniques and philosophy of cognitive-behavioral therapy, principally rational-emotive therapy (RET), can assist those working with these parents. RET provides a rationale for the development of parent-counseling programs based on an empirically derived theory of emotional distress, assessment constructs that allow a clear conceptualization of parents' practical and emotional problems, and a variety of specific therapeutic techniques of proven utility with similar problems in other populations.

JOHN F. MCINERNEY • Director of Pre-School Programs for the Handicapped, Cape May County Schools for Special Services, Cape May Court House, New Jersey 08210.

Parents of exceptional children face many challenges in their daily efforts to meet the needs of their children. The "supportive counseling" so often advocated for such parents, although of some value, makes no attempt to teach parents the relationships among rational thinking, reasonable emotions, and purposive behavior. Although some parents may temporarily feel better with support, they may not as often cope better and, thus, work more effectively with their exceptional child. Parents' distressing negative emotions can result in patterns of behavior that defeat their expressed purposes, which are to stimulate their child for maximum development and to play their part most effectively in the child's total education. As pointed out by Ellis and Grieger (1977, p. 431) cognitive-behavioral approaches, best exemplified by RET, have considerable, although as yet undocumented potential in teaching parents and others working with special children how to manage their own emotions so that they can better meet the child's many requirements for care and stimulation.

Special education and related services are provided within a service delivery system whose critical components include not only parents and children but also special educators and related professionals. The current trends that mandate parent participation, team planning, and teacher accountability are clearly affecting special educators. The parent counseling suggested here will also reciprocally create new challenges for special educators in a given system. They, no less than the parent, seem to experience a variety of distressing negative emotions that can interfere with the effective completion of their important responsibilities. Angry, frequently anxious, or "burned-out" teachers may behave professionally in self-defeating ways that adversely effect their handicapped students, the students' parents, and themselves. Teachers, like parents, however, can be taught to manage their excessive negative emotions and self-defeating behaviors, through individual consultation and group counseling or training experiences based on the principles of a cognitive-behavioral approach such as RET. It is a contention of this chapter that such training has practical utility for special educators, is resource-efficient as "in-service" education, and takes advantage of the demonstrated clinical effectiveness of the RET approach with other populations.

Parents of Exceptional Children

Henry (1981), in his critical review of the literature on parent training, noted that there is an increasing emphasis on efforts to intervene in the problems of children by focusing on working with their parents. A variety of systematic training programs, as well as general theoretical guidelines, have been advanced for helping parents help their children (e.g., Arnold, 1978). To the author's knowledge, none of these approaches have focused on specific techniques for assisting the parents of handicapped children to manage their own thoughts, feelings, and behavior in order to allow them to work better with their child. Within the RET literature, Hauck (1975, 1977), Ellis (1975, 1978), Ellis, Wolfe, and Moseley (1966), and Waters (1980) have provided applications relevant to the problems of parents. Knowledge of these basic contributions is essential to anyone wishing to apply RET and related approaches to the problems of the parents of exceptional children.

BASIC THERAPEUTIC CONSIDERATIONS

Rapport and Relationship Issues

An important initial step in working with the parents of exceptional children involves establishing a relationship in which the parents will honestly share their thoughts and feelings as well as accurately report their behavior. Although RET practitioners do not believe that there is therapeutic magic in "empathic understanding," few would argue that the quality of the relationship is of no initial importance. Many parents of handicapped children have had rather negative experiences with professionals and may be understandably defensive initially. Further, some parents may have misconceptions about therapy, such as viewing it as a treatment imposed on "sick" individuals. Some resent what they see as the implication that they, not their child, require help. It is helpful, then, for the therapist to address these issues from the outset by stating clearly and simply what the parents can reasonably expect from their participation. The following is an example of such a statement:

> Psychologists over the years have found that people don't do difficult jobs very well when they are very upset, angry, or depressed. Your job as a parent of a handicapped child is certainly a difficult one. You'd probably do it better if you learned some proven ways of how to manage your own fears, resentments, and guilty feelings in addition to learning how to stimulate and work with your child. In our work together, I'm going to help you learn to manage your emotions better so you can do a better job with your child.

Statements like this help establish a "self-help" atmosphere. Parents will more readily expect to help themselves by openly discussing their thoughts, feelings, and actions in relation to their child and by sharing ideas on how to change them, because they see a purpose in it.

If parents at least tentatively agree to this effort, then a therapeutic contract can be assumed that gives the therapist permission to proceed with action-oriented, directive therapy toward this goal. In future work, this contract can be reviewed as is appropriate or as is indicated. The author has found group counseling quite effective because discussion among parents with similar practical and emotional difficulties encourages this self-help climate and maintains the focus of the basic contract. It has also been found that voluntary parent participation is most appropriate. Practical considerations that encourage voluntary participation, such as convenient scheduling and transportation, may need to be addressed. One might also find it necessary to try strongly to persuade a given parent to participate in the interest of the child, but requiring parental participation as a condition for service is ultimately self-defeating.

In the interest of initial rapport, it is often useful to reinforce verbal self-disclosure. This can be done in various ways, including direct encouragement through specific discussion topics, personally modeling self-disclosure, and reinforcing self-statements by active listening or an empathic restatement of the parents thoughts and feelings (Walen, DiGiuseppe, & Wessler, 1980, p. 29). A respect for the parents' thoughts and feelings is also communicated by statements accepting them unconditionally as facts, although one may later suggest how they might be changed. Verbalizations that promote the parents' view of the therapist as both credible and trustworthy (Wessler & Wessler, 1980, p. 16) also help to establish rapport. The therapist can state in various ways that he or she has knowledge and expertise relevant to the parents' concerns. It is also important to express and evidence genuine concern about the parent and the handicapped child's progress *per se* without being dependent on this progress. This "trustworthiness" is further aided when the therapist plays other roles in the child's total program and when the parent views the therapist as an "expert" with training and experience in work with handicapped children. As in other applications of RET, the therapist can be most persuasive when seen as an "expert" with relevant training and experience who shares with the parents a genuine concern about the child's and the family's developmental progress.

Disputation

Teaching individuals to recognize and dispute their irrational self-statements, as well as persuading them to do so vigorously and often, is the core of RET. As pointed out by Wessler and Wessler (1980), disputation or "dissuasion" is a matter of both technique and therapeutic philosophy. The inaccurate stereotype of the argumentative RET practitioner not withstanding, the main focus of RET with parents of handicapped children is to persuade them effectively to think and feel differently about the facts of their lives so that they can act in a more satisfying and effective fashion with their child and for their own sakes. Clearly, simply trying to argue parents out of their feelings is shortsighted. Given appropriate attention to relationship issues and the establishment of a contract to proceed, RET with these parents is not significantly different from work with other types of clients. Often the A's, in RET terminology, are different and are often objectively quite painful for the parent, but the philosophy and the techniques of disputation, including cognitive, behavioral, and imaginal strategies (Walen, DiGiuseppe, & Wessler, 1980, p. 96), are essentially the same. Given the often dreadful facts involved in the lives of these parents and their children, philosophically there is even more reason to use all of one's persuasive skills and the most proven methods available to help them learn to minimize their distress and, thus, to cope better with the practical problems of daily living.

Many parents of handicapped children are rather sensitive to what they see as criticism of themselves or their child. Disputation, therefore, is best done sensitively, with attention to both the content and the timing of therapist disputes. Directed, socratic dialogue is ideal for this purpose. Initially, experiential and cognitive disputation of the "inelegant" but pragmatic variety in this context are more effective. At times, parents misperceive disputation as (1) an attempt to get them to deny their strong emotions; (2) a dismissal or trivialization of the emotion (e.g., "How dare he say it's not awful! How would he know how hard it is!"); and/or (3) disapproval of the person for having the distress in the first place. These misperceptions need to be listened for, particularly when disputation fails, and to be corrected either directly or through further dialogue. Sometimes, these reactions, once confirmed, may indicate that some of the relationship issues previously mentioned could use maintenance efforts or that the therapeutic contract requires reexamination. In other cases, it may indicate not so much that disputation has not worked as that it has not worked yet. Persistence is required. In order to maintain interest, while providing sufficient trials to criteria, disputes can be varied in type and content.

The following are some practical suggestions for disputation found to be effective with parents of exceptional children:

1. Use rational self-disclosure to model the disputation process, particularly at the initial stage.

2. When presenting the disputational process didactically (e.g., the ABC-D model), use relevant examples of practical value to the parents in themselves.
3. Use pragmatic, relevant, although "inelegant," cognitive disputes before more abstract philosophical ones.
4. Build in generalization by providing the connection between the disputation process and the content from various practical problems. Use questions to encourage conclusions about generalizations and new applications.
5. Ask for feedback and listen for misperceptions. Be flexible and use all types of disputation, particularly when one approach is unsuccessful.
6. Do not hesitate to use the dissonance between expressed parental values (e.g., "It is important to stimulate my child") and self-defeating ones (e.g., "It should be easy") in disputation.
7. Be persistent, although a "hard-sell" approach seems to be easily dismissed by many parents.
8. Use homework assignments as well as reading oriented toward self-help to augment disputation.

Assessment

DiGiuseppe (1981) pointed out the importance of proper assessment in cognitive therapy with children and their parents. It seems no less important in individual and group work with the parents of exceptional children. One can begin assessment by asking open-ended questions like "What are your major concerns about your child?" Given a modicum of rapport and a supportive atmosphere, most parents will initially tell you things like "I worry about his health" or "I am concerned about her lack of speech." Further guided discussion will help define the dimensions of the parents' concerns. The second question to ask is whether these concerns are reasonable as defined by their effects or whether they are excessive and self-defeating. Considerable judgment on the therapist's part must be exercised here in order to avoid work on "nonproblems" in the parents' frame of reference. A hypothesis-testing approach is recommended whereby data from multiple sources on the frequency, amplitude, and duration of target, hypothesized irrational thoughts, negative feelings, and ineffective or self-defeating behaviors can be elicited. These data can be used to define operationally the cognitive, emotional, and behavioral meaning of the parents' concern and to allow its subsequent exploration. For example, parents may "worry" about their handicapped child's health, meaning cognitively, emotionally, and behaviorally having a realistic concern about a sick child's many physical problems and requirements for medical care. On the other hand, a parent may mean by *worry* excessive preoccupation with an objectively, minor health problem to the point that awfulizing about it creates excessive, dysfunctional fear that prevents the parent from handling and stimulating the child. This type of worry creates distress that is self-defeating, in that the parents' more general goal of helping their child develop as fully as possible is being undermined.

Assessment ought also to address the parents' motivation for change as well as the resources available to assist them, so that intervention can be planned appropriately, with realistic expectations. Initially, many parents are relatively unwilling to give up feelings, even excessively negative ones, that they think they "should" have under the circumstances. They often say something like "You'd feel this way too if your child had brain damage," or "I have to worry all the time; if I don't, nobody else will care." An important determination here is to assess whether the parents are content with their feelings or not. One can ask in a variety of ways, "What are these feelings costing you?" Can these parents, at least intellectually, accept the idea that the other ways or degrees of feeling are possible and desirable for practical reasons? If not, intervention may need to start with very concrete experiential disputes of the parents' belief in the inevitability of their negative emotions. Often, this can be done by introducing these parents to other, more experienced parents with similar children whose feelings are less self-defeating. A realistic inventory might also be made of the resources available for change. For example, is one parent in a couple more open to change than the other? In single-parent situations, are there others involved, such as the grandparents? These others might be involved productively in the counseling process. In other cases, arrangements can be made for support services, or practical problems can be solved so that the parents can participate more actively.

Therapist Variables

As mentioned previously, therapist expertise is an important element in using a persuasive approach like RET. Some degree of training and experience in work with handicapped children and their families, as well as minimum competence in cognitive-behavioral approaches such as RET, is highly desirable. Experience in one or the other area by itself may not be sufficient. Fortunately, such experience is available "on the job," and training in basic RET is readily available through a variety of sources, as well as through personal supervision. Although training and experience clearly improve effectiveness, there is no evidence to the author's knowledge that carefully thought-out implementation of the suggested approach has significant iatrogenic potential even when used by a relatively inexperienced therapist. More than likely, parents will simply dismiss the inexperienced therapist's efforts, which ought to alert the sensitive professional to the need for more training.

A variable of equal import is the therapist's attitude toward the handicapped and their parents. Parents seem to quite easily detect therapist discomfort about the difficult issues encountered. Some are predisposed to say "You can never understand us" and thus dismiss the therapist's efforts. Some honest thought should be given by the therapist to his or her attitude toward the difficult issues likely to be encountered, such as institutionalization; the terminally ill child; controversial "cures" for handicapped children; aggressive, sometimes overtly antiprofessional expressions of parental rights; and strongly critical opinions of other professionals. Factually based opinions appropriately expressed, about any of these or other issues, are not a problem, but unexamined irrational attitudes about what parents of handicapped children "should" be or do usually are. These demands often result in negative emotions in response to some parents, which interfere with communication as well as presenting a model inconsistent with RET.

In addition to this rational self-analysis, therapists would do well to honestly acknowledge their discomfort to parents. Parents value honesty. It can be therapeutic, after rational thought, to forthrightly "own" appropriate discomfort about difficult issues (e.g. "I don't know what I think about putting your child in an institution. I feel uncomfortable when I don't have an answer but I don't have one right now"). After all, this is one of the things we are trying to encourage in parents. Also, parents will more readily accept an honest "I don't know" than a defensively obscure statement. Although some parents may appear to demand an answer for everything, giving them one does not necessarily meet the demand. Even the most difficult factual information about the child can be presented simply and honestly with some forethought and attention to one's own attitudes and emotions about it. Saying, in effect, "I should not tell them what I really think because it will devastate them" is self-defeating because (1) it presents an irrational model inconsistent with the goals of therapy; (2) it often generates excessive negative emotions in the therapist; (3) it reduces "trustworthiness" when the objective facts are ultimately known (e.g., "Why wasn't I told this before?"); and (4) it is often seen as condescension by the parents, as well as ultimately failing to spare their feelings. Clearly, this is not to suggest that parents be indiscriminately confronted with opinions about how badly off they or their child "really" are in the naive hope that these will lead to acceptance. Rather, it suggests rationally and objectively sharing all relevant information, particularly when asked for it.

Programmatic Issues

Program planning requires an assessment of the service delivery system's characteristics and resources in addition to an assessment of parent and therapist variables. Clearly, this context may limit the professional time and resources allocated to a therapeutic program. Although the approach presented here is applicable within an individual consultation or group format, practical considerations might determine which format is selected. The author's preference for structured, time-limited group counseling in combination with brief individual consultation was initially established to accommodate both perceived parent needs and a specific system's resource priorities. A realistic appraisal of the limits of the service provided will help parents, other staff, and the therapist to set realistic goals and expectations. In addition, it can be used to develop guidelines for referral to other therapeutic resources, such as mental health clinics or private practitioners, where appropriate. None of us can be or do everything for everyone. This is particularly true of those of us employed within public settings, such as schools or treatment centers, where funding is limited.

It is further recommended that the therapeutic experiences suggested not be viewed in isolation. Changes in parents will affect other system components and vice versa. An artificial distinction between therapy issues and "school" or "treatment" issues is not helpful. The therapy experience can provide the therapist with valuable information about the system's needs that can have practical import. The author finds no conflict in the therapist's becoming a parent advocate for change, providing that this activity does not replace the parents' own efforts to change the things they can change, that expectations are kept reasonable, and that such activity presents a rational model. These experiences can also suggest training needs in other system components (e.g., special educators, administrators, and community agency personnel). Work with parents can have a maximum impact if such ecological factors are considered, although not to the exclusion of the basic purpose of the therapeutic experience, which aims at individual change.

COMMON THEMES IN WORK WITH PARENTS OF EXCEPTIONAL CHILDREN

Experience in using RET, both in groups and in individual consultation, with parents of younger handicapped children indicates that there are several common problem themes or cognitive road blocks to these parents' more effective work with their children. These themes are, of course, by no means unique to parents with special children, but they seem to occur with somewhat greater frequency and around certain practical issues common to this group. These common themes include self-defeating cognitions surrounding the following issues: denial versus acceptance; fear versus active concern; anger versus rational assertion; and guilt versus self-acceptance.

Denial versus Acceptance

Many authorities suggest that the most common initial response of a parent to having a handicapped child is denial (Cunningham & Sloper, 1980). The psychoanalytic conception of grief and mourning (Solnit & Stark, 1961) is often used descriptively in this context. This view postulates that there are stages of grief that the parents need to work through before being able to "accept" the child. Many parents of handicapped children (Featherstone, 1980) describe initial shock and disbelief as a reaction to their child who is handicapped, but in most cases, this seems gradually to dissipate with time and experience. It seems unwarranted for the therapist to assume that all or even most parents have difficulty accepting their special child after this initial shock. In the author's experience, sometimes the concept of acceptance is misused to explain the child's or parents' lack of progress. Overwhelmed, uncooperative, or simply less able parents are sometimes blamed for this lack of progress by being labeled as unaccepting of their child. Legitimate questioning of professional opinions and authority is at times, similarly punished and dismissed with this label. Misuse of this concept is untherapeutic and self-defeating and is to be avoided. Parents justifiably resent it.

Careful assessment is required to determine if problems in this area exist. This assessment can be done best by looking at the presumed denial's practical consequences. A problem with acceptance might manifest itself most overtly in a parent's reluctance to interact with the handicapped child. In the extreme, this reluctance may constitute child neglect because it prevents the child from receiving needed care and services. Unreasonable reluctance to discuss the child or his or her needs with professionals or family members might also be evident. At times, parents seek numerous "second opinions" in search of a "cure," at the expense of programmatic progress for the child. Further, although some minimization of the child's handicap might be natural in the initial stages and is not necessarily a self-defeating defense, prolonged disregard of the extent of the handicap may cause distress. In all of these instances, it is important to assist parents in looking at the logical consequences of their behavior and in clarifying their thoughts, both rational and irrational, about the child's problem. Denial does produce self-defeating distress for some parents, but rarely are these problems the result of a simple denial of the facts. Often, there are secondary emotional dimensions, such as anger, guilt, or depression, that also require identification and treatment.

The irrational self-statements typical of problems with acceptance include the following: "My child does not have a problem," or "They are wrong; it's not that bad." In one case, the facts are disregarded; in the other, their implication is denied. Often, misinformation or irrational beliefs about the child or in general about people who are handicapped are at the root of these thoughts. Sometimes involved is the irrational belief that children or people who are different are "worthless" as people. Also, the tendency to catastrophize about the handicap may play a part here, for example, "Being handicapped is so awful, such an enormous problem, that I can't think about it." As in most therapeutic problems of denial, after it is ascertained that the facts are known, misconceptions about the facts are best corrected first. For example, all children with cerebral palsey *do not* end up in institutions. Misconceptions can be corrected didactically or experientially. Similarly, irrational attitudes (e.g., "It's awful to be handicapped") can be disputed cognitively and behaviorally. Providing such parents with guided experiences in interacting with their handicapped child, as well as with the parents of other handicapped children, can help counter both basic misconceptions and the "awfulizing" inherent in the problem. Other parents and handicapped adults can present models of acceptance in a way that the didactic presentation and cognitive disputes of the therapist probably cannot. Both their words and their actions can demonstrate that disability does not mean disaster or an inevitably worthless existence.

In experiential disputation, it is probably better not to leave generalization to chance. Providing rational self-statements for the parent by way of clarification and for emphasis promotes generalization. For example, one might say, "You seem to be saying that you can accept your child better and more easily, do what needs to be done, when you say to yourself, 'Well this condition is bad but it's not the end of the world.' In what other situations would that thought help you?" Also, the therapist can provide a model for antiawfulizing self-statements by therapeutically disclosing his or her own ways of thinking about and accepting difficult situations. It is also useful to help the parent question the practical utility of denial. One might ask, "Does it help you in the long run to deny your youngster's condition?" or "Suppose you refuse to see your child as having a problem. How would you be likely to feel and act?" Finally, it is appropriate to discuss acceptance as the frank acknowledgment of those aspects of reality that can not be changed so that one can work on the things that can be changed. This attitude may be approached through directed discussion or in exercises that ask the parents to define the thoughts, feelings, and actions that characterize acceptance. This philosophical attitude, which encompasses the "elegant solution," is a desired long-term goal, albeit one that will never be perfectly achieved and will require daily effort as the parent confronts each new challenge in raising an exceptional child.

Fear versus Active Concern

Featherstone (1980, p. 13), in her unique work, pointed out various types of fear experienced by the parents of handicapped children. She further pointed out that although they are debilitating, they are not necessarily neurotic (p. 24). Many parents, in the author's experience, are quite sensitive about this issue because they see their fears for their child as based on reality. They also, at times, see their fears as a necessary motivator of action in their child's interest. Hara (1975) expressed the outrage felt by many parents of exceptional children when they are told by professionals to "stop worrying." Often, parents seem to see professionals as too easily dismissing their fears as signs of the parents' neurotic maladjustment rather than as an important element in the parents' active concern, which will help the child progress. The cognitive-behavioral approach presented here can be most useful in dealing with this issue because it makes a clear-cut distinction between fear that is excessive—and, as such, debilitating—and concern, which is appropriate and motivating. When properly presented, this approach can teach both a technique for managing self-defeating fears and a philosophy of assertive and active concern.

The RET perspective on fear has been well described by Hauck (1975) and others. It is most important, at first, to encourage an open discussion of fears and to ascertain the parents' perspective on their fears. Then, a didactic but practical presentation can be made of the nature of fear and the role of "awfulizing" thoughts in its genesis. It is then often worthwhile to help the parents to reexamine their fears in the light of this perspective and to begin to make judgments about fear's utility. Open-ended questions about how fear interferes with day-to-day tasks can be helpful. It is important to help establish in the parents' minds the generally "debilitating" nature of excessive fears about the child, while reassuring them that overconcern is human and not "crazy" or "sick" but not always necessary nor useful. Concrete examples from personal experience, as well as from the experience of other parents, can be useful here. Directing parents to various books and articles about the experiences of parents of exceptional children (e.g., Featherstone, 1980; Greenfeld, 1972, 1978) can also be useful at this stage, as can standard works by RET practitioners on the topic of parents' fears (Ellis, 1975; Ellis et al., 1966; Hauck 1972, 1975; Waters, 1980).

Therapy, then, consists of helping parents learn to confront and actively dispute the irrational self-statements behind their fears. A most practical dispute involves variations of the idea that fear, in itself, rarely prevents the feared event from happening. In fact, extreme or constant fear interferes with effective parenting behavior in a variety of ways, which, and in some cases, actually increase the probability of the feared event's occurring. A good example to use might be the parents who fear that their child will be hurt at play with other children and therefore deny the child play experiences. The socially inexperienced or overprotected child is more likely to be hurt by other children. When this child is hurt, the parents' fears are confirmed, and the fear-motivated overprotection increases, with increasingly debilitating effect. The issue of "overprotection" must be dealt with sensitively with parents of exceptional children because, in many cases, a degree of protection beyond what would be appropriate for other children is justified by the objective reality of the child's disability. The concept of *normalization* with regard to maximizing the social development and independence of the handicapped child can be a helpful context within which to present the problem of overprotection. Most parents are in complete agreement with normalization, and the cognitive dissonance between it and fearful, overprotective behavior can be therapeutically utilized.

A misconception about fear held by some parents of handicapped children is that it is a necessary motivator of their behavior. Some appear to believe that, without fear, they would not be motivated to care for or stimulate their child. It is important to point out that this is not the case: few parents would stop caring for their child if their fear were reduced. Also, in some cases, this misconception is the result of confusion over the psychological meaning of the word *fear*. It is useful throughout all RET-oriented work with parents to teach ways of discriminating degrees of emotional experience. Teaching parents a simple 1-to-10 "discomfort" scale for their emotional experiences, including fear, can be helpful in illustrating a psychologically meaningful discrimination between "concern" and "fear." Although this scale is individual for each parent, it can be used as an individual or group exercise quite concretely. On this scale of emotions, 7 through 10 are labeled "excessive fears," 4 through 6 might be called "realistic concerns," and 1 through 3 "small concerns." Parents can be asked to supply feared events for each number of the scale and can then be encouraged to identify the thoughts behind their "excessive fears." The often-used inverted U-shaped gradient depicting the relationship between anxiety and performance can be used to demonstrate that, in many human learning and performance tasks, moderate anxiety, or "realistic concern" on our scale, results in the best performance. Excessive and pervasive fears are not synonymous with the best care of a child.

Helping parents openly discuss and then label and scale their fears is a major therapeutic undertaking in itself, but it is not complete without a demonstration of how to dispute the awfulizing thinking behind the "excessive fear." Awfulizing, put most simply, is taking an anticipated, objectively bad or undesirable event and thinking that it is the worst possible occurrence or more than 100% bad. When fearful, we often grossly overestimate the probability of the dreaded event's happening, incorrectly assume that our fear will prevent its occurrence, and view the event as truly catastrophic, in the same order of magnitude as the very worst tragedies of history. Parents of exceptional children can be encouraged to reexamine the likelihood of feared events' occurring. Although possible, they are rarely certainties. Further, as previously pointed out, excessive fear will not prevent them. Finally, even objectively horrendous events, such as the child's institutionalization or death, are only made worse by awfulizing about them. Even in extreme cases, most parents can think of something worse happening, which, although a small comfort in itself, can help scale down an "excessive" fear to a "realistic concern."

In the author's experience, the fears of the parents of a severely handicapped child are a highly personalized issue. The irrational thinking behind the fears must be disputed sensitivity if one is to avoid trivializing the parents' concerns. Only cognitive-behavioral therapies like RET provide the therapist with the tools for this work. The therapist's work requires considerable empathy with the parents' fears and also the courage and conviction to point out that excessive fears are debilitating and to insist firmly that they are not an inevitable consequence of having even the most severely handicapped child. Human beings have been able to find meaning in even the most dreadful of circumstances, as the experiences of many parents of handicapped children testify (Featherstone, 1980). Empathy is appropriate; sympathetic pity that encourages further awfulizing is therapeutically self-defeating. Such sympathy is rarely appreciated by the parent in the long run.

Once the parents, even tentatively, enter a therapeutic contract to scale down their fears concerning their child, the more practical and forthright the suggestions and practice in doing so, the better. In this context, the ABC-D paradigm of "rational self-analysis" has practical import as well as commonsense appeal to most parents. While fearful thoughts are being extinguished, care should be taken that more rational thinking and problem solving are reinforced. A variety of related cognitive-behavioral techniques can be used as adjuncts in extinguishing fearful thoughts and self-defeating behaviors. Variations of techniques such as systematic desensitization, thought stopping, and implosion or paradoxical intention may be demonstrated, practiced, and suggested as assignments. Rational assertiveness training, to be discussed in more detail in the sections on anger and guilt, is also most useful in providing the behavioral component for expressing realistic concern as an alternative to debilitating, excessive fear.

Anger versus Rational Assertiveness

Anger is a major issue for many of the parents of exceptional children. The enormity of the "injustice" visited on parents by the birth of a handicapped child can, and often does, activate considerable rage. They seem to cry out for someone or something to blame for the injustice. Although this anger at life's unfairness may be a common stage in the grieving process mentioned earlier, it can nonetheless be troublesome for individuals and families. Then, too, people in our society all too often disregard the needs of the handicapped, and discrimination as well as disregard is a fact of life. Thoughtless people ignore, criticize, and pity handicapped children and their parents; each parent's day-to-day experience is full of examples. Medical professionals and educators are objectively "wrong" in their opinions at times. On more occasions, although well meaning, they are not completely open or are thoughtless and condescending in their communication with parents. Institutions are understaffed and school programs underfunded. If extreme anger were an inevitable result of injustice in our imperfect world, then the cosmic as well as the daily injustice experienced by the parents of the handicapped should result in their being in a virtually perpetual state of rage.

Most parents of handicapped children, however, are not in a perpetual state of rage. Like most humans, they anger themselves most frequently when other people are not as they "should" be and, therefore, merit punishment. They mistakenly think anger works when, in reality, it most often generates anger and resentment in others and often guilt in themselves. Parents of exceptional children are not, as a group, less tolerant of frustration than others. They simply are confronted with many more frustrating circumstances, far more frequently. As a result of their personal learning histories, some parents of exceptional children, of course, are unable to tolerate frustration well and frequently upset themselves, whereas others may only periodically get very angry and behave in self-defeating ways. As in other areas, dealing successfully with the anger issue requires a careful assessment of the frequency, the amplitude, and the duration of the response, as well as its pervasiveness, so that intervention may be appropriately directed. But it is an issue of wide applicability in any therapeutic work in this area.

Initial therapeutic work on anger with parents of exceptional children best focuses on creating conditions in which the parent can express anger and resentment openly. Some parents do not allow themselves to express their anger, and others too frequently express it or do so in a displaced way. Some parents are angry at their child but fail to recognize or acknowledge this fact, with self-defeating consequences. The central message to convey at this point is that anger is a natural and human response to frustration, but that it is not inevitable and is often self-defeating. It is important to explore the costs of anger, or many parents may incorrectly confuse anger with "standing up for your rights" and see it as desirable. Anger that is extreme or pervasive (1) has distressing psychosomatic consequences (e.g., high blood pressure and headaches); (2) interferes with problem solving and interpersonal communication, thus leaving frustrating practical problems unsolved after the anger dissipates; (3) interferes with family relationships, particularly when the anger is misdirected or displaced and/or when an angry parental model encourages anger in other family members; and (4) leads to undesirable secondary emotions, such as guilt and depression (Ellis, 1977; Waters, 1980). All of these "costs" can be concretely illustrated by discussion, personal example, and directed role-playing of concrete situations common to the parents' experience.

Once parents see practical reasons for addressing their anger, the rational-emotive psychology of anger (e.g., Hauck, 1974; Ellis, 1977) can be presented. This is done best with practical examples of how we upset ourselves. Rational-emotive imagery can also be used to demonstrate both that it is not events *per se* that upset, because in imagery no "real" events occur, and that demanding, irrational thoughts are largely responsible for our anger. It is important to discuss real-life anger issues whenever possible. If parents are encouraged to make explicit their self-talk in anger situations, they can become further aware of the relationship between one's "shoulds" for people and things and anger. As noted previously, role playing can also be a useful technique in this context. Simple scripts about common, frustrating experiences—such as a visit to the medical specialist, a teacher conference, criticism from a neighbor, or pity from a relative—can be developed by the therapist and played out with instructions for angry and nonangry self-talk. Videotaping these role plays for later discussion has been used with some success. Discussion can focus on the self-talk leading to the anger, the likely logical consequences of the anger, and alternative thoughts and behaviors.

In disputing the angry self-talk of parents of exceptional children, it is often most useful to stay with the concrete facts of a given situation. On a practical, day-to-day level, most parents "stand" a great deal that, at other times, they define as intolerable. Self-talk like "This is awful; I can't stand it," which gives rise to anger, simply is not consistent with the facts, nor is it practical. It is a demand that things or other people not be as they are. The fact that parents in these circumstances do "stand" as well as cope successfully with many things that would drive less experienced individuals into paroxysms of rage can be persistently pointed out. Coping with frustrations by giving up demanding that they not exist, rather than eliminating frustration or anger, is the appropriate focus. Ultimately, a philosophical acceptance of reality is the goal. Abstract discussion about the problem of evil, however, does not seem to further this end significantly; rather, it is mainly through the experience of coping with frustration and injustice with less anger that most parents of exceptional children seem to achieve the frustration tolerance to accept their reality.

It is often important to point out to parents that acceptance of unjust reality does not mean approval of it. Rather, it allows effort, often spent in blaming others, to be spent in more constructive activity to change injustice. Even "righteous anger" can be costly in personal terms and is often self-defeating, no matter how "just" the cause. Therapeutic treatment of anger is not complete without providing experience and practice in rational assertion as an alternative to anger. Rational, assertive behavior can be encouraged through the well-established techniques of rational assertiveness training described in detail in several sources (Hauck, 1979; Jakubowski & Lange, 1978; Lange & Jakubowski, 1976). The situations used in this training can easily be tailored by the therapist to reflect experiences common to the parents of exceptional children. With thought, concrete assignments for trying out rational assertive behavior can also be developed. It should be emphasized that annoyance, not rage, most often results in assertive behavior. Also, assertiveness is no guarantee of getting what one wants, but it generally feels better and works better than angry demands.

Guilt versus Self-Acceptance

Many parents of handicapped children report feelings of guilt about their child's handicap, particularly early in the child's life. Some parents believe quite strongly that they could have and should have done something to prevent the child's disability. Despite the uncertain etiology of many handicapping conditions, some parents believe that their child is being punished because of their own inadequacy. This initial struggle with guilt may be a time-dependent part of the grieving process discussed earlier, but in some cases, the problem generalizes to other areas and results in one or both parents' exhibiting symptoms of clinical depression. Because of this danger, frank discussion of the problem of guilt from the RET perspective ought to be included in virtually all therapeutic work with parents of exceptional children. More than the other negative emotions, the irrational self-talk at the root of guilt seems to respond only to vigorous, persistent, and pragmatic disputation (Ellis & Harper, 1975).

The present emphasis on parent involvement in important aspects of the exceptional child's treatment may also unintentionally contribute to the parents' feelings of guilt and inadequacy. Some professionals contribute to what Featherstone (1980) called the "fantasy of parental omnipotence" not only by blaming parents for their child's problems, but also by demanding too much involvement from them. For parents who already tend to be self-blaming, this added blame is often clearly iatrogenic. Parental responsibilities for their child are a reality and are best treated as such. When a parent believes that he or she is responsible for virtually everything that happens to the child, then guilt seems inescapable. Parental involvement is important—and, in many cases, critical—to a child's maximum development, but there is simply no evidence that this responsibility justifies self-blame or blame by others for a child's performance. On a practical level, guilt is a notoriously poor motivator of behavior. It simply has too many other costs to be effective in the long run. It is important in this regard, then, to help both parents and other people in the service delivery system to learn to think rationally about the concept of responsibility.

Rational thinking about responsibility can be reinforced in a variety of ways. Didactic exposition of RET perspective on depression (Ellis & Harper, 1975; Hauck, 1973) and the psychological difference between guilt and responsibility is useful. Responsibility can be explained as a concept descriptive of the relationship between identifiable actions and their probable consequences. Further, responsibility also implies that the consequences of actions are usually identifiable before hand, and that actions are the subject of some choice on our part. When people fail to live up to these types of responsibilities, the logical consequences constitute the major cost of acting irresponsibly. Guilt, on the other hand, implies much more than responsibility. Guilt is a metaphysical and absolutistic concept. It implies that human beings should omnipotently know the right thing to do in every situation and invariably do it. When they do not, they have done something so awful that they lose all worth or value as persons and are in effect "damned" for all time.

Some of the things that the parents of exceptional children feel guilty about result from misinformation about their child's disability. More often, guilt results from an impossibly broad definition of their responsibilities. Through therapeutic dialogue, misconceptions can be factually corrected, and a more realist conception of responsibility can be developed. For example, parents sometimes say, "I feel guilty because I'm not doing enough for my child." It is useful, then, to question concretely what they mean by "enough." Often "enough" in the parents' frame of reference means "everything." In a variety of concrete ways, the impossibility of doing virtually everything can be pointed out. Ask the parent to list "everything." You can always suggest one more thing for the list. Further, the self-defeating nature of obsessing about doing everything can be made readily apparent to most people. "Do you want to spend all your time and energy thinking about everything that you should have done but haven't or in doing those important things that can be done?" Even when the inevitable mistakes are made, there is no utility in making a bad situation worse by feeling guilty about it. An attitude of self-acceptance whereby the parent learns to evaluate his or her behavior only in terms of its usefulness rather than for what it is incorrectly assumed to say about their personal worth ought to be reinforced.

Many parents are not aware of all that they are doing to cope. An assignment to keep a "coping log" in which they are instructed to list in simple behavioral terms all their daily accomplishments for the child, the family, or themselves can be useful. This and other variations of Beck's pleasure and mastery technique (Beck, Rush, Shaw, & Emery, 1979) can be most useful, because, in many cases, the daily accomplishments of parents of exceptional children are objectively quite remarkable, although often disregarded or devalued by themselves. The "coping log" provides evidence that contradicts their belief that they are "failures." Most parents accomplish a host of other things not directly related to the handicapped child. They care for other children in the family. They hold full- or part-time jobs. They run a household. Why are these less important accomplishments? Clearly, it all depends on the view one takes of them. That, of course, is the major point to get across: it does depend largely on how one chooses to view them.

Some problems of guilt do not directly involve the exceptional child; they are focused on other family members. The spouse or the other children who get less attention because the requirements of the special child's care or treatment are the focus. In some cases, this attitude is the result of an unstated choice to tolerate this "lesser guilt" rather than guilt resulting from doing even a little bit less for the exceptional child. Sometimes this guilt is the result of an exaggerated view of the effect of this presumed neglect on other family members. Encouragement to view this effect more objectively and to test it out by objective discussion with other family members can be helpful. In another sense, this type of guilt presents a classic "double bind," which hinges on the parents' excessive demand on themselves that they do virtually everything for everyone. The objective impossibility of this irrational demand can be pointed out as suggested earlier. Further, the self-defeating practical consequences of this "damned if you do, damned if you don't" situation can be concretely explicated by exercises in consequential thinking.

It should also be pointed out, as an alternative approach to this problem, that, in some cases, parents' guilt-driven obsession to do "everything" for their exceptional child does lead to a relative neglect of other family members. The self-defeating long-range consequences of those choices need to be explicated. The self-defeating imbalance in the distribution of attention in the family of the exceptional child can be best addressed by focusing on both reducing the guilt-driven overinvolvement in the exceptional child and providing behavioral assignments to redistribute attention. Although resistance can be expected, the likely reduction in distressing guilt and family tension provides its own reinforcement once the process is begun.

Parents troubled by problems of guilt in relation to their exceptional child have most often lost perspective on their own value as persons. They often do not see themselves as being of any value except in relation to their role as agents for the exceptional child. Such a view may be accompanied by the clinical symptoms of depression. Sexual, marital, and family adjustment problems are also related considerations. In these extreme cases, the cognitive-behavioral approaches used in the treatment of depression are most appropriate. The self-defeating nature of depression and its helplessness often need to be concretely and vigorously pointed out. The contradiction involved in devaluing oneself to the point of dysfunction, which prevents the accomplishment of the original goal of helping the exceptional child to develop fully, can be made explicit. This overinvolvement to the point of clinical depression can also be disputed experientially by homework assignments to "be good to yourself" while explicating the important psychological difference between "selfishness" and "self-interest." Even with parents relatively little troubled by depression, there is some prophylactic value in dialogue concerning this psychologically meaningful discrimination.

Summary and Conclusions

The techniques and philosophy of the cognitive-behavioral perspective, particularly those of RET, can be successfully applied to the problems presented by the parents of exceptional children. Their value stems from the following: (1) these approaches make no assumption of psychopathology on the part of the parent and no absolutistic value judgments about what parents of exceptional children "should" do for themselves or their families; (2) because of their educational and directive emphasis, including both didactic and experiential disputation of self-defeating thoughts, feelings, and actions, they are readily integrated into a "self-help" format acceptable to parents; (3) because of their relative emphasis on directly teaching practical skills of thought and emotion, most parents view these approaches as being of practical value in day-to-day life; (4) because these approaches help to shape psychologically meaningful discriminations between excessive, self-defeating emotions and realistic but strongly felt concern that impels action, they are consistent with often-needed assertion on the part of parents; and (5) because of their straightforward content and technique, these approaches are most amenable to time-limited individual and group approaches to treatment and are cost effective in a variety of service delivery contexts.

The cognitive-behavioral techniques and philosophy of treatment presented in this section are by no means unique; rather, they are independent variations of others present in the literature on the practice of RET (Hauck, 1980; Walen *et al.*, 1980; Wessler & Wessler, 1980). Some of the ideas suggested (e.g., scaling "worry" or other negative emotions, role-playing anger as well as rational concern and assertion, and the "coping log") have been of considerable practical utility in the author's practice with the parents of exceptional children. At present, no controlled empirical research on the relative merits of the approach suggested is available. The author considers the preliminary application of these techniques encouraging and believes that they warrant further systematic research. Current efforts are being focused on the development of a treatment manual to assist in independent and systematic investigation in this area of application.

Teachers of Exceptional Children

Special educators, although usually technically competent in their area of expertise, appear to have received relatively little training for the emotional demands of their complex role. Special-education teachers today are expected not only to plan and implement individualized classroom instruction for assigned students but also to participate with parents, administrators, and various diagnostic specialists in team planning and decision making. As in many interpersonal communication and decision-making situations, this is often no simple process. At times, the ultimate goal of the process is obscured by the irrational demands of the participants on each other and the excessive negative emotions generated, as well as the self-defeating patterns of verbal behavior evidenced. Special educators have been committed to "in-service" training for staff for some time, but the issue of emotional survival skills has been rarely addressed. Continuing professional development is often mandated by sources of funding. If training or therapeutic experiences based on RET are of value to parents of exceptional children, they are also likely to be of value to the educators working with these same children.

Experience as a consultant to both teachers and parents of special children has suggested that they share several emotional and practical problems. Teachers, like some parents, occasionally find it hard to motivate themselves to follow through consistently on simple, often commonsense behavioral recommendations. Teachers' attitudes and the self-defeating emotions that may be generated (Grieger, 1972) are important if often neglected variables in the success of educational consultation, just as they are in work with parents. When one talks frankly to special educators about their feelings about themselves and their jobs, they describe feelings not unlike those experienced by the parents of their students. These feelings include fear of criticism, their own fear of failing the child, guilt over not doing "enough," anger at the "injustice" of the child's condition, and anger at those others who seem to expect so much but who do not do all they "should." Like the parents of special children and other helping professionals, they run a higher than average risk of burnout, with its deteriorating job performance and symptoms of depression. The burnout issue alone, particularly today when it is so topical in education, justifies providing for special educators therapeutic experiences like those previously described for parents. Most of us who use RET or other cognitive-behavioral techniques professionally have also found them personally relevant and powerfully therapeutic in personal stress management. The results ought to be similar for special educators, with concomitant improvement in consistent job performance, self-reported job satisfaction, and efficiency in service delivery.

Therapeutic and Programmatic Considerations

Experience in teaching RET to special educators in individual consultation as well as group counseling experiences suggests that a few basic considerations should be addressed in addition to those already outlined for parents. Not unlike the parents of exceptional children, special educators are pragmatists. They seem to be most receptive to training when they see it as of immediate relevance to their day-to-day jobs. For that reason, it is important to establish clearly the relationship between the therapeutic training experiences provided and better or more satisfying work with their students. Practical examples will illustrate the self-defeating nature of excessive negative emotions and particularly how they can interfere with effective teaching. The author has had some success with this approach in the context of sessions on stress management or burnout. Most special educators have had experiences that help them to relate to this phenomenon. It is, of course, rather important to establish a supportive atmosphere and adequate rapport in order to encourage teachers to openly discuss their "distress." Therefore, the consultant's role in the therapeutic training process may need to be clearly established, particularly when the consultant either has or is viewed as having some supervisory responsibilities in the service delivery system. Further, the consultant ought to be comfortable with self-revelation in order to encourage it in others.

The training suggested appears to be quite efficiently and effectively done in a group setting. The group setting lends itself to the development of a supportive atmosphere and also allows an efficient use of scarce resources, particularly teachers' time. It is also probably best if participation in the group is voluntary. It is rather absurd to "force" people to learn to manage their emotions. Teachers whose burnout or job dysfunction is such that job action is imminent are supervisory problems that ought to be appropriately referred to the service delivery system's employee-assistance program or to a private therapist. The author has found it useful to make a clear distinction between the training being provided and what most staff see as psychotherapy. Although the distinction is somewhat artificial and is a matter of degree from the perspective of RET, the clear message that the experience being provided is oriented to job performance and job problems rather than "personal problems" or "deep personality conflicts" seems to encourage participation. For similar reasons, a time-limited format with some established agenda of topics to structure participation has been found most effective. A solely didactic approach using a lecture format has had less impact than a group in which content, process (including didactic and experiential disputation), and experience applied between group sessions have been balanced. A job-problem-centered, time-limited RET group also has the flexibility to include training in other cognitive-behavioral skills, such as rational assertiveness, relaxation training, and behavioral self-management.

The basic technique and philosophy of cognitive-behavioral therapy, chiefly RET, can also be effectively applied in individual consultation with special educators. They can be taught in a relatively short period of time to think more rationally about the problem under discussion. This initial focus in consultation on the "problem about the problem" (e.g., excessive anger at a hyperactive, behaviorally disturbed child) must be done tactfully, lest the teacher view it as criticism. But in the vast majority of cases, reduced negative emotion assists in practical-problem solving. Single-session intervention of this type can be quite successful, particularly within the context of systematic group training in the rational management of negative emotions and self-defeating behaviors. In both individual and group work, much of what has already been said about parents concerning disputation, assessment, and relationship issues also applies to special educators.

Common Themes Expressed by Teachers

Special teachers often experience self-defeating fear when they believe that they are being evaluated negatively. They appear to fear criticism because of three somewhat distinct irrational self-statements: (1) "I must be approved of at all times, I've earned it by my care for the handicapped child"; (2) "Criticism is so devastating that I can't stand it"; and (3) "I really must fear this devastation in order to prevent it." These self-statements can be disputed by directed dialogue, including questions concerning the absolute need for approval, its presumed catastrophic effect on a person, and the value of worry in preventing criticism. The idea of the special educator as "suffering servant" who has somehow earned complete remission from criticism also needs to be disputed. These self-statements can also be disputed experientially by role-playing common situations in which criticism occurs (e.g., supervisory conferences, parent conference, and critical comments by colleague), with irrational instructions as well as more rational coping self-statements. Cognitive-behavioral rehearsal for rebutting criticism might also be practiced. Specific homework assignments to do an ABC analysis of several criticism situations and later to discuss them are important. Paradoxical instruction to go out and "collect" minor criticism while covertly disputing its catastrophic effect might also be carefully suggested.

Anger is a frequently discussed issue. Teachers often anger themselves at colleagues, administrators, parents, and their students in a variety of contexts. The irrational self-statements behind this anger are (1) "They should not do this"; (2) "I can't stand it when they do"; and (3) "They should be punished for being so evil, and so they won't do it again." The basic disputes for these ideas are well known (Bard, 1980; Ellis, 1977; Waters, 1980); suffice it to say, that special teachers no less than the rest of us often need to be most vigorously persuaded that anger is self-defeating. It is very important to stay with the inelegant solution with questions like "Did your anger change his behavior?" and "Did she ever criticize you again?" until the logical consequences of anger are appreciated. This is important because, let's face it, anger does sometimes work in the short run. Some attention to the long-range personal consequences of frequent, excessive anger in terms of psychosomatic distress, fatigue, impaired interpersonal experiences, and guilt feelings—in short, all the symptoms of burnout—ought to be focused on. It has also been found to be successful to very concretely discuss alternatives to anger in terms of both rational thinking and assertive behavior. There is a host of frustrations involved in special education, and therefore, coping with frustration philosophically and behaviorally is an all-important skill.

Related to anger is the problem of blame. Other-blaming results in anger, and self-blame or self-damning begets guilt and depression. The rational alternative to blame is acceptance of reality while trying to change what can be changed. This is a philosophical point best presented both didactically and from a practical perspective. The essential point here is that human beings largely create their own emotions, an idea that can be demonstrated effectively through rational-emotive imagery and other examples. One is responsible for one's own emotions. This important point, once acknowledged, allows a more complete consideration of the anger–guilt cycle that results in distress for many special educators, particularly when they anger themselves at people whom they "should" not get angry, most especially their handicapped students. Unacknowledged anger at the child is often misdirected at the child's parents. The guilt stemming from this self-defined unacceptable anger leads to a variety of self-defeating compensations that have practical consequences for the child's behavior and adjustment. Unconditional self-acceptance is the elegant solution to the problem. On a more immediate level, less self-rating or self-damning for one's shortcomings can break up the anger–guilt cycle (e.g., "I am angry; I'd better calm myself down" rather than "I'm such a rotten teacher and person for being angry at this poor kid").

As noted, self-acceptance is the antidote for depression and guilt. In a realistic way, this means giving up self-rating as well as rethinking the concept of self-esteem. Many special educators, as achievement-oriented, educated individuals, have difficulty with this. A useful dispute with many has been found to direct their attention to their implicit conception of human worth. By their actions, specifically their work with and care for the handicapped, they evidence an implicit unconditional regard for human beings. Some work long hours, because "it's the right thing to do," with a severely disabled child who clearly is never going to amount to much in the eyes of the world. They do not as often apply their overwhelming demands on themselves to their students. Performance does not equal "worth" for the child, but it does for the teacher. Explicating this double standard can provide a dispute of self-damning tendencies. If it is done sensitively but forthrightly, it can create cognitive dissonance, which can be directed toward a more self-accepting attitude. Sometimes this approach backfires with extreme perfectionists, who then tell themselves, "Well, of course, I have to expect more of myself because I can do more" and proceed to damn themselves for doing anything less than virtually "everything." Practical disputes about the futility of this attitude (e.g., "Is it possible to do everything?" "What is enough?") and its limited utility (e.g., "How does demanding more of yourself and damning yourself for anything less than perfection help you do more?") are most appropriate in these instances. Self-acceptance is, after all, a choice, but one to be highly recommended because of its practical consequences.

A final area of some import for special educators involves strategies for rational problem-solving. These can be presented in a structured way, with emphasis on removing the largely emotional "problem about the problem" through rational thinking prior to tackling the practical issue. For example, a teacher who is facing an objectively very difficult parent conference becomes quite anxious and defensive. This reaction clearly has the potential to make an already difficult situation far worse.

Instruction and practice in dealing with this and similar situations can be provided.

SUMMARY

Special educators, like the parents of exceptional children, appear to benefit from group training and individual consultation grounded in cognitive-behavioral techniques like RET. This approach has the advantage of efficiency; flexibility as to the problems focused on; practical value as seen by participants; and demonstrated effectiveness with other populations. It is amenable to use in the satisfaction of existing requirements for staff training and provides a methodology that addresses staff concerns about burnout and stress management.

FUTURE DIRECTIONS

Future applications of the principles of cognitive-behavior therapies like RET to the problems of those working with handicapped children might fruitfully focus on integrating the therapeutic experiences provided for both parents and special educators in order to facilitate parent–teacher communication and joint-problem-solving skills. Parents could be used in teacher training and vice versa within the RET context in order to clarify each one's role and points of view. The systemwide consequences of this approach ought to be evaluated for its effectiveness in improving parent–teacher educational planning, for changes in attitude toward the handicapped, and for its ability to implement systemwide educational innovation, such as efforts to remove inappropriate labels from special children. Related applications in areas involving staff supervision, employee assistance programming, the training of parents as volunteers, and therapeutic experiences for the siblings of handicapped children can also be explored. These applications merit full exploration because, in these days of diminishing resources in special education, making the most of what resources are available and committed—namely, parents and teachers—is increasingly important.

REFERENCES

Arnold, L. E. (Ed.). *Helping parents help their children*. New York: Brunner/Mazel, 1978.
Bard, J. A. *Rational emotive therapy in practice*. Champaign, Ill.: Research Press, 1980.

Beck, A. T., Rush, A. J., Shaw, B. F., & Emery, G. *Cognitive therapy of depression.* New York: Guilford Press, 1979.

Cunningham, C., & Sloper, P. *Helping your exceptional baby—A practical and honest approach to raising a mentally handicapped child.* New York: Pantheon, 1980.

DiGiuseppe, R. Cognitive therapy with children. In G. Enery, S. D. Hollon, & R. C. Bedrosian (Eds.), *New directions in cognitive therapy.* New York: Guilford Press, 1981.

Ellis, A. *How to live with a "neurotic."* New York: Crown, 1957. Rev. ed., 1975.

Ellis, A. *How to live with and without anger.* New York: Reader's Digest Press, 1977.

Ellis, A. Rational-emotive guidance. In L. E. Arnold (Ed.), *Helping parents help their children.* New York: Brunner/Mazel, 1978.

Ellis, A., & Grieger, R. The present and the future of RET. In A. Ellis & R. Grieger, (Eds.), *Handbook of rational-emotive therapy.* New York: Springer, 1977.

Ellis, A., & Harper, R. *A new guide to rational living.* Englewood Cliffs, N.J.: Prentice-Hall, 1975.

Ellis, A., Wolfe, J. L., & Moseley, S. *How to raise an emotionally healthy, happy child.* Hollywood, Calif.: Wilshire, 1966.

Featherstone, H. *A difference in the family—Life with a disabled child.* New York: Basic Books, 1980.

Greenfeld, J. *A child called Noah.* New York: Holt, Rinehart & Winston, 1972.

Greenfeld, J. *A place for Noah.* New York: Holt, Rinehart & Winston, 1978.

Grieger, R. M. Teacher attitudes as a variable in behavior modification consultation. *Journal of School Psychology,* 1972, *10,* 279–287.

Hauck, P. A. *The rational management of children.* Roslyn Heights, N.Y.: Libra, 1972.

Hauck, P. A. *Overcoming depression.* Philadelphia: Westminster Press, 1973.

Hauck, P. A. *Overcoming frustration and anger.* Philadelphia: Westminster Press, 1974.

Hauck, P. A. *Overcoming worry and fear.* Philadelphia: Westminster Press, 1975.

Hauck, P. A. Irrational parenting styles. In A. Ellis & R. Grieger (Eds.), *Handbook of rational-emotive therapy.* New York: Springer, 1977.

Hauck, P. A. *How to stand up to yourself.* Philadelphia: Westminster Press, 1979.

Hauck, P. A. *Brief counseling with RET.* Philadelphia: Westminster Press, 1980.

Hara, V. Stop worrying? Nonsense! *The Exceptional Parent,* Jan.–Feb., 1975, *5,* 12–15.

Hayden, A. H., & McGinness, G. D. *Educational programming for the severely retarded.* Reston, Va.: Council for Exceptional Children, 1977.

Henry, S. A. Current dimensions of parent training. *School Psychology Review,* 1981, *10*(1), 4–14.

Jakubowski, P., & Lange, A. J. *The assertive option: Your rights and responsibilities.* Champaign, Ill.: Research Press, 1978.

Lange, A. J., & Jakubowski, P. *Responsible assertive behavior: Cognitive-behavioral procedures for trainers.* Champaign, Ill.: Research Press, 1976.

Solnit, A. J., & Stark, M. H. Mourning and the birth of a defective child. *Psychoanalytic Study of the Child,* 1961, *16,* 523–537.

Walen, S. R., DiGiuseppe, R., & Wessler, R. L. *A practitioner's guide to rational-emotive therapy.* New York: Oxford University Press, 1980.

Waters, V. *Rational stories for children—Rational Parenting Series.* New York: Institute for Rational Living, 1980.

Wessler, R. A., & Wessler, R. L. *The principles and practice of rational-emotive therapy.* San Francisco: Jossey-Bass, 1980.

15

Helping Teachers Cope With Stress
A Rational-Emotive Approach

MICHAEL E. BERNARD, MARIE R. JOYCE, AND
PAMELA M. ROSEWARNE

> *Do you like your job?*
> Yes, I do. (But) I find it a big strain.
> *What is it about it (that is) a strain?*
> I find—the psychological and even physical confrontation with kids constantly. In the first year of teaching, the strain is immense, if you care at all about what you are doing the strain is immense. And I truly felt at one stage at least during my first year that I was really going insane—I mean that quite seriously. I was losing my sense of judgment. Tiny little incidents became terrible catastrophes, and I really was beginning to go off the rails mentally and emotionally. I would feel like bursting into tears at the drop of a hat.
> (From Connell, Ashenden, Kessler, & Dowsett, 1982, pp. 102–103)

There is little question that teaching is an extremely stressful profession. The short-term signs (e.g., absenteeism) and long-term effects (e.g., burnout) of stress are in evidence throughout all levels of our educational system. It is also clear that there are wide individual differences in the way teachers handle the same sources of stress. Some teachers, for example, find maintaining control of the classroom an excruciatingly demanding task, whereas others regard discipline as a responsibility that they handle routinely with only a minimum of hassle. Our observa-

---

MICHAEL E. BERNARD • Department of Education, University of Melbourne, Victoria, 3052 Australia.   MARIE R. JOYCE • Department of Education, University of Melbourne, Victoria, 3052 Australia.   PAMELA M. ROSEWARNE • Counseling, Guidance and Clinical Services, Victoria Education Department, Victoria, 3052 Australia.

tion of teachers is that they vary a great deal both in terms of the types of pressures, responsibilities, and conflicts that occasion stress and in the frequency, intensity, and duration of the stress they experience. Moreover, teachers are remarkably different in their capacities to tolerate stress. Although there have been several programs developed to help teachers acquire the teaching and interpersonal skills that will enable them to handle stressful situations more effectively, very few current programs that we know of are designed to provide teachers with an understanding of and techniques for reducing their tension and stress.

We believe that rational-emotive therapy (RET) provides teachers with a basis for coping with stress so that they are able to function more effectively in their jobs. This chapter presents a framework that mental health practitioners (e.g., school psychologists and counselors) can use to introduce the principles and practice of RET to teachers. Specifically, we show how RET can be introduced both as a part of teacher education and in in-service staff-development programs. We introduce our program by presenting a RET analysis of teacher stress.

THE STRESSES OF TEACHING

The reader may be interested in knowing that the area of teacher stress has not been heavily researched. Although there has been a variety of studies over the past 50 years that have examined emotional problems in teachers (e.g., Hicks, 1933), few studies have examined the effects of "psychologically based" interventions in reducing teacher anxiety. In a comprehensive review, Coates and Thoresen (1976) reported that 78% of 2,290 teachers surveyed by the National Education Association in the United States in 1967 indicated that they experienced stress at a moderate or considerable level. These authors chose to follow historical precedent by defining teacher stress in terms of anxiety—a tradition we shall depart from. In their article in the *Review of Educational Research*, they indicated that the source of anxiety in classroom teachers differs in terms of the number of years of teaching experience (see Tables 1 and 2). In summarizing the studies they reviewed, they concluded that (1) anxiety appears to occur with considerable frequency and is an important concern among beginning and experienced teachers; (2) teacher anxiety appears to be associated with a variety of personal, social, and physical conditions; (3) the specific effects of teacher anxiety on other teacher behaviors and on student actions, although widely studied and apparently important, remain unknown, largely because of the measuring

TABLE 1. Summary of Beginning Teachers' Reported Sources of Anxiety

Handling problems of pupil control and discipline	Introducing new ideas to stimulate discussion
Adjusting to deficiencies in school equipment, physical conditions, and materials	Cheating by students
	Relations with parents
	Methods of evaluating teaching
Adjusting to teaching assignment	Knowing enough to teach units
Adapting to needs, interests, and abilities of pupils	Personality conflicts with supervising teachers
Motivating pupil interest and response	Difficult relations with students
Contractual stipulations	Concerns with self
Orientation to school system	Method of providing feedback about teaching
Faculty relations	
Grading papers	Viewing teaching performance on videotape
Arguing over test answers	
Restlessness of students	
Attending college and doing student teaching at the same time	

Note. Adapted from Coates and Thoresen (1976, pp. 162–164).

operations employed; and (4) systematic desensitization and instruction in teaching techniques may reduce the teacher anxiety (pp. 175–176). In addition, these authors suggested that cognitive rational restructuring holds a great deal of promise for helping teachers to manage personal stress and tension that might otherwise interfere with effective teaching. We hope that this chapter begins to fulfill this promise.

TABLE 2. Summary of Experienced Teachers' Reported Sources of Anxiety

Classroom interruptions: bulletins, announcements, special events	Incompatible relationship with supervisor
Individualizing instruction	Assignment of paraprofessional duties
Promotion standards	Discipline problems
Clerical activities	Obtaining funds for purchase of extra classroom aids
Size of individual class	
Type of pupil	Finding time for creative teaching
Inadequate school facilities	Ability to understand pupils' capacities, to specify objectives for them, to assess their gain, and to determine pupils' difficulties and gains
Extracurricular responsibilities	
Instructional planning	
Inadequate salary	

Note. Adapted from Coates and Thoresen (1976, pp. 166–167).

RET Analysis of Teacher Stress

Stress is a very broad construct that can be viewed from an RET perspective in terms of three dimensions of human experience: cognition, emotion, and behavior. In terms of cognition, *stress can be seen as a function of an individual's interpretation of a situation as demanding or threatening, of the individual's expectation of being able to cope with the perceived demand or threat, and of the individual's appraisal both of the initial perception of a demand or threat and of the personal and interpersonal consequences of the demand or threat.* The intensity of a stress reaction can be explained in terms of the ratio between the magnitude of the perceived demand or threat to the perceived coping resources, as well as the strength of the individual's belief that failure to cope is intolerable and unacceptable. Self-defeating and emotion-arousing appraisals derive from an individual's faulty belief system in general and from specific irrational beliefs in particular. The individual's "philosophy of life" and the extent to which the individual rigidly and unconditionally imposes absolutistic demands (shoulds, oughts, and musts) can be seen to be at the root of stress.

The interpretation of a situation as demanding may be based on *external circumstances* that can be seen objectively to require the individual to perform, act, and adapt in a certain way (e.g., work "demands"). Alternatively, "demands" may have a largely internal origin stemming from the individual's own self-perceived personal needs, standards, and expectations, which translate into demands that the individual makes of himself or herself, others, or the world. Perceived "threats" can be either physical or psychosocial. Although we accept that certain stresses involving physical deprivations and pain may directly lead to stress reactions, we believe that most psychosocial stress derives from the manner in which the individual thinks about and appraises a situation. Ellis (1978b) wrote:

> A fundamental premise of RET (and many other forms of cognitive-behavior therapy) states that stressful conditions do not exist in their own right but vary significantly in relation to the perceptions and cognitions of those who react to these conditions. This does not mean that *no* set of circumstances has intrinsically stressful predicaments attached to it, for a few almost unquestionably do. . . . In the case of ordinary or moderate "stressful" situations, people choose, decide, or create their own feelings of anxiety, depression, and self-downing (which occur at point C) by picking a certain kind of Belief system (at point B) about the situations, or Activating Events, that happen to them (at point A). Their disturbed reactions—or emotional Consequences—at C follow directly from their Beliefs; and although what happens to them at A significantly *contributes* to it, it hardly *causes* C. (pp. 210–211)

A more thorough discussion of the ABC's of RET is presented later in this chapter.

Stress reactions can be observed in the emotional arousal that accompanies and largely derives from the individual's interpretations and appraisals. In this sense, stress reactions can be equated with emotional arousal. Unhealthy emotional reactions lead to behavioral patterns that interfere with the individual's achievement of short-term and/or long-term goals. Emotional overarousal and associated behavioral problems (e.g., drinking) can also be seen to lead to adverse health consequences.

There are two types of stress reactions that RET recognizes. First, there are reactions that arise from specific antecedent events. Second, there is stress that is occasioned by nonspecific and general demands for high levels of work-related and personal performance that severely "tax one's system." In this chapter, we are mostly concerned with the former type, though we do spend some time analyzing the irrational beliefs of teachers that underlie both types of stress.

Let us consider the stress reaction of anger as expressed in a teacher, Mr. Russell. Mr. Russell frequently gets extremely angry when students do not comply with his instructions. His anger is unhealthy because he tends to blow his wind into his students' sails by arguing and yelling. He has a reputation with the principal of not being able to control his class. Several complaints have been raised by parents—specifically, the number of times their children get sent out of the room. Mr. Russell's health can be described as "fragile." He experiences frequent tension headaches and has been taking more and more time off from school. The origins of his stress can be observed in the way he thought about Chris, who continued to talk to his neighbors in class even after Mr. Russell asked him not to do so. Mr. Russell interpreted Chris's noncompliance as follows: "Chris is deliberately disobeying me again. He's upsetting me as well as the rest of the class. This is unfair. If I don't shut him up, the rest of the class will think I'm weak. He's got no right to behave that way. I'll show him and everyone else who's boss." The external threat in this situation was having to confront Chris, and the demand was to establish classroom control. Mr. Russell's appraisal of his interpretation was "Chris should behave properly and fairly at all times, and when he doesn't, I can't stand him and I find him intolerable." This appraisal escalated into extreme anger the irritation he experienced as a consequence of his interpretation. Underlying his appraisal was an overall belief that his self-worth as a person could be defined by his teaching performance, that any person who does something wrong deserves to be blamed and condemned, that other people control his emotions, and, most probably, that life should be pleasant and without frustration.

We do not mean to imply that all stress is unhealthy. We believe stress may motivate, arouse, and fuel the intellectual machinery. For tasks that demand extreme effort and persistence (e.g., writing a chapter), there appears to be, as Clark Hull (1951) has hypothesized, a linear relationship between stress and performance. On the other hand, for interpersonal tasks that require spontaneous problem-solving, interpersonal sensitivity, and flexibility (e.g., maintaining classroom discipline), we endorse the old Yerkes-Dobson inverted-U hypothesis, which associates too little or too much arousal with poor performance, whereas optimal performance is associated with moderate levels of stress.

RET maintains that rational beliefs lead to realistic appraisals of reality and, as a consequence, emotions (sorrow, disappointment, displeasure, irritation, annoyance) that help the individual to make his or her life more satisfactory when he or she finds it unsatisfactory. The irrational beliefs that are at the source of extreme stress almost always consist of what Ellis (1978b) called "*musturbation*—the devout and quite untenable belief in some absolutistic or dogmatic form of *should, ought* or *must*" (p. 212). In his discussion of work and stress, Ellis (1978b) enumerated three main musturbatory or absolutizing beliefs that lead people to overreact to stressful situations and to create emotional distress and behavioral disturbance: (1) the dire need for success and approval; (2) the dire need for considerateness and justice; and (3) the dire need for immediate and constant gratification and ease. These beliefs are elaborated on shortly.

A distinctive contribution of RET in the area of stress is what we call *secondary stress*. Secondary stress reactions derive from how humans interpret and appraise their own stress reactions. It is often the case that people increase their own emotional upset by getting angry, anxious, or depressed about how they reacted initially to a stressful event. Ellis described this tendency as being anxious about one's anxiety, depressed about one's depression, angry about one's aggression, and so forth. The third-grade teacher may upset herself further by downing herself for getting angry by telling herself something like "I *must* not react angrily with my students, because other teachers would not act that way, and I really *should* know better. Because I overreact to stress and I shouldn't, I think it *awful* that I act that way; *I can't stand* my own overreactivity, and *I am a pretty rotten person* for behaving so poorly."

> In other words: people not only partly create (or conceptualize) the original "stressors" they experience but they also bring about their own over-reactions to these "stressors." Then, to crown their self-imposed inequity, they

damn themselves for damning themselves—and this immensely escalates their "stress." A vicious circle—or endless spiral, if you will—that seems to have no finish line! (Ellis, 1978b, p. 214)

As in all stress, we find that the teachers who experience the most stress endorse a variety of irrational beliefs that relate to their role as teachers and their relationship to students and that derive mostly from Ellis's original discussions of irrational beliefs (Ellis, 1962). We have not the space to list the total number of irrational beliefs that underlie teachers' unhealthy emotional and behavioral responses to stressful situations. In Figure 1, we present the Teacher Idea Inventory which assesses a number of the irrational beliefs of teachers. A discussion of these and other beliefs, along with illustrations of techniques for disputing them, is contained in the following sections.

FIGURE 1. Teacher Idea Inventory.

Instruction: This is an inventory of the way you feel and think about various things which happen at school. Answers are to be circled to indicate the extent of your agreement or disagreement. Strongly Agree (4), Agree (3), Disagree (2), Strongly Disagree (1), No Opinion (0).

Do not dwell too long on any one item. First impressions are generally the best.

Be as honest in answering the items as possible; do not mark how you think you should feel.

Try to avoid the No Opinion or "0" answer as much as possible. Select this response only if you really cannot decide.

Please answer all items.

Name _____ Date _____

School _____ Grade taught _____

1.	It is very important that other teachers approve of me.	0 1 2 3 4
2.	I strive very hard to be a perfect teacher.	0 1 2 3 4
3.	Students should behave properly at all times	0 1 2 3 4
4.	I get *extremely* upset when I see schools being unfair.	0 1 2 3 4
5.	I find it very difficult to motivate myself to do unpleasant tasks at school.	0 1 2 3 4
6.	I generally need someone's advice at school to help me overcome problems with students.	0 1 2 3 4
7.	You can really judge the worth of students by their behavior.	0 1 2 3 4

(continued)

FIGURE 1. (Continued)

8.	Teachers are extremely limited in what they can achieve with a student who has been unsuccessful at school in the past.	0 1 2 3 4
9.	Students can make me upset.	0 1 2 3 4
10.	I can become very upset when I see a student having a personal problem.	0 1 2 3 4
11.	I seem to worry a great deal about things that happen at school.	0 1 2 3 4
12.	I work hard to find the perfect solution to problems I have at school.	0 1 2 3 4
13.	I put off making decisions at school.	0 1 2 3 4
14.	As a teacher, I must have the power to be able to make my class do what I want.	0 1 2 3 4
15.	Parents are frequently to blame for the problems of their children.	0 1 2 3 4
16.	It is most important to me that students approve of me.	0 1 2 3 4
17.	For me to feel worthwhile, I should know how to solve each problem I encounter with a student.	0 1 2 3 4
18.	It is easier to avoid problems or difficulties that may arise during the course of the day than it is to confront them.	0 1 2 3 4
19.	Teachers who are unfair to students are "unfit" and ought to be severely disciplined.	0 1 2 3 4
20.	I feel quite uncomfortable when students are being unpleasant.	0 1 2 3 4
21.	I often feel "unable" to solve problems and hassles at school on my own.	0 1 2 3 4
22.	Deep down, I believe that students who achieve poorly are somehow of less value than high achievers.	0 1 2 3 4
23.	It is almost impossible for teachers to change the way they handle a problem.	0 1 2 3 4
24.	I have little ability to control my feelings when something at school upsets me.	0 1 2 3 4
25.	Parents should know how to raise their children better.	0 1 2 3 4

(*continued*)

FIGURE 1. (*Continued*)

#	Item	Scale
26.	I worry a lot about how much others approve of me.	0 1 2 3 4
27.	I frequently feel down when I don't handle a situation at school as well as I would like to.	0 1 2 3 4
28.	I get quite upset when other teachers do not act professionally.	0 1 2 3 4
29.	Students who do wrong are blameworthy and deserve whatever they get.	0 1 2 3 4
30.	Students should not be frustrated.	0 1 2 3 4
31.	Before reaching a final decision at school about how to deal with a problem, I generally consult someone else.	0 1 2 3 4
32.	The worth of teachers can often be determined by their effectiveness with students.	0 1 2 3 4
33.	Students "misbehavior" is frequently caused by bad things that have happened in the past and that can never really be overcome.	0 1 2 3 4
34.	I seem to worry a great deal about the difficulties I see students experiencing.	0 1 2 3 4
35.	I get extremely upset with parents who should be taking more responsibility in the raising of their child.	0 1 2 3 4
36.	I concern myself a great deal about how successful I'll be in the future.	0 1 2 3 4
37.	It is possible to find perfect solutions to the problems of students.	0 1 2 3 4
38.	When I have a conflict with a student, I tend to avoid discussing it in the hope that it will go away.	0 1 2 3 4
39.	It is most important for me to have control of my students at all times.	0 1 2 3 4
40.	I feel that worrying about the future will somehow do some good.	0 1 2 3 4
41.	Hard work will eventually lead to the right answer.	0 1 2 3 4
42.	I think to myself "how awful" it is when students are rude.	0 1 2 3 4
43.	I should have the respect of my students at all times.	0 1 2 3 4
44.	I can't tolerate it when I see a student being treated unfairly.	0 1 2 3 4
45.	Other teachers can upset me.	0 1 2 3 4

In our discussions with teachers in workshop settings and in direct consultation situations, we have identified a variety of situations that occasion teacher stress. In our teacher education programs, we emphasize the three major emotional stress reactions of anxiety, anger, and depression (self-downing), which generally arise in certain situations and not in others. In Tables 3, 4, and 5, we list these different situations involving either teacher–student or teacher–staff interactions, along with typical stress reactions reported by teachers. It had better be emphasized that whereas these situations are likely to occasion the specific emotion indicated, we find individual variation both in terms of which stressors a teacher is likely to react to as well as differences in emotional and behavioral reactions.

We now describe how RET can be used to improve the affective and interpersonal functioning of teachers. The goal of our teacher-stress-reduction programs is to embrace teachers' adjustment and effectiveness so that they are in a better position to manage the current and future problems of their students.

A Stress Reduction Program for Teachers

We have introduced RET to teachers in the context of initial training as well as in in-service education. Although the problems discussed in

TABLE 3. Situations at School That Occasion Anxiety in Teachers

---

Teacher–student interactions
 Student stressors
Teacher anticipating: physical threat, walking into class unprepared, students not achieving objectives, disruptive classroom behavior, not being liked by students, students being angry and "turned off," students' reactions to being given poor grades, whether the teacher will be asked a question she or he cannot answer.

 Teacher stress reactions
Procrastinating, lack of concentration, failing to discipline, overpreparing, overcontrol of student behavior, being weak, not preparing, being intolerant when students do not try.

Teacher–staff interactions
 Staff stressors
Teacher anticipating: Poor exam results of students and others' finding out, conflict situations and disagreement with staff, being judged negatively by staff, criticism by principal or other member of staff.

 Teacher stress
Apathy, lack of assertion, not sticking up for "rights," not speaking up, being overly polite, being submissive, not doing what teacher really wants to do.

TABLE 4. Situations at School That Occasion Anger in Teachers

Teacher–student interactions
Student stressors
Not doing homework, disobeying teacher's instructions, tattling, bullying, talking back, inappropriate talking in class, throwing objects, swearing, showing disrespect to each other, excessive noise, daydreaming, not understanding, lying, lack of trust of teacher.

Teacher stress reactions
Yelling, sarcasm, criticism, inconsistency, humiliation, unfair punishment, excessive and unfair homework, picking on students, putting students on "D" list, walking out, physical contact, throwing student out, calling up parents, talking negatively of student to others.

Teacher–staff interactions
Staff stressors
Disruptions outside class, not being treated professionally by other teachers, differences in the manner in which teachers relate to and teach students, equipment not being returned, students dribbling into class, unfair timetabling, authoritarian decision-making, preferences in teaching load, public disagreement in disciplining a student, unfair share of duty, having "worst" students, slackness of administration in ordering material, special arrangements frustrated, cliquishness, lack of personal and professional cooperation, unfair teacher dismissals.

Teacher stress reactions
Yell at students, keep them back after class, direct verbal aggression, back stabbing, poor morale, noncommunicativeness, not volunteering, withdrawal of support, planning another conflicting activity, turning others against teacher.

TABLE 5. Situations at School That Occasion Self-Downing in Teachers

Teacher–student interactions
Student stressors
Being compared by students to more successful teachers, a "sea of blank faces," students not responding to discipline, lack of enthusiasm, not being efficient in individualizing instruction, personal comments about teacher (e.g., "This is boring"), students not showing up for an elective.

Teacher stress reactions
Absenteeism, moodiness, lack of enthusiasm, lack of lesson planning, withdrawal of emotional support, not caring, "knocking" students or school, being late, letting class out early, withdrawal from staff, public crying.

Teacher–staff interactions
Staff stressors
Public criticism thought by teacher to be correct, exclusion from social groups after school, being ignored, poor exam results of students made public, not being promoted, someone else selected to go on a conference, another program or teacher receiving greater support.

Teacher stress reactions
Withdrawal from contact, transfer, quitting, lack of enthusiasm, not caring about school activities, apathy and listlessness, taking days off.

an in-service program differ somewhat from those of concern to neophyte teachers, the goals of RET remain the same: (1) to help the participants to develop an understanding of how emotions work; (2) to decrease the irrational beliefs associated with stress among the participants; and (3) to provide the participants with techniques to help themselves manage their own emotional and behavioral stress reactions more effectively.

It is possible to introduce RET in 10–12 sessions of 1½–2 hours apiece. If one chooses this organization, one can sequence the content of sessions along the lines proposed by Forman and Forman (1980).

> Session 1. The Nature of Rational-Emotive Therapy and Rational-Emotive Education
> Session 2. The ABC's of Emotions
> Session 3. What Is Rational?
> Session 4. Rational Self-Study
> Sessions 5 and 6. Common Irrational Ideas
> Session 7. Dealing with Anger and Hostility
> Session 8. Dealing with Fear and Anxiety
> Session 9. Dealing with Guilt
> Session 10. Building New Thought Habits

In this program, the general logical sequence of introducing RET to a group is in evidence. Topics not covered, such as "Building an Emotional Vocabulary" and "Dealing with Depression" could also be included. The issue of how much material should be included in order to expose teachers adequately to an analysis of problems of children and adolescents as well as strategies for using RET directly with students both as preventive planning and during problem episodes is an open one. Time places a major constraint on how much material can be covered. Applications of RET directly with students can sometimes be dealt with in a follow-up staff-development program.

We now present material from a manual we have developed entitled *A Staff Development Program for Primary and Secondary Level Teachers: A Rational-Emotive Approach*. The detail provides mental health practitioners with sufficient background information and practical activities to enable them to carry out an RET mental-health program tailored to the requirements of their population of teachers.

In our program, teachers are given the opportunity to identify those irrational beliefs that may be impeding their job effectiveness and teacher–student relationships, and they are helped to modify these beliefs. Teachers are encouraged to examine and discuss how their attitudes toward themselves, their students, and classroom management practices influence the degree of stress they may experience in teaching children. The goal of the process is to enable teachers to solve their problems as the result of abandoning irrational ideas that prevent them from functioning effectively. The result should be that the teachers manage their students more effectively and therefore function more effectively in the future.

The content of the program tha follows is largely adapted from the work of M. E. Bernard, *A Manual for Rational-Emotive Group Counselling* (1979); M. E. Bernard and M. R. Joyce, *Rational-Emotive Therapy with Children and Adolescents: Theory, Treatment Strategies, Preventative Methods* (1984); W. J. Knaus, *Rational-Emotive Education: A Manual for Elementary School Teachers* (1974); and R. E. McMullin, I. Assafi, and S. Chapman, *Cognitive Restructuring for Families* (1978).

Because of limitations in space, we have not been able to cover other units that we employ, including "Irrational Beliefs of Children and Adolescents," "Irrational Beliefs and School Problems," "Challenging Feelings of Anxiety, Depression and Anger," "Learning and Mistake-Making," "Catastrophizing," "Demanding," and "Blaming." We are also in the process of developing materials that are designed to assist teachers directly in applying RET with their students.

Introducing RET to Teachers: Background Concepts for the Program Leader

What is RET?

Rational-emotive therapy (RET) is a cognitive-behavioral approach to psychotherapy pioneered and developed by Albert Ellis (1962). It is widely used by counselors, psychotherapists, and psychologists to help people to learn how to solve their problems and to live more effective lives:

> In addition to being a comprehensive approach to the emotional and behavioral aspects of human disturbance, RET places a great deal of emphasis on the thinking component. One of the major tenets of Rational-Emotive Therapy—that we feel the way we think—is based on an observation made over two thousand years ago by the Stoic philosopher, Epictetus, who noted that much of man's misery results more from man's view of events than from the actual harshness of the events. (Knaus, 1974, p. 3)

According to RET, people demonstrate deeply ingrained thinking patterns that exert an influence on and are observed in the predictable ways that people react emotionally and behaviorally:

> Ellis has expanded the idea that our emotional reactions are caused by our conscious and unconscious interpretations, philosophies, and evaluations, e.g., that upsettedness comes from upsetting perceptions or happiness from happy perceptions, into a highly powerful and effective psychological technique. (Knaus, 1974, p. 3)

The regularity and consistency of human behavior and emotion can best be understood by analyzing the characteristics of the cognitive structure (beliefs) and cognitive processes (perception and reasoning abilities) of the individual.

Ellis (1971) defined RET in the following way:

> Rational-emotive psychotherapy (RET) is a method of treating emotional disturbance that follows the educational model, instead of the commonly used medical, psychodynamic, or other models. Although it integratively employs emotive-evocative and behavioristic-activity methods, it somewhat uniquely teaches people, through many different kinds of educational modalities, that they basically cause their own emotional upsets and by forcefully changing their thinking and actions they can make themselves emote differently and thereby overcome their psychological hangups. (p. 62)

Thus, "RET is based on the hypothesis that it is not facts or events themselves, but the way people view facts or events, that causes emotional disturbance. Our emotions are caused by our thoughts, and emotional disturbance is caused by irrational thoughts" (Forman & Forman, 1978, p. 401). According to Maultsby (1975), thoughts and behavior are rational if they

1. are based on objective reality,
2. are life and health sustaining,
3. produce or do not defeat personally defined goals,
4. or reduce or avoid significant external and/or emotional conflict. (p. 8)

Goals and Objectives of RET

The primary *goal of RET* is "to help people lead non-self-defeating, happier, self-actualizing lives so that they can truly *get* better, rather than simply *feel* better because emotions are understood and expressed" (Knaus, 1974, p. 3). Ellis has described the main goals of RET in terms of emotional and cognitive outcomes:

> My main goals in treating any of my psychotherapy clients are simple and concrete; to leave the clients, at the end of the psychotherapeutic process, with a minimum of anxiety (or self-blame) and of hostility (or blame of others and the world around them) and just as importantly, to give them a method of self-observation and self-assessment that will insure that, for the rest of their life, they will be minimally anxious and hostile. (Ellis, 1973, p. 147)

In addition, he has repeatedly expressed the concept that for a therapy to prove effective, the clients had better not only feel and think better, but, perhaps more important, *behave* in non-self-defeating ways that maximize their own personal-goal attainment. Therefore, Ellis has pointed out that a final goal of his therapy is that people function more effectively in their own environment and not just in the office of the therapist. This is one main reason that RET qualifies as a *cognitive-behavioral* form of therapy.

The *objectives of RET* are

1. To help people recognize inaccuracies and self-defeating qualities in their thinking and acting.
2. To assist them in developing a realistic view of themselves and their environment.
3. To help them to modify their behavior accordingly.

Philosophy of RET

"Ellis' system has its foundations in the philosophy of science, particularly in the scientific method of understanding. The system is concerned with examining and understanding the way attitudes, beliefs and values influence feelings and perceptions" (Knaus, 1974, p. 3). RET helps people to examine their personal philosophies and understandings with a view to changing those that are antiempirical and unscientific. It teaches people to become both better investigators of reality and better hypothesis-testers. The reason that this epistemological position is so central to RET is that many of the hypotheses, assumptions, and conclusions that people hold about the world and that cause them to become and remain upset are either invalid or inverifiable. Our hypotheses and conclusions are always open to disconfirmation and are conditional on our current state of knowledge. Therefore, RET is a thinking or rational system that emphasizes looking at human problems in a straightforward manner.

Rational-emotive therapy is a therapeutic and preventive approach "by which children can be taught sane mental health concepts and the skills to use these concepts" (Knaus, 1974, p. 1). RET is currently being applied with different populations concerned with and responsible for the mental health of the child; for example, psychiatrists, psychologists, counselors, social workers, parents, and teachers. It has been increasingly employed in schools by teachers as a form of preventive and therapeutic treatment of emotional disturbances that follows an educational model. RET was initially introduced into schools in the early

1960s, is currently being used with both elementary- and secondary-level students in the United States, and is being increasingly applied at the primary and secondary levels in Australia, England, and other countries in Western Europe.

Rational-Emotive Education (REE)

In 1974, William Knaus, the chief consulting psychologist and psychotherapist at the Living School, located at the Institute for Rational Emotive Therapy, wrote a manual for elementary-school teachers in which he presented a series of rational-emotive curriculum units that can be used by teachers to introduce RET and REE in their classrooms. Since then, a number of other manuals and handbooks have appeared (Bernard & Joyce, 1984; Gerald & Eyman, 1981; Vernon, 1980). The logic of these materials parallels the basic principles of RET. Children are initially taught a vocabulary to describe their own emotions along with conceptual skills for understanding that feelings may vary in intensity from strong to weak. Children are also taught to discriminate their own as well as the feeling states of others. Depending on the age of the children, they are taught, to various degrees of complexity, where feelings come from and the relationship of thoughts to feelings. Older children are taught the differences between assumptions and facts as well as between rational and irrational thoughts and beliefs. There is generally extensive dramatic role-play as well as didactic instruction in helping children both to judge the rationality of their thoughts and to challenge and change their thoughts. Once these basics are acquired, the teacher is able to select from a number of different topics, including self-concept, stereotyping, overcoming anger, overcoming worry, and overcoming sadness.

Concerning the Living School, Dr. Virginia Waters (1981), Director of Children's Services at the institute, has written in *RETwork*, a newsletter published at the institute:

> The Living School was designed to teach the skills of rational thinking and problem solving as an integral part of their academic curriculum. As time went on, the staff and teachers began to realize that although Rational-Emotive Education proved to be effective and viable in the classroom setting, the program was only reaching about 22 students each year. In order to have a greater impact in classrooms both in the community and across the country, The Living School was transformed in 1975 into the Rational-Emotive Educational Consultation Service [and] provides: (1) in-service workshops for teachers and counselors; (2) consultations to schools, classes, and teachers wishing to implement a program of REE; and (3) materials and techniques for use in classrooms and/or school counseling settings. (p. 1)

Why RET is Useful for Teachers

There are a number of reasons that RET is suited for use in schools by teachers:

1. It enables teachers to solve their own personal problems in order that these problems do not interfere with the teaching of children:

> An important component of problems in a classroom or school is incorrect or distorted perceptions and/or thoughts of school personnel in dealing with children's behavioral or learning problems. From this perspective, RET concepts and techniques can be useful in addressing consultation problems encountered by psychologists in the schools. (Forman & Forman, 1978, p. 401)

2. As a result of being exposed to the principles of RET, teachers are in an ideal situation to introduce RET to individual children at the time when these children actually experience emotional distress and exhibit over- or underreactions. Such therapy helps children to surmount personal crises, to overcome disabling emotions and behavior, and, over time, to acquire RET coping strategies that enable them to exercise self-control and to independently solve their own problems. RET has been used with children who manifest different emotional and behavioral problems that are listed in classification schemes of childhood psychopathology. RET has been employed with individual children and adolescents referred with problems of acting out, violent, destructive and disruptive behavior, impulsivity, stealing, cheating, social withdrawal and depression (general unhappiness), public speaking, test-taking and social anxieties, fears and phobias related to school, truancy, underachievement and learning disabilities, poor motivation and procrastination, parent–child and student–teacher discord, and a variety of other problems of childhood adjustment, including sexual behavior, sleep disorders, and over- and undereating.

3. RET can be employed preventively by teachers on a group basis (rational-emotive education) to further the socioemotional and personal growth of participating children. It is argued that allowing

> a youngster to down himself or herself, and to become afflicted with needless anxiety, depression, guilt, hostility, and lack of discipline, and then taking that individual later in life and attempting to intensively "therapize" him or her in one-to-one encounters or small groups, is indeed a wasteful, tragically inefficient procedure. Far better, if it can be truly done is to help this youngster to understand, at an early age, some of the general principles of emotional health and to teach him or her to consistently apply these principles to and with self and others. This is now one of the main goals of RET. (Knaus, 1974, p. xii)

4. RET views its main purpose as educational and focuses on teaching students a model for helping themselves to resolve their own prob-

lems. It utilizes educational techniques such as critical thinking and the application of the scientific method to self-understanding and behavioral change. Activities include guided discovery, experimentation with problem solving, structured experiences, didactic presentation, homework assignments, structural role-play, assertion training, behavioral rehearsal, shame attacking, risk-taking and emotion-evoking exercises, and a variety of other exercises, activities, and methods that are compatible with the educational process and will help the child deal more readily with everyday events.

5. Another related advantage of employing RET in schools is that the approach that RET takes in working with students is one that reinforces many of the goals of independence, such as positive self-acceptance, responsibility, and self-reliance, which are endemic to the whole purpose of education.

6. RET can be readily adapted to a variety of educational systems and can be used with whole classes or special groups, or individually. RET can be taught to children in the same manner as other subject areas in the course of their regular classroom activities, in addition to the fundamentals of academic education. Studies of both small groups taken out of their classroom and entire classes that have received instruction in RET principles have shown these methods to be equally effective (Knaus, 1974). RET can be adapted to suit the structure and needs of the classroom. It can be taught as a

> self-help and human problem-solving philosophy to all children no matter how they have been categorized (normal, special, slow, advanced, etc.). Because didactically presented concepts may or may not help children deal with some of their everyday problems, it is important for the teacher to be on the alert for live classroom situations in which the concepts may be advantageously illustrated. This kind of experiential use of rational concepts will not only serve to improve problem-solving skills, but it will also emphasize that there are many ways to solve problems. (Knaus, 1974, pp. 4–5)

The initial introduction of RET can be formal or informal, brief or extensive.

7. The RET program "is parallel to the learning theories of some of the more humanistic and enlightened educators who are aware that knowing or learning as directed inquiry, learning as participation and as cognitive action, is clearly the most effective kind of education" (Knaus, 1974, p. 4). Unlike orthodox psychoanalytic and classic behaviorist views, the cognitive perspective places people at the center of their universe, in charge of their emotional state, and accords them a large amount of responsibility for creating their own emotional disturbances and for determining their destiny (Ellis, 1973).

RET Is Effective

Experiments with rational counseling have shown that children can be taught to guide their actions through rational thinking. RET and other approaches that derive directly from Ellis's theory (rational-behavior therapy, rational-emotive education, rational self-counseling) have received support as being effective with primary- and secondary-level children as both a preventive (i.e., with children who do not present with any specifiable problem) and an interventionist (i.e., with children who have severe emotional problems) approach (for reviews, see DiGiuseppe, Miller, & Trexler, 1979; Knaus, 1977).

What Are the Ideas Stressed by RET?

1. *Ellis has elaborated an ABC theory of emotional disturbance that describes how a person becomes upset.* The ABC's of RET suggest that thinking, feeling, and behaving are mutually interdependent functions with cognition providing a major role in the creation of feelings and the guidance of behavior. RET starts with an emotional and behavioral consequence (C) and seeks to identify the activating event (A) that appears to have precipitated C. Although the commonly accepted viewpoint is that A causes C, RET steadfastly maintains that it is the individual's beliefs (B), which are evaluations about what happened at A, that determine C. Figure 2 indicates how this position has been summarized by Ellis.

An example of the ABC theory of emotional disturbance is seen

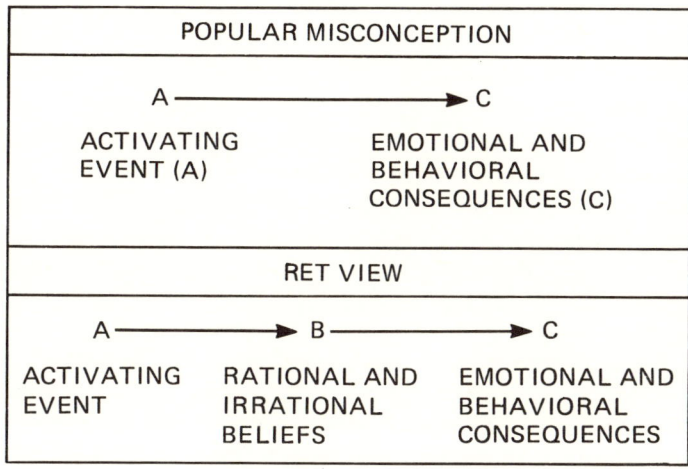

Figure 2. The ABC's of RET.

with 11-year-old Paul, a sixth-grader, who screams in anger and thumps down hard on his desk because his teacher failed to call on him when he had his hand raised. As illustrated in Figure 2, the common misconception is that A, the activating event of being ignored, caused Paul to feel angry, to scream, and to bang his desk (C's). However, if just at the moment Paul is being ignored and before he gets angry, we could somehow get him to forget and erase completely from his mind the memory trace of being ignored, we would observe a boy who is neither angry nor screaming. Therefore, Paul's reaction is dependent on the way he evaluated the incident, that is, his beliefs about it (B). Thus, A does not cause C; B causes C. Otherwise all people when confronted with the same situation would respond in the same way. Likewise, teachers may feel differently (C) in the same situation depending on their beliefs (B) about the activating event (A).

2. *Human beings can think rationally or irrationally.* RET hypothesizes two major subclasses of beliefs or belief systems, which Ellis has described as rational and irrational beliefs. The word *rational* is defined by the dictionary as "reasonable, sensible, intelligent, wise, judicious, sane, lucid, having sound judgement, having good sense" (Gerald & Eyman, 1981, p. 5). The word *irrational* means "without clear thinking or good sense" (Gerald & Eyman, 1981, p. 61).

According to Ellis, the cognitive apparatus of the individual is handicapped by a biological and hereditary propensity for irrationality, which works against the attainment of a person's basic values, purposes, goals, and ideals. This propensity can be seen both in the tendency to misrepresent reality and in faulty reasoning processes. Bernard and Joyce (1984) believe that maladaptive (and adaptive) cognitive content, processes, and structure are largely transmitted to children in the language and other communication patterns of adults. Parenting styles have an enormous influence in shaping the behavior and affectivity of children. As a result of differences in parenting styles (permissive-loving vs. authoritarian-cold), it is believed that children acquire different beliefs and evaluations of themselves and the surrounding world. Of particular relevance to teachers is the view held by Bernard and Joyce that teaching styles can strongly influence the cognitive characteristics of children, thus suggesting a learning-perspective view of human psychological disturbance.

The distinction between rational and irrational beliefs is important because, in trying to effect a change in the personal philosophy (cognitive view or thought) of a person, the irrational beliefs are the target of therapeutic change. These concepts are defined as follows:

- *A rational belief is true.* The belief is consistent with reality in kind and degree; it can be supported by evidence; and it is empirically verifiable.

It is logical, internally consistent, and consistent with realities.
- *A rational belief is not absolutistic.* Instead, it is conditional or relativistic. A rational belief is usually stated as a desire, hope, want, wish, or preference, and thus reflects a desiring rather than a demanding philosophy.
- *A rational belief results in appropriate emotion.* Thus, rational beliefs lead to feelings which may range from mild to strong but which are not upsetting to the individual.
- *A rational belief helps you attain your goals.* Thus, rational beliefs are congruent with: satisfaction in living, minimizing intrapsychic conflict, minimizing conflict with the environment, enabling affiliation and involvement with others, and growth toward a vital absorption in some personally fulfilling endeavor. (Walen, DiGiuseppe, & Wessler, 1980, pp. 72–73).

Irrational beliefs are defined in terms of a set of opposite characteristics:

- *An irrational belief is not true.* It does not follow from reality; it may begin with an inaccurate premise and/or lead to inaccurate deductions; it is not supported by evidence; and it often represents an overgeneralization.
- *An irrational belief is a command.* As such, it represents an absolutistic rather than probablistic philosophy and is expressed as demands (versus wishes), shoulds (versus preferences), and needs (versus wants).
- *An irrational belief leads to disturbed emotions.* Apathy or anxiety may be debilitating at worst and nonproductive at best.
- *An irrational belief does not help you attain your goals.* When one is tied up in absolutes and shackled by upsetting emotions, one is hardly in the best position to work at the ongoing business of life of maximizing pleasure and minimizing discomfort. (Walen, et al., 1980, pp. 73–74)

3. *In terms of the ABC model, irrational thinking results in emotional disturbance much of the time.* Irrational beliefs lead to extremely stressful emotional consequences (intense anxiety, anger, depression) and behavioral reactions (aggression, withdrawal) that make it quite difficult for individuals to improve their situation. Humans become disturbed and malfunction mainly because of their erroneous and irrational beliefs, attitudes, values, and philosophies. Rational beliefs generally lead to moderate emotional consequences that enable people to achieve their future goals by facilitating constructive behavior: "Generally, when human beings think rationally, they are more effective, happy and competent. They can work better and they can play better" (Gerald & Eyman, 1981, p. 6).

4. *"Helpful" versus "hurtful" emotions.* It is important to emphasize to teachers that not all negative emotions are harmful and that RET does not try to rid people of all emotions. "Hurtful" emotions such as depression, extreme anger, and anxiety are thought of as frequently negative because they often lead to behavior (avoidance, aggression) that does not help one to attain one's goals in a situation. "Helpful" feelings, such

as irritation rather than anger and concern rather than anxiety, are functional emotions because they help to motivate the individual to try to solve a problem, rather than to exacerbate a problem by acting destructively. RET attempts to teach people to temper and control excessive emotionality through rational self-analysis and rational thinking and to acquire a less negative and more adaptive repertoire of emotions.

IRRATIONAL BELIEFS

Throughout the writings of Ellis are a number of important irrational beliefs that are held by many individuals in our society who have emotional and behavior problems. Ellis has pointed out that many people live according to these powerful irrational thoughts, beliefs, and assumptions, which cause them much unhappiness and which therefore prevent them from leading relatively enjoyable lives. The goal of the rational-emotive educator is to help teachers to identify the irrational assumptions and thoughts that lead to emotional upset. The teacher may wish to spend a great deal of time discovering and analyzing rational and irrational thought-statements that activate emotional upset using the ABC model. The step of identifying the irrational thoughts of teachers is not an easy one, but it is critical, for if a teacher cannot identify irrational words, sentences, and beliefs, he or she will be unable to see why it is that he or she is upset, and, as a consequence, will be less likely to alter his or her view of the antecedent events.

The irrational beliefs contained in the General Idea Inventory (Figure 3) derive from the recent writings of Ellis (1977a,b), Ellis and Harper (1975), Bard (1980), and Walen *et al.* (1980) and can be rated individually at the beginning of a teacher education program. Teachers are able to examine which irrational beliefs they endorse. These irrational beliefs appear to have core irrational concepts that are apparent in one of the following four types of statements.

1. Awfulizing statements, reflecting the belief that there are terrible and horrible things in the world.
2. Need statements, reflecting the belief that the client must have things to be happy.
3. Should statements, reflecting the belief that there are universal musts.
4. Human worth statements, reflecting the belief that people can be rated. (Walen *et al.*, 1980, pp. 115–116)

AN INTRODUCTION TO DISPUTATION (CHALLENGING)

The most important and distinctive RET approach for helping people to examine and change their irrational beliefs is disputation (D), or as we and others refer to it in practice, *challenging*. In disputation, indi-

Name:_____

People have different ideas. Your opinions and ideas regarding the following statements are of interest. Circle the number that best reflects your beliefs about each of the ideas.

$$1 = \text{Agree (A)}$$
$$2 = \text{Uncertain (U)}$$
$$3 = \text{Disagree (D)}$$

		A	U	D
1.	I must be loved and approved of by every significant person in my life.	1	2	3
2.	I am not worthwhile unless I am thoroughly competent, adequate, intelligent, and achieving at least most of the time in at least one major area.	1	2	3
3.	Things must go the way I would like them to go, because I need what I want; and life proves awful, terrible, and horrible when I do not get what I prefer.	1	2	3
4.	People (the world) must treat everyone in a fair and just manner; and if they act unfairly or unethically, they amount to rotten people and deserve damnation and severe punishment.	1	2	3
5.	Life should be entirely pleasant and enjoyable, and any frustration, discomfort, and pain would be unbearable.	1	2	3
6.	I desperately need others to rely and depend on.	1	2	3
7.	It is possible to measure human worth and to assign a global value rating to individual persons.	1	2	3
8.	It is the past and all its bad experiences that continually ruin the present and that can never really be overcome.	1	2	3
9.	Emotional disturbance comes almost completely from external pressure, and I have little ability to control my feelings.	1	2	3
10.	One should be very upset over the problems and disturbances of other people.	1	2	3
11.	When dangers of fearsome people or things exist in my world, I must continually preoccupy myself with and upset myself about them; in that way, I will have the power to control or change them.	1	2	3
12.	I must find correct and practically perfect solutions to my problems and other problems.	1	2	3
13.	I must be able to control the attitudes and affections of other people.	1	2	3
14.	It's easier to avoid than to face life's difficulties.	1	2	3

FIGURE 3. General Idea Inventory.

viduals debate with themselves their own different irrational beliefs and the antiempirical statements that they have detected. Disputation can involve any technique that demonstrates to people "how their reasoning is faulty and why their beliefs are false" (Bard, 1980, p. 56). The aim of disputation is for individuals to acquire a more flexible, sensible, and nonabsolutistic view of themselves and their world. The outcome of disputation is the person's achieving a new philosophy or *effect* (E). Disputation requires the client to internalize the following view of human disturbance:

1. If I am upset, I am largely responsible.
2. There is something about what I am saying to myself and how I am evaluating this situation that is causing me to be overly upset.
3. I had better be prepared to accept another point of view about what is going on.
4. And I had better be prepared to question my thoughts and beliefs about the world and not rigorously hold on to those (whatever they might be) that do not have any relationship with reality (and particularly with my goals). (Bernard & Joyce, 1984)

The widely employed method of cognitive disputation consists of a set of direct, verbally persuasive strategies for convincing people of the irrationality of their beliefs. A RET practitioner who assists teachers to verbally dispute irrational beliefs requires a clear understanding of why certain concepts (awful, need, should, self-worth) and beliefs are irrational. A brief rationale for the disputation of these concepts is presented below (adapted from Walen *et al.*, 1980).

1. *Awfulizing statements* are generally disputed on the basis of semantics. For when one says that something is awful, what she or he really means is that some state of affairs is horrible, terrible, more than 100% awful—so awful, in fact, that the individual cannot stand it any longer. So people are also helped to view their evaluations of events in relation to other possible events. The practitioner combats low frustration tolerance (LFT) by challenging the person to prove that she or he cannot stand it.

2. *Need statements* are irrational because they imply that we must have things that, in fact, we do not need for survival or happiness. The first step in disupting need statements is to clarify the meaning of the word *need* and to define it in terms of the things we really require in life for survival. When clients state that they need something other than the essential requirements of life, they are assuming something that is not true. There is no evidence that we know of that indicates that we need such things as love, approval, certainty, success, and fidelity. Disputation would involve among other things helping the person to distinguish assumptions ("I need X") from facts ("I want X").

3. *Should statements* are irrational because they imply that somehow people have control over the way they think things should be, others should be, and the world should be. They appear to strongly believe that the world revolves around them and that, because it does, when they want something, they should get it. There is, however, no evidence that would support such a belief. People have to accept that things are the way they are and that it is pointless to demand that they be otherwise.

4. *Self-worth statements,* as we indicated earlier, are based on arbitrary definitions of *worth* and *worthless*. Ellis has argued that much human disturbance is based on people's rating themselves and others wholly good or bad and he has stressed that human beings are not ratable, for there are no universally accepted guidelines for judging the worth of people. Therefore, when we describe someone as being good, bad, weak, strong, dependent, independent, or loyal, we are overgeneralizing because, if someone were, for example, described as honest, she must never have misrepresented the truth as she knew it to be at the time. This proposition would therefore be very difficult to prove. Ellis would argue that although it is appropriate for people to rate their own traits and behaviors (in order to determine goal attainment), people have no rational basis for rating themselves. This point is an important one for parents and teachers, as blaming children for misbehavior imparts the notion that they can be rated as bad.

In assessing the irrational aspects of teachers' thought, it is important to be on the lookout for one of the most debilitating of all irrationalities: low frustration tolerance (LFT). There appear to be two types of LFT: one leads to anger and hostility, the other to anxiety, procrastination, or avoidance behavior. The older conceptualization of LFT focused on people's tendency to become angry when they are frustrated or thwarted. Ellis has made the point that anger and hostility do not stem directly from frustration, but from people's inability to tolerate being frustrated (LFT):

> When you feel furious, your basic view consists of the idea that whatever frustrates you *should* and *ought* not to exist, that it not only proves unfair, but this unfairness, again, *must* not prevail, that you *can't stand* frustration, and those that unduly balk and block you amount to almost vermin who, once again, should not act the way they indubitably do. (Ellis, 1977a, p. 185)

In situations where people perceive that their basic needs have been blocked, LFT sometimes leads to depression rather than anger.

Ellis's (1980) newer view of LFT revolves around the irrational belief that people should be confortable and without pain at all times. The inability to tolerate "discomfort anxiety" is revealed in a variety of maladaptive behavioral patterns that generally involve refusing to put in the effort that is required to accomplish some task. People who procrastinate because they find the effort that is required to do something that is in their best interests "too painful" (giving up food, going to the library) demonstrate LFT. Phrases that indicate disconfort anxiety include "I can't bear it," "I can't live with (or without) it," "I can't stand it," and "I can't tolerate it" (Walen *et al.*, 1980, p. 138). Ellis has defined discomfort anxiety as emotional hypertension that arises when people feel (1) that their life or comfort is threatened; (2) that they *must* not feel uncomfortable and have to *feel* at ease; and (3) that it is awful or catastrophic (rather than merely inconvenient or disadvantageous) when they don't get what they supposedly must.

Ellis (1977b) has developed a strategy that can be used to *detect* irrational thoughts and beliefs. He suggested that irrational beliefs can be detected by *asking* oneself the following four questions:

> 1. Look for your awfulizing. Ask yourself: "What do I think of as *awful* in connection with the antecedent event?" (Awfulizing statements).
> 2. Look for something you think you can't stand. Ask yourself: "What is it about the antecedent event do I think I can't bear?" (Need statements).
> 3. Look for your musturbating. Ask yourself: "What *should* or *must* I keep telling myself about in this situation?" (Should statements).
> 4. Look for your damning of yourself or others. Ask yourself: "In what manner do I damn or down anyone in connection with what went on at A?" (Human worth statements). (p. 10)

Therefore, it is possible to ascertain which of the above four kinds of irrationalities a person's unhappiness stems from.

It is helpful when introducing RET to provide a set of rationally restated beliefs. The list that follows is parallel to the set contained in the General Idea Inventory presented earlier. Some rational belief statements have been collated from other sources (Ellis, 1977b; Ellis & Harper, 1975; Walen *et al.*, 1980).

> 1. It would be desirable and productive to concentrate on self-respect, on winning approval for practical purposes, and on loving instead of being loved.
> 2. It is more advisable to accept oneself as an imperfect creature with human limitations and fallibilities. It is better to do than to do well.
> 3. Things are exactly the way they should be. Although I prefer things to go my way, there is nothing awful about not getting what I want.

4. The world is often unfair. People often behave stupidly and unethically, and it would be better if they were helped to change their ways.
5. There's seldom gain without pain. I can tolerate discomfort although I might not like it.
6. Although I enjoy the company of intimate others, I do not need anyone to help me get along in life; I can always rely on myself.
7. People are extremely complex. It is impossible to measure self-worth.
8. I can overcome the effects of past experience by reassessing my perceptions of the past, and by reevaluating my interpretations of its influence.
9. I am largely responsible for my own emotional upsets. I can control my feelings by changing the way I view and evaluate events.
10. The only way I am going to be of any help to others is by remaining calm and making a judgment of the situation to see what I can to to help; if nothing can be done, I will not surrender my personal peace to an impossible situation.
11. Worrying will not magically make things disappear. I will do my best to deal with potentially distressful events, and when this proves impossible, I will accept the inevitable.
12. The world is an uncertain place to live. To enjoy life fully, I will have to make decisions and take risks without having any guarantees.
13. Although I would like to have the affection and respect of others, there is no law of the universe that says that everyone must like me and follow what I say.
14. Problems seldom go away if I stick my head in the ground.

Irrational Beliefs of Teachers

There are derivations of general beliefs that have a particular relevance to teachers. Teachers often operate on the basis of irrational beliefs or assumptions that can work against their goals and prevent them from functioning effectively by using their skills and knowledge in a problem situation. Therefore, it is necessary to focus on and to deal with the teachers' irrational beliefs and thoughts about the problem situation, instead of providing them with direct solutions to the problem situation itself. A list of common irrational beliefs of teachers are provided in the Teacher Idea Inventory (see Figure 1). Examples of effective disputational approaches to some of these irrational beliefs include the following:

1. Those irrational beliefs that indicate that teachers are worried about having constant approval from significant others, such as other teachers or students, could be challenged by such statements as:
   a. The teacher has no way of knowing what everyone will think of him or her.
   b. Excessive "approval seeking" leads to excessive worry interferes with one's interpersonal effectiveness.
   c. It is very likely that most other people aren't thinking bad things about him or her at all.
   d. If someone does not approve of you, or has negative thoughts, there is no reason to get uspet, as it is impossible to please everyone all the time.
   e. The teacher is irrationally equating his or her self-worth with someone's opinion of the teacher.
   (Adapted from Forman & Forman, 1978)

2. Those irrational beliefs that imply a "should" statement—such as "To be an effective teacher I must have total control of my class at all times," "Children must behave appropriately at all times," and "It's awful when things do not go the way I demand they should"—could be challenged by statements such as:
   a. The statement that something should not be, when it obviously is, is an irrational thought.
   b. Demanding that something should not exist when it obviously does exist only causes one to be angry, upset, unhappy, depressed, etc.
   c. Being overly upset, angry, or depressed does not help one to solve problems and stops one from functioning effectively.
   d. If one does not like things the way they are, it is in one's best interest to calmly pursue one's goal of changing things or to accept things that cannot be changed.
   e. Exaggeration is self-defeating. It may be unfortunate or inconvenient if things are not the way one wants them to be, but it is only a catastrophe if one believes it to be one.
   f. When one turns anger or frustrations into a catastrophe, one is less likely to focus on appropriate problem-solving strategies because one spends too much time and energy awfulizing and feeling sorry for oneself or blaming others.

g. If one wants students to change their behavior, it is best to arrange conditions so that they will learn to behave differently, rather than just demanding that they behave differently.
(Adapted from Forman & Forman, 1978)
h. Forman and Forman (1975, p. 405) suggested the following as examples of questions that teachers can ask to prevent themselves from getting angry and to encourage rational problem-solving.

> "Why *should* these kids behave this way?"
> "Am I just sitting here demanding that things change without doing anything to change them?"
> "What, specifically, do I want these kids to do?"
> "Is it reasonable to try to get kids of this age to behave in this manner?"
> "What are the possible reasons for their not behaving this way?"
> "What will I do in order to teach them this new behavior?"

3. The irrational belief that school ought to be fair can be challenged by statements such as:
   a. Schools will be unfair from time to time, and to insist that they shouldn't be is unrealistic.
   b. Demanding that schools be fair leads one to become angry and at times give up.
   c. It is more healthy to accept that schools will be unfair and to work to change those aspects that are unfair.
   d. A rational view would be "I would prefer school to be a fair place, but if it isn't, it's not the end of the world."
4. Challenging the irrational belief that students should not be frustrated involves recognizing that:
   a. Frustration is a natural part of life, and it is the responsibility of schools to teach students how to cope with it.
   b. Students who never fail may be ill prepared to cope with failure when they leave school.
5. The irrational belief that people (students, teachers) who misbehave, do wrong, or act unfairly are blameworthy and deserve severe punishment can be disputed by recognizing that:
   a. It is often the case that people misbehave out of ignorance. It would be better to educate at these times than to punish.
   b. Severe punishment frequently does not teach a lesson and, often, only exacerbates the problem.
   c. To blame people for their misdeeds presumes that they have total control of themselves and the situation and are operating premeditatively. Such is not always the case.

d. Assigning blame frequently leads to putting the whole person down. This irrational overgeneralization may create—in students, especially—feelings of inferiority and worthlessness.
6. Teachers who avoid tasks and interpersonal situations at school that they find unpleasant demonstrate low frustration tolerance and endorse the belief that "life should be entirely without discomfort and frustration at all times." The following points can be made:
   a. Life wasn't meant to be easy.
   b. By avoiding unpleasantness, teachers frequently diminish both their teaching effectiveness and the potential pleasure of overcoming hardships.
   c. "I-can't-stand-it-itis," which frequently underlies LFT, can be disputed by pointing out that objectively teachers can stand just about anything.
   d. Discomfort anxiety comes from making hassles into horrors and from making mountains out of molehills.
7. Those teacher beliefs that involve having to rely on another to solve personal and interpersonal problems at school can be challenged by statements such as:
   a. Although it appears to be sensible to consult an authority *at certain times,* total reliance on another prevents one from ever learning to function independently.
   b. "Needing" someone else's help is irrational because one can still make a decision if one has to.
   c. Excessively relying on others may lead others to view a teacher as "dependent" and may work against professional advancement.
8. Beliefs that equate a person's self-worth with teaching or academic performances are irrational and can be challenged by reminding teachers that:
   a. Students and teachers are complex. To judge them on a limited aspect of their behavior is an overgeneralization.
   b. Students who perform poorly in school may later on be extremely successful in life.
   c. Rating the worth of a teacher on the basis of teaching behavior may demean that teacher in the eyes of others and may lead to the reinforcement of teaching ineffectiveness.
9. Teachers who believe that the past of a student (or themselves) makes change impossible can be shown that:

a. Students with a history of academic and/or behavior problems may bloom in the right school environment.
b. Students can be taught to correct their ways.
c. Motivation changes over time.
d. Teachers can learn to employ alternative and more affective ways of dealing with problem situations.
10. The irrational belief that the feelings of teachers are caused by other teachers, students, or the problem situation can be challenged by statements such as:
   a. Feelings are caused by thoughts. The problem itself does not make teachers upset.
   b. Teachers can control their emotional upset by changing their thoughts.
   c. Believing that others control one's feelings leads one to be more upset than when one takes emotional responsibility.
11. Teachers who believe that it is "unbearable" for students to be treated unfairly or to have problems can be shown that:
   a. Getting *too* involved in and upset about a student often interferes with a teacher's helping constructively.
   b. Teachers who become "too upset" about a student's problems frequently lose sight of their own goals.
   c. "Unfairness" and "unhappiness" are facts of life that had better, when necessary, be accepted.
12. Challenging the belief that teachers must be in total control of their class at all times involves making the following points:
   a. One will never have total control and to insist that one should is only counterproductive.
   b. Total control and obedience are not *necessarily* a good pedagogic principle.
   c. Students are different; some will like and respect a teacher, and others will not. To insist (rather than prefer) is irrational and self-defeating.
13. The irrational belief that "I must find the perfect solution to all problems" can be challenged by statements such as:
   a. There is generally no perfect solution.
   b. It is best to work hard to find a "reasonable compromise."
   c. Striving to find a perfect solution can drive one crazy.
14. Teachers who blame parents for the problems of their children can be shown that:
   a. Blaming is frequently a cop-out that absolves one from doing anything about the problem.

b. Parents frequently act out of ignorance in raising their children. Mistakes will happen. To demand otherwise and to condemn do little to improve the situation and frequently turn the teacher against the parent.
c. It is more helpful to the student if the teacher tries to understand why the student is having a problem rather than automatically assuming that, the parents are at fault.
15. Those irrational beliefs that imply that "I must be a perfect teacher and never make mistakes," or "I should know how to handle every problem with every child," can be challenged by statements such as:
    a. No one can be a perfect teacher.
    b. Everyone makes mistakes.
    c. Even if one makes a mistake, one will not be a failure.
    d. One has probably solved many problems successfully—every teacher has done something right.
16. The irrational belief that it is easier to avoid problems or difficulties that arise during the course of a teaching day than to confront them can be challenged by such statements as:
    a. It is usually harder to continue with the problem than to do something about it.
    b. Wishing hard or complaining about the problem will not make it disappear.
    c. Things are not likely to change merely because one wants them to change.
    d. Usually, some further action is required for things to change.

Sample RET and REE Methods, Activities, and Techniques for Teacher Education

The following section provides teachers with a linguistic grounding in the basic "emotional concepts" that are necessary to acquire the conceptual skills of rational thinking and problem solving. Teachers can be given practice in questioning their irrational ideas through the presentation of hypothetical situations; through the disputation of irrational beliefs, teachers will learn to think more reflectively, to exhibit more adoptive emotional reactions, and, therefore, to manage the stresses and strains of teacher–student and teacher–staff interactions more effectively.

Teacher Activity 1: Experiential Demonstration of the ABC's of RET

Purpose

The purpose of this activity is to demonstrate that teachers may have different reactions to the same event. In this activity, the group leader has the opportunity to explain different emotional reactions in terms of differences in thinking and beliefs. The leader may use this opening activity to introduce any number of basic RET insights, such as the difference between physical and psychological feelings and between facts and assumptions, and such as that feelings vary on a continuum of intensity from strong to weak. This activity involves some "deception." The leader is advised that certain teachers may take offense. If the teachers are angered, the leader may wish to deal with the irrational demand that life should be fair.

Procedure

1. The content of this activity is in a sense irrelevant to its aims, which are to elicit as many different and reasonably intense emotional reactions in the group of teachers as possible, so as to be able to illustrate any RET concepts one wishes to cover. We use the following scenario to start the program but any one will do, as long as it produces the desired effect.

2. Inform the group of teachers that, in a few minutes, you will be asking one of them to sit in front of the group and answer several questions posed by you concerning those problems that the teacher has in working with students or in relating to staff and that the teacher would like to have answered during the course of the program. Say that the teacher will not be asked anything personal—although you would like her or him to be as candid as possible. Announce that you will give the teachers two minutes to reflect on the question.

3. After the two minutes have transpired, indicate that before someone is asked to answer the question, you would like to get an idea of what people are feeling. On the board, list the different feelings that the teachers provide (worry, anger, curiosity, happiness) and, if you wish, ask each one to rate the intensity of his or her feeling on a scale of 1 to 10, with 10 being the point at which they could not feel any more of the feeling, and 0 being no feeling at all. When it is clear that there are many differences in emotional reactions, inform them that no one will, in fact,

have to answer the question, and that you were trying to dramatize a certain idea.

4. It is at this stage that the leader has the freedom to make whatever point she or he wishes, starting with the question: "Why did the same situation lead to so many different reactions?" and "Is it possible that situations are the direct cause of people's emotions?" After some discussion, you may wish to describe the different cognitions underlying different emotions (e.g., *anger:* "I shouldn't have to do any such thing; it's unfair and awful to have to; he deserves to be condemned and punished;" *anxiety:* "He'll definitely pick on me, and I'll say something or seem stupid; I couldn't bear that; I'd be a total fool"; *depression:* "I'm hopeless at doing this sort of thing; I always fail at amking a good impression and I always will"; *guilt:* "If only I had not been so lazy and had prepared better for this class, I wouldn't be having such a bad time; I'm worthless").

Teacher Activity 2: Group Discussion of Teacher Stress

Purpose

The purpose is to enable the leader to learn some of the concerns of teachers with regard to their work and stress and to emphasize the basic principles and insights of RET.

Procedure

1. Define the word *stress* (see the introductory section of this chapter) and ask the teachers to take a few minutes to anonymously write down situations at school with staff and students that seem to occasion their anger, anxiety, and depression. If it is desired, the Teacher Stress Questionnaire presented in Figure 4 may be distributed and used for this purpose.

2. Collect the information and, referring both to it and the other information concerning sources of teacher stress and teacher stress reactions (see Tables 1, 2, 3, 4, 5), discuss with the teachers their individual reactions and how they are largely brought about by different beliefs as expressed in their thoughts and *self-talk.* Explain that the basic aim of the program is to give all teachers insight into the relationship between teacher stress and their thinking and, more particularly, how their beliefs concerning schools, other teachers, and students influence their interpersonal relationships and teaching efficiency.

FIGURE 4. Teacher Stress Questionnaire.

The purpose of this questionnaire is to find out: (1) The extent to which personal problems at home influence your feelings and behavior at school; (2) The manner in which your feelings influence the way you interact with students and staff.

Can you be as specific as possible in answering those questions that ask you to: (1) Describe ways in which your emotions influence your behavior with students and staff; (2) List situations at school that upset you (make you feel angry, worried, or down).

As this questionnaire is to be completed anonymously, please be as candid as possible.

Thank you for your help.

1. How often do you arrive at school in the morning feeling angry, worried, or down because of personal problems at home? (Check one.)

   Every day _____   Once or twice a week _____   Once or twice a month _____   Hardly ever _____

2. Which of the following feelings do you experience at these times most often? (Write 1 = most often; 2 = middle, 3 = least often.)

   Anger _____   Worry _____   Down _____

3. When you arrive at school feeling upset, how do your feelings influence the way you relate to students? Please describe the different ways in which you behave (examples: "I tend to raise my voice, be impatient, teach poorly").

   I tend to _____

   I never let my emotions interfere with my relationships with students _____

   How do your personal problems and feelings influence the way you relate to staff? (Examples: "I don't talk, become short-tempered, stay by myself.")

   I tend to _____

   I never let my emotions interfere with my relationships with staff _____

4. How often do students say or do things at school during the day that make you feel angry, worried, or down?

   More than twice a day ___   Once a day ___   Once or twice a week ___   Once or twice a month ___   Never ___

   Please list those things students do or say that make you feel *angry*. Can you also briefly describe how you react to students at these times?

(continued)

FIGURE 4. (*Continued*)

> I never get angry with my students. _____
>
> Please list those things that students do or say that make you *worry* (*about yourself and your future*) and briefly describe how you react at these times.
>
> My students never make me worry about myself. _____
>
> Please list those things that students do or say that make you feel *down* and describe how you react at these times.
>
> My students never make me feel down. _____
>
> 5. How often do other staff members do or say things at school during the day that upset you (make you angry, worried, or down)?
>
>   More than twice a day _____ Once a day _____ Once or twice a week _____
>
>   One or twice a month _____ Never _____
>
>   Please list those specific things that they might do or say to cause you to be upset. Describe how you react to them.
>
> 6. When you feel upset at school because of what may have happened at home or at school, how often do such feelings interfere with the way you communicate with and teach your students?
>
>   Almost never _____ Some of the time _____ Most of the time _____ Almost always _____
>
> 7. When you feel upset at school because of what happened at home or at school, how often do such feelings interfere with the way you communicate and interact with staff?
>
>   Almost never _____ Some of the time _____ Most of the time _____ Almost always _____

Teacher Activity 3: The General Idea and Teacher Inventories

Purpose

The purpose is to provide teachers with an introduction to the nature of beliefs and to reveal to them which "ideas" may be creating their own "problems."

Procedure

Ask the teachers to fill out each inventory and indicate that they will be using their own answers as a basis of self-examination and analysis over the following sessions. These forms may be filled in as "homework."

Teacher Activity 4: Feelings

Purpose

The purpose is to help teachers define and identify their feelings; to show that people express their feelings differently; and to demonstrate that feelings are generated by thoughts and beliefs. The teachers will state the words that describe common feelings and understand that feelings can vary in intensity from strong to weak. This activity is adopted from Knaus (1974).

Procedure

1. Ask the teachers for examples of feelings and list these.
2. If the group has contributed what amounts to two lists, one of physical feelings and the other of psychological feelings, ask them why they think you made two different lists. Elicit and emphasize the distinction between psychological and physical feelings. Erase the list of physical feelings, and ask the teachers how they feel when they are happy, sad, or angry. To illustrate and emphasize that psychological feelings have certain physical manifestations and reactions, you may want to give an example: "When I'm excited about some good news, my head feels light, and I have so much energy that I feel like jumping or clapping. When I'm sad because I've received some very bad news, the inside of my chest feels very heavy, and I feel as if there are weights on my body; sometimes I cry and sometimes I don't have much energy." Go through the psychological feelings list and ask the teachers to contribute some of the ways they feel when they are happy, sad, angry,

etc., and let them list their responses next to the psychological feelings on the board (Knaus, 1974, p. 18).

3. Additions may be made to the list of psychological feelings. Some inclusions may be

> the irrational nagging feelings of anger, hate, depression, inferiority, worthlessness; the rational unpleasant feelings of frustration, annoyance, disappointment, sadness, unhappiness, perplexity; and the rational pleasant feelings of joy, enthusiasm, calmness, curiosity, contentment, and excitement. (Knaus, 1974, p. 18)

Examples may also include the following: down, tense, all right, crazy, ashamed, hanging in, happy, scared, fascinated, confused, messed up, guilty, low, freaked out, in love, wiped out, arrogant, cheerful, uptight, funny, flying, weird, turned on, turned off, terrific, excited, thrilled, sorry, nervous, OK, upset, relaxed, anxious, faded out, cool, zonked, determined, together, envious, in a buzz, groovy, hopeful, trusting, bad, embarrassed, afraid, hostile, great, silly, blue, concerned, worried, confident, lonely, high, naughty, distraught, apathetic, hot (Gerald & Eyman, 1981).

4. Ask the teachers which feelings they consider pleasant and which they consider unpleasant, and label these + or − accordingly. Rational and pleasant feelings (such as happiness, joy, love, enthusiasm, excitement, curiosity, relaxation, and confidence) and irrational and unpleasant feelings (such as anger, hate, sadness, depression, fear, guilt, worthlessness, loneliness, frustration, disappointment, anxiety, and annoyance) are differentiated at this point.

5. Ask the teachers to relate a real or imagined event associated with some of these feelings.

6. List the events and associated feelings given by the teachers in the following way: (A) event, (C) feeling.

7. Establish that feelings do not just happen but are responses to events (i.e., a relationship exists between events and feelings). Here are some circumstances or events that might be associated with some of the feelings listed above. An A is placed in front of the event and a C in front of the feeling:

1. (A) Event   I got a promotion.
   (C) Feeling   I felt happy.
2. (A) Event   Mark disrupted the class.
   (C) Feeling   I felt angry.
3. (A) Event   I gave a bad lesson.
   (C) Feeling   I felt depressed.

> 4. (A) Event   I made a mistake.
>   (C) Feeling   I felt inadequate.
> 5. (A) Event   I had to make a speech in front of the staff.
>   (C) Feeling   I felt anxious.

Establish that there are different feelings for the same event.

Six other feelings are listed on the board. Volunteers make up an event that may be associated with each of these:

> 6. (A) Event   _____
>   (C) Feeling   I felt hurt.
> 7. (A) Event   _____
>   (C) Feeling   I felt embarrassed.
> 8. (A) Event   _____
>   (C) Feeling   I felt proud.
> 9. (A) Event   _____
>   (C) Feeling   I felt envious.
> 10. (A) Event   _____
>   (C) Feeling   I felt disappointed.
> 11. (A) Event   _____
>   (C) Feeling   I felt frustrated.

Teacher Activity 5: The Feeling Thermometer

Purpose

The purpose is to help teachers realize that feelings vary in intensity from strong to weak and also to help them to think about the relationship between thoughts and feelings.

Procedure

1. Ask the teachers to describe the meaning of the words *angry*, *down*, and *anxious*. Explain that anger is a feeling that one experiences when one is frustrated by something and believes that the source of frustration (e.g., a person who seems to be causing the frustration) should not exist (that it's unfair). People feel down when they rate their self-worth in a negative fashion after they have failed at something, made a mistake, or have lost something they valued. Depressed people tend to have a negative view of the past, themselves, the present, and the future. Anxiety or worry occurs when one is anticipating and predicting that something awful will happen in the future (being rejected or failing) and that one will not be able to cope very well with the impend-

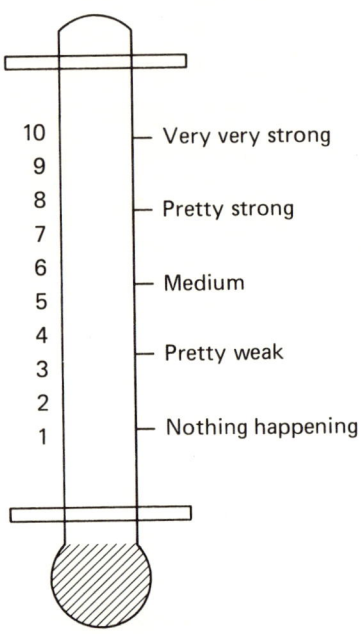

FIGURE 5. The feeling thermometer

ing disaster. Explain that different people may experience different degrees of the same emotion, depending on what they are thinking, and that the same person can change the intensity of his or her feelings (from very angry to annoyance) by changing his or her thoughts.

2. Provide the teachers with copies of the feeling thermometer (Figure 5). Tell them that they are going to rate the intensity of their feelings on the 10-point feelings scale.

anger	1	2	3	4	5	6	7	8	9	10
down	1	2	3	4	5	6	7	8	9	10
anxious	1	2	3	4	5	6	7	8	9	10

3. Ask the teachers to rate their feelings on the appropriate scales for the following thoughts (adapted from Knaus, 1974):

   a. It would be awful if all the teachers on the staff did not approve of me.
   b. I can't stand it when that nuisance, Susan, acts up in class.

c. I wish that my students and I could get along better.
d. I think I would be a good choice to be the middle-school coordinator, but it would be a disappointment if the principal didn't choose me.
e. It is unfair for me to have so much work to correct; I'm so angry I could scream.

TEACHER ACTIVITY 6: THE EVENT–THOUGHT–FEELING + BEHAVIOR DIAGRAM (ETFB)

Purpose

The purpose is to help the teachers visualize how they react to events and to further show that feelings are generated from thoughts. Teachers will state in their own words that pleasant thoughts cause pleasant feelings and that unpleasant thoughts cause unpleasant feelings. Teachers will demonstrate, by providing examples, how their own pleasant thoughts cause them to feel pleasant and how their own unpleasant thoughts cause unpleasant feelings.

Procedure

1. Begin by drawing an ETFB diagram on the board (see Figure 6). Indicate that feelings and behavior can be looked at this way:

Event (1) – *Thought* (2) – *Feeling* (3) + *Behavior* (4)
1. Something happens to you.
2. You think about what happened.
3. The thought you have leads to a feeling.
4. Your feeling affects how you behave.

By changing your thoughts, you can change your feelings.

EVENT	THOUGHT	FEELING	BEHAVIOR
Late for class because mislaid class test	Hope the class is still there to take the test	Annoyance	Hurried to class

FIGURE 6. Blackboard illustration.

2. Again, the relationship between the A's (events), B's (beliefs or thoughts) and C's (feelings and behaviors) is emphasized. It is people's thoughts or beliefs that cause feelings and behavior to occur. In order to highlight the difference between feelings and the thoughts as self-statements that lead to feelings, have the teachers complete the following activity. Ask volunteers to suggest possible B's for the following event and feeling:

Teacher A
A I got a promotion.
B
C I felt happy.

The B's suggested may include:

1. I worked hard for that promotion and I deserve it.
2. Now I'll get the attention I want.
3. I think other teachers will respect me.
4. I always knew that I was a good teacher, and this proves it.

Establish again that different people have different thoughts about the same event and that the same person may have different feelings about the same event. If people's thoughts were different, their feelings would change. With reference to the above example, "I got a promotion; I felt happy," why did Teacher A feel happy? Because Teacher A had told himself at B: "I worked hard for that promotion, and I deserve it." But suppose Teacher A had said to himself something else at B, for example, "Now I will have to take up a position of responsibility and move to another school." Then Teacher A might say, "I got a promotion; I felt anxious."

3. Have the teacher write down their thoughts when they are happy, angry, depressed, or anxious. Ask them to describe the event (E), thought (T), feeling (F), and their behavior (B). This activity will further establish that feelings come from thoughts and that they feel the way they think. The teachers are asked to record this activity on an ETFB worksheet similar to the one drawn on the blackboard.

4. Ask volunteers to record some of their examples on the board, leaving the thought column empty. Figure 7 shows examples of different feelings and related behaviors.

5. Ask why Alan (June, Jim) was depressed (anxious, angry). What thoughts made each of them feel that way? List the possible thoughts in the thought column.

EVENT	THOUGHT	FEELING	BEHAVIOR
Lost class test results (Alan)	The coordinator is going to think I'm hopeless. I can't stand it.	Depressed	Avoided the coordinator
Opportunity to talk at a staff meeting (June)	I would make an awful speech and make a fool of myself.	Anxious	Found an excuse to avoid speaking at the staff meeting
Student misbehaving in class (Jim)	That student deserves to be punished.	Angry	Refuse to help and yell at student

FIGURE 7. Blackboard illustration.

TEACHER ACTIVITY 7: FIND THE THOUGHTS CAUSING YOUR FEELINGS

Purpose

The purpose is to help teachers find which thoughts are creating their feelings. One way of doing this is to record significant A's, B's, and C's that occur daily over a period of one week (see Figure 8) (adapted from McMullin *et al.*, 1978).

Procedure

1. Choose a regular time each day for recording. For many teachers, right before or after recess, lunch, or a regular free period is the best time.
2. During this time, record the major negative feeling experienced by you in the previous 24 hours. Write this feeling next to C.
3. Describe the event or situation you were in when the feeling occurred. Write this situation next to A.
4. Find your thoughts about the event or situation that might have generated your feeling. Listed below are some common emotions that are caused by common thoughts:

Emotion	Thought
Anger	"Someone is not fulfilling my demands, as they should."
Fear	"Someone or something is dangerous to me, as it shouldn't be!"
Depression	"Things are terrible, and they will never get any better."
Resentment	"They shouldn't have done it."
Hate	"Everything about them is no good."
Offense	"It's unfair. It shouldn't be this way."
Emptiness	"There is nothing to live for."
Guilty	"I should have and could have prevented it."
Inferiority	"Everything about me is no good."

(McMullin et al., 1978, p. 37)

5. After the above activity is completed, each teacher will have a list of common B's that cause problem feelings and behavior: "These common thoughts are called "core beliefs" because we think of them in a variety of situations" (McMullin et al., 1978, p. 38).

Teacher Activity 8: The First Step in Challenging

Purpose

The purpose is to help teachers identify rational beliefs (rB) and irrational beliefs (iB) (refer to material presented in the background RET concepts section) (adapted from Knaus, 1974).

Procedure

1. Ask the teachers to define the word *challenge*, and write these definitions on the board. Explain that they are going to question and challenge some of their thoughts by using the ETFB diagram. Definition of key words:

Challenge:	To question yourself to see if your thought is rational or irrational.
Rational thought:	A sensible and logical idea that seems to be true.
Irrational thought:	An unreasonable or absurd idea that is false.

How to find out if a thought is rational or irrational.

Ask yourself, "Is there enough evidence for me to say the thought is true?" YES or NO. If YES, the thought is rational. If NO, the thought is irrational.

Daily time to record _____
Example: A Diana has failed her mathematics test. B I should have taught her better. It's my fault. C Guilt.

Monday   A _____
             B _____
             C _____

Tuesday   A _____
             B _____
             C _____

Wednesday A _____
             B _____
             C _____

Thursday A _____
             B _____
             C _____

Friday   A _____
             B _____
             C _____

Saturday A _____
             B _____
             C _____

Sunday   A _____
             B _____
             C _____

A = Situation   B = Thought   C = Feeling and Behavior

FIGURE 8. Find the Thoughts Causing Your Feelings Worksheet. (Adapted from McMullin et al., 1978.)

2. Have the teachers take out their EFTB worksheets and select examples of rational and irrational thoughts. Have volunteers write a selection of these on the board. Two examples are seen in Figure 9 (from Knaus, 1974, p. 24).

3. Have the teachers identify statements that lead to anger, and have them explain why.

EVENT	THOUGHT	FEELING	BEHAVIOR
Talking in front of school staff and making a mistake.	I wouldn't like making a mistake and getting laughed at. If that happened it would make me a fool and that would be awful.	Unhappy Frightened Anxious Feel inferior	Won't talk in front of the school staff.
Talking in front of the school staff.	I'll try to do my best, and if I make a mistake it's too bad. It's no big deal.	Mild displeasure at the thought of making a mistake.	Get up in front of the staff and say what you want.

FIGURE 9. Blackboard illustration.

4. Explain that an unreasonable or absurd idea is called an *irrational belief or an iB*. Give as an example: "Nobody in the world will ever by my friend." Explain that a *rational belief (or rB) is a sensible logical statement that seems to fit reality*, for example, "Humans are capable of making mistakes" or "Mistake-making tendencies do not make us worthless human beings" (Knaus, 1974, p. 24).

5. Ask the teachers to differentiate between rational beliefs and irrational beliefs from the examples on the board.

6. Discuss the above example in Figure 9, which includes a rational belief and an irrational belief. This may include the following:

> _____ has two different ideas: one is that he wouldn't like to make a mistake in front of the staff. If he only had that thought, he would feel sad or unhappy if he *did* make a mistake and others laughed. But _____ also believes something else: that he would be a fool if he made a mistake, and with that idea, he would feel nervous and frightened and he would put himself down. The first idea, "I wouldn't like to make a mistake," is a rational belief, an *rB*. _____ and _____ also have these ideas. The statements: "I would be a fool if I made a mistake" and the "situation is awful" are irrational beliefs (iB's). (Knaus, 1974, pp. 24–25)

HELPING TEACHERS COPE WITH STRESS 461

TEACHER ACTIVITY 9: NEGATIVE CONSEQUENCES

Purpose

The purpose is to enable teachers to become aware of the negative consequences of irrational thinking. Irrational thoughts may make teachers feel anxious and unhappy and may lead to inappropriate teacher behavior. Furthermore, teachers' irrational beliefs may produce negative feelings and/or behavior in students (adapted from McMullin *et al.*, 1978).

Procedure

Ask the teachers to write an irrational thought and to list a number of negative consequences that have happened to teachers as a result of this thought.
Example: (adapted from McMullin et al., 1978)
Irrational thought: "A teacher must have an ideal class."

Negative consequences of this thought:

1. Normal classroom problems were not accepted or tolerated.
2. Real problems were ignored because the teacher avoided acknowledging that the class was not perfect.
3. The teacher was too strict and inflexible.
4. The teacher was fearful that he or she, or the students, would make mistakes.
5. The students feared punishment for normal classroom problems and became anxious and secretive.

TEACHER ACTIVITY 10: COUNTER CATASTROPHE

Purpose

"Most of our thought problems are caused by mental exaggeration. When something unpleasant happens, our minds build the problem into an earth-shaking catastrophe. Counter catastrophizing can help bring your emotions back to reality" (McMullin *et al.*, 1978, p. 46).

Procedure

1. Instruct teachers that every time they are upset by a school problem, they should examine their mental exaggerations. Have them shout,

"Stop," to themselves. Remind them that, at these times, they are making "mountains out of molehills." To reduce their exaggeration, have teachers get things back into proportion by thinking of counters to reduce the exaggeration.

2. Example:

Situation	Exaggeration	Counter
Another teacher disagreed with my proposal.	She thinks I don't know anything.	Not true. She only disagrees with that particular proposal.
John cannot read yet.	As an adult he will never get a job.	He'll learn, albeit slowly.
Jane does not attempt new tasks.	Jane is withdrawn.	She's unsure of herself.

3. Have teachers form small groups and ask them to list other situations, exaggerations, and counters. These are later shared with the whole group.

TEACHER ACTIVITY 11: DIRECTED DAYDREAM

Purpose

The purpose is to prepare teachers for a future situation that will be likely to upset them. This activity is useful as a homework exercise

Procedure

1. Provide the teachers with the following instructions: Pick a room where you can lie down, be comfortable, and, most important, have no interruptions. Close your eyes and spend several minutes imagining that you are actually in the situation that you fear will happen. Instead of thinking of all the bad things that might occur, imagine you are handling the situation in exactly the right way. Picture yourself thinking nothing but realistic thoughts, feeling only appropriate emotions, and acting only in constructive ways.

2. Example: If you anticipate a confrontation with a student over his disruptive behavior in class, you could create this daydream:

> I am talking to the class. The student begins to disrupt the class. I ask him to sit down and stop what he is doing. He becomes angry and throws a tantrum. I can visualize myself explaining to the student how I want him to behave in class. I am rational, emphatetic, and firm. I don't lose my temper. I am not angry, bitter, or guilty. I act exactly as I wish.

3. *Practice:* Have teachers begin practicing the directed daydream daily. Encourage them to picture the situation and their responses in as much detail as possible.

TEACHER ACTIVITY 12: ARE YOUR THOUGHTS HELPFUL?

Purpose

The purpose is to determine whether the thoughts of teachers are rational or irrational, realistic or unrealistic: "We have enough problems in our lives without believing in all kinds of irrational thoughts, particularly when these beliefs cause us pain" (McMullin et al., 1978, p. 58).

My thought: _____
Situation—when the thought occurred: _____
Feeling generated by the thought: _____

	Evidence	Circle	
1.	Do *all* other teachers always feel this emotion in this situation?	Yes	No
2.	Do *you* always *feel* this way in this situation?	Yes	No
3.	Does thinking this way help solve the problems you are having with your students?	Yes	No
4.	Do the thought and feeling improve your relationship with your students?	Yes	No
5.	Do you have *conclusive* evidence that the thought is correct? By *conclusive* evidence we mean (A) the evidence is objective (not just your opinion); (B) your evidence for the thought is stronger than your evidence against it.	Yes	No
		Total Yes____	
		Total No ____	

Rule: Your thought is realistic and useful if you answer all the questions yes.

FIGURE 10. Is My Thought True and Useful Worksheet. (Adapted from McMullin et al., 1978, p. 59.)

This exercise will enable teachers to logically analyze their thoughts (adapted from McMulin *et al.*, 1978, p.60).

Procedure

1. Using some of the thoughts that the teachers have generated during the course of the program, analyze each thought by completing the worksheet titled "Is My Thought True and Useful? (Figure 10).

2. The teachers may ask themselves the following questions with regard to this activity.

Question 1: Do all other teachers always have this feeling? If all teachers feel the same way in a given situation, then your thought is more likely to be normal and reasonable. If not, then it is just something you are telling yourself, and you don't have to believe it.

Question 2: Have you always had this feeling in this situation? If not, then this situation did not generate the feeling.

Questions 3 and 4: Is the thought helpful? If a thought that does not help solve problems or does not improve the teacher's relationships, then it is not useful to have the thought.

Question 5: Do you let your feelings tell you whether your thoughts are true? Don't! For many centuries, people's feelings told them the world was flat, and they were wrong.

Teacher Activity 13: Rational Self-Analysis

Purpose

The purpose is to assist teachers to undertake a complete *rational self-analysis*.

Procedure

1. This exercise can be used during the day or as a part of homework. Have each teacher select a problem situation at schol in which she or he became upset with either a staff member or a student. Ask each teacher to fill out all the information requested on the rational self-analysis form. Discuss any problems the teachers may have had in analyzing thoughts. Watch out in particular for those thoughts that the teachers describe as irrational and that, in fact, are rational. Remind them (and yourself) that hidden just behind a rational thought (i.e., "I'm not prepared for this class") is often an unspoken, irrational one (i.e., "I'm a total failure as a teacher when I'm not prepared").

Name: _____

Directions: Use the ETFB method to analyze an unpleasant situation that happens to you this week.

1. Event or situation (write down an unpleasant experience):
   _____
   _____
   _____

2. Your thoughts about the event (write down as many as you can think of):
   _____
   _____
   _____

3. Your feelings (write down as many as you can):
   _____ 1 2 3 4 5 6 7 8 9 10
   _____ 1 2 3 4 5 6 7 8 9 10
   _____ 1 2 3 4 5 6 7 8 9 10
   _____ 1 2 3 4 5 6 7 8 9 10
   _____ 1 2 3 4 5 6 7 8 9 10
   Feeling   Medium   Extremely
   nothing   feeling   strong feeling

4. Your behavior (write down what you did):
   _____
   _____
   _____

5. Challenge your irrational thoughts (identify your irrational thoughts from your list of thoughts and write them down):
   _____
   _____
   _____

6. Change irrational thoughts to rational thoughts (rewrite them):
   _____
   _____
   _____

7. Your new feelings (write down how you felt after you changed your thoughts):
   _____ 1 2 3 4 5 6 7 8 9 10
   _____ 1 2 3 4 5 6 7 8 9 10
   _____ 1 2 3 4 5 6 7 8 9 10
   _____ 1 2 3 4 5 6 7 8 9 10
   _____ 1 2 3 4 5 6 7 8 9 10
   Feeling   Medium   Extremely
   nothing   feeling   strong feeling

8. Your new behaviors (write down whether you behaved any differently after your thoughts and feelings changed):
   _____
   _____
   _____

FIGURE 11. Rational Self-Analysis Form. (From Bernard, 1979.)

References

Bard, J. A. *Rational emotive therapy in practice.* Champaign, Ill.: Research Press, 1980.
Bernard, M. E. *A manual for rational-emotive group counselling.* Unpublished manuscript, University of Melbourne, Department of Education, 1979.
Bernard, M. E., & Joyce, M. R. *Rational-emotive therapy with children and adolescents: Theory, treatment strategies, presentative methods.* New York: Wiley, 1984.
Coates, T. J., & Thoresen, C. E. Teacher anxiety: A review with recommendations. *Review of Educational Research,* 1976, 46, 159–184.
Connell, R. W., Ashenden, D. J., Kessler, S., & Dowsett, G. W. *Making the difference: Schools, families, and social division.* Sydney: George Allen & Unwin, 1982.
DiGiuseppe, R. A., Miller, N. J., & Trexler, L. D. A review of rational-emotive psychotherapy outcome studies. In A. Ellis & J. M. Whiteley (Eds.), *Theoretical and empirical foundations of rational-emotive therapy.* Monterey, Calif: Brooks/Cole, 1979.
Ellis, A. *Reason and emotion in psychotherapy.* New York: Lyle Stuart, 1962.
Ellis, A. An experiment in emotional education. *Educational Technology,* 1971, 11, 61–64.
Ellis, A. *Humanistic psychotherapy.* New York: McGraw-Hill, 1973.
Ellis, A. *How to live with—and without—anger.* New York: Readers Digest Press, 1977. (a)
Ellis, A. The basic clinical theory of rational-emotive therapy. In A. Ellis & R. Grieger (Eds.), *Handbook of rational-emotive therapy.* New York: Springer, 1977. (b)
Ellis, A. The rational-emotive approach to counseling. In A. M. Burks & B. Stefflre (Eds.), *Theories of counselling.* New York: McGraw-Hill, 1978. (a)
Ellis, A. What people can do for themselves to cope with stress. In C. Cooper & R. Payne (Eds.), *Stress at work.* New York: Wiley, 1978. (b)
Ellis, A. Discomfort anxiety: A new cognitive behavioral construct. *Rational Living,* 1980, 15, 25–30.
Ellis, A., & Harper, R. A. *A new guide to rational living.* North Hollywood, Calif.: Wilshire, 1975.
Forman, S. G., & Forman, B. D. A rational-emotive approach to consultation. *Psychology in the Schools,* 1978, 15, 400–406.
Forman, S. G., & Forman, B. D. Rational-emotive staff development. *Psychology in the Schools,* 1980, 17, 90–95.
Gerald, M., & Eyman, W. *Thinking straight and talking sense.* New York: Institute for Rational Living, 1981.
Hicks, F. P. *The mental health of teachers.* New York: Cullman and Ghertner, 1933.
Hull, C. L. *Essentials of behavior.* New Haven, Conn.: Yale University Press, 1951.
Knaus, W. J. *Rational-emotive education: A manual for elementary school teachers.* New York: Institute for Rational-Emotive Therapy, 1974.
Knaus, W. J. Rational-emotive education. In A. Ellis & R. Grieger (Eds.), *Handbook of rational-emotive therapy.* New York: Springer, 1977.
Maultsby, M. C. *Help yourself to happiness through rational self-counseling.* New York: Institute for Rational-Emotive Therapy, 1975.
McMullin, R. E., Assafi, I., & Chapman, S. *Cognitive restructuring training for families.* Lakewood, Colo.: Counselling Research Institute, 1978.
Vernon, A. *Help yourself to a happier you: Emotional educational exercises for children.* Lanham, Md.: University Press of America, 1980.
Walen, S. R., DiGiuseppe, R., & Wessler, R. L. *A practitioners guide to rational-emotive therapy.* New York: Oxford University Press, 1980.
Waters, V. The living school. *RETwork,* 1981, 1(1), 1.

16

Rational-Emotive Education

ANN VERNON

In recent years, there has been increased recognition of the need to foster the development of the "total" child—attending to emotional and social as well as cognitive growth. School personnel who are concerned with the mental health of children have advocated the use of affective, or emotional, education programs to help prepare children for life.

The purpose of this chapter is to provide a rationale for emotional education as well as an understanding of rational-emotive education (REE), one of the existing mental-health programs. The unique characteristics of this model are described. In addition, a brief review of the research that attests to the efficacy of REE is discussed, along with specific examples of how REE can be used to help children and adolescents.

RATIONALE FOR EMOTIONAL EDUCATION PROGRAMS

Over the past several years, we have witnessed a steady increase in adolescent suicide, drug abuse, and pregnancy. Those of us who work with young people are forced to acknowledge the reality that these behaviors are one kind of escapism for those who feel as if they can no longer cope with a challenging existence. In addition to the rather dramatic statistics produced by the above-mentioned behaviors, children and adolescents continue to experience alienation, stress, guilt, anger, and anxiety with enough severity and frequency to be referred for therapy.

Because a limited number of professionals is available to provide mental health services, probably many of those needing help will not

---

ANN VERNON • Department of Educational Administration and Counseling, University of Northern Iowa, Cedar Falls, Iowa 50613.

receive it. In addition, the effectiveness of the "cure" approach is somewhat questionable. These factors, coupled with the recognition that people may need more coping mechanisms to contend with a fast-paced, increasingly complex society, have resulted in the development of alternative approaches to helping people.

In advocating an alternative, Pothier (1976) stated that we should strive to prevent problems before they arise. She indicated that we are in danger of wasting one of our major resources unless we initiate and support preventive as well as remedial mental health programs. According to Pothier, 80% of children needing mental health services have encountered conflicts arising from normal developmental tasks or from the effects of life experiences such as death or divorce. This group, it seems, could benefit from a preventive mental-health program in which the goal is to promote positive cognitive, social, and emotional growth. Pothier suggested that the mental health of children be a top priority. She indicated that preventive mental-health programs should be implemented in the schools as a way of ensuring that all children are provided with a learning environment that fosters their socioemotional development.

A Description of Emotional Education

To some extent, the need to develop preventive mental-health programs has been recognized by educators and psychologists, and various programs are now in operation (Bessell & Palomares, 1970; Dinkmeyer, 1973; Knaus, 1974; Spivack & Shure, 1974; Vernon, 1980). The basic goal of programs of this nature is to create learning experiences through which children can gain knowledge about themselves and their feelings and can learn how to apply this knowledge in solving problems and coping with situations throughout life. In essence, emotional education is geared toward the development of the "whole" child—the social and emotional as well as the cognitive dimensions.

Emotional education is typically thought of as being preventive in nature. The purpose is to help children learn about themselves so they can use this knowledge to "nip problems in the bud." Preventive programs also serve as a foundation of knowledge that can be drawn on to enhance oneself and one's interactions with others in a crisis or in a day-to-day living.

Although emotional education programs are usually based on a psychological theory, most programs in some manner emphasize the following concepts:

1. Awareness of self—values, beliefs, strengths, and weaknesses.
2. Awareness of feelings—what feelings are, where feelings come from, and how feelings are expressed.
3. Awareness of self in relation to others—what behaviors attract or detract in relationships and how effective interaction with others can be enhanced.
4. Problem-solving and decision-making skills—evaluating and assessing alternatives and consequences in a realistic manner.

Rational-Emotive Education

Basic Assumptions of REE

One of the emotional education programs that has proved effective with children is rational-emotive education. REE is derived from rational-emotive therapy (RET), a cognitive-emotive-behavioral system of therapy. RET is based on the assumption that emotional problems result from faulty thinking about events rather than from the event itself. Ellis (1973) identified an ABCDE paradigm that explains the rational theory. A is the activating event, which in itself does not create disturbance; rather it is B, the belief about the event, that causes the emotional reaction. There are two types of beliefs: rational and irrational. Rational beliefs contribute to reasonable, moderate emotions, whereas irrational beliefs result in depression, anger, guilt, and other such debilitating feelings. Rational theorists have identified 11 common irrational beliefs, which fall into the three basic categories of shoulds, oughts, and musts. These beliefs represent demanding and unrealistic perceptions of how things should be, such as "awfulizing" statements, which reflect an exaggeration of the event, and statements of blame directed at the self and others. C, the consequence, is the emotional reaction to the event, influenced by the belief. D is the disputation of the irrational beliefs, which then results in E, a new effect, feeling, or behavior as the rational beliefs replace the irrational ones.

RET is a comprehensive form of therapy, not simply a Band-Aid approach to problem solving. Its comprehensive nature is due to the fact that by exploring irrational beliefs, clients become aware that the feelings persist if the beliefs are not challenged. With RET, clients not only express feelings, thereby experiencing some temporary relief, but also gain an understanding of how to prevent further unhappiness by challenging their own thinking.

RET has been used successfully with children, as the case of Roxanne illustrates.

This 11-year-old came to the counselor upset because one of her friends had not been sitting by her and was ignoring her. Roxanne was sure that her friend no longer liked her. Thus, the event lead to her being angry and hitting and pushing her friend in retaliation. As the counselor worked with Roxanne, it became apparent that the angry feelings resulted from the demands Roxanne was placing on the friendship. Once she was helped to separate facts ("My friend didn't sit by me") from beliefs ("She's ignoring me because she no longer likes me"), Roxanne's feelings changed from anger to disappointment. She realized that there was no reason that her friend should always sit by her. By replacing her irrational demands with more reasonable beliefs, she was able to see that it wasn't the end of the world if one friend ignored her. After all, she did have other friends, and maybe if she stopped pushing, this friend might even like her better.

As the example illustrates, an understanding of the connection between thoughts, feelings, and behaviors, along with a challenge of one's irrational beliefs, can result in a more positive feeling.

Basic REE Concepts

RET seeks to help the client help herself or himself. Because of its educative nature, RET readily lends itself to a preventive mental-health model: rational-emotive education. REE is based on the assumption that it is possible and desirable to teach children how to help themselves cope with life more effectively. Specifically, the importance of preventing emotional disturbances by providing children with "tools" with which to cope is the basis of rational-emotive education.

The basic concepts that can be covered in REE preventive programs are listed below. To date, only a few sources have activities based on RET theory for children (Knaus, 1974; Kranzler, 1974; Vernon, 1980), but activities can be developed by educators if the following ideas are elaborated on.

Self-Acceptance

It is important for children to develop a realistic self-concept, including an awareness of strengths as well as weaknesses. Although many affective education programs stress self-concept development, there is a tendency to emphasize only the positive aspects of self. The result is that children begin to belittle themselves if they make a mistake or do something wrong. They had better learn to accept the fact that positive and negative qualities exist in each of us. RET posits that unconditional self-acceptance is essential, but that this does not imply that a person has to like everything that he or she does. A person does some bad things and some good things, but this does not affect her or his self-worth. Who a person is should not be equated with what she or he does.

Other related concepts include accepting oneself as a fallible human being who makes mistakes and can learn from them, accepting compliments and criticism, and understanding that acceptance of self is not contingent on other people's acceptance.

Feelings

Understanding the connection among thoughts, feelings, and behaviors is the essence of REE. Children also need to learn to differentiate between appropriate and inappropriate expressions of feelings and how feelings relate to beliefs. That having feelings is all right, that some emotions are stronger than others, and that feelings change are important concepts for children to learn. Helping children see that the same event can result in different feelings, depending on who experiences it, is also an integral part of REE.

Beliefs

A key component of REE is that there are two types of beliefs, rational and irrational, and that the irrational beliefs result in negative feelings that disturb individuals. The beliefs listed below are a modified version of Ellis's (1962) common irrational beliefs, adapted for children by Waters (1982) of the Institute for Rational-Emotive Therapy. The common irrational beliefs of children are as follows:

1. It's awful if others don't like me.
2. I'm bad if I make a mistake.
3. Everything should go my way; I should always get what I want.
4. Things should come easily to me.
5. The world should be fair, and bad people must be punished.
6. I shouldn't show my feelings.
7. Adults should be perfect.
8. There's only one right answer.
9. I must win.
10. I shouldn't have to wait for anything.

For adolescents, the following irrational beliefs were identified by Waters:

1. It would be awful if peers didn't like me. It would be awful to be a social loser.

2. I shouldn't make mistakes, especially social mistakes.
3. It's my parents' fault that I'm so miserable.
4. I can't help it, that's just the way I am, and I guess I'll always be this way.
5. The world should be fair and just.
6. It's awful when things don't go my way.
7. It's better to avoid challenges than to risk failure.
8. I must conform to my peers.
9. I can't stand to be criticized.
10. Others should always be responsible.

Many problems experienced by children and adolescents are related to these irrational ideas. If children recognize the pervasiveness of these beliefs and understand that the shoulds, musts, and awfulizing can be replaced with more rational beliefs, they will experience fewer debilitating emotions. For example, an adolescent who continually mopes around because he thinks it is the end of the world if he is not liked by all his peers is only going to end up depressed and more hopeless. Eventually, he may start blaming himself because others don't like him. In contrast, the adolescent who knows that it is not awful if everyone doesn't like him learns to appreciate those friends he does have. He feels good about himself even though some people do not like him.

It is important that children understand the difference between facts and beliefs and the role that exaggeration plays in this difference. How many times have you heard a child say, "Nobody likes me" (with the emphasis on *nobody*)? Challenging a child with this exaggerated belief ("*Nobody* likes you?") is a way of helping her realize that she might not be seeing the problem for what it really is. It is necessary to acknowledge the problem as perceived by the child, as well as to clarify the actual issue.

Challenging or Disputing Beliefs

This premise relates to the notion that irrational beliefs can be challenged and can be replaced with rational thoughts. Before beliefs can be challenged, however, children must thoroughly understand the connection among thoughts, feelings, and behaviors. Once this groundwork has been laid, irrational thoughts can be disputed. Their replacement with rational beliefs leads to a new feeling and/or new behavior.

For example, through questioning, children can be helped to see that a situation might not be as bad as it seems. Kristina, after having her eyes examined, was worried because she had to have glasses. Her main concern was that she would look ugly and that friends would call her "four eyes." Her mother asked her if she thought other people who had glasses were ugly. Kristina's reply was "Of course not." Her mother said that although she realized that some people might call Kristina "four eyes," she didn't understand how this would reflect on her as a person. Kristina thought about this and decided that getting glasses was not the worst thing that could happen to her and that it would just take some time and patience to get adjusted to them.

Exaggeration can also be a means of helping children recognize the reality of a situation. Twelve-year-old Tammy was convinced that her parents were the meanest in the world because they "never" let her go out with friends. When her mother and father started to berate themselves, however, exaggerating the incidents and stressing how horrible they were, Tammy began to laugh, realizing that she had overplayed the awfulness of an infrequent restriction.

With very young children, it may first be necessary to provide some rational statements. For example, a child who is fearful of the water can be taught to repeat a statement such as this: "Even though I'm afraid of the water, there really isn't anything to be afraid of. The water is not deep, and there are people here to watch me." The child can understand that some fear is natural but that he will miss out on a lot if he doesn't try new things. This can be achieved through challenging questions, as in the following illustration:

CHILD: But I'm afraid to swim. The water is cold.
TEACHER: Have you got in? How do you know it is cold?
CHILD: Well, I just think it is.
TEACHER: Does it look as if the other children think it is too cold to have fun?
CHILD: No.
TEACHER: Do you want to miss out on that fun?
CHILD: No, but I'm afraid.
TEACHER: All of us are afraid of things sometimes. But if we never try new things, we'll miss out on something that might be fun. Will it hurt you to get in the water?
CHILD: No, but I'm still scared.
TEACHER: You can be scared and still go in the water. Then you can see for yourself if it is fun or not.
CHILD: I guess I'll try.

After the child has tried an experience, it is important to discuss with her or him what it was like. Was it fun? Was it as bad as she or he thought it might be? Was it better to try it than maybe miss out on something good? Reinforcing the child for being a risk taker is desirable:

"I bet you feel proud of yourself for doing something that you were first afraid to try."

IMPLEMENTING REE

The Informal Approach

There are three basic approaches to emotional education programs. In the first, which is informal, concepts related to emotional well-being are taught to children as they experience situations and need help in working through issues.

For instance, Scott, a fourth-grader, frequently got upset when trying something new. He would throw down his pencil and wad up his paper while he muttered under his breath, "I'll never learn this—I can't do anything right." Reassuring Scott that it was all right to make mistakes and that it would take patience to learn new ideas did not help the situation. Eventually, the teacher began to use RET principles with Scott. She helped him to see that his frustrations resulted from self-statements such as "I have to get this right the first time, and if I don't, I'm not smart," or "Everything should come easily for me." Once these ideas were disputed, the teacher was able to help Scott learn some problem-solving skills. He then had some alternatives when he was confronted with a real challenge. Ultimately, Scott was able to ask for help rather than tearing up his paper, and he could verbally express his frustration to the teacher. She, in turn, could help him to dispute his irrational thoughts. It is interesting to note that the teacher initially had to use RET principles on herself so that she wasn't overly critical of herself because of her lack of success with this child.

To help children in this manner, a thorough understanding of the basic ABC's of RET is desirable. In addition, it is important to realize that although it is often easier to tell children how to feel or what to do to solve a problem, it is advisable that they be allowed to work things out for themselves. Children can make choices and solve problems once they are helped to look at the alternatives and the consequences of behavior. Youngsters should be involved in the problem-solving process. Instead of simply telling them that there is nothing to be afraid of, for example, it is better, through questioning, to get them to express fears and to challenge these. In other words, through adult guidance, the child comes up with her or his own conclusions and understandings.

Structured Lessons

The second approach is a formal series of structured emotional-education lessons that can be presented to a small group of students or to a total class. In lessons of this nature, there is generally a good deal of student involvement and group interaction. Understandings are deduced from the use of simulation games, role playing, bibliotherapy, discussions, and student–teacher dialogues. The lessons are typically experiential in that there is involvement in and experiencing of the concepts. In addition, time is spent discussing the activity so that, through questions, children can master the content. The goal is to provide students with lessons that enhance their understanding of their social, emotional, and behavioral selves.

For example, through the use of puppets, first-graders were presented with a variety of feeling words such as *worried, frustrated, upset,* and *nervous*. These words helped them to expand their feeling-word vocabularies. Several weeks later, when involved in an argument with a friend, a child told her teacher that she was "upset" because she and her friend weren't getting along. Prior to the lesson on feeling words, *happy* and *sad* were the only words this child had been able to use. This is just one example of how an affectively oriented lesson can have some long-term effect on enhancing a child's total development.

Emotional education lessons, in contrast to subject-matter lessons, are not graded, because much of the content is of a personal nature and is unrelated to right and wrong. Although REE posits that there are better ways of thinking (rational as opposed to irrational), the purpose is not to make a child feel wrong if he or she is irrational, but rather to help him or her learn how to deal with situations more rationally.

In conducting emotional education lessons, an atmosphere of trust and group cohesion should be established, because children are encouraged to look at themselves and to share and learn from classmates with regard to emotional adjustment. Because much of the content is presented through role playing, simulation games, or discussions and is somewhat personal, sensitivity can be exercised by listening carefully to children's responses, supporting their struggles to gain new insights, and encouraging their attempts to acquire REE concepts.

REE lessons can be readily developed by creating learning experiences based on the major REE components previously identified: self-acceptance, feelings, beliefs, and challenging beliefs. It is advisable to have a sequential progression, so that concepts can be introduced and expanded upon. For example, in a feelings unit, awareness that everyone has feelings and that it is all right to have them precedes the more difficult concept of where feelings come from. Likewise, when dealing with beliefs, a first level would be to distinguish facts from beliefs before moving on to the notion of rational and irrational beliefs, for instance.

The following is an example of a lesson based on the concept of feelings. The lesson is designated for children in the intermediate grades.

In a game similar to bingo, students in groups of four to six are given a board with nine blank squares and a set of cards with one of the following feeling words on each card: *angry, worried, scared, jealous, sad, happy, shy, hurt,* and *excited.* The players lay their cards face up at random on their boards. One person becomes the "caller" and he or she selects a feeling. The other players are asked to share an experience with that feeling and then to turn that card face down. For example, if *worried* was the feeling word, one player might say, "I was worried because I was late for school." Another might respond, "I was worried when my mother was sick." Although the object is not to win the game, the first person who turns over all the cards in a row is then out. After the game is finished, discussion with the total class should focus on the different experiences that people have had with the same feeling. (The students should be asked to reiterate some examples.) Other areas of discussion could include why it is important to realize that people can feel the same way about different experiences. As children participate in this activity, they learn that it is all right to have feelings and to talk about them.

Obviously, in this type of activity, it is important that students respect each other's expression. The facilitator of the activity has the responsibility for seeing that this minimal rule is respected so that children will feel comfortable in sharing. At the elementary level, this is generally not a problem, but as adolescence approaches, students become more self-conscious and hesitant. A nonthreatening classroom atmosphere helps to assure the success of the emotional educational experiences.

One of the advantages of emotional education programs is that the content can be used in coping with future frustrations. To illustrate, Mike, a third-grader, had participated in a simulation game aimed at helping children distinguish between facts and beliefs. Several weeks later, he told his teacher that a classmate had called him names. He said he felt awful because he was dumb and stupid. By referring back to the activity, the teacher was able to help Mike see that it was a fact that someone had called him a name, but it was not a fact that the name applied to him. Mike felt better, and so did his teacher because they had some concrete areas to draw on to work through this event. Showing children how to apply rational techniques in problem situations is an important means of enhancing their development.

Once the basic REE components—self-acceptance, feelings, beliefs, and challenging—are understood, these basics can be expanded on. Specific lessons can be developed that are geared to topics pertinent to children at particular stages in their development. For example, adolescents can benefit from applying RET principles to boy–girl relationships or peer acceptance issues. One series of lessons designed for junior-high students focuses on coping with on-again, off-again relationships, a source of frustration and anxiety for many teens. A short vignette serves to stimulate a discussion about peer relationships. When students express concern about rejection from friends, they are reminded that one's acceptance of oneself is not based on acceptance by others. Through questions that challenge their thinking, students begin to see that it is unnecessary to be critical of themselves if someone doesn't accept them. The concept of overgeneralizing and how it frequently results in conflict is also discussed. A game is played that enables the participants to realize that appearances can be deceptive. Thus, when someone doesn't wave or smile, it does not necessarily mean that the person does not like the other individual. It simply could mean that the person was preoccupied, didn't notice the other, and so forth. The point is that assuming something without finding out the truth can result in problems. Assertive communication concepts are also introduced through the use of Pat Palmer's *The Mouse, Monster and Me* (1977) booklet. Students use role playing to act out assertive ways of dealing with peers. Combined with rational self-talk, this activity makes them better equipped to deal with peer relationships.

A very useful way of ascertaining the extent to which children have learned REE concepts is to have them write their own rational stories. Third-graders enjoyed listening to selections from *Color Us Rational* (Waters, 1979). Then they were asked to write their own stories. One child wrote about learning that it doesn't do any good to mope around and feel sorry for yourself because your parents are divorced. Another girl wrote that she realized she didn't have any friends because she hadn't been trying hard enough to make friends, not because she was ugly. Another child wrote about being a good sport and not throwing tantrums if a game was lost. It was apparent on reading the papers that many students clearly understood the rational concepts.

Homework assignments can also be used very effectively. After a lesson on awareness of feelings, fourth-graders were asked to keep a feeling chart for identifying a specific feeling experienced at different times throughout the day. This activity was a good way to encourage children to be aware of the variety of feelings they experienced and the fact that feelings do not remain the same. Another homework assignment was related to fears. First-graders heard a story about being afraid and afterward were taught some rational self-statements. They were then encouraged to walk with a sibling or a friend into a dark room at home so that they could see that the only thing to be afraid of was the possibility of tripping over something they couldn't see. The parents were informed about this procedure and the purpose of the lesson. Several reported that it was an effective approach to helping their children overcome a fear of the dark.

Other means of introducing concepts include "experiments." A favorite is one in which each child is asked to juggle tennis balls. Because most children cannot do this well, the discussion centers on how they feel when they try something and don't succeed, what it says about them if they do fail, and whether it is better to try than not to take a risk at all. The point is that no one is perfect, and that everyone makes mistakes and can learn from the experience.

Another successful strategy is rational-emotive imagery (REI), which is useful in assisting children with fear and anxiety. Huber (1981), in adapting adult REI techniques for use with children, introduced the concept of the "hero." After children identified their fear and the circumstances under which this fear occurred, they were asked to think of a hero, such as the Incredible Hulk, Wonder Woman, or Spider Man. They were then to imagine that this hero was experiencing the same fearful sequence of events. Next, the child imagined that she or he was the hero who could approach a situation without fear. If this activity is carried out in a classroom setting, several children can volunteer examples, and those who may be unwilling to share can gain understanding from the others how to cope with their fears.

Bibliotherapy can also be used very effectively in helping children to gain insight into productive ways of looking at situations and working through problems. Rational stories can be original, or commercial sources may be used. *I Have Feelings* (Berger, 1971) is an excellent book, which can be used to acquaint children with a variety of feelings. The story can be read to children, followed by activities such as having the children draw pictures of situations in which they have experienced a particular feeling, or having them act out in small groups a play about a feeling. A book can also be given to a child to read on her or his own when an adult senses that the child could benefit from learning that others have similar feelings. The parent or teacher may want to follow up with a brief discussion with the child about her or his reaction to the book. This reaction could also be expressed in writing, depending on the grade level of the child.

The *Color Us Rational* stories (Waters, 1979) are also excellent for this purpose. These stories introduce a variety of rational concepts, such as overcoming fears, realizing that the world can't be perfect, coping rationally with teasing by realizing that what others say about you isn't what you are, and understanding that everyone makes mistakes. After the stories are read to children, questions can be used to clarify and reinforce the concepts presented. These questions should stimulate thinking about what was addressed in the story as well as apply the content to real life. After discussing the content of a story about teasing, personalizing questions such as the following could be asked:

- How do you feel when someone teases you?
- What makes you feel this way?
- If someone teases you, does this mean that you are what they say you are?
- Do you suppose that anyone goes through school without being teased?
- How can you learn to handle yourself when others tease you?

Questions of this nature help the child apply concepts to her or his own life.

Careful consideration needs to be given to the books selected for bibliotherapy. It is important that the RET concepts of self-acceptance and feelings related to beliefs be presented, in addition to positive ways of coping with problems. Stories in which the characters rely on "fate" to solve their problems, believe that they cannot control their life or their feelings, or equate their self-worth with what they do are obviously anti-RET and must be considered poor selections.

Integration into the Curriculum

A third approach to emotional education is to integrate the concepts into an existing subject-matter curriculum. When teaching literature, teachers could select and discuss stories that present characters solving problems rationally or expressing feelings in a healthy manner. Topics for themes could be related to self-awareness, such as making mistakes, strengths and weaknesses, handling problems in a constructive manner, or overcoming fears. Vocabulary and spelling lessons could include feeling-word vocabularies and definitions. Social studies lessons could focus on personal and societal values, on a rational understanding of the concept of fairness as it applies to societal groups or to law and order, or on cultural beliefs and the way in which these affect feelings. Students experiencing math anxiety could be helped to overcome it through cognitive restructuring. This approach is often less direct than a more structured lesson. However, with appropriate debriefing, children can see the application of the concepts, and this can be an effective means of enhancing emotional development.

The optimal manner in which to introduce emotional education is through a formal, structured lesson at least once a week, with emotional education concepts integrated into the curriculum whenever feasible. In addition, parents and teachers should be prepared as situations arise to help children to get in touch with what is bothering them, to identify the feelings and the beliefs behind them, and to cope with the problem by challenging the irrationalities. Given these efforts, children will repeatedly be exposed to information that should assist them in working through problems.

Efficacy of Rational-Emotive Education

It is apparent, based on the paucity of REE materials for children, that these strategies are underutilized with young children and adolescents. However, there is evidence to attest to the efficacy of this approach. Knaus (1977) reported on two pilot studies by Albert, designed to examine the effectiveness of rational-emotive education lessons. The two studies were conducted during the same time period. In the first study, fifth-graders with overt signs of emotional disturbance were divided into a rational-emotive group and an attention-placebo group. The subjects in the second group were also fifth-graders from the same school who exhibited no signs of emotional disturbance. They, too, were divided into rational-emotive and attention-placebo groups. The subjects in the rational-emotive groups received REE lessons four times a week for five weeks. The lessons were one hour long. The children in the rational-emotive groups demonstrated significantly less test anxiety and more positive classroom behaviors than the students in the attention-placebo groups.

Knaus and Bokor (1975) measured the effectiveness of REE lessons in influencing the self-concept and test anxiety of sixth-graders. As predicted, they found this method to be effective in self-concept enhancement and the reduction of test anxiety. DiGiuseppe and Kassinove (1976) studied the effects of REE on fourth- and eighth-graders. They concluded that the REE lessons reduced irrational thinking in both the fourth and the eighth grades, although the effects were stronger with the younger children. In addition, they found that the acquisition of RET concepts increased emotional adjustment. DiGiuseppe and Kassinove stressed the desirability of further research of a longitudinal nature to determine the effect of REE as a preventive program.

In another study, Miller and Kassinove (1978) conducted an investigation to determine which components of REE are most effective. Their results indicated that REE plus behavioral rehearsal and homework were superior to any one component in isolation. Miller and Kassinove indicated that even though further research is desirable, REE can be recommended as an effective mental-health program for children.

Limitations of REE

As Huber (1981) noted, cognitive-behavioral approaches such as RET have not been utilized extensively with young children because of the misconception that their cognitive capabilities are limited. Therefore, it is felt that the environment should be changed—rather than the child—so that the child can function more effectively.

In reality, perhaps some environmental manipulation had better occur, depending on the situation. However, cognitive coping strategies can also be used effectively. What must be realized, however, is that strategies suitable for adults cannot be applied to a younger population. Significant modification may be necessary to adapt strategies that younger children can grasp. For example, it may take repeated efforts before a child can see the distinction between thoughts and feelings. Groundwork has to be laid carefully and concepts must be modified so that connections can be made. Patience on the part of the adult is also required.

However, as the case of Eric illustrates, young children can learn to think rationally:

> Eric was angry because his parents said that he had to wear his brown shoes, not his tennis shoes, to school. His declaration that everyone wore tennis shoes was challenged by his mother, who asked him if everyone in the room really wore tennis shoes. In rethinking this, Eric said no, but he still thought it was awful that he had to wear the brown shoes and that his parents were mean. When asked if anything worse than this could happen, he replied that it would be worse if his dog died. His mother, indicating that he would need to wear the brown shoes, asked how he would deal with the problem. "Not look at my feet so I won't see the shoes" was his reply! The following day, there was no incident over the shoes, and Eric remarked that it really wasn't a big deal if he had to wear them.

In using REE with children, it is important to keep in mind that young children live very much in the "here and now." Repeated efforts may be needed to help a child overcome a fear, for instance, because simply challenging a fear one night may not carry over to the next. Also, children rely heavily on the concrete presentation of concepts. For this reason, it is good to use puppets, games, stories, or dramatization when presenting REE lessons. Involvement in activities is essential; what is designed must be intriguing, challenging, and varied in format so that the concepts can be reintroduced and built on. In this way, children can continually be exposed to a productive way of thinking and feeling that they can ultimately apply to themselves. If these approaches are used appropriately and if accommodations are made for the age of the child, the effects of cognitive therapies with children need not be as limited as some profess.

Further Applications of REE

Although REE lessons can be very effective in helping children and adolescents learn to cope more effectively with life's frustrations, one important consideration is the extent to which rational living is an inherent part of a young person's experience. Surely, a daily or weekly 30-minute REE lesson will not assure healthy emotional development unless the concepts can be practiced and reinforced in the environment. Of basic significance is adult modeling. If children can see parents and teachers handling situations in a rational manner, the likelihood is greater that they, in turn, will react rationally.

As Waters (1980) noted, however, it is difficult to develop a rational stance toward life when surrounded with a great deal of irrationality. Therefore, as parents and teachers observe poor role modeling on television, in books, or in real life, a discussion of more rational, appropriate ways to handle a situation could be initiated in order to create a constructive learning experience for children. Talking about how to express anger other than "punching someone out," or asking children to imagine what life would be like if everyone were as violent as Popeye and Bluto, is a way of redirecting children's thinking about what they routinely observe on television. Song titles are also fraught with irrationality (Waters, 1980). Discussing rational equivalents of irrational song titles would be a productive exercise. For instance, the song "I Can't Live If Living Is without You" reinforces the notion that one is helpless in the face of events and that unpleasant situations cannot be tolerated. A rational approach, on the other hand, is that unpleasant situations are tolerable even though not desirable, and that one has the power to take charge of this event. Pointing out these distinctions is a viable way of establishing the difference between healthy and unhealthy living.

Encouraging children's independence in problem-solving situations is a goal for parents and teachers. A child who is having a conflict with another person should be encouraged to take responsibility for it, as opposed to the adult's intervening to solve the problem. Depending on the age of the child, adult guidance may be necessary. For example, John and Andrew, age 5, were arguing about what to play. Instead of telling them what to do, John's father introduced a brainstorming technique, in which both boys were asked to indicate quickly all of the things they could think of that they might like to play. After a minute, with the parent as the recorder, the list was read back to the boys, and they were each to decide which one thing sounded best. John said "store" and Andrew said "cat." The father asked if there was any way that they could choose one of those or combine the two. Quickly, they arrived at having a pet store! In time, a procedure of this nature can be initiated by the children themselves.

It is also important to reinforce assertive interaction and expression of feelings. If a child is unsure of how to approach another person assertively, an adult can role-play the situation with the child, modeling a constructive means of interaction. The child can then practice her or his own version and the adult can assume the role of coach, giving suggestions about how to improve the confrontation. Understanding that they are responsible for their feelings and that seldom things are as bad as they seem are also important concepts to teach to children.

Conclusion

Rational-emotive education is still in its infancy. Although REE appears to be a viable preventive mental-health program, further efforts are needed to ensure that teachers will receive proper training in RET and in the application of the emotional education approach.

As stressed previously in the chapter, equipping children with emotional "tools" that they can use in coping with situations throughout life is imperative. The implementation of rational-emotional education can be one means of facilitating healthy emotional development.

References

Berger, T. *I have feelings*. New York: Human Sciences Press, 1971.
Bessell, H., & Palomares, A. *Methods in human development: Theory manual and curriculum activity guide*. San Diego: Human Development Training Institute, 1970.

DiGiuseppe, R., & Kassinove, H. Effects of a rational-emotive school mental health program on children's emotional adjustment. *Journal of Community Psychology*, 1976, *4*, 382–387.
Dinkmeyer, D. *Developing understanding of self and others*. Circle Pines, Minn.: American Guidance Services, 1973.
Ellis, A. *Reason and emotion in psychotherapy*. Secaucus, N.J.: Lyle Stuart and Citadel Books, 1962.
Ellis, A. *Humanistic psychotherapy*. New York: McGraw-Hill, 1973.
Huber, C. H. Cognitive coping for elementary age children. *RETwork*, 1981, *1*, 5.
Knaus, W. J. *Rational-emotive education: A manual for elementary school teachers*. New York: Institute for Rational-Emotive Therapy, 1974.
Knaus, W. J. Rational-emotive education. In A. Ellis & R. Grieger (Eds.), *Handbook of rational-emotive therapy*. New York: Springer, 1977.
Knaus, W. J., & Bokor, S. The effect of rational-emotive education lessons on anxiety and self-concept in sixth grade students. *Rational Living*, 1975, *10*, 7–10.
Kranzler, G. *Emotional education exercises for children*. Eugene, Ore.: Cascade Press, 1974.
Miller, N., & Kassinove, H. Effects of lecture, rehearsal, written homework, and IQ on the efficacy of a rational emotive school mental health program. *Journal of Community Psychology*, 1978, *6*, 366–373.
Palmer, P. *The mouse, the monster and me*. San Luis Obispo, Calif.: Impact Publishers, 1977.
Pothier, P. C. *Mental health counseling with children*. Boston: Little, Brown, 1976.
Spivack, G., & Shure, M. *Social adjustment of young children*. San Francisco: Jossey-Bass, 1974.
Vernon, A. *Help yourself to a healthier you: Emotional education exercises for children*. Lanham, Md.: University Press of America, 1980.
Waters, V. *Color us rational*. New York: Institute for Rational-Emotive Therapy, 1979.
Waters, V. *Teaching children to light up their own lives: The power of rational thinking*. New York: Institute for Rational-Emotive Therapy, 1980.
Waters, V. Replies to frequently asked questions. *RETwork*, 1982, *1*(2), 3.

17

Working with Children in Groups

ALLEN ELKIN

Historically, the field of child group therapy has received comparatively little interest from the professional community. Like a forgotten relative, it has watched with envy the fuss and attention paid to its more prestigious kin. While the adult therapies and even individual child therapy gave gone on to develop exciting new approaches and methodologies, group work with children has remained relatively stagnant, clinging to models and methods long abandoned by others.

This is no longer the case. In recent years, there has been a growing recognition of the value and importance of working with children in groups (Ellis, 1973). In part, this interest is a response to a need for more preventive programming that reaches a greater number of children. Much of this renewed interest, however, stems from another less obvious development.

Within the last decade, we have witnessed the growth and acceptance of newer models of human behavior, models that provide a better understanding of how people become emotionally disturbed and act in self-defeating ways. With these models has come an impressive array of strategies and procedures to treat dysfunction. The results, although preliminary, seem equally impressive. We are finding that more can be done in less time, and that change can be achieved by those who have less than years of professional training as child therapists. We are also learning that these innovative approaches work well, if not best, with groups.

ALLEN ELKIN • Department of Psychology, Empire State College on Long Island, State University of New York, and Clinical Psychologist in Private Practice, 110 E. 36 St., New York, New York 10016.

This chapter explores these newer directions. It aims to provide the reader with a selection of ideas and tools with which existing programs may be improved or new programs started. The hope is that the reader will come away with some of the excitement and challenge that I have found in applying these concepts to children in groups.

A Cognitive-Behavioral–Skills-Training Approach

With the advent of behavior therapy in the 1960s and 1970s came the introduction of an important number of treatment approaches that changed the face of therapy. Concepts and procedures such as modeling, behavioral contracting, desensitization, aversive conditioning, and so on have become part of the professional vocabulary. Even those who do not share the underlying behavioral philosophy are finding a place for behavioral techniques in their treatment package.

However, with its restrictive emphasis on overt behavior, behavior therapy fell short of its initial promise as a comprehensive method of treatment. What was lacking was a consideration of cognitive behaviors: the thoughts, images, and ideas that make up the inner life of the individual.

More recently, theorists concerned with psychological functioning have been paying more attention to the role that these cognitive processes play. The term *cognitive-behavior therapy* represents a significant extension of the behavioral approach. It focuses on the ways we think, our images, beliefs, and attitudes, that is, what we "say" to ourselves.

A cognitive-behavioral perspective gives a central role to self-talk, be it at a conscious or an unconscious level. It holds that such cognitive behavior mediates and largely determines how we feel and how we act. Dysfunctional behavior and feelings stem largely from distorted thinking, irrational belief systems, and a lack of appropriate self-talk. Getting better means finding ways of modifying these cognitions to make them more realistic, rational and, adaptive.

Implicit in a cognitive-behavioral approach is an emphasis on a functional analysis of behavior, that is, the systematic analysis of a complex task for the specific psychological abilities that are required to perform that task. Put another way, such an analysis asks the question: What skills or knowledge must be available to the child for that child to perform effectively in that situation?

Most of life's problems and challenges are complex, and adequate psychological adjustment demands that we possess a variety of skills, both practical and psychological. Just as riding a bicycle requires skills of balance and coordination, making a new friend or handling a frustrating situation demands that the child possess specific interpersonal and emotional skills. As adults, we may take such skills for granted, seeing these abilities as something that the child will master sooner or later. Unfortunately, many children develop them slowly, if at all, and the emotional and behavioral consequences of an early deficiency may be difficult to reverse.

Fortunately, many, if not most, of these psychological skills can be and have been taught in schools, in clinics, and in the home. But until now, the focus has been almost exclusively on behavioral skills. Although such skills are important and necessary, they provide the child with a limited set of tools that do not adequately meet his or her needs in coping with a difficult world.

A cognitive-behavioral analysis gives a more complex picture of psychological functioning and suggests a number of skills and abilities that underlie the child's psychological adjustment. These may be usefully grouped into the following categories: (1) rational-emotional skills; (2) problem-solving and self-instructional skills; and (3) interpersonal behavioral skills. Given the important role they play in assessment and treatment, it is worthwhile to take a closer look at each of these three sets of skills.

RATIONAL-EMOTIONAL SKILLS

If thinking plays such an important role in mediating a child's feelings and behavior, then teaching that child to think differently becomes the primary goal of child group therapy. Teaching children to think rationally means helping them develop a variety of skills and abilities that will allow them to see themselves, their world, and others in it in a realistic, adaptive, and meaningful way. It means not only learning to think more logically and clearly but also formulating a set of attitudes and beliefs about questions of human worth, personal values, and life goals.

These rather complex skills and abilities can be analyzed and presented in a simpler form, one that can provide direction for assessment and treatment. They include the ability to:

1. Recognize and identify feelings.
2. Assess the appropriateness of such feelings.
3. Recognize and identify behavioral response patterns.
4. Assess the appropriateness of such actions.

5. Understand the relationships among thoughts, feelings, and actions.
6. Recognize the existence of irrational beliefs and distorted thinking.
7. Challenge and dispute such irrational thinking and correct distorted thinking.

These specific rational-emotional skills reflect the contributions of a number of cognitive-behavioral theorists, particularly the thinking of Albert Ellis and Aaron Beck.

Ellis (e.g., 1962, 1973; Ellis & Harper, 1975) has maintained that most psychological disturbance is a direct result of the individual's irrational beliefs. An example would be the belief, "I must have the approval of others to be a worthwhile person," or, "It is horrible and awful when things do not go the way I want them to!" For Ellis, the major goal of therapy is to uncover these irrational beliefs and to begin to replace them with more rational and realistic ones.

Beck's analysis (e.g., Beck, 1976) differs somewhat from that of Ellis but again gives a prominent place to cognition in producing emotional disturbance. Beck has placed greater emphasis on the stylistic qualities of the person's thinking than on belief systems. These appear as cognitive distortions where the rules of logic and realistic thinking are violated in some fashion. Spilling a few drops of coffee on the sofa and yelling, "My whole sofa is ruined!" would be an example of *magnification*, exaggerating the extent and meaning of an event. *Dichotomous thinking* is another form of distortion. Here, the person sees people or events as falling into two classes only—all good or all bad, all right or all wrong—not recognizing that much of real life can be described on a continuum.

Both Ellis and Beck have maintained that learning to uncover irrational belief systems and correcting distorted thinking styles are skills that can be taught and learned. Such skills training plays a major role in the group treatment programs.

Problem-Solving and Self-Instructional Skills

If the presence of irrational or distorted self-talk is detrimental to healthy psychological functioning, so is the *absence* of other forms of self-talk. More and more, we are coming to appreciate the role that healthy self-talk plays in directing and controlling feelings and behavior. Whether spoken or hidden in the form of thoughts, self-talk can provide the child with a set of directions or road maps that he or she can use to cope with and solve the personal and interpersonal problems that may arise. We know that many children lack the appropriate self-statements to tell them what to do when confronted with a problem and that lacking directive self-talk can produce emotional and behavioral difficulties.

A number of researchers and clinicians have attempted to describe very specifically the kinds of self-statements and the related cognitive skills that are needed for problem-solving and problem-coping behavior (e.g., D'Zurilla & Goldfried, 1971; Spivack, Platt, & Shure, 1976; Meichenbaum, 1977). These include the ability to:

1. Recognize that a problem exists.
2. Conceptualize problem solving as a systematic process.
3. Generate alternative solutions for presenting problems.
4. Articulate the means and methods by which a particular goal can be realized.
5. Be aware of the consequences and impact of actions.
6. Be aware of how others might view the problem.
7. Use coping self-statements when faced with a problem or a distressing situation.

INTERPERSONAL BEHAVIORAL SKILLS

Not all the skills necessary for adequate social adjustment are cognitive. Many children lack the behavioral patterns and repertoires called for in daily living. These behaviors can range from highly complex interactions, such as cooperation and assertiveness, to more simple interactions, such as smiling and saying "hello." Why children fail to learn such skills or why they learn them poorly is not answered easily. We do know that such skill deficiencies, especially in the area of social acceptance, can play an important role in later psychological adjustment.

Much work has gone into specifying and describing these behavioral socialization skills, and this aspect of the child's functioning will be the most familiar to the reader. Although behavioral skills not the major focus of this chapter, any group treatment program with children that neglects them is incomplete. A listing of the major interpersonal behavior skills would include the ability to:

1. Approach, greet, and converse with others.
2. Assert oneself, be able to make requests, give compliments, and express disagreements.
3. Share and cooperate with others.
4. Deal with disapproval, criticism, and rejection.

Having identified and described, at a theoretical level those cognitive and behaviorial skills needed for successful personal and interpersonal functioning, it now remains to assess levels of ability in these areas, and to develop and implement programs in the group sessions that will address these skills. However, before considering assessment and treatment, a number of more practical questions and concerns warrant discussion.

Forming the Group

The Group Therapist

Who should lead the group? A number of people besides the professionally trained therapist are potentially capable of doing child group therapy along the lines described in this chapter, for example, educators, child-care workers, nurses, concerned parents and others who regularly interact with children (Ellis, 1973). But the prospective group therapist had better possess—or aim to possess—a variety of skills, abilities, and knowledge, such as:

- Understanding the theory of cognitive-behavior therapy and having some knowledge of its applications.
- Understanding developmental processes in childhood, particularly in the areas of cognition and socialization.
- Experience in working with children presenting emotional and/or behavioral problems.
- Experience in working with, and programming for, groups of normal children of different ages.

In addition, it is hoped that the therapist will possess some childlike qualities, that is, that he or she is able to play, imagine, and take chances.

Using Cotherapists

If there are relatively few child group therapists, it is probably because of the mixture of skills and experience required. One answer to the problem of the need for multiple skills and knowledge is sharing the resources of two or more individuals, each contributing his or her areas of expertise. This sharing can take several forms. In the *consultant–therapist model,* the consultant might possess the theoretical knowledge and assist in diagnosis, designing programs and evaluation. The therapist would run the group sessions and apply the programs.

In the *co-therapist model,* two people lead the group, each contributing his or her own strengths. This model is especially recommended, as the demands of orchestrating materials, content, and behavior can be overwhelming for a single therapist.

Types of Groups

Groups, like shoes, come in all types and sizes. In *problem-* or *population-focused groups,* the group members share either a common set of skill deficiencies, a common presenting problem, or some common defining trait. Examples are socialization groups, assertiveness-training groups, anxiety and relaxation groups, groups of physically handicapped children, children with learning disabilities, or children of recently divorced parents.

Mixed groups contain a variety of presenting problems and group-member characteristics. Most therapists who run mixed groups do so for the most part because they do not have the luxury of picking and choosing members from a larger pool.

The advantages of problem-focused groups are clear. Given similar profiles, programming can be more specific and more extensive. Problems can be more narrowly defined and more thoroughly explored. But mixed groups are not without their advantages. Having six acting-out 12-year-olds in a group may make for more efficient programming, but there is also a greater chance that the children will learn new acting-out behaviors. By providing a broader range of behavioral skills, a mixed group offers more opportunity for a child to learn positive behavior from others.

Group Size

The size of the group may vary widely, depending on the age and types of problems of the children and the resources of the setting. Five children with behavior problems can be more difficult to cope with than ten children with presenting problems of withdrawal and shyness. The ages of the children are also a factor in group size. Younger children require more structure and individual attention. Having a cotherapist allows some expansion of the group.

One method of determining group size and membership is to use the first few group meetings as assessment sessions. Assessment in this case means looking not only at cognitive-behavioral skills but also at how the children are functioning as a group. Is it a cohesive group? Are one or more children too disruptive for the group. Is a child too young? Too old?

Number of Sessions and Session Length

An additional consideration is whether the group is to be ongoing or time-limited. In most settings, reality demands that groups have a fixed starting and stopping point in time. The school-year calendar is perhaps the best guide as to when to begin, to have breaks, and to complete the sessions. If need be, the same group can be continued for another block of sessions.

With older children, especially adolescents, sessions once or twice a week generally work well. With younger children, more frequent sessions are suggested.

The length of each session is variable, depending on the ages of the children, the number of sessions per week, and the total number of sessions programmed. Because a large part of each session involves play in some form, the sessions are usually longer than one-to-one therapy sessions.

New Members

Given the curricular model of treatment presented here, with its emphasis on sequential learning, it is not advisable to add members once the sessions have started. It is better to hold the new member until a new group starts. It is much like having the child start a new school in the middle of the term—not impossible but often awkward for both the child and the group as a whole.

Therapeutic Balance

When the composition of the group is unsatisfactory (or additional members are needed but unavailable), introducing "nonproblem" children into the group might be considered. These members can be friends, classmates, or relatives of children in the group. The therapy group can be viewed as an attractive after-school activity with potential therapeutic rewards for its members. The inducements for such participation is (1) not charging the child's family and (2) providing the parents with a complete explanation of the program, its goals, methods, and results. By establishing a better therapeutic balance, modeling and role-playing techniques are more effective, and overall chances for positive learning within the group are enhanced.

MAINTAINING INTEREST AND MOTIVATION

Unlike in adult therapy, most children come to the group because they were told to by a parent, a teacher, or a court official. The question of what motivates the child to participate in the group becomes a primary concern. For the group to succeed, the child's level of interest must be sufficiently high to maintain active participation in the process.

One answer, and an important one, is to make the sessions fun. The therapist must discard any semblance of aloofness and passivity and become more childlike, outgoing, and dynamic. The children's attention has to be engaged, their curiosity aroused. Materials should be inviting. As much as possible, the therapeutic programming should be packaged as games, puzzles, and other challenges. Stories and role plays should be age-appropriate, and examples should be taken from recognizable and appealing sources. This may mean that the group leader will have to watch some Saturday morning television or spend some time in a computer-game arcade.

Motivation can also be maintained by incorporating behavioral reinforcement systems into the sessions. A relatively simple token economy can be established whereby children are rewarded with "participation points" for taking part in the group—answering discussion questions, volunteering for a role play, etc. "Behavior points," on the other hand, are earned by complying with certain rules and guidelines describing appropriate behavior for the group—no hitting, yelling, etc. The specific behavior rules can be decided on by the group itself during an initial therapy session. Children may save their earned points for a small concrete reward, or points can be totaled for the group as a whole. When a certain number is reached, an activity chosen by the group can serve as the reward.

ASSESSMENT STRATEGIES AND PROCEDURES

Assessment provides the group therapist with the kinds of directions needed for effective programming. It also provides the group therapist with a way of evaluating the therapeutic effects of such programming. While supplying this information, a cognitive-behavioral assessment adopts strategies and procedures that frequently differ from traditional approaches. These differences reflect a greater interest in describing cognition and affect—the way the child thinks and feels. This is not to suggest that traditional assessment procedures have no place in child therapy. It is meant to suggest, however, that such approaches may need to be modified.

Using the Traditional, Nontraditionally

Assessing children in groups combines traditional assessment approaches with the new cognitive-behavioral procedures. The standard psychometric test, the clinical interview, and the meeting with parents, teachers, etc., all have a place in the assessment strategy. However, these more traditional devices are used somewhat differently.

For example, watching a child assemble a puzzle tells one something not only about his or her abilities in dealing with spatial relationships but also about the child's cognitive-behavioral skills. Thus, assessors should ask themselves additional questions when administering traditional devices:

- How does the child go about solving this problem?
- How does the child deal with frustration?
- How does the child deal with success or failure?
- What kind of self-talk is involved?
- What can be said about the child's cognitive style?
- What are the child's underlying belief systems?
- What are the child's more common affective responses?
- What are the child's defensive behaviors?

This orientation extends to the clinical interview, observing the child in the home or the school, discussions with parents and teachers, and any other opportunity for information gathering. Asking the child what he or she thought about receiving a poor report card is as important as knowing that the child is doing poorly in school.

Although traditional approaches can be usefully extended, there is also a need for additional techniques that focus more directly on cognitive-behavioral skills. Such techniques do exist and can work well in a group setting.

Cognitive-Behavioral Techniques

The number of techniques assessing cognitive-behavioral skills in children is rapidly growing. Many have been in existence for some time now, particularly measures of overt behavior and, to a lesser extent, measures of affect (e.g., Walker, 1970). Several measures in the form of self-report inventories and questionnaires have been developed specifically to assess cognition (e.g., Murphy & Ellis, 1976; Knaus, 1974). Many of these approaches can and should be used in the group.

The most promising cognitive-behavioral assessment techniques, however, are just now being developed and put into practice (Merluzzi, Glass, & Genest, 1981; Kendall & Korgeski, 1979; Cartledge & Milburn, 1980). For the most part, these approaches fall into the categories of semiprojective or reconstructive methods. These more flexible procedures are well suited to the gathering of information about the way the child thinks and feels.

The *sentence-completion technique,* for example, can supply a wide sample of cognitive, affective, and behavioral responses. The group leader can readily construct a series of incomplete sentences that will elicit the most relevant information for a particular child or group of children. Such sentences might begin:

When I do poorly on a test at school, I think . . .
The best way to make new friends is . . .
When I don't get my way, I . . .

The cognitive-behavioral skills elicited can include coping self-statements, irrational beliefs, problem-solving skills, affective responses, and so on. This technique can work quite well in a group, with the incomplete sentence being directed to the entire group. The children can either write down their responses or complete the sentences out loud. Looking at responses to the same stimuli after a period of treatment provides a useful measure of change.

An extension of this approach is the *storytelling technique.* The materials and methods can be very simple. Pictures from magazines can be gathered, forming a set of semistructured stimuli that elicit stories rich in content and information. Should the storyteller go blank or run dry, prompts can be used:

"What's going on in this picture?"
"Tell me what you think she's going to do?"

Such prompts can be very specific, zeroing in on particular cognitive-behavioral skills:

"How is she feeling?"
"How will the little girl get out of this situation?"
"What do you think she was thinking?"

In a modified approach to storytelling, the group-leader begins the story and has the group members either complete the story or fill in missing thoughts, feelings, and action on the part of the character. For example:

> Michael is the goalie for the local Pee-Wee Hockey team. Up against a stronger opposing team, they lose, 6–0. In the dressing room, Michael overhears a teammate complaining to another friend, "We would have won if we had a decent goalie!"

Follow-up questions could include:

"How did Michael feel when he heard this?"
"What was he saying to himself?"
"What did he do?"

Like the sentence-completion techniques, stories can be focused to elicit specific skills. The following vignette assesses problem-solving abilities:

> David and Jordy both want to watch TV. David wants to watch the football game on Channel 2, and Jordy wants to watch cartoons on Channel 7. What could they do?

One format I have found useful in classifying the content obtained from incomplete sentences and storytelling material is the "four-column" technique (Figure 1).

As Figure 1 illustrates, this recording technique is useful in other ways, linking specific cognitions with certain inappropriate emotional responses and/or self-defeating behavior patterns.

George Spivack and his co-workers have produced a standardized set of stories designed to measure specific interpersonal-problem-solving skills in children. *The Pre-school Interpersonal Problem Solving Test* assesses the child's alternative thinking skills. A sample story-situation illustrates the approach:

> Here's Jeff and here's Dick. Jeff is playing with this truck and has been playing with it for a long time. Dick wants a chance to play with the truck, but Jeff keeps on playing with it. Who's been playing with the truck for a long time? You can point. That's right, Jeff. (*Point to Jeff.*) Who wants to play with it? That's right. Dick. What can Dick do so he can have a chance to play with the truck? (after Spivack & Shure, 1974, p. 194)

The *What-Happens-Next Game* measures the child's consequential thinking skills, that is, his or her ability to anticipate consequences:

> Here's Gerry and this is Mrs. Smith. Gerry saw Mrs. Smith's little poodle dog on her porch and took it for a walk. But Gerry did not ask Mrs. Smith if he could take it. What might happen next in the story? (after Spivack & Shure, 1974, p. 198)

The *Means–Ends Problem-Solving Test* assesses means–end thinking,

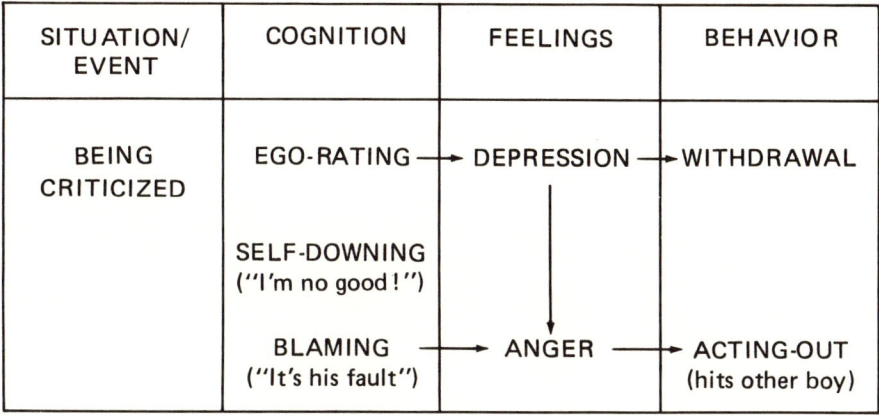

FIGURE 1. The four-column technique.

or the skill with which the child is able to conceptualize the means to reach a particular goal. One story in the test depicts a child who would like to make more friends:

> Al has moved into the neighborhood. He didn't know anyone and felt very lonely.
> The story ends with Al having many good friends and feeling at home in the neighborhood. What happens in between Al's moving in and feeling lonely, and his ending up with many good friends? (after Spivack, Platt, & Shure, 1976, p. 65)

Spivack's work is a good example of the kinds of techniques that characterize a cognitive-behavioral assessment approach.

The *think-aloud* and *thought-sampling* approaches suggest a related, but slightly different, assessment technique. Here, the child may be given a puzzle, a game, or any task or problem of some complexity. The child is asked to work on this activity and to think out loud at the same time. For example, the children in the group can be given paper-and-pencil mazes, the goal being to start at the beginning and reach the end point without lifting the pencil. Samples of typical self-talk might sound something like:

> OK . . . I'll start here . . . better look ahead a few steps . . . darn it! . . . I went too fast. I can't do this . . . (etc.)

Some initial cognitive modeling may be needed, but children quickly grasp the idea. This sampling of verbal responses gives the observer a measure of the quality and quantity of the child's self-statements.

A "thoughts, feelings, and actions diary" is a good way to have some of the cognitive assessment done as homework. Here the children

WHAT HAPPENED	WHAT I THOUGHT	WHAT I FELT	WHAT I DID

FIGURE 2. The thoughts, feelings, and actions diary.

in the group are given small notebooks, with the pages looking something like Figure 2.

Each child in the group is asked to record several episodes that have occurred after which they have found themselves angry, upset, anxious, etc. This diary provides the therapist with a fairly clear picture of common cognitive, affective, and behavioral patterns.

Role-playing techniques play a valuable part in assessment, especially assessment in a group setting. Using one variant of this approach, the group leader constructs a situation that would elicit a range of cognitive-behavioral skills. For example:

> Laura, I want you to pretend that this is your first day at a new school. Abby, Jonathan, and Andrew, I want you to pretend that it's recess and you three are playing a game together. Laura, you would like to join them. . . . Think for a minute about what you're going to do, and then we can begin.

Or:

> Adam, this time we're going to pretend you are overweight. One day at school, some kids begin to tease you. Who would like to play the "teasers"? OK. Chris and Billy. We'll give you a minute to get ready, and then we'll start. This time, though, I want you to think out loud as you try to figure out what to do.

Role plays can be used with great flexibility and specificity to replicate problems and situations common in children's lives. As with the other techniques discussed, responses can be recorded and coded so that they provide information about current skill-levels and the effects of programming.

Treatment Strategies and Procedures

In a very real sense, treatment begins with assessment. The very act of having the child think about what he or she is going to do in any situation is the beginning of the change process. The child may only now recognize that any thinking was going on or that a problem could be evaluated without an overt response. Similarly, seeing other children act differently provides the child with new options. Understanding the consequences of these options may lead to new strategies and new behaviors.

Implicit in a cognitive-behavioral-skills-training orientation is a strategy for treatment: developing or strengthening those cognitive, affective, and behavioral abilities that are lacking or are judged deficient, but that are important to the child's psychological adjustment. Assessment provides the direction and determines the content of each session. The skills to be addressed and the intensity of the programming are a function of the needs of the group members, the time constraints, and the availability of professional resources. The treatment plans for one group differ from those for another. However, common to every group is a concern about meeting certain broader goals. The therapist not only is guided by a desire to help the child adjust to a particular problem or situation but also has the hope that the child will be able to deal with future situations and solve new problems when they arise. This means giving the child a set of skills or tools with which he or she can better understand why a psychological or practical problem exists and what can be done to cope with or to eliminate that problem. In the broadest sense, the goal of therapy is to teach the child the skills of getting better. The child is learning how to become his or her own therapist.

In the sections that follow, I have selected a sampling of cognitive, affective, and behavioral skills to illustrate the kinds of procedures and techniques that have worked well with children in groups. Although the discussion is far from exhaustive, hopefully it will convey the form and flavor of programming and treatment.

Teaching Rational-Emotional Skills

The process of emotional change requires that the child be able to recognize feelings and label them correctly. Often children, especially younger children, need some help in this area. They need to be taught how to become aware of the facial and bodily cues, as well as the contextual variables, that accompany different feelings.

There are a number of ways this skill can be taught. In the "feelings game," for example, the children in the group are handed small cards with the names of feelings printed on them. In younger groups, the feeling names are whispered to the children. When her or his turn comes, each child is asked to act out that feeling, using only bodily and facial gestures. The leader asks the other group members to guess what the feeling is and to explain why they chose that feeling. Other related techniques could include:

- Showing the children pictures of "emotional" faces and having them guess what the feelings are and why they think so.
- Having them draw faces that show different emotions.
- Having the therapist model an emotion and the children not only try to guess the name of the feeling but also "rate" the extent of the feeling on a 10-point scale.

- Having the children suggest the appropriate emotion for various situations, for example, not getting the present one wanted or being teased.

Board games can be created and used to teach the group members how to identify feelings and gauge their intensity. In one such game, when a player rolls the dice and lands on a square marked "Pick-a-Feeling," he or she takes a card from the center of the board and acts it out. The card will have the name of a feeling written on it and an intensity rating, for example, "Anger (7)." The player next in order has to give the name and the intensity of the feeling.

In a variation of this game, a situation or circumstance is written on the card, for example, "You come home hoping to watch some TV and find that the set is broken. You feel———( )." The "guesser" has to suggest and portray an appropriate emotional reaction. The answer is used as a focus for group discussion.

Teaching children that thoughts can produce feelings and the way in which this happens is a more complicated task. An approach that I have found useful with groups of children is one that combines concepts taken from Ellis's rational-emotive therapy with some ideas central to Beck's cognitive therapy. With this approach, the children are taught to recognize their "thinking errors." These are labels or descriptions that quickly capture the essence of an irrational belief or a style of illogical thinking. Some examples of thinking errors are *can't-stand-it-itis* (the irrational belief that it is *unbearable* when things do not happen the way we would like them to), or *mind reading* (assuming, without any real evidence, that people are thinking in certain ways), or *ego rating* (equating your worth or esteem with the approval of others, your performance, or your traits). Other errors include *awfulizing, catastrophizing, fairness-itis, keyholing,* and *blaming*. The errors, as well as their names, change with the age of the children in the group. Thus, with older children (12 and above), I would use the name *magnification* to describe the error of exaggeration. With younger children, the term *ballooning* would be used to convey the same distortion. These thinking errors are systematically taught and illustrated with various examples and descriptions.

One game that can help teach these concepts is "what's my error?" Here, a series of cards are handed out and read to the children. One such card reads:

> Yesterday Ben was given a new electronic game for his birthday. He turned it on but found that it didn't work. The battery was dead. Ben became very upset and started crying, "Nothing I get ever works right! It's not fair!"

The children in the group are asked to guess the thinking error (or errors) that best describes the irrational thinking portrayed in the vignette. The child with the correct answer gets to keep the card, and the winner of the game is the child with the most cards. An advanced version of this game has the child correct the thinking error by supplying the more rational self-talk.

The use of *rational worksheets* is suggested as a technique for strengthening rational thinking skills. One such worksheet that I find works well in groups looks like Figure 3 when completed.

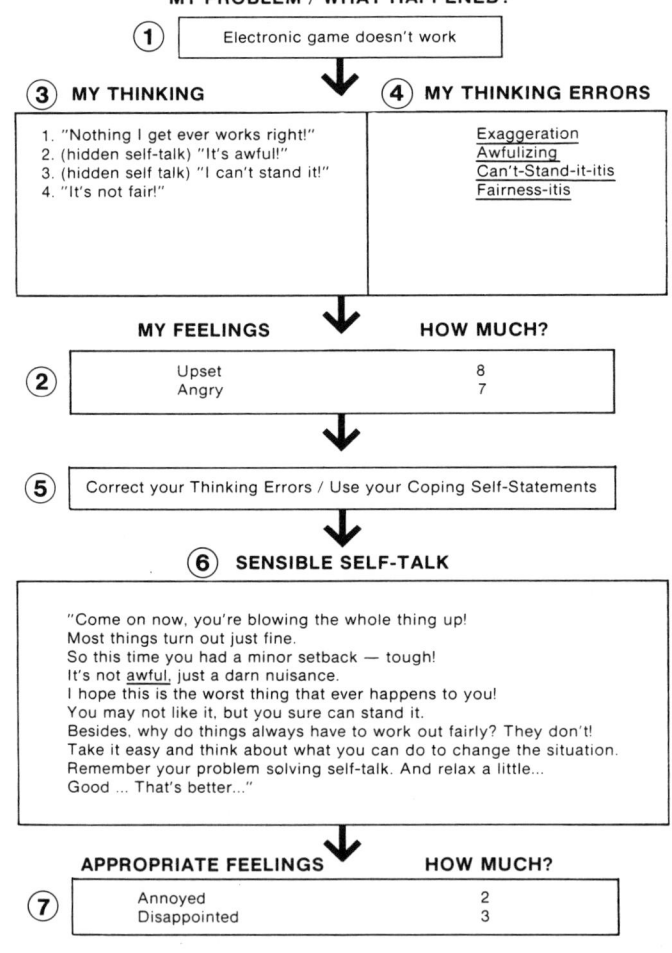

FIGURE 3. Children's rational worksheet.

WORKING WITH CHILDREN IN GROUPS 503

During the sesssions, group members are given practice in using the worksheets to analyze either hypothetical problems or actual problems that the group members introduce.

Teaching Problem-Solving and Self-Instructional Skills

A major goal of treatment is teaching the child how to approach any problem in a systematic fashion. This means being able to articulate what the problem is, generating possible options and their consequences, coming up with a plan, carrying it through, and finally evaluating the results. Although the skill can be taught in a variety of ways, techniques using some cognitive modeling procedures seem especially useful. Camp and Bash (1981) suggested a way in which the problem-solving sequence just described can be made more age-appropriate. The child learns to ask:

1. "What is my problem?"
2. "How can I solve it?"
3. "Am I using my plan?"

And finally:

4. "How did I do?"

To illustrate how this technique can be applied to an actual problem, the group leader may begin with an impersonal problem, such as putting together a jigsaw puzzle. Modeling the appropriate problem-solving self-statements, the therapist thinks aloud:

> *What is my problem?* . . . I have to get these pieces together to complete the puzzle. . . . *How can I do it?* . . . Well, I could go by the colors. . . . I could put all these green pieces together. . . . Or I could start by looking at shapes . . . or even use both shapes and colors. . . . That's it! I think I'll use both. . . . Now I need a blue piece with two arms and one pocket. . . . Here it is. . . . *Am I using my plan?* Yes, I think so. I'm going by the color I need and the shape of the piece next to it. (*Later.*) *How did I do?* I did fine! It's a good idea to follow a plan. Good for me!

Simple problems can quickly be replaced by more complex interpersonal ones. "Problem-solving cards" can be made, presenting the group members with a problem such as:

> Beth wants to buy her mother a present for Mother's Day, but she is short of money. What are some things she could do in this situation?

Or:

> Joshua has a test tomorrow, and he should study if he wants to do well. His friend has tickets for the hockey game tonight and has just called him on

the phone to ask him if he wants to come. What should Joshua do in this situation? Why?

Here, children are asked to think out loud about how they would handle the situation. Again, the emphasis is on internalizing a set of self-statements that would guide the problem-solving process.

Many of the child's problems involve some personal distress, and additional strategies need to be taught to deal with it. By using cognitive modeling and role-play techniques, the appropriate self-talk needed to cope with circumstances can be developed. For example, the group therapist may begin:

> My problem-solving card says, "You are in the dentist's office and it's your turn next to have your tooth pulled." OK, let me give it a good try. . . . Take a deep breath . . . and slowly let it out. . . . Remember the relaxation exercises you learned . . . tighten your muscles . . . good . . . (etc.). . . . Now don't blow this up . . . you won't die from this. . . . There might be some pain, but you can take it . . . and probably not so much pain as you imagine. . . . Don't think of the worst that can happen. . . . Calm down. . . . You're doing fine. . . . Relax. . . . Good.

Related techniques for teaching problem-solving and self-instructional skills include:

- Using puppets as characters for cognitive modeling situations, and having them model appropriate problem-solving and coping statements.
- Creating picture books or storybooks in which the characters think rationally about their problems and use adaptive self-talk.
- Using creative videotaped "programs" in which appropriate problem-solving and coping skills are modeled.

Homework assignments can be used to complement and strengthen the skills learned in the group. A pocket-sized "problem-solving diary" can be used by the children to record and monitor the week's problems and how they handled them. The problems can also serve as material for the next therapy session.

Teaching Interpersonal Behavioral Skills

The procedures of choice in teaching interpersonal behavior skills are social modeling, role playing, and coaching. Like self-instructional training, these three procedures are often combined in a therapeutic sequence. To teach sharing and cooperative behaviors for example, the therapist can begin by raising a number of questions for discussion, such as:

"Why is it good to share?"
"What are some things you just can't do by youself?"
"What would the world be like if nobody helped anyone else?"

Modeling can then be introduced, with the therapist beginning:

> Let's pretend I'm having my lunch, and today my mother has given me two extra cookies for dessert. I see that my friend, who is sitting next to me, has no dessert. . . . Now, Peter, you come up and pretend you're my school friend. . . . The rest of you watch what I do.

Modeling can be done by other group members as well as the therapist. Puppets can be used, and characters in books, stories, etc., can serve as valuable models.

Videotape is an extremely useful tool for behavioral modeling. It is a realistic medium that children find engrossing. Videotapes can be prepared ahead of time, and the tapes can be stopped at any point for clarification or for an "instant replay" reviewing the learning. Following the modeling, the therapist initiates further discussion and coaching along the following lines:

"What did I do?"
"How did Peter feel when he asked if he wanted to share?"
"What are some other things that could have been done?"

At this point, the therapist could ask for solutions and have the group members role-play the same situation. New situations can be role-played as they are suggested, and these can be videotaped, replayed, and discussed.

Many other techniques are possible as well. Games that teach socialization skills can be excellent teaching devices. In the board-game format introduced earlier, for example, a player throws the dice and, landing on a square marked "Take a Card," picks one from a pile in the center of the board, which reads:

> Ask the person next to you if he or she would like to share a treat with you at the next session. You now get a free roll of the dice—and don't forget the treat!

The therapist can devise creative play and activities that require a variety of interpersonal skills, for example:

- Having two children type a letter, with each child having access to only one side of the keyboard. Make this a game by timing it and subtracting five seconds for each mistake.
- Have the children run in relay races or potato-sack races, which require one child to be dependent on another.

- Do a "blind walk," in which one child is blindfolded and a second child leads the other around, preventing him or her from bumping into things.

Contingency reinforcement is another technique that can help teach socialization skills. Here, children are rewarded with social and/or concrete reinforcers for appropriate socialization behaviors.

Games, puzzles, books, pictures, etc.—the content and range of programming is limited only by one's imagination. Should this run dry, additional sources for ideas and materials are listed under "References" at the end of the chapter.

Working with Younger Children

Much of the programming described here is aimed at the latency-age child and the young adolescent. This is not to suggest that group work with younger children using a cognitive-behavior–skills-training approach is inappropriate or ineffective. Such group work with children in the preschool years has worked, and worked well. However, some important modifications should be considered.

With younger children, far more attention is given to the readiness skills necessary for cognitive, affective, and behavioral growth. The therapist should ask such questions as:

- Does the child have a vocabulary of feelings?
- Is the child able to understand concepts of relationships and such terms as *why, if,* and *because*?
- Is the child able to follow simple directions?
- Is the child able to attend for sufficient periods of time?

In treatment, there is far less emphasis on cognitive restructuring techniques and much more attention given to coping self-statements and self-instructional skills. Socialization is more important at the younger ages, and socialization goals are modified to reflect more basic deficiencies, for example, the ability to make eye contact, activity levels, and impulse control.

The treatment techniques, although similar to those used with older children, are emphasized differently. Concrete and social reinforcement programs are more commonly used. Modeling, for both cognitive and behavioral responses, is very important, but the models shift from live models to stories, puppets, etc.

Parents and teachers are given a more active role in the treatment. Their attendance at sessions is encouraged, and they are taught the procedures and approaches used in the group wherever possible.

The Challenge

This chapter has explored some of the richness and potential available to those working with children in groups. The ideas and approaches are relatively recent in their development. Although the findings are far from complete, initial results point with promise to their therapeutic value. Clearly, there is a need for greater experimentation and the acquisition of additional skills on the part of group therapists working within this framework. Even now, however, there is a feeling of excitement that comes from knowing that we are moving in an important new direction.

Suggested Readings

Developmental Groups for Children edited by J. A. Duncan and J. Gumaer (Springfield, Ill., Charles C Thomas, 1980).
Cognitive-Behavioral Interventions edited by P. C. Kendall and S. D. Hollon (New York, Academic Press, 1979).
Treating Children in Groups: A Behavioral Approach by S. D. Rose (San Francisco, Calif., Jossey-Bass, 1972).
"Review of Social-Cognitive Problem-Solving Interventions with Children" by E. S. Urbain and P. C. Kendall (*Psychological Bulletin*, 1980, 88, 109–143).

References[1]

Beck, A. T. *Cognitive therapy and the emotional disorders.* New York: International Universities Press, 1976.
*Camp, B. W., & Bash, M. A. *Think aloud.* Champaign, Ill.: Research Press, 1981.
*Canfield, J., & Wells, H. C. *100 ways to enhance self-concept in the classroom.* Englewood Cliffs, N.J.: Prentice-Hall, 1976.
*Cartledge, G., & Milburn, J. F. (Eds.), *Teaching social skills to children.* New York: Pergamon Press, 1980.
D'Zurilla, T., & Goldfried, M. Problem solving and behavior modification. *Journal of Abnormal Psychology,* 1971, 78, 107–126.
Ellis, A. *Reason and emotion in psychotherapy.* New York: Lyle Stuart Press, 1962.
Ellis, A. Emotional education at the Living School. In M. M. Ohlsen (Ed.), *Counseling children in groups.* New York: Holt, Rinehart & Winston, 1973.
Ellis, A., & Harper, R. A. *A new guide to rational living.* Hollywood, Calif.: Wilshire, 1975.
*Gerald, M., & Eyman, W. *Thinking straight and talking sense.* New York: Institute for Rational-Emotive Therapy, 1981.
Kendall, P. C., & Korgeski, G. P. Assessment and cognitive behavioral interventions. *Cognitive Therapy and Research,* 1979, 3, 1–4.

---

[1]References preceded by an asterisk were found to be especially useful to providing practical programming ideas and resource materials.

*Knaus, W. *Rational emotive education*. New York: Institute for Rational-Emotive Therapy, 1974.
*Meichenbaum, D. *Cognitive-behavior modification*. New York: Plenum Press, 1977.
Merluzzi, T. V., Glass, C. R., & Genest, M. (Eds.), *Cognitive assessment*. New York: Guilford Press, 1981.
Murphy, R. J., & Ellis, A. Rationality scales: A bibliography. New York: Institute for Rational Living, 1976.
*Spivack, G., & Shure, M. B. *Social adjustment of young children: A cognitive approach to solving real-life problems*. San Francisco: Jossey-Bass, 1974.
*Spivack, G., Platt, J. J., & Shure, M. B. *The problem-solving approach to adjustment*. San Francisco: Jossey-Bass, 1976.
Walker, H. *Problem behavior identification checklist*. Los Angeles: Western Psychological Services, 1970.
*Young, H. S. *A rational counseling primer*. New York: Institute for Rational Living, 1974.

18

Research Perspective for the Mental Health Practitioner

KAREN SUTTON-SIMON

INTRODUCTION

Cognitive-behavioral approaches to child pathology and treatment are indeed "new kids on the block" (DiGiuseppe, 1981, p. 50), whose permanent residence within the psychotherapy community is still uncertain. Although the clinical acceptance of cognitive-behavioral interventions has been enthusiastic, the literature describing their applications to childhood problems, as well as empirical evaluations of their efficacy, remains sketchy. A simple remedy for these circumstances is to call for increased clinical and research activity. However, the cognitive-behavioral perspective offers a novel conception of the nature and amelioration of psychological problems, and therefore I believe that it warrants a novel approach to research. It is the purpose of this chapter to initiate such an approach, first by identifying the unique issues posed by cognitive-behavioral therapy with children, and then by formulating research questions that follow from these issues. In considering directions for research, I will attempt to maintain a focus on questions that hold significance for clinical practice.

To accomplish these goals, I first provide a brief overview of the empirical literature relevant to cognitive-behavioral therapy with children in order to determine where initial research reports are available and where they are lacking. I refer the reader to several recent excellent reviews for in-depth evaluations of this work (see, for example, Karoly, 1977; Kendall & Finch, 1979b; Little & Kendall, 1979; Meichenbaum &

KAREN SUTTON-SIMON • Department of Psychology, Oberlin College, Oberlin, Ohio 44074.

Asarnow, 1979). Next, I examine closely those areas that lack research, and I begin to articulate the questions they pose. Where appropriate, I will also raise issues relevant to conceptualizing cognitive-behavioral research and the methodological problems specific to the cognitive orientation. Throughout this chapter, I offer suggestions for possible empirical investigation in an effort to spark the reader's thinking as well as to provide templates for the development of future research. To further assist the clinician contemplating research, I review the guidelines for conducting research in clinical settings and suggest ways to prepare for and cope with the exigencies of conducting research in such settings. It is my hope and intention that these discussions will offer the clinician sufficient guidance and encouragement to initiate clinically meaningful yet empirically rigorous examinations of cognitive-behavioral therapy with children.

Review of Research

The empirical literature concerning cognitive-behavioral therapy with children has concentrated on two clinical problems: impulse control (Kendall & Finch, 1976, 1978, 1979a; Kendall & Wilcox, 1980) and social adjustment (Platt, Scura, & Hannon, 1973; Platt, Spivack, Altman, Altman, & Peizer, 1974; Spivack, Platt, & Shure, 1976; Spivack & Shure, 1974). The literature relevant to impulse control consists primarily of therapy outcome studies and includes reports of the development and application of cognitive interventions for hyperactivity (Bornstein & Quevillon, 1976; Douglas, Parry, Marton, & Garson, 1976); self-control (Meichenbaum & Goodman, 1971); aggressiveness (McCullough, Huntsinger, & Nay, 1977); disruptive classroom behavior (Drummond, 1974; O'Leary, 1968; Monohan & O'Leary, 1971); and an impulsive cognitive tempo (Camp, Blom, Herbert & Van Doorninck, 1977; Finch, Wilkinson, & Nelson, 1975; Kendall & Finch, 1978; Kendall & Wilcox, 1980). The literature concerning social adjustment problems also consists primarily of therapy outcome reports and presents and evaluates cognitive interventions for interpersonal cognitive problem-solving skills (Shure & Spivack, 1978; Spivack *et al.*, 1976; Spivack & Shure, 1974); role taking (Chandler, 1973; Douglas *et al.*, 1976; Little, 1978); and interpersonal self-control (Huntsinger, 1979). Cognitive treatment techniques have recently been extended to children's academic skills, and several writers have described how self-instructional training and related cognitive techniques can be used to teach children the process of learning (Brown,

1983; Kestner & Borkowski, in press; Meichenbaum & Asarnow, 1979; Turnure, Buium, & Thurlow, 1976).

The subject groups to which cognitive-behavioral techniques have been applied in the above-mentioned research include some clinically relevant samples, such as impulsive children (Meichenbaum & Goodman, 1971); hyperactive children referred for psychiatric treatment (Bugenthal, Whalen, & Henker, 1977; Douglas *et al.*, 1976; Palkes, Stewart, & Freedman, 1972); emotionally disturbed children (Finch *et al.*, 1975; Spivack & Levine, 1963); and delinquents (Huntsinger, 1979; Williams & Akamatsu, 1978). However, major segments of the child population seeking therapy have not yet appeared in cognitive-behavioral research reports. For example, we lack information about the development and effectiveness of cognitively oriented treatment programs for severely disturbed and psychotic children and for children with impaired intellectual functioning. In addition, current research has not yet extended cognitive interventions to the full spectrum of pathology that clinicians encounter when working with children. Descriptions of cognitive approaches to such common childhood problems as social isolation, shyness, depression, fears and phobias, and sexual problems are just now appearing in the literature (see Chapters 4 through 11). Finally, the cognitive techniques that have been applied to children in the current literature are limited to self-instructional training (Kendall & Finch, 1976, 1978; Douglas *et al.*, 1976; Robin, Armel, & O'Leary, 1975); training in search and scan strategies (Bender, 1976; Egeland, 1974; Zelniker, Jeffrey, Ault, & Parsons, 1972); training in alternative and means–ends thinking (Bowman, 1979; Robin, Kent, O'Leary, Foster, & Prinz, 1977; Spivack *et al.*, 1976); and the modeling of cognitions (Cohen & Przybycien, 1974; Douglas *et al.*, 1976; Meichenbaum & Goodman, 1971; Ridberg, Parke, & Hetherington, 1971). Although additional efforts to develop and apply the full range of cognitive interventions to children's problems are under way, to date we lack systematic evaluation of such well-established cognitive-behavioral approaches as rational-emotive therapy (Ellis, 1962) and cognitive therapy (Beck, 1972).

From this brief overview, it is apparent that research in cognitive-behavioral therapy with children has a long way to go. There are major areas of therapy development and application for which we lack even initial evidence of effectiveness. In these areas, our task is to initiate the process of empirical evaluation. However, in areas in which empirical investigation is under way, major questions concerning the comparative efficacy and the relative efficiency of treatments, the contribution of various treatment components to outcome, and the preventive potential of cognitive interventions have not yet been addressed in research. Additionally, whole segments of the therapeutic process, such as assessment and the transfer of treatment objectives to the natural environment, have received scant research attention. Finally, issues of theoretical significance, such as the nature of the cognitive process involved in children's pathology, also wait empirical examination. I now examine these neglected areas to identify some of the specific research questions that need to be raised, as well as to determine how they might be investigated both to enrich the practitioner's clinical skills and to provide a sounder data base for future clinical applications.

Areas for Research

Assessment of Cognitive-Behavioral Interventions

Although accurate and relevant assessment is critical in planning treatment, research on assessment for cognitive-behavioral interventions with children has lagged far behind that on therapy outcome. One segment of the available research reflects an interest in developing content-oriented psychometric scales that attempt to assess subjects' cognitions directly. The best researched example of these is the Ideas Inventory (Kassinove, Crisci, & Tiegerman, 1977), derived from assumptions of rational-emotive theory (Ellis, 1962; Ellis & Harper, 1975). Accordingly, it attempts to measure children's irrational beliefs. A measure similar in format and objective is the Rational Behavior Inventory (Shorkey & Whiteman, 1977), which, in one version, can be used with children as young as 9. It, too, purports to measure the nature and degree of children's irrational thinking.

Although there is some evidence to suggest that these scales assess variables related to mental health (DiGiuseppe & Kassinove, 1976; Kassinove *et al.*, 1977; Shorkey & Saski, 1981), more extensive research is needed to establish their validity and their clinical utility. For example, we lack empirical investigations of the functional relationships between constellations of irrational beliefs in children as measured by these scales and specific childhood disorders, although rational-emotive theory is rich in hypotheses on this subject. Additionally, we have no data to indicate the utility of these scales in predicting the success of cognitive treatment or in facilitating the development of novel cognitive interventions. Validity determinations for these instruments could also be improved measurably by their use with children drawn from clinically representative samples.

Beyond these pragmatic concerns, however, we need research to establish the construct validity of these measures by identifying the uniquely cognitive nature of the dimensions they assess. We assume that because the content of these scales is derived from cognitive-behavioral theory, they, in fact, measure cognitions, yet we lack even suggestive evidence for this crucial assumption. Although we believe that children can be excellent sources of information about themselves, it is possible that on scales that assess the content of cognitions, we may be asking for information beyond their awareness, or worse, we may be asking them to mold their cognitions to fit our theoretical preconceptions. Undoubtedly, the clinical convenience and face validity of content-based, self-report measures are compelling. Nonetheless, it is unwise to allow convenience to overshadow our concern about methodological and conceptual validity. Simply put, we need research that demonstrates that content-based self-report measures do, in fact, assess cognitions. In light of the ephemeral nature of cognitions and the difficulties in measuring them, we might be wise to generate research on a variety of assessment strategies that would enable us to measure cognitions from several methodological as well as conceptual viewpoints. Additionally, we might also initiate research on the mediational processes that we assume underlie particular cognitions, and we might also attempt to measure the behavioral and affective products of cognitions. One assessment tool developed to tap the behavioral products of cognition is the Kendall Self-Control Rating Scale (Kendall & Wilcox, 1979), which measures behavioral self-control in extratherapy settings following self-instructional training for nonimpulsive behavior.

As I suggested above, the cognitive assessment of children need not be confined to the currently available self-report, content-oriented scales. Indeed, the structure and the inflexibility of these scales relative to other cognitive assessment procedures argue against their use with children. We would do well to remember that a child's cognitive world is not as closed to others as an adult's. For example, children often engage spontaneously in overt private speech and are frequently encouraged to guess what someone is thinking as a part of play. Additionally, children are often taught to solve academic problems by thinking them through out loud. From experiences such as these, several cognitive assessment procedures developed for use with adults may already be familiar to children. Thus, clinical researchers might adapt think-aloud methods and thought-listing assessment procedures for use with children, because children should be as least as able as adults to report on their cognitive worlds.

One means of adapting cognitive assessment techniques for use with children is suggested by an exploratory investigation by Weston and Glass (1980). Based on the play therapy model, Weston and Glass (1980) had children use puppets to respond to vignettes containing interactional problems. After the children put thinking caps on their puppets, they were able to report what the puppets were saying to themselves about the problem situations. Research with these additional assessment strategies may serve both to expand our ability to assess an individual child's cognitive dysfunction and to extend our knowledge of dysfunctional cognitions.

The question raised earlier of what is being measured by cognitive assessment scales is related to a larger issue confronting cognitive-behavioral therapies, namely: What is the most appropriate object of assessment? Clinical researchers might rightly question whether we should even attempt to assess cognitions. That is, do our efforts to evaluate the gains of cognitive-behavioral therapy and to develop a better understanding of pathology from a cognitive perspective depend on our ability to assess cognitions? If cognitive-behavioral therapists consider behavioral indices the *sina qua non* for therapy evaluations and identification of pathology, then a case can be made for the alternative strategy of confining our measurement efforts to specifiable performance differences. Under these circumstances, cognitive therapists might then face the unique and perplexing situation of attempting to account for performance improvements following cognitive interventions without invoking changes in cognition. On the other hand, if therapists view cognitive change as an index integral to therapy evaluation and include cognitive assessment in treatment posttesting, they might then be called on to account for changes in cognition for which there are no concomitant changes in behavior. Would such an outcome be considered successful therapy? In light of clinical reports that suggest that behaviors and cognitions do not always change in the same direction or to the same extent as a function of cognitive-behavioral therapy, in future research we must also attempt to determine how our cognitive indices are related to measures of affect and performance. Clearly, research in cognitive assessment needs to address both theoretical and applied issues to answer questions of what to assess as well as how to assess. We anticipate that research in this area will bear on how we describe pathology in cognitive terms, as well as on how we measure the outcome of cognitive interventions.

Although the most obvious research question in the area of assessment is how best to measure cognitions, research in cognitive assessment can also address clinicians' questions concerning the cognitive mediational nature of the underlying pathology. Cognitive-behavioral theory conceptualizes psychopathology as being the result of either excesses of dysfunctional cognitions or deficits of adaptive ones. However, little research has been geared to identifying these processes in children. One notable exception is in the area of lack of self-control, which can be assessed by the Kendall Self-Control Rating Scale (Kendall & Wilcox, 1979) mentioned above. This scale was developed to tap the cognitive dimensions of deliberation, problem solving, planning, and evaluation. The research strategy of employing assessment methods to attain a better understanding of the nature of the cognitive problem appears ripe for further investigation in light of the continuing development of cognitive models of child pathology (see Chapters 1 and 8). For example, clinical experience suggests that school underachievement results from cognitions similar to "It doesn't matter whether or not I do the work; I always fail anyway," that is, cognitions that both elicit negative affect and interfere with or inhibit adaptive responses. Thus, an assessment that involves attempts to identify this cognitive content prior to or during the execution of school assignments might provide us with information not only about an individual child client but also about the cognitive nature of the problem of school underachievement. In the long run, this research strategy may have implications for treatment development.

Many psychotherapy approaches have grappled with questions of the compatibility between treatment methods and children's abilities. Alternate treatments, such as play therapy, have arisen from the belief that children lack the ability to participate in the traditional therapy format. Similar concerns have been voiced by practitioners of cognitive-behavioral therapy (DiGiuseppe, 1981; Kendall & Finch, 1979a,b), yet research to date has not explored this issue. This is especially surprising for cognitive-behavioral therapy not only because the interventions presuppose a level of cognitive development sufficient to follow treatment, but also because they seek to affect changes in cognitive content and process. Assessment research geared to analyzing a child's level of cognitive development could be employed to determine whether a child has the cognitive capacity to profit from a particular cognitive intervention. Research on assessment viewed from this perspective would have a twofold purpose. First, by focusing on assessment of the individual, it could provide the clinician with information about the "therapy readiness" of a particular child client. Second, by accumulating information across children, it could facilitate the development of general guidelines for the application of various cognitive interventions to given age or development groups. This latter purpose would seem especially important for atypical children, such as those who are retarded or have learning disabilities. In this broad definition of assessment, I am suggesting that it would be useful to the cognitive-behavioral therapist to have information about a child's cognitive strengths as well as weaknesses and that research on cognitive assessment can aid in this process.

Research on Therapy Content and Process

For the mental health practitioner, the most pressing research questions often concern the effectiveness of treatment. The empirical answer to the question of whether a therapy has succeeded is more likely to bear directly on a therapist's actual practice than any other research. Unfortunately, this emphasis may deflect attention away from research questions concerning the substance of therapy or what occurs during sessions. There are costs to overlooking research on therapy content and process. First, without such research, we are not able to modify currently available techniques and procedures to make them more effective. Second, we cannot enhance therapy efficiency because we are unable to specify which client should receive which intervention under a given set of conditions. These drawbacks may be felt most keenly by practitioners of cognitive-behavioral treatments because the conceptual system is so new and the interventions are so diverse that we have few concrete guidelines for the applications of various techniques. In an effort to encourage a sharpening of the prescriptions for cognitive-behavioral interventions, we devote this next section to considering issues of psychotherapy content and process. I hope that an empirical examination of these issues will contribute to the development and application of more effective and efficient cognitive treatment for children.

Psychotherapy process research indicates that therapists' expectations of clients often influence the course and outcome of treatment. Within the cognitive-behavioral scheme, the influence of therapists' expectations of child clients may be especially important to examine because these expectations may include crucial assumptions about the child's cognitive abilities. Whether we consider children cognitively mature enough to understand a particular cognitive intervention determines whether we include that technique in treatment. For other therapies, therapist expectations may lead to a modification of some aspects of the treatment plan, but generally, the basic treatment modality is itself unchanged. Only with cognitive-behavioral interventions do we encounter therapist expectations that may require us to change the content of treatment. As a general consideration, we would be wise to examine the effects of therapist expectations that err in both directions, those that underestimate as well as those that overestimate a child's cognitive capacities.

Although cognitive-behavioral therapy posits the source of therapeutic influence in the cognitive change techniques rather than the personality of the therapist, we may expect some dimensions of therapist style to interact with the techniques and thus to have a bearing on the outcome of cognitive treatment. For example, we might examine whether a child is more likely to be receptive to disputing irrational beliefs when the therapist presents disputation in a challenging dialogue or when the therapist teaches disputation didactically. Additionally, we might examine whether self-instructional training is more effective for children when presented with a coping content or with a mastery content. Although I do not believe that a therapist's personal style is sufficient to attain positive behavior change, I also caution against dismissing issues of style and manner as irrelevant to developing effective cognitive-change techniques.

Children as well as therapists bring expectations to treatment. The popular image of psychologists and psychotherapy probably leads children to expect a "talking cure" conducted by a passive therapist. Cognitive-behavioral treatment and therapists are likely to depart from these expectations, but with what effects on the course and outcome of treatment? Does the problem-solving, goal-oriented format of cognitive-behavioral interventions require a pretherapy educational phase to help children shift their expectations? Does the inclusion of such an educational phase enhance the efficiency of cognitive treatment? On the other side of the coin, does the cognitive-behavioral therapist's active, directive style mislead children to expect to be passive recipients of treatment, and if so, how does this attitude influence outcome? How might it be overcome? These are some examples of the myriad empirical questions we might generate regarding the effects of client variables on therapy outcome.

I would argue that practitioners of cognitive-behavioral therapy, to a greater extent than practitioners of other treatments, must be sensitive to the verbal abilities of their child clients. Cognitive-behavioral interventions face the unique challenge of attempting to teach child clients to report on their covert cognitive processes. To accomplish this, we must teach them to monitor and then articulate their thoughts. We need research to determine what minimal level of verbal ability is required for children to understand and participate in this complex process. Additionally, we need empirical demonstrations that the language of cognitive interventions is comprehensible to children. If necessary, we may need to develop ways to modify this language to match the child's verbal skills more closely.

I have already pointed out several areas in which child clients' cognitive abilities raise important research questions unique to the cognitive orientation. This is especially true for research on the therapy process. We may be able to improve significantly the effectiveness of cognitive-behavioral interventions if we can match treatments to the child's cognitive abilities. It has been suggested that, prior to treatment, therapists undertake an analysis of the child's level of cognitive development (Kendall & Finch, 1979a; DiGiuseppe, 1981) to determine whether a particular cognitive intervention is suitable for that child. Although such a strategy may enable clinicians to enhance therapy effectiveness for individual children, it may also have an additional long-range benefit. Relevant research findings accumulated over individual children may enable therapists, first, to identify the therapy-task-relevant cognitive abilities generally possessed by children of a given age or level of intellectual development and, second, to modify standard techniques and generate novel ones that would capitalize on the cognitive capacity of children at those levels of development. For example, such process-oriented research might examine children's ability to learn to estimate accurately the likelihood of the occurrence of a negative event, a cognitive skill that Beck (1976) suggested is necessary for countering depressogenic thoughts. If research indicated that young children were able to learn the logical skills required to evaluate the probability of negative events empirically, we would then be encouraged to develop and incorporate procedures to teach this skill in a treatment program for depression in young children.

Another aspect of the child client's functioning relevant to research on the process of cognitive therapy concerns psychological test data. By and large, cognitive-behavioral practitioners do not emphasize information provided by tests of psychological dimensions. Yet, such data, especially as they indicate "psychological-mindedness," might enable practitioners to develop better cognitive treatments. For example, we might examine children's tendencies to experience anxiety cognitively rather than physiologically in order to determine whether such differences affect the children's suitability for cognitive treatment. Or we might examine whether children make internal or external attributions of their success and failure experiences to determine whether differences on this dimension have bearing on the course of cognitive treatment.

Another large segment of therapy process research concerns the structure of the therapy session. Research in this area of cognitive-behavioral interventions could be geared to determining how best to teach cognitive skills by varying such facets of the session as the use of treatment time on different tasks; establishing session goals; employing adjuncts to therapy sessions such as homework assignments and readings; and relying on therapy assistants in school and home for additional treatment. The possibilities of developing a more effective therapy process are limited only by practitioners' imaginations and their sensitivity to what seems most effective in their clinical experience. Research relevant to the content and the process of cognitive-behavioral interventions may prove to be the richest source of treatment innovations.

Research on the Outcome of Cognitive-Behavioral Therapy

Many cognitive therapies with children have not yet been exposed to enough empirical scrutiny to provide the data necessary to establish their efficacy. Outcome studies are sorely needed to put to rest questions of the therapeutic legitimacy of these cognitive interventions. However, some of the most clinically meaningful therapy research goes beyond determinations of outcome alone to examine more specific questions of measurement and maintenance of treatment effects and comparative contributions of treatment components to outcome. For cognitive interventions for which a body of outcome research exists, it is appropriate to consider these issues. The next section covers both these avenues of research—the beginning outcome studies where none exist, and the more complex issues relevant to outcome—in an attempt to examine the issue of efficacy for the entire range of cognitive-behavioral interventions.

Initial Investigations of Therapy Effectiveness

Although several of the principles and techniques of rational-emotive therapy have been extended to apply to children, we lack empirical demonstrations of its effectiveness with child clients. Descriptive reports are available for clinical samples of children, but the research assesses rational-emotive education with normal children. Thus, we await the first empirical evaluation of rational-emotive therapy with disturbed children. In planning studies for this treatment approach, investigators might wish first to conduct exploratory examinations to develop an initial estimate of the most effective rational-emotive techniques to use with children as well as the best means of presenting them. Such studies could be conducted by means of an own-control design (Goldstein, Heller, & Sechrest, 1966; Hayes, 1981) before undertaking complex and expensive group-comparison studies. These initial examinations might assess, for example, whether young children can learn elegant or philosophical disputing reasonably well or whether rational-emotive treatment for children should emphasize empirical or inelegant disputing. With answers to such questions, researchers could undertake the more costly group comparisons using only the most effective techniques in a rational-emotive treatment for children.

Cognitive therapy, as developed by Beck and his colleagues (Beck, 1976; Beck, Rush, Shaw, & Emery, 1979) has a research history with children similar to that of rational-emotive treatment. Clinical applications are described (Bedrosian, 1981) and effectiveness is reported, but no empirical data are available. Thus, research on cognitive therapy needs to begin with demonstrations of the effectiveness of such techniques as teaching children to identify their automatic thoughts and to engage in hypothesis testing. As previously suggested, it would be advisable to begin therapy evaluations with the less costly outcome designs of own-control or time-series studies.

This discussion of interventions in need of initial outcome research is far from exhaustive. However, I hope it provides a framework and some examples to guide the practicing clinician with interests in assessing the effectiveness of particular cognitive interventions with children. Of course, much work needs to be done with other cognitive approaches, and I now discuss some of these additional avenues of research.

Measuring the Outcome of Cognitive-Behavioral Therapy

The question of how we should evaluate the outcome of cognitive-behavioral therapy has two meanings: (1) What are the variables we should assess to establish the efficacy of cognitive interventions? And (2) what are the best tools for assessing those variables? A related consideration is which measures we believe are most appropriate for use with children. As indicated in the section on assessment, cognitive-behavioral therapy poses a unique problem because of the possible independence of the cognitive, affective, and behavioral dimensions. Cognitive-behavioral therapy with children raises a further complication because of the possibly of an interaction between cognitive changes due to maturation and those attributable to therapy. In the discussion of assessment, I questioned whether we could assess the success of a cognitive therapy by examining only the behavioral dimensions. Conversely, I also questioned whether improvement along a cognitive dimension alone would be sufficient evidence of a treatment's efficacy. Until we have a better understanding of the relationships among cognitive, affective, and behavioral variables, our best strategy might be to incorporate several outcome measures that are conceptually, as well as methodologically, independent. Thus, we might include two or more distinct cognitive measures, such as a scale of cognitive distortions and a thought-listing procedure, as well as affective rating scales, behavioral observations, standardized measures of mental health, and peer or therapist ratings. With regard to the special problem of assessing therapy outcome with children, we would have either to determine that our assessment instruments were tapping therapy gains rather than age-related changes or to develop age norms for our assessment measures.

Although the strategy of relying on a broad base of assessment tools to measure therapy outcome enables us to cope with the question of what to assess, it cannot help us to arrive at unequivocal determinations of treatment effectiveness when we are faced with equivocal findings on those measures. For example, would we consider a cognitive therapy successful if we found behavioral improvement but no cognitive change? On the other hand, would we be satisfied with a cognitive treatment that resulted in cognitive improvement but no behavioral change? The answers to these questions depend on several factors, including the specific targets of the interventions, the relative significance of the variable in the constellation of the symptoms, and our sophistication in measuring the variables. This issue of measuring cognitive therapy outcomes becomes even more complex when we undertake comparisons between cognitive and noncognitive interventions. Presumably, each treatment is the most effective in modifying those variables that it targets directly. This supposition could leave us with difficult decisions regarding conclusions about comparative treatment effectiveness.

Questions concerning the measurement of therapy outcome have yet another facet, one that involves the time dimension. When we evaluate treatment, we must also consider when to measure the outcome. Thus, we must address questions concerning the maintenance of therapy effects.

Maintenance of Therapy Outcome

It is generally agreed that the quality of therapy outcome research is improved significantly when it includes follow-up reports. Follow-up reports enable us to determine not only that the therapy has resulted in improvement, but also that the improvement is not an epiphenomenon. Nonetheless, most posttesting is conducted immediately upon completion of treatment, and conclusions about treatment effectiveness are frequently based on data collected while the therapy proscriptions are still fresh and the client's optimism and self-esteem are high.

Few cognitive-behavioral outcome studies report follow-up assessments. Therefore, we are unable to compare the maintenance of therapeutic gains for cognitive-behavioral and other interventions. However, because cognitive approaches emphasize developing cognitive coping skills and strategies that we presume can be applied across situations, it can be argued that cognitive-behavioral interventions should result in better maintenance. Therefore, it is imperative that future cognitive-behavioral outcome research include follow-up assessments. Researchers might wish to vary both the time since treatment and the nature of the follow-up data collected across studies, in an effort to accumulate the most extensive and meaningful information about the maintenance of treatment gains. For example, for a study involving disruptive school behavior, the research might concentrate follow-up on monthly school observations but collect self-report scales only at three-month intervals. In general, follow-up strategies can be adapted to what makes most sense for the individual child and the particular problem.

Once cognitive-behavioral researchers begin to gauge the durability of their treatments, they might then be ready to examine the conditions under which maintenance can be enhanced. We might then wish to focus on particular facets of treatment to ask whether there are ways to restructure it to enhance maintenance. Alternatively, we might investigate whether there are ways to work with child clients to modify their environments to make maintenance more likely. The larger issue here is to formulate outcome research questions that enable us to improve our available treatments by strengthening their effectiveness and efficiency.

Generalization of Treatment Effects

No cognitive treatment, despite its durability, is very useful to practitioners if its positive effects are limited only to the situations and the tasks specifically targeted in the treatment. Indeed, because the emphasis in cognitive approaches is on variables that we presume have cross-situational impact, cognitive treatments for which we cannot demonstrate generalization are disappointing. Thus, another research issue of great significance for the mental health practitioner pertains to demonstrating the generalization of cognitive-behavioral treatment effects. In developing therapy outcome studies, we need to build in opportunities to determine whether the treatment yields positive changes in extra-therapy situations. For example, in an outcome study examining the effectiveness of self-instructional training in modifying children's impulsive cognitive style on academic tasks, we might also observe interpersonal behavior to determine whether there are related improvements in peer relationships.

Information about the generalization of treatment effects can assist clinicians in several ways. First, in identifying failures of generalization, it can enable us to develop more effective treatments by focusing future research and development on the variables that might foster generalization. Second, it can provide a truer picture of the significance of cognitive treatment effects by indicating the breadth of the real-life impact of therapy. Third, information concerning generalization provides assessment data that may indicate what areas other than the targeted ones seem to have improved and what areas still require therapeutic attention.

Finer Specification of Therapy Outcome

Although it is important for clinicians to know that a given cognitive treatment is more effective than no treatment or an attention control, this comparison rarely reflects the choices facing the clinician. More typically, a therapist must choose from among several treatment plans, each of which includes cognitive and noncognitive elements. Thus, more realistic therapy-outcome questions concern the relative effectiveness of treatment approaches and the contribution of various treatment components to outcome. Therefore, I would suggest that a more effective research strategy would compare and analyze the effects of several cognitive-behavioral approaches in a single outcome study.

Because it would make sense to keep comparative outcome studies close to the available data base, investigators might formulate outcome questions involving one or more well-researched cognitive-behavioral treatments, one or more cognitive-behavioral treatments for which little research exists, and at least one active noncognitive treatment. Although this design is certainly expensive, it may afford some long-term savings. For example, if the untested cognitive-behavioral treatment did not result in treatment effects at least as powerful as the other treatments, we would then drop it from further clinical and research consideration for that particular child population with that particular disorder. That is, for our untested cognitive treatment, the issue is not whether it is effective but whether it is more effective than the other available treatments.

I offer the following as an example of this strategy: We have a base of evidence for the effectiveness of self-instructional training in developing self-control in children. However, the technique of disputing distorted perceptions of reality has not been empirically tested for this target problem. For the clinician to select the rational-emotive approach, he or she needs evidence that disputing is at least as effective as self-instructional training but perhaps somewhat cheaper to administer. Additionally, self-control is a target skill for which reasonably effective behavioral procedures are available. The practitioner-researcher could construct a fairly sophisticated outcome study from these three treatments that would yield information about the relative merits of (1) the cognitive and behavioral approaches and (2) the two cognitive approaches. Furthermore, this research model permits the investigator to examine the increase in the size of effects when children are exposed to a combined treatment. Continuing this example, if posttesting indicated that both a cognitive and the behavioral treatment were effective, the clinician could then expose a subset of children in each group to the other treatment to determine whether a combined treatment program substantially increases the effects of either treatment alone. Clearly, this methodological conception permits a more important question than whether a no-treatment control group, later treated, shows improvement to the level of its companion treatment group.

The standard controls and safeguards for internal and external validity that apply to all outcome research apply, of course, to the research strategy outlined above. However, the nature of this model (comparing tested and untested cognitive and noncognitive treatments in a single design) requires some additional considerations. For example, the investigator must be particularly attentive to presenting untested treatments in their strongest forms to give them a fair trial. It would be unfortunate to dismiss as "less effective" a treatment that was, in actuality, poorly applied. Additionally, it is helpful if there is either a clinical or a theoretical basis for the particular treatment comparisons included in a study. Thus, an investigator may choose to compare two treatments because clinical experience leads him or her to suspect differential treatment effectiveness. Alternatively, predictions of differential treatment success may be derived from theory. The empirical or theoretical basis that provides the rationale for making particular treatment comparisons enables researchers to formulate unambiguous hypotheses and also serves as a framework for organizing and understanding the obtained data. Both of these results are crucial to developing and executing meaningful therapy outcome research.

I have focused this section on research that compares the effectiveness of various treatments. In many cases, research projects that assess the contribution of treatment components to outcome will be similar in conceptualization and design. In these instances, we might think of a treatment component as a small-scale independent treatment. However, there are other cases in which a components analysis departs substantially from this model and, for this reason, is worthy of its own discussion.

For some cognitive therapies for children, treatment can be broken down into separate phases or independent tasks that are not treatment by themselves but that function as part of a larger therapeutic venture. Concrete examples might illustrate this point. Almost every cognitive-behavioral treatment for children includes an educational component whose goal is to impart the cognitive conceptualization of pathology and treatment. The usual rationale for including the educational component is to ensure that both child client and therapist will share a similar view of the child's problem and will speak the same language in therapy. Although the educational component is separate from and independent of other treatment tasks, it is unlikely that any therapist would employ it as a separate treatment. For a more subtle example of this analysis, consider the following: A verbal self-reinforcement component is typically included within self-instructional training. No researcher has yet suggested that training a child to emit such statements as "Hey, I got it right. Good job!" is, itself, responsible for therapeutic effectiveness. However, most researchers assume that such statements facilitate the positive changes that follow from self-instructional training. Similarly, children's treatment focusing on skills in solving interpersonal cognitive problems (Spivack et al., 1976) often includes training in causal thinking, the ability to see a purposeful relationship between an event and its outcome. However, it has not been suggested that training in causal thinking alone can enhance interpersonal skills. More typically, it is assumed that a child needs certain "cognitive equipment" before he or she can engage in interpersonal-problem solving; causal thinking is seen as one of several cognitive tools.

In each of the above examples, the components are presumed to be necessary for effective treatment, although, by themselves, they are not viewed as sufficient for a positive outcome. Components analysis research would attempt to determine the contribution of such components by conducting several variations of a single treatment. The variations would differ by the inclusion or the exculsion of given components. The components contained in the most effective version of treatment could then be viewed as accounting for the major portion of the treatment effects. This research would thus enable the practitioner to offer more efficient treatment by emphasizing the most effective components and by omitting components that do not contribute substantially to outcome.

Components-analysis outcome research has another rationale within the cognitive-behavioral approach. In some research and clinical undertakings, cognitive techniques have been treated interchangeably because of their endorsement of similar conceptions of pathology and its modification. This circumstance has resulted in the development of treatment packages that are cognitive-behavioral smorgasbords: some training in the empirical examination of beliefs; some training in alternative appraisals; some work on coping self-instructions, etc. Although such a technique grab-bag may be formulated into a highly successful treatment package, the absence of a systematic development prevents both practitioner and researcher from determining what components account primarily for the positive effects, and thus, it foils attempts to make further improvements in treatment. Under these circumstances, a components analysis helps to untangle the unique contributions of each technique or, alternatively, to demonstrate that the treatment package is, in fact, more effective than the sum of its parts.

Research on the effectiveness of cognitive-behavioral interventions with children is an area of burgeoning research reports. However, from this review, it would appear that cognitive-behavioral researchers have many additional avenues of research to follow to answer questions concerning the effectiveness of treatments.

Cognitive-Behavioral Interventions as Education and for Prevention

Because of the pressing human needs, most mental-health practitioners treat child clients whose dysfunctional behavior has already brought them to the attention of adults. For this reason, the majority of research questions concerning treatment effectiveness tend to be geared to meet the needs of this population. However, initial research reports (DiGiuseppe & Kassinove, 1976; Knaus & Bokor, 1975), as well as some creative treatment innovations (Knaus, 1974; Shure & Spivack, 1978), suggest that cognitive-behavioral interventions may also be used for education and primary prevention. I would now like to turn to a consideration of the research questions posed by such novel applications of cognitive therapy with children.

The first question to be researched in this area is whether cognitive interventions can, in fact, be used to prevent psychological problems. Early reports (DiGiuseppe & Kassinove, 1976; Knaus, 1974) indicate that cognitive principles can be acquired by normal schoolchildren and that such acquisition is related to decreased anxiety and neuroticism as measured by psychometric tests. However, these reports do not explore fully the preventive potential of cognitive interventions for two reasons:

first, only rational-emotive principles were examined, and second, no follow-up assessment was made to determine the incidence of the development of psychological problems in the treated group. Therefore, no statement can be made about the program's ability to prevent psychological difficulties.

Obviously, later follow-up is the key for research to assess the preventive value of cognitive programs. We need to formulate research questions that will enable us to determine not only whether children can acquire the cognitive skills but also whether doing so immunizes them from developing problems later.

Additional avenues for research on the preventive value of cognitive interventions are suggested by questions concerning the role of cognitive skills in the child's behavioral repertoire. For programs aimed at prevention, we might formulate research questions that seek to identify the areas of functioning that benefit most from prevention. For example, we might develop a self-instructional program that provides training in search and scan strategies using training tasks of both interpersonal and task-oriented content. We might then conduct a study to determine whether this training improves children's interpersonal as well as task-oriented behavioral expressions of self-control. As another example, we might offer training in means–ends thinking employing interpersonal content and more formal examples of logic. We could then examine the benefits of such a program by assessing children's interpersonal skills, as well as their ability to engage in critical thinking. As indicated by these examples, research on the preventive value of cognitive-behavioral training might attempt to determine how the acquired cognitive skills innoculate the child against stress or enable her or him to cope with its effects. Although this issue is relevant to the question of the generalization of treatment effects, it also opens up another area of inquiry concerning how treatment effects operate. Thus, empirical studies of prevention programs would enable us to ask why cognitive training enables the child to cope more successfully, and how its effects interface with the child's affective and behavioral repertoires. Research along these lines begins to address the nature of the operation of mediational processes.

One important aspect of programs for prevention and education is their flexibility: they can be developed for those who work with and care for children as well as for the children themselves. For programs developed for those who work with children, we could generate research concerning both the direct and the indirect effects of training. For example, we could formulate research to determine to what extent teachers and parents exposed to cognitive-behavioral therapy are more effective as the result of their own enhanced psychological functioning (direct effects). Alternatively, we could ask to what extent teachers and parents are more effective in their roles because of their use of cognitive-behavioral principles in teaching, disciplining, and interacting with children (indirect effects). In the first set of research questions, the parent or teacher is viewed as the client who develops enhanced cognitive skills. In the second set of research questions, the parent or teacher is viewed as a vehicle for conveying the cognitive skills to children. Nonetheless, in both sets of research questions, our ultimate interest is the effects of such programs on children. Thus, we would ask not only "Can teachers be trained to use cognitive-behavioral skills in their classrooms?" but also "Do children in such classrooms show enhanced interpersonal and academic functioning?"

Research on programs of prevention and education can be particularly appealing to the mental health practitioner in that it extends the conception of treatment beyond the setting of the clinic and makes it possible to do large-scale group research where it would not otherwise be feasible.

Conducting Research in Clinical Settings

In the foregoing sections, I have discussed possible directions for research on cognitive-behavioral therapy with children. My overriding objective was to encourage mental health practitioners to undertake clinically relevant investigations by identifying areas that either lack an empirical data base or pose questions unique to the cognitive-behavioral perspective. Throughout this discussion, I have assumed that practitiones are eager to become involved in clinical research and that it is possible, although certainly not easy, for them to conduct research within clinical settings. However, judging from the fact that the modal number of research publications for clinicians is zero (Kelly, Goldberg, Fiske, & Kilkowski, 1978), it would seem that clinicians' enthusiasm for research could profit from further bolstering. To make it more likely that practitioners engage in research on cognitive-behavioral therapy, I offer the next section on guidelines for conducting research within clinical settings. I will first review the traditional experimental approach to clinical research and then identify the difficulties encountered when this approach is applied to real-life settings. Next, I will discuss alternative models for clinical investigations when the obstacles to traditional research are either too imposing or are philosophically at odds with the clinical undertaking. My task here is not to provide the practitioner with a detailed and exhaustive examination of research design and methodology, but to remind the practitioner of the empirical possibilities and problems encountered when we move from the lab to the clinic.

Traditional Clinical Research Strategies and Guidelines

Experimental designs relying on between-group comparisons constitute the most popular format for clinical research. Designs that employ between-group comparisons enable researchers to build in controls sufficient to conclude that a treatment (used here in its generic meaning of environmental intervention), rather than extraneous factors or idiosyncratic reactions, accounts for the changes observed in or the differences measured between clients. However, the effectiveness of these controls in clinical research depends on several requirements specific to clinical investigations. Let us examine some of these now.

Meaningful between-group comparisons require substantial numbers of clients who are similar in some way, usually in the symptom picture that they present. It is impossible to generate specific numerical guidelines for including clients in treatment groups because this decision is affected by such practical considerations as the availability of clients and the per client cost of the intervention, as well as such methodological considerations as the size of the clinical effect aimed for and the size of the risk of failure to obtain an effect that the researcher will tolerate. Nonetheless, conventions have evolved in the clinical literature, and it now appears that clinical researchers are satisfied with a minimum of 20 subjects per study, 10 per group for a treatment–control trial (Fletcher & Fletcher, 1979; Kraemer, 1981). Similar conventions have evolved for such other aspects of clinical research as therapists and treatments. With regard to therapists, it is suggested that to control for the nonspecific effects of the personality of the therapist, at least two therapists of approximately similar backgrounds and levels of experience should participate in outcome studies, with each therapist offering each treatment. With respect to treatment sessions, although many outcomes studies offer as few as 6 exposures, most clinical researchers agree that 8–10 sessions is the minimum treatment time required for demonstrating effects. Of course, the treatment must be standardized, and the provision of a detailed therapy manual for each condition makes this more likely. Conducting treatment in groups, rather than individually, is another means of ensuring standardization of treatment.

As discussed earlier in this chapter, a good case can be made for utilizing a standard assessment package that measures several aspects of functioning by methodologically independent instruments. To further increase methodological control, researchers might also assess subjects' status on such presumably extraneous variables as IQ and socioeconomic status, which might affect response to treatment. This additional assessment can be used to match subjects prior to assignment to treatments to increase the homogeneity of the groups. Because clients' expectations of treatment as well as their perceptions of their therapist can contribute to their receptivity to treatment, clinical research often includes a measurement of these variables as well.

Even with the most careful planning, the clinical researcher often encounters unexpected problems. Some of these are so commonplace that conventions have arisen concerning how to handle them. For example, most clinical researchers prepare for client drop-out either by including more clients than their minimum requirements, by having others waiting in the wings, or by instituting a means of minimizing the dropout rate. Requiring a monetary deposit that is refundable only on completion of the treatment research has been moderately effective. Similar safeguards can be planned when clients miss sessions. The research procedure might permit makeup sessions either by listening to a tape of the regular session or by working with the therapist at an alternate time. Of course, any departure from the study's standard procedure detracts from the methodological rigor of the research. Nonetheless, these are compromises that the clinical researcher often is willing to make.

Despite their adaptations of traditional and experimental models to include additional methodological controls and their tolerance of departures from standard procedure, clinical researchers nonetheless encounter major obstacles to conducting research within clinical settings. It has been argued (Barlow, 1981) that no number of additional resources can overcome these obstacles because they arise from a basic incompatability between the methods and philosophy of research and the nature and values of the clinical undertaking. For example, the large number of clients required to compute the between-group comparisons is often not clinically feasible. Clients, especially child clients, who present with similar disorders simply do not appear at mental health agencies in sufficient numbers for research projects. Even when they can be identified, because of the size of the agency or the incidence of the disorder, or through advertisements for clients with a particular disorder, they often cannot be matched on important background characteristics. Frequently, the clients' targeted disorder is only one facet of their overall dysfunctional affect and behavior. On occasion, clients refuse to participate in the necessary research procedures. Additionally, the scale of most clinical research requiring many clients, several therapists, numerous sessions, extensive assessment, and the personnel to orchestrate the project and collect the data is beyond the capabilities of most mental-health agencies. Finally, one of the most difficult issues that clinical researchers face is the ethical problem of withholding treatment from control groups or assigning clients to placebo groups, where it is assumed that they will receive less effective treatment.

As if these problems were not sufficient to discourage even the most enthusiastic practitioner from undertaking clinical research, the philosophical differences between research and clinical treatment present yet other obstacles. Researchers continue to rely on statistical significance as the means of identifying treatment effects. Most practitioners are unimpressed by statistical significance because it tells them nothing about either the size of the effect as it is expressed in real-life contexts (Carver, 1978) or the likely effect of that particular treatment on any particular client (Hersen & Barlow, 1976). Additionally, researchers attempt to develop standardized treatments and assessment procedures to enhance methodological rigor. Clinicians, on the other hand, attempt to develop procedures that are tailored to the needs of the individual client. Because these points limit the applicability of research findings to clinical practice, many practitioners fail to incorporate research findings into their clinical repertoire. At the same time, most clinical researchers do not become involved in practice because of the amount of time and energy they must devote to research. Hence, we have the origins of the scientist–practitioner split (Joint Commission on Mental Illness and Health, 1961), an unfortunate development for the field of clinical psychology.

As an alternative to either struggling through the enterprise of traditional clinical research or not undertaking clinically relevant research at all, another research strategy has recently been suggested for clinical investigation. This strategy is known by a diversity of terms, *including intensive local observation* (Cronbach, 1975); *single-case design* (Hersen & Barlow, 1976); and *time-series design* (Glass, Wilson, & Gottman, 1975). In these designs, every therapist–client pairing is the unit source of data, and every individual therapy treatment constitutes an outcome study. The data are accumulated over clients. It is argued that this approach to data collection can provide knowledge about the efficacy of clinical interventions that is more clinically meaningful and that can be more widely generalized. To draw valid conclusions and make the clinical application possible, time-series designs require, at a minimum, the standard repeated measurement of a client's behavior over time in treatment; the clear specification of the intervention applied to the client; and the replication of the treatment outcome with other clients (Barlow, 1981; Hayes, 1981; Hersen & Barlow, 1976).

In addition to avoiding the problems created by the scale of traditional clinical research, time-series designs have the advantage of being flexible enough to reflect the actual therapeutic venture more accurately. For example, if a particular intervention technique does not appear to be having the desired effect, it can be discontinued, and that phase of the outcome study can be ended without too great an expenditure of resources. After another round of assessment to reestablish behavioral baselines, the clinician can introduce another therapeutic approach. The systematic nature of assessments, the record keeping, and the concrete specification of interventions alone distinguish time-series designs from actual clinical practice. It is argued that, because of this enhanced similarity, empirical studies built on time-series designs hold more potential to influence the future course of clinical treatment than traditional clinical research. The relative simplicity and flexibility of time-series designs may make it more appealing for practitioners to become involved in the process of clinical research in their "natural" settings.

The approach to clinical research offered by time-series methodology appears to hold special promise for evaluating cognitive-behavioral therapy with children. For example, the objects of therapeutic change (cognitions and mediational processes) can be so idiosyncratic and the techniques of affecting change so diverse that the amount of research that might be required to identify the most effective client–therapy or pathology–therapy matches might not be feasible. The flexibility to institute and discontinue treatments and to tailor treatment to the individual child's needs during therapy may serve to cut the task of outcome research down to manageable proportions. Thus, a time-series approach to research might enable clinicians to generate guidelines for the effective application of cognitive-behavioral therapy far more efficiently than traditional clinical research. Additionally, the notorious variability of cognitions across situations and time, the weakness of our current tools for measuring them, and the absence of point-for-point relationships between cognitions and other aspects of functioning have presented serious measurement problems for cognitive-behavioral outcome research. The requirement of repeated measurement in time-series experimentation may improve our ability to assess change, because frequent repeated measurement is more likely to make stable patterns noticeable. Hence, time-series studies may provide a more effective methodology for assessing cognitive treatments.

Conclusion

This chapter has sought to identify potential significant avenues for research on cognitive-behavioral therapy with children. The objective was to encourage mental health practitioners to undertake clinically relevant research by identifying questions relevant to cognitive-behavioral assessment, treatment, and prevention of disorders. I attempted to temper my enthusiastic encouragement of clinical research by reviewing some drawbacks and difficulties of conducting research within clinical settings. Despite these difficulties and the sizable resources that must be committed to clinical research, I concluded that research relevant to the needs of clinicians could be conducted with careful planning and reliance on novel experimental designs. I would like to end this chapter on a positive note. To the extent that cognitive-behavioral therapy is well grounded in a body of psychological knowledge and involves clearly specifiable therapeutic procedures, I believe that it warrants continued research efforts to improve its effectiveness and efficiency. At the same time that I encourage clinicians to become involved in investigations of cognitive approaches to child therapy, I also implore them to undertake the task with creativity, so that, as practitioners, they might examine the questions that, as researchers, they might have overlooked.

References

Barlow, D. On the relation of clinical research to clinical practice: Current issues, new directions. *Journal of Consulting and Clinical Psychology*, 1981, *49*, 147–155.

Beck, A. *Depression: Causes and treatment*. Philadelphia: University of Pennsylvania Press, 1972.

Beck, A. *Cognitive therapy and the emotional disorders*. New York: International Universities Press, 1976.

Beck, A., Rush, A., Shaw, B., & Emery, G. *Cognitive therapy of depression*. New YorK: Guilford Press, 1979.

Bedrosian, R. The application of cognitive therapy techniques with adolescents. In G. Emery, S. Holland, & R. Bedrosian (Eds.), *New directions in cognitive therapy*. New York: Guilford Press, 1981.

Bender, N. Self-verbalization versus tutor verbalization in modifying impulsivity. *Journal of Educational Psychology*, 1976, *68*, 347–354.

Bornstein, P., & Quevillon, R. The effects of a self-instructional package on over-active preschool boys. *Journal of Applied Behavior Analysis*, 1976, *9*, 179–188.

Bowman, P. *A cognitive-behavioral treatment program for impulsive youthful offenders*. Unpublished manuscript, 1979.

Brown, A. Development, schooling and the acquisition of knowledge about knowledge. In R. Anderson, R. Spiro, & W. Montague (Eds.), *Schooling and the acquisition of knowledge*. Hillsdale, N.J.: Lawrence Erlbaun, in press.

Bugenthal, D. Whalen, C., & Henker, B. Causal attribution of hyperactive children and motivational assumptions of two behavioral-change approaches: Evidence for an interactionist position. *Child Development*, 1977, 48, 874–884.

Camp, B., Blom, G., Herbert, F., & Van Doorninck, W. "Think aloud": A program for developing self-control in young aggressive boys. *Journal of Abnormal Child Psychology*, 1977, 5, 157–169.

Carver, R. The case against statistical significance testing. *Harvard Educational Review*, 1978, 48, 378–399.

Chandler, M. Egocentrism and antisocial behavior: The assessment and training of social perspective taking skills. *Developmental Psychology*, 1973, 9, 326–332.

Cohen, S., & Przybycien, C. Some effects of sociometrically selected peer models on the cognitive styles of impulsive children. *Journal of Genetic Psychology*, 1974, 124, 213–220.

Cronbach, L. Beyond the two disciplines of scientific psychology. *American Psychologist*, 1975, 30, 116–127.

DiGiuseppe, R. Cognitive therapy with children. In G. Emery, S. Hollon, & R. Bedrosian (Eds.), *New directions in cognitive therapy*. New York: Guilford Press, 1981.

DiGiuseppe, R., & Kassinove, H. Effects of a rational-emotive school mental health program on children's emotional adjustment. *Journal of Community Psychology*, 1976, 4, 382–387.

Douglas, V., Parry, P., Marton, P., & Garson, C. Assessment of a cognitive training program for hyperactive children. *Journal of Abnormal Child Psychology*, 1976, 4, 389–410.

Drummond, D. *Self-instructional training: An approach to disruptive classroom behavior.* Unpublished doctoral dissertation, University of Oregon, 1974.

Egeland, B. Training impulsive children in the use of more efficient scanning techniques. *Child Development*, 1974, 45, 165–171.

Ellis, A. *Reason and emotion in psychotherapy.* Secaucus, N.J.: Lyle Stuart, 1962.

Ellis, A., & Harper, R. *A new guide to rational living.* Englewood Cliffs, N.J.: Prentice-Hall, 1975.

Finch, A. J., Wilkinson, M., Nelson, W., & Montgomery, L. Modification of an impulsive cognitive tempo in emotionally disturbed boys. *Journal of Abnormal Child Psychology*, 1975, 3, 47–51.

Fletcher, R., & Fletcher, S. Clinical research in general medicine journals: A 30-year perspective. *New England Journal of Medicine*, 1979, 301, 180–183.

Glass, G., Wilson, V., & Gottman, J. *Design and analysis of time-series experiments.* Boulder: University of Colorado Press, 1975.

Goldstein, A., Heller, K., & Sechrest, L. *Psychotherapy and the psychology of behavior change.* New York: Wiley, 1966.

Hayes, S. Single case experimental design and empirical clinical practice. *Journal of Consulting and Clinical Psychology*, 1981, 49, 193–211.

Hersen, M., & Barlow, D. *Single case experimental designs: Strategies for studying behavior change.* New York: Pergamon Press, 1976.

Huntsinger, G. *Teaching self-control of verbal and physical aggression to juvenile delinquents.* Unpublished manuscript, 1979.

Joint Commission on Mental Illness and Health. *Action for mental health.* New York: Science Editions, 1961.

Karoly, P. Behavioral self-management in children: Concepts, methods, issues and directions. In M. Hersen, R. Eisler, & P. Miller (Eds.), *Progress in behavior modification* (Vol. 5). New York: Academic Press, 1977.

Kassinove, H., Crisci, R., & Tiegerman, S. Developmental trends in rational thinking:

Implications for rational-emotive, school mental health programs. *Journal of Community Psychology*, 1977, *5*, 266–274.

Kelly, E., Goldberg, L., Fiske, D., & Kilkowski, J. Twenty-five years later. *American Psychologist*, 1978, *33*, 746–755.

Kendall, P., & Finch, A., Jr. A cognitive-behavioral treatment for impulse control: A case study. *Journal of Consulting and Clinical Psychology*, 1976, *44*, 852–857.

Kendall, P., & Finch, A., Jr. Analyses of changes in verbal behavior following a cognitive-behavioral treatment for impulsivity. *Journal of Abnormal Child Psychology*, 1979, *7*, 455–463. (a)

Kendall, P., & Finch, A. Developing nonimpulsive behavior in children: Cognitive behavioral strategies for self-control. In P. Kendall & S. Hollon (Eds.), *Cognitive-behavioral interventions: Theory, research and procedures*. New York: Academic Press, 1979. (b)

Kendall, P., & Wilcox, L. Self-control in children: The development of a rating scale. *Journal of Consulting and Clinical Psychology*. 1979, *47*, 1020–1029.

Kendall, P., & Wilcox, L. Cognitive-behavioral treatment for impulsivity: Concrete versus conceptual training in non-self-controlled problem children. *Journal of Consulting and Clinical Psychology*, 1980, *48*, 80–91.

Kestner, J., & Borkowski, J. Children's maintenance and generalization of an interrogative learning strategy. *Child Development*, in press.

Knaus, W. *Rational-emotive education: A manual for teachers*. New York: Institute for Rational-Emotive Therapy, 1974.

Knaus, W., & Bokar, S. The effects of rational emotive education on anxiety and self-concept. *Rational Living*, 1975, *10*, 7–10.

Kraemer, H. Coping strategies in psychiatric clinical research. *Journal of Consulting and Clinical Psychology*, 1981, *49*, 309–319.

Little, V. *Developmental role-taking deficits in institutionalized juvenile delinquents*. Paper presented at the meeting of the Southeastern Psychological Association, Atlanta, March 1978.

Little, V., & Kendall, P. Cognitive-behavioral interventions with delinquents: Problem solving, role-taking, and self-control. In P. Kendall & S. Hollon (Eds.), *Cognitive-behavioral interventions: Theory, research, and procedures*. New York: Academic Press, 1979.

McCullough, J., Huntsinger, G., & Nay, W. Self-control treatment of aggression in a 16-year-old male. *Journal of Consulting and Clinical Psychology*, 1977, *45*, 322–331.

Meichenbaum, D., & Asarnow, J. Cognitive-behavioral modification and metacognitive development: Implications for the classroom. In P. Kendall & S. Hollon (Eds.), *Cognitive behavioral interventions: Theory, research, and procedures*. New York: Academic Press, 1979.

Meichenbaum, D., & Goodman, J. Training impulsive children to talk to themselves: A means of developing self-control. *Journal of Abnormal Psychology*, 1971, *77*, 115–126.

Monohan, J., & O'Leary, K. Effects of self-instruction on rule-breaking behavior. *Psychological Reports*, 1971, *29*, 1059–1066.

O'Leary, K. The effects of self-instruction on immoral behavior. *Journal of Experimental Child Psychology*, 1968, *6*, 297–301.

Palkes, H., Stewart, M., & Freedman, J. Improvement in maze performance of hyperactive boys as a function of verbal-training procedures. *Journal of Special Education*, 1972, *5*, 337–342.

Platt, J., Scura, W., & Hannon, J. Problem-solving thinking of youthful incarcerated heroin addicts. *Journal of Community Psychology*, 1973, *1*, 278–281.

Platt, J., Spivack, G., Altman, N., Altman, D., & Peizer, S. Adolescent problem-solving thinking. *Journal of Consulting and Clinical Psychology*, 1974, *42*, 787–793.

Ridberg, H., Parke, R., & Hetherington, M. Modification of impulsive and reflective cognitive styles through observation of film-mediated models. *Developmental Psychology*, 1971, *5*, 369–377.

Robin, A., Armel, S., & O'Leary, K. The effects of self-instruction on writing deficiency. *Behavior Therapy*, 1975, *6*, 18–187.

Robin, A., Kent, R., O'Leary, K., Foster, S., & Prinz, R. An approach to teaching parents and adolescents problem-solving communication skills: A preliminary report. *Behavior Therapy*, 1977, *8*, 639–643.

Shorkey, C., & Saski, J. Comparison of rational beliefs of blind, deaf, and non-handicapped high school students. *Perceptual and Motor Skills*, 1981, *52*, 751–754.

Shorkey, C., & Whiteman, V. Development of the Rational Behavior Inventory; Initial validity and reliability. *Educational and Psychological Measurement*, 1977, *37*, 527–534.

Shure, M., & Spivack, G. *Problem solving techniques in child rearing*. San Francisco: Jossey-Bass, 1978.

Spivack, G., & Levine, M. *Self-regulation in acting-out and normal adolescents*. (Rep. M-4531). Washington, D.C.: National Institute of Health, 1963.

Spivack, G., & Shure, M. *Social adjustment of young children: A cognitive approach to solving real-life problems*. San Francisco: Jossey-Bass, 1974.

Spivack, G., Platt, J., & Shure, M. *The problem-solving approach to adjustment*. San Francisco: Jossey-Bass, 1976.

Turnure, J., Buium, N., & Thurlow, M. The effectiveness of interrogatives for promoting verbal elaboration productivity on young children. *Child Development*, 1976, *47*, 851–855.

Weston, J. B., & Glass, C. R. *A cognitive-behavioral analysis of children's social skills in peer interactions of middle childhood*. Unpublished manuscript, Catholic University, 1980.

Williams, D., & Akamatsu, T. Cognitive self-guidance training with juvenile delinquents: Applicability and generalization. *Cognitive Therapy and Research*, 1978, *2*, 285–288.

Zelniker, T., Jeffrey, W., Ault, R., & Parsons, J. Analysis and modification of search strategies of impulsive and reflective children on the Matching Familiar Figures test. *Child Development*, 1972, *43*, 321–335.

Index

ABC's of RET, 13, 214, 433
  with adolescents, 94
  and rational-emotive education, 469
  in treating anxiety, 234–235
  in treating conduct disorders, 115, 135
  working with parents of exceptional children, 401
  working with special educators, 411
  working with teachers, 426, 447–448
Academic underachievement
  definition, 189–191, 193–195
  and impulsivity, 159
  irrational beliefs of adolescents, 195
  as psychopathology, 191–193
  and self-concept, 142
  treatment, 196–207
Acting-out behavior, 112–113, 159. See Conduct disorders
Anger, childhood
  and conduct disorders, 73, 78, 104, 116–118, 135
  and impulsivity, 178–180
  and low frustration tolerance, 139–146
Anger, parental, 345–347
  and conduct disordered children, 61, 130–132
  and exceptional children, 402–403
Anxiety, childhood
  assessment, 230–231
  cognitive distortions, 222–227
  definition, 213
  discomfort anxiety, 226–229
  ego anxiety, 223–225
  treatment, 29, 232–237
Anxiety, parental
  cognitive distortions, 219, 347–350
  disturbed parenting styles, 220–222

Assessment methods, general, 25–26, 122–123, 227
  for adolescents, 92–94
  for children, 60–66, 230–231, 338
  for children's groups, 493–499
  for parents, 230, 336–338, 371–373
  for parents of exceptional children, 392–395
Attributional retraining, 33–35, 62

Battered child, 153–156
Behavioral treatment approaches, 27, 67–69, 102, 379. See also Self-instructional training
  anxiety, 69
  conduct disorders, 115–116, 121–122, 127, 133
  impulsivity, 166–168, 179
  obesity, 281, 284–285, 288–292
  social isolation, 263
Beliefs. See Irrational beliefs, childhood; Irrational beliefs, general

Challenging. See Disputation
Childhood maladjustment, 18–24, 49–50, 213–218
Cognition. See Childhood maladjustment; Inferences, incorrect/antiempirical interpretations; Irrational beliefs, childhood; Irrational beliefs, general
Cognitive ecology, 303
Conduct disorders
  assessment, 122, 125
  diagnosis, 111–115
  irrational beliefs of children, 117–118
  treatment, 121–122, 127–136

Critical thinking skills, 70–72, 235–236

Daydreaming, 142–143, 228, 250
Depression. *See also* Self-esteem, childhood
  childhood, 73–77
  conduct-disordered children, 118
  parent, 341–344
Developmental limitations, 19–21, 58–60, 265, 295, 481–482
Discomfort anxiety, childhood, 226–229. *See also* Low frustration tolerance, children
  conduct disorders, 117, 134–136
  impulsivity, 180–182
  low frustration tolerance, 139–146
  underachievement, 199–207
Discomfort anxiety, parental. *See also* Low frustration tolerance, parental
  and conduct disordered children, 61, 132–133
  general irrational beliefs, 350–353
Disputation, 11, 55, 436–441, 472–473
  with adolescents, 94–101
  with children, 56–57, 78–86
  with parents, 128–133
  with parents of exceptional children, 390–407
  with special educators, 410–413
  with teachers, 441–446, 458–460
Drug and alcohol abuse, 201
DSM-III
  conduct disorders, 144, 163
  impulsivity, 163
  low frustration tolerance, 144

Emotional problems, 27, 51, 71, 336–338
Emotions
  and child awareness, 26, 56, 64–65, 70, 223
  and cognition in children, 19–22, 45–48, 56, 113, 178–180. *See also* Childhood maladjustment; Irrational beliefs, childhood; Irrational beliefs, general
  RET conceptualization, 47–48
Empirical analyses and solutions, 51–52. *See also* Inferences, incorrect/antiempirical interpretations
Encopresis, 61
Enuresis, 155

Fear
  childhood. *See* anxiety, childhood
  general irrational beliefs, 347–348
  and parents of exceptional children, 398–399
Frustration. *See* Low frustration tolerance, children; Low frustration tolerance, parental

Generalization of treatment, 71, 99–101, 184–185, 236, 397, 522. *See also* Homework, RET
Grief, 396
Guilt
  child, 224–225
  parent, 113, 128–130, 359
  parents of exceptional children, 404–407

Hitting. *See* Conduct disorders
Homework, RET, 71, 100–101, 124, 151, 379
Hyperactivity. *See* Impulsivity

Impulsivity
  behavioral correlatives, 162
  cognitive-behavioral interventions, 163–174
  and conduct disorders, 112, 116
  definition, 160–161
  early influences, 161–162
  and emotionality, 178–179
  and low frustration tolerance, 144, 155
  psychiatric classification, 163
  research, 510–511
Inferences, incorrect/antiempirical interpretations, 14, 48, 73, 216
  adolescents, 89, 91, 98
  assessment, 62
  childhood anxiety, 219–222
  children, 48, 51–52, 73
  children's sexual problems, 324–327
  and emotional problem solving, 51–52
  and emotions, 47–48
  and parents of exceptional children, 397–407
  treatment, empirical solutions, 52, 72–78, 78–87, 98, 397
Interpersonal cognitive problem solving, 27, 31–33
  and child group work, 489

Interpersonal cognitive problem solving (cont.)
  and children, 31–33
  and conduct disorders, 118–120
  and impulsivity, 161
  and obesity, 303
  research, 510–511
  and social isolation, 247
Irrational beliefs, childhood
  of adolescents, 20, 94–98, 471–472
  of children, 19, 53, 471
  and conduct disorders, 117–118
  and discomfort anxiety, 226, 228–229
  and ego anxiety, 224–225
  and low frustration tolerance, 143
  and obesity, 298
  and underachievement, 195–196
Irrational beliefs, general, 11–15, 33, 335–336, 434–437
Irrational beliefs of parents
  anger, 130–132, 345–347
  depression, 341–344, 374
  discomfort anxiety, 132–133
  of exceptional children, 397–407
  fear, 347–348, 374
  guilt, 113, 128–130
  procrastination, 124, 350–351
  related to family dysfunction, 375
  and resistance, 376–377
Irrational beliefs of special educators, 410–412
Irrational beliefs of teachers, 421–423

Living school, 17
Low frustration tolerance, children. *See also* Discomfort anxiety, childhood
  conduct disorders, 117
  contributing factors, 144–146
  definition, 139–141, 350
  signs and symptoms, 142–144
  treatment, 146–153
Low frustration tolerance, parental. *See also* Discomfort anxiety, parental
  and conduct disordered children, 124
  and procrastination, 350–353

Manipulative behavior, 336–337, 353–355. *See also* Practical problems
  important insights for parents, 355–360

Motivation. *See* Discomfort anxiety, childhood; Discomfort anxiety, parental; Impulsivity; Low frustration tolerance, children; Low frustration tolerance, parental; Self-esteem, childhood

Nightmares, 228
Noncompliance, 62, 111, 114, 116, 117. *See also* Conduct disorders
Nonmanipulative behavior, 336–338, 340. *See also* Emotional problems

Obesity, children and adolescents, 144, 229, 271
  adolescents, 300–305
  assessment, 276–277
  behavioral treatment, 288–292
  children, 294–300
  cognitive treatment, 292–294
  etiology, 273–275
  treatment considerations, 277–288

Parent emotions
  anger, 130–132, 345–347, 402–403
  anxiety/fear, 219–222, 347–350, 398–401
  depression, 341–344
  discomfort anxiety, 132–133
  guilt, 113, 128–130, 359, 404–407
  low frustration tolerance, 124, 350–353
Parenting goals, 369–370
Parenting styles, disturbed, 23–25, 113–114, 126–127, 197–207, 220–222
Parent interview, 126–127, 230, 319, 338, 371–373
Parents, 23–25, 215
  and childhood anxiety, 219, 234–236
  and childhood impulsivity, 184–185
  and childhood low frustration tolerance, 145, 219
  and childhood obesity, 279, 283–284, 294
  and childhood sexuality, 312–318, 324
  and conduct disordered children, 113–114, 125–132
  and underachievement, 197–207
Patient uniformity myth, 36, 180–182
Phobia, childhood. *See* Anxiety, childhood
Piaget, 20–21, 46, 58–59, 181

Practical problems, 51, 62, 70–71. *See also* Manipulative behavior
Psychosomatic complaints, 68, 225, 228

Rapport building, 61
  adolescents, 90–92
  children, 53, 61, 123–124
  parents of exceptional children, 389–390
Rational beliefs. *See* Irrational beliefs, childhood; Irrational beliefs, general
Rational-emotive education, 6, 17, 148–153, 430
  basic assumptions, 469–472
  informal approach, 431–432, 474
  integration into curriculum, 479–480
  limitations, 481
  and low frustration tolerance, 151–153
  rationale, 467–468
  research, 480–481
  structured lessons, 146–147, 475–479
  and underachievement, 209
Rational self-talk, self-statements, 21, 26, 62, 70
  as inner speech, 10–11, 28
  treating anxiety, 236
  treating conduct disorders, 63, 135
  treating obesity, 304
  treating social isolation, 259–263
Response cost, 68, 124, 167
RET
  definition, 427–429
  elegant, 8, 52, 72, 115
  philosophy, 429–430
  rationale for use with parents, 334
  rationale for use with teachers, 431
  versus CBT, 8–10, 178–180

School phobia, 228
SCIENCE, 302
Self-disclosure, 54, 69–70, 390
Self-esteem, childhood. *See also* Depression
  adolescents, 97
  anxiety, 216–217, 224–225
  conduct disorders, 118
  low frustration tolerance, 148–151, 155
  obesity, 287
  parental blame, 23
Self-instructional training, 27–30, 34, 50

Self-instructional training (*cont.*)
  and child group work, 487–489, 503–504
  and conduct disorders, 120–121, 135
  developmental limitations, 58
  and impulsivity, 164, 168–169, 174
  and obesity, 295, 296, 304
  research, 164–174, 510–511
Sexuality, childhood
  assessment, 322–323
  developmental considerations, 314–319
  sex education, 312–314
  suggested readings, 327–329
  treatment, 319–322, 323–327
Social isolation, childhood
  assessment, 224, 252–257
  behaviors, 183, 249–251
  child group work, 489–490
  cognitions, 245–249
  definition, 241–245
  and impulsivity, 183
  treatment, 259–263
Stress
  and low frustration tolerance, 141
  secondary, 420
  and teachers, 418–425, 448–451
Stress inoculation training, 30–31, 135

Teachers
  disputation, 441–446
  of exceptional children, 408–413
  irrational beliefs, 436–441
  stress, 416–425, 448–451
  use of RET, 431–432
Temper tantrum. *See* Anger, childhood
Therapist variables, 53–55, 382–383, 393–395. *See also* Rapport building
Treatment methods, general, 15–16, 26–27, 67–69
  for adolescents, 94–100
  allied cognitive-behavioral approaches, 27–35
  in child group work, 499–506
  for children, 72–74
  for parents, 92, 234–235, 340, 368–369
  for teachers, 441–446
Truancy, 103

Underachievement. *See* Academic underachievement